Scottish Literature
an introduction

ALAN RIACH

Luath Press Limited
EDINBURGH
www.luath.co.uk

First published 2022

ISBN: 978-1-80425-063-1

The author's right to be identified as author of this book
under the Copyright, Designs and Patents Act 1988 has been asserted.

Typeset in 11 point Sabon LT Pro by
Main Point Books, Edinburgh

© Alan Riach 2022

ALAN RIACH is a poet and teacher. Born in Airdrie, Lanarkshire, in 1957, he studied English literature at Cambridge University from 1976 to 1979 and completed his PhD in the Department of Scottish Literature at Glasgow University in 1986. His academic career has included positions as a research fellow, lecturer, Associate Professor and Pro-Dean in the Faculty of Arts at the University of Waikato, New Zealand, and he has given scholarly lectures, keynote addresses and public talks and poetry readings at universities, festivals and other venues internationally. He has introduced and taught Scottish and other literatures in four continents and two hemispheres, from Bengal to Bucharest, from Singapore to Montenegro, the USA, Australia, China, France, Poland and Spain. The publication of *Scottish Literature: an introduction* in the centenary year of the first appearance in print of Hugh MacDiarmid and on the 10th anniversary of the long overdue formal provision of the literature of Scotland into Scottish schools, consolidates a working lifetime's commitment to the subject he professes, and celebrates its subversive endurance despite institutional neglect and hostility. It was prompted by a conversation with Paul Henderson Scott of the Saltire Society in 2005 and brings together the astonishing diversity of Scotland's national literature, in language, geography, historical periods, literary expressiveness and sheer quality.

Other books by Alan Riach:

Poetry
This Folding Map
An Open Return
First & Last Songs
From the Vision of Hell: An Extract of Dante
Clearances
Homecoming
Wild Blue: Selected Poems
The Winter Book

Translations
Duncan Ban MacIntyre, *Praise of Ben Dorain*
Alasdair mac Mhaighstir Alasdair, *The Birlinn of Clan Ranald*

Criticism
Hugh MacDiarmid's Epic Poetry
The Poetry of Hugh MacDiarmid
Representing Scotland in Literature, Popular Culture and Iconography: The Masks of the Modern Nation
Arts of Resistance: Poets, Portraits and Landscapes of Modern Scotland (with Alexander Moffat and Linda MacDonald-Lewis)
Arts of Independence: The Cultural Argument and Why It Matters Most (with Alexander Moffat)
Arts & the Nation: A critical re-examination of Scottish Literature, Painting, Music and Culture (with Alexander Moffat and John Purser)
The Edinburgh Companion to Twentieth-Century Scottish Literature (co-editor)
The International Companion to Edwin Morgan (editor)

'Teaching is probably the noblest profession in the world – the most unselfish, difficult, and honourable profession, but it is also the most unappreciated, underrated, underpaid, and under-praised profession in the world.'
Thus wrote Leonard Bernstein in his book *Findings*.

This book is for the teachers, and of the best of my own: Edward Stead, Tim Cribb, Helena Shire, Marshall Walker and Douglas Gifford, in partial repayment of a debt I'll never want to close.

Contents

	This is where we begin	13
	Preface	17

PART ONE: THREE QUESTIONS

1	Why read Scottish literature?	20
2	What is literature?	26
3	Was there ever a 'British' literature?	33

PART TWO: SCOTLAND EMERGENT

1	The Gaelic tradition: the Three Great Cycles	44
2	The Gaelic Otherworld	53
3	Merlin, Arthur and Calgacus	57
4	The Picts, *The Gododdin* and Columba	62
5	From *The Dream of the Rood* to the Norse sagas	69

PART THREE: APPROACHES

1	Performing Scotland: plays, drama and theatricality	76
2	Poetry: how to read and what to read	84
3	Stories and novels	89

PART FOUR: AUTHORS AND WORKS

1	Early Gaelic poetry: the Dean of Lismore and the MacMhuirichs	98
2	Thomas Rhymer and Wyntoun's *Cronykil*	103
3	*The Bruce, The Wallace, Bannockburn* and the *Declaration of Arbroath*	106
4	Love is all you need: James I, *The Kingis Quair*	113
5	The rule of compassion: Robert Henryson	118

6	Not energy ordered, energised order: William Dunbar	124
7	Poet and translator: Gavin Douglas	128
8	Early plays, *Philotus* and David Lyndsay's *Satyre of the Thrie Estaitis*	133
9	The Latin tradition and George Buchanan	145
10	The Latin tradition and Arthur Johnstone	154
11	Defy them all: Elizabeth Melville	159
12	Mark Alexander Boyd and the 'Castalian Band'	163
13	Sorrow in a deadly vein: William Drummond of Hawthornden	168
14	The Border Ballads, Robert Kirk and the Marquis of Montrose	171
15	Oddfellows: William Lithgow and Thomas Urquhart	176
16	Gaelic poetry of the 17th century	183
17	Gaelic poetry of the early 18th century	189
18	More Gaelic poetry of the early 18th century	194
19	Scottish Enlightenment authors: Stewart, Hume, Smith, Hutton, Ferguson	197
20	In the eye of the storm: Alasdair mac Mhaighstir Alasdair / Alexander MacDonald	205
21	The ecological eye: Donnchadh Bàn Mac an t-Saoir / Duncan Ban MacIntyre	213
22	Gaelic poetry of the later 18th century	217
23	James Macpherson and *Ossian*	222
24	Ramsay's *The Gentle Shepherd*, Home's *Douglas* and Carstairs's *The Hubble-Shue*	231
25	Tender strengths: Robert Fergusson	245
26	The politics of song: Robert Burns	249
27	Poetry in English: from Thomson to Byron	258
28	The doctor's expeditions: Tobias Smollett	263
29	What can this thing be?: James Hogg	268
30	Divided loyalties, sympathies unbound: Walter Scott	273
31	Domestic politics, fanatic extremes: John Galt	293

32 The Tavern Sages and Ferrier, Baillie, Brunton, Oliphant, Cockburn and Reid	298
33 Victorian Sages from Thomas Carlyle to Margaret Oliphant	304
34 Gaelic poetry of the 19th century	310
35 Prophet of modernity: Robert Louis Stevenson	315
36 Stevenson's contemporaries: from Charles Mackay to Florence Dixie	322
37 Writers of the Industrial Revolution: from Thomas Campbell to Arthur Conan Doyle	327
38 Gaelic poetry: from 19th century to the 20th century	332
39 Beyond the Kailyard	338
40 The internationalists: from R.B. Cunninghame Graham to Violet Jacob	352
41 Gaelic poetry of the early 20th century	357
42 Playwrights and plays: from Joanna Baillie to John Brandane	363
43 Renaissance: Hugh MacDiarmid	369
44 Questions of language: William Soutar and Edwin Muir	383
45 Thin ice and voluminous works: Compton Mackenzie and Naomi Mitchison	389
46 The morning star: Lewis Grassic Gibbon	394
47 Matters of spirit: Neil Gunn	399
48 Tragedy and comedy: Fionn Mac Colla and Eric Linklater	404
49 Self-determinations: Catherine Carswell, Nan Shepherd and Willa Muir	409
50 Playwrights and plays: Joe Corrie, James Bridie, Joan Littlewood and Ewan MacColl	413
51 Edinburgh and Lochinver: Robert Garioch and Norman MacCaig	421
52 Love and war: Somhairle MacGill-Eain / Sorley MacLean and Sydney Goodsir Smith	425
53 Scouts of the limits: W.S. Graham and Deòrsa mac Iain Dheòrsa / George Campbell Hay	430
54 Folk song and the dance of the intellect: Hamish Henderson and Edwin Morgan	437
55 Deadliness and grace: Robin Jenkins and Muriel Spark	443

56	Lords of the Isles: George Mackay Brown and Iain Mac a' Ghobhainn / Iain Crichton Smith	448
57	Gaelic poetry of the later 20th century	458
58	Playwrights and plays: from Robert McLellan to John McGrath	463
59	Literary fiction: from George Friel to Jessie Kesson	469
60	Scotland and America: Alexander Trocchi and Gordon Williams	473
61	Bestsellers: from Annie S. Swan to Nigel Tranter	476
62	Resisting repression: James Kennaway, Agnes Owens, Archie Hind and Alasdair Gray	481
63	An awkward squad: from David Lindsay to Andrew O'Hagan	485
64	Gaelic prose fiction: from the 16th to the 20th centuries	489
65	Gaelic prose fiction in English and the Ùr-sgeul initiative	493
66	Modern Gaelic prose fiction: a flood of new novels	497
67	Possible dancers: Irvine Welsh, Carl MacDougall and A.L. Kennedy	500
68	Risky desires and natural needs: Iain Banks and Janice Galloway	505
69	Scotland and further: James Robertson, Ali Smith and Alan Warner	509
70	Forms of revival: Allan Massie, James Kelman and Alan Spence	513
71	Scotlands (plural): from Janet Paisley to Kirstin Innes	517
72	Gaelic fiction in the 21st century: satires, vexations and vicissitudes	522
73	Playwrights and plays: from Robert Kemp to Liz Lochhead	527
74	Plays: future prospects and past performance	533
75	Plays in Gaelic: on the page and on the stage	541
76	Plays, theatres and drama: a good night out	548
77	Lowlander and Gael: Stewart Conn and Aonghas MacNeacail	553
78	Three kinds of poet: Douglas Dunn, Tom Leonard and Liz Lochhead	557
79	Nothing in uniform: from Veronica Forrest-Thomson to Jackie Kay	562
80	Worlds of difference: from Tom Buchan to Kathleen Jamie	566

PART FIVE: DIVAGATIONS

1. Languages, literature, humanity and tragedy — 572
2. Big themes and new approaches — 578
3. Mongrel nation: freedom, history and geography — 583
4. Modernity and war: visions beyond violence — 588
5. Genres and forms: crime, science fiction, children's literature, song — 594
6. Scottish literature at play — 600
7. Psychology, flyting, philosophy and speculation — 607
8. Religion and sport — 612
9. Radio, film and TV — 617
10. New media — 622
11. Travel writing — 628
12. Diaspora — 633

PART SIX: A LOOSE CANON

1. The idea of a canon — 640
2. What a canon is — 644
3. What a canon is for — 649
4. A loose canon: significant authors and works of Scottish literature — 654

PART SEVEN: A GAZETEER OF SCOTTISH LITERATURE

Map — 676
101 places to visit — 677

Further reading — 709
A select bibliography of histories of Scottish literature — 711
Endnote — 715
Acknowledgements — 716
Index of author names — 717

This is where we begin

The painting on the front cover of this book depicts a mountainous landscape, sensually presented in vivid colours, with deep seawater and freshwater lochs, long straths of land forming bays and peninsulas around inlets: a natural and ancient world, but with a scattering of houses: a populated landscape, far from cities but occupied by the lives of people, their loves, concerns, and particular dispositions through generations. The painting is 'The Cuillins, Evening, April 1964' by John Cunningham (1926–98). The great Gaelic poet Somhairle MacGill-Eain or Sorley MacLean (1911–96) ends his poem 'The Cuillin' like this:

> Thar lochan fala clan nan daoine,
> thar breòiteachd blàir is strì an aonaich,
> thar bochdainn, caitheimh, fiabhrais, àmhgair,
> thar anacothruim, eucoir, ainneairt, ànraidh
> thar truaighe, eu-dòchais, gamhlais, cuilbheirt,
> thar ciont is truaillidheachd, gu furachair,
> gu treunmhor chithear an Cuilithionn
> 's e 'g èirigh air taobh eile duilghe.

Here are the lines in MacLean's English translation:

> Beyond the lochs of the blood of the children of men,
> beyond the frailty of plain and the labour of mountain,
> beyond poverty, consumption, fever, agony,
> beyond hardship, wrong, tyranny, distress,
> beyond misery, despair, hatred, treachery,
> beyond guilt and defilement: watchful
> heroic, the Cuillin is seen
> rising on the other side of sorrow.

The poem was written in 1939, at the beginning of the Second World War. MacLean saw the rise of Fascism in Europe and imagined the mountain range of his native place as a geological opposition to human brutality, a permanent symbol of hope. He was born on the island of Raasay, beside Skye, and grew up looking over towards these mountains, climbing them as a young man.

By the 20th century most of Scotland's population was living in cities – Glasgow, Edinburgh, Aberdeen, Dundee. So we might begin with a recognisable image of Scotland as a place of natural beauty and symbolic authority, but we must deepen our understanding with a sense of the historical complexity of

Scotland's national identity before we can begin to fully encounter the richness of Scottish literature. The geological physicality, the potent imagery, the experience over many generations of both country and city, the religious histories of Catholic and Protestant dominions, the political priorities of communal or profit-based economies, and most recently the doubleness of British imperial and independent Scottish identities, and above all the interpretations made possible by different, but overlapping languages, pre-eminently Gaelic, Scots and English – all these help form the particular kaleidoscope of singularity we call Scotland.

'Scotland' is a word that names a particular nation, defined by geographical borders. In the early 21st century, since the union of the crowns of Scotland and England in 1603 and the union of the parliaments of Edinburgh and London in 1707, this nation exists within the political state of the United Kingdom and Northern Ireland, with its global legacy of British imperialism. Scotland might be imagined in two different dimensions: as part of a political state with its imperial political legacy, and as a single nation of separate, multi-faceted cultural distinction, along with other nations in the world. As the American poet Charles Olson puts it in 'Letter 5' of *The Maximus Poems*:

> Limits
> are what any of us
> are inside of

For people who grow up and live within the borders of this nation, certain things may be conferred by languages, geology, terrain, climate and weather, architectural designs, current behavioural habits and a history of cultural production, that might be different from such things elsewhere. The languages in which most Scottish literature is written – Gaelic, Scots and English – confer their own rhythms, sounds, musical dynamics, and the relations between them create their own character in the priorities of expression in speech and writing.

Geography creates another range of characteristics. Growing up speaking in different languages and living in different parts of Scotland, generates different prospects and perspectives. In the Borders, you might look south to England; along the east coast, you might look across to other northern European nations. Things look different again in the archipelagos of the north, Orkney and Shetland, and of the west, the Inner and Outer Hebrides; and different again along the west coast of mainland Scotland, or in the north in Caithness and Sutherland, or in the central fertile farmlands of Perthshire and Kinross, or in the central belt where most people in the country now live, the industrialised, now post-industrial, Glasgow, and Scotland's capital (or 'capital-in-waiting'), Edinburgh. All these locations suggest the diversity of perspectives Scotland – and Scottish literature – presents. Each one creates different ways of seeing. And such ways of seeing are not only a birth-right. They may also be learned. But as Hugh MacDiarmid points out:

> It requires great love of it deeply to read
> The configuration of a land...

Where did this nation begin?

Over half a millennium, from before Columba's time in the 6th century, through Kenneth MacAlpin in the 9th century and Malcolm Canmore in the 11th century, different groups of people of different languages and cultural preferences got to know more about each other and began to live together in a comity of identity. Before them, there was birdsong. Before that, there was the ice.

Identity is a function of position, and position is a function of power.

This is where we begin.

Preface

THIS BOOK IS mainly concerned with retrieving and renewing, history brought into the present, the dead returned to the living. But above all it is a personal introduction. Its investment has been quite a lot of my life. It rests on a formidable quantity of scholarship, but it's written with immediate attention to primary texts, and with relatively little reference to secondary critical material. Scottish literature has over long eras been neglected or deliberately obscured, so securing its place in the firmament is a kind of redress, a reclamation. To paraphrase a fictional character of diabolical intent, 'Revenge is sweet, mine extends over centuries, and time is on my side.' And all poets, as we know, are of the devil's party.

In this overview of major periods, themes, authors and works of Scottish literature, I have chosen to emphasise certain authors, works, avenues of approach and aspects of consideration, which seem to me at this point in history to warrant emphasis. I hope the overarching story is accurate enough to the enormous and varied terrain, and I hope that what I say here works in the recognition that the terrain itself is always shifting, never entirely fixed, always open, never completely closed.

Some people, over many generations, have denied the validity of Scottish literature as a worthwhile area of study and attempted to tell the story of literature across the centuries as if there were only one central story to be told. For a long time, Scottish literature has been a neglected subject in our educational institutions. But as the great Scottish artist William Johnstone says in his book *Creative Art in Britain* (1950): 'It is idle to blame teachers. My criticism of educational methods is aimed at certain consequences of the prevalent attitude to experience.' And as Ezra Pound puts it in his *ABC of Reading* (1934): 'the value of old work is constantly affected by the value of the new'. There is always a need to reassess work which the current 'attitude to experience' – especially as represented in most media every day – is urging us to neglect.

I have not written exclusively for professional scholars and critics but for people who enjoy reading, looking at paintings and sculptures, listening to music, and learning about things. I have included reference details in the body of the book, giving only date of publication for works that are easily identified, and place, publisher and further information as well as dates for specific works whose details are less accessible. Dates for the lives of authors are given where they first appear or where their works are discussed extensively. I have not used notes in the hope that the book might be read fluently, and such information as may be needed is provided in the main text. I think it was A.R. Orage who advised writers for his periodical, *The New Age*, to read their work out loud before submitting it. If it doesn't work read aloud, it shouldn't be printed. Good advice.

Marshall Walker, in his book *Scottish Literature since 1707* (1996), confessed a 'partiality for a view of literary works as incontrovertibly human products' created 'by real people with visions to impart according to more or less ascertainable aesthetic devices. Such works come from authors, not merely from other texts, but all texts are related in some way to a *Zeitgeist*.' I agree with him.

Angus Calder, in his book *Russia Discovered* (1976), wrote of the authors of that country words that apply just as well to those of Scotland: 'These great writers have so much to teach us about the use of time, the search for the full potential of every second, and the obligatory rage against whatever denies that to us. And no other reading, surely, is less a waste of time.'

My book is primarily concerned with such writers and makers of literature whose quality Calder describes but it is also 'a view of literary works' as Walker puts it, and therefore one among many acts increasing the possibility and extent of awareness of Scotland's culture. A.P. Cohen, in an essay which ultimately addresses the relation between human awareness and ecology, 'Oil and the Cultural Account: Reflections on a Shetland Community', *Scottish Journal of Sociology*, 3 (1978), notes as follows: 'Once one has become conscious of culture, it must be perceived and handled in a different way than previously.'

Here's hoping.

Alan Riach, Alloway
April 2022

PART ONE

Three Questions

I

Why read Scottish literature?

THE ARTS ARE maps. They show us the terrain of life, contours, cliffs and coasts, they chart our deepest oceans and their rivers run like arteries across arid plains. But maps also tell us that human landscapes are always changing, and they require a special understanding, a training in how best they might be read. In answer to a question about the nature of art, the American novelist and poet Robert Penn Warren once said to a friend of mine, 'Ah believe it's just gettin' yore reality shaped a little better.' We have to learn how to make reality shapely.

The work of all the arts is to represent and interpret the world.

Represent and *interpret*.

Representation might suggest approval or even celebration, and interpretation might imply criticism or even satire. Art resists the numbing of the senses. It helps us to live more fully, engaged with the world and critical of it.

The function of all the arts, and especially of literature, is, at the same time, both representation and critique. Mimesis – the representation of reality in art – might give us a recognisable scene. But to articulate that scene in an aesthetic form is also to imply a selection and arrangement of material. And this involves a distancing from lived reality. The painting has its frame and space from the viewer, the pages of print have their book or magazine covers, the page is held at a distance from the understanding of the reader. The reader works to go through it and takes pleasure in that work. Music performed to be listened to addresses the listener in a different way from that performed to be danced to. For any writer or artist, the given world is never to be merely accepted and used, but celebrated and criticised, built upon or demolished. In this lies the fundamental manifesto of all writers and artists.

All art slows you down and quickens you at the same time. You have to take the time to stop and look and see, and listen, and hear, and read, what the world is, if you're going to change it for the better.

But in an age of crass commercialism, the arts are disadvantaged, partly because the training that is needed to help us comprehend them is so vulnerable. The vanity of rampant managers and the strafing heartlessness of advertising clog up the channels of contemplation. In 'Criticism, Art, Letters', collected in *The Best of Myles* (1968), Flann O'Brien is only mildly exaggerating a popular philistinism when he declares:

> There is no excuse for poetry. Poetry gives no adequate return in money, is expensive to print by reason of the waste of space occasioned by

its form, and most of it is bad. Nobody is going to manufacture a thousand tons of jam in the expectation that five tons may be eatable.

He has a point, hasn't he? You can imagine certain ministers of education coming out with this sort of thing without a trace of irony and getting knighthoods for the damage they do to generations.

The arts look after themselves. The creative force that produces them is so essential, so profoundly necessary, that they are as inevitable in human life as the desire for shelter, food and procreation. And sometimes, even when you're not looking for it, the necessary thing will find you. A long time ago I came across an audio cassette in a drawer in a desk in an office I was using in a university I was visiting, and on it, hand-written, was the name of the American poet William Carlos Williams, and when I played the recording, I heard his voice on the tape say this:

...because the purpose of the artist, whatever it is, is to take the life which he sees, and raise it, raise it up, to an elevated position where it has dignity, just the same as a Navajo Indian puts a mark around a clay water pitcher and makes it distinguished, so the artist's purpose in life, what he's for, why he's been preserved for the ages as he has been, the most, the imperishable thing, the one imperishable thing, that the world never lets die, is the work of art. Cities are wiped out, civilisation is wiped out, Homer persists. England will disappear. Shakespeare will be there. It's that. The race cherishes that, cherishes the work of the artist. He's the most important creature in any generation.

The arts – all the arts – are as inseparable from being human as the dance is from the dancer, as W.B. Yeats says in his poem 'Among School Children'. But as the American critic Guy Davenport points out in his essay, 'Do You Have a Poem Book on E.E. Cummings?', in *The Geography of the Imagination: Forty Essays* (1981), if the purpose of journalism is to inform and disseminate, it isn't doing its job: 'Thirty years of liberal twiddling with the lines of communication have made it almost impossible to broadcast anything but received propaganda.' And so, 'what's happening in the minds that keep other minds alive and give them the courage to live is reported, if at all, in a dangerously denatured and official trickle of news.' When the arts are neglected or obscured, people suffer from ignorance and their lives are made dull.

The purpose of the arts is to help people to live. Yet new technologies change how things may be perceived and understood. They change the context in which we read anything. In the 1960s, Marshall McLuhan saw the way things were going and argued in his book *The Gutenburg Galaxy* (1962) that the print-based, book-reading culture that had characterised the western world since the 15th century was changing forever. At the start of the 17th century, at the time of the union of the crowns of Scotland and England in 1603, there were around 2,000 books in print. In the early 21st century, there are at least 15 million books available online. The problem we face with the digital archive is not the availability of material but how to select from it profitably, critically, happily: how to find what we need to spend our time on.

So much for generalisations. I would like to close in now on Scottish literature with some personal data that I hope will be relevant.

My parents encouraged my reading when I was a boy, and my grandfather especially encouraged me. I have a particular memory of my grandfather's gigantic bookcase and what appeared to be hundreds of books, encyclopaedias, guides to world literature, titles like *Races of the World*, *Everyman's Encyclopaedia*, the collected works of Shakespeare, Scott, Burns, Keats, Shelley and Byron. It was so big you could literally almost climb inside it when I was a wee boy. When I was about ten, my father gave me a copy of *Huckleberry Finn* and the notion of floating downriver on a raft still pleases me; then he gave me a copy of *Moby-Dick* and I still remember the shock I felt when I read the final chapter, when Ahab goes over the side. It took my breath away.

Great writing has this power. It helps you through all your life, one way or another. All the arts do this, I think, but literature is the greatest of them all because it gives you such a range and depth of experience of lives, languages, places, politics, and histories, other than your own.

Literature is the most liberating of all the things human minds have ever created.

The journalist Ryszard Kapuściński in his book *The Other* (2008) eloquently describes how every person is twofold: one is a human being like the rest of us, with joys and sorrows, good days and bad, desires and disappointments, the other is a carrier of culture, beliefs, language-systems, particular forms of expression, aspects of identity that differ in place and time. Both these aspects of every single person are always changing, dynamic, mobile, partial, variable. Yet this relation between what human beings have in common and what gives every one of us relations through nationality, history, tribe, family, religion, class and so on, is what gives us our potential. If we fully acknowledge what we have in common, we have secure ground for exploring and enhancing all those things that make us different. Understanding this fact and exploring its full complexity is above all the provenance of literature.

And literature arises from two basic human forms of expression: stories and songs. All else comes from these.

But literalism is always a danger. I remember a particularly egregious member of staff at a university English department meeting who suggested in all seriousness that *Heart of Darkness* should be taken off the curriculum because Mister Kurtz was not a very good role model for the students.

The proper reply was given, quick, merciful and ruthless: 'Neither is Lady Macbeth!'

Of course the Macbeths are not role models: they are the embodiments of our human potential *at its worst*. The arts propose not literal but metaphoric truths. In his autobiography, *Theme and Variations* translated by James A. Galston, (1947), the conductor Bruno Walter defines this:

> History! Can we learn a people's character through its history, a history formerly made by princes and statesmen with an utter disregard of, frequently even in opposition to, its interests? Is not its nature disclosed rather by its poetry, by its general habits of life, by its landscape, and by its idiom? Are we not able more deeply to penetrate into a nation's soul through its music, provided that it has actually grown on its soil? Is anyone entitled to speak with authority of the Russians who has not become familiar with Pushkin, Lermontov, Gogol, Dostoyevsky, Tolstoy, and Gorky, and has not listened to the music of Mussorgsky, Borodin, and Tchaikovsky? I have preserved the unshakable conviction that man's spiritual accomplishments are vastly more important than his political and historical achievements. For the works of the creative spirit last, they are essentially imperishable, while the world-stirring historical activities of even the most eminent men are circumscribed by time. Napoleon is dead – but Beethoven lives.

Or, to paraphrase, Henry Dundas (1742–1811) – the immensely powerful Scottish Tory politician who was known as King Harry the Ninth or the 'Great Tyrant' – is decidedly dead, but in a different sense, his contemporary Robert Burns, in his poems and songs, lives on. Or Joseph Stalin (1878–1953) – the tyrannical Communist Party leader after the death of Lenin in 1924 – is dead, but his contemporary the Scottish poet Hugh MacDiarmid, in his works, lives on.

The foregoing is preliminary to the more specific answer to the question, 'Why read Scottish literature?' So let's come to that now.

I was born in Scotland. I left when I was four and went to school and university in England, then returned to live in Scotland from 1979 to 1986, completing a PhD at Glasgow University. I went to New Zealand in 1986. New Zealand was absolutely central in world politics to my view at that time. The country was nuclear-free and the Greenpeace ship the *Rainbow Warrior* had just been blown up by French spies, with murderous loss of life. Teaching across the range at the university where I worked, the University of Waikato (it is the Maori name for the area and the river that runs through it), I was able to initiate courses in Scottish, Irish and 'Postcolonial' literatures and Creative Writing and to teach courses on English and American literatures and convene the big first-year 'Introduction to Literature' courses. I was thinking about how best to introduce what really mattered to me to students who might have no prior knowledge about these things to draw from.

I was asking myself, 'What are the important things about Scottish literature you have to know about, to get a sense of the shape of the terrain, the character of the country, its national history, its music, languages, the major writers?' And a number of key moments were clearly of massive importance in providing crucial aspects of the country's myths and its actual history. There is the prehistory of Scotland, stories and songs from the Celtic and early Christian worlds, there were the Wars of Independence, then there was the Reformation, the Union of the Crowns in 1603 and of the Parliaments in 1707, the Enlightenment, Romanticism, the Industrial Revolution, world wars and revolutions, the rise of mass media: how should we approach literature in these contexts? Literature has its own special value but also, of course, it is connected and inter-related to other arts and across historical eras.

The historical depth of Scotland goes back to long before the word Scotland was used. Starting from any contemporary position, what would be the predominantly governing factors in appreciating an identity we could legitimately call 'Scotland'? And would these factors apply equally well in other countries? What would they be if they were applicable anywhere? Could they yield descriptions of identity specific to particular countries?

I'd like to suggest two: geography and language. By which of course I mean in their pluralities: geographies and languages.

First, how should we begin to acquire a comprehensive understanding of the geographical variety of Scotland?

One example was set by the great American poet Walt Whitman in the 19th century. The essential principle is to start from wherever you are. Whitman begins one poem, 'Starting from fish-shape Paumanok, where I was born...' You begin by looking out the window, walking out the door. Whatever is immediately around you is where you begin from. Think of James Joyce and *Dubliners*, William Faulkner and Yoknapatawpha County, Lewis Grassic Gibbon and the Mearns of Kincardineshire in the north-east of Scotland. And it does not imply sentimental attachment, blind, flag-waving loyalty or any lack of irony. Consider Edward Dorn's brilliant little poem, 'Success?':

> Success? I never had to worry about success.
> Coming from where I come from,
> You were a success the minute you left town.

The Borders are a long way from Shetland, the Hebrides are a long way from Edinburgh, but all the different places of Scotland deliver a sense of complementarity, of plurality, of the relativity of cultural value, which is not the same thing as the sense of a single trajectory, a unified imperial history. This sense of diversity is matched by a sense of profundity, the depths from which our culture arises, the insights it can give us today.

And how should we think of the languages of Scottish literature?

The 18th century saw a flourishing of poetry and song in Gaelic, sometimes drawing from the same sources as James Macpherson, whose poems and stories of Finn and Ossian rise from pre-Christian myths, but they also deal directly with contemporary events, from the Jacobite rising of 1745 to the consequences visited upon the Highlanders after Culloden in 1746, and the Clearances, the enforced depopulation of Scotland, which has continued to this day. Two major poems not directly related to these events but still with astonishing immediacy and vibrant attraction are 'Praise of Ben Dorain' by Donnchadh Bàn Mac an t-Saoir / Duncan Ban MacIntyre (1724–1812), which describes a deer hunt across a wooded mountain, and 'The Birlinn of Clanranald' by Alasdair mac Mhaighstir Alasdair / Alexander MacDonald (c.1695–c.1770), which describes a sailing ship or birlinn, crossing through a storm on a journey from Scotland to Ireland. Both these major works draw on the Gaelic tradition common to both Scotland and Ireland, but there are also influences and affinities with English-language poems such as James Thomson's *The Seasons* (1730) and the Scots-language poems and songs of Robert Burns and others. The name of Robert Burns should never be mentioned without also acknowledging the greatness of his contemporaries writing in Gaelic, and his great predecessors in the Scots language, Allan Ramsay and Robert Fergusson, and the English-language dominated writings of the Enlightenment, which preceded and continued through his lifetime.

Therefore, with a living sense of the diversity of terrain in the geography of Scotland, the Borders, the Highlands and Islands, the cities, the farmlands, the mountains and moors, the rivers and lochs and lochans; and with an acknowledgement of the vitality of living languages – pre-eminently in both our history and currently, Gaelic, Scots and English, but also in the acknowledgement of languages that have arrived and are in use more recently, we can imagine a set of co-ordinate points or magnetic poles or centres of gravity of one kind or another by which it may be possible to navigate our way through the whole theatre of Scottish literature. It's an impossible voyage, of course. And since literature is one among many arts, each one interrelated, we should begin with the knowledge that the cradle of our understanding holds more potential than could ever be fulfilled.

And yet, isn't that all the more reason to set it gently rocking, not just into sleep but towards a further awakening?

When I worked in New Zealand, we had a visit from the President of Ireland, Mary Robinson. The line she delivered then has haunted me ever since: 'The arts are the genius of your country, and education is the key with which you unlock the door.'

Let's open the door.

2

What is literature?

LANGUAGE, STORIES AND music are the basic components of literature, from the simplest memorised nursery rhyme to the most subtle and sophisticated of written texts. The most complex modern novels still arise from our sense of what makes a good story – bewilderment, discovery, finding out about things, where you are, where love can be found, what forces are working against it. The study of literature is based on the development of sensitivity to language and enhances the enjoyment of stories about people in different places, relationships, situations of difficulty or pleasure. The visual patterns of writing to be seen on a page or parchment and the sounds of speech in the air as they are uttered in voices suggest the two different but overlapping areas of sensual apprehension involved in the appreciation of literature: the visual and the aural. These are portals to reality. The advantage of literature over some other arts or popular media is the detail with which it sensitises such appreciation and the depth of engagement it invites with the difficult areas of human experience. It doesn't solve problems, but it can help understanding.

The question, 'What is literature?' might be answered in a multitude of ways, none of them final or absolute. They would be suggestions, propositions, ideas that might be discussed. Here are seven.

LITERATURE IS A WORD SIGNIFYING ONE MAJOR ACTIVITY OF THE CREATIVE ARTS

Essential to its creation are language and stories. Stories can be told in various media, with or without words, but literature usually tells stories through words. (Sometimes it can be through only letters, or sounds.)

Words can be broken down and reassembled in their constituent parts, in letters (aesthetically precise visual signs, thus connected to drawing and painting) and sound (thus connected to music). Grammar normally implies narrative, as understanding moves along the line of the sentence. However, sentences might be held in the mind simultaneously and rhyme, metre, patterns of various kinds, can imply a kind of simultaneity in the musical coherence of a work of literature. The English poet Edmund Spenser (1552–99) imagined that his long poem *The Faerie Queen* (1590–96) might be held in the mind in its entirety and visualised like an enormous stained glass window in a cathedral, constructed, not in the assertive image of the poet, but rather for the glory of God. He hoped that what you might see through this vast, wondrous window, would not be him, but God.

In English, the word music is connected to the Greek Muses, quasi-divine figures who gave inspiration of one kind or another. In Scots Gaelic, however, the word for music is *ceol* and it has nothing to do with the Greek Muses. This word refers to the musical sounds made in piping, originally through bird-bone flutes (bird-bones being hollow). You can hear this when you pronounce it. In literature, poetry and music (*ceol*) are always connected (except in some examples of experimentalist poetry which deliberately try to reject the component of human tonality in utterance. Some reject the human voice and use computerised sound and non-standard grammatical effects of language. Generally, though, the infusion of music in poetry is clear: in songs and ballads, opera libretti, even in the rhythms and musical movement of verse that has no immediate instrumental accompaniment, and in the longer narrative rhythms of stories and novels, the musical component is always present. The American poet Ezra Pound tells us that poetry withers and dries out the further it is removed from music. This might be self-evident in the essential vocal function in the oral tradition, as well as in plays and theatres, whether performed to the most vulgar public, to the hypersophisticated sensibilities of a courtly audience, or to the rhetorical superclasses of the Kirk (of whatever disposition) but it is also present in the musical structures, rhythms and shapeliness you can feel in short stories and novels.

LITERATURE IS WRITTEN ART IN THREE PRINCIPAL GENRES: POETRY, FICTION, PLAYS

But other forms of writing may be read effectively as literature – the Bible or the Koran, philosophy, letters, diaries, journalism – all writing may be read and considered carefully by a trained literary sensibility, though that doesn't mean that all writing is literature. Moreover, a literary sensibility brings good critical reading to work in other media precisely because we can train ourselves to appreciate storytelling and the languages of representation sensitively.

The various products of cinema, radio, television and comic books may all be read best by people not only specialised in their own discipline but also familiar with what literature can teach. This is also true of painting, sculpture and music in all its forms. In so far as a literary training shows you clearly how language works, it's also very good help in seeing how professional politicians, advertisers and journalists manipulate language in their speeches, articles, adverts, reports and manifestos. The modern western world is saturated with the images, languages and sounds of commercialism. All advertising is heartless. It is trying to get something from you. Unlike advertising, literature is about touching. It is there to give you something.

To the degree that literature is the work of the creative imagination, its priority or emphasis of purpose is distinct from philosophy. But the writers of the Scottish Enlightenment – pre-eminently David Hume, James Hutton, Adam Ferguson and Adam Smith – are also masters of literary essay-writing and we should accommodate them within the remit of Scottish literature. Similarly, other forms of writing should be taken into account: essays, diaries, travel writing, 'life-writing' or autobiography, and so on. For example, William Lithgow (1582–1645) is one of the very first international world-travellers in his time, going from his native Lanarkshire as far afield as Africa and Constantinople, now Istanbul. A poet and prose writer fired by curiosity and the desire to wander through the world and see as many aspects of it as he could, he is a singular figure in our literary history.

In contemporary terms, there are other contexts for literary production than that of the published book. Scottish literature includes radio drama, television drama, film texts and inter-disciplinary works which bring together literary and other artistic forms. There is a long tradition of song in Scottish literature; not only of traditional ballads and folk songs but of more self-consciously artful song-settings of Scottish poems (the work of Burns and George Thomson, and of MacDiarmid and F.G. Scott, for instance). Further, the classical tradition of orchestral and chamber music has many examples of work inspired by or in dialogue with literary texts, such as Hamish MacCunn's opera *Jeanie Deans*, based on Walter Scott's novel *The Heart of Midlothian* or William Sweeney's tone-poem based on Lewis Grassic Gibbon's *Sunset Song*. If our primary concern is with poems, plays and prose fiction, we should keep ourselves receptive to all these other forms of literary writing too.

LITERATURE IS WORDS ARRANGED TO MAXIMUM EFFECTIVENESS AS ART

This prompts the question: What is art for?

I have given my answer already. The arts are there to help people to live. The arts are not leisure activities. They are essential. They are the best maps we have of human experience. Our poets and artists are our best guides to the worlds around us. In an era of distraction, the best of them address the things that matter. Technologies change and sciences progress. Discoveries are made, new things are found or formed. But the work of the artist is always *current*. As William Carlos Williams says in his poem, 'Asphodel, that Greeny Flower' (the lines in the original are italicised):

> *It is difficult*
> *to get the news from poems*
> *yet men die miserably every day*

> *for lack
> of what is found there.*

In his novel *Lanark*, Alasdair Gray writes that Glasgow is 'the sort of industrial city where most people live nowadays but nobody imagines living.' This is what literature, and indeed all the arts, help us to do: to imagine how our lives might be, how they might be better, deepened, more beautifully curved or patterned, shaped, adventurous, enriched, enjoyed, made gamesome and quickened.

LITERATURE IS A CO-ORDINATION OF THREE INTERSECTING ENERGIES, FOUND IN PERSONALITY, HISTORY AND SUBSTANCE

By *personality* I mean the writer, who he or she is, individually, linguistically, socially, their mind, disposition, determination, character.

By *history* I mean the times they live through, actually – a war poet speaks of war, a sea poet goes to sea – or imaginatively: the artist can imagine anything, often more accurately than one whose experience of the same thing is lived and actual. But experience is real and valuable: Ezra Pound once said that Gavin Douglas's translation of Virgil's *Aeneid* was better than the original because Douglas had heard the sound of the sea. The creative imagination has its own history, and some eras offer imaginative insights others might foreclose. It was the inception of the Jacobean era in 1603 that allowed Shakespeare the possibility of writing his greatest tragedies.

By *substance* I mean the words themselves. They have gravity, weight, energy, history, component parts like syllables, vowels, consonants, letters, connectedness, music and visual import. Words are the actual material of the writer's art.

LITERATURE IS A FORM OF COMMUNICATION, A NEGOTIATION THAT TELLS TRUTHS

Literature works between history and myth (or philosophy, including religions). It is not tied to documentary evidence about how people lived (the limitations of history), nor to the structures of systems of belief that seem to validate themselves as ideology (the limitations of myth). The Canadian critic Northrop Frye in his book *Fables of Identity* (1963), tried to argue and insist that all literature is grounded in such mythic structures. He was wrong.

History is a process of engagement with verifiable data and our interpretation of it. Myth arises from commitments of belief. More than in either, literature is always a negotiation of meaning, its language is always active. It can never be merely recording. It can never be merely formulaic. It is alive.

Negotiating, interrogating, finding balance is what literature does. It activates argument in the endlessly moving spaces *between* history (data, fact, scientifically verifiable information, documentary objectivity, interpretation validated by what can be proven) and myth (or religion, or ideology, or any belief systems, questioned or unquestioned, validated ultimately only by faith). Literature comes to life between these two areas. And by doing so, it brings things, engaging thoughts, curious questions, to life *unpredictably*. Literature is human existence come to life. It is therefore open, never closed. It is an act, as well as a product of aesthetic sensibility. It is an action, as well as an enactment of formal pleasure. It is an intervention.

The various languages in which Scottish literature has been composed are a major distinctive quality of the subject. Unlike English literature, Scottish literature immediately demands the recognition of the value and validity of different tongues. An important ecclesiastical tradition of writing in Latin includes poems attributed to St Columba (c.520–597) and the *Life of Columba* by Adomnán (c.624–704) through to the writing of George Buchanan (1506–82) and Arthur Johnstone (c.1579–1641).

The Gaelic tradition includes poems directly engaged with aspects of Scottish Highland history such as the Jacobite risings and the Clearances, and in the poem 'Praise of Ben Dorain' there is a distinct understanding of landscape, nature and human presence which is sharply different from contemporary English Romantic ideas of the sublime.

Since at least the 18th-century Enlightenment, Scottish literature has been written extensively in English. Enlightenment philosophers tried to remove the most distinctive Scots aspects of their diction from their writing and in the 19th century a gulf opened up between the authority of English as a language for narrative or storytelling in novels and the vernacular Scots spoken by characters acting in the story – often eccentric, comic or exaggerated characters. However, by the late 20th century, the use of the English language by Scottish writers had developed in distinctively Scots tones. In the poetry of Norman MacCaig, for example, the English is as close to the modulations of the speech of a Scottish voice as in any major English-language Scottish poet of the period.

The Scots vernacular tradition is one of the richest literary resources and most distinctive linguistic forms, both accessible to English-language readers and characteristically distinct from English-language literature. The Scots language in Scottish literature opens a door to one of the great linguistic mediums of European writing. Both Scots and English have common roots but they developed through different local, national and imperial histories and through different literary traditions. Scots is as ancient a language as English and has at least as many spoken varieties across the country. It would be as absurd to call Scots a dialect of English as it would be to call English a dialect of Scots. And since the range of languages spoken and written in Scotland continues to extend beyond those pre-eminently used over past centuries of literary production, it's worth emphasising the validity of any language as a potential medium of Scottish literature.

A sensitivity to the fact that Scottish literature has been written in a number of languages establishes the sense that aesthetic and literary understanding is never absolutely singular. It is always engaged in dialogue. In this multi-vocal world, there can be no simple assertion of superior value in any single language, setting out to dominate all others with imperial certainty. There is always more than one way of seeing, more than one way of representing something, more than one way of interpreting it. In any language, communication may be direct, but there is always more than one story to be told. Each language does it differently and reveals different parts of the world. Every single one is only partial. But in a work of literature, it becomes communicable.

LITERATURE IS THE WRITTEN EXPRESSION OF REVOLT AGAINST ALL ACCEPTED THINGS

It is a form of resistance. The act, the expression, of literature, is to resist the vanity of all efforts to bind and contain imaginative life. It is to resist the mechanical excess of systematic meaning. It is to teach that intelligence and sensitivity reside with an irreducible openness, never with the closed.

LITERATURE IS A LONG CONVERSATION, USUALLY WITH THE DEAD; BUT IT IS A LIVING DIALOGUE

It is what happens between the work of art and the reader, just as the creation of the work of art by the artist is the moment of its formation. The pen on the page, the brush on the canvas, all the complex processes between the score of a piece of music and the bow coming down on the catgut, the ears listening to what sounds fill the air at that moment of its beginning. An Australian aboriginal blows pigment from his mouth onto his hand on a rock in the desert and the shape of the hand stays there, surrounded by colour: this is the moment of creation another will read, noting if the tip of a forefinger up to a certain joint is missing, what that might mean, what group that man might belong to. Aesthetics are a social code.

Or put it like this. Literature is a community – it could be a community of people who read books or who respond as they do at a certain time – but it's not the book that is literature, or the people, it's what happens *between* the book and the people, or even a single poem and a single solitary person reading it, that forms a community, a literature, an engagement with each other and possible readings, other readers who might also be imagined. That's also what literature is: a reason to read, to carry on reading and enjoying the pleasure of that. This involves both play and seriousness, both close, inquisitive reading and liberating opposition to conventions and complacencies. It can help us to imagine and create a better world.

3

Was there ever a 'British' literature?

THIS BOOK IS concerned mainly with Scottish literature, but as we have seen, that national identity has been formed, been independent, been part of a British state and imperial expansion in different parts of the world, and continues to reinvent and reconstitute itself.

Reading Scottish literature takes you back before the British state or the United Kingdom, and it indicates ways forward beyond that.

In many other parts of the world, a convenient way of approaching the literatures of the different nations of the United Kingdom is to describe them as constituting a 'British Literature' – although this is no guarantee of homogeneity. More often, the word 'British' simply means 'English'. What does our reading of Scottish literature contribute to an answer to the question, 'Was there ever a "British" literature?' In his poem, 'The Difference' Hugh MacDiarmid was characteristically forthright:

> I am a Scotsman and proud of it.
> Never call me British. I'll tell you why.
> It's too near brutish, having only
> The difference between U and I.
> Scant difference, you think? Yet
>   Hell-deep and Heavenhigh!

T.S. Eliot, in a famous review in the periodical *Athenaeum* of 1919, asked 'Was there a Scottish Literature?' and concluded that there had been once but there was no longer. This was part of a strategic politico-literary move to oust Matthew Arnold from his central place as arbiter of taste in English letters and instate Eliot himself as critic-magus. His individual talent would realign 'Tradition' and coalesce American and English literature in English-language writing. Scottish literature had been a valid contributor along the way but had no contemporary currency, according to Eliot. For him, Burns was the last example of a decadent tradition.

Eliot, more English than the English, came from Missouri to High Anglican London. He followed a different path from Ezra Pound, who also abandoned America for London, but then abandoned London for European high culture and abandoned the botched civilisations of the west for the Classics of ancient China. In retrospect, Pound's ever-expanding intellectual career looks more like one of cultural inclusiveness and accommodation, rather than anything narrowing, even if the last *Cantos* are desperately moving in their lyrical self-portrait of loneliness and exhaustion. But compare Eliot and William Carlos Williams. In his autobiography, Williams said that Eliot's betrothal to Anglocentric letters and academic élitism in *The Waste Land* stopped him in his tracks, set him back 20 years, as it seemed to be opposed to the 'primary impetus, the elementary principle of all art, in the local conditions.' Eliot's poem was 'the great catastrophe' – not too strong a term for Williams, a poet who had to rediscover and redescribe 'the American grain' – a distinctive tradition in American literature, a vernacular voice local to that place, 'rooted in the locality which should give it fruit.' When Eliot disparaged the contemporary viability of Scottish literature, he was only echoing what had been said a hundred years before him about American literature itself: Was there any? Robert Creeley told me that the poet George Barker once asked Williams the same question. Williams in America, like Hugh MacDiarmid in Scotland, was trying to make a poetry that would be nourished by its own geography, its own history. Eliot, supreme craftsman and pervasive influence, seemed intent to abandon that commitment and priority.

In this light, consider the violent argument between Edwin Muir and Hugh MacDiarmid in 1936. Lewis Grassic Gibbon and MacDiarmid were commissioning editors of a series of books about contentious issues in Scotland and Edwin Muir was invited to write about Walter Scott and Scotland but he turned in a book which effectively attacked the achievement of writers who had written in the Scots language. What he said was that the great Irish writers – pre-eminently Joyce and Yeats – had won international acclaim and achieved great literary worth through writing in English and this was the way forward for Scottish writers too. More than that. He said it was the *only* way forward for Scottish writers. He wrote: 'Scotland can only create a national literature by writing in English.'

Muir asserted that the chief requirement for a national literature was a homogeneous national language and that Scots was no use for that. Only English would do. In this Muir was merely echoing Eliot, who in the 1919 *Athenaeum* essay had written: 'The basis for one literature is one language.' By which, he meant his own brand of the English language. There was no place for Scots in this dispensation. When Muir declared that Scottish literature could only go forward in English, MacDiarmid was enraged. MacDiarmid's whole point was that there are different languages in Scotland, different voices – not only English but also Gaelic as well as Scots, voices of women as well as of men, and they all needed to find articulation in literature. He responded to Muir by editing *The Golden Treasury of Scottish Poetry* (1940), which includes poems translated not only from Gaelic but also from Latin, as well as poems in Scots and English – and nothing by Muir.

But Muir had a point too. The Irish writers *do* have an international cachet – a readership, especially in English and American universities – which is usually denied the Scots writers. And this is at least partly because the language allows them to be accommodated more quickly.

But is that a good enough answer?

'All dreams of imperialism must be exorcised,' MacDiarmid wrote once. '... Including linguistic imperialism, which sums up all the rest.'

The long hand of the law continues to finger your collar.

In Michael Alexander's *A History of English Literature* (2000), we read: 'Now that English is a world language, this history needs to be supplemented by accounts of other literatures in English...' So far, so open-minded. However (next paragraph), 'This volume is not a survey of present-day writing in English, but a history of English literature.' The national identity has very quickly become coterminous with the national language. Next sentence: 'The author, an Englishman resident in Scotland for over 30 years, is aware that a well-meant English embrace can seem imperial even within a devolving Britain.'

Good intentions are not enough. The consequences of this approach lead to Robert Louis Stevenson being listed in the book under 'Minor fiction': we are told that he was 'once famous' but 'his work faded'. *Dr Jekyll and Mr Hyde* 'makes a bonny film' says Professor Alexander, but 'has dated' and 'disappoints adult re-reading'. The word 'bonny' there is perhaps intended as affectionate but it carries a strong whiff of condescension delivered from a superior height of judgement. It may be well-meaning but it feels imperious. Alexander does not concur with the opinion of the great novelist Henry James: *Jekyll and Hyde*, said James, is 'the most serious' tale, 'endlessly interesting, and rich in all sorts of provocation, and Mr Stevenson is to be congratulated on having touched the core of it.' And how does Hugh MacDiarmid fare in this *History of English Literature*? Professor Alexander tells us that MacDiarmid 'would not want house-room in a Sassenach literary history' – and ostensibly honouring MacDiarmid's putative wishes, Professor Alexander gives him none. Readers are introduced to Seamus Heaney and Derek Walcott but are told next to nothing about MacDiarmid.

Incidentally, the American scholar Nancy Gish has an excellent essay on Stevenson in the online *International Journal of Scottish Literature* (no.2), which rightly sees *Jekyll and Hyde* as prophetic of Modernism and 20th-century concerns as much as Conrad's *Heart of Darkness* and Wilde's *Dorian Grey*. But Alexander's relegation of the Scots takes its part in a long tradition that goes back at least as far as Samuel Johnson responding to James Boswell's suggestion that he could teach the good Doctor the Scots language so that he could enjoy Allan Ramsay's play *The Gentle Shepherd*. Johnson said no: 'I won't learn it. You shall retain your superiority by my not knowing it.' This was a tactic of reversal. Promising Boswell 'superiority' meant that Johnson maintained his own. Instead of learning Scots (or trying to learn anything about the tradition of written Gaelic), Johnson authorised English and the Enlightenment followed his example and our education system followed theirs. Boswell, meanwhile, compiled his own Scots language dictionary, but this was not published and the manuscript was only discovered in 2011. The authority of English, in writing and speech, oppressed that of Scots for centuries. English was legitimate and valid; Scots was illegitimate and invalid. As a language, Scots appeared for the first time on a national census in 2011. It is officially recognised as a European minority language and the first formal educational courses on the language were offered by the Open University in 2019.

Michael Alexander's selection of authors therefore is one of privilege not based on literary merit but political provenance.

One more example. In Neil Corcoran's *English Poetry since 1940* (1993), we meet W.S. Graham and Douglas Dunn alongside numerous familiar suspects from Ireland, and the tutelary spirits are Louis MacNeice and – guess who? – Edwin Muir. But again, scarcely a mention of MacDiarmid.

It's not that Alexander and Corcoran are bad critics but that the political context of these books and many others, and the ideology that sustains the publishing and education industries that help produce them, are not innocent.

The whole matter of curriculum development is normally a vexed history of vested interests, warring clans and factions, protected properties and proprieties, and personal animosities. James Joyce was excluded from the English literature curriculum until such time as it might accommodate him. Now his work has generated a massive academic industry. A further accommodation might be noted in the shift from the distinctive category 'Anglo-Irish Literature' (as described by A. Norman Jeffares in the 1970s and defined in his 1982 book of that title as 'written in English by Irish authors') to an inclusive category called 'Irish Literature' that brought consideration of Anglo-Irish writing and writing in Irish Gaelic together, even when the latter could only be encountered in translation, exemplified in Seamus Deane's *A Short History of Irish Literature* (1986).

Deane's effort to include a sense of linguistic, cultural, social and political difference in his comprehensive sense of national identity is not the same thing as the imperial example that settles on the slippery elision of 'English' as language and nation.

Which bring us back to the 'British' question.

Seamus Heaney, who is the last writer considered fully in Alexander's book and takes a major place in Corcoran's, famously wrote a poem entitled 'An Open Letter' to the editors of *The Penguin Book of Contemporary British Poetry* (1982), Blake Morrison and Andrew Motion, who had included him. Heaney admits he was hesitant and doubtful whether he should complain, because he knew that since he published in the *London Review of Books*, the *Times Literary Supplement* and *The Listener*, and his books were published by Eliot's publisher Faber and Faber, his readership was inevitably (though not exclusively), 'British' but he insisted that he must 'demur' because 'My passport's green': 'No glass of ours was ever raised / To toast *The Queen*.' He immediately qualifies this: 'No harm to her' but 'from the start her reign...would not combine / What I'd espouse.'

This gentle, friendly retreat from the UK flag evoked by the book's title is a lot more deferential than the attitude summed up more wittily in MacDiarmid's poem 'The Difference', quoted above. To British readers, perhaps Heaney's is a more attractive, less challenging attitude. Like Heaney's, MacDiarmid's poem was also occasional, prompted by the invitation to contribute to a special weekend edition of the traditionally Unionist Edinburgh newspaper *The Scotsman* put together for the Sir Walter Scott centennial celebrations (and was published in it, 14 August 1971, p.3).

Given the diversity of traditions and languages in Scottish literature, the provenance of 'English literature' and 'British literature' seems increasingly narrowing, a pinching encroachment. Imperialism is founded on ignorance of otherness, grounded on fear and the power of assertion. In the small town, village and rural worlds so beautifully described by Jane Austen and George Eliot, questions of nation and empire rarely seem relevant. Assumptions prevail, normally unquestioned. Charles Dickens, in *Bleak House*, has Mrs Jellyby more concerned with the shortcomings of life in Borrioboola-gha than with what's happening in her own home, even when her babies are bouncing head-first down the stairwell. This is fair and funny satire, but it risks foreclosing the international view in favour of the domestic. Something of the poignancy of the predicament had been perfectly caught by Wordsworth in 'The Solitary Reaper' where he asks us to consider the plight of his own ignorance: 'Will no one tell me what she sings?' The detailed study *Field Notes: 'The Solitary Reaper' and Others* (2007), by J.H. Prynne, is an exhaustive exploration of this problem of the circumscription of the English language. Wordsworth's poem about his own ignorance of Scots Gaelic is a more appealing confession of inadequacy than Johnson's dismissal of Boswell's offer to teach him Scots.

But where does that leave us now, those of us still limited by our language, who would nevertheless like to read more deeply in Scottish literature and study its distinctive traditions?

With a lot of work still to do. While Irish literature is widely recognised as a valuable area of study it is still possible for people all over the world to be simply ignorant of the story of Scotland's distinctive literary history. Alongside this there is an international recognition of Scotland's icons – instantly recognisable images: tartan, kilts, bagpipes, heather, whisky and Mel Gibson in *Braveheart* (although, happily enough, this film is fading in the memory of new generations).

The icons all have their history, connected with the obscurity into which our literature fell. That history is rooted in the 19th century, when two things happened to Scotland: it became identifiable by the images instantly signifying Scottishness – and yet, at the same time, it became invisible, part of a greater state, the British Empire. Scotland was Scotland all right, but it was often referred to rather as 'North Britain'. My grandfather worked as a manager for a Co-operative store in Lanarkshire in the 1950s and I remember seeing his official notepaper headed with the address of the store and the designation 'North Britain'. At the time, I was puzzled but the meaning is clear.

Throughout the 19th century, the role of the people of Britain – or rather, the British subjects – was one of imperial service, pre-eminently in the fields of industry, engineering, ship-building and agriculture, in world dominion. Their education was designed to provide reliable schooling for stalwart generations who would lead in the international exercise of imperialism. This also was what Britain's natural resources were used for. In the same century, the country was rapidly industrialised. Glasgow was known as the Second City of the Empire – only after London in importance. At the beginning of the 19th century, most Scottish people lived in the country, as they always had done – a rural, agricultural economy prevailed. By the end of the century, most people lived in the industrial cities, especially Glasgow. What encouraged this rapid growth was Scotland's position in the British Empire and to grasp that you have to go back a few hundred years, first to 1603 and then to 1707, when two different events deepened and cemented a union with England.

In his speech at the British Labour Party conference of 2007, the then Prime Minister Gordon Brown, a Unionist Scot, used the word 'British' or its cognates about 81 times. It seemed a little too obviously insistent, evidently prompted by the success of the Scottish National Party (SNP), who, in the 2007 election in Scotland, became the leading party by one vote and went on to manage as a minority government. In the next Scottish election, in 2011, the SNP gained an outright majority and continued in government, delivering their promise to hold a referendum on Scottish independence. That took place on 18 September 2014, and the result was 45 per cent in favour of independence, 55 per cent against it. The turnout of voters was exceptionally high, at 85 per cent of the eligible population of Scotland. Writers of all kinds took part in the political debates that surrounded this referendum, engaged with the ideas explicitly in their work and also in public forums throughout Scotland. Almost all were in favour of independence. The relation of literature and politics, clearly, is much closer and more complex than any exclusively 'literary' account will allow.

We can think of this in another context.

Ask most readers who the greatest English writer of all time is and they'll probably say Shakespeare. Why? Three reasons. One is simply that he was Shakespeare – inimitable. But there are two others that allowed him to be himself. One was the theatre. He had a medium that allowed him to write plays. The other was the political climate he lived through. That changed radically when in 1603 the Elizabethan world (you might say, the late medieval and early Renaissance world) shifted suddenly into the Jacobean (or early modern) world. In this new dispensation, Shakespeare wrote *Macbeth* and *King Lear* and his later plays. They all owe something to the new sensibility that was coming to prevail in the world he experienced. After 1603, Scotland had no court but it still had its parliament. But the Scottish parliament voted itself out of existence in May 1707. Robert Burns was to write that we had been 'bought and sold for English gold' and that the Scots who had approved the Union were 'a parcel of rogues'.

There was resistance. The Jacobite rising of 1745 led by another Scottish icon, Bonnie Prince Charlie, posed a massive threat to the frail young economy of the recently United Kingdom. This is why the reprisals against the Highlanders after Culloden in 1746 were so severe. At the beginning of the 19th century, when Walter Scott wrote the first of his novels, *Waverley* (begun in 1805, published in 1814), he gave it the subtitle *'Tis Sixty Years Since* – in other words, enough time had elapsed for people on both sides of the border not to feel violent. We could read about events rather than draw swords. When Scott orchestrated the visit of King George IV to Edinburgh in 1822, he persuaded the king to wear a kilt, thus demonstrating royal approval of Highland clothing as characteristically Scottish 'fancy dress'. By the late 19th century, all the iconic images – kilts, bagpipes and so on – became internationally known through mass media – first through postcards and paintings by such as Edwin Landseer ('The Monarch of the Glen' looks proudly independent but in T.S. Eliot's words, is 'bred for the rifle'). Later came the exaggerations of radio, film and television. Scotland became well known, but these images did not represent the industrial cities and there was no place for deeper studies of Scottish literature or any other more serious forms of artistic production.

To begin to grasp the story of Scottish literature, we need to go much further back.

There is an ancient theoretical model which helps to sum all this up: the X axis and the Y axis. Let's say the X axis is a horizontal plane on which lots of things happen in relation to each other. The study of literature on this axis is relational or comparative. For example, you read Stevenson alongside Henry James, Bram Stoker and Conan Doyle, or Lewis Grassic Gibbon beside Joyce and Proust. And that's fine. But then there's the Y axis, which is vertical, and goes deep down. On this axis, you can link Gibbon back to Stevenson, Stevenson to Scott and Burns, Burns to Fergusson and Ramsay and Ramsay back to Dunbar and Henryson. At any point on the Y axis you can stop for an X axis moment but you have to have an emphasis on the sense of traditions that go into the past, and come forward from it, from Stevenson forward to MacDiarmid, Edwin Morgan and Liz Lochhead. There's no reason why both shouldn't be available. So long as a British – or any other – imperium isn't foreclosing the choices and pleasures involved and leaves room for the loose ends and origins to be visible. The American poet Charles Olson deliberately evokes the graininess and rootedness of the sense of the local in his poem, 'These Days':

> whatever you have to say, leave
> the roots on, let them
> dangle
>
> And the dirt
>
> just to make clear
> where they came from

So what's the answer to the question, 'Was there ever a British Literature?' Well, there was certainly a British Empire, and you can read a literature in the English language in a trajectory that might describe the arc of empire, but would its authors and works be most deeply understood in the context of that history, or would they be more fully understood in their own national contexts too, outwith British imperial identity even while they are component parts of it? If so, then what can we say of literature in the indigenous languages of the islands of the north-west European archipelago, the Welsh novels of Kate Roberts, the Gaelic poetry of Duncan Ban MacIntyre, the Scots poems of William Soutar, for example? How can we be fair to work that does not subscribe to the imperium of the English language?

The Welsh poet David Gwenallt Jones (1899–1968), whom people refer to simply as Gwenallt, was an exact contemporary of MacDiarmid and Eliot and Williams. How many readers of these poets know Gwenallt's work? Very few of his poems have ever been translated and I know only those in *The Penguin Book of Welsh Verse* (1967), translated by Anthony Conran. One poem, 'Rhydcymerau', is freighted with the authority of responsibility for family, people, places, a language and a culture. 'Rhydcymerau' seems to be a place-name but it also means 'the ford where the waters meet'. I don't know, but the word also has the suggestion to me of another meaning: 'the crossing-over place of the Welsh people' – the ford of the Cymru. He talks about the forestry plantations of trees and the imposition of imperial financial power onto the area and family he came from. He talks of his grandparents, an uncle and cousin, and the place where they lived. This is how the poem ends:

> And by this time there's nothing there but trees.
> Impertinent roots suck dry the old soil:
> Trees where neighbourhood was,
> And a forest that was once farmland.
> Where was verse-writing and scripture is the south's bastardised English.
> The fox barks where once cried lambs and children,
> And there, in the dark midst,
> Is the den of the English minotaur;
> And on the trees, as if on crosses,
> The bones of poets, deacons, ministers, and teachers of Sunday School
> Bleach in the sun,
> And the rain washes them, and the winds lick them dry.

This is very different from the image of the alienated artist we're familiar with from Eliot and even Joyce. The artist is not 'refined out of existence' but bears the weight of conscious connection with his or her society, family, language and national history. And this is to do with a feeling for home or belonging. The Scottish Gaelic word for this feeling or idea is 'dùthchas'. We shall come back to this word.

Andrew McNeillie has a fine poem called 'Cynefin *Glossed*'. Now, 'Cynefin', I'm told, means a sense of belonging, at-homeness. And McNeillie has his own mixed loyalties – his father, John McNeillie, who also wrote under the name Ian Niall, was a novelist from Galloway in Scotland, but he moved south. Andrew McNeillie grew up in Wales but also lived in Ireland for a long time, so his own experience leads him exactly to what this poem is asking us to consider. Here it is:

> What is another language? Not just words
> and rules you don't know, but concepts too
> for feelings and ideas you never knew,
> or thought, to name; like a poem that floods
> its lines with light, as in the fabled
> origin of life, escaping paraphrase.
> So living in that country always was
> Mysterious and never to be equalled.
> For example, tell me in a word how
> you'd express a sense of being that
> embraces belonging here and now,
> in the landscape of your birth and death,
> its light and air, and past, at once, and what
> cause you might have to give it breath?

The political structure of 'British' identity does not allow for the specific, national loyalty voiced by MacDiarmid or Gwenallt. And something more than Britishness produced McNeillie's profound question about language and identity. Poets intuitively understand this. The evidence is there. But as scholars and teachers whose business is research and recovery, teaching and conveying the information that matters, even simply as good readers (which is all that critics are), we are required to look more deeply into national traditions and areas of work that have been covered up or forgotten.

If the category of 'British' literature obscures the depths and subtleties, traditions and major themes of literatures ostensibly contained within it, we need to dismantle it thoroughly and put the pieces together again in a more responsible way. This is what Walter Benjamin (1892–1940) insisted that we must never forget, in his 'Theses on the Philosophy of History' (1940): 'Only that historian will have the gift of fanning the spark of hope in the past who is firmly convinced that *even the dead* will not be safe from the enemy if he wins. And this enemy has not ceased to be victorious.'

The dead always demand this of the living.

PART TWO

Scotland Emergent

I

The Gaelic tradition: the Three Great Cycles

THE GAELIC TRADITION is the longest and most continuous literary trajectory in Scotland. It predates Christianity and comes forward vitally into the contemporary world, but at least since the 18th century, there are violent shifts, breaks and reconfigurations in the story.

This is an overview that gives emphasis to the continuity, while indicating clearly where the violent disruptions happen. The story should be read alongside our understanding of literature in Scots and English. Anyone claiming authority in the story of 'British' literature is a mere chancer if they're ignorant of the Gaelic tradition. Nobody can claim the excuse that it's too difficult because of 'otherness' since there are fine bilingual anthologies and English translations of Gaelic poetry, and easily available English-language accounts of Gaelic literature.

But ignorance is far more powerful than knowledge. Without some knowledge of the Gaelic language, we who are limited by English can only go so far. Yet it is surely worthwhile to attempt to approach an understanding of Gaelic traditions, authors and works even without knowing the language. Many English-language readers are familiar with the great works of Russian, French, Italian and Greek literature through translations. Why not Gaelic?

Let me put my cards on the table from the start: I have no fluent knowledge of Gaelic but my name – the word Riach – is a Gaelic word (*riabhach*, often with the *bh* silent) and has its own specific meaning. The point is this: my father spoke no Gaelic and he told me his father didn't either, so you'd have to go back at least three or four generations in our family to find people who spoke the language of our name. That's part of Scotland's story too. Many Scots are like this. Most of us have no Gaelic. Many of us have lost the language of our names.

A major part of this book is an attempt to introduce Gaelic literature, predominantly poetry, to English-language readers, by someone who has studied Gaelic a little, but has gained what knowledge he has mainly from English-language sources and from Gaelic-speaking people. No doubt I'll make mistakes. I'll be glad to correct them. But I think it's an attempt worth making.

There's a good, if dangerous, precedent for this: the best introduction to Russian literature I know is *Russia Discovered: Nineteenth-Century Fiction from Pushkin to Chekhov* (1976) by Angus Calder (1942–2008), who begins by noting that he has no Russian at all but writes from his reading of the great Russian authors in their English translations. These chapters, like Calder's book, should demonstrate at least what predominantly Anglophone readers might have access to, straightforwardly. Let's be possessed by the intrinsic optimism of curiosity.

As far as we can tell, much of the earliest literature arising in what we now call Scotland is found in the Gaelic stories and songs that were there before writing. These come from people who lived before, during and after the coming of Christianity. These stories of Celtic heroes and lovers have usually been associated with Ireland but they are profoundly part of a shared Celtic identity. Their presence in Scotland should be known much more deeply and much more widely, here, in Scotland, now.

The three major cycles of early Celtic stories and songs have been the source of many retellings, both solemn and subversive. The earliest of the three cycles of ancient Celtic stories and songs tells of the first mythological age, recounting the conflict between the Fomorians and the Fir Bolg and the arrival of the Tuatha Dé Danann. It is as wild, fantastic and outlandish as any cinematic epic like *Star Wars*, *Lord of the Rings* or *Game of Thrones*. Brilliant visual interpretations of these figures include the bizarre characters depicted by John Duncan (1866–1945) in his painting 'The Fomors (or The Power of Evil Abroad in the World)' (c.1939) and J.D. Fergusson (1874–1961) in 'Danu, Mother of the Gods' (1952). Danu is the mother goddess of the Tuatha Dé Danann, among whom the pantheon includes Dagda, father-god of wisdom, fertility and agriculture, the Morrigu, raven god of destiny and war, Bride, goddess of dawn, spring, healing, poetry and smithcraft, whose festival day is 1 February, and Lugh, god of arts, truth and law, a sun-god whose harvest festival is 1 August, known as Lughnasa. This is the word – and festivity – celebrated in the title of the poignant play *Dancing at Lughnasa* (1990) by Brian Friel (1929–2015). But all these gods, goddesses and mythical figures have their rites and roles in a panorama of shifting provenance.

Next are the tales of the Red Branch, among which are the stories of Cuchulain and Skaaha, Deirdre and Naoise, and other characters in a fantastic Iron-Age world of martial arts, chariots, duels and outlandish humour. From the point of view of urban people, inhabitants of towns or cities, these are the wilderness people, 'others', hunters, wild and untameable. The central epic of this second cycle is *The Táin Bó Cúailnge* or *The Cattle Raid of Cooley,* and the life of the hero Cuchulain is central to the many stories elaborately unfolding in this cycle in multiple, interconnected ways.

Then there are the tales of Finn and the Fianna or Féinn, the Fenian cycle, dialogues, songs and stories of the outlaws: 'outlaws' here in the sense of characters loyal to legitimate rulers, and not to usurpers and false authorities. Finn in this sense prefigures Robin Hood: opposing the usurper, loyal to a higher legitimacy. There are numerous instances, traces and echoes of Cuchulain in traditional Scottish Gaelic stories and songs but more generally, this third, Fenian cycle, whose central characters are Finn and Ossian, is as much a part of Scottish Gaelic as of Irish literature, tradition and lore. Its local roots are in almost every part of the Highlands and Islands of Scotland. Local place names were and continue to be explained by reference to these stories and ballads, their events, loves, conflicts and characters. As William Power puts it: 'Scotland had a full share in the Fenian cycle'.

They have their own cast, ethos and trajectory, markedly different from the more aristocratic players of the second, Red Branch cycle, even though they sometimes overlap. It's significant that where W.B. Yeats preferred Cuchulain and the warriors and ladies of the second cycle, James Joyce, subversively endorsing the virtues of a far more common humanity, took Finn as his totemic figure, morphologically changed into the title of his last work, *Finnegans Wake* (1939). Joyce's irreverence is at its most riotous in *Ulysses* (1922), when the mild, dogged, heroic Mr Bloom enters Barney Kiernan's pub and encounters the one-eyed cyclops, the 'Citizen' and his hound, the 'bloody mangy mongrel, Garryowen' waiting 'for what the sky would drop in the way of a drink.' The parody here is supreme:

> The figure seated on a large boulder at the foot of a round tower was that of a broadshouldered deepchested stronglimbed frankeyed redhaired freely freckled shaggybearded widemouthed largenosed longheaded deepvoiced barekneed brawnyhanded hairylegged ruddyfaced sinewyarmed hero.

Joyce's crazy exaggerations are only just beginning. He continues:

> From shoulder to shoulder he measured several ells and his rocklike mountainous knees were covered, as was likewise the rest of his body wherever visible, with a strong growth of tawny prickly hair in hue and toughness similar to the mountain gorse (*Ulex Europeus*). The widewinged nostrils, from which bristles of the same tawny hue projected, were of such capaciousness that within their cavernous obscurity the fieldlark might easily have lodged her nest. The eyes in which a tear and a smile strove ever for the mastery were of the dimensions of a goodsized cauliflower. A powerful current of warm breath issued at regular intervals from the profound cavity of his mouth while in rhythmic resonance the loud strong hale reverberations of his formidable heart thundered rumblingly causing the ground, the summit of the lofty tower and the still loftier walls of the cave to vibrate and tremble.

After that, you have to remind yourself that this is simply a bully of a bigot in an inner-city Dublin bar on 16 June 1904. After an increasingly riotous account of his clothes, and the company of great ancient heroes and heroines engraved upon a girdle of 'seastones' dangling around him, including Cuchulain, the Last of the Mohicans, Muhammed, Patrick W. Shakespeare, Lady Godiva and the Rose of Tralee, it comes as a rude and sudden interruption when the narrator returns us to the realistic context: 'So anyhow Terry bought the three pints Joe was standing and begob the sight nearly left my eyes when I saw him hand out a quid.' – 'And there's more where that came from, says he.'

The legacy of the Celtic stories and songs is a recollection of heroism at one level but pomp calls for satire and subversion, and Joyce supplies it. His zany humour is complemented by his love and respect for the virtues of affection, human grace, lust for life and the art of giving. These are embodied in Mr Bloom's sympathy and care, his sensitivity and humour, and his quiet determination not to give way to the authority of the power of violence. Heroism, for Joyce, means something else.

Yeats was always more ambivalent about this. In his poem, 'The Statues' (1938), Yeats asks: 'When Pearse summoned Cuchulain to his side, / What stalked through the Post Office?' The Easter Rising in Ireland signified a moment in recent history for Yeats, in which, he said, 'a terrible beauty' was born. The poem brings the image of Cuchulain into a contemporary political confrontation. The violence that actually happened is neither endorsed nor condemned by the poem but left in a condition of ambiguity and questioning. Yet the poet seems to have no ambiguity when he calls upon 'We Irish, born into an ancient sect / But thrown upon this filthy modern tide' to climb 'to our proper dark' that the beauty of 'a plummet-measured face' may be seen in full understanding. Such beauty arises from the depths of history and the poem implies the sad, bitter question of who might be capable of seeing and appreciating it fully these days? And if its prospect has been made possible by violence, isn't there an even greater urgency to respond to its value?

The mysteries in these lines are multiple but there is surely a palpable commitment to both heroic aspiration and genuine humility. If there is nobility here, it is vulnerable.

Joyce's preference for Finn was shared by Hugh MacDiarmid. In his autobiography *Lucky Poet* (1943), MacDiarmid says that if he were asked to describe in a sentence the life he has led, he would reply: 'It's all just a matter of a Hjok-finnie body having a ride on a neugle.' A 'neugle' is a mythical Shetland water horse but is similar to many wild animal-gods, while a 'Hjok-finnie body' MacDiarmid glosses as 'a buried Finn up again', one of those 'who were adept at recovering things lost in the sea which to ordinary mortals were irrecoverable'. More prosaically he explains, 'My life has been an adventure, or series of adventures, in the exploration of the mystery of Scotland's self-suppression.'

MacDiarmid's quest to retrieve from the depths a sense of self-worth, beyond all imperial scorn and disdain, to restore what's worthwhile, to give us the chances we are always in need of, is heroic in ways that Yeats, Joyce and Mr Bloom himself might approve.

William Power (1873–1951), in his book *Literature and Oatmeal: What Literature Has Meant to Scotland* (1935), wrote this:

> Gaelic has had a far bigger and longer run in Scotland than Scots or English. Teutonic speech is still a comparative upstart, and its sweeping victory did not begin till well on in the 17th century. A conscientious Chinaman who contemplated a thesis on the literary history of Scotland would have no doubt as to his procedure. 'I will learn a little Gaelic, and read all I can find about Gaelic literature from the oldest Irish poets down to Ban MacIntyre; and nearly a third of my thesis will be on Gaelic literature.' He would be rather mystified when he discovered that historians of Scotland and its literature had known and cared as much about Gaelic literature as about Chinese, and that they had gone on the remarkable assumption that the majority of the Scots were Anglo-Saxons and that their literature began with Thomas the Rhymer, in the reign of Alexander III.

That was written in 1935. It is salutary to think about both how much and how little has changed since then.

Gaelic ballads were concurrent throughout the tradition, among them 'Deirdre's Farewell to Alba', one of the loveliest of all songs. After nine happy years in Scotland with her lover Naoise, spent in and around Glen Etive, Deirdre prepares to leave with Naoise and his two brothers, Ainle and Ardan, for their native Ireland and towards the culmination of their tragedy. The story is the basis of J.M. Synge's play, *Deirdre of the Sorrows* (1910). In the song, her leave-taking is essentially a list of the names of all the rivers and valleys and mountains she knows she will never see again: immediately evocative, lasting images. The poem comes at the very beginning of the anthology *Scotlands: Poets and the Nation* (2004), I co-edited with Douglas Gifford and a version for voice and clarsach is recorded on John Purser's two CD-set *Scotland's Music* (LINN CKD 008). This is my own version:

Deirdre's Farewell

That is the land I love,
Borne east from the land of my birth,
To this, in the west fold of Scotland,
The loveliest world on earth –

In every location, looking around,
The air is so clear, wonder is breathing –
My love brought me here, nine short years ago,

Now only for him am I leaving –
I love the safe ground,
Looking out from the fortress,
The Island of Thorns,
The Fortress of Sweeney –

The ocean of forest around them,
Where Prince Ainle roamed the sad shores,
There, between tides, that ambivalent ground.
Our years here all past in an instant.

Glen Restful I loved,
To sleep in safe haven, deep in the shelter
Of that strong rock.
Food there was plentiful, rich, good fish –

In the Low Glen supplies were abundant:
Fat from the badger, venison fresh –
In Glen Masson, wild garlic grew tall,
The green grass incredibly bright –

And up where the trees look over
The river mouth, safely,
We gently rocked ourselves to sleep,
Undisturbed, untroubled –

I built my first house in Glen Etive,
The trees a protection at dawn,
And the cattle-fold there
Filled always with sunshine –

Glen Orchy was straight
As a young sapling's spine,
The ridges above it
Always in sunlight –

My love in his youth was proud,
As proud as any as young –
Glendaruel, I love still,
For all who are born there are happy –
The cuckoo's sweet call, double-throb,

> From up there, on that bending bough,
> Concealed in high branches of trees,
> Echoing down from above –
>
> And Blackthorn Island's beach stays firm,
> Clear water runs over pure sand –
> I would never have come here and never have left,
> Were it not for my one true love –

The first two cycles seem to depict pre-Christian times and the Finn Cycle evokes the arrival of Christianity in the form of St Patrick, so the whole arc extends through the first, second and third centuries AD and begins to close with the dialogue between Finn's son the bard Ossian and the Christian St Patrick. It's been argued that this is a late medieval invention, but it's also arguable that many of these stories and songs have roots that go back at least as far as the early medieval period and some perhaps much further.

One essential turning point in the third cycle is the story of Ossian, who spends his younger years with his father Finn MacCoul and the warriors of a heroic age, then journeys to the land of the ever-young, returning after a long absence to a Christianised world from which his former companions have all departed. One legend has it that Ossian's mother was a deer, indicating the non-hierachical connection between humankind and animals, evident too in the totemic names of clans (as in, Clan Chattan of Caithness, the Province of the Cat). Similarly, the proverbial 'three jewels of the ocean' connect different species: they are lobster (crustacean), mackerel (fish) and seal (mammal), and the seal is also the transformative, shape-shifting selkie. This relation between people and the natural world is evident too in the landscapes of the Gael. Most Gaelic myths and stories take place in identifiable territories rather than a mythical otherworld (not so much 'Sherwood Forest' as the Homeric Aegean). The stories of Deirdre and Naoise, for example, occupy the actual Glen Etive and its environs. And the land is still with us.

The image of 'Ossian after the Fianna' – the survivor from an earlier age now in a new world where all the old, high virtues have gone – is one of the most significant evocations of haunting and loss that underpin many depictions of the Gaelic world, all the way to the 20th century and Sorley MacLean's poem about the cleared township of Hallaig on his native island of Raasay. Such an evocation survives because it has perennial human application. To be clear: 'perennial human application' is what we find in Homer, Shakespeare, Melville, Dickinson, Dickens, George Eliot or James Joyce.

Here is my own free translation of poem III from *Heroic Poetry from the Book of the Dean of Lismore*:

I am Ossian

I looked on them once, the household of Finn
Nothing feeble or faint was their way
I see them all in my memory's eye
I follow the men of yesterday

I lived with them once, the household of Art
He who would love sweet song to begin
Nobody ever was better than he
He lived in the household of Finn

If you with your eyes had seen what I saw
Those men and those women, my friends and my kin
What you never have seen, you never will see
I have been in the household of Finn

May mercy this evening fall gently
Upon what is mine, every sin
May my soul be spared now from all torment
I have lived in the household of Finn

Also collected in *The Book of the Dean of Lismore*, the dialogues of Ossian and St Patrick foreshadow those of a number of crucial confrontations in modern Scottish literature, most notably between Fearcher and Maighstir Zachairi in Fionn Mac Colla's novel about the Highland Clearances, *And the Cock Crew* (1945). Fearchar, the secular bard of the community, cannot understand Maighstir Zachairi's compliance with the British authorities set upon evicting the people and ending their way of life. The minister discusses the question with him, all the time knowing guiltily and troublingly that his side of the argument will win by armed force and not by spiritual conviction and lived practice. A similar confrontation is also at the heart of the conflict between the Old Woman and the Minister in Iain Crichton Smith's beautifully lucid short novel *Consider the Lilies* (1968).

A fourth cycle, tales of the traditional kings of Ireland, seems more deeply rooted in that country: the kings include Cormac mac Airt, Niall of the Nine Hostages, Conn of the Hundred Battles, and so on, yet they overlap with what seem to be earlier stories. Cormac, for example, is described in one story as the ruler who employed Finn and the Fianna. Nothing seems fixed here except the lasting and liminal significance of the stories themselves.

How can we gauge the truths the stories and songs convey? Are they literally connected to place and time? Do they carry truths that might apply in different locations, adapted to different places and times?

These are impossible questions to answer. All stories are provisional. In the end, historians, archaeologists, textual and linguistic scholars can't verify much about any of them. They are there for you to find and hear or read and enjoy thinking about. We must not be credulous but we shouldn't be exclusivist either. We shouldn't foreclose possibilities that are open to revision. And we should keep in mind what is really powerful and haunting about them, what has kept them part of a living tradition over millennia.

Why do I believe these stories and songs are worth our attention?

Because they tell you things about what it is to be human, to feel love and fear and loyalty and betrayal, birth and death, being old or young, what 'beautiful' is, what 'horrible' means, comedy and tragedy – and the exhilaration of living bodily in a physical world. And they speak of the world of their terrain – both Ireland *and* Scotland – what it's like, its landscapes, wildernesses, sunny folds, the waterways between them, rivers, lochs and seas, hard or pleasant weather, places exposed to wind and rain, places of shelter and warmth, days of dark storm or bright sunshine.

They are all about being alive. We have so much to learn from them.

NOTE
There are many different versions of the older Celtic stories and songs that comprise the three major cycles of the Celtic myths that prevail in Scotland and Ireland. All are related to each other. Their written forms are partial, none of them definitive or comprehensive. They extend from early books in Gaelic such as the 12th-century Irish *Book of Leinster*, the 16th-century Scottish *Book of the Dean of Lismore*, through Samuel Ferguson's *Lays of the Red Branch* (1897), Charles Squire's *Celtic Myth & Legend* (1905) and Aodh De Blácam's *A First Book of Irish Literature* (1934) to Frank Delaney's *Legends of the Celts* (1989), Marie Heaney's *Over Nine Waves* (1994), Seamus Heaney's *Sweeney Astray* (1983), and Thomas Kinsella's version of *The Tain* (1969) or the same work in a new version by Ciaran Carson (2007). One concise and accessible summary of them (as well as those of Wales, Cornwall, the Isle of Man and Brittany, and the larger British and European context), is *Celtic Myths & Legends* (2013) by Martyn Whittock, which also valuably provides lists of the earliest written and published sources. Above all I would recommend *Window to the West: Culture and Environment in the Scottish Gàidhealtachd* by Meg Bateman and John Purser, which Ronald Black has described as 'a richly-illustrated history of the people of the Highlands and Islands over the past 2,000 years, including their language, literature, folklore, beliefs, artefacts and music. [...] The book's stated purpose is that it 'asks whether there is anything distinctive about how the Gaels through the ages have looked at the world'. This is modest to the point of self-effacement. *Window to the West* is nothing less than a rounded portrait of Scottish Gaelic civilisation. It is as far as possible permanently and freely available from the publisher, Clò Ostaig, on the internet: www.smo.uhi.ac.uk/files/PDFs/Window-to-the-West.pdf

2

The Gaelic Otherworld

THERE ARE VARIOUS accounts of the Gaelic 'otherworld' not always matching each other, as is appropriate for the shapeshifting, identity-loosening, explorative explications it offers. It is the bureaucrats' ultimate nightmare. Among these accounts are *The Secret Commonwealth of Elves, Fauns and Fairies* by Robert Kirk (c.1641–92). This was said to have been published in 1691 but no copy of such a first edition is known. Walter Scott claimed to have read it and he published an edition in 1815. It was republished in 1893 with an introduction by Andrew Lang, dedicated to Robert Louis Stevenson. The 2007 edition has an introduction by the feminist scholar of religion, myth, fairy tales and art, Marina Warner. We'll be coming back to Robert Kirk.

There is also *Survivals of Belief Among the Celts* (1911) by George Henderson (1866–1912), who collected material from the Outer Hebrides, particularly South Uist. Henderson was a graduate of Edinburgh and Vienna universities, becoming a lecturer in Celtic Studies at the University of Glasgow from 1906 until his early death. *Survivals of Belief* tracks three areas: 'The Finding of the Soul' considers 'internalised' belief: religion and ritual, speech and spells, charms and names, the Evil Eye, the significance of blood, and the 'Gessa' or taboo. 'The Wanderings of Psyche' takes us through outward manifestations: the 'theriomorphic soul' in its forms as hand or weapon, bird or bee, animals of various kinds (not least of interest, the Boobrie, which might be bird, water-horse or water-bull), trees and stones. And 'The Earthly Journey' considers rites of healing, illumination, fire, water, milk, magic stones, sacrifices, faith, caves, lochs and wells. The book concludes with discrimination between 'folk-consciousness' which 'thinks in pieces' and 'a sovereign content of existence' which comes with Christianity. Among many other studies of folk belief and supernatural matters, there is *The Magic Arts in Celtic Britain* (1945) by the poet Lewis Spence, an older contemporary of Hugh MacDiarmid.

But I'd like to spend some time here with John Gregorson Campbell (1834–91), a Gaelic-speaker from Appin, a minister of Tiree, and one of the major folklorists of the 19th century. The material he collected c.1850–74 was published in two volumes, *Superstitions of the Highlands and Islands of Scotland* (1900) and *Witchcraft and Second Sight in the Highlands and Islands* (1902). The dating suggests that some of his informants were born in the 18th century and some stories seem to predate the Jacobite rising of 1745, drawing from earlier, more traditional Gaelic society. Folklore collecting was international, with the brothers Grimm in Germany, Robert Kirk and later Walter Scott in Scotland, Thomas Crofton Croker and later W.B. Yeats and Lady Gregory in Ireland. William Grant Stewart was the first collector in the Scottish Highlands, followed by James Napier in the Lowlands and Walter Gregor in the north-east. But Gregorson Campbell is a key figure.

Revised, collated, introduced and annotated by the Gaelic scholar Ronald Black, his books were republished as *The Gaelic Otherworld* (2008; reprinted 2019). This new edition invites a review of the whole sense of the 'otherworld' in traditional Gaelic story and song.

More than that: Black draws out clearly the ways in which the folklore itself has contemporary application, in psychological, political, social and other spheres of life. Far from being 'quaint' or 'esoteric', there is vital application of the material, both as arresting narrative and imaginative revelations of metaphoric understanding. We need to think again about this 'otherworld' as something more than merely 'superstition'.

Black identifies in Gregorson's work not one but three otherworlds, peopled respectively by fairies, spirits and witches.

The world of the fairies is secular, suggesting what has since been delivered by science: the ability to fly, Freudian psychiatry, moral quandaries, the mix of reason and instinct, the tension between intellectual self-apprehension and animal desires, evident in creatures that cross a hierarchy of life in the animal kingdom, from the 'uruisk' (a Highland monkey), to mermaids and water-horses.

Then there is the world of spirits, ghosts and second sight. This is the home of the dead, where we encounter the omens of death and other premonitions. This sphere is grim, often violent, forced upon our attention by the fact of mortality and foresight, or simply self-knowledge of what the future inevitably holds for each one of us.

The world of witchcraft and the devil is 'the religious otherworld'. Polarities – good and evil, God and the Devil, healing and harming, medicine and mistreatment, high hopes and missed chances – are characteristic, and they generate both or either comedy and tragedy.

Each otherworld engages the mysterious and unanswerable questions of time and space, reality and dream, what is above or beyond our knowledge, past visible horizons, what can be seen on the face of the earth, and what lies below (underground, underwater). A visit to an otherworld usually involves some distortion of time. As Black points out, 'Rip Van Winkle is a migratory legend of Celtic origin, claimed by Orcadians to have come from Washington Irving's father, who was born and bred in Shapinsay'. But time has practical meaning in the divisions of the Celtic Year, with quarter-days, Gaelic names for different kinds of wind, festivals, the seasons and what happens in each of them, an annual calendar of turning-points to be marked and acted upon.

Start with the fairies: where did they come from?

The Catholic tradition in Scotland reports that the fairies are supposed to belong to the angelic order of beings, who remained neutral in the revolt of the Angels and had to undergo a trial on earth after their leader Lucifer had been expelled from Heaven and fallen into Hell. When God commanded the angels to cease fighting, those who fell to earth became fairies, those who remained in the sky became the northern lights, those who fell on rocks became echoes, those who fell in the sea became seals. Yeats and Lady Gregory were informed that there were two kinds of fairies, the Tuatha Dé Danann, or the Peoples of the Goddess Danu, who were good, and the Fir Bolg, or Men of Bags, 'more wicked and more spiteful': these are 'the two races of the Sidhe' (pronounced, 'shee'). According to Lady Gregory, one is tall, handsome, given to jesting and playing pranks, riding on horseback at night-time in large companies and troops or in carriages decked with flowers; the others are small, dark, malevolent and big-bellied. The idea that each carries in front of them a bag suggests to Ronald Black that perhaps they were wearing sporrans. But the general implication of succession is clear: 'the fairies of any one race are the people of the preceding race – the Fomors for the Fir Bolgs, the Fir Bolgs for the Dananns, and the Dananns for us.' When the old races die they don't depart into absence, they become fairies, spirits, and look on, to hinder and distract, sometimes to help.

Robert Kirk of Aberfoyle, author of *The Secret Commonwealth*, was described as a 'walker between two worlds' and Black confirms the justice of this appellation, 'but not in the sense in which it was intended'. The two worlds Kirk walked between were the Gaelic-speaking world of the parish of Aberfoyle in Perthshire, where he preached, and the Scots- and English-speaking worlds of his parents and background in Edinburgh. As a churchman, he was more than familiar with Latin but it is his immersion and integration into the Gaelic world which validates the description. Black notes:

> This is a truly 'secret commonwealth' with a discernible organisational principle, and indeed the traditions of the Church upon which the Roman Catholic doctrine of purgatory is based were themselves substantially inherited from eschatologies of this kind, including those of the Celts and the Greeks.

In a sense, the Gaelic otherworld is purgatory. And all these terms are metaphoric, which is to say, while they take narrative, literary forms as stories, in imagery, with tension and a powerful sense of risk and danger, they are not mere whimsy or fancy, but rather generated out of realities which anyone might understand immediately in the material, secular universe.

Metaphor is what we use when we don't have an immediately applicable vocabulary for certain things. Black gives an example: 'Every so often in Gaelic literature we notice a poet or writer groping for familiar words to express an alien concept.' A 16th-century woman calls a gun 'a slender powder of poison', as if it were a snake; a 20th-century writer mentions the trolley of a Glasgow tram looking 'like a lobster's antennae'.

Take this further and the stories of the Gaelic otherworld, whether of fairies, spirits, or witches and demons, might be decoded as psychic constructions that would help make sense of things otherwise inexplicable, or most stiflingly fearful. What cannot be spoken of directly might not dictate silence, but rather parallel forms of expression besides the literal. And these might help people make rules for living well, avoiding danger, observing moral priorities and social equilibrium in a dangerously changing world. Such rules of guidance might apply in domestic as much as political contexts, from housekeeping to childcare, from bereavement and separation to relocation, migration and exile, from pregnancy to alcoholism, sickness and death.

The conflation of aspects of Christian religion with pagan superstition and folk-beliefs may seem strange but an immediate, sharp understanding of how this works is supplied by the Welsh poet and clergyman R.S. Thomas (1913–2000). As noted in his biography by Byron Rogers, in an interview given in his 87th year, Thomas was asked by a journalist from the *Daily Telegraph* what sort of God he believed in, and replied: 'He's a poet who sang creation [and] He's also an intellect with an ultra-mathematical mind, who formed the entire universe in it.' Further: in a TV film of 1972, Thomas said this: 'The message of the *New Testament* is poetry. Christ was a poet, the Resurrection is a metaphor; and I feel perfectly within my rights in approaching my whole vocation as a priest and preacher as one who is to present poetry'. And he elaborated on this, saying that the disciples, 2,000 years ago, 'experienced something' and then had to 'convey it by means of manuscripts, or whatever they used, in language. And we have to take their account in language, but there are aspects of language which are most successfully conveyed by metaphor, and the risen Christ, the resurrection, to me, as I said, is metaphor. It's an attempt to convey an experience of a kind of new life, an eruption of the deity into ordinary life, a lifting up of ordinary life into a higher level...'

Or, to put it another way, to acknowledge and describe (if not always to understand) the forces at work below the surface of things, that erupt into daily material life, and those that surround us, from above and far away, invisible, ineffable, metaphor is vital. In this, the imagination is not merely helpful, but necessary. As Hugh MacDiarmid puts it in his poem, 'On a Raised Beach': 'What the seen shows is never anything to what it's designed to hide'. The premise of the Gaelic Otherworld is within this understanding.

3

Merlin, Arthur and Calgacus

THE POEM, *The Gododdin* gives us what seems to be the earliest reference to King Arthur. We're not sure exactly when it was composed, maybe anywhere between the 6th and the 11th centuries. And we're not sure when the events it refers to happened, or when or if the characters it refers to ever lived. Another work, entitled *Vita Merlini Caledonii* (c.1150) by Geoffrey of Monmouth (c.1100–55), tells the story of the mad prophet Lailoken and his meetings with Kentigern or Mungo, patron saint of Glasgow. Lailoken is Myrddin. Myrddin is identified with Merlin and thus connected to the Arthurian legends. Things get hazy very quickly.

One helpful book here is Tim Clarkson's *Scotland's Merlin: A Medieval Legend and Its Dark Origins* (2016). Although there are numerous Scottish locations with Arthurian references (Dunadd in Argyll, Iona, Ben Arthur in the Trossachs, Edinburgh's Arthur's Seat and the Roman Fort at Trimontium, at Melrose, in the Borders), the stories themselves, linked in different cycles to Cornwall, Wales and Scotland, like the composite character of Merlin, evade any singular definition. Yet Merlin or Myrddin is firmly present in the lore of the Scottish Borders and his grave is said to be where the Powsail burn runs into the river Tweed at Drumelzier, near Peebles.

In 1889, John Veitch published *Merlin and Other Poems*, which delves into the wizard-poet's wanderings in the Borders and his meetings with St Kentigern or Mungo – in other words, his moving between the pagan world of the forest and the world of early Christian settlement. It's a similar moment to that in which Ossian meets St Patrick. So much in both these worlds slips between verifiable history and uncertainty. Merlin is legendary but something in his story was surely actual. Myth is almost always founded in some kind of reality. The title poem in Veitch's collection is a conversation between Merlin, Gwendydd (the Dawn, his twin sister) and Hwimleian (The Gleam, his early love). Merlin sets the scene 'in the Glen, and on Drumelzier Law':

> All night I've wandered in the glen, 'mid hum
> Of hidden waters moving in the gloom,
> And eerie sound, strange voices from th' unseen,
> And things have shaped themselves upon the air,
> Some mocking me, and some soliciting
> My evil will; – dim, weird sprites, that pass
> 'Twixt sky and earth in dark hours ere the morn, –

> Form after form in crowding mystery,
> Where none can mark the mien of living thing,
> Or pause upon a face for love or light;
> But all that seems to be doth also pass
> In mockery of show to mortal eye.

Veitch was professor of Logic and Rhetoric at Glasgow University, author also of *The Tweed and Other Poems* (1875) and historical and critical books, *The Feeling for Nature in Scottish Poetry* (two volumes, 1887) and *The History and Poetry of the Scottish Border* (two volumes, 1893). His bas-relief sculpted portrait can be seen in the stairwell in the main building of the university going up to the Bute Hall. For many years it was surrounded by oil paintings of past principals and luminaries, and when these portraits were distributed to various neighbouring rooms since they formed too weighty a preponderance of austere, elderly, dead white men, Veitch's portrait was the only one to remain because it had been sculpted into the wall itself.

The mysterious magician haunts modern Scottish literature too. Edwin Muir, in his book *Journeys and Places* (1937), begins his poem addressed to him like this: 'O Merlin in your crystal cave / Deep in the diamond of the day…' and the title of Hugh MacDiarmid's poem 'Esplumeoir' refers to the mythical retreat into which Merlin has disappeared for the time being. The poem is a series of metaphors for eternity, some comic and banal, others weird and almost incomprehensible. Eternity, MacDiarmid tells us, is like a jellyfish seen in the water from a boat, which, when you try to hook it, slips away, ungraspable. Or it's like a beady-eyed parrot that doesn't say much but cocks its head at you and seems to imply that if it wished it could tell you 'a thing or twa'. Or, finally, it's the space in a building under a royal blue canopy which must be entered through a door, beside which is a pearl button. You push the button and hear delicate chimes but there's a bulletproof mirror and behind it a white-haired black man named Tutti-Frutti Forgle. He is inspecting you, and he 'kens his business':

> Aince past Tutti, you check your hat
> In a quiet soft-lit anteroom,
> Syne the haill place is yours.

And with that, the poem ends. It's a marvellous evocation of uncertainty and our nervous approach to inexplicable mystery. The shifting territory between history and fabulation is the provenance of Merlin and the Arthurian stories.

One of the most enjoyable navigations of this territory is Alistair Moffat's *Arthur and the Lost Kingdoms* (1999), which considers the relation between the Welsh, Scots and Gaelic-speaking peoples, particularly between the Antonine

Wall and Hadrian's Wall in the period around the retreat of the Romans from the Borders. Moffat has little hard factual historical evidence to rely on but speculates provocatively on the meanings of place names, the significance of geographical terrain and its relation to the human economy, and the ideological significance of nationalities in Britain as they were beginning to find forms. He argues that Arthur's base of operations was in fact in the Scottish Borders, along with more famous sites in Wales and Cornwall, and ventures to infer that the original location of what we think of as Camelot was Roxburgh.

Moffat concludes that Arthur 'defined the nations of Britain and in doing so set the dynamic of our polity'. His victories 'allowed Scotland to remain a nation for another thousand years' after his death (which Moffat gives as 517 AD), 'long enough for its memory to be strong and to allow its rise again in the next millennium.' Meanwhile, 'Wales formed itself behind Offa of Mercia's dyke and resisted the English for 700 years, long enough to remember its beautiful language to help us understand Britain as it was before the Romans came. The Irish fared worst,' Moffat concludes, and remained 'still bleeding through ancient wounds.' Fanciful as these speculations are in any historical analysis, the fact that Arthur and Merlin informed the imagination of Europe is indisputable. Their legacy in the work of the greatest poet of the First World War, David Jones, is evidence enough in itself to insist that we pause to recognise that stretch, reach and tenacity.

When Hugh MacDiarmid edited *The Golden Treasury of Scottish Poetry* (1940), the first anthology of Scottish poetry to emphatically include translations from Gaelic and Latin, he wrote in the introduction that he agreed with the speculation of Dr Agnes Mure Mackenzie that *Sir Gawain and the Green Knight* was probably written by one Hucheone of the Awle Royale, Sir Hugh of Eglinton, who died in 1381. This may have been the 'Sir Hugh of Eglinton' to whom William Dunbar refers in his 'Lament for the Makars'. Andrew of Wyntoun also refers to 'Huchown of the Awle Ryale' (or 'the Palace Royal') as the author of stories of the Arthurian adventures of Sir Gawain. Now, the Gawain poet has never been identified but the language of that poem is a form of Middle English connected to speech forms in Cheshire and the reference in it to the wilderness of the Wirral clearly indicates territories now referred to as Cheshire and Derbyshire. Folk tradition places the Green Knight's chapel in the Peak District.

There are further intricacies but the main thing I'd like to emphasise here is that there's an important distinction between the southern literary tradition embodied by Chaucer, which runs its magnificent and grandiloquent course through Shakespeare, Milton, Wordsworth, all the way to Derek Walcott and on, and the northern alliterative tradition, of which Gawain is a part, which breathes a different air.

The point is not to claim the Gawain poet as 'English' or 'Scottish' but to understand that the Gawain poem is part of this northern tradition, and therefore relates to contemporary and later Scots-language poems in different parts of Scotland.

The onset of the north European winter invites us to encounter the metaphysics of spring, a hard-won renewal that comes at a cost. Its universal significance is the assertion of human value in the face of mortality. If there is a central symbol of hope in Scottish literature in an act of defiance in the face of innumerable odds or inevitable defeat, it may be found in the force that drives Gawain on, enduring the ferocities of winter and hard nature, on his inexplicably successful quest. An affinity may be found in the image of defiant resistance fighters standing against a greater military might or overwhelmed by an imperial ethos. The image pertains to the hunters and fighters of Gaelic antiquity, the Fianna, whose pagan world is superseded by Christianity, leaving only one survivor, Ossian, to speak of an earlier, less pious culture. It is there also with the small band of Caledonians led by Calgacus at the battle of Mons Graupius in the Grampians, described by Tacitus (c.56–120 AD) in the *Agricola* (98 AD), and later again in the closing sentences of the *Declaration of Arbroath* (1320). The Christian formulation of this symbolic confrontation, of course, is the story of David and Goliath.

Neil Ross, editor of the 1939 edition of *Heroic Poetry from the Book of the Dean of Lismore*, quotes Kuno Meyer: 'The Fian were "often men expelled from their clan (éclaind); or landless men (dithir); sons of kings who quarrelled with their fathers; men proscribed; or men who seized this means to avenge some private wrong by taking the law into their own hands." The singular number is Fian, a warrior band, and the plural Fianna means a number of such bands.'

This is a familiar image. Think of the lonely band of warriors in the classic Japanese film, Akira Kurosawa's *Seven Samurai* (1954) or its Hollywood version, *The Magnificent Seven* (1960), or the damned but determined outlaws in Sam Peckinpah's *The Wild Bunch* (1969). Such renegades, highly trained in martial skill, were to become the material of legend and song, and their outlaw status has an affinity with the sense of opposition you feel in *The Gododdin* and the resistance to imperial Roman militarism voiced by Calgacus in the *Agricola*. There are many other examples but the *Agricola* is a lastingly resonant work. Here is my own version of Calgacus's speech:

We are the last men on earth, the last of the free. We have been shielded till now by the distance and remoteness of the place where we live, on the edge of what is unknown. But today the border is revealed to us like a line made by a sword drawn on the earth. Beyond us is nothing, waves and rocks on one side, Romans on the other. They are the thieves and spoilers of the world. They ruin the land with their plunder and they ransack the ships of the sea. They look upon wealth and feel only greed. They look upon poverty and feel nothing but lust for power. East and West have not satisfied them. Their grasp is all the world and they are strange, for they will attack the poor as violently as the rich. Robbery, slaughter and rape, these liars name Empire. They make a desert, and they call it Peace.

Many of the poems I've been talking about in these chapters on 'Scotland Emergent' can be found in the anthology, *The Triumph Tree: Scotland's Earliest Poetry AD 550–1350*, edited by Thomas Owen Clancy (1998). Edwin Morgan's review of this book is also worth reading in *The Times Literary Supplement* (12 March 1999).

The violence of war, the priorities of peace, the pathos of the struggle, the different languages and customs of human behaviour, all come into the spectrum of the earliest stories and songs that characterise what we now call Scottish literature. Perhaps the same may be said of any literature, in any language, but what's singular here is the encounter of the languages and the geography itself, the terrain, the archipelagic identity of Scotland. That creates something essential to what Scotland is now and could be, connected to all the world, but not like anywhere else.

That impulse to violence and that longing for peace, that pathos, pity and indeed the glory of the human engagement in these struggles are exemplified in the literatures in Gaelic, Norse, Latin, Old Welsh and northern alliterative Old English and Scots. These languages are all part of what Scottish literature began with, and from which it arises.

4

The Picts, *The Gododdin* and Columba

IN SCOTLAND, AS anywhere, literature emerges from a number of languages and cultural identities that come into close relation with each other over centuries, or indeed, over millennia.

If you go right back to an era before Scotland itself began to take form, there are identifiable diversities of language, a range of separate but overlapping idioms, tongues and forms of speech. The speech doesn't come down to us. Recordings are only recent inventions. Yet who's to say that some practices of voice don't come down the line in our voices today? Usually, forms of speech are created not only by what our culture accustoms us to but also by the physical properties of our bodies, our throats and mouths and vocal chords, and these are created partly by our parents, as they were by their forebears. So maybe our forms of speech do come from the distant past and should be valued accordingly. The sounds we make with our voices arise from biological structures as well as practices of habitation, and there are structures of intonation, the physics of throat and jaw, the design of our bones. All these have evolved through time. If we look at the written sources, though, we can see that evolution at work, and with such evidence, we might be on surer ground.

As we've noticed, Scotland and Scottish literature come from a part of the world inhabited thousands of years ago by a number of different peoples with different languages and ways of life, long before Christianity and our current way of giving dates to time began. We can sketch a few of these languages and peoples that have been important influences on many writers who come later.

The earliest stories and songs we might consider in a constellation that shines into the beginning of an identifiable tradition of Scottish literature are Celtic. The earliest languages we know of are Pictish, Gaelic, Norse, Old Welsh (Cymric), Old English (Anglian) and Latin. These are all parts of the cultural diversity we begin with.

Nothing that we might call literature comes down to us in Pictish but there are a handful of names that suggest a verbal context of syllabic subtlety. The names are caught in 'The Picts', a poem by Edwin Morgan, from his sequence *Sonnets from Scotland* (Glasgow: Mariscat, 1984). It begins:

> Names as from outer space, names without roots
> Bes, son of Nanammovvezz; Bliesblituth
> that wild buffoon throned in an oaken booth;

wary Edarnon; brilliant Usconbuts;
Canutulachama, who read the stars.
Where their fame flashed from, went to, is unknown...

And there is the Ogam alphabet, in which letters are grouped phonetically, with five groups of five letters each taking their names from trees (as Gaelic still does). As John Purser writes in his book, *Scotland's Music* (1992; revised edition 2007), 'The arrangement of Ogam letters suggests their sound value was crucial.' So the essential connection in literature between music and vision is significant here. Ogam was used as the basis for drawings and designs by the artist J.D. Fergusson (1874–1961) to accompany the first editions of Hugh MacDiarmid's long poem *In Memoriam James Joyce: from a Vision of World Language* (1955). In this poem, the varieties of languages throughout the world are celebrated, not as heralding a globalised uniformity or simplified communication but rather as the basis for a global human culture of difference, distinction and the sympathetic understanding of subtle relationships between people of all nations.

The text of the earliest Scottish poem we know of, *The Gododdin*, is written in Old Welsh or Cymric. It has been dated to anywhere between the 6th and 11th centuries and survives in a manuscript from the 13th century. *The Gododdin* is attributed to Aneirin, a court poet at Din Eidyn, the settlement that was to become Edinburgh. It assumes a knowledge of the story behind its words, of how the ruler of the Gododdin (the Lothians) brought together a company of 300 warriors to Din Eidyn / Edinburgh. They spent a year preparing for battle by feasting and drinking, then rode south and engaged in a massive fight against the southron forces at Catterick in Yorkshire where all but a handful of them were killed. The 83 fragments in the A-text scatter abstractions and concrete images together. This is my own version of the first one:

Think of the courage of these young men, eager to get into battle –
The thick hair waves of the manes of the stallions riding –
The young men gripping their horses' bellies with strong legs, riding –
Each with a light shield strapped over the rump of his horse –
Swordblades shine blue. Their clothes have gold fringes –
I praise them: Too young to be married, but old enough to fight and be killed –
On a field all sodden and puddled with blood, there, they were eaten by crows –
Before they could bury him, Owen was lying there covered in ravens –
Who can say where in the field was old Mark's only son hacked down?

In 563 AD Columba sailed from Ireland to Iona, establishing a Christian community. He was not the first to try this. Before Columba, Nynia, or Ninian, had begun his missionary work at Whithorn, in Galloway, in the south-west of Scotland. But arguably, there seems to have been a different ethos at work. Nynia seems to have been devout to the centrality of the church in Rome. Columba, no less devout, seems to have been dedicated to the idea of locality. It would appear that for Columba, missionary worth could only be proved by dedication to the people you lived among, rather than by reporting to an imperial authority. Celtic Christianity seems to be related to Syrian and Egyptian Christianity, with an emphasis on monasteries and hermits in areas remote from centres of power. To scholarship, the life of Columba (521–597) is documented to a certain extent, but its meaning is tantalising, suggestive, and invites literary interpretation and speculation. In various popular versions of Columba's story, there is a convincing humility about the realisation of these missionary ideals, because the faith they invoke arises from human conflict, violence, remorse, penitence and a dedication to trying to make better the lives of others.

The folklorist F. Marian McNeill (1885–1973), in her book *Iona: A History of the Island* (London & Glasgow: Blackie & Son, 1920), tells the story that in Ireland, where he was born and grew up, Columba was caught copying a Bible. He wanted more copies of the book to be available more widely, to spread the word. But the owner demanded the copy and the chief in charge decreed: 'To every cow belongs her calf, and to every book its copy!' In other words, he should keep the Bibles together in one place, and thus be able to secure all the authority to himself. Columba was angered by this. It was a judgement against Columba, personally, but it was also a decree that prevented people from finding out more for themselves. Columba appealed to his friends – powerful men – and this coincided with growing conflicts on a political front. When Columba made his appeal it triggered a terrible battle in which many people were killed.

Remorseful, he decided to leave Ireland and devote himself to missionary work. His name – Columcille, in Ireland – means 'The Dove of the Church' and his example of peaceful living is potent partly because it possesses this history of moving away from violence, towards penitence and peace. Scholarship since McNeill has speculated on this story, and McNeill herself admitted: 'This narrative is not reliable.' In their scholarly introduction to *Iona: The Earliest Poetry of a Celtic Monastery* (1995), Thomas Clancy and Gilbert Márkus describe it as something 'about which we would like to know much more'. They leave the question unanswered but allow for speculation and wondering.

It is possible that Columba himself was the author of the 'Altus Prosator' – a magnificent song in praise of 'The Maker on High' – but he may also have been involved in the compositions of the Columban plainchants collected on the CD *Scottish Medieval Plainchants: Columba, Most Holy of Saints* (CD GAU 129) performed by Cappella Nova under Alan Tavener. A sample from this plainchant tradition, 'O Columba', is also available on John Purser's *Scotland's Music* double CD-set.

Columba, his church and the productions of Iona – including the Book of Kells (c.800s), that beautifully illuminated manuscript work held on display in the library of Trinity College in Dublin – have sometimes been described as purely Irish. But Columba had to leave Ireland and be out of sight of it before he began his work, so we have to reclaim him as a figure who once again brings Ireland and Scotland together.

When he reached Iona, you would like to think that it was as it often is there: bright turquoise seas under cerulean skies and high white clouds, a walkable island of pink rocks and emerald grass seen in a light so intense against a horizon so broad, that the wealth of detail in wave and cloud and terrain conveys a precision of focus and a brightness of colour that helps you to see things more clearly than anywhere else in the world. These qualities can be seen in the paintings of Iona by F.C.B. Cadell (1883–1937) and Samuel Peploe (1871–1935), and before them, the coming of Columba to Scotland was a key subject for William McTaggart (1835–1910). The artists knew very well the significance of their subject in Scottish history, cultural identity and mythic authority, and the Book of Kells should be equally secure in that arc of Scotland's artistic production.

Adomnán (c.624–704), abbot of Iona (679–704), was the author of the *Life of Columba*, probably written around 697–700, a hundred years after Columba's death. This book differs from many other lives of saints because it's full of good stories and glimpses of stories that aren't fully fleshed-out. Of course, there is no psychology, but the characters are strong. It is not mere hagiography. One story has Columba traveling to the north of Scotland and meeting people on the shores of Loch Ness who are being terrorised by a monster from the deeps. When it heaves itself out of the water, Columba confronts it and banishes it to the depths of the Loch. What is described might have been a bear but who can say it was not a young Loch Ness Monster, and Columba its nemesis? One report has it that Columba could speak quietly to a small group of friends but when required his voice could rise like a lion's roar and he could address a vast assembled crowd in full volume and utter clarity. Another story tells of him as an old man, knowing his death is near, and welcoming the tender acknowledgement of his old white horse, who walks over and gently lays its long head on Columba's shoulder on the day of his death.

Columba is a foundational figure in the development of a myth of kinship among the different peoples of Scotland. His travels to the north of the country to the territory of the Picts (whom scholarship suggests were also Celtic) might be described as original in the tradition of 'peregrination' – the wandering missionary – but they also resulted in the legacy of stories about the traveler whose various encounters suggest an affinity between the different peoples he meets. Through Columba's story, many differences become related to each other, all threaded on the line of his journeying, from his birthplace in Ireland and across the geographical diversity of Scotland. This is one of the virtues of Adomnán's biography: about 140 different stories illuminate different aspects of Columba's character.

Of the poems attributed to Columba, the 'Altus Prosator', written in Latin, was translated by Edwin Morgan. He catches the rolling, emphatic rhythms and rhymes of the original and follows its structure, each verse beginning with the letters of the alphabet, taking you from A to Z as you go from Creation to Fall to Last Judgement, including a vision of Hell. This is the last stanza:

> Zabulus burns to ashes all those adversaries
> who deny that the Saviour was Son to the Father
> but we shall fly to meet him and immediately greet him
> and be with him in the dignity of all such diversity
> as our deeds make deserved and we without swerve
> shall live beyond history in the state of glory.

That phrase, 'the dignity of all such diversity' gives us the clue to it all. Following the alphabet but reinventing the story in fresh poetry is also a balanced way to answer the question between the priorities of predestined structure and the exercise of free will.

There is a great deal of early work in this tradition from Iona and elsewhere but Columba's influence extends into contemporary and later work in Gaelic. Dallán Forgaill, who flourished around 597, in his 'Elegy for Columba' memorably says in that language that the world without him is like a harp without a key – as if the world itself were a musical instrument and Columba's great capability was to allow its music to sing out, appropriately tuned, exact in its tension and playability.

If Columba is widely known as an adopted Scot arriving from Ireland, it's less widely acknowledged that St Patrick was quite possibly a Scot who moved to Ireland. Here, though, all I'd like to do is highlight the famous dialogues between St Patrick and Ossian, which refer back to the heroic days of the Celtic warriors. They describe a confrontation between the ancient, secular, pagan world and the modern, pious, sacralised world. The old world is viewed with more than nostalgia: it is a land of youthful self-confidence, stamina and appetite, as any old person might recollect. The new world might give little comfort to this act of aged remembering but the evocation of the old world in some of the poems from these dialogues remains as crystal-clear as the sea around Iona on a good day.

The Columban church and the Celtic Christianity it embodied seems to have been confronted by the centralising orthodoxy of the Roman Catholic church after Columba's death. Some would say that the dispute was essentially about the dating of Easter and the proper way to have your hair cut but there was surely more to it than that. John Purser notes:

> the Celtic church was distinct in philosophy, organisation, language use, literary style, aspects of order of service, calendrical calculation, physical appearance of its monks, appearance of its script, form of the cross, and, now, the character of its music in so far as it has survived in the *Inchcolm Antiphoner*.

Whatever the intricacies of its distinctive identity, the outcome of the confrontation with the increasingly centralised religious structure was that the establishment orthodox Roman church prevailed and the priorities of Celtic attention to the local were put under pressure. But literature – any art worth having – always comes from real people in actual places, never from centralised dictat. The lesson is there for us, clear to see.

Columba was one of a number of characters whose lives became the subjects of hagiographies or proto-biographies in later centuries. These include, from the 12th century, lives of St Nynia or Ninian, St Kentigern or Mungo, and St Margaret. These figures all still have specific local associations in Scotland. The Holy Island, off the coast of Arran near Lamlash, was the home of St Molaise (or Laisren, to give him his Irish name) and his cave can still be visited and you can drink from the well of pure water beside it. In Glasgow, when you visit the Cathedral, you can go down to Mungo's crypt. When you travel west along the Clyde to Dumbarton Rock, the ancient capital of Al Clud, later called Strathclyde, you will be standing where Mungo is supposed to have met Merlin. In legend, the Rock is also associated with Mordred, villain of the Arthurian stories. The name Dumbarton means the fortress of the Britons, that is, the Celts who spoke Old Welsh or Cymric, the language of *The Gododdin*. Modern research has unearthed music and texts from the early Christian periods and recordings have been made of Columban plainchant and the vespers and matins for the feast of St Kentigern. In the 20th century, the composer Thomas Wilson (1927–2001) in his *St Kentigern Suite* (1986), beautifully commemorated the legends depicted in the crest of the city of Glasgow:

> This is the bird that never flew
> This is the tree that never grew
> This is the bell that never rang
> This is the fish that never swam

In the stories of Mungo, each of these negative images registers a problem which the saint solves. Wilson's music intensely and understatedly represents exactly that: each piece gives us a knotted problem and then, its resolution. Edwin

Morgan, in a poem that is chiselled into the pavement in Candleriggs, a street in the Merchant City just south-east of Glasgow's George Square, takes these images and makes strange affirmations of them:

> Praise for the tree that growled but grew
> Praise for the bird that fainted but flew
> Praise for the bell that rusted but rang
> Praise for the fish that sighed but swam

When Morgan collected the poems written when he held the appointment of poet laureate of Glasgow in the early 21st century, he published them in a book called *Cathures*, the name by which Jocelyn of Furness referred to Glasgow in his 12th-century biography of Mungo. These early Christian figures have a long legacy in Scottish literature.

5

From *The Dream of the Rood* to the Norse sagas

THE DREAM OF THE ROOD is an old poem that represents Christ's human sacrifice through words delivered as if spoken by the cross itself. It is an extraordinary act of sympathetic imagination, telling us what it was like to bear the weight of the man who died to save humankind. As Edwin Morgan puts it in his *TLS* review of *The Triumph Tree*, it speaks of 'the pain and shame as the nails are driven through Christ's body and into its own'. Whatever religion you espouse or refuse, whatever humanism you prioritise, should never cut you off from such a work of inspired perception.

Around the year 700, someone who had a particular love for this old poem had words and phrases from it etched into a tall stone sculptured cross, and if you travel to Ruthwell, near Dumfries in the south of Scotland, you can still see the Ruthwell Cross. The fragments of the poem are in Anglian, which has been confusingly described as 'North-West Northumbrian Old English' or 'South-Eastern Dumfriesshire Old English'. The language relates to modern Scots as Saxon does to modern English. Edwin Morgan described the Ruthwell Cross as solid Dumfriesshire red sandstone, weathered but preserved, and the crucifix it is modelled on is a tree of victory: 'Christ conquers death, but poetry conquers silence and gives a voice to dead wood [or in this case, to stone], and the book (made from wood) gives a voice to forgotten traditions.' The poem is a memorable evocation of the human sacrifice crystallised in the image of Christ's crucifixion. And understanding the meaning of that does not require a commitment to Christianity.

A century on, a major figure in the tradition of Christian philosophy is Johannes Scotus Eriugena (c.815–77), whose great work, *De Divisione Naturae*, appeared c.867. Eriugena worked out his own understanding of the divisions of nature and attempted to define the constitution of the universe in four categories, beginning with God as origin and concluding with God as the end to which all things return. The orthodox considered this pantheistic. At the heart of the whole thing is a problem later millennia returned to in the question of predestination and free will. God is perfect, by definition, but to create the universe and everything in it, including people, He must have moved, because you can't create without moving. This is admitted. But God, being perfect, can't move because perfection can't change. This is also admitted. So there's a problem.

The answer, maybe, is that perfection *can* change, be different in different parts of the world, for different peoples, and at different times – but that would allow a human dimension to the word. But this is not allowed. Then there really is a problem.

Perhaps we should recollect that phrase from Edwin Morgan's translation of Columbus's 'Altus Prosator': 'the dignity of all such diversity'. That 'dignity' is the provenance of Heaven, the gift of God, in this imagination. The notion of perfection accommodates it all. Perhaps. Morgan himself draws on the argument in his trilogy of plays on the life of Christ, A.D. (2000), where he has Christ explain: 'The kingdom of heaven is not a thing, / Nor is it a place, it is alive, it grows.'

The problem had been considered in multiple permutations by the early 6th-century Roman philosopher Boethius, in *The Consolation of Philosophy* (523–34), which asks hard questions about free will and predestination: How can people be happy in an unreliable world? What is the value of the work of the mind? In 2015, a manuscript copy of the book dating from 1130–50 in Glasgow University Library was identified by researcher Kylie Murray, not as English, as had been believed, but rather closely resembling work from Kelso Abbey in the Scottish Borders, from the era of the Scots Kings David I (1124–53) and Malcolm IV (1153–65). This manuscript was a product of the Scottish kingdom. Boethius was being read in Scotland 300 years earlier than previously thought, proof of a flourishing intellectual and literary culture in a Scotland many would like to caricature as backward and impoverished. Boethius wrote the original in prison, awaiting execution (in Pavia, in what would become northern Italy): the problems he addressed were close, pressing and real. They are political and human as much as theological, and they are always with us.

Another major figure in the philosophical-religious tradition is Duns Scotus (c.1266–1308), born as his name indicates in Duns, Berwickshire, in the Borders (there's a statue of him in the Public Park there, dating from 1966). Contemporaries knew him as Johannes Duns. Educated at Oxford and possibly at Cambridge too, he lectured at the University of Paris then went to Cologne around 1307, where he died quite suddenly the following year.

The central tenet of his philosophy has exerted enormous influence in the 20th century: 'haecceity' or the 'thinginess' of things, otherwise called 'thisness'. This 'thisness' underlies the dictum of the American poet William Carlos Williams (1883–1963), 'No ideas but in things' – in other words, abstractions are useless unless they are earthed in reality, arise from or come out of material objects, facts, things. Scotus's theological argument about 'univocity of being' endorsed the idea that words used with reference to God must have meaning with reference to human understanding, so that when you say, 'God is good' the word 'good' means the same as it would if you said, 'That man over there is good.' Others, including Thomas Aquinas, argued that such words when applied to God could only be analogies for anything that applied to human beings. Words applied to God are different. Their meaning is different because God is different. Scotus rejected this and held that such notions as goodness, power, reason, were 'univocally' applicable. When the philosopher Gilles Deleuze developed the idea in the 1990s, he emphasised that far from endorsing conformity in this 'univocity', what the term actually signified was that the one characteristic of all being is difference. Things are different from other things. Or as the poet Charles Olson put it, paraphrasing Heraclitus, 'What does not change / is the will to change.' Again, it's that idea of the dignity of all diversity.

Scotus gave his last name to Scotism, essentially a method of learning which emphasises dialectical reason (thesis, antithesis, synthesis), inference and the acceptance and resolution of contradictions. His first name was used by his opponents to label people they deemed incapable of learning much at all: the 'dunce's cap' (an inverted cone) was used in schools where the practice was to stigmatise and shame less able scholars publicly. Without going more deeply into the details of religious philosophy in arguments that have continued over centuries, or the ideas associated with what the philosopher Martin Heidegger called 'onto-theology', it's enough to note here that modern thought from the 1960s on saw Scotus as moving away from the beliefs of Aquinas, and that the heart of this shift, in some complex respects, foreshadowed the division defined in Scotland in 1560 by the Reformation. The American Edward Dorn has a pertinent short poem called 'The Protestant View' whose meaning is every bit as political as it is religious:

> That eternal dissent
> and the ravages of
> faction are preferable
> to the voluntary
> servitude of blind
> obedience.

You don't have to agree with that preference to see what he means.

Then there were the Norse. The ravages of faction were most violent when the Norsemen came south, round the northern coast of Scotland and into the western islands. Iona was terrorised in 795, again in 802 and 806, and in the following years most of the community left for Kells in Ireland (hence the name given to their most beautiful book).

A god who walked on water without getting his feet wet was no match for gods devoted to fighting, seafaring and cunning. Yet the stories and images that come down to us from both worlds are equally haunting. The crane, exhausted by flying through storms and violent winds, is nursed back to health by Columba in an image redolent of Christian charity and consolation. The ravens, blood-gorged in the Norse fields of slaughter, embody a different portent. One mythic world speaks of the creation and sustaining of peace and healing, the other of the necessity of sacrifice and the natural inevitability of violence. Both are contemporary, in their time and in ours.

The sagas tell stories of people who inhabited various places and moved around from the Norse countries, through the northern seas, to island archipelagos – Orkney, Shetland, Faroe – north to Iceland and Greenland, west to America and south to the Hebrides and the Scottish mainland, and west again to Dublin. One of the greatest of all, *Njal's Saga*, written in Iceland around 1280, tells of its characters holding parts of Ross, Moray, Sutherland and Caithness (Njal is the Gaelic name Neil). *Njal's Saga* is one of the great works of literature, with its evocation of a world where wrongs and grievances cross generations and no matter what efforts good people make to prevent the worst from happening, bad things befall people anyway. The burning of the house which Njal and his family are defending is one of the most horrific episodes. No-one describes the depth of the darkness of the northern night as accurately as the author of this saga.

The Norse presence in Scotland is extensive. *The Orkneyinga Saga* refers to Norse connections with Galloway, in south-west Scotland. The historian Alfred P. Smyth in his book *Warlords and Holy Men: AD 80–1000* (1989) wrote: 'this Scottish tradition in Icelandic oral history is of far greater antiquity than the 13th-century saga age, and it was so strong that it survived for centuries'. Both *Laxdaela Saga* and *Eyrbryggja Saga* begin with accounts of the Hebridean origins in Scotland of the great families of the western fjords of Iceland: 'a group of stubborn Vikings settled in the Hebrides' in the 860s and 870s. This genealogy was as important to its Icelandic audience 'as the Book of Genesis was to the Hebrews'.

Certainly, for George Mackay Brown in Orkney in the late 20th century, the significance of *The Orkneyinga Saga* (written in Iceland c.1200) was undisputed. According to Mackay Brown, the two great undertakings of the 'most intriguing character' in the saga, Rognvald Kolson, Earl of Orkney, were a crusade with 15 ships to Jerusalem in 1151–54 and the building of Kirkwall Cathedral in honour of his uncle, St Magnus (begun in 1147). Magnus's story haunted Kolson all his life. It also haunted Mackay Brown. He returns to the theme in numerous poems and most powerfully in his novel *Magnus* (1973), where the events of Magnus's martyrdom are related to the violence of the Nazis during the Second World War. The paradox of a good man, Magnus, being killed by his own brother, knowingly sacrificing himself to allow peace to reign free of rivalry and social contention is one of the most violent yet also Christian stories. In his earlier novel, *Greenvoe* (1972), Mackay Brown gets to the heart of this matter:

And I would not have you think either that love is all sweet desire and gratification, and thereafter peace. The essence of love is pain; deep in the heart of love is a terrible wound. Yes, and though a man should grow wise and quiet at last, yet if he hath trafficked in love but once, he shall be borne to his grave with the stigma of suffering on him. His monument shall bleed.

There are unforgettably gruesome images from *The Orkneyinga Saga*, like the severed head of an enemy exacting its revenge upon the victorious warrior who was carrying it on horseback, tied to his saddle, by opening its mouth with the movements of the horse and gnawing with its teeth the warrior's leg, giving him a wound which, seeming negligible, festers, suppurates and causes his death.

Before George Mackay Brown, another modern Orkney writer had been profoundly influenced by the sagas: Eric Linklater (1899–1974). In its very title, his first novel, *White-Maa's Saga* (1929), makes the connection and in *The Men of Ness* (1932) and elsewhere, the mythic dimensions of the narratives and the personal qualities of characters, of courage, tenderness and an understanding of violence are important components of his work. This is vivid in the autobiographical episodes from World War One in the early chapters of *Magnus Merriman* (1934) and in the World War Two novel *Private Angelo* (1946). The struggle to find a way to build a life worth having in the 20th century, after the bloody conflict and psychological trauma of two world wars, is an epic effort in which Linklater's writing draws as much valuable knowledge from his readings of the sagas as from his own personal experience.

For a long time, the northern archipelagos, Orkney and Shetland, and the Outer and Inner Hebrides in the western sea, were all identified with Scandinavian centres of authority rather than with the kingdom of Scotland. But the sea is an open road. In the second half of the first millennium it was as open as the skies have been in the second half of the second and beginning of the third: murderers, pirates, colonists and settlers arrive and go as they will with their different purposes.

Some things don't change. Matter and mortality are our condition, however we might value the spirit. The Christian, pre-eminently Latin tradition, and the Norse sagas are both ancient forms of understanding the world. Both made deep contributions to the development of the literary and cultural vision to be found distinctively in Scotland.

PART THREE

Approaches

I

Performing Scotland: plays, drama and theatricality

SIGNS OF SCOTTISH identity have become famous clichés throughout the world. Kilts, tartan, heather, whisky are among the most obvious examples. To wear a kilt is intrinsically a performance, both in the immediacy of its action and in the history of cultural oppression from which it emerges. To some degree, history always characterises how a society performs itself to itself, and how it enacts its identity to people in other nations, in other societies. So is Scotland a 'performance culture'?

Clothing is only one of innumerable outwardly visible examples of national identity in cultural 'performance' evident in countries all over the world. Language, accent and vocal register are among the most intimate. But is there something particular to Scotland's history which qualifies this distinction of the country as a 'performance'? It's essential to the country's history, from pre- to prospectively post-Union times. 'Britishness' is a performance – and what a performance! To many, its worst exaggerations are wretched and pathetically comical, or gloriously colourful spectacles of (rather costly) pageantry. They can seem unavoidable, beamed at us almost every day. How is 'Scottishness' different? And how has our culture been presented in theatres, in plays, in specific occasions designed to be staged?

Marshall Walker in his book *Scottish Literature since 1707* (1996) sums up a general perception: 'Drama is the genre in which Scottish writers have shown least distinction.' This is qualified, however: 'There is no shortage of Scottish theatrical heritage, but there is a shortage of durable Scottish plays.' Yet in the decades since that was written old works have been rediscovered, new works have appeared, and new ways of reading them have been developed. Ways of understanding Scottish drama and theatre (two different things) and evaluating cultural performance and specific plays (two very different things) have changed. Maybe we should start with a clear sense of what 'theatricality' means. Trish Reid begins her little book *Theatre & Scotland* (2013) like this:

> The theatre is everywhere, from entertainment districts to the fringes, from the rituals of government to the ceremony of the courtroom, from the spectacle of the sporting arena to the theatres of war. Across these many forms stretches a theatrical continuum through which cultures both assert and question themselves.

Theatre in Scotland has a long, rich history, and the history of performance is especially dramatic if you include church history as theatre. After all, a pulpit is a site of performance, and a Kirk is intrinsically a theatrical building. For generations there was at least one in every parish, where moral pronouncements, Biblical stories and songs (hymns) were more or less taken up regularly by attentive and participating or disengaged and dozy congregations. The long history of sonorous monologues delivered within the solemn walls of churches is a clear indication of theatricality. Direct address to an audience, enacted public moral retribution for sinful behaviour, parable fiction, poetry, vocal music of lament or celebration, pious humility or militant evangelism, storytelling, both tragic and comic, complex or light, moralistic and assured or questioning and challenging – all these have been essential to the life of the Kirk, whatever the orthodoxy. They all have their stars: the minister in the pulpit, spotlit by God, is only the most obvious.

This point is made forcefully by James Shapiro in his book *1606: Shakespeare and the Year of Lear* (2015): 'We tend to think of plays as the main site for exploring sensitive issues of authority in Shakespeare's day. But for King James, sermons – both those for public consumption at Paul's Cross and those delivered before him at court – better served that purpose, and for every play he saw James may have heard half-a-dozen sermons.' James's preachers, Shapiro comments, were also 'the king's men':

> they just engaged in a different sort of writing and public performance, and they too turned to the distant past to explain the present. In ways now lost to us, these two popular literary forms, both of which explored the divisive issues of the day, were in conversation with each other.

The dramatic and directly political engagement of the Kirk in Scotland for centuries has been passed over too easily without comment. This is surely one reason why the disruption of 1843 was such a crucial moment not only in Scottish church history but also in the performed political history of moral priorities in a world like our own, where ownership is power. The contest between material and spiritual possession was being starkly enacted.

When 474 ministers broke away from the established Church of Scotland what was in question was the authority of Church and State over social morality and justice. The authority of the land-owning patron to install a minister of his choice was in direct conflict with that of the Church to maintain independent 'spiritual jurisdiction'. In 1834, the evangelical party, with a majority in the General Assembly of the Church of Scotland, had passed the 'Veto Act', giving the people of any particular parish the right to reject a minister nominated by their patron. The matter of who legitimised and confirmed the appointments of ministers would be crucial in the broader social context. State power was being challenged.

When the Court of Session ruled that the established church was a creation of the State, the Church's sense of its own identity and spiritual independence was challenged in turn. This is what led to the disruption of 1843. Rather than denigrate the church as puritanically anti-theatrical, seeing it like this is more revealing. Its lessons, after all, are not confined to theological doctrine.

Two questions are pressing, though. If the establishment of the Free Church was initiated by such a radical act of self-determination in defiance of secular class power and the authority of the owners of land and material wealth, what went wrong? How did it become known as the orthodox religion of repression so familiar in clichés and caricatures?

And secondly, why is there so little fiction, poetry and indeed drama addressing this conflict? The most compelling exceptions are the novel by Robin Jenkins (1912–2005), *The Awakening of George Darroch* (1985) and the novel *Johnnie Gibb of Gushetneuk* (1871) by William Alexander (1826–94), which has the Disruption as its background. But what else is there?

These mysteries are only answerable within the cultural performance of Scotland's history. If the Kirk is the repository of 'pure' theatre, might we characterise politics as the arena of 'impure' theatre'?

The Declaration of Arbroath of 1320 has been considered an influence upon the American Declaration of Independence of 1776. It is perhaps more apt to describe the influence going the other way around. The Arbroath document was not familiarly known as a 'Declaration' until long after 1776, although it's true that among its signatories were John Witherspoon, formerly a minister of the Laigh Kirk, Paisley and James Wilson, a Fife lawyer who, in Edward J. Cowan's phrase, was thought to have 'contributed the crucial concept of the sovereignty of the people' and who on more than one occasion referred to 'essential liberty, which... we are determined not to lose, but with our lives'.

Cowan, in his essay 'Declaring Arbroath' in *The Declaration of Arbroath: History, Significance, Setting*, edited by G.W.S. Barrow (Edinburgh: Society of Antiquaries of Scotland, 2003), quotes a contemporary, writing of Witherspoon and Wilson:

> Both strongly national & can't bear any thing in Congress which reflects [badly] on Scotland. [Witherspoon] says that Scotland has manifested the greatest Spirit for Liberty as a nation, in that their History is full of their calling kings to account & dethroning them when arbitrary and tyrannical.

Cowan then asks the question: 'In this assertion may there lurk the shade of "Arbroath"?' The answer is yes it may, but in the judgement particular to Scots law, it is 'not proven'.

What is true is that the Arbroath document was not so much a Declaration as a letter, or specifically, a petition, to Pope John XXII in Avignon, to request, or rather, to ask emphatically or politely demand that Robert Bruce be recognised as the King of Scots and that therefore Scots must not be ruled in perpetuity by the English monarchy. The letter, and its purpose, its ideals and political meaning, had the approval not only of the signatories, the Scots nobles, but also of the church leaders.

And this is the point. To quote the historian Alexander Grant, in *Independence and Nationhood: Scotland 1306–1466* (London: Edward Arnold, 1984), as well as the conviction of the Scots nobles:

> The attitude of the Scottish Church was also significant at this time. Most of the bishops were staunch nationalists, who had stocked their dioceses with like-minded relatives and dependants. Not all of them actively supported Robert I, but few were directly hostile. On the whole the Scottish Church, unlike the nobility, attached more importance to the national cause than to the way Robert had seized the throne; it did not condemn, let alone excommunicate, him for his sacrilegious murder of John Comyn in a church.

So the church, as well as the nobility, was embroiled in what remains one of the most dramatic political statements in history. David Annand's arresting sculpture on the edge of Arbroath shows the figures of both Bishop and King, raising the document into the air above and in front of them, one hand on each side, as if it were a shield guarding not the individuals holding it but the realm beyond and behind them, not only Scotland (not as property but as a place in which to live) but also, and as a priority, the Scots, a people to live among and be part of. Factions of support raged around both John Balliol and Robert Bruce as potential kings but the cause of independence in this era was profoundly endorsed by the church, beyond individual leaders.

And today?

The assertion of self-determination embodied in the Declaration of Arbroath is and remains a theatrical statement, performance culture at its most dramatic. Yet the question of whether Scotland might be described as a 'performance' culture in this way is counterbalanced by a more familiar sense of Scotland as a culture of repression, tight-lipped silence and self-suppression. Both are exaggerations, of course, and both have some truth, but the balance, or oscillation, or bagatelle, between these ideas of how the pre-eminent characteristics of a culture might be presented – or represented – are suggestive. Asked to comment on the prevailing mood of the country in early 2021, with the condition of a global pandemic and the prospect of remaining within the United Kingdom or choosing independence in a referendum, one observer, after a moment's reflection, said: 'Half of the people are scared, the other half frustrated. It's a conundrum.'

Religious and moral conviction is everywhere in the political imperatives dramatised in David Lyndsay's *Satyre of the Thrie Estaitis*, where comedy and political address come together in social satire and critical engagement. The play is an immediately entertaining performance of ideas about religion, social morality and statecraft. The context of complex religious conflict is crucial to its political purpose, its display of human motivation, and its vision of a just society.

But in the years since screen media have come to dominate visual experience in the western world, live theatre has had to renegotiate its presence and value. David Hutchison, in his essay on 'The Experience and Contexts of Drama in Scotland' in *The Edinburgh Companion to Scottish Drama* (2011), sums up an essential quality of all play performances like this: 'Liveness is of the essence of the theatrical experience.'

The problem, he points out, is that since the days of the music hall, screen media has contested the attractiveness of 'liveness'. The music hall's 'largely working-class audience abandoned liveness for the spectacle and exoticism of recorded images'. The boom in cinema-going between the wars, the establishment of radio, the infiltration of television and now online technology, all these mechanisations of spectacle are in competition with liveness, especially when the ground rules for engagement are commercial priorities. Hutchison reminds us there are many opportunities made possible through screen and sound media for representing (in both senses) plays and literary works of various kinds, and for renewing critical engagement with them.

Examples abound in the under-researched history of Scottish radio drama: John Purser, Stewart Conn and Iain Crichton Smith all wrote memorable plays for radio; Gerda Stevenson's radio version of Walter Scott's novel *The Heart of Midlothian* is the best quick way to get an accurate summary of that huge, complex work because Stevenson deeply understands not only its language, historical moment, characters and lasting significance but also the literary-philosophical and dramatic-theatrical values inherent to its narrative structure. Television drama like John Byrne's *Tutti Frutti* (1987), or the television adaptations of literary fiction by George Mackay Brown, Lewis Grassic Gibbon, George Douglas Brown, Walter Scott and Robert Louis Stevenson broadcast in the 1970s and 80s, or Troy Kennedy Martin's *Edge of Darkness* (1985) and David Kane's *Jute City* (1991) remain to be rediscovered and learned from in the 21st century. Hutchison concludes that 'important as radio, television and film are for the understanding and experience of Scottish drama' nevertheless 'live theatre remains crucial to its existence and success.'

Performance, live communication, performativity in actual, staged production, demands a particular kind of respect, in Hutchison's words:

The writer is important, but is one of a team whose efforts combine, sometimes in a workmanlike fashion, sometimes even in a dull fashion, but sometimes to magical and mesmerising effect.

But the question remains, who writes the scripts for the London government at Westminster? That is surely 'impure theatre' at its most unenjoyable. Keeping both political and church history in mind as examples of theatricality in action, how might we approach 'real theatre' in Scotland, with plays, actors performing playscripts or improvising on their basis, buildings and stages, with lights, sound effects and music, and a quality of unpredictable liveness that makes every visit different?

At moments of revolutionary upheaval, the best writers are usually quick to grasp how important live dramatic performance can be. Their work frequently precedes and imagines what might follow. In Ireland, in the Easter Rising of 1916, Irish patriots occupied the Dublin Post Office, the most significant symbolic site for the exchange of information. This had been preceded by the foundation of the Abbey Theatre in 1903, itself a development of the Irish Literary Theatre which had been founded by W.B. Yeats, Lady Gregory and others in 1899. The theatre wasn't built with the idea of prefiguring bloody revolution opposing the British Empire but in retrospect, questions arise. Much later, reflectively, Yeats asked himself rhetorically in his 1938 poem, 'The Man and the Echo' whether the sentiments he expressed in his play *Cathleen ni Houlihan* (first performed in Dublin in 1902) inspired revolutionary action: 'Did that play of mine send out / Certain men the English shot?'

And that's the difference. What happened in the Post Office was not theatre. Its performers were not actors, playing their parts. Yeats's play, *Cathleen ni Houlihan* was a staged production and its performers were indeed playing. Yeats's perhaps guilt-burdened recognition of the possibility of fatal influence marks the distinction. The consequence of a play might be action. Its possible influence should certainly be considered in a contemplative period of time. The results of action risk the destruction of that space of contemplation which all art opens out. This is not to deny that sometimes action must be taken. Rather, it is to acknowledge a distance between theatricality and theatres.

The Disruption of the Kirk in 1843 and the Declaration of Arbroath in 1320 were dramatic events, but they were not plays. Had there been plays written and performed about those events since their occurrence, we might understand them better. And perhaps have a better idea about where we're going next.

When I was last in a Court of Law it was to take a group of language students to the public gallery to witness the proceedings. Everyone in front of us was very evidently acting – except the people who came to stand in the dock. For them, there was nothing at play. Their reputations, savings and even liberty were seriously at stake. Theatricality is present in all sorts of ways but the traditions of theatre as a genre of writing and live performance overlap with but are different from these social instances. That's partly why a trial usually makes great drama in the theatre. *Twelve Angry Men* (1954) by Reginald Rose (1920–2002) can be utterly compelling on the stage and directed by Sidney Lumet with Henry Fonda and a cast of serious actors it made an impressive film in 1957: not a courtroom drama but a post-trial deliberation on the verdict to be delivered. The greatness of *The Caucasian Chalk Circle* (1944–54) by Bertolt Brecht (1898–1956) is partly due to its enactment of a trial in front of the characters and at the same time the audience in its concluding scene, where a child's life is at stake. The future is held in the balance. The neglected Scottish playwright C.P. Taylor (1929–81), in his play *Good* (1981), made into a compelling film (2008), charts the drift into fascism of a schoolteacher at the time of the rise of Nazism in Germany. As the story unfolds it might be described as evidence in the case of a quiet man becoming inescapably trapped in a despicable political regime, compromising himself into an ultimate position of complicity with murderous, genocidal results. The audience is his judge.

Both the historical political moment, the literary depth and vitality, and the stage-performativity of the plays of Yeats, J.M. Synge and Sean O'Casey have kept them in the repertoire of theatres and the libraries of readers of literature, ever since their earliest productions. Similarly those of Rose, Brecht and Taylor. Each playwright was committed to the art of writing as well as to professional theatre performance – but this is writing for performance, not only for reading. Their work was produced in the context of developing conventions in both state-subsidised and commercial theatres, including experimental drama on the one hand, music hall and pantomime, on the other. Their plays have lasted and earned international esteem.

In Scotland, there is a broad sense that while there is plenty theatrical 'heritage', there seems to be a comparative shortage of lastingly valuable Scottish plays. Scholarship and research since the 1990s has altered this assumption. Historical questions remain, of suppression and censorship associated with the Reformation, the removal of the court to London in 1603 and the Licensing Act of 1737. Broad judgement has been that despite figures such as Allan Ramsay, John Home, Joanna Baillie, and the vitality of folk, music-hall and variety theatre, nothing much happens between David Lyndsay in the 16th century and the 'return' of Scottish drama in the 20th century, with J.M. Barrie, James Bridie and John McGrath. As an appraisal of the whole complex story, this is too simple. So much more has been discovered and made public through the last decades of the 20th, and first decades of the 21st centuries, that a fresh overview is required.

The Kirk often supported theatrical activity, to some degree shaping it to its own ends, but often encouraging the development of drama, especially in schools.

Folk plays flourished and ceremonial dramas had their place in religious contexts. As Ian Brown notes in *The Edinburgh Companion to Scottish Drama* (2011), the 'performative theatrical culture of Scotland has seemed to lack playwriting stars to match Shakespeare, Congreve or Sheridan' and yet George Buchanan's plays were models for Corneille and Racine, and other Scots playwrights, minor as they may be, indicate a neglected theatrical culture in Scotland.

Scottish playwriting had different roots and kinds of social prominence from that of England, and there was a lot of it. As Brown notes, for centuries,

> whether we think of folk drama, Kirk drama, street drama, rural drama, or the theatrical drama of the urban middle and upper classes, whether in Gaelic, Scots, English and even Latin, a wide range of theatrical forms was available.

It is still being retrieved and reinterpreted.

2

Poetry: how to read and what to read

HUGH MACDIARMID'S CONVICTION that Scotland's poetic tradition was multi-vocal was confirmed by the generation of poets who began writing through the Second World War. Many of them were in the desert campaign in North Africa: Edwin Morgan, G.S. Fraser, Hamish Henderson, George Campbell Hay and Sorley MacLean. MacLean's first book was published in 1943, during the war, and marked a crucial new beginning for modern Gaelic poetry. This book, *Dàin do Eimhir agus Dàin Eile / Songs to Eimhir and Other Poems*, included poems of love and war, bringing the Gaelic tradition into a poetic constellation connected to T.S. Eliot, Ezra Pound, W.B. Yeats and MacDiarmid.

In 1955, MacDiarmid published *In Memoriam James Joyce*, a book-length work said to be only part of an ultimately unfinished poem on an epic scale, similar to Pound's *Cantos*. The central theme of the work is the endless variety of languages in the world, the diversity of poetic and artistic expressions of human creativity, the limitations placed upon expression by political power and imperialism, and the need to balance energy and form. It is essentially a celebration of difference:

> The effort of culture is towards greater differentiation
> Of perceptions and desires and values and ends,
> Holding them from moment to moment
> In a perpetually changing but stable equilibrium...

After the Second World War, Scottish poetry shows more than ever how rich this diversity is, each of the major poets of this generation drawing strengths from their favoured places. Through and since the 1970s, women have been pre-eminent among the finest modern poets, drawing on the gains and potential made evident by earlier generations.

All poets – or almost all – draw on the work of their predecessors, not to emulate but to learn from. Before we come to the late 20th- and early 21st-century poets we might pause to take account of the diversity and range of different kinds of poem that have appeared in Scotland across centuries. The idea of a multi-vocal and multi-lingual identity in the traditions of Scottish poetry which MacDiarmid emphasised so strongly was already well-established long before the 20th century – long before the 17th century, in fact. English is only one of our languages.

Many people find poems a bit scary. Stories and novels are fine but there's something special about poetry that can make people think it's either pretentious – a pompous thought expressed in flowery language – or else just plain difficult. What does it mean? What's it about? Simple questions that demand simple answers, at least to begin with.

There's an ancient device for helping you to get inside a poem quickly and not to be afraid of it: SIFT. The idea is that you 'sift' the poem, let its meaning drift through the mesh of your mind softly and carefully.

How do you do this? Follow the letters.

S stands for 'Subject': what's it about? Answer the question as simply and straightforwardly as you can.

I stands for 'Imagery': what are the most vivid images in the poem? What are they doing? Are they attractive or repulsive or what? How do they work alongside each other? Are they comfortable together or do they rub up against one another? Do they harmonise or clash?

F stands for 'Form': How would you describe the form of the poem? Does it rhyme? Is there a regular rhythm in each line? Do the sounds of vowels make assonance? Do the sounds of consonants create alliteration? What does the overall structure or form contribute to the meaning of the poem?

Some key questions about the forms that poems take are: can you identify a Sonnet? What would be a Ceremonial (court) poem, as opposed to an Occasional (social) poem or an Occasional (individual) poem? How would you describe a Lyric poem or an Epic or a Concrete poem? What sort of poem is a Satire? How might form itself be used ironically? What especially characterises a Ballad or a Song? What are the special qualities of a Monologue or a Dialogue? Who is or are the personae, the characters in the poem? Who is the persona, the first person singular, the 'I' in a poem (it is not always simply the person who wrote it)? Think about Narrative poems, poems that tell stories. There are various kinds of narrative poem: for example, fables or fantasies or dramatic stories with characters and tension and confrontation and resolution.

T stands for 'Tone': What is the tone of voice in the poem? Who is speaking and who is being addressed? What sort of tone of voice is suggested by the language of the poem? What tone is conveyed by the form? Is the tone in tune with the subject or does it grate against it? How is tone of voice related to the imagery in the poem?

If you start asking any of these questions about any of the poems listed below, you begin to open them up and open your own mind to them. But you should always remember that a poem works through the *movement* of the words in it. The language of a poem is *moving*. To understand a poem you need to listen to it. Read it out loud. Repeat it in your head. Memorise it. You could memorise any of the poems below and enjoy them, think about them, just to yourself wherever and whenever you want to. Or quote them to people who might care to hear them.

There are a few other questions you might consider. How do these poems represent places in Scotland, the languages of Scotland, the people of Scotland – women and men – and what we might describe as major themes in Scottish literature? How do they connect to the historical trajectory of Scotland, to specific political or historical events? Where do they belong in terms of particular traditions? And how are these traditions determined by, or reach across to each other from, their different languages, Gaelic, Scots and English? What is their relationship with other major international movements? Do they show characteristic aspects of Medieval Literature, Romanticism or Modernism? How do they connect with the other arts of their time? For example, music (with reference to William Dunbar and the choral church music of his contemporary the composer Robert Carver, or to the Ballads, or to particular song-settings? Or paintings, sculpture, architecture or film?

We shall return later to the idea of major themes in Scottish literature but there are major themes in all the literatures of the world that come up again and again. I'm thinking of the themes of Love, Death, War, the Journey, the Quest, Satire, Celebration, Praise, Lament, Cursing and Condemnation, Leavetaking on Departure, Welcome on Arrival, the Dance, Marriage, Nature, the Country and the City, Exile, Homecoming.

What follows is a short list of some recommended Scottish poems which can be found easily in most anthologies of Scottish poetry or online. Ask questions about what they show you in terms of their poetic form and with reference to the big questions some of them address. Ask yourself as you browse through these poems, can they help? How useful are they? If you think you might find them useful, pass them on. When my oldest uncle died, I wanted immediately to read the last few pages of a poem by the Welsh writer David Jones, called 'The Sleeping Lord' and one by the American poet Wallace Stevens, called 'Waving Adieu, Adieu, Adieu'. Now I think of MacDiarmid's version of a poem from the German poet Stefan George, 'You Know Not Who I Am…' which is about spirit – that which animates matter – something essential that cannot be defined or captured. 'Spirit' may be a contentious word but less so when it's plural. When I read Norman MacCaig's poems, I know I can rely on any one of them – let's say, 'literally' – to lift my spirits.

Since the following list covers a whole history of Scottish poetry, it might be described as a 'wee canon' of Scottish poems (a culverin, perhaps). We shall return to the idea of 'the canon' and 'canonicity' towards the end of this book, but here it is introduced as a proposition not necessarily to be agreed with, but only with the promise that each of the poems listed below has tested, lasting value.

EARLY, MEDIEVAL AND RENAISSANCE

1. Anonymous Gaelic Song, 'Deirdre's Farewell'
2. Columba, 'Altus Prosator'
3. Robert Henryson (c.1430–1505), 'The Testament of Cresseid'
4. William Dunbar (c.1460–c.1520), 'To a Lady' and 'The Dance of the Sevin Deidly Synnis'
5. Gavin Douglas (1474–1522), Prologue to Book VII of 'The Eneados'
6. Alexander Scott (c.1515–1583), 'To love unluvit'
7. Alexander Montgomerie (c.1555–c.97), 'Ane Lang Gude-Nicht'
8. Dòmhnall mac Fhionnlagh nan Dàn / Donald son of Finlay of the Poems (fl. end of the 16th century), 'Òran nan Comhachaig' / 'The Song of the Owl'
9. Mark Alexander Boyd (1563–1601), 'Cupid and Venus'
10. Anonymous Ballads, 'Thomas the Rymer', 'Sir Patrick Spens' and 'The Twa Corbies'

ENLIGHTENMENT AND ROMANTICISM

11. Sìleas na Ceapaich / Cicely MacDonald of Keppoch (c.1660–c.1729), 'Alastair à Glengaradh' / 'Alexander from Glengarry'
12. Allan Ramsay (1684–1758), 'Lucky Spence's Last Advice'
13. Alastair mac Mhaighstir Alasdair / Alexander MacDonald (c.1695–c.1770), 'Birlinn Chlann Raghnaill' / 'The Birlinn of Clanranald'
14. Donnchadh Bàn Mac-an-t-Saoir / Duncan Ban MacIntyre (1724–1812), 'Moladh Beinn Dobhrain' / 'Praise of Ben Dorain'
15. Jean Elliot (1727–1805), 'The Flowers of the Forest'
16. Robert Fergusson (1750–1774), 'Ode to the Gowdspink'
17. Robert Burns (1759–1796), 'Now Westlin Winds' and 'Tam o' Shanter'
18. Sir Walter Scott (1771–1832), 'Proud Maisie'
19. Allan Cunningham (1784–1842), 'The Sun Rises Bright in France'
20. Màiri Nic a' Phearsain, Màiri Mhòr nan Òran / Mary MacPherson, Big Mary of the Songs (1821–98), 'Nuair a Bha Mi Òg' / 'When I was young'

VICTORIAN AND MODERN

21. James ('B.V.') Thomson (1834–82), 'The City of Dreadful Night'
22. Robert Louis Stevenson (1850–1894), poem XI from 'Songs of Travel'
23. James Young Geddes (1850–1913), 'Glendale & Co.'
24. John Davidson (1857–1909), 'The Testament of a Vivisector'
25. Violet Jacob (1863–1946), 'Hallowe'en'
26. Edwin Muir (1887–1959), 'The Good Town'

27. Hugh MacDiarmid (1892–1978), 'Milk-Wort and Bog-Cotton' and 'On a Raised Beach'
28. Robert Garioch (1909–81), 'The Puir Faimly'
29. Norman MacCaig (1910–1996), 'Five minutes at the window'
30. Somhairle MacGill-Eain / Sorley MacLean (1911–1996), 'Hallaig'
31. Sydney Goodsir Smith (1915–1975), 'Under the Eildon Tree'
32. Deòrsa mac Iain Dheòrsa / George Campbell Hay (1915–84), 'Bizerta'
33. W.S. Graham (1918–1986), 'Loch Thom'
34. Edwin Morgan (1920–2010), 'Trio' and 'For the Opening of the Scottish Parliament'
35. Ruaraidh MacThòmais / Derick Thomson (1921–2012), 'The Herring Girls'
36. George Mackay Brown (1921–96), 'Hamnavoe'
37. Iain Mac a' Ghobhainn / Iain Crichton Smith (1928–98), 'Poem of Lewis'
38. Liz Lochhead (b.1947), 'Something I'm Not' and 'Mirror's Song'
39. Jackie Kay (b.1961), 'Pride'
40. Kathleen Jamie (b.1962), 'Crossing the Loch'

3

Stories and novels

IN HIS ESSAY, 'The Storyteller' (1936), collected in one of those essential books, *Illuminations*, edited with an introduction by Hannah Arendt, translated by Harry Zohn, Walter Benjamin (1892–1940) explores various aspects of the relation between stories and novels, oral and print-based cultures, which were of pressing concern to him at that time in the context of escalating fascism and approaching war. Stories we tell others and to ourselves create understandings of identity and are caught up in every way in the conflicts of power and the contest of priorities. The American poet Diane di Prima (1934–2020), in a poem entitled 'Rant' from the book, *Revolutionary Letters* (London: Long Hair Books, 1969), says this: 'The only war that matters is the war against the imagination / All other wars are subsumed in it.' Insofar as the work of the imagination inhabits all the arts, storytelling and novels as well as poems, and every other form, Benjamin's observations have bearing not only on fiction, orality and print in general but may be applied to all aspects of Scottish literature.

As the literary form of the novel developed, the oral culture of storytelling directly contributed to it. This is especially important in Scotland in the 18th and 19th centuries, in the work of James Hogg and Walter Scott, who collected oral tales, ballads and songs, transcribed them and wrote them up to be published in books. And in the 20th century, Hamish Henderson became dedicated to the collection of oral tales and songs, recording them for the archive of the School of Scottish Studies at Edinburgh University. He worked not only as an archivist and historian, but also wrote original songs himself which were taken up by soldiers and singers more generally during and long after the Second World War. These have circulated in print as well as in the mortal memories and through the living voices of people across generations. As with songs, oral storytelling was not superseded by print culture: they co-existed and co-exist. But the development of print culture fostered the commercial economy of the novel in a different way from that of the oral culture of storytelling. Nevertheless, many 20th-century and 21st-century Scottish novels play with conventions of oral storytelling.

And the Land Lay Still (2010) by James Robertson (b.1958) is much concerned with the relations between oral culture and written literature, as well as photography and other forms of art. An epic novel, its narrative spans half a century of life in Scotland, from the end of the Second World War to the end of the millennium. Storytellers are among its cast of characters. Walter Benjamin's essay relates directly to this and other novels: 'Experience which is passed on from mouth to mouth is the source from which all storytellers have drawn.' Benjamin identifies two kinds of storyteller:

> 'When someone goes on a trip, he has something to tell about,' goes the German saying, and people imagine the storyteller as someone who has come from afar. But they enjoy no less listening to the man who has stayed at home, making an honest living, and who knows the local tales and traditions.

Benjamin's two kinds of storyteller, the stay-at-home and the wanderer, are both present in *And the Land Lay Still*. In Part Two, 'The Persistence of Memory', the novel's account of the history of the 1950s is delivered by an anonymous omniscient reporter summarising both the experience of living through that decade and the overview that might be taken of it in retrospect. But the narrative introduces a large cast of characters. One, Jack, is a wanderer, and we are introduced to a variety of locations through his journeying across Scotland. Another character, Saleem, is an immigrant to Scotland in the aftermath of Indian independence and the partition of India and Pakistan in 1947. In Part Four, 'Scenes from Olden Days', he is discussing the history of his journey from Delhi, India, to become a shopkeeper in Scotland, with his friend Don, a more conservative political unionist. Their conversation, set in the 1960s, concludes with Saleem telling Don, 'I think you had better hurry up here in Scotland or you will be the last ones out of the British Empire and if that is the case, well…' Don replies, 'Well what?' and Saleem ends the dialogue: 'Well, you will look pretty bloody stupid.'

Don himself and other characters are long-term residents of particular places in Scotland, others yet are natives of Scotland but long-term residents of London or elsewhere. The novel gathers them all in a kaleidoscopic vision of the nation in all its differences. Some are more or less severely limited by their own singular perspectives, but each one overlaps with another, or more than one other, so that a collective sense of communal vision is palpable.

As Benjamin says,

> If peasants and seamen were past masters of storytelling, the artisan class was its university. In it was combined the lore of faraway places, such as a much-travelled man brings home, with the lore of the past, as it best reveals itself to natives of a place.

Foreign places and home form a dichotomy held in balance, but so do past and present, history and the prospect of a future yet to be built. The novel explores these themes, beginning in the aftermath of the Second World War, with some characters returning from Europe and a sense of their role in rebuilding the nation.

But which nation? The British state or an independent Scotland? Benjamin's emphasis upon the distinction between oral and print-based cultures highlights the fact of historical process with which the novel is so concerned.

> The earliest symptom of a process whose end is the decline of storytelling is the rise of the novel at the beginning of modern times. What distinguishes the novel from the story (and from the epic in the narrower sense) is its essential dependence on the book. The dissemination of the novel became possible only with the invention of printing. What can be handed on orally, the wealth of the epic, is of a different kind from what constitutes the stock in trade of the novel. What differentiates the novel from all other forms of prose literature – the fairy tale, the legend, even the novella – is that it neither comes from oral tradition nor goes into it. This distinguishes it from storytelling in particular.

And the Land Lay Still is a novel but it is concerned with the art of storytelling and depicts it especially in the character of Jean Barbour, in Part One, 'The Mouth in the Box'. The novel is made up of many stories, each of which might have been developed into a novel in itself. In this extract from Benjamin's essay a connection is made between storytelling and 'the wealth of the epic' as traditional epics were and are orally transmitted. This was as true of the Homeric stories as of the Celtic cycles of stories and songs in Scotland and Ireland.

> Every morning brings us the news of the globe, and yet we are poor in noteworthy stories. This is because no event any longer comes to us without already being shot through with explanation. In other words, by now almost nothing that happens benefits storytelling; almost everything benefits information. Actually, it is half the art of storytelling to keep a story free from explanation as one reproduces it.

This comment bears emphatically upon the development of constant media news programming. There is a continual stream of news through mass media and relatively little informed reflection upon it.

> There is nothing that commends a story to memory more effectively than that chaste compactness which precludes psychological analysis. And the more natural the process by which the storyteller forgoes psychological shading, the greater becomes the story's claim to a place in the memory of the listener, the more completely is it integrated into his own experience, the greater will be his inclination to repeat it to someone else someday,

sooner or later. This process of assimilation, which takes place in depth, requires a state of relaxation which is becoming rarer and rarer. If sleep is the apogee of physical relaxation, boredom is the apogee of mental relaxation. Boredom is the dream bird that hatches the egg of experience. A rustling in the leaves drives him away. His nesting places – the activities that are intimately associated with boredom – are already extinct in the cities and are declining in the country as well. With this the gift for listening is lost and the community of listeners disappears. For storytelling is always the art of repeating stories, and this art is lost when the stories are no longer retained.

There is a deep truth here. It should have become more obvious since Benjamin wrote it, but it has become more obscured, just as Benjamin implied: we make noise, we don't listen.

The essential definition of a short story is that it's short, and it's a story. Benjamin sees this as a merit in that its brevity and lack of commentary can help make it memorable and literally can help us memorise it and keep it in mind and be able, willing and keen to retell it. The gift and skill required is also in the listening. He's suggesting that if there is a gift in creating a memorable story, there is also an art in listening, before we can memorise anything.

In Robertson's novel, the characters have various professional occupations, and their stories arise from these occupations. The shopkeeper (who trades in the marketplace), the photographer, the spy, the poet, the nurse, all these people engage in and prioritise forms of work and each form of work informs the perspectives they have and the judgements they make. If the novel is a gathering of stories and storytellers, each of them is related in an epic complexity. Here's Benjamin again:

> A man listening to a story is in the company of the storyteller; even a man reading one shares this companionship. The reader of a novel, however, is isolated, more so than any other reader. (For even the reader of a poem is ready to utter the words, for the benefit of the listener.) In this solitude of his, the reader of a novel seizes upon his material more jealously than anyone else. He is ready to make it completely his own, to devour it, as it were. Indeed, he destroys, he swallows up the material as the fire devours logs in the fireplace. The suspense which permeates the novel is very much like the draft which stimulates the flame in the fireplace and enlivens its play.

The storyteller is present, literally, telling the story, and his or her presence vouchsafes a security. The novelist, by contrast, is (normally) absent. The printed book circulates without the presence of its author. But doesn't a novel also bear 'the handprints' of the author?

Such a sense of the 'handprints' on printed texts and manuscripts is nowhere more available than in the collection of the Martin Bodmer Foundation in Geneva, one of the most marvellous and comprehensive public museums of manuscripts in the world. Three thousand years of books and manuscripts may be visited and seen here, from a Greek manuscript of the Gospel of Saint John on Egyptian papyrus dating from the 2nd century and transcriptions of Homeric texts to a copy of the Folio edition of Shakespeare's plays, and on to manuscripts and first editions of work by Jane Austen, Walt Whitman, James Joyce and Franz Kafka. I know of no other museum where the feeling for the authors' physical presence is so palpable in our examination of the paper and ink they used, and the books that were made of their writing. Print culture is perhaps not quite so anonymous as Benjamin suggests. And in the writing of particular Scottish novels the living presence of voices, sometimes even with musical annotation, and the vivid emphasis upon the work of the storyteller's imagination, is deliberately incorporated into the printed book.

If we were to compare the trilogy of novels, comprising *Sunset Song* (1932), *Cloud Howe* (1933) and *Grey Granite* (1934) published together as *A Scots Quair* (1946) by Lewis Grassic Gibbon (James Leslie Mitchell, 1901–35) with *Lanark* (1981) by Alasdair Gray (1934–2019) and place them alongside *And the Land Lay Still*, we might describe them as three 'epic' works made up of almost innumerable individual overlapping stories.

These might be nominated the three major works in prose fiction in Scottish literature of the last hundred years. I've called them 'works' because they're bigger than what's normally thought of as 'a novel'. *A Scots Quair* is three 'novels', *Lanark* is four 'Books' and *And the Land Lay Still* is six 'Parts'. But each novel, book or part is an integrated component of the whole work, and each whole work has its own singular integrity, on a grand scale.

In *A Scots Quair*, a single central character, Chris, navigates her way through the three novels, from farm and rural community to small town, to industrial city, and although she is increasingly moved away from the central position she occupied in the first novel, *Sunset Song*, in each successive novel she remains the main character around whom different kinds of social worlds are depicted, and different stories are told.

With *Lanark*, again, the individual central character, Duncan Thaw, or Lanark (he is the same character, but different, in the separate 'books' that make up the whole), is in continual relation with the communities that surround him. He is a part of these communities but also alienated from them, whether the realistically depicted Glasgow or the dystopian nightmare city of Unthank.

The poem placed near the end summarises the autobiographical nature of experience both as an individual defined by solitariness and as a human being living in a community or social world with its threats and dangers, virtues and values:

> I STARTED MAKING MAPS WHEN I WAS SMALL
> SHOWING PLACE, RESOURCES, WHERE THE ENEMY
> AND WHERE LOVE LAY. I DID NOT KNOW
> TIME ADDS TO LAND. EVENTS DRIFT CONTINUALLY DOWN,
> EFFACING LANDMARKS, RAISING THE LEVEL, LIKE SNOW.

These lines might suggest a way of reading *A Scots Quair*, *Lanark* and *And the Land Lay Still*. These are three epic works in which individuals and society change through historical time and the overlapping, coinciding trajectories of human lives are depicted at length and in complex detail. They take us to the heart of the question of literary form in the idea of the story and the novel. Benjamin is wonderfully helpful in identifying the differences between these forms and the distinctions they embody but there is also the proximity of each to the other.

Each of these works is epic by design. That is, they are not novels in which the narrative develops haphazardly, driven by the energies animating the characters of the scenes or events. *A Scots Quair* was deliberately planned to take the reader from rural, farming Scotland, to small-town Scotland, and from there into the industrial city, following the course of Scotland's economic history through pastoral farming communities which existed for millennia, through the rise of small communities to the massive and rapid industrialisation of the 19th century, towards the wars of imperialist conflict of the early 20th century.

Lanark was deliberately planned as four 'books', two written in realist form, depicting a young artist growing up in Glasgow in the 1950s and 1960s, two in a parallel universe in which Glasgow and its characters are transformed into a dystopian, nightmare vision of an industrial city where all the vicious liabilities of capitalist exploitation are highlighted or exaggerated and portrayed in non-realist, nightmarish, sometimes surrealist forms. And more than this, *Lanark* was designed to be read in a deliberate sequence, beginning with the non-realist 'Book Three' then following that with the realist 'Book One' and 'Book Two' and then ending with 'Book Four'. The bewilderment of Lanark (the character) at the beginning (Where is he? Where am I?) is 'explained' in the central Books before returning the reader to the strange world of Unthank for the conclusion. The proposition the novel makes and delivers so powerfully is that life is a constant renewal and renegotiation of imagination and reality, connected by a Moebius strip of twisting, turning, mortal consequence. This structure was planned and intended.

And the Land Lay Still is similarly deliberate, intended and planned. But its structure is fundamentally different from *A Scots Quair* and *Lanark*. Its structure is defined by historical sequence and chronological time. Its epic nature is partly defined by the scale of the period of history it encompasses, the enormity of change that occurs within this period, and arguably the unended argument of the novel, the idea that the future is handed over to the reader: the novel's retrospective summary of 50 years is given to the reader to decide what to do with, where to take it, what happens next.

The word 'epic' is one of the woolliest of literary terms. It usually just means a long poem with some fighting in it. It's often also used to describe a foundational narrative which depicts events leading to the creation of something new: a city, a society, a confirmation of belief and development, a rising from ruins. And it also suggests scale: something big.

All these ideas apply in various ways to *And the Land Lay Still*. It begins in the aftermath of the Second World War, and perhaps its core subject is the slow creation of a new society. It involves conflicts of perception, sometimes confrontationally, in terms of class or race conflicts, sometimes in terms of assumption, or presumption, in terms of feminist and patriarchal authority. If the core conflict involves an opposition to ignorance and the obliteration of memory, the core values prioritise recuperation of memories, the revival of forgotten connections and the affirmation of virtues that have been neglected or obscured. And unquestionably, it's a big book. As an epic of Scotland, it holds in balance not only the population of Scotland but the land beyond demographics, the territories of Scotland, depopulated wildernesses, forests, moors and beaches, coastal grounds and borderlands.

One of the results of this is an emphasis on the natural resources of Scotland. Since the novel was published, awareness has grown of the potential wealth in Scotland's natural resources, for power generated by wind and water: green energies. These are of value as naturally renewable resources beyond the carbon-based wealth extracted from coal and oil. Such potential is suggested in Robertson's novel but not emphasised or developed. There are always new stories to be told.

Stories, novels, poems, plays: the generic forms of literature are universal, and particular in Scotland to all that Scotland is.

There is a Gaelic word for the idea of the relations between land, people, and culture. That is, 'land' in the sense of all the terrains and territories of Scotland, including island archipelagos, different groups of islands in themselves and in relation to each other, farmlands and mountains, Borders and Highlands, alluvial plains and estuaries, rivers and hills, the places in which cities and towns and villages have been built over time. And 'people' as in all living human beings who lived, have lived or will live upon this land, in all their variety and wherever they have come from, and their relationships with each other, with the land and with all other living creatures in nature. And culture, meaning what has been created, naturally or by human intention or design, generated, manufactured, imposed or developed, grafted on or grown up into, thus inclusive of the cultivation of militarist or patriarchal or politically subservient culture as well as feminist, independent, linguistically distinctive national culture or the culture of mass media, habits of life, from how we use cutlery and crockery to what kinds of clothes we wear and how we wear them. These three things: land, people, culture, are inter-connected. The Gaelic word for this is 'dùthchas'. We shall return to it.

PART FOUR

Authors and Works

I

Early Gaelic poetry: the Dean of Lismore and the MacMhuirichs

GAELIC WAS ONCE spoken almost everywhere in Scotland. When the difference between Highland, Gaelic-speaking people and Lowland, Scots-speaking people, was noted, it was predicated on an engagement between them – an interface, a proximity, or even an intermingling. Members of the same families might be fluent in both Gaelic and Scots, and many knew Latin and French as well. Especially after the Wars of Independence in the 14th century, Gaelic identity was interwoven with other distinctive linguistic and cultural aspects of Scotland. Gaelic was spoken familiarly as far south as Ayrshire, Galloway and Dumfriesshire. In the 16th century, William Dunbar satirised his Gaelic-speaking contemporaries but he was familiar with their language, hearing it at the court of King James IV. His 'Flyting' with the Gaelic-speaking Walter Kennedy indicates not only antipathy but also familiarity and proximity. And Kennedy was an Ayrshire man.

To some degree, Gaelic identity in the Hebrides developed in a continuing relation to the Norse and Scandinavian presence in the late medieval period, and this has continued ever since. In the 21st century, there's still a strong sense of Norse identity, especially in Lewis. In some respects, Scotland may be accurately described as an intrinsically 'Nordic' nation. Orkney and even more clearly, Shetland, preserve and celebrate aspects of this inheritance but the Hebrides, over centuries, established Gaelic as the dominant linguistic and cultural ethos, while maintaining the Nordic as part of the culture. Certainly, there was and is no sense of 'pure' cultural identity in any of these archipelagos. Identity is made up of different things. Again, the connection with Gaelic Ireland is of profound importance in the development of this story.

A selection of written Gaelic texts was collected by James MacGregor, in *The Book of the Dean of Lismore*, between 1512 and 1542 in Fortingall in Perthshire, although the earliest Gaelic text from Scotland is to be found in the *Book of Deer*, written around 1150 at a Columban monastery in northeastern Aberdeenshire, which indicates how far Gaelic extended into the north east – much further across Scotland than it does in the early 21st century. *The Book of the Dean of Lismore* collects songs, ballads and stories in verse which evidently arose from the bardic tradition and relate the adventures of heroes and lovers more conventionally attributed to Ireland. Most of the works in the book are in Gaelic, but in the manuscript there are also a number of texts in Scots and Latin, including extracts from poems by William Dunbar and Robert Henryson.

In the 12th century, the profession of poetry was separated from the churches in Ireland and secular bardic schools developed, where poets would learn strict forms and styles. Religious works continued to be composed but the principal work of the bards was to legitimise and authorise their aristocratic patrons. Major events and occasions – domestic (weddings, births and deaths) or political (battles or conflicts) – were their subjects, so their poems can take us through the history and society of their times, demonstrating the communal values they shared.

Their work is social and conservative. Romantic ideas of individualism and the agony of creativity are foreign to it. It is deeply embedded in a loyalty to, and responsibility for, family and community, and this legacy comes right through to poets in the 20th- and 21st-centuries speaking and acting on behalf of the people of Scotland, whether they asked for it or like it or not. This is evident in Hugh MacDiarmid's poetry, prose and public interventions as a political candidate and journalist, or in Sorley MacLean's invocation of bardic authority in his poems not only about his own people, cleared from their lands, but also about the threat of nuclear devastation in the modern era. It is also evident more generally in the approval of Scottish independence by almost all of our country's major writers in 2014. This is one way in which the history of Scottish writing – and especially Gaelic poetry – is different from more conventional ideas of Anglophone Romanticism and Modernism, where the lonely, isolated artist is a familiar image.

The most enduring hereditary family of poets was the MacMhuirichs. In Derick Thomson's book *An Introduction to Gaelic Poetry*, we read: 'The MacMhuirich bardic line is the most remarkable by far in Scotland'. In the early 1200s, 'the Irish poet known as Muireadhach Albanach or Scottish Murray came in flight to Scotland' and the family line continued throughto the late 1700s, with professional poets working through 15 generations, and their poems recorded across 500 years. Such poems were associated with conflicts like the Battle of Harlaw (1411) and the Battle of Sheriffmuir (1715), praise of chieftains and occasions of celebration or mourning.

We will always need more translations of Gaelic poems. The more translations there are, the more intriguing their language itself should be understood to be, both by those of us who are familiar with it and those still limited by our ignorance of it.

Traditional Gaelic bardic poets used specific forms and familiar repertoires. For example, comparisons for a chief's excellence might be made with eagles or salmon but never with sparrows or pike. The praise-poem therefore would be composed from familiar images carefully coded in social understanding, so the ability of the poet was tested by the sharpness and freshness of the composition. Public presentation was normal but we know little about the specific performances of poetry in early Gaelic Scotland. Poets may have relied upon a professional actor to recite or sing the work, and there may have been musical accompaniment, with a clarsach or an instrument similar to the lyre. This was professional work, serious entertainment, and had to earn its appreciation. Throughout later Gaelic poetry, especially in the 17th, 18th and 19th centuries, the voices of women are conspicuous and strong, but this is less true of the earlier period.

In the major anthology of early Gaelic poetry, *Duanaire na Sracaire / Songbook of the Pillagers: Anthology of Scotland's Gaelic Verse to 1600*, edited by Wilson McLeod and Meg Bateman (2007), Bateman's translations give a vivid sense of linguistic vitality and the immediacy of tone and sense. There are two main traditions represented: the Learned Tradition and the Song Tradition, both including ballads, songs of satire, religion, elegy, humour, love and incitement. Numerous poems stand out, to be returned to. Of religious poems, many were composed as if in the persona of Columba. In 'A Blue Eye Turns' we see the homeland of Ireland disappear under the horizon as the saint travels to Scotland. In 'O Great Mary, Listen To Me' the sensual attractions of drinking and feasting, the visual delight of gold curled locks and the baby suckling the virgin's white breast demonstrate a characteristic balance of physical and spiritual understanding. This is a complement to the more ascetic tone of contempt for the world and the virtues of abstinence which characterises much religious verse. 'A Little Poem', first printed at the start of John Carswell's *Book of Common Order* (1567), includes the stanza confirming the myth of egalitarianism, a major theme in Scottish literature generally. Here is my version of it:

> There is nothing to fear from the children of Adam,
>   all who would love what is right –
> Nestle with them, find your place there –
>   Go far, little book, from morning to night.

This too connects with the impetus to satirise and undermine pompous authority and thus endorses the best ideals of the Reformation. But what may be termed the religious poems rest in an integrated way with the Panegyric tradition, the learned work of professional poets in a firm social order, in which praise, satire and celebration have their distinct places and traditions.

However formal this structure is, it does not preclude the vibrant individuality of single poems, such as the extremely personal elegy by Muireadhach Albanach (c.1200–30), 'M'Anam do Sgar Riomsa A-Raoir' / 'My Soul Parted from Me Last Night' or the earliest poems in Gaelic attributed to a woman, 'A Phaidrin Do Dhúisg mo Dhéar' / 'O Rosary That Woke My Tears' by Aithbhreac inghean Coirceadail (c.1470) and 'Atá Fleasgach arm o Thí' / 'There's a Young Man in Pursuit of Me' by Iseabal Ni Mheic Cailéin (c.1500), a courtly noblewoman. And Marion Campbell's 'Cumha Ghriogair MhicGhriogair Ghlinn Sreith' / 'Lament for MacGregor of Glenstrae' (c.1570) was described by Sorley

MacLean as 'one of the greatest poems ever made in Britain'. The tenderness and intensity of such poems complements the robust, ribald sensuality of satires such as 'Bod Brioghmhar Atà ag Donncha' / 'A Potent Prick Has Duncan' (an unembarrassedly detailed description). If some songs appear to endorse sexual appetites generally, others demonstrate more conventional misogyny, as in 'Tánaig Long ar Loch Raithneach' / 'A Ship Has Come on Loch Rannoch' where the vessel is constructed from brambles, thorns and cables of reeds, delivering a supernatural visitation of evil women, inimical to men.

This book includes quotations from Gaelic poems and translations or versions of them into English, of greater or less proximate literal accuracy. Occasionally complete poems are given. I made these without fluent, familiar knowledge of the language but I studied each poem in its original Gaelic as closely as I could and I read as many English-language versions as I could find, including those by Gaelic scholars and poets. The major anthologies of Gaelic poetry with facing-page English translations are also quoted sometimes. All the translations I read worked in part, in different ways, and have fascination, but none of them seemed to carry the poems fully into the English language. To do so is impossible, of course, and many studies have been written about the virtues and liabilities of literal and non-literal translations and what extremes of accuracy and approximation are permissible. I read essays, historical accounts, critical material relating to both the individual poems and their authors, their historical and cultural contexts. I went through many of them closely with people who knew Gaelic, and who knew the poems, what they are about and how their rhythms, music and idioms work. But my versions are my own and all the liabilities, failures and affrontery involved in their presentation are mine. My principle is that it is better to have some indication of the quality of the work rather than none at all. Some will disagree.

So try this poem, in praise of the island of Arran. It was recorded in the 13th century (though it is possibly much earlier, suggesting the interaction of Gaels on either side of the Sea of Moyle). My English-language version begins like this:

Arran, on high, running: a company of stags,
The cloak of the sea is ultramarine, around the island's shoulders rippling –
The green mountains bountiful, giving to warriors nourishment,
And the hunt to the high stone ridges ends with blue spearheads made scarlet –

Deer running wild on the ridges,
And in bushes in valleys, the soft fruit of berries is ripening –
Clear, cold water, in fast, sunlit streams, champagne goes gurgling through glens,
Strong oak-trees rise tall, weigh heavy with acorns in forests –

This is the favourite hunting-ground of the Fianna, rich in game and with fish and fruit in abundance. Some stories tell that Finn's wife is buried in Machrie Moor, on Arran, one of the most significant bronze-age locations in Scotland, where the standing stones mark the centre of a marvelously variegated amphitheatre of gently rising fields, tall mountains in the north and coasts within walkable distance to the west, south and east.

Go there and you can still imagine their presence. It is not far away.

2

Thomas Rhymer and Wyntoun's *Cronykil*

THE GAELIC WORD for the country our literature inhabits is Alba. The word Scotland has its own history, and the idea of national identity as it is understood in the 21st century, arguably came into being in the era through the reigns in the 9th century of Kenneth MacAlpin and in the 11th century of Malcolm Canmore. We have been looking at a whole range of literary forms, in different languages, produced in various locations and circumstances, outwith what we would describe as a modern 'nation'. In literary terms, that sense of national inhabitation rises into the Gaelic world in territories that include parts of what we now call Scotland and Ireland. From the death of Alexander III of Scotland in 1286 to the 14th-century poets writing in the wake of the Wars of Independence, a more coherent idea of what Scotland is and what Scottish literature might be comes into play.

On the night of 18 March 1286, King Alexander III left Edinburgh and set off on horseback to Kinghorn in Fife, to spend the night with his wife Queen Yolande, whose birthday was the following day. Separated from his guides, he came off his horse and his body was found at the foot of a steep rocky bank on the way. This left Scotland vulnerable, without the King or the assurance of certain succession. Factions were growing around rival claimants to the throne, John Balliol and Robert Bruce and others, and King Edward I of England was invited to adjudicate these claims. When he claimed legal authority as overlord, and then asserted his own hereditary right to the throne of Scotland, opposition to his authority began to lead to the Wars of Independence.

On the same night that Alexander III set off from Edinburgh, in the village of Earlston (or Ercildoune), Thomas Rhymer (c.1220–98), whose name presumably signified his job (like Baker or Carter), had been summoned to dine with the Earl. On being asked what he thought the morning would bring, he prophesied that the worst tempest Scotland had ever known was coming the next day. When news of the King's death arrived, Thomas's reputation as a prophet was confirmed. His reputation as a poet rested on an epic narrative, *Sir Tristram*, and apparently remained high for centuries and as another of Alastair Moffat's books, *The Borders: A History of the Borders from Earliest Times* (2007) tells us, there are good grounds for considering him 'the forerunner of Henryson and Dunbar'. But we should note that much uncertainty remains about the security of attributions and identifications from such an antiquity.

Some things seem fairly certain, though. Economically, Scotland had been prospering until, after the death of Alexander III, the resistance to King Edward I of England led to civil strife. This context is the basis for one of the earliest surviving verses written in Older Scots, recorded in 1424 in the *Oryginale Cronykil of Scotland* by Andrew of Wyntoun (c.1350–c.1425). It's a lament for Scotland after Alexander's death, but it's also an invocation of what prosperity might mean and why it was longed for:

> Quhen Alexander our kynge was dede
> That Scotlande led in lauche and le,
> Away was sons of alle and brede,
> Off wyne and wax, of gamyn and gle.
> Our golde was changit in to lede.
> Christ, borne in virgynyte,
> Succoure Scotlande, and remede,
> That stade is in perplexite.

There is certainly a direct line from Thomas through the songs and poems of the Scottish Borders to Walter Scott's collection of ballads, *Minstrelsy of the Scottish Border* (1802–03), and from there to Nigel Tranter (1909–2000), whose novel *True Thomas* (1981) offers a realistic explanation for Thomas's mysterious disappearance and whose narrative is peppered with poems and prophecies. The long poem 'Sir Tristrem', often ascribed to Thomas, was revised and reprinted by Scott in the early 19th century, as was the traditional ballad of 'Thomas the Rhymer' (ostensibly a poem about the poem's author).

With more than 600 years between these poems and Scott, and nearly 200 between Scott and Tranter, the authenticity of such stories and their authors becomes, at least, uncertain. On the one hand, 'Thomas the Rhymer' is a traditional ballad of the otherworld, in which Thomas, lying on a grassy bank, encounters the Queen of Elfland and rides off with her into a twilight zone, the Celtic land of the ever-young, and returns after seven years, which seem like no time at all to him. The ballad is full of mysterious suggestions of wondrousness and difficulty, sexual implication and insight, the cost of bloodshed and the virtues of love. When Thomas returns to his human world, he has acquired the gift of prophecy. So much for the ballad, whose events we cannot date or verify. But on the other hand, Thomas seems to have been a real man who lived and wrote and whose verses and prophecies survive from the early 1400s, referring to his adventures in a first-person narrative that names actual places such as Huntlie Bank and Eildon, near Melrose.

What are we to make of all this?

Perhaps we should simply acknowledge the fact of ambiguities in this world, and that there are things we cannot see. The reality of that immaterial world, that gives rise to ideals that cannot be presented as material goods, surely lies behind the words of the Declaration of Arbroath. Such immaterial reality is what vitalises poetry and makes life more than mere existence. This is why the clay grows tall.

3

The Bruce, The Wallace, Bannockburn and the Declaration of Arbroath

THE BATTLE OF BANNOCKBURN, 1314, is normally marked as the defining moment of victory for Bruce and the Scots and the turning point in the Wars of Independence, but in fact it was followed by many years of further warfare and even the Declaration of Arbroath in 1320 did not bring the threat of English domination to an end. The First War of Independence is usually dated 1296–1328, ending with the Treaty of Edinburgh-Northampton. But the second War of Independence followed, 1332–57, and did not end until the Treaty of Berwick. So the historical complexities of the time are not easily defined. But Wallace and Bruce occupy a key position in both history and literary tradition.

John Barbour (c.1320–95) was born around the same year as the Declaration was written and his epic poem, *The Bruce* (c.1375), was composed only 60 years or so after the events. While Latin was the language of international politics, *The Bruce* was written in vernacular Scots for a local – including courtly – readership, drawing on stories Barbour had heard, some no doubt from eye-witnesses. Barbour had become Archdeacon of Aberdeen in 1357, travelled to study at Oxford and Paris, and was a man of high authority in both church and civil law, Auditor of the Exchequer to King Robert II, grandson of the Bruce, from whom he received a regular pension after 1378, partly in recognition of his writing *The Bruce*.

The poem is a masterpiece: hyper-tense stories, of course, but everything propelled by radical declarations of strong resolution and high hopes. Its most famous exclamation comes in Book 1, after a description of the brutish English occupation of Scotland. This is when the call in praise of 'Freedom' rings out:

> A! fredome is a noble thing!
> Fredome mayss man haiff liking,
> Fredome all solace to man giffis;
> He levys at ess that freely levys.

We meet various characters, including Bruce's close friend, the ferocious fighter Sir James of Douglas. (Incidentally, this is the precedent for the relation in *Trainspotting* between Renton and Begbie.) After Bruce kills the Red Comyn, we follow him on the run, through various battles, over the sea to his refuge on Rathlin Island, and to his hiding out in the mountains, taking shelter.

Episodes of lurid violence flash through the poem, as when the 'Douglas Larder' is described: Douglas captures a castle, eats his fill and throws all the goods his soldiers can't carry into the cellar with his prisoners, then takes savage revenge:

And the prisoners that he had tane,	And the prisoners he'd taken,
Richt tharin gert he hed ilkane.	He there had beheaded, every one.
Syne of the tunnys the hedis out-strak,	And then the wine tubs he did smash
A foul melle thair can he mak;	And made a foul and bloody mash.
For meill, malt, blude, and wyne	For meal and malt and wine and blood
Ran all to-gidder in a mellyne...	Ran all together in a flood...'

One of the most climactic stories is the Battle of Loudoun Hill. On the edge of Ayrshire and Lanarkshire, south-east of Glasgow, as the main north road from Carlisle to Edinburgh cuts overland from south-west to north-east, Loudoun Hill still sits like a couchant lion near the road running up the Irvine valley. English soldiers advancing from the south wouldn't have been able to see the preparations Scots troops might have made for them, the trenches and dykes Bruce orders constructed in the poem. The English would have narrowed their front to proceed by the river Irvine, so that a smaller opposing force might tear through them fast and gain the advantage before the strengths of the invading army could be properly mustered. By the end of the fight, 'The feld wes weill neir coverit all / Bath with slayn hors and with men...'

When we come to the Battle of Bannockburn, as the troops are drawn up on either side, a David and Goliath scenario is enacted with a small army facing much larger forces. As Bruce is encouraging his soldiers before battle begins, riding up and down in the field in front of them on a small, light horse armed only with a battle-axe, the English knight Sir Henry de Bohun emerges from the English ranks, a big, black-bearded man with heavy lance on a huge, heavy charger. De Bohun spurs the horse onwards, lowering and pointing his lance, intending to skewer the Scottish king and end the battle before it begins. Bruce, seeing the danger at the last moment, stays steady then suddenly wheels his small horse round, evading the lance and swinging his battle-axe with all his strength, bringing it down as de Bohun hurtles by, splitting through his helmet and cleaving his skull to the neck-bone. As the big Englishman hits the ground, Bruce holds up what remains of his weapon and drily complains that he has broken the hand-shaft of his good battle-axe.

A different kind of realism is encountered in Robert Baston's poem of Bannockburn, recorded in Walter Bower's Latin history of Scotland, *The Scotichronicon* (1440–47). The occasion of the poem is rich with irony. The English King Edward II sent Baston, a Carmelite monk and prior of the abbey of Scarborough, with his army to Bannockburn, with instructions to write a poem about the great victory over the Scots he was certain they would win. After Bannockburn, the Scots held on to Baston and agreed that he should indeed write the poem. To the credit of the Scots, and Baston, and the Latin poem's 21st-century translator, Edwin Morgan, what comes across clearly is not smug triumphalism but the physical horror of the murderous clash and the pain of its aftermath. If the battle was indeed worth fighting, this measures something of its cost.

'This is a double realm' Baston tells us, noting that the urge to dominate and subjugate has led to the slaughter he witnessed:

> Hence this waste of men, crossed out by war's black pen,
> Whole peoples sunk in the fen, still fighting, again and again,
> Hence white faces in the ground, hence white faces of the drowned,
> Hence huge grief is found, cries with which the stars are crowned,
> Hence wars that devastate field and farm and state.

Drawing on vernacular tradition like *The Bruce*, *The Wallace* (c.1477) by Blind Harry (c.1440–92), is one of the most popular Scottish literary works of all time, also abundant with gory effects, close-up accounts of blood-letting, split heads and limbs chopped off in battles. Like *The Bruce*, it's an accumulation of stories, many of them showing perspectives and episodes which reveal Wallace and his struggle in the light of personal as well as national significance. There is unaffected, unsentimental poignancy in Harry's representation of Wallace's unflinching, broadsword-slicing vigour. This was probably a touchy subject: King James III was trying to establish peace with the English when the poem was written. Harry claimed to be following a Latin text written by Wallace's chaplain but the poem breathes vernacular Scots immediacy on every page.

It embodies the myth of Wallace as a man of the people (even though he was a knight's son) who had to be knighted himself to be allowed to join the aristocratic men directing the Wars of Independence. He was made 'Guardian of Scotland' and led the Scots to victory most memorably at the battle of Stirling Bridge. He was let down by his own aristocratic supporters and betrayed by the Earl of Menteith, taken to London and tried for treason. He pointed out that he never swore allegiance to the King of England so could not be tried for treason, but this was no defence and his public execution made him a martyr. At the heart of the poem, Wallace's brief marriage allows a poignant moment of domestic respite which must be left behind for the greater struggle ahead. When Wallace's wife is killed, the national purpose melds with the motive of personal vengeance to heighten the story's urgency.

Just as Barbour's Bruce travels through Scotland, Harry's Wallace crosses the terrain of the nation and further, into England for the siege of York. Unlike the hero of Barbour's poem, however, Harry's Bruce is compromised by his wavering loyalty to King Edward, and a haunting image pictures him after the battle of Falkirk, where he had fought on the English side against the Scots. He sits to eat at the table without washing, and is mocked by his English peers: 'The South'ron lords did mock him in terms rude / And said, "Behold yon Scot eats his own blood!"' From this moment, Bruce begins to realise which side he should be on.

Wallace is heroic but vulnerable, not only as revenge deepens and twists his personal motivations but also as cruelty sometimes escalates his actions. He promises 'Rivers of floating blood, and hills of slain!' and the poem delivers. But also, in Book v, Wallace is haunted by the ghost of one of his victims and runs from a blazing castle with a headless corpse in pursuit. The extremes of atrocity and repulsion are matched by dedication and righteousness, so that when Wallace is left for dead at one point, women nurse him back to health, one of them suckling him at her breast.

After Baston's Bannockburn poem and behind both Barbour's *Bruce* and Harry's *Wallace*, there is a different kind of historical document which retains immense authority, one of the most lastingly influential pieces of writing in Scottish literature, the *Declaration of Arbroath* (1320).

It is literature in the sense of composed writing, rhetoric, an artifice of language, not in the sense of fiction or play. It was originally a letter, written in Latin, attributed to Bernard de Linton (d.1331), the King's chancellor, and signed by a number of Scottish earls and barons, addressed to the Pope, appealing to him to approve their cause above the oppressions of the English. Yet it is not merely a political gesture generated by religious or military strategy, nor is it simply the product of relatively wealthy people with vested interests who might have cared nothing for the people who lived on the land they claimed as property. The point about this document is that it articulates ideas that have quickened the sense of value people have and their – and our – desire to want better. The same can be said for any great work of literature, music or art. The abstract ideas – the nation, rule of law, truth, liberty, honesty – are generalities that always have specific reference. Essentially, they are about self-determination. They are the ideals whose endorsement is the means to bring about the freedom to effect that self-determination. It is not a call to attack, conquer, colonise and rule other people elsewhere, but a defence of the right to choose your own form of government. It is anti-imperialist and lies at the heart of a vision of social justice that need not be exaggerated into caricature or denigrated as merely idealistic. This is how it concludes:

> Yet if he [Robert the Bruce, King of Scots] should give up what he has begun, and agree that we or our kingdom should be subject to the King

of England or the English, we should exert ourselves at once to drive him out as our enemy and a subverter of his own rights and ours, and make some other man better able to defend us our king; for, as long as one hundred of us remain alive, never will we be brought under English rule. It is in truth not for glory, nor riches, nor honours that we fight, but for freedom – for that alone, which no honest man gives up except with life itself.

In a pamphlet, *On the Declaration of Arbroath* (Edinburgh: Saltire Society, 1951), Agnes Mure Mackenzie wrote: 'We fear, and we try to counter, material weapons, that have never been so formidable as now. We do not fear enough the mental weapons, that make the most devilish of the material as mild, by comparison, as a small boy's squirt. To counter these, we must clean the poisoned minds, and feed the healthy, clear-cut knowledge, precisely fashioned shapes of human freedom.'

As Dauvit Broun says in an essay in the book *The Declaration of Arbroath: History, Significance, Setting*, edited by Geoffrey Barrow (Edinburgh: Society of Antiquaries of Scotland, 2003): 'The account of Scottish origins in the Declaration of Arbroath, as the pedigree of Scottish self-determination, was not a statement of biological descent or ethnic affiliation. It was the pedigree of an allegiance'. This was an allegiance to an authority characterised by responsibility to the people who were pledging their allegiance. In other words, an act of loyalty not merely to a state or kingdom or an area on a map, but to an idea which has its own history, in Broun's words: 'an idea which people have engaged with, recreated and adapted.'

This idea in its articulation in 1320 may have had little in common with what we understand today by the word 'democracy' or with the meaning of that word as applied to the slave-owning societies of ancient Greece and Rome or of the United States in the 18th and 19th centuries.

Nevertheless, in the evolution of the priorities of giving voice to those denied representation, and to listening and acting upon what those voices speak of, the intrinsic idea is a thread through many labyrinths of social, political and geographical circumstance, and widely far-apart territories.

In 1967, when a Scottish National Party member gained a Westminster parliamentary seat and the nationalist 1320 Club was founded, the interpretation of the Declaration as an affirmation of independence was established. Of course, the document's historical data and context insist that we must read the letter in its own time and place, but equally, its power as an assertion of priority has mythical status, about which we are wise to be careful, but from which, also, we might draw strength.

For it is not only a document from history, nor a prismatically shapeshifting text at the mercy of its exploiters of whatever disposition. It is rather a work of literature, words organised by laws of both self-conscious rhetoric and emotional intuition, which, as much as it demands to be located specifically in itself and in the uses identified in its deployment, also commands literary respect and imaginative engagement.

The judge and historian Lord Cooper (1892–1955), in an address to the Scottish History Society in 1949, indicated in detail the formal use of Latin prose rhythmic structures in the original document, the 'ars dictaminis'. As he says in his book *Supra Crepidam: Presidential Addresses delivered to the Scottish Historical Society* (London: Thomas Nelson, 1951), these would have been familiar to the papal chancery to whom the original letter was addressed. Cooper describes three patterns of words arranged to effect emotional meaning, structures that generate cadences, arts of persuasion that have to be convincing. They cannot be merely manufactured, but they have to fit what he calls 'the substance of the message'. The three 'primary forms' as he calls them, or the 'three keys' are as follows: the 'Cursus Planus' for narrative (as in 'servants departed'), the 'Cursus Tardus' for solemn invocation (as in 'perfect felicity') and the 'Cursus Velox' for passages of deep urgency or strong feeling (as in 'glorious undertaking'). These rhetorical devices signify highly developed literary sensibilities at work in the document's composition and that it was designed for an intensely literate reading.

Also, there is a subtle modulation of a crucial quotation from Sallust (Gaius Sallustus Crispus, 86–35 BC, a Roman historian, politician and opponent of the old Roman aristocracy). In his work, *The War with Catiline* (probably written between 44 and 40 BC), we read:

> At nos non imperium neque divitias petimus, quarum rerum causa bella atque certamina omnia inter mortalis sunt, sed libertatem, quam nemo bonus nisi cum anima simul amittit.

Or in English, as translated by J.C. Rolfe, from the Loeb edition:

> But we are seeking neither power nor riches for the sake of which all wars and strife arise among mortals, but rather freedom, which no upstanding man gives up except together with his life.

The literary sophistication at work here is an extraordinary example of what writing can do. Cooper describes it as a 'remarkable manifesto':

> Read it again, and judge for yourselves whether it does not deserve on its merits to be ranked as one of the masterpieces of political rhetoric of all time.

Agnes Mure Mackenzie's distinction between 'material weapons' and 'healthy, clear-cut knowledge' is perennially important, and the diagnosis that a poison of imagination is even more deadly, far more deadly, in fact, in Walter Scott's words, a 'weapon formed for slaughter', filling veins with 'death instead of life', is as accurate in the 21st as it was in the 14th century. So that 'mortal venom' (drawn from fear itself, sometimes, and its origin, ignorance) needs to be opposed by a self-determination given to affirming identity through allegiance rather than, or beyond, the social strata into which you were born, your place of birth and upbringing, your given world. Your affinities are elective as well as given. It's not only an insistence, it's also your choice. And the context of requirement in any act of self-determination is always present tense.

Beyond the given, the only allegiance worth making comes through knowledge and wisdom, which is why education is crucial, and the dignity of diversity in cultural identity, always and everywhere, is the only real diplomacy that works.

In the public debate at Oxford University on 3 December 1964, Hugh MacDiarmid spoke alongside the black American revolutionary Malcolm X, who was assassinated in 1965, to approve the motion that 'Extremism in the defence of liberty is no vice; moderation in the pursuit of Justice is no virtue.' MacDiarmid quoted the last sentences of the *Declaration* and then said, 'My people, the Scottish people, have done little but betray that oath ever since.' Yet 1964 is not the end of the story.

See *The Bruce*, translated into modern English verse by Archibald A.H. Douglas (Glasgow: William MacLellan, 1964). The best modern scholarly edition is *The Bruce*, annotated and introduced by A.A.M. Duncan (Edinburgh: Canongate, 1999). And *The Wallace*, edited and introduced by Anne McKim (Edinburgh: Canongate, 2003). And Robert Baston's *Metrum de Praelio apud Bannockburn / The Battle of Bannockburn*, translated by Edwin Morgan (Edinburgh: Scottish Poetry Library, Akros and Mariscat Press, 2004).

4

Love is all you need: James I, *The Kingis Quair*

WHEN THE YOUTHFUL King James I of Scotland (1394–1437) was taken prisoner and held in England, in Windsor Castle, he saw from a tower window the beautiful Joan Beaufort walking in the garden below, and decided there and then that she was the woman for him.

So the story goes.

The Kingis Quair (c.1424) is the poem attributed to James, written in an elegant, gentle and well nigh unique 'Anglo-Scots', and it survives in a manuscript collection from the end of the 1400s, now held in the Bodleian Library in Oxford. 'Quair' simply means 'Book' but it also suggests 'Choir', a collection of voices raised in harmony. The poem is beautifully eloquent, sustaining itself through various different kinds of writing: straightforward description, lyrical song, praise, complaint, prayer, lucid instruction, dream-allegory and moral adventure. It's made up of 197 seven-line stanzas, each rhyming ababbcc, a form that is itself an emblem of sustained poise, and prompted the description 'rhyme royale' because of King James's use of it here.

Its genre, the dream poem, is traditional, and in Scots poetry runs all the way through to MacDiarmid's *A Drunk Man Looks at the Thistle*, and on. In the dream in King James's poem, the lover makes his case to Venus before an assembly of peers who have known the pain of being in love, and asks about destiny and free will in a context where love's liberating idealisation provides an escape from the poet's physical imprisonment. The poem's imagery is bright: singing birds, crystal waters, little fish and the shifts of fortune men and women suffer all have their places. Birds are closer to God and blessed with voices for songs of their own, literally flying higher than the silent but beautiful wee fishes, who, while lower in the scheme of things, and voiceless, are nevertheless equally part of God's world. So the poet, caught between them, birds on high and fish below, suffers on Fortune's wheel –

> the nature of it is evermore,
> After ane hicht, to vale and give a fall

– but this is a love poem with a happy ending, tense but ultimately buoyant, emotionally immediate without sentimentalising anything.

James I did indeed marry Joan Beaufort but the poem is also wise about luck. Implicit is the sense that Fortune's wheel may turn again, as indeed for James it did, but the formal closure of the poem allows it to remain finally a work of art, a lasting pleasure.

James I in this poem was decidedly Chaucerian in form but his successors, including Robert Henryson, William Dunbar and Gavin Douglas, were a very different lot. The fine English critic A.C. Spearing, in *Criticism and Medieval Poetry* (1964; reprinted 1972), notes that 'what they take undergoes an often radical transformation, since they also draw on a vigorous and non-Chaucerian tradition' and 'there is a far more individual life in their work than is to be found in their English contemporaries.'

But let's stay with *The Kingis Quair* and savour it a bit more. It takes off, as many poems of its era do, with reference to the poet's reading of another book. This is most familiar from Henryson's *Testament of Cresseid* (c.1485), where the poet begins in winter by withdrawing to his warm fireside with Chaucer's *Troilus and Criseyde* (c.1385), but then taking up 'another' book and wondering if Chaucer told the whole story truthfully, or whether there isn't more to say. Similarly, *The Kingis Quair* is prompted by reflection on *The Consolation of Philosophy* (c.523) by Boethius (c.477–524). The poet recollects how Fortune's wheel turned badly for Boethius, but the *Quair*'s story is of Fortune bringing good things, beneficence, blessing, love. It's an affirmation. The variety of forms it demonstrates is partly a healthy exercise of poetic ability, a happy showing-off of expertise, but its deeper purpose is a demonstration of life's variousness, as the wheel carries you into a happier position.

With the great wheel of interstellar, intergalactic creation turning around him, the lonely poet wakes in a solitary bed, his mind restless, thinking of 'this and that' – so he takes a book to read. The poem begins like this:

>   Heigh in the hevynnis figure circulere
>   The rody sterres twynklyng as the fyre,
>   And, in Aquary, Citherea the clere
>   Rynsid hir tressis like the goldin wyre
>   That late tofore in fair and fresche atyre
>   Through Capricorn heved hir hornis bright,
>   North northward approchit the mydnyght,
>
>   Quhen, as I lay in bed allone waking,
>   New partit out of slepe a lyte tofore,
>   Fell me to mynd of many diverse thing,
>   Of this and that, can I noght say quharfore,
>   Bot slepe for craft in erth myght I no more,
>   For quhich as tho coude I no better wyle,
>   Bot toke a boke to rede apon a quhile...

Structurally, the poem is in five parts. Part One introduces the poet and sets the scene. It's important to remember that the poem itself is written by an older, wiser man than the one presented in the prison, for this helps us understand that the imprisonment is both literal and allegorical. James is imprisoned in the tower but also in solitude: he is loveless. Love, marriage and wisdom will bring him freedom. The poem is a foundation myth and, if we're lucky, speaks of a reality as crucial as that of Wallace, Bruce and Independence.

Part two recollects James's capture and imprisonment by the English, of how he came to the sorry state he's in:

> With doutfull hert amang the rokkis blake,
> My feble bote full fast to stere and rowe,
> Helples, allone, the wynter nyght I wake,
> To wayte the wynd that furthward suld me throwe.
> O empti saile, quhare is the wynd suld blowe
> Me to the port, quhar gynneth all my game?
> Help, Calyope, and wynd, in Marye name!

And as the sea becalms his ship, 'enemies' capture him and his companions:

> The bird, the beste, the fisch eke in the see,
> They lyve in fredome, everich in his kynd;
> And I a man, and lakkith libertee!

Yet even in despair and loneliness, he can see from the window in his prison tower a

> gardyn fair, and in the corners set
> Ane herber grene with wandis long and small
> Railit about

and he calls out in a hymn to love and love's mercy, and looks out once more:

> And therwith kest I doun myn eye ageyne,
> Quhare as I sawe, walking under the tour,
> Full secretly new cummyn hir to pleyne,
> The fairest or the freschest yong floure
> That ever I sawe, me thoght, before that houre;
> For quhich sodayn abate anon astert
> The blude of all my body to my hert.

There is little of what we would call realistic narrative detail in the poem, which makes the sight of the beloved from the window all the more memorable. The woman departs from the garden and the poem takes us through a vision of the gods, and the poet's prayer to the goddess of love.

Part three is the dream. There are three 'dreamscapes' and a god for each one: Venus, Minerva (wisdom) and Fortune. First we travel to the heavens and meet all sorts of lovers, and Venus herself, who gives the poet Hope, who takes him to Minerva, after being admitted to her realm by the porter, Patience. Venus commands the poet to remember the moment of vision and the motivation of love, and to make her authority a priority among all those he will come in time to rule:

> 'Quhen thou descendis doun to ground ageyne,
> Say to the men that there bene resident
> How long think thay to stand in my disdeyne
> That in my lawis bene so negligent
> From day to day, and list tham noght repent
> Bot breken louse and walken at thair large?
> Is ther none that therof gevis charge?
>
> 'And for,' quod sche, 'the angir and the smert
> Of thair unkyndenesse dooth me constreyne,
> My femynyne and wofull tender hert,
> That than I wepe, and to a token pleyne,
> As of my teris cummyth all this reyne
> That ye se on the ground so fast ybete
> Fro day to day, my turment is so grete!...'

After leaving Venus with Hope, Patience and Wisdom return him to earth, dream-walking through an ideal landscape with a flowing river filled with fish, blossoming plants and lively animals of all kinds. Fortune is turning her wheel and invites the poet to climb on, for the wheel can carry folk up as well as down. Then she pinches his ear and he wakes up: she

> by the ere me toke
> So earnestly, that therewithal I woke.

The tiny detail of the goddess nipping his ear to bring him out of the dream is an example of how the allegory is kept sharp and lively.

In Part four, the poet, the lover, is now awake and more worried than ever by the thought that only dreams can bring him to what he desires. But then he looks out the window once again. What he sees reaffirms his sense of the authority of love:

> In hye unto the wyndow gan I walk,
> Moving within my spirit of this sight,
> Quhare, sodeynly, a turtur quhite as calk
> So evinly upon my hand gan lyght,
> And unto me sche turnyt hir full ryght,
> Of quham the chere in hir birdis aport
> Gave me in hert kalendis of confort.

The white turtle-dove (the turtur) alights, bringing him a scroll on which 'gillyflowers' (like carnations) are depicted and a poem announces that heaven has decreed he shall have his wishes granted. The poet's purpose is confirmed: to serve love, and to write the poem and send it into the world to do its work, as he will return to liberty, marriage and Scotland independent and at peace.

In Part five, the story concludes. The courtship was successful, and the poet gives thanks to the gods and to the earlier poets from whom he learned his skills. *The Kingis Quair* itself is sent out into the world to tell its tale and spread the word.

Marriage, in this poem, is freedom. The harmony of all things is the affirmation of all the celestial and earthly realities we have encountered. In *The Allegory of Love* (1936), C.S. Lewis said of this poem:

> In it the poetry of marriage at last emerges from the traditional poetry of adultery; and the literal narrative of a contemporary wooing emerges from romance and allegory. It is the first modern book of love.

We live and learn.

5

The rule of compassion: Robert Henryson

THE BIOGRAPHICAL ACCOUNT has it that after studying church law at Glasgow University, Robert Henryson (c.1435–c.1505) became a schoolmaster attached to the Benedictine Abbey in Dunfermline, whose manuscript collection was a crucial resource. His poems embody the great themes of literature: the need for moral reform, the vanity and the vulnerability of living things, the desire for justice and fairness in a world crossed by violence, the reach beyond the self, the quest for harmony. There are three major achievements in his work.

In his version of Orpheus and Eurydice, Orpheus travels through Heaven and Hell looking for his beloved Eurydice, to restore human sexual order to the harmony of the planets in their orbits. The mathematical precisions of his journey through the stellar system in search of lost love are a contrast with the poem's human message: search as methodically and thoroughly as you will, but you won't find Eurydice in Heaven. You have to take the risk of a journey into Hell to find her.

The story is pre-Homeric, from the world of Greek myth, before the siege of Troy or the travels of Aeneas and the founding of Rome, or Odysseus's voyages, first home to Ithaca, and then his final journey to the west. Myth is the key: Orpheus is masculinity, looking for his female counterpart. He embodies the principle of song: his only weapon is music. When he finally discovers Eurydice in the deepest reaches of Hell, he persuades her captor that she must be released. But not forever. On the way back to earth's surface, Orpheus looks at Eurydice, and she is taken down once again, into the shadowlands. But she returns each year to the earth, for a limited time.

The story enacts the rhythm of the seasons: Eurydice is spring. Song brings her back to the world and she stays, happily, through summer, till autumn starts to send her back to earth and earth's depths, once again. The cycle is also a metaphor: procreation, regeneration. The rhythm is repeatable, as the mathematical precisions of the poem show, when Orpheus journeys through the stars – but there is always a risk, always an uncertainty, always something human to care about, to yearn for, something that demands the risk be taken.

Henryson's second great achievement is his reworking of 13 of Aesop's *Fables*, transferring their location to distinctively Scottish farms and small towns and surprising the reader with unpredicted moral explanations. The general point made by each of them is that to judge only by external appearances is disastrous. Each fable describes an encounter and then delivers a 'Moral' at the end, which might overturn all reasonable expectations. In 'The Cock and the Jasp' a cockerel spots a jewel on the dungheap, finds it inedible and walks away. He seems to have taken the wise decision but the Moralitas tells us that the jewel is all the difficult wisdom,

> perfite prudence and cunning,
> Ornate with mony deidis of vertew...

So we should respect and acknowledge the quality of the jewel above 'the sempill corne' or we are no better than fools, scornful of science and ignorant of learning.

The moral endings surprise us when they reinterpret what's gone before but the fables are engaging because of Henryson's vivid depictions and visual immediacy. His language is attentive to both narrative subtleties and visual impact, and he writes dramatic dialogue, with the animals engaged in eyebrow-raising quizzical responses to what's around them and to each other. However, in 'The Wolf and the Lamb' no amount of rhetorical persuasion can save the lamb from the wolf's hungry jaws: when they come to a river, they both drink:

> bot not of ane intent:
> The wolfis thocht wes all on wickitnes,
> The selie lamb was meik and innocent.

The wolf 'drank his blude and off his flesche can eit'. And the moral?

> The pure pepill this lamb may signifie – [poor]
> As maill-men, merchandis and all laboureris, [small tenant-farmers]
> Of quhome the lyfe is half ane purgatorie
> To wyn with lautie leving as efferis; [To win their livelihood honestly and aptly]
> The wolf betakinnis fals extortioneris
> And oppressouris of pure men – as we se –
> Be violence or craft in facultie. [manipulating human nature]

In 'The Paddock and the Mouse' an ugly-looking toad offers to ferry a mouse across a river, arguing that 'Thow suld not juge ane man efter his face'. Halfway over, the toad tries to kill the mouse – so appearances sometimes can in fact be revealing of deeper reality. A kite flies down and carries them both away. The Moralitas is categorical: the mouse is the soul, the toad is the body, the kite is death. Meaning is not secure and violence always threatens social civility or religious piety. The distractions of surface delights can kill sensitivity to deeper, unseen or obscure meanings.

> Ane fals intent under ane fair pretence
> Hes causit mony innocent for to de.
> Grit folie is to gif over-sone credence
> To all that speiks fairlie unto the.

Read in sequence, the 13 fables explore increasingly dark and violent situations. Some are comic and all have the liveliness of tales where the main characters are figured as anthropomorphised animals with tell-tale human characteristics. The prayer for peace which underlies them all is energised by compassion and sympathy every bit as much as by the authority of church law – perhaps more. People are always vulnerable. So, beyond the conventions of allegory, there is a human sense of touching.

And touching is at the heart of Henryson's masterpiece. *The Testament of Cresseid* is one of the great works of world literature, a proto-humanist tragedy with intensely realised characters and a pantheon of inhuman gods. The essential story of *The Testament* comes from the Homeric tales of the war when the Greeks besieged Troy. Troilus and Cresseid were on opposite sides, brought together, fell in love, parted by dictates of conflict, and their separate lives run different courses to death. In Chaucer's version (c.1382–86), they are fully human characters subject to the authority of Chaucer's own belief-system. In Henryson's, Troilus and Cresseid look upon each other searchingly, yearning for recognition. Beyond the self, each wants the other to confirm their own past love and show some human sympathy in the face of the truth that time has turned rotten. But Cresseid in her leprous blindness cannot see, and Troilus cannot recognise her any more. Each tries to reach beyond their own identity and their failure is human failure, not dictated by cosmic schema or medieval church preordination. This is what touches us.

The poem begins by linking the weather, the character of the poem and the state-of-mind of the poet:

> Ane doolie sessoun to ane cairfull dyte
> Suld correspond and be equivalent:
> Richt sa it wes quhen I began to wryte
> This tragedie – the wedder richt fervent...

The poet is alone in his study, looking out:

> The northin wind had purifyit the air,
> And sched the mistie cloudis fra the sky;
> The froist freisit, the blastis bitterly
> Fra Pole Artick come quhisling loud and schill...

The poet reflects that he had once trusted Venus, Queen of Love, to keep him warm-hearted and youthful, but now he must retire to the fire in his private room. He has known love and the end of love and now builds up the fire, pours himself a drink and takes down a book, Chaucer's story of Troilus and Cresseid. But then, he tells us,

> To brek my sleip ane uther quair I tuik,
> In quhilk I fand the fatall destenie
> Of fair Cresseid, that endit wretchetlie.

And he asks, 'Quha wait gif all that Chaucer wrait was true?'

After Troilus and Cresseid have loved and parted, she takes up with another lover, Diomed, and then suddenly we are moved into the story with the word 'When...' ('When' is always a great way to begin a dramatic story because it leads to at least two things happening at the same time: 'When this was happening, that was also happening...') When Diomed has had his fill of Cresseid, he abandons her. She withdraws into her own private room, echoing the introspective movement of the poet, and cries out her regret that she ever believed in Venus and Cupid, also echoing the poet's disillusionment with love. Another 'When':

> Quhen this was said, doun in an extasie,
> Ravischit in spreit, intill ane dream scho fell...

And in this dream, the gods appear: cold, omnipotent Saturn, with chattering teeth, blue lips and lean, thin cheeks: 'Out of his nois the meldrop fast can rin'; burly, golden-haired Jupiter, 'richt fair and amiabill' but carrying a spear in his right hand; Mars, 'With reid visage and grislie glowrand ene'; Phebus, 'lanterne and lamp of licht'; Venus, come to answer Cresseid's charge:

> Bot in her face semit greit variance –
> Quhyles perfyte treuth and quhyles inconstance...

Mercurius, 'eloquent and full of rethorie'; and finally, Lady Cynthia, the lovers' moon, portentously dark because all her light is taken from the sun: 'Hir gyse was grey and ful of spottis blak', foreshadowing the leprosy that will disfigure Cresseid. Cupid appears and condemns Cresseid for her curse on him and his mother. The Gods confer and pass judgement, Saturn's gentleness belying the cruelty of the sentence: she is to be excluded from fairness and mirth, denied the health she has enjoyed, live in pain and suffering, and die a beggar.

'The Complaint of Cresseid' then follows, a beautiful lament for the passing of youth and life's cruelty: 'Thair is na salve may saif the of thy sair' she acknowledges: 'Nocht is your fairness bot ane faiding flour'. But the poem has a further twist to deliver. Cresseid, finally in the company of lepers, lifts up her blind head towards Troilus, riding by, who almost recognises her:

> Than upon him scho kest up baith her ene –
> And with ane blenk it come into his thocht
> That he sumtime hir face befoir hid sene.
> Bot scho was in sic plye he knew hir nocht;
> Yit than hir luik into his mynd it brocht
> The sweit visage and amorous blenking
> Of fair Cresseid, sumtyme his awain darling.

Cresseid speaks of herself as a warning to all others of the uncertainty of love and makes her final testament, surrendering her 'corps and carioun' to be torn apart and eaten by worms and toads, whatever gold she has to be given to the leper-folk and to return the ring given her by Troilus. Her spirit she says she would leave to the goddess Diana, to 'walk with her in waist woddis and wellis'. The irony of the promiscuous woman bequeathing her spirit to the goddess of chastity is both hard and heartbreaking. Troilus receives the ring, remembers Cresseid and collapses in sorrow, but he pulls himself together to console himself with perfunctory judgement: 'Scho was untrew and wo is me thairfoir.'

In Shakespeare's *Troilus and Cressida* (c.1602), the rottenness of politics and warfare corrupts all innocence and silence seems the only appropriate response. The two young lovers remain ambiguous characters: how deep is their commitment? How far is the expedient move dictated by force of circumstance? The sharp poignancy of crushed idealism that persists somewhere in their story may have been drawn directly from Henryson, as Shakespeare almost certainly read Thomas Speght's 1598 or 1602 edition of Chaucer's works, which included Henryson's poem. Henryson's version has all of Shakespeare's ambiguity and more piercing poignancy than Chaucer. In Henryson, Troilus and Cresseid are prophetic of those fully-realised, psychologised, physically palpable characters of 19th-century fiction, yet they're inescapably also medieval depictions, signals, forms.

The big question is to what degree you think Henryson's sympathy lies with them. Troilus is the more conventional figure because of his fixed role, and yet, when the chink in the armour appears, and he almost sees the leprous Cresseid for what she once was, he thinks of what love was, for a moment, and drops her some money. For that moment, he is both pathetic and the kind of person anyone might be. Cresseid is far more severely blasted by judgement.

The poem's ending might seem to uphold an orthodox medieval view of women as sinful corruptors, daughters of Eve. The rule of the gods, whom Cresseid defies both courageously and petulantly, is vicious. You can't help thinking that Henryson himself must have had some sympathy with her. No sensitive reader could fail to allow her spirit, freed from suffering, its place beside Diana, wandering through woods, by woodland rivers. But Henryson cuts short indulgence in such sentiment: 'Sen scho is deid, I spek of hir no moir.'

The poem ends without reassurance, except of what humanity is. Maybe this is the real reason it speaks to us across centuries: whether you're Catholic or Protestant, Christian or Muslim, atheist or agnostic, American or European, anything else or unaligned, it doesn't matter. None of these things makes you superior. What the poem gives us of Cresseid's humanity, her suffering, aspiration and hope, is what counts. It matches anything in Chaucer or Shakespeare. It bites so deep at the heart.

These are the poem's last two stanzas:

> Sum said he maid ane tomb of merbell grey,
> And wrait hir name and superscriptioun,
> And laid it on hir grave quhair that scho lay,
> In golden letteris, conteining this ressoun:
> 'Lo, fair ladyis! Cresseid of Troyis toun,
> Sumtyme countit the flour of womanheid,
> Under this stane, lait lipper, lyis deid.'
>
> Now, worthie Wemen, in this ballet schort,
> Made for your worschip and intructioun,
> Of cheritie, I monische and exhort:
> Ming not your lufe with fals deceptioun.
> Beir in your mynd this schort conclusioun
> Of fair Cresseid – as I have said befoir.
> Sen scho is deid, I speik of hir no moir.

6

Not energy ordered, energised order: William Dunbar

WILLIAM DUNBAR IS not simply to be read as a poet of the distant past, irrelevant to modern times, but rather as a major figure at the foundations of Modernism. Just as Charles Rennie Mackintosh went back to the architecture of medieval castles to design the Glasgow School of Art, just as the artist J.D. Fergusson in Paris from 1907 to 1914, embracing Cubism, looking at Picasso and Braque, stated boldly that Modernism was simply a matter of getting back to fundamentals, and went looking for copies of Dunbar's poetry to read in this context, just as Stravinsky's quintessential modernist work, *The Rite of Spring*, is subtitled 'Pictures from Pagan Russia', going back even further than Dunbar, the great artists, writers and composers of the Modern movement regenerated their work through return to their earliest sources.

Dunbar lived from around 1460 till around 1520. He was a churchman, a chaplain at the great Renaissance court of James IV, and seems to have been widely travelled in England, France, Denmark and elsewhere. His poems range just as widely as Burns's. Formal poems for state occasions, squibs and satires of daily life at court, playful, topical, colloquial poems, verbally dexterous, 'enamelled' verse or vulgar, downmarket rhymes of more popular purpose. He moves from the flippant comedy of 'How Sir John Sinclair Began to Dance' (one foot always gets it wrong) to the steady, heavily-paced 'Lament for the Makars', a lengthening list of predeceased poets and friends, written in the pressing knowledge of his own mortality, from the most carefully poised love poem:

> Sweet Rose of virtue and of gentleness,
> Delightsome lily of every lustiness,
> Richest in bounty and in beauty clear
> And every virtue that is dear
> Except only that ye are merciless...

to the hell-dance vision of the 'Dance of the Seven Deadly Sins', from the sexually explicit 'Twa Marriet Wemen and the Widow', where three ladies discuss the relative merits of men, to the sheer ferocity of the religious poems in praise of God and condemnation of evil.

Sins are awful realities in Dunbar's poems, and their meanings apply today as much as ever. When temptation rises, prompting greed, lechery, drunkenness, violence, the threats are as much with us now as they were in the 16th century.

Date rape, drunk driving, bullying, gluttony. The sensual apprehension of the attractiveness of self-indulgence is vivid in Dunbar, and countered by the shields of self-knowledge and active defence against its allure. This is central in his poem 'The Golden Targe', where male desire is roused by the approach of a host of beautiful women.

The value he puts upon the ideals of social justice is central to 'The Thrissil and the Rose', the poem he wrote in celebration of the marriage of King James to Margaret Tudor of England in 1503. The union he affirms can only be maintained, he says, if the king himself is virtuous, as the lion, king of beasts, the eagle, king of birds, or the thistle, crowned above all plants. He must 'do law alike to apes and unicorns' and is in Dame Nature's charge, at her ultimate command. With hindsight, of course, we know how that union failed, James leading his army to slaughter at Flodden in 1513. But the ideals remain, brilliantly expressed in Dunbar's poem.

Hugh MacDiarmid recommended Dunbar to his contemporaries in the 1920s, in two slogans: 'Not Burns – Dunbar!' and 'Back to Dunbar!' He was saying that not only is there another poet of vision and technical brilliance equal to Burns, but that there is a whole history, a tradition of Scottish poetry that opens its doors to all sorts of human experience. To celebrate only one poet in this tradition is not good enough.

More than that, he was indicating a rich culture in Scotland that common popular currency neglects, ignores, or even suppresses. And its tradition extends much further back into history than the 18th century.

In his 1943 book, *Modern Scottish Painting*, J.D. Fergusson described his attempt to buy a copy of Dunbar's poems:

> I went to every bookshop in Paris, London, Glasgow and Edinburgh, and got the only one existing at a reasonable price in Edinburgh, and of course *not at all complete*. This means that the Calvinists have kept the work of Dunbar from the poor student of Scottish poetry, from the time of the Reformation till the time I asked for it – from say 1565 till 1914.

It is not only Calvinists who suppress one's knowledge of the arts, though.

In MacDiarmid's beautiful poem, 'Homage to Dunbar', he notes that anyone can visit the graves of Burns or Walter Scott, but nobody knows where Dunbar is buried, lost in an older Scotland, abandoned, unexplored. Like Atlantis drowned beneath the ocean, Dunbar and his Scotland remain almost unknown. And yet, as if from the bells of the cathedral under sea, sometimes a strange sound can indeed be heard across the distance:

> Still, like the bells o' Ys frae unplumbed deeps,

> Whiles through Life's drumlie wash your music leaps
> To'n antrin ear, as a'e bird's wheep defines
> In some lane place the solitude's ootlines.

There is even more than that. The phrase, 'Not Burns – Dunbar!' suggests a different way of approaching poetry, culture, and all the arts. As a medieval and early Renaissance poet, Dunbar lived in a world where nearly all art was didactic. Paintings, music, architecture, poetry: all art was made to teach, seriously. Serious lessons all folk need to know, about what virtue is, about what hurt and pain will come when certain temptations are surrendered to. The arts, in this understanding, are not merely entertainment. We underestimate their worth at our peril.

This is neither pious nor solemn, neither sentimental nor sanctimonious. Rather, it is an affirmation that poetry and all the arts are there to help people to live, to tell us things we need to know about immaterial life. Economic realities are not the only ones. There are these qualities of what, for want of a better word, we might call the spirit. They can raise things up, as in 'high spirits' (and Dunbar can be a very funny poet indeed), they can help with formal occasions of great moment, or they can help us deal with grief at times of irreparable loss.

Dunbar's 'To a Ladye' is a different kind of poem from Burns's 'My love is like a red, red rose' but it's every bit as poignant, sharp, yearning, and subtle in its suggestion of material and emotional realities. 'Rew' is a pun on the word 'rue' or sorrow, regret, pity, and the same word meaning the evergreen garden-grown herb, supposed to repel venomous snakes, diminish amorous desire in men, and encourage it in women. The phrase 'that I of mene' signifies, 'of which I speak'.

To a Ladye

> Sweit rois of vertew and of gentilnes,
> Delytsum lyllie of everie lustynes,
> Richest in bontie and in bewtie cleir
> And euerie vertew that is deir
> Except onlie that ye ar mercyles.
>
> In to your garthe this day I did persew.
> Thair saw I flowris that fresche wer of hew,
> Baithe quhyte and rid, moist lusty wer to seyne,
> And halsum herbis vpone stalkis grene,
> Yit leif nor flour fynd could I nane of rew.
>
> I dout that Merche with his caild blastis keyne
> Hes slayne this gentill herbe that I of mene,

NOT ENERGY ORDERED, ENERGISED ORDER: WILLIAM DUNBAR

Quhois petewous deithe dois to my hart sic pane
That I wald mak to plant his rute agane,
So confortand his levis vnto me bene.

NOTE
See *The Poems of William Dunbar,* edited by Priscilla Bawcutt, 2 volumes (Glasgow: Association for Scottish Literary Studies, 1998)

7

Poet and translator: Gavin Douglas

GAVIN DOUGLAS (C.1475–1522) was a younger son of the Earl of Angus, head of a prominent family ensuring the poet a privileged upbringing. Like his contemporary Dunbar, he attended St Andrews University, but unlike Dunbar, he attained high office in the church quite quickly. He was provost of St Giles's Kirk in Edinburgh's Royal Mile, and was there at the time of King James IV's marriage to Margaret Tudor in 1503, for which, as we noted, Dunbar wrote his poem, 'The Thistle and the Rose'. Douglas must have known this poem and surely knew Dunbar, 16 years his senior, another churchman but in a different position in the hierarchy. Douglas's poetry was written in Edinburgh at this time, mainly during the reign of James IV. In 1516, during the reign of James V, Douglas was appointed Bishop of Dunkeld and became fully occupied by church, court and political business, diplomatic negotiations and intrigue. He could be outspoken and made enemies as well as friends. His father's successor, the sixth Earl of Angus (whom Douglas called a 'witless fuill') tainted Douglas in a conflict with the king. Douglas moved to London, fell victim to the plague and died in 1522.

Where Dunbar's poetry is characteristically energised and dynamic, 'ordered energy, not energetic orderliness' in Edwin Morgan's memorable phrase, and Robert Henryson's is sustained by a quality of character, compassionate, curious, with a tempered sense of judgement, Douglas's is typically rich with an unusual vocabulary and a thick texture. He slows you down but the rewards are great. He's a thoughtful, meditative poet, engaged by ideas of value and worth. 'The Palice of Honour' (c.1501) is an introspective meditation on virtue and heroism, remarkable for its valorisation of poetry as a valid calling and music as vital. Douglas identifies musical polyphonic techniques that would be familiar to the great composer Robert Carver (1485–1570):

> In modulatioun heard I play and sing
> Fauxbourdon, pricksang, descant, countering,
> Cant Organe, figuratioun and gemmel,
> On croud, lute, harp, with mony gudlie spring...

Complex rhythms, vocal inter-connections, soaring voices and onward drive are carried to levels of brilliance in Carver's choral music as in Douglas's poetry.

> Soft relischingis in dulce delivering,

Fractionis divide, at rest, or close compel.

Other short poems, 'King Hart' (whose authorship is contested) and 'Conscience' take similar delight in allegorical meanings and rich linguistic brio.

Douglas's greatest achievement is his translation of Virgil's *The Aeneid*, which he called *The Eneados*, completed in 1513, just before the battle of Flodden. It's one of the first vernacular translations of a major classical work, forerunning Arthur Golding's translation of the *Metamorphoses* of Ovid (1567) and Christopher Marlowe's translations of the *Elegies* of Ovid (c.1580s). Douglas translates all 12 books of *The Aeneid* (and the conclusion by the Italian humanist Mapheus Vegius, from 1428) but he also introduces his own descriptions of Scotland and Scotland's landscapes and weather into the prologues to each section of the poem, relocating the Virgilian world within his own. The translation is across more than languages. According to the *Oxford English Dictionary*, *The Eneados* also contains the first use of the word 'wow'!

Douglas's translation, like Henryson's Aesop in the 1480s or Urquhart's Rabelais in the 1650s, is a recreation, a revisioning of the earlier text, a transposition of that text into a different context. The old stories are told anew. And this is how art works. Read the tragic love story of Aeneas and Dido and then listen to the English composer Henry Purcell's setting of Nahum Tate's 'Dido's Lament' from their opera *Dido and Aeneas* (c.1688). It's another kind of transposition. You can sense the pathos that carries across cultures and time.

This is how Douglas opens the poem:

> The battelis and the man I will descruive
> Fra Troyis boundis first that fugitive
> By fate to Italie come...

Eneas has suffered 'grete payne in batteles' and arrives in what we now call Italy, by 'force of goddis' to found the city now called Rome.

An excellent translation into modern English prose of *The Aeneid* (London: Penguin Books, 2003) is by another Scot, David West, and it helps to be familiar with Virgil's poem before immersing yourself in Douglas's version. There's also an immediately accessible modernised Scots version by John Law and Caroline Macafee.

The epic begins with Aeneas and his fleet fleeing from devastated Troy, caught up in a storm and wrecked on the coast of Libya, where Dido, Queen of Carthage, helps them and falls in love with Aeneas. There's a long recollection of the siege of Troy and the six years' travelling that has brought them to Carthage. Then in Book 4, Aeneas, committed to going further, to following his destiny, moves on, leaving Dido to curse him and die heartbroken. Book 5 includes the funeral games in honour of Aeneas's father, and Book 6 brings him to Italy, where he goes into the underworld to see his father. Here, he also meets Dido again. Finally sailing up the Tiber and setting up camp on the river's bank, Aeneas encounters the native inhabitants, the local people of Latium. The Latin Prince Turnus leads the war against the new arrivals. After various bloody conflicts, the gods leave the scene and Aeneas and Turnus settle things with a one-to-one duel. Defeated, Turnus begs mercy for his father's sake; Aeneas hesitates, but then sees the belt Turnus stole from the dead Pallas, whom the boy Aeneas had pledged to protect. Enraged, Aeneas kills Turnus mercilessly. David West describes the whole epic as: 'a dramatic representation of ordinary human relations and of the unpredictable in life, the place of justice in the world, the limits of human effort and understanding and the inscrutable splendour of the universe'.

In English or modern Scots that can be felt keenly, but going back to Douglas's words is to experience the forces at work in the human world and the natural world twiced. The more effort you put into reading and rereading the work, the greater it becomes.

Descriptions in Douglas are tense, exciting and vivid, whether of battles or of individual portraits, such as those of Charon the ferryman who takes dead souls across the river into Hell, or of Venus dressed as a huntress in Book 1, 'Her skirt kiltit til hir bair kne'. They stay in the mind. Try this one, of a storm at sea:

> Ane blasterend bub, out fra the narth braying,
> Gan ouer the foirschip in the bak sail dyng,
> And to the sternys up the fluide can cast,
> The ayris, hatchis, and the takillis brast,
> The schippis stewyn frawart hir went can writhe
> And turnit her braid side to the wallis swythe
> Heich as ane hill the jaw of watter brak,
> And in ane heip come on thame with ane swak.

This is my modern English version:

> A blustering storm brays out from the north in a gale –
> Hurls itself over the prow and slams the back sail –
> And the flood swell beneath casts the ship's stern up to the stars
> And all bursts into bits, the oars and hatches and tackle and spars
> And the prow and then the whole vessel writhes and twists and slides
> And turns her broad flank on to the ocean's leaning walls, their sides,
> As high as a hill, a jaw of water breaks open and crack!
> A mountainside of water falls down upon them, whack!

The English is immediately accessible but the poetry is in the Scots. It was the American poet Ezra Pound who championed Douglas in the 20th century. In his essay 'Landor' (1917), Pound says that Douglas improved on Virgil 'whenever the text touches the sea or the elements.' And in his *ABC of Reading* (1934), Pound writes: 'the texture of Gavin's verse is stronger, the resilience greater than Chaucer's' and he admits, 'I get considerably more pleasure from the Bishop of Dunkeld than from the original highly cultured but non-seafaring author.'

The poetry of Gavin Douglas also marks a key moment in Scottish literary history with regard to the Scots language. The development of Scots as a language for literature, as well as a spoken language for many people, signifies a turning point that distinguishes it from English in a specific way, and Douglas notes it emphatically.

In the court of James IV, Gaelic, Latin, French, Spanish and English were all familiar. Dunbar called the language in which he wrote his poems 'Inglis' and acknowledged the authority of Chaucer while writing poetry of an intensity that Chaucer could never have mastered. But when Gavin Douglas marked the distinction by saying explicitly that his language was not 'Inglis' but 'Scottis' he was aligning the language we now call Scots with the status of the other languages known to him, identifying it as a vernacular tongue with a validity as convincing and comprehensive as the Latin from which he was translating Virgil, and as the Gaelic he would have heard regularly. Most crucially, he was distinguishing it from English by asserting the validity of political national self-determination: 'This buke I dedicait' he wrote, 'written in the language of the Scottis natioun.' Similarly, the 'Dedication' in *The Complaynt of Scotland* (a work whose authorship remains disputed, published in 1549, and a major source of information about the Scots Ballads, their language and provenance), includes this passage:

> Nou heir I exort al philosophouris, historiographours, ande oratours of our Scottis natioune, to support and til excuse my barbir agrest termis: for I thocht it nocht necessair til hef fardit ande lardit this tracteit vitht exquisite termis, quhilkis ar nocht daly vsit, bot rather hef vsit domestic Scottis langage, maist intelligibil for the vlgare pepil.

This aligns the use of Scots in literature with Dante's essay of c.1305, 'De vulgari eloquentia' ('Of Eloquence in the Vulgar Tongue'), written in Latin but focusing on the question of the relation between Latin and vernacular Italian as spoken by most folk.

The language we call Scots is close to English but different from it. Before, through and since Douglas's time it has been spoken by people who breathed different air, worked different terrain, saw different landscapes and different people in them, than their English contemporaries. English and Scots – people and languages – have lived through different histories and this is part of how their languages work. The journalist Paul Kavanagh wittily wrote in the newspaper *The National* ('There's nae need tae cringe', 9 January 2016): 'The most common complaint about Scots is that it's not a language at all. People whose knowledge of linguistics fills a dictionary from A to Aa all of a sudden turn into Noam Chomsky when the subject is Scots.'

Douglas's identification of the Scots language in the early 16th century as something different from English prompts us to consider all the resources of Scotland, all the differences that make the nation, their potential complementarities and conflicts. Understanding these differences is essential to understanding what Scotland has been, is and might be. This is very different from suggesting that a single dominant language is needed for a single nation, and that such a language is superior to other languages. All the languages of Scotland live relative to each other. Some need more support than others. But none is singularly adequate to the experience of Scotland. Scottish literature itself is a testament to this sense of need. We need all the words we are given, all the words we can use, to express the world in which we find ourselves. Above all other arts, literature is what helps us to do this.

The court of James IV with all its Renaissance glories of poetry, architecture and music, especially the music of Robert Carver, came to an end in 1513 at the Battle of Flodden. James IV and most of his courtiers were killed. It's likely that Dunbar survived beyond this date and Douglas certainly did, but the culture that allowed them to thrive was devastated. Carver himself was around 30 at the time of Flodden and continued writing music for another half century, through to the Reformation of the 1560s. That is, he lived and continued working through profound and far-reaching cultural and political changes.

While we can see the radical extent of the disruptions, we should also recognise the continuities and progressions. The human stories always need to be carried, in translations, transpositions, new forms, across such drastic fractures in history. This is the work our writers, composers and artists always bear. Douglas, while marking new literary and linguistic identity ('the language of the Scottis natioun') was also marking a continuity in human sympathy and understanding, from classical Rome and Greece before that, to 16th-century Scotland, and from then to us now.

NOTE

See *Glory and Honour: The Renaissance in Scotland* by Andrea Thomas (Edinburgh: Birlinn, 2013), a beautifully illustrated account of Scotland's contribution to Renaissance culture, in architecture, the arts, music, education, literature, chivalry, pageantry and warfare. It demonstrates beyond doubt the European provenance of Scottish culture in the 15th and 16th centuries and annihilates the myth that nothing of value pertained here before 1707 as ruthlessly as Aeneas did Turnus.

8

Early plays, *Philotus* and David Lyndsay's *Satyre of the Thrie Estaitis*

ON GOOD FRIDAY 1535, a pre-Reformation play, *History of Christ's Passion* by John Kyllour (or Keillour), was performed on Stirling playfield in front of the King, Court and senior church figures. It seemed to connect Christ with the Protestants, the former opposed by the Pharisees the latter by the Catholic bishops. These were intolerant times. Kyllour was burned at the stake in Edinburgh in 1539.

Meanwhile James Wedderburn (c.1495–1550/53), after travelling in France, returned to Scotland where two of his plays were performed in the open air in Dundee around 1539–40: one a tragedy culminating in the beheading of John the Baptist, and the other a comedy entitled *Dionysius the Tyrant*. They have not survived, but references to them imply that they caused considerable offence to establishment church figures. James had to flee into exile. The Scottish hierarchy tried to prosecute him but they failed to extradite him from Rouen and Dieppe where he sought refuge. While he and his brother Robert remained in the Catholic community, another brother, John, was more drawn towards the Reformation, collecting popular ballads and revising them as Protestant protest songs. After circulating informally for years, they appeared as 'Godly and Spiritual Songs' in 1565 and later came to be familiarly known as *The Gude and Godly Ballads*.

These examples of the relations between the establishment's powers, authors, written and printed play and song texts and performances in public or private buildings or streets, might extend into Scottish culture of much later date. Few Scottish play-texts survive from before 1650. Yet among those that do are astonishments still awaiting modern professional production, including two mighty tragedies in Latin by George Buchanan, which we'll look at in the next chapter.

After the Reformation, Buchanan returned to Scotland where he wrote further plays for Queen Mary's court as well as becoming tutor to the young James VI. John Burel's *Pamphilus* (1590), based on a Latin text from the early 12th century, was used in schools throughout Europe. And later, William Alexander (c.1567–1640) wrote 'closet dramas' not intended for public performance, including a series of tragedies on Julius Caesar and other classical figures. Such play-texts, performed or 'presented' in the homes of the wealthy, were among a number of performance genres, including farce, guising, masque and mumming.

The public theatre of the era was organised principally by three key institutions: the Kirk, the Burgh and the Court. The churches had regular ceremonies, towns and villages held pageants, holy fairs, Robin Hood summer processions and the 'Crying of the Fair' on festival days. Drama was staged in educational institutions. At Court, there were tournaments and spectacles. And later, in the 17th century, performances were regular at the Tennis Court Theatre at Holyrood.

Throughout this era, religious, political, moral and social priorities were enmeshed with educational playwriting, song-writing, performances and poetic compositions of all kinds. The relations between the virtues of theatrical play and mortal consequences made all performance a risky business. But we have one memorable comedy from this time, a life-affirming celebration: the anonymous *Philotus* (published 1603, written possibly 1567). Its cast (foolish old men and young lovers), and plot (mistaken identities, cross-dressing and confusion), testifies to the familiarity of both elite and popular forms, European and local themes, and theatrical traditions employing both eloquence and vulgarity in effervescent liveliness, brevity and speed. It's a fantastical Scottish early Italianate Renaissance comedy and a shining illustration of Scotland's repertoire of unperformed wonders.

Dr Jamie Reid-Baxter has persuasively argued that although the play was published in 1603, it may have been written much earlier, perhaps as an epithalamium and entertainment for the court wedding of William Maitland of Thirlstane and Mary Fleming in 1567, and possibly hinting that the estranged Queen Mary and her king-consort Lord Darnley might reconcile. But we do know that in 1564, Reformer John Knox, who denounced Catholic Mary from his high pulpit, was over 50 years old when he married the 17-year-old Margaret Stewart, a distant relation of the Queen. To many, this was scandalous, and Maitland himself was another older man obsessed with one of the Queen's young ladies-in-waiting, the 'Four Maries'. The play's subtext and satire would have been instantly topical. The mix of the courtly and the physical, the politically loaded and sexually charged, the spiritual and creatural aspects of the play, and specific references and indications in the text itself, endorse Reid-Baxter's argument. This would give it a context of festive merriment and formal appropriateness exemplified in the story's method and morality, its healthy, vigorous mixing of sexual appetite, social justice and fundamental human goodness. It's fast but also very robust. In fact, it's a riot. And it's a play of reconciliation, with a happy ending. Its closing passages suggest to Reid-Baxter that an ethos of Catholic and Protestant co-existence is invoked, with Biblical imagery from the Old Testament and echoes of psalm-singing.

The plot is far too preposterous to recount in detail, but here goes. Philotus is an 80-year-old lecher whose lust for a 14-year-old maiden, Emily, is backed up by his wealth, so his approach is approved of by the young woman's father, Alberto. Emily's long-lost lookalike brother Philerno appears from abroad, setting up the prospect of male/female guising. Conjunctions of old and young are threateningly proposed. Philerno (in Emily's clothes) and Philotus are married, not entirely by mistake, and Philotus has a disillusioning wedding night but Philerno finds his wife in the shrewd, practical Brisilla, Philotus's daughter. Finally we reach a conclusion in which youthful wisdom and nimbleness happily outmanoeuvre the fumbling geriatrics and their wobbly bad intentions. Emily has found her husband in Flavius, a young man given to exaggerated proclamations of his love. The names themselves highlight the ironies: 'Philotus' means 'The Lover' and 'Philerno' means 'the lover of the offspring'. Edwin Morgan, in his essay 'Scottish Drama: an overview' published in the Association for Scottish Literary Studies' periodical *ScotLit* 20, 1999 says this: 'In the end there are two pairs of young lovers successfully brought together, with Philotus lamenting his solitary state and warning other old men to keep their eyes off young lassies. The play is both sophisticated and coarse, in a peculiarly Scottish way.'

Two new characters introduced to the story maintain velocity in both action and language: Plesant (a scurrilously commentating jester) and the Macrell (a bawdy go-between who tries to convince Emily to take advantage of Philotus's lust and indulge her sexual appetites with other young men while waiting for the old man to die so she can inherit his money). Their interventions and verbal brio keep things lively beyond the formulaic.

Morgan quotes an 18th-century English theatre historian, who wrote of the play:

This delectabill treatise [as it's called on the title-page] is by far the most offensive drama ever produced... These words so frequently scribbled in chalk on walls and shutters are here printed at full length; a sufficient proof of the barbarous state in which Scotland remained till civilised by its intercourse with England.

In the 21st century, it's high time we moved beyond such nonsense. Who wouldn't much rather see a production of this play, fully-funded and properly mounted, than anything by Andrew Lloyd Webber?

For all that much work has been done and continues retrieving and exploring the plays, theatres and performance culture of pre-17th-century Scotland, there remains one major figure who comes through the centuries with one overwhelmingly engaging and vital work: David Lyndsay (c.1486–1555) and *Ane Satyre of the Thrie Estaitis*.

Lyndsay was a much younger contemporary of Robert Henryson, then more immediately of William Dunbar and Gavin Douglas. Born in the last years of the reign of James III, he lived through those of both James IV and James V, and was in service to James V's second wife and widow, Mary of Guise (mother of Mary Queen of Scots). In 1513, the year of Flodden, Lyndsay had a tenement flat in Edinburgh's High Street while Douglas was provost of St Giles's Kirk. After the death of James IV at Flodden, Lyndsay's commitment was to keeping safe the 15-month old James V, and encouraging him in his education. Moral authority is clearly pre-eminent in Lyndsay's writing, and characteristic of his poem 'The Dreme' (c.1526). He wanted the young king to learn morality's worth.

In 1529, Lyndsay was appointed Lord Lyon King of Arms, one of the most senior judicial posts in the country, especially in days when the rights to family inheritance were crucial to wealth and social and political power. In the 1530s, he was sent on diplomatic travels, especially to France, partly to ease trade agreements but also to negotiate for a future wife for James. He stayed close in the King's affection: the two of them exchanged at least one courtly flyting, insulting each other in rhetorically flamboyant verse. Lyndsay's 'Answer to the King's Flyting' (c.1535–36) reprimands James for his sexual adventures:

> Thocht ye rin rudelie, like an restless ram,
> Schutand your bolt at mony sindrie schellis, [various targets]
> Belief richt weill, it is ane bydand gam. [a waiting game]

He advises the king to 'tak tent, and your fine powder spair, / And waist it nocht'.

By 1540, Lyndsay was looking after the envoy of Henry VIII, sent from England to encourage James V to follow the English king's ideas about church reformation. In that year, Lyndsay wrote an 'Interlude' presented in the Great Hall of Linlithgow Palace in the presence of the royal court, including this envoy, attacking church corruption in what appears to have been a first and shorter version of his great play, *Ane Satyre of the Thrie Estaitis*. The Scots King valued Lyndsay, awarding him and his wife financial support, and in 1542 referring to him as 'knycht' as well as 'Lyon King of Armes' assuring him of a pension for the rest of his life. Lyndsay lived on as the drive towards Reformation intensified its focus. He died in 1555, only a few years before that focus concentrated and erupted in irrevocable action, though he'd encountered the violence and tension of his era. After the reformers who killed Cardinal Beaton held St Andrews Castle in 1546, Lyndsay went to negotiate with them during the siege. He spent time in Denmark in 1548 again looking for a trade deal and the promise of help against English hostilities. Denmark was by then officially Protestant: Lyndsay's commitment to reformation was informed by such international experience.

Having come from a landed family in Fife, Lyndsay was a prolific poet at court, continuing to write poems throughout his life, work such as 'The Testament of the Papyngo' (1530) and 'The Tragedie of the Cardinall (1547), which ends with the exhortation:

> I counsale everyilk christinit kyng
> With in his realme mak reformatioun,
> And suffer no mo rebaldis for to ryng
> Abufe Christis trew congregatioun.

Lyndsay's later works include 'Squyer Meldrum' (c.1550), a semi-pastiche chivalric romance, and 'Ane Dialog betwix Experience and ane Courteour' (1553), nothing less than a history of the world. All his poems are fascinating in their own right and if he had produced nothing else he would still be an important writer, but his masterpiece is not a poem but a great poetic play, an epic work in more than one sense. Like Gavin Douglas's *Eneados*, it is radical, vibrant with immediacy and action, and politically, nationally, foundational.

Ane Satyre of the Thrie Estaitis (1552, based on a 1540 'Interlude' and revised and expanded in 1554), is a large-scale political satire portending Reformation and demanding political and ecclesiastical self-correction. The drama is generated when the quasi-allegorical figures of King and Church are led astray by self-indulgence and the attractions of sin. At this point, Divine Correction enters to begin to set things straight again. But Lyndsay insists that the answer is not only that King and Kirk must mend their ways in the social structures of their era but also to pay attention to the complaints of the common people – John the Commonweal speaks up eloquently when he and 'The Poor Man' enter in the second half of the play. The immense hinterland of the unrepresented people of Scotland is finding its own voice and being heard, loud and clear.

In Part One, the young King is beset by the corrupting temptations of the vices: Wantonness and Sensuality are opposed by Good Counsel and Chastity. Chastity and Verity are put in the stocks at the most threatening moment for the King. In this world, the attractiveness of the temptations is real, and the danger of the conflict is theatrically immediate. Something similar is seen in Dunbar's poem 'The Golden Targe'.

The key figure to keep in mind for modern reference is Bertolt Brecht (1898–1956), whose theory of 'alienation' in the theatre is exactly applicable. Brecht's idea that an audience was going to think as well as enjoy what they were seeing was Lyndsay's prerogative too. The 'Interlude' of 1540 was performed to King James and his court at Linlithgow and the play of 1554 to his widow the Queen Regent, Mary of Guise. The 1552 production in Cupar and the 1554 production at the Edinburgh playfield, in the open air, were performed to the court but were also open to the public generally. So it wasn't an elitist production for an intimate theatrical space addressed exclusively to a courtly audience; rather, it was a public spectacle designed to entertain as well as enlighten and challenge. The royal household, courtiers and sophisticates, and commoners of all professions, were among the audience, all at the one time.

Immediate pleasures were joined to the urgency of the message, in national, religious, economic and social terms.

Reading the play now you can see how valuable that mixed address was, how much Lyndsay could get away with in terms of sophisticated representations of dramatic conflict and coarse humour that hits the sensitive spots with merciless precision and force. The 1554 performance lasted from 9am till 6pm. You could stay through the whole day, or drop in and out of parts of the play as you wished. In a very Brechtian way, the play is a series of open questions, and in this sense it remains unfinished. It's not an aesthetically 'complete' and tightly structured story, like a domestic tragedy by Ibsen or Strindberg; it's a vast quarry of possibilities ready for adaptation at any point. Modern productions have taken advantage of this. More could be done. After all, the circumstance of Lyndsay's work is not that far away from us. Scotland in 1552 had been at war with England on and off for eight years, the economy was depleted and politically it was a divided country. The corruption of church elders was symptomatic of a wider need for reform and social change. Lyndsay's demand for reformation was as much political as religious.

The Three Estates were the Church (the clergy and churchmen), the Nobility (the knights, aristocrats and courtiers) and the Burgesses (the merchants of the 'middle class' who ruled the towns). All three, the play shows, are in need of reform. When John the Commonweal and the Poor Man break into the play in a proto-Brechtian style they represent the rest of the community in need of what such reform must deliver.

At the end of Part One, the court is cleansed by the imposing figure of Divine Correction, but in Part Two, when the figure of the Poor Man comes out of the audience and enters the play's action, and John the Commonweal speaks up for the real world beyond the court, beyond the allegorical functions of the play and beyond the moral certainty Lyndsay endorses, a truly revolutionary intervention is taking place. Where the figures in Part One are allegorical, those in Part Two are drawn from social types. All can be rendered as vividly individuated characters in a good production, leavened with topical references to place and moment. The intrusion of representatives of people in society at large, pushing into a foreordained structure and demanding its change, a social reformation, is Lyndsay's great dramatic strength, and a vision that he passes on to later generations. What is the rule of law and kingship for, if not the welfare of the people?

Let's sample some of the text and listen to how Lyndsay organises the voices, setting them against each other and binding together all the political, social and religious arguments. Here are the words of Good Counsel, advising the King:

> Sir, if your Highness yearns lang to ring, [long to reign]
> First dread your God above all other thing.

> For ye are but ane mortal instrument
> To that great God and King Omnipotent.

Having reminded the mortal King that there is the Kingdom of God, in which he is merely another single living creature, Good Counsel then advises him how to exercise his authority in the social world:

> The principal point, sir, of ane king's office
> Is for to do to everilk [every] man justice,
> And for to mix his justice with mercy,
> But [without] rigour, favour, or pairtiality.

In this respect, if he does well, lives and rules wisely, the record of his rule will be held in memory in high regard as exemplary:

> For every prince after his quality, [according to his nature]
> Though he be dead, his deeds shall never die.
> Sir, if ye please for to use my counsel,
> Your fame and name shall be perpetual.

In lines 2056–2673 of the play, Good Counsel begins by stating that the purpose of the coming reformation is to benefit 'the Commonweal': in other words, to help people to live. When poor folk are exploited by the high rents insisted upon by corrupt landlords, things need to be changed. The Poor Man agrees, and Divine Correction sets out to make this an order. Then John the Commonweal himself speaks up, advising that if the change is to be meaningful at all, it must begin at the border. That is, start the Reformation at home, in Scotland. Scots would never be able to defend themselves against England if the Scottish landowners continue to impoverish the people who live here. We must first bring an end to 'our own Scots common traitor thieves'.

My worthy Lords, sen ye have tain [since you have taken] on hand
Some reformatioun to mak into this land,
And als ye know it is the King's mind, [intention]
Wha to the Commonweal has ay been kind,
Though reif and thift were stanchit weel enow, [robbery and theft were ended]
Yet something mair belongs to the plough. [remains to be done]

The Pauper agrees:

> Sir, by God's bread, that tale is very true!

> It is weel kenned I had baith nolt and horse, [cattle, horses]
> Now all my gear ye see upon my corse. [body]

Divine Correction takes the point and decides to turn this into law: 'Or I depart I think to mak ane order.' And John the Commonweal speaks up:

> I pray you, sir, begin first at the border.
> For how can we fend us [defend ourselves] against England,
> When we cannot within our native land,
> Destroy our own Scots common traitor thieves,
> Wha to leal [honest] labourers daily does mischiefs.
> Were I ane king, my Lord, by God's wounds,
> Wha-ever held [tolerated] common thieves within their bounds [lands],
> Where-through that daily lealmen might be wrangit, [wronged]
> Without remeid their chieftains [landowners] should be hangit,
> Whidder he were ane knight, ane lord, or laird,
> The De'il draw me to Hell and [if] he were spared.

Temporality asks John 'What other enemies has thou? Let us ken.' John's reply is stunning, exhaustive, even-tempered and yet blazing with restrained force:

> Sir, I complain upon the idle men,
> For-why, sir, it is God's own bidding,
> All Christian men to work for their living.
> Sant Paul, that pillar of the Kirk,
> Says to the wretches that will not work,
> And been to virtuous labour laith: [have been loath to work virtuously]
> *'Qui non laborat non manducet.'* [II Thessalonians 3:10]
> This is, in English tongue or leit, [language]
> 'Wha labours not, he shall not eat.'
> This been against the strang beggars, [those who could work but
>   choose to beg instead]
> Fiddlers, pipers, and pardoners,
> Thir jugglers, jesters, and idle cutchers, [idle gamblers]
> Thir carriers and thir quintacensors, [sycophants, alchemists]
> Thir bauble-bearers and thir bairds, [fools ('bards' as in tabloid journalists)]
> Thir sweer swingeours [bold villains] with lords and lairds
> Mair than their rents may sustain,
> Or to their profit needful been,
> Whilk been ay blithest of discords,
> And deadly feud amang their lords.

John is attacking the hordes of superfluous sycophants such as might be hanging around the households of the wealthy. If there were no feuds, the bards wouldn't get the chance to praise their patrons or scorn their opponents.

> For then thir slouchers mun be treatit,
> Or else their quarrels undebatit.
> This been against thir great fat freers [friars],
> Augustines, Carmelites, and Cordeleirs,
> And all others that in cowls been cled,
> Whilk labours not and been weel fed.
> I mean not labourin' spiritually,
> Nor for their living corporeally, [physically]
> Lyin' in dens like idle dogs,
> I them compare to weel fed hogs!

John carries on for more than 20 lines listing the hypocrites, sycophants and wastrels whose sloth and idleness, greed and gluttony, are all a constant drain upon the virtues of the common working people. As if that was not enough, Divine Correction invites him to carry on: 'Whom upon mair will ye complain?' And he does: 'Marry, on mair and mair again'. He denounces the thieves and wasters in high office, in church and government, all of whom are in dire need of serious 'correction'. He goes on:

> Ane peggrel [petty] thief that steals ane cow
> Is hangit; but he that steals ane bow, [a whole herd]
> With als mickle gear as he may turse, [as much property as he can take]
> That thief is hangit by the purse. [that is, merely fined]
> Sic picking peggrel thieves are hangit,
> But he that all the world has wrangit, [wronged]
> Ane cruel tyrant, ane strang transgressor,
> Ane common public plain oppressor,
> By buds may he obtain favours [bribes]
> Of treasurers and compositors. [accountants]
> Though he 'serve great punitioun, [deserves]
> Gets easy composition: [an easy (financial) settlement]
> And through laws consistorial, [consistory court laws]
> Prolix, corrupt, and partial, [over-complicated]
> The common people are put sae under,
> Though they be poor, it is nae wonder.

In lines 2894–2911, Good Counsel opens the question of how prelates and priests ought to be remunerated for their work. For these 'prelates and priests' today we might read, advisors and public authorities, people who should be telling us truths and giving us wisdom, people in public office, politicians indeed:

> My Lords, there is ane thing yet unproponit, [still to be discussed]
> How prelates and priests oucht to be disponit. [provided for]
> This bein' done, we have the less ado. [less to do]
> What say ye, sirs? This is my counsel, lo,
> That, or we end this present Parliament,
> Of this matter to tak ripe advisement. [mature advice]
> Mark weel, my Lords, there is nae benefice
> Given to ane man but for ane good office.
> Wha taks office and syne they cannot use it,
> Giver and taker, I say, are baith abusit.
> Ane bishop's office is for to be ane preacher,
> And of the law of God ane public teacher.
> Right sae the parson unto his parichon, [parishioners]
> Of the Evangel [Gospel] should lear [teach] them ane lesson.
> There should nae man desire sic dignities,
> Without he be able for that office.
> And for that cause I say, without leesing, [lying]
> They have their teinds, [taxes] and for nae other thing.

What makes the play so exceptionally valuable in European terms is not only that its dramatic urgency combines universal allegorical figures in an unfolding story that delivers both high moral certainty, coarse, snappy comedy and sheer theatrical adventure, but also that the voices of the poor and dispossessed are heard resounding in the full context of the authorised social arbiters of power.

Lyndsay's play was published in full in Edinburgh in 1602 and then in a slightly altered version in London in 1604. It would certainly have been read by Shakespeare, just when the English playwright was writing *King Lear* (c.1603–06). Was there a direct influence? It's certainly possible. As John Corbett says, Lear 'mistakes flattery for true love' and 'rejects the good counsel of his faithful servant, Kent' while Cordelia 'combines the virtues of chastity and verity.' Flattery and sensuality are there in her sisters and flattery and deceit are there in Edmund. The *Satyre* is a lively and ultimately vitalising work, hopeful that corruption might be corrected, against all the odds. Shakespeare's play is one of the most terrible visions of the corruption moral evil brings and its consequent political, social and familial devastation.

Shakespeare's brilliance needs no emphasis but two specific things fuelled his genius: the popularity of theatres when he flourished provided him with a medium and a technology he could not have enjoyed nor so characteristically exploited at any other period in history, and the death of Queen Elizabeth and the accession of the Scot, James the VI and I, turned his world into something other than what it had been. It's impossible to imagine that Queen Elizabeth would have allowed *King Lear*. It is too dangerous and too close to home. But the Scots King James VI and I not only gave his permission, he and his country and his fellow Scotsman's great play may have helped prompt it, and the Jacobean world enhanced the visionary portent of both plays, Lyndsay's and Shakespeare's.

Lyndsay offers hope in 'Divine Correction' but Shakespeare's play has none of that. Both *Lear* and the *Satyre* are there to help us still, after 500 years. The visions which both hold forth are complementary, and remain horribly pertinent. The National Theatre of Scotland might think of a season in which productions of both might be seen, back-to-back. Epic theatre, indeed.

Theatre critic and commentator Joyce McMillan described the *Satyre* in *The Guardian* (17 November 1986) as

> a magnificent, rounded, humorous and serious morality pageant about the state of the nation, the abuses of power, and the art of good government under God. Dating from the last century of Scotland's existence as a nation in its own right, it combines a mature and confident grasp of universal political realities with a uniquely brilliant and complete evocation of the character of Scotland itself.

David Lyndsay wrote on the eve of the Protestant Reformation but still from a position within the Catholic Church. In Scotland in 1560, a Reformation Parliament rejected the authority of the Pope, the celebration of the Mass and the influence of French religious and political pre-eminence. John Knox (1505–72), leader of the Reformation in Scotland, opposed the rule of Catholic Mary of Guise and Mary Stuart (Mary Queen of Scots, the spelling of whose family name in the French style predominated after her childhood spent in exile in France). Knox's pamphlet *The First Blast of the Trumpet against the Monstrous Regiment of Women* (1558) set out to denounce them ('how abominable before God is the Empire or Rule of a wicked woman, yea, of a traiteresse and bastard').

Knox's writings display more character, salt and sting than most of the ministers' sermons I remember listening to when my mother had the power to insist I went to church. Yet they rumble away in ponderous and portentous tones, shoving the prose along like so much slow-flowing sludge. Memorable as some of Knox's writings are, in parts, the value of their literary merits might be disproportionate to the effort you'd have to make finding them. But you never know. Reading Knox with that in mind is, I suppose, an argument against predestination. But it's no guarantee. Keenly reading Lyndsay and Shakespeare, however, does guarantee an invigorated sense of human value. Try it. Be reminded. Reform.

And as we reform ourselves, keep the liveness of the experience in sharp focus. Lyndsay's *Satyre* is exceptional in the whole European context. Its dramatic urgency combines universal allegorical figures in an unfolding story driven by high moral certainty, coarse, snappy comedy and sheer theatrical adventure. And further: the voices of the poor and dispossessed are heard cutting through the authorised social arbiters of judgement. There is nothing quite like it.

Its greatness arises not only from the moral force I've described but from the balance of authority and humour, passion and ribaldry, an understanding of what temptations are and a sympathy with our mortal inclination towards them.

When I went to the Assembly Hall in Edinburgh in 1984 with my parents to see the Tom Fleming production, performed by almost all of Scotland's greatest actors of that era, it was a revelation to me of what large-scale theatre could do. From Andrew Cruickshank (some will remember old Dr Cameron, Dr Finlay's mentor) as the Abbot to Gregor Fisher (better known on TV as Rab Nesbitt) as Falsehood, the performances were impeccable. When the Poor Man (Phil MacCall) threw the Pardoner (Walter Carr) off the stage for his lying duplicity, he landed in a heap of limbs on the floor right in front of my mother. Gathering his robes, he rose to his feet still holding what was obviously a big cow's jawbone which he'd been trying to sell to the poor people in the play as a relic of Christ. He glanced at my mother, pointed to the bone and said, 'Hi, Missus, could ye no' mak' a great pot o' soup oot o' that?' The laughter was spontaneous, wonderful and everywhere. Carr skipped off before anyone could catch him.

That's the play: the immediacy of riotous humour, verbal speed, serious morality, delivered through brilliant acting and direction, full scale production quality and, without banality or obviousness, the sheer power of contemporary application. Neglect it at your peril.

NOTE
The most accessible, succinct and information-packed introduction to the *Satyre* is John Corbett's *Sir David Lyndsay's A Satire of the Three Estates* (Glasgow: Association for Scottish Literary Studies, Scotnotes series, 2009), available direct from the ASLS. The most scholarly edition easily available is that edited by Roderick Lyall, published by Canongate in 1989 in the 'Canongate Classics' series. The ASLS also publishes the definitive edition of the *Selected Poems of David Lyndsay* edited by Janet Hadley Williams (2000). See also Joyce McMillan, *Theatre in Scotland: A Field of Dreams*, edited by Philip Howard (London: Nick Hern Books, 2016).

9

The Latin tradition and George Buchanan

THE TRADITION OF Scottish literature in Latin goes back to very ancient times, and it comes forward across centuries. There are various major sources for literature in the Latin tradition, including pre-eminently the *Scotichronicon* (1440–47) by Walter Bower (1385–1449), written in 16 books, and the *Scotorum Historiae*, published in Paris in 1527, written by Hector Boece (c.1465–c.1536), and including the *Agricola* of Tacitus. But Latin has a long tradition in Scottish literature. Historical accounts include the *Rerum Scoticarum Historiae* (Edinburgh, 1582), by John Leslie (1527–96), Catholic bishop of Ross. But its greatest flourishing is in the era of the Renaissance in Scotland, detailed lovingly in *Glory and Honour: The Renaissance in Scotland* (2013) by Andrea Thomas.

Thomas points out that the European Renaissance was manifested in Scotland through a mixture of foreign and domestic influences. Italy, France, the Low Countries, England, Germany and Scandinavia, as well as indigenous preferences, all had significant bearing. The imperial theme was important as Roman history and mythology were adapted into the Scottish cultural landscape. Crucially, alongside this imperial theme, humanism came to prominence as an educational and cultural priority, with its academic disciplines of *studia humanitas*: poetry, grammar, history, moral philosophy and rhetoric in Latin and Greek. As Thomas memorably puts it:

> Humanists believed that their studies could identify deep universal truths of great moral force, so they promoted an active engagement in public life by intellectuals.

Humanist scholarship was seen to have practical application in social life, encouraging peaceful citizens to be reasonable, prizing dignity, eloquence and education for the laity as well as the clergy, endorsing the scientific method of close observation, spreading knowledge and cultivating discrimination. In the 16th century, humanist priorities were given local application by public intellectuals, among whom perhaps the most distinguished was George Buchanan.

George Buchanan (1506–82) was one of the most significant literary and political figures of the 16th century: poet, playwright, historian, intellectual humanist scholar, teacher of the French essayist Michel de Montaigne (1533–92), Mary Queen of Scots and later of her son, the boy who was to become King James

VI of Scotland and I of Great Britain.

As Andrea Thomas says, Buchanan had 'a towering scholarly and literary reputation of European proportions. He taught at universities in France and Portugal and translated many texts from Greek and Hebrew into Latin' and 'his plays, *Jephthes* and *Baptistes* (written in France, 1539–43), were very influential in the later development of European Renaissance drama.' They take their biblical subjects and construct them as neo-classical tragedies modelled on Euripides and Seneca. He also translated Euripides's *Medea* and *Alcestis*. More light-hearted are his works for the royal court, including his verses for court pageants at Holyrood, with Darnley portrayed as a heroic figure. Buchanan's birthday ode for James is modelled on Virgil and classic tropes of the king-to-be who will restore a Golden Age. All this, of course, was before Mary's demise and James's repudiation.

Buchanan travelled widely: to Paris, at 14, serving as a soldier with the French army, fighting against Henry VIII's English invading forces, returning to enrol at the University of St Andrews. He worked as a tutor to nobility and in the 1550s, embraced the Reformation, in Robert Crawford's words, going well beyond his contemporary David Lyndsay 'in his open support for Protestantism and, later, his sometimes furious denunciations of papal power.' He placed himself in danger in a political and religious culture where people were being burned at the stake for professing their beliefs. He went to London and then to a teaching position in Bordeaux, where he taught Montaigne and wrote his most lastingly famous plays, both formal tragic dramas exploring the risks and values of commitment: *Jephthes*, centred on the question of loyalty to God, and *Baptistes*, a consideration of the story of John the Baptist. Writers of the Scottish Enlightenment recovered Buchanan: William Tait (schoolmaster in Drumelzier in the Scottish Borders) made an English translation of the *Tragedy of Jephthah* (1750) and in the 20th century, Hugh MacDiarmid and Robert Garioch both translated Buchanan's work.

Buchanan's plays were performed across Europe at least until the end of the 18th century, providing models for the great French playwrights Corneille and Racine.

Dr Jamie Reid-Baxter is one of the few whose meticulous scholarship, understanding of history and sensitivity to languages are brought to bear on the priority of living performance. As scripts, plays are as dead as musical notes in a manuscript: just waiting for production. But imagination is primary: how can we imagine them? In his essay, 'Drama out of the "Closet": Buchanan on Stage' from *George Buchanan, Poet and Dramatist*, edited by P.I. Ford and R. Green (Classical Press of Wales: December 2009), pp.237–252, Reid-Baxter describes an actual performance of *Jephthes* in Aberdeen University Theatre in 1983, which tells us a great deal about what kind of play it is and what kind of production it demands.

The Biblical story itself is gripping. In, Judges 11: 30–40, Jephtha, judge of Israel, vows that if he wins the next battle, he'll sacrifice the first thing he sees afterwards. He does. It's his daughter. What follows is tragedy. What caused that tragedy is also part of it. The bitter pathos of mortal consequence is at the story's core.

The production, without any excess lighting or sound effects, brought out the play's power, translated from Latin into English. Reid-Baxter's description of the production explains something of this:

> The use of tragic masks, precluding use of facial expression, forced actors and audience to concentrate on the words being spoken. The lack of living faces to look at also heightened the impact of each of the gestures or moves made. These were minimal.

Thus, the tension between strict form and volcanic emotional content' was given full effect, leading 'inexorably to the harrowing, desolate and terribly human ending, with Storge [Iphis's mother] alone with her grief on the vast stage of the world.

Although this translation was in English, Robert Garioch's Scots language version surely warrants production. Here's a passage from the Second Chorus, full of what Reid-Baxter calls 'rolling grandeur':

> Oh, ruler o the gowden licht,
> sun, wha swees the lyft [sky] aroun,
> swith [swiftly] returning day and nicht,
> wha bear your never-bydand flame,
> pairting the seasons for the warld,
> eftir twenty darksom years
> nou we see your blissit licht,
> Isaac's sons at laist set free
> frae the dule o slavery.
> Jephthah's strang richt haund has brak [broken]
> Ammon's hairt for aa his pride,
> the reiver reivit o his gear. [the thief stripped of his possessions]

But alas, as Reid-Baxter notes, 'the Aberdeen University Theatre actors, although all Scots-born and bred, baulked at the idea of acting in Scots'. It's as if our very language were sacrificed by the strong and foolish priorities of tyrannical rule. Still, the actors' 'passionate lyricism' ensured that 'Jephthes on stage was very moving indeed' and remains a profound human tragedy and – potentially – terrific theatre. Indeed, the moral applies now, to climate ruination and the health of a nation's population. For what gain would you sacrifice your daughter?

Buchanan's other, equally unfamiliar play is *Baptistes*. Based on the story of John the Baptist, beheaded by Herod's command as demanded by Salome, it's a bitter satire on political corruption and an affirmation of virtue in the face of despicable misuse of power. Reid-Baxter comments:

> I have long thought of *Baptistes* in terms of a lavish, pageant-like production, not least because the more sumptuous the royal and ecclesiastical personages and their surroundings, the starker the contrast both with the unworthiness of their motives, and with the Baptist himself.

Robert Garioch's Scots version is as tight as the original Latin and gives a flavour of the play's power:

> But we, betrayit by opinions an errors,
> while fleeing fate, rin foolishly on fate.
> The fire may spare us, we droun in the sea;
> if we perish nae be water, the plague will kill us;
> the war's survivor is wastit by slaw disease.
> God may defer, but doesna cancel our fate,
> and we pey daily interest for daith's delay
> in dule and danger, trauchle and disease.
> Nor is a lang life ocht but a lang chain
> o evils: even to the term o daith,
> linked in a langsome series. We are laith to think
> we are in thralldom, thirlit to yon chain;
> an the outgait frae whilk we micht win free
> skars us mair nor the slavery.

Some critics have suggested that *Baptistes* could be read as an allegory with political parallels for its own time, so that John the Baptist could be Thomas More, and the villains would be Henry VIII, Anne Boleyn and Archbishop Cranmer, and the daughter (Salome, or 'The Lass' in Garioch's version) would be Elizabeth Tudor. The correspondences don't work exactly but the point is eternal:

> as a drama, it shows the human difficulties of conforming oneself to the absolute demands of the moral law when a tyrant rules, the priesthood adapts, and the non-evil, prudential elements of society beg for compromise.

The idea of a priesthood 'adapting' to tyrannical rule might be like our 21st-century mass media following establishment rules and endorsing the status quo, no matter how corrupt, incompetent and homicidal it becomes. Modern priests might be celebrities and newsreaders. As Reid-Baxter says:

> Costume and staging could be used to telling effect in any production of this timeless text, which denounces tyranny, calumny, self-deceit and moral hypocrisy in the material world, and contrasts them with the unsettling integrity of the Baptist, committed to truth and to a spiritual vision of human existence. While overly specific – and hence anecdotal – topicalities all too often prove merely distracting and confusing in modern stage productions of older texts, I believe that a fully thought-through application of contemporary allusion to a production of Baptistes could greatly increase the impact of the play on a modern audience, for many of whom John the Baptist, let alone Herod, would not be a familiar figure.

Of course Buchanan's play could have powerful contemporary performance. It requires that combination of scholarship and imagination that Reid-Baxter brings but it's entirely possible.

As well as his plays, Buchanan was a virtuoso of poetic forms, a master not only of odes, elegies and epigrams but also of rude and irreverent poems, secular and bawdy verse, energetic evocations of a sexual nature. While resident in Portugal, he was once again taking risks with his mockery of royal authority.

Robert Crawford's translation of 'De Sphaera' / 'On the Planet' gives a sense of Buchanan as a poet of scientific exposition:

> This poem is to show how different
> The universe's parts are, and explain
> In a unifying theory its discordant
> Primordial elements.

He promises to show forth how the planet moves, how day and night, heat and cold, sun and moon, all have their role in time, and prays that 'God, the sacred parent of all being' will approve the poet's

> Project to outline to the planet's peoples
> All you have made, and while we try to scan
> Your magnum opus, bless us, so we humans,
> Ignorant of the truth, may raise sky-high
> Our plodding, unenlightened intellects,
> And, as the human mind's amazed to see
> The planet's stellar zones, and how the seasons
> Recur in their great predetermined course,

> The mind may sense the Author of it all,
> Who powers the mass of matter with his strength,
> Controls it with his everlasting laws,
> And who by his sure plan makes it conform
> To an infinity of good designs.

By contrast, Jamie Reid-Baxter's translation of 'In Rusticum' is a good example of Buchanan's bawdy:

> Splitting logs for the winter, a country swain
> Went 'hah!' as he struck again and again;
> 'Does it help, all this hah-ing?' his wife enquired,
> And the man said it got him truly inspired
> To strain every sinew and nerve in his back
> And helped drive the wedge deep into the crack;
> Remembering this as they sported in bed,
> 'Drive it home with a hah!' the country-wife said –
> 'There's no need for that, wife' no hah-ing for you,
> I just want to poke you, not split you in two!'

Buchanan was arrested and interrogated by the Spanish Inquisition in 1550–51, and appropriately, terrified of what might be made of his writings and his transgressions of Church rules by his inquisitors. In Crawford's rendering of Buchanan's Latin paraphrase of Psalm XXIII, the circumstances of his interrogation by the Inquisition are palpable:

> Rabid dogs, why waste your time on me?
> Envy, why carry on with your corruption?
> As a shepherd leads sheep, so the Lord leads me
> And I shall want for nothing at his side.

His 'Epithalamium' for Mary Queen of Scots and Francis of Valois, the Dauphin, was composed in 1558, when the subtext of contemporary politics included the prospect of allying the realms of Scotland and France and overcoming Queen Elizabeth of England's Protestant nation with the Catholic priorities of both her northern and southern neighbours. Beyond its historical context it draws into its evocation of the promise of the delights of marriage both personal and social pleasures and virtues. Addressing Francis, Buchanan promises that Mary's beauty is incomparable. In Hugh MacDiarmid's translation:

> See the great nobility of her brow, what charm through her winsome

cheeks is suffused, how ripe a flame from eyes how lovely flashes its lightnings, in what friendly alliance harmonises with fresh youth mature seriousness, and soft, easy gracefulness with queenly dignity! No whit behind her body is her brain, being well-trained in the employments of Pallas, and, as it has received the culture of the Muses' arts, so tranquillises her moods as to render them gentle and obedient to wisdom's rule.

For dowry, Buchanan emphasises, Francis will have 'these war-brave hearts, the Scots' and the poem then extols the splendour and resources of the nation, fertile land, bountiful in fruit, fish and deer, hills and glens, and imbued with 'the holy spirit of friendship' and an ingrained resistance to being 'made subject to a foreign yoke'.

This is an echo of the *Declaration of Arbroath* in its insistence that Scotland has held at bay the attempted conquests of Angles, Saxons, Danes, Normans, Romans, indeed any attempted invasions. But then, crucially, the poem affirms another value:

And think not that, so accustomed as they are to cruel Mars' pursuits, their hearts have attained not to the refinement of the cultural arts. Scotland too, when barbarian invasions shook the Roman world, almost alone among nations gave hospitality to the banished muses.

As a humanist, Buchanan insists upon the worth of 'the arts and humanities' in this most politically volatile of circumstances. The poem concludes with conventional priorities confirmed, even if presented in vivid metaphor: as land and sea war against each other in storms and kiss each other in peace, as ivy obeys the strength and security of the tree it climbs upon, 'So too in marriage, submission is the woman's role.' But more than this, what's celebrated is the marriage of Scotland and France:

those whom sea with waves, and sky and earth by huge distances sunder, unity of purpose unites into one people, unity of purpose destined to endure as long as the everlasting fires of the stars.

Of course the stability of personal and political commitments endorsed by the poem is wishful, as Buchanan's later denunciation of Mary demonstrates.

Buchanan returned to Scotland, tutored Mary and read Latin with her, and was appointed Principal of St Leonard's College, St Andrews in 1566. Contemporary Scottish poets writing in Latin were encouraged by Buchanan and their work was collected by Arthur Johnstone in the next century. In Robert

Crawford's formulation, 'in most of his prose and all of his poetry Buchanan used the language of the Romans against Rome.'

Among the coins in use in James's currency was a £20 gold piece which along with the portrait of the king carries the motto: *In utrunque paratus* (Prepared for either [war or peace]), and the legend *Parcere subiectis et debellare superbos* (To spare the conquered and defeat the proud), both, Thomas tells us, probably devised by Buchanan. Buchanan dedicated his Latin psalm paraphrases to James and translated Thomas Linacre's *Rudiments of Grammar* from English to Latin, and it became a 'bestseller'. Scottish education in the classics throughout this era was on a par with any in Europe.

Latin remains one of the great, neglected languages of Scottish literature. As Robert Crawford says in the introduction to his book, *Apollos of the North: Selected Poems of George Buchanan & Arthur Johnston* (2006), 'For a thousand years it was Scotland's most important written medium, and until at least the 18th century it remained a vital cultural channel, an engine of the Scottish Enlightenment.' English is 'a relative newcomer.'

Latin was 'the international language of long-distance communication, the language of art, knowledge and international diplomacy that linked Scotland to Europe and beyond'. Latin is the language of Columba's 'Altus Prosator' and of the *Declaration of Arbroath*. It was the voice of Europe, drawing directly from Virgil, Ovid, Seneca and Tacitus, and was beloved of Buchanan and generations of Scottish poets. But it was a learned language, and when the priorities of the Protestant Reformation insisted upon direct access to the Bible in a vernacular tongue, the stigma of elitism became attached to it and has never entirely gone away. Yet it's worth quoting the West Indian poet Derek Walcott explaining his regret that the teaching of Latin should have gone from Caribbean schools, and evoking his delight in his own education, which enabled him to read Ovid's *Metamorphoses* in the original 'while eatin' a mango': 'it's two different sensualities'. And the precisions, sharpness, firm delineations, forceful ambiguities that can be felt in such poets as Douglas Young, George Campbell Hay, Norman MacCaig and Ian Hamilton Finlay, all owe something to their Latin learning.

Yet it's equally important to remember that Buchanan was a native Gaelic speaker from near Killearn, near lower Loch Lomond, who was deeply impressed that the Gaels had held onto their language and culture for more than two thousand years. He was a Catholic who committed himself to the Reformation, joined the Reformed Protestant church in the 1560s and published *De Iure Regni apud Scotos / On the Law of Kingship among the Scots* in 1579.

This is one of the most important books in (what shall we say? – all British? – or all European?) literature. It is arguably the most essential text in our understanding of the constitution and the state. How many of us have heard of it, let alone read it? It follows the *Declaration of Arbroath* (1320) in saying that all political power resides in the people, and it must reside in the people, and that it is lawful and necessary to resist kings (or queens, or, we might say, all rulers, and all their minions and myrmidons) if they become tyrants. Buchanan was basing his argument at least partly on his understanding of the clan system. There were numerous attempts to suppress this work in the century following its publication, not least by the king he had tutored. In 1582, Buchanan's *Rerum Scoticarum Historia / The Matter of Scottish History* reminded James once again that royal power was legitimately constrained by the will of the people. Buchanan had condemned Mary Queen of Scots after her downfall as a tyrant deposed by her godly people, but Mary's son was unpersuaded by the argument. In Andrea Thomas's words, James 'would reject this radical political philosophy outright'.

In his later years, Buchanan lived in and near Edinburgh. Tradition tells he was housed finally in Holyrood itself, before his death in 1582. The poet and novelist James Robertson (b.1958), in 'George Buchanan in Old Age' from the sequence *Stirling Sonnets* (Newtyle: Kettillonia, 2001), writes that he 'foresaw / where stupid Stewart vanity would lead' and suggests the practice of the 'Democratic Intellect' he embodied:

> Well-wishers, calling in his dying days,
> found him, far from complacency or sleep,
> teaching a servant how to read, and still
> the intellect flashed in his icy gaze:
> 'Far better this,' says he, 'nor stealing sheep,
> or sitting idle, which I count as ill.'

In the 18th century, the Latinist scholar Thomas Ruddiman (1674–1757) published Gavin Douglas's Scots translation of Virgil's *Aeneid* in 1710, and an edition of the major Scottish English-language poet, William Drummond of Hawthornden, in 1711; he followed these with a new edition of Buchanan's poetry. By republishing, retrieving and renewing the work of these poets, Ruddiman was regenerating understanding of Scotland's multilinguistic literary traditions, and this was taken forward by Allan Ramsay, in his anthology *The Ever Green* (1724). We'll return to that but it is important to note the confraternity of all these writers and the centrality the Latin tradition held for them.

10

The Latin tradition and Arthur Johnstone

ARTHUR JOHNSTONE (C.1579–1641) was born near Inverurie in Aberdeenshire, and took patriotic pride in the association his family and territory had with Scottish battles of the past. His family was related to different branches of local aristocracy and his sense of the landscape of his birth and childhood encompassed a social hierarchy and pastoral capaciousness. The mountain dominating the area is Bennachie and the tributaries of the river Don, the Urie and Gadie, were familiar to him as he was growing up. He went to school in Kintore and to the University of Aberdeen, and from there to the continent, the Casimir College of Heidelberg, where he published his early poems. He taught at the University of Sedan, in France and then travelled to Padua, in Italy, befriending another Scottish Latin poet, Andrew Melville (1545–1622). Around 1620, Johnstone left for Paris and published more poetry there. He visited the courts of James VI and Charles I in London then returned to Scotland, to Aberdeen, with his first wife Marie de Cagniol. When she died, he married Barbara Johnstone, became a burgess of Aberdeen in 1622, was friendly with both the poet William Drummond of Hawthornden, and Scotland's first major portrait painter George Jamesone. Where Buchanan was renowned as a poet of Virgilian magnitude, Johnstone's affinity was more with Ovid; in Robert Crawford's words, Johnstone 'has a more charming and gentle strain than Buchanan; his more moderate work is perhaps easier to love and is devoid of the Presbyterian Reformation harshness that can give certain Buchanan poems extra bite.'

Johnstone edited the major anthology of Scottish Latin poetry in the same year that he was elected Rector of the University of Aberdeen, 1637, at a time when complex political and religious machinations were bearing down on academic life as King Charles I, son of James VI and I, was exerting his authority on the Scottish Reformed Kirk and incurring the ferocious opposition of the Covenanters. In 1641, Johnstone went south, to London and Oxford to visit his daughter, married to an English clergyman there. He became ill and died there.

Among the distinctions of his poetry are 'Epigrams in Honour of Some of the More Famous Cities and Towns of Scotland'. As Crawford points out, Johnstone melds local knowledge with learned Classical references so that it is sometimes difficult to tell the degree to which he is seriously honouring Scotland's towns and the extent to which a sense of humour is being implied, as when he sets Dundee above 'The pyramids of Memphis,' which 'count for nothing, Compared to you.' Johnstone's humour is light but earthed in understanding of his native topography as well as wide classical learning. He marks the distinction of the capital (in my own version) like this:

> The Tiber terrifies Rome, Venice is scared of the sea
> But Edinburgh smiles serene on things like that, with dignity.
> It's true: there is no city on this earth more fit
> To hold a sceptre and to rule with it.

His vision of Glasgow is no less enthusiastic: 'The gods see you and all turn effervescent / Sea, earth, air conspire to make you luminescent.' Stirling, whose castle has proven the most unconquerable in Scotland's history, is also extolled:

> Who could speak of Stirling fairly, nursery of kings,
> Who built their fortress strong upon its height,
> Security of stone in clean air sings
> On high, with towers of strength and light.

As Crawford says, Johnstone's 'series of poetic landscapes has a unique place in Scottish verse'. It sets a precedent for more familiar 'landscape poetry' produced in the 18th century by James Thomson, and is a distant relation of the poetry of place in the Gaelic tradition, such as Duncan Ban MacIntyre's 'Praise of Ben Dorain' from the 1750s. The differences between Johnstone's Latin cityscapes and the poetic evocations of landscapes in English, Gaelic and Scots traditions are many and deep but their relations and similarities would be well worth further exploration.

Perhaps Johnstone's best-known poem is 'A Fisher's Apology', which begins by distancing the poet-fisherman from the prescriptions of the Kirk. In Hugh MacDiarmid's translation, this runs: 'Minister, why do you direct your artillery against my nets? Why am I forbidden to fish on the Sabbath day?' The logic pursued in the argument is insistent: if on Sunday it is forbidden to work, then among the ancients, fishing was not work but sport, and so it is for the poet today. The enthusiasm with which Johnstone depicts the fisherman turning from nets to rods, with 'bronze barbs' covered 'with the treacherous dainties' and the delight of luring the salmon to the catch, is contagious:

> Now he rushes downstream, now flies back against the
> current, now darts through the waters by a cross-path.
> Sometimes he whirls round and struggles in the water, making
> it somewhat turbid. Sometimes he gapes his mouth, and, too
> late, shakes his throat vainly.

> Worn out by a thousand meanders, he at length leaves the
> stream, and, on the dry shore, captive, lies dead.

After the exhilaration of fishing and catch, the poem neatly turns back to become an inquisition on the suppression of such pleasures by the Church and its ministers, pointing out that if it were not for such lively and healthy temptations as fishing, 'unrespectable young men' and 'those great chatterboxes, the old women' would probably turn to drink. The poet and the fisherman extols the virtues and pleasures of 'the light of Heaven and the life-giving water' and prays that his epitaph on his gravestone might read: 'There are fish in the Heavens; there are rivers in Hell; either region affords, now his day is done, the means of sport.'

In the introduction to *The Golden Treasury of Scottish Poetry* (1940), where the first English translation of this poem appeared, MacDiarmid insisted that

> it is one more delectable example of the extent to which our poets and our clergy have always been at variance, and of that mock-serious poetic gibing at the Puritan régime which characterises so many of Scotland's best poems (no matter in what tongue) throughout the whole range of our literary history.

MacDiarmid notes that this accords with the adage he attributes to the English writer Frederick Rolfe (Baron Corvo, 1860–1913), that 'Life is Mind out for a lark' and intrinsically opposed to 'the strait-waistcoats of dull platitudes'.

The Humanist tradition of Buchanan and Johnstone and the Latin poets continued through to the philosopher George Davie. It underpins Davie's seminal book *The Democratic Intellect* (1961), and its discussion of the value of the four-year degree in Scottish education. Davie also produced direct translations from the Latin which MacDiarmid used in his versions of poems by both Buchanan and Johnstone in *The Golden Treasury of Scottish Poetry*. By insisting on having such translations in his anthology, MacDiarmid was demonstrating the multi-lingual nature of Scotland's literary history, a fact that has been accepted by later anthologists but rarely taken up in general education or mass media.

While George Buchanan and Arthur Johnstone are the most familiar names in this Latin tradition, and Buchanan is certainly a major figure in the European cultural context, they are not the only ones. The field is rich, and still to yield many treasures. Among them, the physician, Episcopalian and Jacobite Archibald Pitcairne (1652–1713) wrote poems in Latin. His elegy for John Graham of Claverhouse, Viscount Dundee, was translated by John Dryden. His play in English, *The Assembly or The Phanaticks* (written 1692, not published until

1722), is a satire on Presbyterian rhetorical humbug centred on the General Assembly of the Church of Scotland. He places himself consciously in the tradition of David Lyndsay's *Satyre of the Thrie Estaits*. Edwin Morgan, in his essay 'Scottish Drama: an overview' from the Association for Scottish Literary Studies' periodical *ScotLit* 20, 1999 tells us that: 'The main targets are fanaticism, bigotry, and hypocrisy; there's a theological main plot which is well dovetailed with a love subplot; and the play is written in racy colloquial prose, a mixture of English and Scots, with much word-play and double-entendre.' The verse prologue suggests Pitcairne's regret and even anger at the lack in the culture of plays that might deliver some healthily derisive laughter to an establishment prioritising its own self-righteousness:

> The Author gently doth bespeak and pray,
> The Criticks['] Favour for his first Essay.
> Our Northern Country seldom tastes of Wit,
> The too cold Clime is justly blamed for it:
> Nothing our Hearts can move, our fancy Bribe,
> Except the Gibberish of the canting Tribe.
> 'Tis a long while since any Play hath been,
> (Except Rope Dancing) in our Nation seen:
> Yea, but in this our all reforming Age,
> We have a Play, the Pulpit turn'd a Stage!
> And Jack the Actor, doth appear Devout;
> The only Way to catch the senseless Rout…

Pitcairne refers to 'Rope Dancing' and implies the lively popular entertainments Morgan describes: 'tightrope dancing and acrobatics, often of a remarkable order of skill, were great crowd-pullers, especially in the streets of Edinburgh'. Pitcairne knew the theatrical practices of 'buskers of all sorts, ballad-singers, storytellers, musicians, and those unfortunate persons with physical disabilities who were paraded as freaks'. But he had something else in mind:

> The antics and theological acrobatics of the black hoodiecraws in the General Assembly were just as much 'theatre' as what you saw in the streets and squares of the city. As Pitcairne said, 'We have a Play, the Pulpit turn'd a Stage!'

But *The Assembly* went unperformed. Morgan notes: 'There was no theatre to put it in, and even if there had been, its subject would have made it virtually impossible of acceptance. […] There is, by the way, a nice irony in the fact that a proposal to stage *The Assembly* in the Assembly Hall during the Edinburgh

Festival of 1965 was turned down by the church authorities, who said such a bawdy and blasphemous play was totally inappropriate for such a holy building. So Pitcairne rests his case, even three centuries on! They haven't changed, you can hear him say.'

The 17th century has most often been characterised as relatively barren for Scottish literature, an era in which religious faction and political violence was rife, but the achievement of the Latin authors speaks of a different cultural quality altogether. Mark Alexander Boyd (1563–1601) was the author of the most memorable sonnet written in Scots, 'Cupid and Venus' to which we shall return. But he wrote most of his work in Latin, and this remains to be fully appreciated.

NOTE

The two major collections of Scottish Latin poetry are the *Delights of the Illustrious Scottish Poets of this Age, Delitiae Poetarum Scotorum hujus aevi Illvstrivm* (edited by John Scot of Scotstarvit and Arthur Johnstone, published in Amsterdam in 1637 in two volumes of almost 1,300 pages), containing the work of 37 poets (excluding Buchanan) and the third volume of *Musa Latina Aberdoniensis* (edited by Geddes and Leask, Aberdeen, 1892–1916), which contains the work of 32 poets.

The *Delitiae Poetarum Scotorum* (1637) has been central to the immense research project undertaken principally by the editors of *Corona Borealis: Scottish Neo-Latin Poets on King James VI and his Reign, 1566–1603*, edited by Steven J. Reid and David McOmish (Glasgow: Association for Scottish Literary Studies, 2020). The resulting electronic resource is the major outcome of this project: Bridging the Continental Divide: Neo-Latin and its cultural role in Jacobean Scotland, as seen in the *Delitiae Poetarum Scotorum* (1637), now available at: https://www.dps.gla.ac.uk/ Check it out.

11

Defy them all: Elizabeth Melville

'THOCHT TIRANNES FREAT, thocht Lyouns rage & roir: / Defy them all and feir not to win out' – or, in English: 'Though tyrants try to intimidate you and lions rage and roar, defy them all and fear not – we will win.'

Fine words from the first woman in Scotland to see her work published in a book of her own: *Ane Godlie Dreame*, printed in Edinburgh by Robert Charteris in 1603. Elizabeth isn't named on the title page. The book is credited to 'M.M. Gentelwoman in Culros, at the requeist of her freindis'. 'M.M.' is Mistress Melville and the epigraph reads: 'Introite per augustam portam, nam lata est via ducit ad interitum', from Matthew 7:13:

> Enter ye in at the strait gate, for wide is the gate and broad is the way, that leadeth to destruction, and many there be which go in thereat.

The two-line quotation above is engraved in the paving stones in the Makars' Court, just off the Royal Mile in Edinburgh, unveiled with a flourish by Germaine Greer on 21 June 2014. Melville is commemorated alongside Burns, Fergusson, Ramsay and many others.

But she stands also in the company of other women, whose poetry too often has been neglected or obscured. No real poet will ever denigrate the value of what might be learnt from other poets – women or men – so the generation of women writing poetry since the 1970s acknowledged the generation of pre-eminent poets, all men, writing immediately after the Second World War. Their names are familiar: MacCaig, MacLean, Morgan, Garioch, Goodsir Smith, Mackay Brown, Crichton Smith.

The names of those women writing great work in the later 20th and early 21st centuries might be equally – some even more – familiar: Liz Lochhead, Jackie Kay, Kathleen Jamie, Meg Bateman, Carol Ann Duffy, Anne Frater, Gerda Stevenson. But as with all our poets and literary history, secure critical evaluation of their work is ongoing.

There is one thing they all share, though: none are disciples. None follow blindly the styles or opinions of their fellows and predecessors. Influence is not the word. But there are climates of experience, attitudes and priorities that change in time like gravitational tides and currents, while certain values stay true. MacDiarmid was an example to all, good, bad, ugly and beautiful, but he was never an idol and deplored the idea of 'followers'. Iain Crichton Smith once remarked that

MacDiarmid's one really important example was to show that it was possible to be a great poet in modern Scotland. It could be done.

So instead of the familiar habits of our day, celebrity culture, the authority of money and media – the broad way through the wide gate – maybe it's worth picking a strait gate and a narrow path to approach some of these less familiar poets. And think of them in their own histories.

In the UK, it was only after the First World War in 1918 that men over the age of 21 and women over 30 were 'given' a vote. Equal franchise at 21 took until 1928. Democracy is a long time coming. In New Zealand it had happened in 1893. In Finland, in 1913. In Saudi Arabia, not until 2015. The political, social and domestic contexts – not to mention sexual, financial and religious assumptions and oppressions – affected the very possibility, let alone the encouragement, of women writing poems, or painting, or composing, until very recently.

And if that's no more than a thumbnail sketch, it's easily forgotten. These simple facts are a context for the long haul towards the acknowledgement that women, as much as men, make works of art as valid as any by virtue not only of experience but also, and equally, of quality of insight and judgement.

It is evident in Elizabeth Melville's poems. In our secular, materialist era, their pervasive religious context might seem at first glance to make them irrelevant. This is wrong, for two reasons: first, religious conviction is everywhere evident even in the 21st century, in its worst aspects of sectarianism and violence. In its assumptions and exclusions it can be as dangerous as patriarchal sexism. In daily practice and social life, religion is always political. It was even more emphatically so in Melville's time. Society is not as secular as it seems.

More important, though, is that in literary terms, any belief system can be read metaphorically. The Welsh poet R.S. Thomas understood this and said so: as a church minister, he got himself into some trouble for saying that he thought God was a poet with a great mathematical mind who dreamed the world into being, and that the Bible was an enormous metaphor. Who can prove he was wrong? Sometimes literalism is the enemy. All literature works by metaphor. That does not mean that it is not grounded in reality or doesn't help us with the literal and lasting truths of what life is. Ultimately, that's why we still read Homer or Dunbar.

London will disappear. Troy did. Shakespeare will survive.

So when we read Elizabeth Melville, we have to understand her work entirely in her own history with its specific religious contexts but we can also appreciate its value in the 21st century. It has application.

Melville, or Lady Culross (c.1578–c.1640), was the second daughter of an aristocratic Fife family, in times when the gulf between rich and poor was not as great as it is in the 21st century. She was an exact contemporary of Shakespeare, and witnessed the departure of King James VI to London to become James I of the abruptly united kingdom.

Her major work is 'Ane Godlie Dreame', a vision-poem taking us on a journey through Hell. She may have been familiar with Robert Henryson's 'Orpheus and Eurydice', in which Orpheus searches for his lost love through Heaven and Hell. It is certainly possible that she had read Dante's *Inferno*. Her poem explores a similar metaphor and its meaning is familiar to anyone: you have to search high and low, untiringly, even though immense difficulties are set against you, to find the truth you're looking for. This is a cliché of cringing pulchritude in Harry Lauder's song, 'Keep Right On to the End of the Road' and politicians will trot out something like it flippantly whenever a soundbite is wanted. But there is a truth in it, and Melville's expression of it has lastingly serious force. Unlike Henryson or Dante, Melville was a staunch Protestant but the imagery and linguistic energy in her poetry are not confined to any single faith.

> Thir ar the dayes that thou sa lang foretold
> Sould cum befoir this wretchit warld sould ende.
> Now vice abounds and charitie growes cald,
> The Devill prevaillis, his forces he dois bend
> Gif it could be, to wraik thy children deir

It is all too familiar in a 21st century where instead of provision for the worst-off folk the prevailing political practice is to rob the poor and fill up the coffers of the richest. For Melville, hope comes in the form of a benevolent angel:

> With siches and sobs as I did so lament,
> Into my dreame I thocht their did appear
> Ane sicht maist sweit, quhilk maid me well content:
> Ane Angell bricht with visage schyning cleir

The Angel asks her, why all this grief, and advises, 'Lift up thy heart, declair thy greif to mee, / Perchance thy paine brings pleasure in the end.' So the journey begins, through an infernal terrain so visually vivid the impression of filmic potential is emphatic:

> Fordwart wee past on narrow brigs of trie
> Over waters greit that hiddeouslie did roir:
> Their lay belaw, that fearful was to sie,
> Maist uglie beists that gaipit to devour.

And when she almost falls in weariness to rest, the Angel pulls her up: 'thou may not sit nor stand, / Hald on thy course and thou sall find it best, / Gif thou desyris to sie that pleasant Land.' But it gets worse:

> I luikit down and saw ane pit most black,
> Most full of smuke and flaming fyre most fell:
> That uglie sicht maid mee to flie aback,
> I feirit to heir so manie shout and yell

The Angel confirms her fear: 'This pit is Hell, quhairthrow thou now mon go, / There is thy way, that leids the to the land'. The essential metaphor of the poem is clear enough: 'The way to Heaven mon be throw Death and Hell.'

Along with the 'Dreame', a selection of Melville's poems recovered from manuscripts by one of the finest scholars of early and Renaissance Scottish music and poetry, Dr Jamie Reid-Baxter, was published in 2010 by Solsequium. This little book, carefully annotated with a glossary for the unfamiliar Scots words, is a treasure of Scottish poetry and a key work in the history of Scottish women's literature. Here, for example, is a 'Sonnet':

> I will be as an elme that still doth stand
> and will not bowe for no kinkynd of blaist
> I will have my affectiouns at command
> and cause them yield to reason at the laist
> In midst of all my paine I will hold fast
> the herb of patience to cure my sore
> No kind of greif sall mak my hairt agast
> nor earthlie cairs torment my mynd no more
> Sould I lament I can not tell quhairfoir
> It will be long or murning may me mend
> altho I sould sit siching evermore
> no sichs nor sobbs can caus my greif tak end
> Rejoyce in god my saull and be content
> then hes thou more than wealthie Cresis rent.

So the story of women writing poetry in Scotland has a long tradition, despite our society's oppressions of it, and it comes to us across centuries. Many, perhaps most, of the great Scottish ballads may have been composed by women. In the 20th century, Violet Jacob (1863–1946), Marion Angus (1865–1946), Helen Burness Cruickshank (1886–1975) and the novelist and translator Willa Muir (1890–1970), warrant reappraisal. As Edward Dorn put it in 1984, 'Poetry is where you find it, not where it says that it's at. Where it says it's at, I don't find a lot of poetry there – very often, mostly none.'

NOTE
See: *Poems of Elizabeth Melville, Lady Culross*, edited by Jamie Reid-Baxter (Edinburgh: Solsquium, 2010)

12

Mark Alexander Boyd and the 'Castalian Band'

THE 'CASTALIAN BAND' is a term used for a group of poets associated closely with and effectively led by King James VI (1566–1625) before, and to a lesser extent after, he became James I in London in 1603. They were immediate contemporaries of Shakespeare. James was a poet himself, alongside Alexander Montgomerie, William Fowler, John Stewart of Baldynneis and others. Before we come to them, one of their older contemporaries warrants attention for his own sake. I'd propose that on the strength of a single poem, he's one of our greatest writers.

Mark Alexander Boyd (1563–1601) was the oldest of three cousins, all literary figures, of the Carrick family of the Boyds of Penkill. Penkill Castle, near Girvan in Ayrshire, their family home, is now privately owned but houses a remarkable stairwell mural depicting scenes from James I's poem, *The Kingis Quair*. Boyd studied at Glasgow University, where apparently he was an insubordinate scholar, leading a rebellion against the Principal, Andrew Melville, and quarrelling violently with his teachers. He travelled to Paris, gambled away his money, joined a troop of horse-soldiers fighting German and Swiss mercenaries and journeyed through France, Italy and the Low Countries, having various adventures. He published a collection of letters and poems in Latin and Greek in Antwerp in 1592, finally returning to Scotland where he died at Penkill in 1601 and was buried in the churchyard at Old Dailly. His biography by Lord Hailes was published in 1783. This is my version of one of his Latin poems, a poem of gratitude addressed to his teacher Patrick Sharpe:

> If you were the first to show me how to see
> The mountains to their topmost peaks, and how to drink
> As deep as earth from replenishing springs –
>   Now, face to face –
> It is not only words, nor poor prayers sent by me,
> Nor fragile flowers, nor the simple strength of my arms, I think,
> But thanks from my soul this poem brings –
>   Now, let's embrace!

'Cupid and Venus' is Boyd's greatest poem and one of the finest sonnets ever written. Ezra Pound, in his indispensable book *ABC of Reading* (1934), wrote of it:

Boyd is 'saying it in a beautiful way'. The apple is excellent for a few days or a week before it is ripe, then it is ripe; it is still excellent for a few days after it has passed the point of maturity. I suppose this is the most beautiful sonnet in the language, at any rate it has one nomination.

By which I take it Pound means that 'Cupid and Venus' is the most beautiful sonnet because it is most perfectly ripe. Fools will quibble.

One of Scotland's greatest composers is Francis George Scott (1880–1958), a major songwriter in the European tradition whose songs for voice and piano, available on *Moonstruck* (Signum Classics, SIGCD096), include wonderful settings of Burns and others, all quite miraculously catching the movements of poetic structures and emotional shifts in language. He uses the piano to evoke a range of experiences from devastating tragedy to comic frivolity.

Scott's setting of 'Cupid and Venus' alone is worth the price of the CD and listening to it delivers deep interpretation of the poem itself. From the opening line, with its lonely, tremulous, cold-fever sense of moving around blindly in circles, pursued and almost overwhelmed by an exhausting, enfeebling 'fantasy' (subtle arpeggios), through the fragility and futility of the sounds of the falling leaf and the reed trembling in the breeze, you know that you are in the company of two masters, the poet and the composer. Sonorous chords of hymn-like resolution support line 5, acknowledging the 'Twa gods' before giving way to mysterious, delicate but strong, hopeful phrasing describing the blind boy Cupid and the love-goddess Venus, the 'wife' engendered by the sea. Perfectly balanced, the last six lines reflect on the preceding first eight lines, musically and verbally, compounding the pain of love's helpless magnetic commitment with the uncertainty or impossibility of predicting a happy outcome. Bad enough to plough sand and sow seed in the air, but such unhappiness is nothing next to the sweeping tonal descent into 'twice unhappier is he...' who feeds his heart with a 'mad desire' and persists in his wild, hopeless, unending quest, led by blind love and taught by childish manger-faith. The unreasoned and inexplicable is perfectly combined with the tenderness of trembling initiation in these closing phrases. It is a masterpiece. The music is in the text already, but if you want to hear it brought out in an interpretation that is both accurate and exquisite, find the CD. Or better still, find the score and play the music for yourself. Here is the poem:

Cupid and Venus

Fra bank to bank, fra wood to wood I rin,
Ourhailit with my feeble fantasie;
Like til a leaf that fallis from a tree,

> Or til a reed ourblawin with the win.
> Twa gods guides me: the ane of tham is blin,
> Yea and a bairn brocht up in vanitie;
> The next a wife ingenrit of the sea,
> And lichter nor a dauphin with her fin.
> Unhappy is the man for evermair
> That tills the sand and sawis in the air;
> But twice unhappier is he, I lairn,
> That feidis in his hairt a mad desire,
> And follows on a woman throw the fire,
> Led by a blind and teachit by a bairn.

Mark Alexander Boyd died two years before the Union of the Crowns, an older contemporary of the 'Castalian Band'. Like Elizabeth Melville, this loose group of poets produced work before and after that historical transition. The flavour of work by Alexander Montgomerie (c.1555–c.97) may be sampled in 'The Solsequium' or the ending of 'A Lang Guidnicht':

> Sen for thy saik Death with his darte me shot
> That I am bot a carioun of clay
> Wha whylome lay about thy snauie [snowy] throt,
> Nou must I rot wha sum tym stood so stay
> What sall I say? This warld will away.
> Anis on a day I seimd a semely sight
> Thou wants the wight that never said thee nay.
> Adeu for ay. This is a lang guidnicht.

Montgomerie's poems deal with love, mortality, parting and commitment and he was deeply embroiled in the political and religious transition through the reigns of Mary Queen of Scots and Elizabeth 1 of England. As a Catholic supporter of Mary, Montgomerie carefully places coded messages in the political and religious allegory of his long poem, *The Cherrie and the Slae* (1597). He is the original 'Enigma Code' man.

Another member of the 'Castalian Band', William Fowler (1560–1612) is remembered for a sequence of 72 sonnets, *The Tarantula of Love* (1587). In his most anthologised poem, 'Ship-broken men', a vivid description of shipwreck effectively carries the metaphoric meaning of sexual desire: 'In hope if anes I be to shipwreck driven, / Ye will me thole to anchor in your heaven.' Code, metaphor, literary devices, symbols of all kinds abound in the work of these poets. Their world of multiple meanings and political import is as fraught with danger, ambivalence, subtlety and imminent violence as anything by John le Carré.

The magnum opus of John Stewart of Baldynneis (c.1545–c.1605) is *Roland Furious* (c.1582–84), a version of *Orlando Furioso* (c.1505–1516) by the Italian court-poet Ludovico Ariosto (1474–1533). Ariosto's poem was influential all across Europe as a racy, adventure-filled, elegant, endlessly-plotted, artfully-poised saga, a kaleidoscope of monsters and fabulous encounters, battles and love affairs, romantic and grotesque. However, its 46 cantos, stretching to 1600 pages, test the most committed Proust-lover's stamina, whereas Stewart's shorter, coarser, more intensely flamboyant abbreviated version in 12 cantos is constantly arresting. Stewart was perfectly capable of elegance and formal poise in his sonnets, but the pacy bravura of *Roland Furious* compels excitement and attention. The battle scenes, in which Roland flourishes his sword 'Durandel' to stunning effect, are action-packed. Here's my own rendering in modern English from the original Scots of the end of the first canto:

> As thunder through the elements runs crazed
> And the little heather blossoms that the wind blows all about
> Like chestnuts split and strewn, eyes wide and all amazed
> So Roland scattered warriors, bold and stout,
> With lots of noise and clamour. So stalwartly he struck,
> Some fled and hid in caves. He simply ran amuk.
> Some crept off, scared of every little thing,
> Such terror Roland was equipped to bring.
> These frightened folk their anguish they endured
> While Roland grew to hot pursuit inured,
> Chasing folk round hollows, valleys, hills and braes,
> Valiant and swift, jumping into frays
> Like a firefly from the firmament, he moves fast
> When Mighty Jove blows up the high winds' blast
> The little daisies growing, all around, just then,
> As Roland looks about him, and suddenly when
> Two horses gallop up and try to bring rescue
> To riders, DURANDEL once more Roland lightly drew
> And swinging it four times, he both men and horses slew.

Yet Stewart could be a marvellously tender poet, as in 'Of a Fountain':

> Fresh fountain fair and springing cold and clean
> As brightest crystal clear with silver ground,
> Close clad about by wholesome herbs all green,
> Those twinkling streams do yield a lovely sound,
> With bonnie trees as shelter all around

From violence of the high sky's brightness there,
And scented leaves suave wind-drafts make rebound
In sweetest breathings of the temperate air –
When the brassy sun above is flaming all aglare
To scorch the earth in ardent heat and flare,
Then, Traveller, if hurt by this, repair
Here to this place: you will refreshment find
Both in the Well, the Shadow and the Wind.

13

Sorrow in a deadly vein: William Drummond of Hawthornden

AFTER THE FIRST major turning point of modern British constitutional history, when Elizabeth I of England died and James rode down to London, Shakespeare's immediate contemporary Ben Jonson (1572–1637), claiming Scottish ancestry, travelled north in 1619 and visited William Drummond of Hawthornden (1585–1649) at Hawthornden Castle, just south of Edinburgh. Drummond's notes on Jonson's conversational comments (whether or not or to what extent they may be apocryphal) are spiky, delightful and illuminate both men's tempers. Drummond notes Jonson's complaints: 'That Shakespeare wanted Art' and that he had 'in a play, brought in a number of men saying they had suffered shipwreck in Bohemia, where there is no sea by some 100 miles.' And Drummond tells us Jonson 'dissueded me from poetry, for that she had beggared him' and yet, 'In his merry humour he was wont to name himself The Poet.' Finally, Drummond sums up his visitor thus:

> He is a great lover and praiser of himself, a contemner and scorner of others, given rather to lose a friend than a jest, jealous of every word and action of those about him, (especially after drink, which is one of the elements in which he liveth)... passionately kind and angry, careless either to gain or keep, vindictive, but, if he be well answered, at himself.

They seem to have enjoyed each other's company.

Drummond, like Mark Alexander Boyd, is not closely grouped with any 'Castalian Band' but he was their contemporary, on the other side of the Union. The quality of his work is carefully assessed in Edwin Morgan's essay, 'How Good a Poet is Drummond?' in *Crossing the Border: Essays on Scottish Literature* (1990), where he reminds us of his satirical, angry and humorous qualities, as in the epitaphs, epigrams, or the savage hate-poem about a former lover, 'For a Ladyes Summonds of Nonentree' where he can be seen, as Morgan puts it, 'striking out like a scorpion':

> Summond not for mee to enter, there's no doubt
> These twice four years and more I have beene out,
> And I it not denie; I did you wrong
> At first, but since could not come in for throng.

> Counts, knights, and Gentilles so hanted your Roome
> Then your kinsmen, yeomen, and evry Groome.

Thus he begins, and it gets much worse: 'Unhapy Kite, doth not thy breath stinke worse / Than that strong matter which Nature doth force / From a turn'd Gutt...' and goes on to ask, 'Are not the Twinnes now of thy withered brest... / Like sodden Haggises...' and resolves: 'Let mee alone, and force mee not to enter / If Hell be into earth its in your Center.'

Morgan notes that Drummond is a little like Yeats: 'Hawthornden was his Thoor Ballylee from which he watched *his* civil war raging back and forth. One remembers also the patents Drummond took out in 1627 for new and fearsome weapons and other military devices; even if these never got beyond the drawing-board, the mere fact that he had thought them up, apparently with some care, presents an extraordinary contrast to any view of him as a delicate lyricist and nothing more.' But he was certainly a delicate and fine lyricist. This is evident in numerous songs, 'madrigals' and sonnets, and especially in 'Song ii':

> *Phoebus arise,*
> *And paint the sable Skies*
> *With azure, white and Red:*
> *Rowse* Memnons *Mother from her* Tythons *Bed,*
>   [Raise dawn up from night]
> *That Shee thy Cariere may with Roses spred,* [carriage (the sky)]
> *The Nightingales thy Comming each where sing,*
> *Make an eternall Spring,*
> *Give Life to this dark Worlde which lieth dead.*
> *Spreade foorth thy golden Haire*
> *In larger Lockes than thou wast wont before,*
> *And Emperour-like decore* [decorate]
> *With Diademe of pearle thy Temples faire:*
> *Chase hence the uglie* Night
> *Which serves but to make deare thy glorious Light...*

Drummond's excellence might be measured by his Sonnet xxviii, 'Sound hoarse, sad lute', a work of immensely skilful literary craft but also one of the most memorable and haunting of all sonnets, and a permanent enactment of the sway, poise and blend of verbal dexterity, musical association and emotional exactness:

> Sound hoarse sad *Lute*, true Witnesse of my Woe,
> And strive no more to ease selfe-chosen Paine
> With Soule-enchanting Sounds, your Accents straine

> Unto these Teares uncessantly which flow.
> Shrill Treeble weepe, and you dull Basses show
> Your Masters Sorrow *in a deadly Vaine*,
> Let never joyfull Hand upon you goe,
> Nor Consort keepe but when you doe complaine.
> Flie *Phoebus* Rayes, nay, hate the irkesome Light,
> Woods solitarie Shades for thee are best,
> Or the blacke Horrours of the blackest Night,
> When all the World (save Thou and I) doth rest:
> Then sound sad Lute, and beare a mourning Part,
> Thou *Hell* may'st moove, though not a Womans *Heart*.

The word 'Consort' in line 8 means musical harmony or accord, but it also puns on 'consorting with' or keeping company, and musical performance in itself suggests an attunement of purpose and desire. The poem's vocabulary as well as its structure beautifully sustains these lovely, poignant ambiguities.

In their writing, the 'Castalian Band' were another 'Consort': sophisticated, erudite, clever, sharp and witty. They could as easily be venomous as festive. If we think of their contemporaries in Elizabethan and then Jacobean London, they hold their own authority. These courtly poets literally had no court in Edinburgh after 1603 but there was another tradition in Scottish literature flourishing around this time, working well beyond the sophisticates of the capital city and its environs: the Ballads.

14

The Border Ballads, Robert Kirk and the Marquis of Montrose

THE BORDER BALLADS are stories in song, and great poems. They're characterised by succinct expression, terrible poignancy and razor-keen humour. As such, they're the ancestors of the best modern crime fiction. But the poetic power in each one comes from their form: the tension between the unpredicted story that unfolds and the metrical regularity with which it's told. In good performance or attentive reading, uncannily, they never tire.

All poems have some relation to song, even simply in the music of the voice, and the ballads have developed this tradition across centuries. They are still memorised and performed in Scotland today. One great medieval ballad, 'Greysteel', survives in a version that would take about two hours to sing, yet when Andy Hunter recorded it for John Purser's radio series *Scotland's Music,* Purser discovered that the hypnotic, incantatory, eerie tune could sustain musical as well as narrative compulsion well beyond a conventional attention-span. This indicates a perhaps obvious yet crucial fact about the impact of oral literature generally: that its effect is uniquely powerful in performance, so we should pay appropriate attention to performance, and not rely only on written accounts. The School of Scottish Studies at Edinburgh University has an extensive archive of this material recorded and collected from a living tradition. Will Scottish television ever make good use of it? Or even the BBC?

Walter Scott, in his *Minstrelsy of the Scottish Border* (1802–03), suggested the ballads could be divided into categories: 'historical' and 'romantic', the latter including what we call the 'supernatural'.

The 'historical' ballads include 'Johnny Armstrong':

> 'To seek het watter beneath cauld ice
> Surely is a great folie
> I have asked for grace at a graceless face
> But there is nane for my men and me.'

This ballad is based on an actual event of 1530, when King James V, who had promised Armstrong and his 36 men safe conduct, hanged them all at Caerlanrig chapel, ten miles south west of Hawick, where a memorial was erected in the chapel graveyard. The ballad survived through the anthology of older Scottish verse called *The Ever Green* (1724) brought together by Allan Ramsay (1686–1758), where it was said to be 'copied from a gentleman's mouth of the name of Armstrang, who is 6th generation from this John'. So the legitimacy and continuity of the story over many generations is claimed.

This suggests how difficult it is to date the composition of the ballads securely. 'Sir Patrick Spens' may be based on events of the late 13th century, though no clear parallel historical episode exists. 'Traditional' ballads may have flourished in the 15th, 16th and 17th centuries, but they're a living component of oral cultures predating Christianity and are still a valid currency today. In each ballad, immediate presence is re-enacted in the moment, whenever it is sung, read or heard. Embellishing, changing, adapting words and tune across generations keeps the matter fresh and alive, and might refashion the significance of the event depicted for different audiences. 'The Battle of Harlaw' exists in numerous versions from different periods, and while it ostensibly refers to a battle of 24 July 1411, the verses aptly leave us in some doubt about whether any side could claim it as a victory:

> Oot o' sixty thoosan' redcoats
> Went hame but thirty-two
> And ninety thoosan' Hielanmen
> Went hame but forty-three.

The descendants of 'The Twa Corbies' can still be seen sitting on fences or branches of trees by the roadside waiting for roadkill. In the ballad, they are waiting to get at a slaughtered knight, talking to each other about how, fortunately for them, not only has his hawk gone to the hunting and his hound left to fetch the wild fowl, but even his lady has taken another husband, thus confirming the fickleness of love and its betrayal. But things are not all bad. The corbies themselves can look forward to an enjoyably uninterrupted meal.

> Mony a ane for him maks mane
> But nane sall ken whaur he is gane
> Owre his white banes when they lie bare
> The wind sall blaw for evermair

Like the knight in 'The Twa Corbies', the historical Bonnie Earl o' Murray will not come riding back in his ballad, and nor will 'Bonnie George Campbell', in whose ballad we are told that this fine and handsome man 'rode oot on a day':

> Hame cam' his saddle a' bluidy tae see,
> Hame cam' his guid horse, but never cam' he.

However they might be categorised, historical, romantic or supernatural, and whenever they might be dated, the ballads embody essential truths, as vividly realised as those of Jacobean drama, and as perennial.

The story of 'True Thomas' refers to the historical Thomas of Ercildoune (now Earlston, near Melrose), but there are other ballads, traditional and more recent, that involve journeys to the other world, including one of 'Orpheus' recorded from Shetland in which the musician and his beloved Euridice return to the surface of the earth from the underworld and thus deliver a happy ending. The mysterious poem 'Kilmeny' by James Hogg (1770–1835), was written at a time when Walter Scott, Hogg himself and not long before them Robert Burns had been taking down songs from the oral tradition and publishing them with their music for performance in polite society in the cities and the drawing rooms of the big country houses. Mysterious travels, mythical locations, grim portents, potent images and narrative tension that keeps resolution suspenseful – all these animate the ballads.

Most clearly 'supernatural' is 'The Wife of Usher's Well': three ghostly sons return to visit their mother after she has heard of their deaths, then have to leave her for a second and final time:

> 'The cock doth craw, the day doth daw,
> The channerin worm doth chide;
> Gin we be missed oot o' oor place
> A sair pain we maun bide.'

The intensity of this last leave-taking cuts deep. As with many ballads, the power of its meaning crosses history and continents. Another pre-eminent example of this is 'The Demon Lover'. The lover seduces the good lady who loved him long ago into following him on board his ship, leaving behind her husband and two small children, only for her to catch a glimpse of his cloven foot before he breaks the ship in two and sinks it to the ocean floor. A remarkable study of this ballad, tracking various versions of it from Scotland to America and back again is *Dylan's Daemon Lover: The Tangled Tale of a 450-Year Old Pop Ballad* (1999) by Clinton Heylin. This follows the song through various permutations, demonstrating its effect in numerous contexts. There's also a brilliant concert interpretation for full orchestra by John Blackwood McEwen (1868–1948) on *Three Border Ballads* (Chandos CD CHAN9241). Likewise transformative, both in subject and application, is 'The Great Selkie o' Sule Skerrie'. The Great Selkie is a man upon the land and a 'selkie' or seal, in the sea, who in human form marries and has a child, and who returns to the sea with the child, knowing that they are likely to be killed by hunters, leaving the widowed mother bereft. Different versions of this ballad and stories related to it are recounted in *The People of the Sea* (1954) by David Thomson.

Supernatural visitation and psychological truth are joined in 'The Cruel

Mither'. A young, unmarried mother kills her two babies at birth, then is tortured to damnation by her own guilt. Looking out at young children playing with a ball, she sees them turn to her and become her own murdered bairns, saying reproachfully: 'For nou we're in the heavens hie, / And ye've the pains o' hell to dree.' In this ballad, the implied patriarchal context of hierarchy, subjection and stigma, a common human world of physical desire and need, the pain of childbirth, the speed and horror of the killing, the long agony of guilt, all are evoked in tiny phrases and chilling, unelaborated, utterly unsentimental construction.

The otherworldliness of the ballads is an essential part of the character of Robert Kirk (c.1644–1692), a distinguished poet in Gaelic, whose famous – or notorious – prose work *The Secret Commonwealth* (1691) delivers an account of the relation between the material world and that of the 'elves, fauns and fairies' who live 'under the hill'. Like the ballads, Kirk's world is social, material, palpable, and even when haunted, earthly. When you go to Aberfoyle, just north of Glasgow, where he spent his final years as a minister, you can visit Kirk's grave, though his remains are said not to be there, and the story goes that in fact he did not die but was taken under the hill himself, shortly after completing his book. No copy of the first edition appears to have survived (if indeed there ever was one). Walter Scott published an edition in 1815 which was then republished by Andrew Lang in 1893 with a dedication to Robert Louis Stevenson. It is a classic 'mysterious book', in which a sense of Christian piety and a rather un-Christian sense of liminality or the numinous potential of life and the aura of locations sit weirdly together. It has a long legacy, haunting the narrative of James Robertson's novel *The Testament of Gideon Mack* (2006). When you walk up Doon Hill at Aberfoyle, the atmosphere is indeed otherworldly.

By contrast, the worldliness and violence characteristic of the border ballads, along with a bold sense of Christian piety, informed the short and bloody life of James Graham, Marquis of Montrose (1612–50). He was a royalist soldier and strategist who fought for King Charles I against the Covenanters, was ordered by the King in 1646 to desist and went into exile in France, but he proclaimed his loyalty to Charles II on his accession in 1649 and returned to Scotland, becoming his captain-general. He was betrayed and captured at Ardvreck Castle on Loch Assynt, taken to Edinburgh and hanged. He had the grace to give orders in 1645 that his fellow-poet William Drummond and his property of Hawthornden should be protected from the ravages of war, and he had the hard-headed realism to face his own death with sanguine equanimity and unintimidated presence of mind. On the eve of his execution, as legend has it, he wrote on the window of his prison cell with the point of a diamond, his 'Metrical Prayer':

> Let them bestow on ev'ry Airth a Limb;
> Open all my Veins, that I may swim

> To Thee my Saviour, in that Crimson lake;
> Then place my pur-boil'd Head upon a Stake;
> Scatter my Ashes, throw them in the Air;
> Lord (since Thou knows't where all these Atoms are)
> I'm hopeful, once Thou'lt recollect my Dust,
> And confident Thou'lt raise me with the Just.

But his most memorable set of lines remain these, from the second stanza of 'Montrose to his Mistress' ('My Dear and Only Love'), a poem which might stand as a dangerous but helpful motto for any one of us on some occasions in our lives:

> He either fears his Fate too much,
> Or his Deserts are small
> That puts it not unto the Touch
> To win or lose it all.

The paradoxical logic here belies the flamboyant sense of rightness and loyalty to something greater than yourself and the self-determined conquest of timidity which the lines convey so convincingly. Hard reality, and the facts of the spirit, what is at stake and what we might risk, are at the heart of the work of Kirk and Montrose, as they are likewise the essence of the ballads. Their truth is always pertinent. Sometimes, you really do have to 'put it to the Touch.'

15

Oddfellows: William Lithgow and Thomas Urquhart

THE FIRST SENTENCE of Rafael Sabatini's novel *Scaramouche* (1921) is one of the best ever written: 'He was born with the gift of laughter and a sense that the world was mad.' The two writers considered in this chapter have something of that quality to them.

So far we have been reading a number of great writers such as Robert Henryson, William Dunbar, David Lyndsay. But there are others who do not seem central as 'major authors' by virtue of the quantity, if not the quality, of their work. It would be a bad mistake to neglect such writers. Sometimes the most non-canonical authors bring unpredicted things and new ways of thinking, insights of unusual character, to our reading. Here are two of them.

First, Scotland's earliest most international traveller, a vagabond, possibly a spy: William Lithgow, otherwise known as 'Lugless Will' (c.1582–after 1645). Then a translator, a chivalrous courtier, a soldier and prisoner-of-war, another traveller and a committed Rabelaisian: Sir Thomas Urquhart of Cromarty (1611–60). Their lives overlapped and extended through the 16th and 17th centuries. Each of them gives to Scottish literature unique and treasurable qualities.

William Lithgow is one of the most unusual characters in all literature, a world-traveller whose most famous work, *The Totall Discourse of The Rare Adventures & Painefull Peregrinations of long Nineteene Yeares Travayles from Scotland to the most famous Kingdomes in Europe, Asia and Africa* (1632) is an exhilarating account of his experiences.

Born in Lanarkshire, educated at Lanark Grammar School, he started travelling early, being possessed of what he calls 'a large infusion of the wandering spirit common to his country-men.' Lithgow's book describes a world of otherness: people, places, cultures, habits and ways of life. He was a tough, seasoned traveller, starting with trips to Orkney and Shetland, and going on to Germany, Paris, and then on the three major expeditions depicted in his *Totall Discourse*, taking him to Italy, Corfu, Greece, Crete, Constantinople, Aleppo, Palestine, Jerusalem, Egypt, Malta, Sicily, Ireland, Rome, Spain (where he was imprisoned as a spy by the Spanish Inquisition and severely tortured), and elsewhere, and finally back to Scotland. It's said that he was known as 'Lugless Will' because at least one of his ears was cut off by the brothers of a young woman he was courting.

Edwin Morgan, in the Edinburgh Book Festival Post Office Lecture of 1990, published in both the periodical *Chapman* and *PN Review*, 'Scotland and the World', drew attention to what Lithgow himself called 'the science of the world':

this is it above all things that prefereth men to honours and the charges that make great houses and republics to flourish, and render the actions and the small words of them who possess it agreeable both to great and small. This science is only acquired by conversation and haunting the company of the most experimented: by divers discourses, reports, by writs, or by a lively voice, in communicating with strangers; and in the judicious consideration of the living with one another; and above all and principally by travellers and voyagers in divers regions and remote places, whose experience confirmeth the true science thereof and can best draw the anatomy of human condition.

He encounters some of the best and worst specimens of humanity. The *Totall Discourse* culminates in his capture by the Spanish Inquisition, who tortured him viciously. His description of this is horrifying: 'Now mine eyes begun to startle, my mouth to foame and froath, and my teeth to chatter like to the doubling of Drummers stickes. O strange inhumanity of Men-monster Manglers!' When he finally made it home, he was crippled for life.

> My destiny is such,
>   Which doth predestine me,
> To be a mirror of mishaps,
>   A Mappe of misery.
> Extreamely do I live,
>   Extreames are all my joy,
> I find in deepe extreamities,
>   Extreames, extreame annoy.

This foreshadows the verse from Hugh MacDiarmid's *A Drunk Man Looks at the Thistle* (1926), inscribed on his headstone at the cemetery in Langholm:

> I'll hae nae hauf-way hoose, but aye be whaur
> Extremes meet – it's the only way I ken
> To dodge the curst conceit o' bein' richt
> That damns the vast majority o' men.

But this experience of life and the world's extremes, and Lithgow's international travels, add depth to his expression of love and affection for his native land, country, county, and town of origin:

> Would God that I might live,
> To see my native Soyle:

> Thrice happy in my happy wish,
> To end this endless toyle:
> Yet still when I record,
> The pleasant bankes of Clide:
> Where Orchards, Castles, Townes, and Woods,
> Are planted by his side;
> And chiefly Lanerke thou,
> Thy countries Laureat Lampe:
> In which this bruised body now
> Did first receive the stampe.
> Then doe I sigh and sweare,
> Till death or my returne.
> Still for to wear the Willow wreath,
> In sable weed to mourne.
> Since in this dying life,
> A life in death I take,
> Ile sacrifice in spight of wrath,
> These solemne vows I make,
> To thee sweet Scotland first,
> My birth and breath I leave:
> To Heaven my soule, my heart King James,
> My corpse to lie in grave.
> My staffe to pilgrims I,
> And Pen to Poets send;
> My haire-cloth roabe, and half-spent goods,
> To wandering wights I lend.

At the end of his book, he bids the reader farewell by acknowledging his own journeying in search of 'the trueth of it':

The general computation of which dimmensious spaces, in my goings, traversings, and returnings, through Kingdomes, Continents, and Ilands, which my payneful feet traced over (besides my passages of Seas and Rivers) amounteth to thirty six thousand and odde miles, which draweth neare to twice the circumference of the whole Earth. And so farewell.

Lithgow's younger contemporary, Sir Thomas Urquhart was born into a family which held the sheriffdom of Cromarty. He shared the Royalist and Episcopalian views of his father, which meant that when the Civil War (1642–51) interrupted everything, he was on the losing side. He was among the 10,000 prisoners taken after the battle of Worcester (1651), imprisoned in the Tower of London and

Windsor Castle, where he wrote copiously to prove his own worth and seek freedom, and began his translation of Rabelais. Tradition has it that he escaped from the Tower, travelled to the continent again, and 'died suddenly in a fit of excessive laughter, on being informed by his servant that the King was restored.'

It is as if Lithgow and Urquhart both had set out to discover and experience for themselves the furthest reaches of human capacity, for good or ill, seriousness and humour, at the risk of their own well-being. I don't know of any other writers quite like these two.

Urquhart's great writing was done in prison. In the *Pantochronachanon* (1652), he traces his genealogy elaborately through 153 generations back to Adam and Eve. In *The Jewel (Ekskybalauron)* (1652) he portrays the Admirable James Crichton (1560–82), the exemplary Renaissance man whose exploits are described to astonish and inspire, mounting what Urquhart calls 'a vindication of the honour of Scotland'. This is made alongside severe castigation of the worst aspects of the Scots abroad, embodied in London bankers:

> There hath been in London, and repairing to it, for these many years together, a knot of Scotish bankers, collybists [usurers], or coine-coursers, of traffickers in merchandise to and againe, and of men of other professions, who by hook and crook, fas et nefas, slight and might, all being as fish their net could not catch, having feathered their nests to some purpose, look so idolatrously upon their Dagon of wealth, and so closely, like the earth's dull center, hug all unto themselves, that for no respect of virtue, honor, kinred, patriotism, or whatever else, be it never so recommendable, will they depart from so much as one single peny, whose emission doth not, without any hazard of loss, in a very short time superlucrate beyond all conscience an additionall increase to the heap of that stock which they so much adore...

Not all their compatriots, Urquhart insists, are similarly 'infected with the same leprosie of a wretched peevishness': Scots are not all 'quomodocunquizing cluster-fists and rapacious varlets'.

To describe *The Jewel* as richly written would be an understatement. When the admirable Crichton and his beloved manage to secure themselves some privacy, Urquhart's prose excels itself in dexterity and ripeness. They find themselves 'not only together but alone with other' and 'transported both of them with an equale kinde of rapture':

> Thus for a while their eloquence was mute and all they spoke was but with the eye and hand, yet so persuasively, by virtue of the intermutual unlimitedness of their visotactil sensation, that each part and portion of

the persons of either was obvious to the sight and touch of the persons of both. The visuriency of either, by ushering the tacturiency of both, made the attrectation of both consequent to the inspection of either. Here was it that passion was active and action passive, they both being overcome by other and each the conquerour. To speak of her hirquitalliency at the elevation of the pole of his microcosme or of his luxuriousness to erect a gnomon on her horizontal dyal, will perhaps be held by some to be expressions full of obscoeness and offensive to the purity of chaste ears; yet seeing she was to be his wife and that she could not be such without consummation of marriage, which signifieth the same thing in effect, it may be thought, as *definitiones verificantur in rebus*, if the exerced act be lawful, that the diction which supposes it can be of no great transgression, unless you would call it a solacisme or that vice in grammar which imports the copulating of the masculine with the feminine gender. [The Latin phrase means 'logical definitions are verified by objects'.]

In *Logopandecteision* (1653) Urquhart describes a vision of a universal language which he promised was 'contrived and published / both for his own utilitie, and that of all / pregnant and ingenious Spirits'. His version of the first two books of the great French writer Francois Rabelais's *Gargantua and Pantagruel* appeared in 1653 and the third book was published posthumously in 1693, the translation later completed by Pierre Motteux. Like James Joyce's *Ulysses* and *Finnegans Wake*, Urquhart's work is 'a farraginous outpouring'. His translation of Rabelais follows the original works in revealing and relishing the bodily world, the physicality of pleasure. It's a celebration of corporeality in all its poise, appetite and propensity for self-extension, redolent with honest recognition of the facts of defecation, corruption and decay, thoroughly robust about the delights of the body.

To understand Urquhart, and have a sense of what he was extending and elaborating upon in his translation of Rabelais, you have to understand something of the great French writer too. He's one of the world's greatest writers, there with Shakespeare, Dante, Cervantes, Euripides and Aeschylus: you name them. Francois Rabelais (c.1494–1553) was a doctor in Lyon whose satirical pamphlets criticising church and civic authority and his great books *Pantagruel* and its prequel *Gargantua* were condemned by the Roman Catholic Church as heretical. No wonder. Here is Gargantua's father, translated by Urquhart:

> Grangousier was a good fellow in his time, and a notable jester; he loved to drink neat, as much as any man that then was in the world, and would willingly eate salt meat; to this intent he was ordinarily well furnished with gammons of Bacon, both of Westphalia, Mayence and Bayonne; with store

of dried Neats tongues, plenty of Links, Chitterlings and Puddings in their season; together with salt Beef and mustard, a good deale of hard rows of powdered mullet called Botargos, great provision of Sauciges, not of Bolonia (for he feared the Lombard boccone) but of Bigorre, Langaulnay, Brene, and Rouargue. In the vigor of his age he married Gargamelle, daughter to the King of the Parpaillons, a jolly pug, and well mouthed wench...

After a little while, to this happy couple a son is born: 'The good man Grangousier drinking and making merry with the rest, heard the horrible noise which his sonne has made as he entered into the light of this world when he cried out, Some drink, some drink, some drink...' And after a large quantity of wine is poured into his 'great and nimble' throat, 17,913 cows furnish him with a milk supply appropriate to his needs. Accordingly, the child is named Gargantua.

Gargantua and his own son Pantagruel are giants who, along with their friends Panurge and Brother Jean, are in search of the Divine Bottle, and food and material comfort adequate to their enormous appetites. One famous passage discusses the best kind of toilet-paper and concludes that a live goose swept between the legs while held by the neck is as close to perfect as human beings can get. Their search takes them to the Abbey of Theleme, which is equipped with swimming-pool, maid service and a conspicuous absence of clocks. The inscription upon the great gate of Theleme begins as follows:

> Here enter not, religious boobies, sots,
> Impostors, sniveling hypocrites, bigots:
> Dark-brain distorted owls, worse than the Huns
> Or Ostrogots; fore-runners of baboons:
> Curs'd snakes, dissembling varlets, seeming sancts.
> Slipshop caffards, beggars pretending wants;
> Fomentors of divisions and debates,
> Elsewhere, not here, make sale of your deceits.
> Your filthy trumperies,
> Stuff'd with pernicious lies,
> (Not worth a bubble)
> Would only trouble
> Our earthly paradise.

Likewise banned from the Abbey are lawyers, demurrers, usurers and goldgraspers, while made welcome are all noble sparks, the brave, the witty, the honest, faithful and true, and ladies all 'of humour gay and free'. Here the inhabitants spend all their lives 'not in laws, statutes or rules, but according to their own free-will and pleasure.'

With luscious ease and shocking familiarity, Rabelais shows how humanity is healthily attracted to sensuality, and exposes the hypocrisy of those who would deny it. Yet the 'creaturality' of his vision is also a moral correction of exploitation. Urquhart embellishes Rabelais and goes further. The translation is almost twice as long as the original, and full of lists. For example, where the Frenchman catalogues the noises of animals that break into the pleasant quiet of the countryside, he names nine of them, including the unlikely calls of elephants and snakes. Urquhart supplies us with the noises of 71 species, including 'the drintling of turkies, coniating of storks,' the 'rantling of rats' and the 'snuttering of monkies'. Which leads one to reflect that Cromarty must have been an exceptionally curious corner of Scotland in the 17th century.

In any case, a national literature that boasts an author who died laughing has something going for it.

16

Gaelic poetry of the 17th century

DOMHNALL MAC FHIONNLAIGH NAN DÀN / DONALD SON OF FINLAY OF THE POEMS,
IAIN LÒM MACDHÒMHNAILL / 'BARE' JOHN MACDONALD, RUAIDHRI MACMHUIRICH,
'AN CLÀRSAIR DALL' / RODERICK MORISON, 'THE BLIND HARPER'
AND MÀIRI NIGHEAN ALASDAIR RUAIDH / MARY MACLEOD

MANY OF THE early Gaelic poems and songs of Scotland are associated with the stories of Finn MacCoul and his band of warriors, the Féinn, or Fianna. One outstanding poem, 'The Glen Beside Me is Glen Shee' relates the consequence of the love story of Diarmid and Grainne, and apparently was only recorded in Scotland, in *The Book of the Dean of Lismore*. Other songs include more popular, less exalted anecdotes or evocations of wild or domestic animals and birds. 'The Song of the Owl' (c.1600) by Domhnall mac Fhionnlaigh nan Dàn is a haunting expression of the idea of unity existing between land, people, all living creatures, nature and culture. As we've noted, the Gaelic word for this is 'dùthchas'.

In the poem, the owl moves through the air, touching on tree after tree, listening to their murmuring, drinking from rivers and circling the mountains, becoming a connecting witness of land, people, nature, generations living across history and conflict. So the poet and the owl become almost indistinguishable. The owl's inheritance is also the human inheritance, contributing to a shared identity, a creation of culture evoked as the verses are sung: this is a musical composition, a confluence of words, sounds and movement.

The importance of this concept of the connectedness and inter-relationships between land, people and culture, held in the word 'dùthchas', cannot be overestimated. It prefigures our 21st-century idea of the need for ecological balance and care and it helps us read more deeply into the literature of Scotland and the social traditions from which it arises.

One example: each of the letters of the Gaelic alphabet is associated with a tree name: Ailm (elm) for A, Beith (birch) for B, Coll or Calltain (hazel) for C, and so on. Like the Scots language, Gaelic puts your body to work as well as your mind. Your intellect is bound up with your physical being: throat, muscles, saliva and lips combine with synapses, insight and structuring intelligence. Nobody should underestimate a language that has a word like 'Bruchlas', meaning the fluttering sound birds make when they land in trees. This is visceral understanding, similar, perhaps, to 'twinkling' or 'splash' but different. It has its own music. Ignorance of Gaelic is merely an invitation to admit your limitations and try to learn more. And this kind of knowledge always brings profit to the wise.

Up until the 18th century, many Gaelic poets were highly trained and performed a defined social function in Scotland and Ireland, attached to clan chiefs and working through generations in a hereditary role, employing a repertoire of poetic forms, devices and phrases. These poets formed a bardic tradition and were maintained by the aristocracy (using that term broadly to mean minor or great lairds or chiefs and their families). The poets' job was to praise or dispraise and to act more generally as civil servants. Among their familiar genres were eulogies, laments, satires and condemnations. These had serious purpose, defining what was socially endorsed, to be celebrated, grieved for, opposed or despised. They were not merely entertainment (though they had to catch your attention). They were essential to the values and worldview of Gaelic-speaking society. The satires were believed capable of causing physical disfigurement or injury.

Formal work undertaken by clan bards is exemplified by 'Latha Inbhir Lòchaidh' / 'The Battle of Inverlochy' by Iain Lòm MacDhòmhnaill / 'Bare' ('Lean' or perhaps, 'Bald') John MacDonald (1624–1710). This is one of the most famous Gaelic war poems, commemorating a crucial victory for Montrose, the Royalists and the poet's own clan against the Covenanters and their supporters, the Campbells, in February 1645. The poem is in a traditional genre but it's vitalised by personal engagement. Iain Lom was at the battle and speaks from experience about bloodshed, severed sinews and stripped corpses. Another formal poem is his panegyric in praise of a chief, 'Òran do Dhòmhnaill Gorm Og MacDhòmhnaill' with its itemising of handsome features, a generous disposition, efficient weaponry, and expertise in combat and seafaring. Such structures of praise invoke an ancient social order that was to be broken in the coming century.

In the 17th century, these poets' hereditary places were being taken by untrained poets and by the early 18th century, they had gone. That trajectory follows the increasing anglicisation of the Highland chiefs, which is lamented and satirised by Ruaidhri MacMhuirich, 'An Clàrsair Dall' / Roderick Morison, 'The Blind Harper' (c.1656–c.1714) in 'Òran do MhacLeòid Dhùn Bheagain' / 'A Song to MacLeod of Dunvegan'. Morison was renowned as a bard who accompanied himself on the clarsach, skilled in the arts of both poetry and music.

There was more than one kind of poet, however. Some were untrained aristocrats, some were the composers of the ballads of the Féinn and some, predominantly women, were composers of work songs. Women were not prominent among the highly-trained bards, whose work was routinely put into writing, but were prominent in every other category. The hierarchy was both social and linguistic, placing the work of the trained poets high and the work songs low. Written, 'approved' forms were held in common in Scotland and Ireland. Scottish Gaelic vernacular poetry was not normally written down until the 18th century: the more demotic the work, the more likely it was to be a product of verbal virtuosity, and the less likely to be recorded.

But there are borders and exclusions everywhere: *The Book of the Dean of Lismore* includes misogyny and obscenity but not work songs; the anthologies of the late 18th and early 19th centuries include ballads of the Féinn but exclude work songs. In 1900, Alexander Carmichael's *Carmina Gadelica* included work songs but when the work stopped being carried out communally, the songs were lost. All we can retrieve are fragments.

It would be wrong not to emphasise that both women and men composed and created songs and poems in the Gaelic tradition but it would be equally wrong not to acknowledge that there were these distinctions, hierarchies and priorities of function, social recognition and practice. And material has been lost everywhere. When a culture is under sustained siege on all fronts, reliance on manuscript tradition is no more a guarantee of survival than reliance on oral tradition.

One of the major poets of the 17th century is Màiri nighean Alasdair Ruaidh (c.1615–c.1707), or Mary MacLeod. She was born at Rodel in Harris and most of her life was spent at Dunvegan in Skye, in the MacLeod chieftain's household. For a time she was exiled by her chief to Mull, perhaps for giving too much praise to his relative, Sir Norman MacLeod of Bernera. She was afterwards recalled to Dunvegan and died there. She is known as one of the more 'personal' Gaelic poets who emerged in the 17th century, eventually replacing the classical Gaelic bards. Even so, her poems extol the virtues of her clan, the MacLeods and their heroism, including deeply-felt elegies at their passing and celebrations of love of family.

The songs and poems of Mary MacLeod possess an ethos less classical or impersonal than immediate. They are guarded yet intimate, open to the world yet engaging with nuance, domestic detail, suggestion as well as assertion. This is clear in her 'Luinneag Mhic Leoid' / 'MacLeod's Song'. As in more traditional Gaelic bardic poetry, the pleasures of deer hunting, the virtue of good weaponry and the qualities of the hero (clear blue eyes, healthy, ruddy cheeks, material wealth along with practical care for the clan) are noted in familiar images here. But there is also the specific location, the woman's presence as poet coordinating her own position in relation to the geography and terrain around her and also to the hierarchies of civil society she is part of, and yearns for, even in her exile. There is a sense of desire, longing and loneliness, beside the admiration of military prowess. Here's my English version of it, with thanks to Ronald Black for pointing out the term 'culverin' (neither a musket nor a cannon but a weapon somewhere between both):

I am here on the hilltop, troubled, bereft,
Looking towards Islay, longing and sad –
Before things changed, I would never have thought
I would come to see Jura from Scarba.

From Scarba now carry my song
To the land in the shadow of that ragged skyline of mountains –
To young Norman the warrior, a man of great worth,
Known in all lands.

In all lands folk speak of your worth,
Your wisdom, your courage, your shrewd understanding,
Courage and spirit, toughness and soul –
No simple thing, to measure your line.

To measure your line in the unbroken blood
Of Lachlan's old kings, straight from the source,
Through nobles and earls of Ireland and Scotland –
No lie but a story that's proven.

Proven your father, open-handed, far-famed,
In his wisdom above all other knights in the wars –
And in peacetime, generous, giving of gifts,
Silver sustaining well-being.

Sustaining well-being and passing it on
To his son, prudent, liberal, free, of good spirit, and strong –
Such is your inheritance, sons of the warrior Roderick,
Fallen, now, so many, the dead and the missing.

The dead and the missing, so many, all gone,
But one yet remains, and I would wish never to hear
Of your death, though I am from you, sundered and parted forever –
Yet your treasure resides in your health, your fair form is flawless.

Your fair form is flawless, heart manly and generous,
The red and the white both become you,
Your clear eye is blue as the berry,
Your cheeks as red as dog-rose.

Red as dog-rose under high curling locks,

Glorious hair, thick as cushions –
Your home holds all required arms on weapon-rack,
Powder-horn, shot-horn, choicest of weaponry.

Choicest of weaponry, sword-blades so slender,
Tapering up from the hilt to the tip,
Beside them, the culverins, and hard bows of yew,
Healthy and tough with their bowstrings of hemp.

Bowstrings of hemp, and culverin-cannon,
Only the best at whatever the cost,
Arrows all polished, thrust down into quivers,
Fledged with the plumage of eagles, and silk thread from
    Galway in Ireland.

Silks from Galway in Ireland, possessed by the hero
I love. May you prosper, dear man –
Your pleasure I know would be hunting out there,
In those mountains, those forests, climbing and seeking.

Climb there and seek out the deer,
Let slip the young hounds and whip up the old ones,
And from that incitement the bristles will rise, the blood of the
    deer will be broken
And flow on white flanks, drenching the mantles of russet, the
    blood of the deer –

Blood of the deer of the lean flanks, at the hands of your good
    noble fellows,
They handle their muskets with skill, they know how to read
    all the signs in the day –
Raising the sail of the ship that would run and speed over the ocean
To the welcoming beach, the haven awaiting, your destination.

  The worlds of the Enlightenment and the Romantic movement we are about to encounter foreground literary and cultural production in the contexts of ideas about social collectivism and rebellious individualism. Even in her place of exile, as in the song above, Mary MacLeod can rely upon a security of order and knowledge, hierarchies of rightness, truths to which her appeal might be made.
  The Gaelic word 'uaisleachd' is conventionally translated as 'nobility' but it signifies more than a hierarchical distinction of social class. It might be used

disparagingly, as in, 'Tha e anns na h-uaislean ach gu dearbh chan eil e uasal.' / 'He is in the nobility but certainly not noble.' And 'na h-uaislean' has a certain negative connotation, referring to overlords, estate owners and so on, but the word on its own has a different authority. It suggests, without any undercutting irony that might come in an age of democratic egalitarianism, 'honourable' or even 'knightly'. But it also conveys gentleness, firmness and stature, sensitivity and care, attentiveness and self-knowledge of righteousness, and self-confidence (but without any of the liabilities of hubris western culture normally associates with these). It's a quality of character. Mary MacLeod gets it in this poem almost effortlessly, suggesting her own admiration without fawning and the virtues of the object of her attention, outwith mere adulation. She indicates her own pride, shrewdness, respect, longing and self-restraint. She also describes his strengths and qualities in a way which brings objectivity and measurement in tune with feelings of attraction. These components of human disposition are all held in careful balance in the poem and are suggested by the word itself. Intrinsically, this suggests a world of different conventions than those more familiar to Anglophone readers. This reading of it might seem idealistic but the world that can be seen through this poem and this word is practical. It is not so much exalted as pre-eminently a visual, tactile, sensual and simultaneously intellectual and emotional apprehension of understanding. It is not mundane but inherently of the earth.

The Gaelic tradition from earliest times to the first half of the 18th century is hardly concerned with the contrast between the social order and the romantic sinner, or the rebel artist in a world of political conservatism. In this tradition, poets occupied a valued place and performed an immediately practical function. But after the mid-18th century poets become more often the 'unacknowledged legislators of the world', in P.B. Shelley's famous phrase from *The Defence of Poetry* (1821). Their role as a witness or recorder of truth takes on in itself a rebellious character when it is distanced from a social order determined to control what that truth is and how it is seen and understood. And this will become increasingly evident in particular ways in the major Gaelic poets later in this era, and in poets writing in Scots and English as well.

NOTE
Essential to our understanding of Gaelic poetry of the 1600s is *Gàir nan Clàrsach / The Harps' Cry: An Anthology of 17th Century Gaelic Poetry*, edited by Colm Ó Baoill with translations by Meg Bateman (1994). This gives us a sense of a coherent tradition in all its complexity, a tradition then broken in the wake of the Jacobite rising of 1745.

17

Gaelic poetry of the early 18th century

IAIN DUBH MAC IAIN MHIC AILEAIN / JOHN MACDONALD,
IAIN MACCODRUM / JOHN MACCODRUM AND
MÀRTAINN MACGILLEMHÀRTAINN / MARTIN MARTIN

MOST OF US in Scotland are tourists in our own country, to a greater or lesser degree still trying to find out about the languages, places and traditions we have inherited.

Most importantly for English-language readers, many of these qualities, inherited from Gaelic, have been caricatured into cliché or romanticised beyond recognition. And yet there are things beyond the superficial images that might immediately hook any reader's imagination: ideas, sound-structures, ways of making meaning that are distinctively expressed in the Gaelic language.

Formal procedures that were regularly employed in Gaelic poetry included such things as personal and local reference, deliberate understatement or exaggeration, lists of adjectives, densely-packed imagery, use of food, drink, colour, sensual detail specific to outdoor or indoor location, and repetition, reference back to motifs noted earlier, and reinterpretation. These are all good literary techniques that can become dull with overuse or predictable employment, but in the imaginative work of a good poet they can deliver the cold shock of insight and the warm assurance of recognition.

Gaelic poets were highly sophisticated composers but not necessarily literate. For example, Duncan Ban MacIntyre and Rob Donn were two major 18th-century poets who composed their works without paper and ink, memorising, reciting or performing them as songs. Their poems were written down by others. Linguistic virtuosity does not rely only upon literacy.

However, as formal clan patronage for poets fell away after 1715 and then conclusively after 1746, the place for regular recitation, singing and storytelling became the ceilidh, a quasi-formal gathering in which what we might call verbal (so, not strictly 'literary') skills could be learned and passed on, through oral, unscripted occasions, where presence, memory and commanding enactment were priorities. Every Highland community had ceilidh-houses and workplaces where oral tradition was normal every day and night, so as soon as a good song was heard it would zip around the country maybe as quickly and effectively as the internet. More so perhaps, for they were created and circulated in a community of shared insight and values, rather than one overloaded with useless or misleading information and priorities of exploitation. They were not 'poems' as we think of words on a page, they were 'words in musical forms': primarily, things to be heard.

After the establishment of the Society for the Propagation of Christian Knowledge in 1709, schools began to be built throughout the Highlands. It would be simplistic to polarise native Gaelic oral and written culture and the educational aspect of the ceilidh against written Christian Anglocentric culture and the church schools, but there is a distinction of preference. And there are tragic consequences. The 18th century saw a gradual transfer of social authority from clan to church.

For example, 'Òran do Raghnall Mac Mhic Aailein' / 'A Song to Ranald of Clanranald' by Iain Dubh mac Iain mhic Ailein / John MacDonald (c.1665–1725), is considered an address to Ronald, clan chief, who was in France in the summer of 1716, in the aftermath of the Battle of Sheriffmuir. The poem laments the length of time that the chief – hawk-noble, steel-strong – has been absent, leaving his people, in Morar, Uist, Eigg and Canna, all over the Highlands and Islands, still unfailingly loyal, but anxious and uncertain. The chief used to look after widows and orphans, the song concludes: what will happen to the poor people now?

Thirty years later, after Culloden, the tradition of Gaelic poetry and song that had run through centuries was broken. The next generation kept contact with the surviving older professional bards, but while they drew on the tradition, they were establishing individual voices that were not sustained by clan family structure, though there was still a prevalent emotional attachment and loyalty, to families, people, particular things and particular places.

This condition is memorably evoked in 'Òran do na Fògarraich' / 'A Song to the Exiles' by Iain MacCodrum / John MacCodrum (1693–1779), which protests against the landowners' increasing dedication to accumulating wealth and neglecting their people in favour of a more profitable population of sheep. They go off to live in comfort in 'a realm without want' and leave behind them poverty, blight and rationing. The judgement and stance resonates into future centuries. What were to become sadly familiar images and tones are, in this song, composed in the early 1770s, fresh with bitterness and sour condemnation.

But there are other ways of approaching the greatness of Gaelic poetry for an English-language reader. For example, consider the poems of Norman MacCaig (1910–96), particularly his poems in the three familiar genres, not only of sorrowing and condemnation but also of celebration. MacCaig wrote exclusively in English, but his Gaelic ancestry was important to him and his poems show clearly how essential these genres are.

Without irony, in 'Praise of a collie' ('She flowed through fences like a piece of black wind'), 'Praise of a boat' ('in still water gurgling like a baby') or 'Praise of a thorn bush' ('an encyclopaedia of angles') he uses metaphors and similes that retain cut-crystal brilliance. His laments (especially in the sequence 'Poems for Angus') show how, with minimum resources of language – no multisyllabic rhetoric, phrases pared down to essentials – the utterance of grief at the death of our loved ones is meaningful on the verge beyond which words become silence. And his hate-poems, condemning the loss of language in the Gaelic world, particularly 'Aunt Julia' and 'Two Thieves', are angry poems that remain forever angry, partly through the skill of their composition (their use of repetition, imagery, argumentative development) and partly because the reason for their anger is still with us.

In fact, simile is relatively rare in Gaelic poetry and metaphor is primarily a form of straightforward identification. So while MacCaig's brilliance of observation and allusion might indicate an essential aspect of Gaelic poetic practice, it is not directly aligned with it. In MacCaig's most explicitly political and longest poem, 'A Man in Assynt' (1967–68), he writes of the Highlanders, asking, has it come to this:

> that this dying landscape belongs
> to the dead, the crofters and fighters
> and fishermen whose larochs
> sink into the bracken
> by Loch Assynt and Loch Crocach? –
> to men trampled under the hoofs of sheep
> and driven by deer to
> the ends of the earth – to men whose loyalty
> was so great it accepted their own betrayal
> by their own chiefs and whose descendants now
> are kept in their place
> by English businessmen and the indifference
> of a remote and ignorant government.

Consider especially that phrase: 'men whose loyalty / was so great it accepted their own betrayal'. There is pathos in that description as well as a kind of modern critical condemnation of outmoded ways of thinking, self-destructive habits of mind and self-sacrificing attitudes of respect and humility.

Yet that ambiguity of feeling begs the question, are these ways of thinking really outmoded? The pathos persists. These lines describe a loyalty that cuts across class distinctions and economic strata, something that may derive from quasi-feudal social structures but seems more profoundly based in the social organisation of all great literary tragedy, and comedy: the family.

And by that I mean not the nuclear but the extended family. From that proposition, this sense of loyalty might embrace a whole society, with a multiplicity of personal identities held in a changing but stable equilibrium of land, people and culture, as held in the Gaelic word, 'dùthchas'. That's the word I emphasised earlier. Land, as in all the territory, including island archipelagos and the waterways connecting them; people, as in everyone who lives here, long generations of residents and new settlers too; culture, as in everything humanly and naturally created, including both that which is of palpable benefit and healthy as well as that which is exploitative and inimical to well-being, and must be opposed, so, whatever is created. All these are interrelated and at best, held in balance.

Is it fanciful to suggest that that was precisely what the clan system really meant?

To read Gaelic poetry of the 18th century, even if only in English translation, we need to go back behind the landscape MacCaig is describing there.

One way to do that is with Martin Martin (c.1669–1718), one of the great early travel writers, who precedes Johnson and Boswell in his account of journeying through the Western Isles. He experienced life in the islands as a native, born near Duntulm, in Skye, from a family of landowners' factors. And yet his travel writing often gives the impression that he was not native: he describes what he sees and encounters as if for the first time, with faux innocence and open-eyed wonder, like a new visitor to unfamiliar territories. He graduated from Edinburgh University in 1681 and mapped St Kilda in 1697, publishing *A Description of the Western Islands of Scotland* in 1703. He entered Leiden University in 1710, taking a doctoral degree in medicine, then living in London till his death. His description of the effects of Scotch whisky is vivid: 'at first taste it affects all the Members of the Body' and 'if any Man exceed' two spoonfuls, 'it would presently stop his Breath, and endanger his Life.' That smacks of faux naiveté to me. I'm certain Norman MacCaig would have agreed.

NOTE

Essential to any reading of the whole range of material in this era are *Gaelic Poetry in the Eighteenth Century* edited by Derick Thomson (1993) and *An Lasair: Anthology of 18th Century Scottish Gaelic Verse* edited by Ronald Black (2001). A handful of books are especially helpful: Derick Thomson's *An Introduction to Gaelic Poetry* (1974) and *A Companion to Gaelic Scotland* (1983), James Hunter's *On the Other Side of Sorrow: Nature and People in the Scottish Highlands* (1995) and *Last of the Free: A Millennial History of the Highlands and Islands of Scotland* (1999), Michael Newton's *From the Clyde to Callander: Gaelic Songs, Poetry, Tales and Traditions of the Lennox and Menteith in Gaelic with English Translations* (1999; reprinted 2010), *A Handbook of the Scottish Gaelic World* (2000), and most comprehensively, *Warriors of the Word: The World of the Scottish Highlanders* (2009). An informed understanding of the whole literary context is *Dùthchas Nan Gaidheal: Selected Essays* by John MacInnes, edited by Michael Newton (2006). A different kind of work but an important contribution is Calum I. Maclean's *The Highlands* (1959), which emphasises aspects of tradition and tradition-bearers. *The Hebrides: An Aerial View of a Cultural Landscape* (Birlinn, 2010) by Angus and Patricia Macdonald offers an overview of the entire territory, where much of its history can be seen in the intimate variety and detail of its geography, the land itself and the seaways and rivers that surround and run through it. The landscape itself can be our primary reference in Gaelic poetry and the Gaelic world.

In this regard, especially valuable are John Murray's books, *Reading the Gaelic Landscape / Leughadh Aghaidh na Tìre* (2014) and *Literature of the Gaelic Landscape: Song, Poem and Tale / Litreachas na Tìre – oran, bardachd is sgeul* (2017). All of these works help take us into the history, economy, social priorities and contemporary potential of the Gaelic world. Like so much else in Scotland, they invite us into a whole library of unfinished stories. They can help us leave tourism behind, and become more fully informed residents, and ultimately better inhabitants of the whole cradle: 'dùthchas' understood.

18

More Gaelic poetry of the early 18th century

NIALL MACMHUIRICH, SÌLEAS NA CEAPAICH / CICELY MACDONALD OF KEPPOCH AND GEORGE MACKENZIE

FOR THE GAELIC world as it had been regenerated for hundreds of years, cataclysmic changes were to be enacted in the 18th century. It might be said that the Battle of Sheriffmuir in 1715 was the beginning of the end, and Culloden in 1746 the end of the end. To go back to the poets of the first half of the 18th century before coming forward into the changed world after Culloden is to go into a more socially coherent and reliably structured literary community, in which praise-songs, laments, riotously funny and physical satires, erotic, comic and playful engagements, tender love songs and poems evocative of season and place all have a vitality and lasting pleasure. Poems were also a way of reminding powerful people of their responsibilities to the less well-off in society. In the 1980s, the American poet Edward Dorn pointed out that certain politicians and economic priorities were going to do bad things:

> 'Where there is wealth,
> let us create excess…
> where there is need,
> let us create hardship,
> where there is poverty,
> let us create downright misery.'

Such cautionary reprimands were also the prerogative of Gaelic poets in the 18th century. If the earlier Jacobite rising of 1715 disrupted that coherence, the role of certain poetic forms at that time remained secure. Among the great laments of the period is 'Òran do dh'Aiolean Dearg' / 'A Song to Red Allan' by Niall MacMhuirich (the last professional bard of the Clanranald MacDonalds). Here is the first verse and Ronald Black's translation:

> Gur e naidheachd na Ciadaoin
> Rinn mo chruitheachd a shiaradh;
> Le leann dubh, 's le bron cianail
> Gun drùidh i trom air mo chrioschaibh –

> Mo sgeul duilich nach iarr mi ur còmhradh
> Mo sgeul duilich nach iarr mi ur còmhradh
>
> Wednesday's news
> Has wasted my frame;
> With regret, wretched mourning
> It struck hard my defences –
> > My sad tale's that I can't seek your converse,
> > My sad tale's that I can't seek your converse.

Similarly deep passion is felt in the equally formal, gestural lament by Sìleas na Ceapaich / Cicely MacDonald of Keppoch (c.1660–c.1729), 'Alastair a Gleanna Garadh' / 'Alexander from Glengarry'. This is one of the great songs of remorse. Here's the opening of the sixth verse with Ronald Black's translation:

> Bu tu 'n loch nach fhaoidt' a thaomadh,
> Bu tu tobar faoilidh na slàinte,
> Bu tu Beinn Nimheis thar gach aonach,
> Bu tu chreag nach fhaoidte theàirnadh...
>
> You were the loch that couldn't be emptied,
> You were the generous well of health,
> You were Ben Nevis above every hilltop.
> You were the cliff that no-one descends...

Recollecting her own bereavement, Cicely thereby puts the death of the heroic chief in a powerfully personal emotional context, going on with tender acknowledgement of the vulnerability of his widow and their surviving son.

There's an unrestrained vigour and freedom of engagement here utterly strange to the English-language tradition. For example, Cicely also composed a very funny response to a lurid comic poem in praise of carnality and the pleasures of copulation. 'The Oobie Noogie' by George Mackenzie (c.1655–post-1730) is an onomatopoeic tour-de-force expressing delight in the joys of sex, in the voices of various women, close cousins to Burns's *Merry Muses*. Various bodily nooks and crannies are happily and eagerly explored in 'The Oobie Noogie' but Cicely, in her response, 'Against the Oobie Noogie', urges caution, an older woman reprimanding younger folks' promiscuous lusts. She and Alasdair mac Mhaighstir Alasdair / Alexander MacDonald, the major poet of the century, occupy the earlier, socially coherent Gaelic world but just as Cicely comes forward to the world after the 1715 rising, Alasdair also crosses into the post-Culloden era.

In the second half of the century, a new strand in Gaelic tradition began to develop, of bards who would be attached to Highland regiments in the British army. This flourished in the 19th century.

And there is another strand in the tradition, that of what we now call folk song. The legacy of this only began to be fully understood in the modern English-speaking world when Hamish Henderson and Calum I. Maclean started recording songs and stories in Gaelic and Scots for the School of Scottish Studies at Edinburgh University in the second half of the 20th century, although among the pioneering champions of Gaelic as a subject for scholarly research, Professor John Stuart Blackie (1809–1895) was pre-eminent. His efforts established the first Chair of Celtic at Edinburgh University in the 1870s. His life and work is the subject of Stuart Wallace's *John Stuart Blackie: Scottish Scholar and Patriot* (2006).

Beyond scholarship, however, remains traditional practice. Puirt à beul (mouth music) can be heard throughout the Gaelic musical world, usually sung unaccompanied. It's there in the ceilidh scene in the film *Whisky Galore!* (1949) and the rock band Cocteau Twins performed or evoked puirt à beul in some of their songs in the 1980s and 1990s. Its most wonderful modern performer is Julie Fowlis (b.1978), born in North Uist in the Outer Hebrides, whose various albums include *Gach sgeul / Every story* (2014) and *Alterum* (2017).

'Puirt à beul' means 'tunes from the mouth' – in other words, vocal production that is musically instrumental in style. Details are in Keith Norman MacDonald's *Puirt à Beul: The Vocal Dance Music of the Scottish Gaels*, with an introduction and historical notes by William Lamb (1901; new edition, Upper Breakish, Isle of Skye: Taigh na Teud, 2012). These tunes were always performed in dance rhythms and all could be danced to, but they were also performed simply for pleasure, for their own sake. Sometimes the vocal line would be meaningless vocables, sometimes words full of humorous intent, incorporating tongue-twisters. The term's significance for literature is that it suggests the close relation between music, sound and poetic rhythms, structures of meaning in poetry that are expressed through metrical and aural organisation. The emphasis is on the subtlety and quickness of the component parts of sound patterns. No greater sophistication or intricacy of understanding exists in any analyses or composition of English-language poetry – not even Norman MacCaig's.

19

Scottish Enlightenment authors: Stewart, Hume, Smith, Hutton and Ferguson

FROM THE MOMENT in 1660 when Thomas Urquhart dies laughing to the publication of Walter Scott's first novel *Waverley* in 1814, Scottish literature becomes increasingly aware of itself. That is, Scottish writers – some of them – become increasingly self-conscious of their own literary ancestors and the idea of national literary traditions. This is brought about centrally in the work of Allan Ramsay (1684–1758), in his anthologies of earlier poets, and in the edition of Gavin Douglas's translation of Virgil's *Aeneid* (1710) published by Thomas Ruddiman (1674–1757), which was probably what Burns was quoting from in the epigraph to 'Tam o' Shanter': 'Of Brownyis and Bogillis full is this Buke.'

It is apt perhaps that the year of Mary MacLeod's death was also that of the Treaty of Union, 1707. Mary MacLeod was one of the last of the traditional, pre-Culloden Gaelic poets, still part of a clan structure in which the role and value of poets were relatively secure. After that Union, and especially after Culloden, people generally and writers in particular, in both the Gaelic world and the Scotland in which Scots and English were the dominant languages, would become increasingly aware of their own distinctiveness.

The turn towards greater self-awareness, the process of questioning and revisioning the formation of national identity and the positioning of that identity in an ongoing struggle for economic prosperity and international colonial and imperial power, is central in the history of Scotland from 1707. It underlies and suffuses the writing of philosophers, politicians, dramatists, novelists, poets, and travel writers. Andrew Fletcher of Saltoun (1655–1716), foremost among those engaged directly in that epochal transition arguing for Scotland's continuing independence, was not only a politican but a political philosopher. To quote William Power (1873–1951), in *Literature and Oatmeal* (1935), 'Fletcher was the first Scot to depart from ecclesiastical and theocratic preconceptions, and apply pure thinking to political and social questions. He initiated a new branch of Scottish literature.' In this regard, Fletcher heralds the Enlightenment and a developing tradition that runs through Carlyle to MacDiarmid and on.

After the Union of 1707, the flourishing of great poetry in the Gaelic tradition that surrounded the Jacobite risings of 1715 and 1745, the poetry linked to the suppression and dispersal of the clans after 1746, and to the later Highland Clearances, the brilliance of vernacular Scots language poetry pre-eminently in Fergusson and Burns, the popularity of radical new departures in

English-language poetry like James Thomson's *The Seasons* (1730) or novels like Tobias Smollett's *The Expedition of Humphry Clinker* (1771) – all these things fermented in Scotland's intellectual life through the course of the 18th century. Underlying them all were questions about the viability of the identity of Scotland itself: a singular nation voiced in multiple and elaborate formulations.

The historical context is crucial for our understanding of Enlightenment and Romanticism. The foundations of both Enlightenment and Romanticism, in Scotland, are a complex mix of social structures and individually exceptional acts. In English literature, and perhaps in Europe generally, the transition is normally thought of as chronological and linear, from the social satire of snappy, crackling Pope, to the socialist individualism of atheist Shelley, hypersensitive Keats, solitary, self-reflective Wordsworth, intensely imaginative Coleridge. Formal, social dance in the grand ballroom gives way to the heaven-bound leap of the individual dancer, soaring above the mob. Patterns observed give way to acts of perception, the violent individualism of moments or characters described, say, in paintings by Goya, or equally, the urgency of the artist's perception itself. Early Haydn gives way to late Beethoven.

In Scotland, the story is more complex, the two kinds of ethos more closely enmeshed. It is not a simple progression but a range of responses to, and developments from, aspects of cultural history that have not always been seen comprehensively. Burns and Scott were both men of the Enlightenment and at the same time, they were both Romantics. Both respected and loved things in their appropriate place and their correct order: in 'Now Westlin' Winds' Burns approves the plover in the mountains, the partridge in the fruitful dells; Scott sees justice in balance, mediation, moderation: rarely is he driven to extremes, never easily. Yet both assert the rights of men and women of whatever social station to a democratic justice of human worth. For Burns, Tam o' Shanter's life is as valid as any king's, for Scott, Jeanie Deans's story in *The Heart of Midlothian* is as vital as the aristocrat Amy Robsart's or even Queen Elizabeth's in *Kenilworth*. This carries the seed of a new and different aesthetic for modern Scottish literature: not the epiphany of perception enacted by an isolated consciousness but an epiphany of participation in a changing social continuity. The isolated individual and the organisation of society are understood to be not opposed, neither 'naturally' nor in historical chronology, but are in continual relation to each other.

So, what is 'The Enlightenment'? What is 'Romanticism'?

To answer these questions we need to understand what precedes them. The prehistory of the Enlightenment is also the prehistory of Romanticism, and the prehistory of both is the Reformation. The Reformation is often thought of as a fundamental cultural fault-line, yet the continuities across it are many. The ideal of education as a birthright, not as a privilege of class or financial status, the provision of schools in every parish in Scotland, were to some degree present before as well as after the Reformation. Protestantism may have endorsed universal religious education for every individual but the institutional foundations to enable that were not new.

Yet if the Enlightenment developed out of a fundamental capacity for understanding, socially enhanced by respect for the intrinsic value of education, it also came out of a period of contest and conflict – intellectual, literary, ethical and religious, as well as social, political and military. Both Enlightenment and Romanticism arise in the wake of the Jacobite risings of 1715 and 1745, where systems of religious belief and social hierarchy, language, cultural practice, socially approved habits of thought and behaviour, sensitivity to the beliefs and sensibilities of others, were ferociously contested. Both arise from a widening experience of cultural relativism and the acknowledgement of independent forms of government and social authority. From the same century and the same mix arise the assertions of new forms of self-government in France and America.

To make a crude distinction, Enlightenment endorses reason as the best human response to the unpredictability of life whereas Romanticism trusts in impulse and intuition, in acts that are beyond reasonable foresight or rational plans. In this figuration, Romanticism may seem to be a reaction to classical Enlightenment, but even in this distinction, both are connected. For Hume, reason serves no end but that of pleasure, desire, instinctual hope; for Burns, one spark of 'nature's fire' is all the learning he wants or needs, but that spark will suffice in place of learning, reason, rationalism itself. So, both Enlightenment and Romanticism arise in the age of the codification and categorisation of knowledge, the age of the first English dictionary and the *Encyclopaedia Britannica*. Yet at the same time they both arise in the age of slavery, in a century where literary culture could not face up squarely to the full meaning of tragedy.

Dr Johnson may have famously compiled the first English dictionary in 1755 but it should be noted that James Boswell set about compiling the first Scots dictionary in the 1760s. The major work of John Jamieson (1759–1838), the *Etymological Dictionary of the Scottish Language*, appeared in two volumes in 1808, and the primary editor of the *Oxford English Dictionary* was another Scot, James Murray (1837–1915). The *Encyclopaedia Britannica* was first published between 1768 and 1771 in Edinburgh, in three volumes, compiled by yet another Scot, a friend of Robert Burns, William Smellie (1740–95), and founded and published by more Scots: Colin Macfarquhar (c.1745–93), Andrew Bell (1726–1809), Archibald Bell (1774–1827) and others.

If slavery involved Scots at every level, the anti-slavery movement involved Scots at every level too: the situation cannot be easily simplified in moral terms, as it prompts neither comprehensive guilt nor self-glorification, neither abjection nor pious superiorism. The liability of the dictionaries and encyclopaedias was that in gathering and categorising knowledge, it might seem that they could encompass human experience, securing knowledge as property and endorsing education as privilege. Equally, to many people, the slave trade was financially lucrative, thus eminently sensible, yet it was also humanly appalling, thus to a growing number of people, utterly reprehensible. If anything, the complex contradictions in lexicography and the arts, international economy and brutality, formed the essential characteristics of the era.

The philosophers and intellectuals of the Scottish Enlightenment lived, usually in comfort, in a context of ideas and conversation, where the articulation of thought was engaged in company as well as in solitude. There were many individuals, in Edinburgh, Glasgow, Aberdeen and elsewhere, whose work contributed to the whole movement. Their favoured literary form was pre-eminently the essay, and any literary reading – supplementing the philosophical, economic, social or scientific aspects of their work – might begin from the point of appreciating their skill as essayists. An excellent selection is available in *The Scottish Enlightenment: An Anthology* (1997), edited by Alexander Broadie, in which contents are arranged by theme: human nature, ethics, aesthetics, religion, economics, social theory and politics, law, historiography, language and science. Broadie's work on the Enlightenment in various books and studies is invaluable. He introduces the book by noting that the most influential account of the nature of Enlightenment is by the German philosopher Immanuel Kant (1724–1804), which he describes as a freedom from the unquestioned acceptance of imposed rules. Failing to take up that freedom is the consequence of laziness and cowardice. It takes courage to use your own reason freely, in public. To do so requires a society of toleration in which ideas are publicly debated – that is, published and discussed – and this requires a degree of education and inculcation to familiarise yourself with the rules of the conversation. These impose their own limitations but they are out there, to be questioned, tested, challenged and, as appropriate, changed. It was not always so. Religious intolerance of freedom of thought had characterised for centuries the public expression of ideas. You could be burned alive for advocating the wrong thing amongst certain people. David Hume was stigmatised by many for his reputation as an atheist but at least his case was there to be discussed, and thus, tolerated. In the Enlightenment, religion and especially Christianity were made subject to reasoned enquiry as never before. Faith was to be questioned. Miracles required proof.

The long history I've sketched leading to the Enlightenment had specific bearing in Scotland. The Scottish universities, St Andrews (founded 1411–12), Glasgow (1451), Aberdeen (1495) and Edinburgh (1583) followed Oxford (1096) and Cambridge (1209) and together were among the oldest established universities in Europe. They carried a long history of the international and national priorities of education, especially in Science, Law and Religion. The international context was essential, exemplified in such thinkers as Montesquieu (1689–1755), Voltaire (1694–1778), Rousseau (1712–78), Kant and Benjamin Franklin (1706–90).

Here I would like merely to draw attention briefly to a small number of the major figures and suggest some of their most lastingly important innovative thinking.

Pre-eminent is David Hume (1711–76), whose importance derives from the sense he conveys that all sciences are inter-related, connected, reciprocal, and specialisations are always connected back to the ultimate benefit of people: they are there to help people to live. Hugh MacDiarmid called him 'Scotland's Greatest Son'.

For Hume, the three main disciplines of ethics, economics and engineering form a unity and all lead to what Hume called 'the science of man'. The train of connections are clear: developments in engineering have economic consequences that give rise to ethical questions. Keep the categories separate and the idea of a good society will be riddled with exploitation and corruption. Good health and well-being is all in the balancing. In summary, Hume's brilliant perception was that so much – if not everything – in our understanding, explanation and reasoning for action depends on the nature of the observer. We see things happen and follow their consequences and think of them as inevitable, products of necessity, not chance. But that sense of inevitabilty is a result of expectation based on repeated events. So if there is a necessary connection between cause and effect that is necessarily a product of the observing human mind. All the moral sciences, ethics, aesthetics, politics are dependent on human nature. Hume's conclusion, which was fundamentally an agreed tenet of the Enlightenment in its entirety, is given in *A Treatise of Human Nature* (1739–40):

> There is no question of importance, whose decision is not compriz'd in the science of man; and there is none, which can be decided with any certainty, before we become acquainted with that science.

While Thomas Reid (1710–96) in his philosophy of 'Common Sense' emphasised that there were limits to scientific enquiry into the human mind and that the words we use in that enquiry and to express the thoughts of that mind themselves have limitations and can be a trap, nevertheless, like all the Enlightenment thinkers, he agreed with Hume's essential proposition. Likewise following Hume, Dugald Stewart (1753–1828) argued for the interconnectedness of all sciences and carried the teaching of moral philosophy into the early 19th century. Through Stewart the ideas of Francis Hutcheson and Adam Smith were taken forward. He taught the young Walter Scott.

Hutcheson (1694–1746) was known especially for his enquiries into 'Beauty,

Order, Harmony and Design' and the affects of the passions and affections on the moral sense, and for his 'Thoughts on Laughter'. These were all written in Dublin before he moved to Scotland in 1729, where he took up the Chair of Moral Philosophy at Glasgow University and was the first professor there to deliver his lectures in English instead of Latin. A magnetic teacher, his work on economics directly influenced Adam Smith, who counted Hutcheson and David Hume as the two most memorable people in his life.

Adam Smith (1723–90) has been popularly characterised – or caricatured – as the foundational economist who sanctioned laissez-faire capitalism but the truth is more complex. His major work, *The Wealth of Nations* (1776), is indeed an exploration of how wealth is generated and how it can be controlled and its benefits regulated, but it hardly offers total sanction to the excesses of late 20th- and early 21st-century Western capitalism. Smith's distinction was to see how the division of labour could effectively generate wealth and interdependence, the stimulation of intellectual engagement and imagination, and thus help the economy to grow. To abandon the moral foundation would have been abhorrent to him, as would many of his modern advocates, the profiteers, tyrants and oligarchs of banks and other multinational exploitative companies. Indeed, Smith's first major work, *The Theory of Moral Sentiments* (1759) emphasises sympathy for others without which the self-interest interpreted as a primary motivation in *The Wealth of Nations* is inadequate and lacking in a necessary human balance.

The major work of James Hutton (1726–97) was 'Theory of the Earth; or an Investigation of the Laws observable in the Composition, Dissolution, and Restoration of Land upon the Globe'. This was read aloud to the Royal Society of Edinburgh in 1785 and then published in their Transactions in 1788, after Hutton had been working on it for around 25 years. It is the foundational work of modern geology, opening speculative thought on the nature of time and change in the formation of the earth and the idea of geological time ('deep time'). When Burns, in 'My Love is like a Red, Red Rose', pledges that his love will last until all the seas go dry and the rocks melt with the sun, underneath this promise is the notion that the rocks will, indeed, one day melt with the sun, and all the seas go dry. All things change, even the geology of earth itself, in the longest measurements of time. Many of the ideas that underlie Hugh MacDiarmid's 'On a Raised Beach' and Norman MacCaig's poems in praise of the mountain Suilven and the north-west corner of Scotland known as Assynt, where the stone is so ancient that it carries no fossils, for it predates cellular life, arise from the world Hutton depicted. As much as by David Hume, human understanding of the world was changed forever by James Hutton.

Adam Ferguson (1723–1816), whose seminal work was *An Essay on the History of Civil Society* (1767), presented historical progress as twofold: natural, created by God and evident in the earth itself, and social, man-made and progressive. This progressive sense of human evolution was based in sympathy, courtesy and civil behaviour, but it went through distinct 'stages' and was therefore known as the 'Stadial Theory of Evolution': human society developed from hunter-gatherer groups, to farming communities, and ultimately to urban civilisations centred in cities. After that, there are the economics of the state, control of capital and government-protected order.

The problem with this theory, of course, is that human societies do not develop at the same rate or in such a simple directional way: hyper-sophisticated cities co-exist contemporaneously with nomadic tribes in different geographies, desert lands. We do not all live in the same time. The most famous example of this in literature is in Scott's novel *Rob Roy* (1817), where the title character is a Highland outlaw but also first cousin to the city-based Bailie Nicol Jarvie. And social regression, as we know too well, is always possible. Some politicians, some forms of media, bring out the worst in people, and the stakes are higher in the 21st century than ever before.

Another proposition underlies the Enlightenment: Dugald Stewart states it as 'an incontrovertible logical maxim that the capacities of the human mind have been in all ages the same' and Hume himself famously wrote: 'Mankind are so much the same, in all times and places, that history informs us of nothing new or strange in this particular'. As Alexander Broadie points out, if this means that people usually deliberate before acting, there is some truth in it, but these generalisations don't help us understand people living in the distant past or in societies radically different from our own. There's a liability in the Enlightenment, an assumption of the privileged viewpoint from which provable and thus conclusive truth can be delivered. This is what limits the virtues of the thinking of these philosophers and permits Hume to express some views, about race for example, that are unacceptable in the 21st century. Yet to understand this does not endorse wholesale rejection of their thought. The freedom to express that thought and to debate it is a virtue they maintained and sets an example to anyone foolish enough to believe only one viewpoint should be taken and all others cancelled. The seeds of self-criticism were there in the arguments they made. Only the enemies of freedom deny them.

Walter Benjamin, in 'Theses on the Philosophy of History' (1940), wrote:

> There is no document of civilisation which is not at the same time a document of barbarism. And just as such a document is not free from barbarism, barbarism taints also the manner in which it was transmitted from one owner to another.

Writing during the Second World War, Benjamin's understanding of the relation between so-called 'barbarism' and so-called 'civilisation' was certainly as acute as that of the Enlightenment philosophers.

Perhaps we should think of them all in two contexts. One is of an optimistic hope for reason. In the 18th century, *King Lear* was revised to provide a happy ending since reason would not surrender itself to tragedy. That indicates a failure in over-reliance on reason to provide a remedy for what the world brings upon us. Knowing that, we might accept its virtues with greater humility and discrimination. But the other context is a world in which tragedy was being enacted every day. In the 20th century, the Nazis didn't bother to rewrite anything, they simply burned the books. The lesson is there.

20

In the eye of the storm:
Alasdair mac Mhaighstir Alasdair / Alexander MacDonald

THE GREATEST SINGLE work by Alasdair mac Mhaighstir Alasdair (c.1695–c.1770) is 'The Birlinn of Clanranald' (a birlinn is a ship, a large galley under sail, which can be rowed by working sailors, a mode of transport that was used around the islands and coasts of Scotland and Ireland for hundreds of years). 'The Birlinn of Clanranald' is a poem which describes its component working parts, mast, sail, tiller, rudder, oars and the cabes (or oar-sockets) they are nestled in, the ropes that connect sail to cleats or belaying pins, and so on, and the 16 crewmen, each with their appointed role and place. It describes their mutual working together, rowing, and then sailing out to sea, from the Hebrides in the west of Scotland, from South Uist to the Sound of Islay, then over to Carrickfergus in Ireland. The work of the crew is presented in detail, their skills of seamanship, their co-ordination and the need for it, the construction and beauty of the boat itself, and the balanced relations in the clan, within the commerce of a sea-based economy.

Although that economy is not mentioned in the poem, the collective work of the crew is crucial and the magnificence of the natural world around them is evoked in the last third of the poem, which vividly describes the storm that almost engulfs them. The devastation of Highland culture and the sorrow at its passing were not only figured literally in stark political commentaries and poignant songs of farewell. In its sensitivity to the natural world, the poem is a counterpart to Duncan Ban MacIntyre's 'Praise of Ben Dorain'. Duncan Ban, in 'Summer Song' and 'Last Leave-taking of the Bens', seems to be directly saying farewell to the older Scotland he once knew, yet 'The Birlinn' and 'Ben Dorain' also have symbolic or suggestive political meaning. Realistic detail in 'The Birlinn of Clanranald' informs an allegorical meaning, as the sailors navigate the ship through the tempest. Their journey from Loch Eynort in the Outer Hebrides to Carrickfergus in Ireland, reconnects these two Celtic countries across the storm of the 18th century. That journey represents a major transition in 18th-century Scottish history, through the Jacobite rising of 1745 to an affirmation of Celtic identity shared by Scots and Irish Gaels. It describes the work of a company of men, a more communal ideal than would have been the story of a heroic captain, master and commander. After the last third of the poem takes us through the horrendous storm, we make it – only just – to safe harbour. The poem evokes what is at stake and counts the cost. Here is the opening of the poem in the original Gaelic:

> Gum beannaicheadh Dia long Chlann Raghnaill
>   A'cheud là do chuaidh air sàile,
> E fèin 's a thrèin-fhir da caitheamh,
>   Trèin a chuaidh thar maitheas chàich,
>
> Gum beannaich an Coimh-dhia naomh
>   An iùnnrais, anail nan speur,
> Gun sguabte garbhlach na mara,
>   G' ar tarraing gu cala rèidh.
>
> Athair, a chruthaich an fhairge
>   'S gach gaoth a shèideas às gach àird,
> Beannaich ar caol-bhàirc 's ar gaisgich,
>   'S cum i fèin 's a gasraidh slàn.
>
> A Mhic, beannaich fèin ar n-acair,
>   Ar siùil, ar beartean, 's ar stiùir,
> 'S gach droineap tha crochte ri 'r crannaibh,
>   'S thoir gu cala sinn le d' iùl.
>
> Beannaich ar racain 's ar slata,
>   Ar crainn 's ar teudaibh gu lèir
> Ar stagh 's ar tarraing cùm fallain
>   'S na leig-s' ann ar cara beud.
>
> An Spiorad Naomh biodh air stiùir,
>   Seòlaidh e 'n t-iùl a bhios ceart,
> 'S eòl da gach longphort fon ghrèin,
>   Tilgeamaid sinn fèin fo 'bheachd.

And this is my version of the opening in English:

> May the great lord god of movement
>   carry us safe,
> on all the choral waters of this world,
> the seas and oceans, currents and streams, enable us,
> take this craft upon them, across them, and cradle us –
>   We are launched on Day One
>   this craft of my clan
>   Each one of the crew
>   being tough, strong and true

> Each man hears this call –
> Bless them all.

It was written sometime around 1751–55 and first published posthumously in 1776. It is, therefore, deeply connected with its historical and political moment, but it has lasting value and meaning beyond that. Alasdair's earlier songs such as 'Song of Summer' and 'Song of Winter' (both from the early 1740s) may have been prompted by Allan Ramsay and by James Thomson's *The Seasons* (1730), the most influential and radically new poem written in English in the first half of the 18th century. What's important to note here is that there was a literary and intellectual commerce between the traditions of Gaelic, Scots and English-language writing that it would be easy to overlook or underestimate. While it may be convenient to see these three traditions as distinct, such influences cross languages and cultural priorities. Alasdair's 'Song Against the Highland Disclothing Act' (1747) comments on the rule of law suppressing the wearing of the tartan kilt. 'A Song for the Prince' (in praise of Charles Edward Stuart) is a rallying call for the Jacobite cause. Refrain and chorus here include meaningless vocables, familiar from traditional 'puirt à beul' and essential in many Gaelic poetic compositions.

Alasdair mac Mhaighstir Alasdair was a teacher and soldier, a Jacobite officer during the rising of 1745 and Gaelic tutor to Prince Charles Edward Stuart. His father was an Episcopalian Church of Scotland minister, who taught the boy and introduced him to Greek and Roman literature. He knew about sea voyages literally, in the Hebrides, but he also read about them in the poems of Homer and Virgil. In his poem, there is clear evidence that the author had experienced the sea, but there is also a supremely literary sensibility at work, especially when we come to the storm, where a wealth of poetic resources of hyperbole and imagery are drawn upon. The modernity of this passage is startling, and it could almost be described as psychedelic or surrealist. This is the opening of the last section in the original Gaelic:

> 'Ghrian a' faoisgneadh gu h-òr-bhuidh
>   As a mogal,
> Chinn an speur gu dùldaidh, dòite,
>   Làn de dh' oglachd,
>
> Dh' fhàs i tonn-ghorm, tiugh, tàrr-lachdann,
>   Odhar, iargalt;
> Chinn gach dath bhiodh ann am breacan
>   Air an iarmailt:
> Fadadh-cruaidh san àird-an-iar oirr',

        Stoirm 'na coltas,
'S neòil shiùbhlach aig gaoith gan riasladh,
        Fuaradh-frois' oirr'.

        Thog iad na siùil bhreaca,
        Bhaidealacha dhìonach,
        Shìn iad na coilpeinean raga,
        Teanna, rìghne
Ri fiodhannan arda, fada
        Nan colg bìth-dhearg;

Cheangladh iad gu gramail, snaompach,
        Gu neo-chearbach
Roimh shùilean nan cromag iaruinn
        'S nan cruinn fhailbheag;

Cheartaich iad gach ball den acfhainn
        Ealamh, dòigheil,
'S shuidh gach fear gu freasdal tapaidh
        'Bhuill bu chòir dha.

'Sin dh' fhosgail uinneagan an aeir
        Ballach, liath-ghorm
Gu sèideadh na gaoithe greannaich
        'S bannail, iargalt';

Tharraing an cuan a bhrat dùbhghlas
        Air gu h-uile,
Mhantal garbh, caiteanach, ciar-dhubh,
        'S sgreataidh buinne;

Dh' at e 'na bheanntaibh 's 'na ghleanntaibh,
        Molach, robach,
Gun do bhòc an fhairge cheigeach
        Suas 'na cnocaibh.

And here is my version of the opening of this last section:

    Hoist sail at dawn on the day of Saint Bride,
    bearing out from the mouth of Loch Eynort, South Uist.
    Furnace-gold, hot-yellow, yolk-yellow, brass-brazen sun, burning

> through fish-nets of clouds, trellises meshed, burning them open,
> emerges, and the clouds burn back, close in once again,
> cover all things, changing, sky becomes ash, blackening, and a blue
> splash there, and then thickening, bulging, effulging,
> turning sick, pale, brown, beige, tawny, impending, bellying
> down, and the fretwork rematches itself, closes in, hue
> thick as tartan, dark weaves, anger flashes, and there high in the west,
> a broken shaft, a dog-tooth of rainbow, colour stripes swelling,
> a fang of sharp colour, clouds moving faster to cover it over, and the winds
> pick up speed, toss the clouds as if showers of boulders,
> grey fragments of stone, chips of earth, avalanching in sky.
>
> They lift up the sail, they spring up to stretch
> the stiff-solid ropes to their places, secure now,
> tough and unbreakable, there from the deck
> to the high, hard, tapering, resin-red point of the mast,
> secure all the knots, faultless all joints, rope connections between
> all bolt-rings and hooks, made impeccable,
> run up and tied down, tense and unflexing as iron,
> assured, reassured, now firmly, secured.

The storm, when it comes, is a nightmare. The Gaelic maintains the rhythmic regularity and metrical density of vowel rhymes under constant consonantal pressure, moving with increasing velocity and impending threat, but to mimic that in English I felt would be to draw attention primarily to that mimicry, as if the translation were an imitation rather than a recreation. This is my version of part of the storm section:

> The sea all lifts up, like a great black coat,
> rising to cover the sky, like a shroud, thrown out,
> soaring up, like a blanket, coarse stuff,
> shaggy its surface, a big horse's pelt in black winter,
> a cataract rising, a waterfall soaring, returning itself to its source,
> unnatural, screaming and screeching and howling and yowling,
> and ocean becomes: mountains and bens and valleys and glens,
> all rough with the forest and bushes and grass.
> Sea opens its mouth, is all mouth, all agape,
> widening, opening, sharpened the teeth, all
> crocodile-strong, hippopotamus tusks, and gripping and turning,
> as if wrestling was fun, forcing over each one –
> Sky shrinks and clenches long ribs on its brow –

> It has turned to ferocity now –
> The fight to the death has begun.

Now, there are neither crocodiles nor hippopotamus tusks in Alasdair's arsenal of imagery but the storm is an assault, a shocking, compulsive imposition of things you could not be prepared for. Its arrival is an attack on what you think of as 'normal'. I stand by my version of the poem for its attempt to approach the truth of what the poem means.

Alasdair attended the University of Glasgow and grew quickly familiar with contemporary and classical literature and culture, Scots, English and European. In 1729, he became a schoolteacher, an English teacher, working in various parts of Moidart and the west of Scotland. In 1738 he was teaching at Kilchoan, Ardnamurchan. One of his most famous songs of this period was the lyrical, 'Allt an t-Siucar' / 'Sugar Burn'. In 1741, Alasdair's *A Galick and English Vocabulary*, effectively the first Gaelic-English dictionary, was published, commissioned by the anti-Catholic, anti-Gaelic, Society in Scotland for the Propagation of Christian Knowledge (SSPCK), to help spread the English language and extirpate Gaelic. Alasdair had worked on it in the belief that it would help take Gaelic forward, but he soon came to oppose everything the SSPCK stood for. Making this book, if anything, confirmed his own commitment to his language and culture. His poems took on increasingly sharp edges. Called to account for satiric and inappropriate writing, it is said that he abandoned his teaching to join the Jacobite rising, and that he was among the first at Glenfinnan when the flag was raised on 19 August 1745. Many of his poems and songs openly extol the virtues of the Jacobite cause and satirise the Hanoverians and their Scottish supporters, the Campbells. He was a captain in the Clan Ranald regiment, in charge of 50 recruits, and, as noted above, taught Gaelic to the Prince himself. He converted to Catholicism, perhaps at this time, but perhaps much earlier. After Culloden, he and his family were fugitives. His house was ransacked by Hanoverian troops.

He and his family settled on the island of Canna in 1749 and stayed there till 1751, when he travelled to Edinburgh to publish a book of his poems, *Ais-Eiridh na Sean Chánoin Albannaich / The Reawakening of the Old Scottish Language*, replete with satires on the Hanoverian succession. In the long poem 'An Airce' / 'The Ark', he promises that the Campbells will be plagued and scourged for their treason to Scotland, while he himself will build a ship of refuge for those Campbells true to the Jacobite cause, and all moderates who, after swallowing an effective purgative of salt sea water, would be willing to reject allegiance to the British crown. The authorities were outraged. There is a richly informative two-volume study by the scholar Ronald Black entitled *The Campbells of the Ark: Men of Argyll in 1745, Volume 1: The Inner Circle* and *Volume 2: The Outer Circle*, replete with biographies, maps, and vital information about the political context (Edinburgh: Birlinn, 2017).

Aware of the threat of prosecution, he moved to Glen Uig but then moved again to Knoydart, then to Morar and finally to Sandaig, in Arisaig. He often visited South Uist, where his friend Iain MacFhearchair / John MacCodrum was bard to Sir James MacDonald of Sleat. The MacDonalds and Clan Ranald were his people, and their family connections extended throughout the west of Scotland and to Ireland, to Carrickfergus.

On his deathbed, his last words were addressed to friends watching over him, who were reciting some poems of their own. Alasdair awoke, corrected their metres and versification, showed them how to do it with some verses of his own, then quietly lay back and drifted away. He is buried in Kilmorie cemetery, Arisaig.

'The Birlinn of Clanranald' is his masterpiece: so visceral and grainy in its depiction of realities, it almost seems hostile to metaphoric interpretation, but, as we shall see with 'Praise of Ben Dorain', the historical context in which the poem was written provides one inescapably.

Both poems were composed in the aftermath of the Jacobite rising of 1745 and the massacre at Culloden in 1746. Necessarily, the poems imply reflection upon this social and human disaster in ways that go further than their literal meanings.

'Praise of Ben Dorain' gives us a mountain, deer, and the hunt for the deer, in a world in ecological balance and a self-replenishing, self-sustaining economy. 'The Birlinn' presents a clan and a crew of men working in extreme co-ordination, disciplined and intuitive, in conditions of knowledge drawn from experience, but they and their vessel are subjected to a storm of unprecedented violence, a natural imposition that calls up inimical forces from well beyond anything that might have been predicted.

In 'The Birlinn', the courage and skills of the crew and the strength of the ship carry them through, but at a cost, and without any sense of inevitability. The safe harbour they come to connects the Celtic worlds of Scotland and Ireland. In 'Ben Dorain', the skills and stealth of the hunter on the mountain carry him through to the kill, but the beauty and treasure of the deer are valued at their true worth, in a world of natural balance sustained by both self-conscious design and intuitive understanding and sympathy.

The journeys both poems take us on are signals of an ancient kinship, across differences, of the Celtic peoples, of the human needs of all people, and of the relations between these and animals, and sea, earth and nature.

They are both emphatically and intrinsically opposed to those hostile forces in nature and the anti-human forces in the political world that intervene to wreak havoc and destruction on us all. Their triumph is in regeneration.

So much depends not only on what our education provides, but also what the current attitude to experience is, what we are encouraged to remember, and what our state of culture insists we should forget.

The kind of education in Gaelic and Scots languages needed in Scotland has never been more effectively summarised than by Ronald Black in a letter to the newspaper *The National* (26 January 2016). It deserves to be quoted:

> The Scotland I want to live in is one in which the speaking of languages other than English is not seen as an affliction of the elderly but as a wonderful gift which benefits the individual and society as a whole. Basic Scots and Gaelic should be taught in every primary school. Advanced Scots and Gaelic should be available in at least one secondary school in every local authority area. Ultimately it should be possible for pupils in any part of Scotland to be taught Scots or Gaelic for the entirety of their educational career. The teaching of English grammar, spelling and literature should also be strengthened. Fluent Gaelic speakers should be tempted into education [...] And generally speaking, this sort of educational background should be sine qua non for applicants to culturally-sensitive posts.

21

The ecological eye:
Donnchadh Bàn Mac an t-Saoir / Duncan Ban MacIntyre

NOW TURN TO Alasdair's younger contemporary, Donnchadh Bàn Mac an t-Saoir or Duncan Ban MacIntyre (1724–1812). Both were immediate contemporaries of Burns (1759–96) but it is impossible to imagine three more different poets.

During the Jacobite rising Alasdair and Duncan Ban had been on opposite sides. The older man, Alasdair, as we noted, fought with the Jacobites. The younger, Duncan Ban, fought on the Hanoverian side but reluctantly: he had to, as he was employed by the Hanoverian Campbells. At the battle of Falkirk, Duncan Ban had had enough though, and famously discarded his sword, which had been lent to him by his chief. He would fight no more.

Duncan Ban MacIntyre was born and grew up in Glen Orchy, near Ben Dorain. He had no formal education. He could neither read nor write. From 1746 to 1766 he was a gamekeeper for the Earl of Breadalbane and then the Duke of Argyll, working among the hills and woods of the area. By 1768 he and his family had moved to Edinburgh; he joined the City Guard (the police), like many Highlanders. Robert Fergusson (1750–74), who was there at the same time, called them 'the black banditti'. Here in Edinburgh, his poems were written down, published and sold well. After Alasdair's death (1770), in 1786, as Robert Burns's poems were being published in the Kilmarnock edition, Duncan Ban and his wife were back in the Highlands and Islands. As Burns was being lionised in Edinburgh, Duncan Ban was being warmly welcomed in the north-west of Scotland. He returned to Edinburgh, left the City Guard in 1793, and was a soldier with the Breadalbane Fencibles, though now in his 70s. He retired in 1806, died in 1812, and he and his family are buried in Old Greyfriars churchyard. In 1859, a monument designed by John Thomas Rochead (1814–78), who also designed the Wallace monument at Stirling, was erected in the hills near Dalmally, overlooking Loch Awe.

Duncan Ban was in Edinburgh precisely when James Macpherson, Henry Mackenzie and Adam Smith were flourishing, Enlightenment and proto-Romantic writers. There is almost no recognition of Duncan Ban's work or indeed of contemporary Gaelic literature in their writing. To English-language readers, the Highlands were becoming recognised – or branded – through the work of Macpherson and later, Walter Scott.

This division of perception is one reason, perhaps, why 'Ben Dorain' and 'The Birlinn' have been neglected. Yet there is another division implicit in 'Ben Dorain' itself, between the vision of the mountain and its plenitude of riches and the traditional Gaelic praise-poem for clan and clan chief. As the clans themselves had been violently put down after Culloden, so the ascendancy of English-language writing, and the gulfs between English, Scots and Gaelic worlds were opening up. These gulfs were not unbridgeable – as we noted above, Alasdair mac Mhaighstir Alasdair was familiar not only with Burns's work but also that of James Thomson, whose *The Seasons* (1730) was the most famous Scottish poem of its time and effectively triggered the tradition of English-language pastoral poetry. However, 'Praise of Ben Dorain' is very different.

It is crucial to remember that Duncan Ban was illiterate. The poem was composed as a song in the poet's mind before it was ever written down on a page. The 'original' is not the written or printed version, nor any of the English-language translations, but something Duncan Ban made in his own head, that he would have made into sound through his own voice. There is no way to get back to that, and no way to replicate it. But when I decided to try to make my own English-language version of the poem, that's what I was trying to represent.

Work like this should not be so hard to imagine. Bagpipe-players learn tunes through 'translating' them from sounds that can be sung by the human voice (canntaireachd) into music played on the pipes. Thus the accuracy of replicating written or printed annotation is of secondary importance to the primacy of conveying meaning through the music, whether in bodily human voice or a fashioned material instrument. This also relates to the teaching or transmission of a tune without written manuscript. So, I argued, the same might apply to the poem.

Its shape is essential to its meaning. It was composed to the musical structure of a pibroch – in Gaelic the spelling is piobaireachd – the classical music of the Highland bagpipe. It is also known as 'ceol mor' or 'big music' or 'great music'. And it is important to remember that the Gaelic word for music, ceol, has nothing to do with the muses, so music is not something 'handed down' as a gift from 'on high' but rather it signifies sound made by breath moving through tubes or pipes, imagined or physical, constructed, bodily. In this configuration, harmony, of one kind or another, signifies health.

The poem is in eight parts, a base theme and variations on it, or journeys around it. (1) The opening gives the main theme or 'urlar': the mountain, the deer, and the first-person singular narrator of the poem, a young man who will hunt the deer, not for sport but for the nourishment of himself and his people; (2) then the first journey takes each of the preceding three main component parts and extends, expands, or elaborates some aspects of them; (3) then there is a return to the main theme; (4) then the second journey; (5) then the main theme once again; (6) then the third journey, or variation; (7) and then the main theme is returned to for the last time; and finally (8) there is the culmination of the entire poem, its crowning or bringing together of all the elements in the onslaught of the hunting dogs and the killing of the deer. In the last few lines there is a confirmation that the poem as given is not enough, and never could be, to encompass everything it sets out to describe.

Seen in this way, there is a cyclical, or seasonal, sense of repetition. The main theme is given four times, each time followed by a transitional 'variation' or journey between them, and at last the 'culmination' brings things to a conclusion, but with the promise of further repetition or regeneration – although, obviously enough, not for the particular individual deer killed in the last section. Yet at the same time, this structure, once experienced, may be read or listened to again and again with an increased awareness of tension. Even on a first reading there are clues that the end will be bloody and climactic. This balance or combining of a regenerating, cyclical structure and a linear, increasingly suspenseful, narrative, is stunningly achieved, and appreciated more deeply after several readings. In my version, this is how it begins, with the 'Urlar' or 'Main Theme'.

First, in the original Gaelic:

> An t-urram thar gach beinn
>   Aig Beinn Dóbhrain;
> De na chunnaic mi fo'n ghréin,
>   'S i bu bhòidhche leam:
> Munadh fada réidh,
> Cuilidh 'm faighte féidh,
> Soilleireachd an t-sléibh
>   Bha mi sònrachadh;
> Doireachan nan geug,
> Coill' anns am bi feur,
> 'S foinneasach an spréidh
>   Bhios a chòmhnaidh ann;
> Greadhain bu gheal céir,
> Faghaid air an déidh –
> 'S laghach leam an sreud
>   A bha sròineiseach.
>
> 'S aigeannach fear eutrom
>   Gun mhórchuis,
> Theid fasanda 'na éideadh
>   Neo-spòrsail:
> Tha mhanntal uime féin,
> Caithtiche nach tréig –
> Bratach dhearg mar chéir
>   Bhios mar chòmhdach air.

And here is my version of the opening in English:

> Praise over all to Ben Dorain –
> She rises beneath the radiant beams of the sun –
> In all the magnificent range of the mountains around,
> So shapely, so sheer are her slopes, there are none
> To compare; she is fair, in the light, like the flight
> Of the deer, in the hunt, across moors, on the run,
> Or under the green leafy branches of trees, in the groves
> Of the woods, where the thick grass grows,
> And the curious deer, watchful and tentative,
> Hesitant, sensitive: I have had all these clear, in my sight.
>
> A herd of the deer: each startles at once,
> And they leap, as if one, and it starts!
> The bounding of bodies, the weight in their forms,
> In movement away, their white rumps up, bobbing,
> Away in a spray, an array:
> They are grace, in their movement, yet skittish.
> Prompted by fear, carried by muscle, charged by instinctual sense;
> Equally so, the shy, sombre stag,
> In his warm brown coat,
> The russet of fur, his antlers raised high,
> Stately and slow, he walks by.

The question remains, whether 'Praise of Ben Dorain' may be read in the 21st century as a poem not only of praise, but also of sorrow, resistance and anger, a permanent protest against the devastation some folk bring upon others. This is not explicitly depicted in the poem, but its historical context implies it: after Culloden and before the denudation and exploitation of the mountain and the land all around it. In the 21st century, most of the deer and the forests, the natural plenitude of Ben Dorain, has gone. It is a beautiful, but bare mountain. In this, perhaps, it is comparable to that other great poem of sorrow, the persistence of memory and the demand for justice, Sorley MacLean's 'Hallaig'. And that gets us to the question of land ownership in Scotland and underlines the powerful pertinence of the poem, its lasting example and quickening sense of what ecological harmony really means.

'Praise of Ben Dorain' is a register of loss: not a praise poem for a chief, hero, leader or clan, but a praise poem for a non-human source of economic health and human well-being, a politically balanced ecology, a mountain that is not simply the 'earth-mother' myth idealised but a reality, a promise of what health is, what regeneration requires. It is sublime, but it is also utterly realistic.

22

Gaelic poetry of the later 18th century

FROM CHRISTIANA FERGUSSON, IAIN RUADH STIÙBHART / JOHN ROY STUART
AND DÙGHALL BOCHANAN / DUGALD BUCHANAN
TO ROB DONN MACAOIDH / ROB DONN, UILLEAM ROS / WILLIAM ROSS
AND SEUMAS MAC AN T-SAOIR / JAMES MACINTYRE

THE BATTLE OF CULLODEN, 1746, is a turning point of Scottish, British and indeed European and world history. The full title of Trevor Royle's book *Culloden* (2016) suggests the extent of the consequences of the event: *Culloden: Scotland's Last Battle and the Forging of the British Empire*. His study begins: 'Drumossie Moor, dawn, Wednesday 16 April 1746' but later chapters move across North America, Canada, the Caribbean and India, before returning to Europe, Scotland and modernity.

The representation in Gaelic literature of Culloden and what it signified makes a study of that literature, even in translation, a vital corrective to that of more exclusively English or Scottish literature in Scots and English. That representation is both explicit, in poems of lament, rage, grief or recuperation, and implicit, in the assumptions from which the compositions themselves arise. There is always a counterpoint between songs and poems that refer to things that are perennial, and those which spring directly from contemporary historical events.

Many of the most piercingly beautiful songs of the Culloden era are anonymous, but one of the sweetest is 'Mo Rùn Geal Òg' / 'My fair young love', by Christiana Fergusson. In *Songs of Gaelic Scotland* (2005), Anne Lorne Gillies comments: 'This is the abiding Gaelic memory of Culloden: a woman left behind, weeping for the husband she has lost and for the life she will now have to lead.' Also rooted in its history is 'Òran air Latha Chuil Lodair' / 'A Song on the Battle of Culloden' by Iain Ruadh Stiùbhart / John Roy Stuart (1700–1752). Here are the fifth, seventh and 11th stanzas of my own English version:

> My grief unrelenting, the pale corpses lie
> On the slopes of the hills, just there, I can see them.
> No shrouds and no coffins.
> No graves and no honour. The dead are just there.
> And those who survived, scattered, in tatters,
> Packed on board ships, tight bound in their confines of flight.

> They got what they wanted, the Whigs.
> Now we are known as the rebels.
>
> I never dreamt or saw into the future
> That things could become as they are.
> At the start of the year, the water in flood, bears all away,
> When new growth is only beginning.
> The wheel turns, has turned, will not turn again
> In my day. This is no justice.
> My God, look down. Look here and give mercy
> On men such as I, for no mercy shows in the enemy.
>
> My sorrow, this land we have come to,
> Lifted to bare desolation.
> No harvest of grain or sweet corn, no store
> For the future in wild fields or farm.
> Hens from their roosts have been stolen.
> The spoons we would eat with are stolen. I curse you,
> Now, with the blossom dried up, the sap all gone wersh,
> The straight sapling twisted from leaf down to root.

And the terrifying magnificence of Dùghall Bochanan / Dugald Buchanan (1716–68) envisioning 'The Day of Judgement' is unforgettable: 'The sky is all scarlet! Now Christ's here and drives / Through black clouds an opening: Judgement arrives!'

In the immediate aftermath of Culloden, Rob Donn MacAoidh (1714–78), in 'Song of the Black Cassocks' connects apocalyptic imagery with specific place and time. The specificity is the poem's prompt: The Disclothing Act of 1746, where we read: 'No man or boy within that part of Britain called Scotland, other than such as shall be employed as Officers and Soldiers shall, on any pretext whatever, wear or put on the Plaid, Philabeg, or little Kilt, Trowse, Shoulder-belts, or any part whatever of the Highland Garb; and that no tartan or party-coloured plaid of stuff shall be used for Great Coats or upper coats.' A first offence was accorded six months' imprisonment, a second, seven years' deportation. The Act was repealed in 1782 but Rob Donn's poem dates from c.1747.

> I am heartsick for Scotland
> The people, so badly divided:
> Motives, desires, the mind of the country,
> All split apart. Nothing binds us together.
> And the Government reads this, starts

> Fanning the flames: encouraging greed
> And the worst competition. The flames will rise up.
> We will tear each other's throats out.

There is hope yet, but it is qualified, strained, and difficult to sustain:

> Your grief has no measure
> Or precedent.
> The best of our falcons
> Is chained to a buzzard.
> The lion will repay the pain
> Its season will come once again.
> If only it will not be muzzled.
>
> Now Prince Charles Edward Stuart
> The hope of the clans:
> We went out to find your true crown
> And the fire roared over the land.
> We now hide away like low snakes in the grass.
> Our skins are cast off.
> But still there are fangs that grow sharper.
> Still we await your return.

The poem is locked into its historical moment, a protest against the prohibition of the wearing of Highland dress. The poet's clan, Mackay, had been on the Hanoverian side in the '45, but here Rob Donn is asserting allegiance with all Highlanders, opposing the Government's tyranny. A universal sense of justice is required: 'The lion will repay the pain. / Its season will come.' But when? And how muzzled has it become since the time of the poem's composition?

Uilleam Ros / William Ross (1762–c.1791) also stands out in the later 18th century. Although he wrote in a range of forms and has been compared to his immediate contemporary Burns, whose work he seems to have known, Ross is inimitable in the intensity of personal utterance, as in 'Another Song':

> I am lost in my grief, a steep pass –
> A dram can do nothing to please.
> The maggot alive in my mind has
> Ended good spirits and ease.
> I see her no more, that beautiful girl –
> As she walked in the street with such grace –
> The gentlest eyes, the loveliest face –

> My confidence, broken and fallen
> Like leaves from the highest of trees.

As with Rob Donn, the individual voice of William Ross, in all its range, arises from a coherent social vision that characterised the Gaelic world before the 18th century, carrying through its ruins traces of what that social identity might yet be again, even in the evocation of its destruction.

Maybe most vigorous satire of the late 18th century, in Culloden's aftermath, is 'Òran don Ollamh MacIain' / 'A Song to Dr Johnson' by Seumas Mac a t-Saoir / James Macintyre (1727–99). Along with Robert Fergusson's poem to Johnson, this ought to be as well-known as Johnson's *Journey to the Western Islands of Scotland* (1775) itself, as necessary counterbalances. Macintyre erupts into fireworks of abuse. These are my own versions of some of the more pungent lines:

> You're dragging your slime-yellow belly, slowly, you big ugsome toad,
> Sluggishly, heavily, crawling, and oozing along the low road –
> A soft slug sleazily slipping, clutching a venomous load as you must,
> A slithering lizard, down in the grass, a slow-worm there on the road, in the
>   dust –
> A bluebottle greedily gripping its rancid pittance of grub, farcical,
> A rabid dog with its eyes on the bone, a badger, its nose turned round up its
>   arsicle –
> I would stuff your mouth full with a gag – big enough for its copious cave –
> It would stay there as long as you live – till the day you will rot in your
>   grave –

One passage in Johnson's journal describes his disdain for certain Highlanders who helped him who could not speak English. Macintyre's premise is the conviction that after enjoying his accommodation among the people of Scotland, Johnson abused their hospitality, returning to England to spread slander and lies about them.

And yet, the story is not so simple. It never is.

Johnson seemed to enjoy the company of Highlanders generally, but not mountains, bogs, bad weather and filthy inns. Moreover, he held an intense animosity to James Macpherson, considering Macpherson's *Ossian* no more than a fraud. Even though it was internationally popular and arguably one of the most influential works ever published, most people have followed Johnson. Among English-language readers, Johnson's judgement maintains potent authority. But Johnson claimed that there were no Gaelic manuscripts above a few decades old, which was absolutely untrue. His perception that the Gaelic tradition was predominantly oral was correct but that in itself could not disprove the authenticity of Macpherson's *Ossian*.

Having been attacked, the honour of Macpherson's *Ossian* became for many synonymous with the honour of Scotland and the force of public opinion in Scotland turned against Johnson. He reacted by attacking Scotland itself: another bad move.

The legacy of Johnson's encounter with Macpherson and Scotland remains an unsettled account, but it brought the persistence and presence of Gaelic literature to the attention of English-language readers. Macpherson's *Ossian* stories remain the most famous representation of Gaelic literature in the 18th century and one of the crucial episodes associated with Gaelic literature internationally. Fame is not everything, and strictly in terms of Gaelic literature itself, Macpherson is the last and least of it. Yet his work introduced many people to that literature's very existence, prompting a healthy curiosity that extended and expressed itself in a multitude of art forms across generations and continents.

23

James Macpherson and *Ossian*

MACPHERSON HAS BEEN described as an unparalleled creative influence and *Ossian* as the foundation of Romanticism, but after two centuries, he is usually unread and frequently dismissed as a forger or discredited as a fraud. Reassessment of his value, historical significance and lasting importance has been taking place but it's a long way between scholarly reappraisal and popular understanding. But bridges are constructions. The poet and translator Peter McCarey reminds us that 'impossible' is a word we should understand 'as seriously as did Robert de Luzarches, whose masons built Amiens cathedral with a plumb-line and a knotted rope.'

MACPHERSON'S FIGURATIONS AND TABLEAUX

As noted above, St Columba, an adopted Scot arriving from Ireland, and St Patrick, quite possibly a Scot who moved to Ireland, both turn to face the future. Both help bring into being new worlds by resolutely moving away from the old. And yet that affinity across difference, the sense that the old world never really lets us leave, the lands of youth always beckon and are always yearned for, is an essential part of the human story.

In the cycles of tales and songs relating Celtic myth and legend, the dialogues between St Patrick and Ossian refer back to the heroic days of the Celts and describe a confrontation between the ancient, secular, pagan world and the modern, pious, sacral world. Accounts differ and verification is always dubious but at the heart of the whole thing is a sharp sense of retrospective grief, not nostalgia but despair at what's lost and never to return.

The old world is viewed with more than merely sentiment: it's a land of youthful self-confidence, stamina and appetite, as any old person might recollect. The new world gives little comfort to this act of aged remembering. But the evocation of the old world in some of the poems from these dialogues remains crystal-clear. The power of this evocation rests on the myth of 'Ossian after the Fianna', returning after the world of heroes has disappeared, to tell his stories to the enquiring St Patrick in the new dispensation of Christianity. Ossian's world is gone. But St Patrick's questioning prompts the telling of the stories and the songs that will continue to commemorate that lost world, and make it a living imagery for the future.

The stories of Ossian, and preceding them, the stories of Cuchulain and

Deirdre, of Finn and Ossian (or Oisin), of the old gods, have been retold many times, notably in Marie Heaney's *Over Nine Waves: A Book of Irish Legends* (1994). But of all the versions of the tales of Ossian, the most lastingly controversial are those by James Macpherson (1736–96).

So who was he?

A blunt answer would be that James Macpherson was a descendant of a Jacobite clan who became a sycophantic Hanoverian toady, a man for the main chance. The conventional description of his versions of Gaelic tales is that they are 'forgeries' pretending to be translations. Neither answer is good enough.

Macpherson was born and grew up in a rural, Gaelic-speaking area of Badenoch within half a mile of Ruthven Barracks, a British Army fort established to enforce London rule after the 1715 Jacobite rising. The traditional oral Gaelic culture of stories and songs about Finn and Ossian, alongside the Hanoverian military authority, surrounded him. Mountains, rivers, caves were named for figures from Celtic myth and legend. James was only nine years old when his uncle Ewan Macpherson joined the Jacobite army on their march south. They returned, burned the Barracks and retreated north to Culloden. The survivors came back to Ruthven before dispersing as fugitives, while the local community was destroyed by the victorious Hanoverian troops. His uncle remained in hiding for nine years. So up to the age of 18, Macpherson lived through, and in close proximity to, one of the most cataclysmic events in modern Europe prior to the 20th century.

He studied at Aberdeen University, reading Caesar's *Commentaries*, where the opposition between the native German tribes and the soldiers of imperial Rome was detailed, and taking in contemporary ideas about the relation between 'primitive' and 'enlightened' societies. He became a teacher back in Ruthven, then a private tutor, growing acquainted with the Enlightenment literati, and was introduced to the idea that local folk lore could be drawn upon for use in sophisticated contemporary literary works. The minister and playwright John Home prompted Macpherson to produce a translation from traditional Gaelic tales and the result was 'The Death of Oscar', which appeared in Macpherson's first publication, *Fragments of Ancient Poetry, collected in the Highlands of Scotland* (1760). This was a slim pamphlet of 15 short pieces, few more than a page in length, each a lament for fallen warriors. The opening paragraph of section VIII gives its characteristic flavour:

> By the side of a rock on the hill, beneath the aged trees, old Ossian sat on the moss; the last of the race of Fingal. Sightless are his aged eyes; his beard is waving in the wind. Dull through the leafless trees he heard the voice of the north. Sorrow revived in his soul: he began and lamented the dead.

Extracts published in *The Scots Magazine* and *The Gentleman's Magazine* were immediately popular and the idea that they were only glimpses of an unrecorded epic took hold. Macpherson set out to find it. He went north in 1760 to find the storytellers from whom he could recover the epic tales of the ancient Gaels. He knew the Gaelic language and he met the local tradition-bearers. What he did in his transcriptions has been the cause of contention ever since.

He is usually scorned by English-language readers as a charlatan. But go closer. He knew Gaelic, he travelled in the Highlands and he talked to Gaelic speakers. To modern eyes, his English-language versions are stilted and 'artificial'. But all works of art are made by artifice. They're often described as a 'fraud' or a 'hoax'. This in itself has been a long-standing hoax of the British establishment, always opposed to the notion of an ancient Scottish Gaelic civilisation predating its own.

As always, priority is power.

There were only three publications: *Fragments of Ancient Poetry* (1760), followed by *Fingal, An Ancient Epic Poem in Six Books* (1761) and *Temora, An Ancient Poem in Eight Books: together with Several Other Poems composed by Ossian, the Son of Fingal* (1763). The first collected edition was *The Works of Ossian, The Son of Fingal* (1765). They are not all 'fabrications'. Many episodes are recognisable versions of traditional tales from Gaelic sources. But their language is distinctively mannered Enlightenment English, and there's a monotonous consistency of diction, posture and address with little variation of tone, despite dramatic battles, deaths and flamboyant gestures.

So what are they about?

Fragments collects 15 items, some inexplicable, allusive, misty, with characters whose names sound vaguely familiar yet elude solidity. Some are clearly based on Gaelic originals to be found for example in *The Book of the Dean of Lismore*. *Fingal* tells the story of an invasion of Ireland by King Swaran of Denmark (confusingly termed 'Lochlyn'). The Irish chief Cuchulaid rallies his people and raging battles follow but Swaran is winning until Fingal, King of Scotland, comes to the rescue, repulses the Danes, reconciles all enemies, and returns to Scotland victorious. *Temora* recounts Fingal's further adventures, again travelling to Ireland to remove a usurper and reinstate the rightful ruler. After a version of a Gaelic ballad appears in Book One, it is the most fabricated of the three books. Added to these 'epics' are a number of shorter items, fragments relating to named places, the deaths of particular heroes, songs and evocations of atmosphere and landscape, nobles, bards and battles. Some are related to Gaelic originals, in varying degrees of proximity.

Each one of Macpherson's accounts of the Gaelic stories is characterised by three things: a mellifluous yet ponderous prose style, a tone of lament, sorrow and poignancy and a visual impression of action suspended in picturesque, vivid tableaux. The style in English is heavy with solemnity, sustaining a sonorous monotone. And descriptions of the action, the fighting and physical gestures of the characters, often seem strangely static, as if carefully designed and presented on a stage. Even when vigorous conflict and bloodshed is presented, the impression is one of slow motion, as if everything is seen underwater or through a thick mist. This is unlike most Gaelic poetry of the era, which is characteristically quick, with a repertoire of conventions of symbolic imagery which is nevertheless slippery with colour and deployed with verbal dexterity in the fast exchange of emotional currency. Macpherson's writings are burdened by an invisible weight. In the proto-Romantic style of Enlightenment drama, this was exactly attuned to popular literate taste for sentiment but emboldened the posture of sadness with a gesture towards deeper grief, the recognition of a culture, homeland, and in fact language, destroyed by design and irretrievably lost. Or so the Hanoverian ascendancy and the political arbiters of 'Enlightenment' might have wished.

The appetite for this epic was keen for more than one reason. A reclamation of Gaelic cultural authority arising from antiquity was effectively a Scottish cultural counterpoint to the post-Culloden military and social devastation. This attraction was a counterpoint to Hanoverian triumphalism and might appeal to any reader. From the strictly 'British' point of view, the outbreak of war with France in 1756 meant that stories of Fingal's heroes defeating invading armies was an inspiring example. In 'polite' or 'genteel' society, the atmosphere of lament for fallen heroes chimed precisely with the sentiment of readers 'of feeling' and fuelled the characterisation of the Celt as emotional, moody and vague, as opposed to the hard-headed practicalities embodied in what could be promoted as the 'Anglo-Saxon' ethos.

When Macpherson heard what he heard in the Scottish Highlands, the people who had gathered the stories across generations may well have adapted them from earlier versions to their own location. In other words, the stories themselves, their characters and actions, had come to inhabit the country of the storytellers. The stories themselves would be immigrants, settled, whose descendants would grow to be natives.

Does that make any difference?

Fiona Stafford summarises the Macpherson legend like this:

> *Fingal* may not be a direct translation of Gaelic poems that had survived intact since the third century, but neither is it a 'fake' or a 'forgery', because of Macpherson's peculiar situation at the confluence of very different cultures.

As a Highlander, he drew on the Gaelic oral traditions, where Ossian was often acknowledged as author; as a university-educated gentleman, he considered the oral tradition unreliable and appealed to his patrons' hopes that the Gaelic tradition matched that of Homeric Greece. Stafford concludes:

> Macpherson's *Ossian* is thus a text belonging exclusively to neither Gaelic nor English culture, and can only be understood sympathetically as an attempt to mediate between the two.

Macpherson's early life and the publication of his Ossianic works in the 1760s are what concern us here, but after this his writing and career took a different turn. His *Introduction to the History of Great Britain and Ireland* (1771) was followed by other works generally endorsing Anglocentric Hanoverian authority: *Rights of Great Britain asserted against the Claims of America* (1776) and *The History and Management of the East India Company* (1779). He became the MP for Camelford in Cornwall but never visited the constituency or spoke in parliament, and died in 1796 on his estate in the Highlands, which he had purchased with wealth accrued in his career.

But both aspects of his life require understanding: his childhood, youth and experience of Scotland at the crucial turning point of the 1740s, and the confluence of his comprehension of his native territory with his ambition and address to wealthy readers and potential patrons. Together, these are the keys to unlock the value as well as the liability of his Ossianic tales.

OSSIAN'S LEGACY

The imagery of Ossian has perennially been the subject for the visual arts. Alexander Runciman (1736–85), John Duncan (1866–1945) and Calum Colvin (b.1961) are among the most famous Scottish artists to have depicted them, while a host of European artists, including Danish Nicolai Abildgaard (1743–1809), French Jean-Auguste-Dominique Ingres (1780–1867), Anne-Louis Girodet (1767–1824), François Pascal Simon Gérard (1770–1837), English J.M.W. Turner (1775–1851) created epic paintings as part of the Romantic movement, alongside a distinguished line of international artists who have ensured that the meanings inherent in the Ossianic tales are re-envisioned and rejuvenated for new generations.

The idea that Macpherson perpetrated a 'hoax' persists. This is unjust and inadequate. Macpherson's *Ossian* is, in Fiona Stafford's words, 'pre-eminently a text of the margins – not in the sense that it is peripheral to serious literary study but because it inhabits the margins of contrasting, oppositional cultures. For Macpherson's "translations" involved acts of interpretation not only between Gaelic and English, but also between the oral culture of the depressed rural communities of the Scottish Highlands, and the prosperous urban centres of Lowland Britain, where the printed word was increasingly dominant.'

The legacy of Ossian, beyond Macpherson's actual works, is immense, deep and surprisingly rich, and not only in the visual arts, in paintings and drawings. The literary influence is there too, and is felt early. Wordsworth (1770–1850), in 'Glen-Almain; or, the Narrow Glen' (1803), as a result of his tour in Scotland, gives us this:

> In this still place, remote from men,
> Sleeps Ossian, in the NARROW GLEN;
> In this still place, where murmurs on
> But one meek streamlet, only one:
> He sang of battles, and the breath
> Of stormy war, and violent death...

Here, Wordsworth tells us, there is 'a spirit turbulent': 'sights were rough, and sounds were wild, / And everything unreconciled'. And then he asks the question:

> Does then the Bard sleep here indeed?
> Or is it but a groundless creed?
> What matters it? – I blame them not
> Whose Fancy in this lonely spot
> Was moved; and in such way expressed
> Their notion of its perfect rest.

And this ethos, this atmosphere, hypersensitive Wordsworth cautiously tells us:

> Is of the grave; and of austere
> Yet happy feelings of the dead:
> And therefore, was it rightly said
> That Ossian, last of all his race!
> Lies buried in this lonely place.

And in 1793, S.T. Coleridge (1772–1834) ended his 'The Complaint of Nina-Thoma' (imitated from Ossian) with this verse:

> A Ghost! by my cavern it darted!
>   In moon-beams the Spirit was drest –
> For lovely appear the Departed
>   When they visit the dreams of my rest!
> But disturbed by the tempest's commotion
>   Fleet the shadowy forms of delight –

> Ah cease, thou shrill blast of the Ocean!
> To howl through my cavern by night.

Ghosts and graves and windy hills and caves are essential parts of the story, as in the short, haunting poem 'Ossian's Grave' by the Russian writer Mikhail Lermontov (1814–41), here given in my own translation:

> In the Highlands of Scotland I love,
> Storm clouds curve down on the dark fields and strands,
> With icy grey mist closing in from above –
> Here Ossian's grave still stands.
> In dreams my heart races to be there,
> To deeply breathe in its native air –
> And from this long-forgotten shrine
> Take its second life as mine.

In the most radically modernist of all Hugh MacDiarmid's books, *Stony Limits* (1934), in his poem 'Lament for the Great Music', a tragic vision of the loss of Scotland's highest cultural traditions, such as that of the classical music of the Highland bagpipe, the pibroch (or to be accurate, piobaireachd or ceòl mòr), we have this:

> To remember the great music and to look
> At Scotland and the world today is to hear
> *An Barr Baudh* again where there are none to answer
> And to feel like *Oisin d' éis na Féine* or like Christ
> In that least homoousian hour.

The word 'homoousian' is a Christian theological term, referring to the belief that Jesus, God the Son, is the same 'in being' or 'in essence' as God the Father. MacDiarmid is saying that Christ's cry upon the cross, the anguish of the forsaken, is a sign of feeling at the furthest remove from the promised coherence of identity and redemption. The Gaelic phrases relate to this. In footnotes, MacDiarmid explains that '*An Barr Baudh*' is 'A somewhat in a state between existence and non-existence.' And '*d'* éis *na Féine*' is 'A withered babbling old man, "Oisin after the Fianna" (i.e. when his love for Ireland made him return to it from Tir-nan-nog) in that immortal phrase which has in it more than Virgilian tears.'

In other words, the evocation of Ossian 'after the Fianna' – after his father and family and companions of high youth, health and vigour, have all gone into the past, leaving him old and alone – delivers a permanent image of tragic and irrecoverable loss, encompassing and predating other ancient religions and civilisations.

And there is no fraud or hoax involved in that. Its permanence is also Ossian's legacy.

Many composers, from Franz Schubert (1797–1828) and Felix Mendelssohn (1809–47) and Niels Gade (1817–90) to James MacMillan (b.1959) wrote music to accompany, illustrate or in response to Ossianic stories, poems or scenes, as discussed in James Porter's *Beyond Fingal's Cave: Ossian in the Musical Imagination* (Rochester, NY: University of Rochester Press, 2019). Porter distinguishes four periods of composition responding to Ossian: the first, from around 1780 to 1815, is dominated by opera, the second, 1816 to 1880, by cantata, the third, 1880 to 1918, and fourth, since 1918, by symphonic poem and instrumental works.

The greatest of all Scottish modernist composers, Erik Chisholm (1904–65), entitled his Symphony No.2 'Ossian' but perhaps the toughest, most distinctive and direct application of Ossian in music is Chisholm's six piano nocturnes comprising *Night Song of the Bards* (1944–51), as John Purser has explored in his monograph, *Erik Chisholm, Scottish Modernist 1904–1965: Chasing a Restless Muse* (Woodbridge: Boydell & Brewer, 2009). The composer draws on a passage at the end of 'Croma: A Poem', from Macpherson's *Works of Ossian* (1765).

At the command of their Chief, himself a poet, five Bards, one at a time, each go out into the October night and then return to the Chief's hall with their different accounts of what the night holds and portends. The first returns to report a sense of mysterious, stormy menace: 'The dead are abroad!' The second tells of potential future violence: 'The rain is past. The dry wind blows. Streams roar, and windows flap. Cold drops fall from the roof. I see the starry sky. But the shower gathers again.' The third tells of his vision: 'A maid sits sad beside the rock, and eyes the rolling stream. Her lover promised to come. She saw his boat, when yet it was light, on the lake. Is this his broken boat on the shore? Are these his groans on the wind?' The fourth speaks of a calm, fair, 'settled' night but a form is approaching: 'Come, let us view thee, O maid!' But 'The blast drives the phantom away; white, without form, it ascends the hill.' The night returns to its settled state: 'calm, blue, starry, bright with the moon'. The fifth Bard tells that more than half the night is past but there is a whirlwind in the forest: 'the mighty army of the dead returning from the air.' And now 'it is dark over all.'

Each evocation is experienced in turn, in a range of visions complementary in their evocation of the lunar, stellar, stormy, haunted night. Then finally they are brought together in the final song of the sixth Bard, the Chief, who acknowledges mystery beyond knowledge: clouds rest on hills, spirits fly, travellers fear, storms descend, the pale moon rises and pours its beams on the mountains: 'The young day returns from his clouds, but we return no more.' So much is familiar, yet the Chief ends the sequence with a call to song and joy, for the company to dance in the candle-lit hall, for Bards to tell the tales of former times, to keep the bows and dogs at hand, to ascend the hills at daybreak and go hunting for the deer. But the tone is still melancholy. Everything in this vision now, as John Purser says, remains 'hovering unresolved' and 'floating out into its own night air.'

Chisholm's musical interpretation of this is a small masterpiece of the modern piano repertoire, with nothing of the vagueness of Macpherson's overwrought language or of romanticism's self-indulgence or wistful nostalgia and comfortable gloom. The composer's modernist idiom effects a hard realisation of an ineffable world in which human beings are lonely and lost. And yet if we live in discomfort, we also persist in defiance. The connection to the Ossianic world is clear and firm. The resources upon which Macpherson opened the door remain vast and inexhaustible. There is much more to be done.

NOTE
Of the wealth of material centred on Macpherson's *Ossian*, the following are especially recommended: Derick S. Thomson, *The Gaelic Sources of Macpherson's 'Ossian'* (1951); Fiona Stafford, *The Sublime Savage: James Macpherson and the Poems of Ossian* (1988); James Macpherson, *The Poems of Ossian and Related Works*, ed. Howard Gaskill, with an introduction by Fiona Stafford (1996); Dafydd Moore, ed., *The International Companion to James Macpherson and the Poems of Ossian* (2017); James Porter, *Beyond Fingal's Cave: Ossian in the Musical Imagination* (Rochester, NY: University of Rochester Press, 2019). Chisholm's music is discussed in John Purser, *Erik Chisholm, Scottish Modernist 1904–1965: Chasing a Restless Muse* (2009).

24

Ramsay's *The Gentle Shepherd*, Home's *Douglas* and Carstairs's *The Hubble-Shue*

THE PARADOXES OF the 18th century are many: the age of slavery and the brutal exploitation of human beings by other human beings, and at the same time, the age of the dictionaries and encyclopedias and the categorisation of knowledge; the concentrated destruction of Gaelic culture, its people and their language, and the cultivation of speculative thought that produced the revolutionary intellectual understandings of the Enlightenment philosophers; the complementary character of writing and debate in ascendancy English and vernacular Scots, in both print and verbal encounter.

These paradoxes or counterpoints were inhabited by Allan Ramsay (1684–1758) in various identifiable ways. He made wigs for a living but what economic acumen he exercised accompanied a commitment to the theatre and the virtues of printed books and libraries. As a poet, he was an urban inhabitant of Edinburgh, a familiar city man of the Old Town, before the division of wealth had been defined by the development of the New Town, north of the loch, but he was also an enlightened Augustan thinker, a poseur, a person of property, propriety and poise, writing in the English language for literary sophisticates. He was also a Scots language vernacular song-writer, a singer and poet of the country or at least the city's hinterland, born in Leadhills, Lanarkshire, and as a 'country poet' he could deploy sentimental and homely comic tones and turns in verse with nimbleness and flair. If he sometimes appears lightweight or superficial in the extent of his various proficiencies he shouldn't be underestimated.

Two of his poems illustrate the paradoxes and exemplify the seriousness in his character. 'Lucky Spence's Last Advice' satirises genteel pretensions as a dying prostitute delivers her judgement on the rotten underworld of Edinburgh's sexual hypocrisy. And 'Wealth, or the Woody' (the 'Woody' is a term for the Gallows upon which criminals were publicly hanged) is another kind of satire, this time focused on the hypocrisy of international mercantile investment culminating in economic collapse and financial ruin, with all its immediate human consequences upon people too poor to have had any stake in the investment. Its final judgement is a vision of the con men rewarded by execution: '…in gardens, park and silent glen, / When trees bear naething else, they'll carry men' who shall 'swing / Aboon earth's disappointments in a string…'

Other poems like 'Tartana, or the Plaid' and especially 'The Vision' offer an assurance of Scotland's national authority as an imaginary reality seen in a dream. The dream is alive but any chance of its enactment is prohibited by political authority, convention and law. Ramsay is a complex and fascinating writer whose anthologies of older Scottish poetry and song, *The Tea Table Miscellany: or, A Collection of Scots Sangs* (Dublin, 1711; Edinburgh, 1723–37) and *The Ever Green: A Collection of Scots Poems, Wrote by the Ingenious before 1600* (1724) were essential acts of retrieval and the renewal of a tradition which English ascendancy was concerned to obscure. He had another way of enacting such a preference for older inherited legacies: literal enactment of their representation in the theatre.

After the closing of the playhouses in 1642, the confluence of priorities of religious and political dogma began to stifle public performance. Nevertheless, productions of one sort or another persisted. Even under the puritanical Cromwellian Commonwealth in Scotland from 1650, folk drama of various kinds still took place, while in 1659 Aberdeen Town Council authorised public play performance. Meantime, drama remained a key part of humanist education, often under the supervision and with the support of the local Kirk, introducing pupils to the pains and pleasures of dramatic performance.

From 1650 to 1800, drama was a highly controversial medium. While churches would endorse performances in schools and universities, they might also assert a right to condemn specific texts, their concern not being with drama as in itself necessarily sinful, but rather with the content being promoted. In 1688, for example, in Lundie, a small village in the Carse of Gowrie, the Dunkeld Presbytery suspended the master, William Bouok, for 'acting a comoedie wherein he mad a mock of religious duties and ordinances'. In the Palace of Holyroodhouse, after the 1660 Restoration, at least by 1662, the Tennis Court Theatre was established. Such a playhouse theatre was very much an elite pursuit, of course, but thus theatre in Scotland began its recovery from Cromwellian oppression. In 1663, William Clark's *Marciano, or The Discovery*, was acted to 'great applause'. Ostensibly set in Italy, the political and romantic intrigues that determine the plot suggest self-conscious deflection of potential censorship: the play is clearly a coded exploration of Cromwell's overthrow of the Stuart monarchy and its restitution. The Tennis Court Theatre survived until 1689, when the arrival of William and Mary in London enforced a stricter radical Presbyterian control of Scottish public life for the rest of the Stuart reign. This was despite the fact that Mary herself, before becoming Queen, had acted in masques at Holyrood before her father James VII, while, as Duke of York, he had stayed there in the early 1680s. Since civic unrest formed the social context in Scotland well into the 1700s, more controversial plays might be written and performed privately, in the form sometimes of closet drama, none the less vibrant, and certainly more subversive, but not being permitted performance on the public stage. Archibald Pitcairne's *The Assembly* (1692, but not published until 1722), for example, satirises pedantic 'obscurantism' in sectarian politics.

The 18th century sees a new kind of play, exemplified for us in the pleasantly posturing pastoral comedy of Allan Ramsay's *The Gentle Shepherd*, loaded with implications about property, propriety, the prim, the primping and the preposterous. And this brings us back to Ramsay. While visiting friends, the Forbes family of Newhall, he found that the protected setting of Newhall House, at Carlops, Penicuik, Midlothian, near Edinburgh, gave him the opportunity to write *The Gentle Shepherd* (1725), a small-scale pastoral comedy, premiered in Edinburgh in 1729 by Haddington Grammar School boys. This should not be taken to imply that the standard of production was what we might call 'amateur'. Drama was central to humanist education and high standards are known to have been achieved. (It was through such performances after all that Shakespeare began his theatrical career: Edward's Boys, a company of current pupils of his old school shows the high quality of such companies involved.) Indeed, Ramsay's premiere was at Skinner's Hall, then Edinburgh's leading professional theatre venue. There is no reason to assume anything but a high standard of production.

The Gentle Shepherd is self-consciously a work of representational artifice. The actors speak or sing their lines in the full knowledge shared among the audience that's what's going on is a fantasy, a fabrication elaborating upon the conventions of the idyllic pastoral scene. A polite rustic homeliness pervades the ethos and the conflicts dramatized are as deliberately designed as any baroque architecture or musical sonata for clavichord. It gives all the appearance of a light, breezy, miniature classical sinfonietta. That artifice gives it an edge and an ambiguity. It may appeal to unquestioning fantasists but it may also be read against its 'natural' grain, as a work exhibiting its own techniques and prejudices.

It opens by setting the scene: under a crag where 'crystal springs' pour forth, two shepherds, Patie (the Gentle Shepherd himself) and Roger (his richer companion), tend their flocks on a May morning. Patie begins the play with a song:

> My *Peggy* is a young thing,
> Just enter'd in her teens,
> Fair as the day, and sweet as May,
> Fair as the day, and always gay.
> My Peggy is a young thing,
> And I'm not very auld;
> Yet well I like to meet her, at
> The wawking of the fauld.

The play is structured by the conventional story of a rich inheritance being lost, and then discovered, to bring about a happy ending – the title gives the clue that the rustic shepherd will be revealed as the inheritor of wealth and claimant to gentility. Although the gentle birth of the shepherd is revealed at the beginning of the play, there is an obstacle to his happy marriage. This is what generates the drama.

Patie, the shepherd, falls in love with Peggy. A richer shepherd, Roger, is in love with Jenny. Sir William Worthy is the absent laird; Symon and Glaud are two of his tenants and an old woman, Mause, seems to be a witch but is in fact simply an educated and independently-minded woman; Elspa, Symon's wife, Madge, Glaud's sister and Bauldy, a farmworker, stand on the side of the action as it unfolds. When Patie declares his love for Peggy, Sir William, now returned, tells him he is in fact his father and forbids the marriage as Peggy is of a lower class. Sir William commands Patie to take a long journey away. But Mause reveals that Peggy is in fact the daughter of Sir William's sister, and therefore not only Patie's cousin, but more importantly, his social equal. Sir William gives his blessing to the marriage.

The plot is not too complicated and the structure is clear enough, but what makes the play perennially fascinating, what gives it both sharpness and charm, is its constant play with social expectations, limitations and parameters, and this is conveyed through a subtle linguistic layering of English and Scots speech, from broad Scots, through genteel Scots, to upper-class English. Mause, speaking of the rustic, Bauldy, suggests the strata of identity Ramsay is layering here:

> This fool imagines, as do mony sic,
> That I'm a wretch in compact with Auld Nick;
> Because by education I was taught
> To speak and act aboon their common thought.
> Their gross mistake shall quickly now appear;
> Soon shall they ken what brought, what keeps me here;
> Nane kens but me, – and if the morn were come,
> I'll tell them tales will gar them a' sing dumb.

As the play approaches its happy conclusion, Sir William has the last spoken word. Good behaviour assured, characters finally secure in their allotted stations, virtue rewarded and all at rights, Peggy brings the play to an end with a love song. Gamesome and acutely observant of language and social class, Ramsay draws out social distinctions in order to emphasise their relations to each other and to assemble them into a coherent balance: a hopeful, and indeed, gentle, shepherding.

The play was a consequence of its historical occasion, arising from the Augustan era that prized order, security and social hierarchy. And yet this era led towards the crucible of Romanticism in its endorsement of vernacular language and common humanity. The play endorses both hierarchies of class and the worth of individuals. That's a contradiction. If you want those hierarchies held secure, there's a liability in approving value in the individual. The play became most popular in the 40 years from 1780 to 1820, with about 160 productions throughout the United Kingdom and in America, and around 120 editions published. That is, just as it exemplified formal neo-classical virtues, its vogue coincided with the Romantic movement. Rather than fall between them, it managed to balance and combine two kinds of vision.

And there's another ambiguity. At first, with its plot concerning the restoration of an older and 'better' order, it carried hints of support for the Stuart cause and Jacobitism. Andrew Hook, in his essay 'Scottish Literary Romanticism and Its American Reception' from his book, *From Mount Hooly to Princeton: A Scottish-American Medley* (2020), says this:

> The plot of the play hinges on the return from exile of a nobleman, a supporter of Charles II, at the time of the Restoration in 1660. The Scottish peasantry rejoice at the restoration of their old master; good times are returned, old buildings restored, the land re-cultivated. The good life is seen to lie in a recreated past, not a revolutionary future. The politics of the play are Tory, aristocratic, and Jacobite. A similar conservatism pervades the ideas of the piece: the values of reason and common sense take precedence over those of feelings and passion.

The pressing question Hook identifies is: 'How could such a work continue to grow in popularity long after neo-classical values were no longer dominant?'

His answer is to emphasise that there is 'a potentially Romantic strain in the play which a changing sensibility could register and bring to the fore.' Just as the play presents a rural Scotland 'increasingly remote from modern, sophisticated society' it also seems 'to take seriously the feelings of simple people' and its language has 'the natural spontaneity of an unpolished vernacular.' Moreover, it incorporates 'versions of about 20 traditional Scots songs.' This was immediately appealing to a growing appetite for, and indeed the invention of, a theatre of spectacle and stage. In other words, the performance took place within a securely identifiable frame of reference, a refined medium, as opposed to a theatre of participatory enactment. Both these aspects of theatre are complementary. The further each strays from the other, the more identifiable its appeal becomes, and the more its audience can be targeted. As the economic structures of live (or later, screened) entertainment changed, both restructured themselves in what came to be accepted as 'Scottish popular culture'.

Ramsay opened The New Theatre in Edinburgh in Carrubber's Close in 1736. In 1737, the Licensing Act, intended to prohibit political satires in London and not directly relevant to Ramsay at all, came into effect, and offered more conservative members of the Kirk and Council a means to close his enterprise. The theatre was closed the year after it opened. Nonetheless, such was the grip Ramsay's theatrical innovations had on Edinburgh folk, very soon a device used in other parts of Britain too was employed: plays were performed accompanied by brief musical concerts where the ticket price paid nominally for admission to the concert allowed the play to be presented 'gratis'. Ramsay himself, however, retired to his house at the top of the Royal Mile on Castlehill, where Ramsay Gardens can be visited today.

Like Tobias Smollett in *The Regicide* of 1749 and *The Reprisal* of 1757 and Archibald Maclaren in *Kenneth, King of Scots* in 1807, Ramsay was a playwright of more than historical significance. So were David Mallet and James Thomson, authors of *Alfred: A Masque*, first performed to music by Thomas Arne in 1740, and now lastingly famous for the song, 'Rule, Britannia'. In performance, it is sung as a duet by Alfred the Great and his wife Eltruda, celebrating their victory over the threatening Danes, anachronistically and metaphorically. Given the date of first performance and with hindsight now of the Jacobite rising that was to happen five years later, fully contextualising the production in its history gives it considerably more dramatic power than we might allow were it read merely as 'text'. Certainly, it formed part of an argument within government and court circles as to whether post-Union Britain should be focused primarily on Hanoverian interests in Europe or instead more on trade and empire, as Alfred and his wife advocate in the play, by ruling the waves. It would be exhilarating to see a new production, appropriately edited, perhaps with a newly-written 'Prelude' and 'Postlude' presenting historical contexts, 1707–40 and 1740–46.

Meanwhile, in Gaelic Scotland, folk drama was flourishing. Oral stories, poems and songs in Gaelic often employ voices and dialogues; animals speak and sing, personae are mutable, drama and dance are reciprocally enabling, there is a profound relation between life, death and the cycle of seasons, tidal returning. All these are embedded in Gaelic culture and all its representations in performance. This also reminds us that there is a different way of reading literature than the 'words on the page' tradition of critical appraisal.

To those of us familiar with Shakespeare and the ancient Greek plays of Aeschylus, Sophocles and Euripides, the matter of tragedy is crucial. In *The Artist's Reality: Philosophies of Art* (posthumously published in 2004), the painter Mark Rothko says that 'the introduction of humanity into the picture, an attempt to relate the representation of the individual emotionality in the terms of universal emotions' is crucial: 'It is significant that such emotionality in relationship to the individual is found only in a tragic emotionality. In comic situations this quality is achieved only in an ironical presentation whose end again is the enhancement of the tragic element through the medium of the tragic doom.'

Rothko's perception is that the art that speaks to the humanity in each one of us most deeply, universally, and unanswerably, is tragic. Or at least, recognises and acknowledges the fact of tragedy as inalienably human. And this knowledge informs even the most defiant, affirming, celebratory works of art, whether in painting, music or literature.

Perhaps the one key characteristic of 18th-century English-language theatrical literature was its inability to fully engage with tragedy. Throughout the century, Nahum Tate's revised *King Lear* was supplied with a happy ending. There are some things the culture of a particular time and place will not allow. We should not judge plays of one era by the conventions of another but these historical contexts also need consideration.

John Home (1722–1808) was most famous for his play *Douglas* (1756). David Hume praised it for having more refinement than 'the unhappy barbarism' of Shakespeare. Like *The Gentle Shepherd*, *Douglas* is a play about inheritance rediscovered, and takes place predominantly through a series of set pieces, rhetorical speeches and gestural moments usually unencumbered by what we might call dramatic tension, as was the theatrical expectation of the time.

And like Ramsay's *Shepherd*, the plot seems complex but is carefully structured. Against her father's wishes, Lady Randolph has married wicked Lord Douglas and a son is born, Young Norval. The baby boy and his nurse are presumed drowned while trying to escape. Norval joins the Scottish army and becomes a hero. Later, he returns, attempts to save his mother from the evil schemes of Lord Douglas and his lieutenant, Glenalvon, but dies in the process, and in her distress, Lady Randolph kills herself by leaping from a tower of the castle. The anguish of the mother and the fated struggle of the long-lost son are joined in the dramatic self-possession with which they meet their noble ends.

At first reading, the gestures and rhetoric seem to be enacted on the surface only, but once again, historical contextualisation supplies a more complex meaning. The play is about what is at stake, what the costs are to families across generations, in a world of civil strife and social division, and ultimately, civil war. It was first performed only ten years after Culloden. Questions of property, loyalty, and the outcome of vexed vested interests are pre-eminent. It is a coded text, imbued with reference to the Jacobite rising of 1745 and its consequences. The popularity of the first productions was enhanced by flamboyant performances by the celebrity Irish actress, Margaret (Peg) Woffington (1720–60) in the part of the matriarch Lady Randolph. The words on the page may not say these things explicitly, but the full context of theatrical conventions and the politics of the time give the play complex power and depth. Presumably this power is what was acknowledged by the member of the audience who, famously if perhaps apocryphally, rose to his feet at the end of the first performance and cried out, 'Whaur's yer Wullie Shakespeare nou?'

The play also resembles Ramsay's *Gentle Shepherd* in that it makes an appeal to sensibility to contemplate in security the re-establishment of order in the universe. Modern literary criticism might argue that both plays emerge from mentalities utterly removed from the destructiveness that characterises tragic drama: in Enlightenment conventions, passion becomes sentiment, despair becomes elegy. Tragedy, in the Greek or Shakespearian sense, is not permitted. This was not the case with David Lyndsay in the 16th century, and would not be the case in the 20th and 21st centuries. And yet it is futile to criticise these plays for their performance conventions: Home's *Douglas* represents a conception of tragedy current in 18th-century theatre, and in its own historical, political and national contexts, the meaning of tragedy, post-Culloden, has a much deeper and broader social context than any single theatre could accommodate. David Hume praised the play for having more refinement than 'the unhappy barbarism' of Shakespeare. Remember Walter Benjamin, in 'Theses on the Philosophy of History' (1940), writing: 'There is no document of civilisation which is not at the same time a document of barbarism.' This is not simply 'a play'. It's a cultural document of a society trapped in its own priorities.

We considered earlier the question of performativity in Scottish society, noting the engagement of church and nobility in the gesture known as the Declaration of Arbroath, and the theatricality of the Disruption of the Kirk in 1843. In both these instances, politics and religion were, if not the same thing, then deeply imbricated with each other. What I am suggesting here is that the political world in which these 18th-century plays were performed is itself part of the drama we need to understand to read them accurately. The coding and context, in both plays, has to be understood before they can be fully appraised.

Moreover, *Douglas* surely marked the triumph of professional playhouse theatre over more conservative elements in the Kirk. Although the Edinburgh Presbytery sought to condemn Home, a minister, for writing his play, and other ministers who had attended its performance, the condemnation was not taken very seriously. A simple apology sufficed to excuse those who had attended and Home simply resigned from the ministry and went off to write for the London stage. The Kirk conflict had been between the more severe Evangelical wing and a Moderate party which included Home. This is the same division of viewpoints that would lie behind the Disruption nearly 90 years later. By that time, professional playhouse theatre was well established at all levels in Scottish society and even by the 1780s, as one report has it, the General Assembly had altered its starting time to allow ministers to attend the theatre to watch the performance of the great star Sarah Siddons.

Quickly following its first performance, the play was published in Edinburgh in 1757 and two further editions appeared in Dublin in the same year. Around 75 editions followed these. By any account of publishing in its era, it was a bestseller.

According to Andrew Hook, in his essay 'Home's *Douglas* and Macpherson's *Ossian*' in his book *From Mount Hooly to Princeton* (2020), after its first American publication, in Philadelphia in 1790, another ten editions appeared by 1821:

> Amédée Pichot would publish a French translation in 1822, and an Italian translation would appear in Genoa in the same year. The play was performed in Philadelphia as early as 1759 and as late as 1825 the *New York Literary Gazette* was referring to it as 'one of the best modern tragedies'.

It became a favourite acting vehicle for most leading British actors: Mrs Siddons, Mrs Crawford (Ann Street Barry), John Philip Kemble, Henry West Betty, John Howard Payne, Charles Kean, Edwin Forrest and the great Scottish actor Henry Erskine Johnston. Both the play's publishing and theatrical history confirm that this conventional, sentimental 18th-century drama 'enjoyed an enduring success far beyond anything achieved by any of the works of contemporaries such as Thomas Otway or Nicholas Rowe.' Andrew Hook asks: 'Once again the question is why?'

We have summarised the plot, but the ethos and atmosphere of the play is worth pausing on. It is set in a vaguely historical medieval period when Scotland is threatened by Danish military and naval forces, and while the particular named Scottish locations – Edinburgh, Lorn, the river Teviot, the Grampian mountains, the Bass Rock – give a kind of topographical veracity to the landscape, the characters seem to come from a heroic world where aristocratic virtues are not tied so much to social hierarchy as to moral authority. More than money, nobility is power. And in this world, the indulgence in melancholy is characteristic.

Very soon, this would characterise the tales of Ossian which James Macpherson would present as authentic translations from original Gaelic sources. Feelings of loss, suffering, loneliness and sorrow are the emotional sustenance of the characters. Macpherson's first 'Ossian' collection, *Fragments of Ancient Poetry*, was published in 1760, only four years after the premiere of *Douglas*, and in fact it was John Home who had encouraged Macpherson to collect the fragments and present them to the public.

In his essay, Andrew Hook makes a pertinent point about the relation between Home's play and Macpherson's early poems 'The Hunter' and 'The Highlander'. The critic Fiona Stafford has noted that both poems are examinations of 'the idea of the prince raised in obscurity, proving his worth through deeds rather than merely inheriting his power. In both, the military interest of Scotland being close to defeat but emerging victoriously is mingled with a romantic tale of love and marriage'. Hook's point is that while 'the parallel here with the story of

Douglas is far from exact' nevertheless 'the similarities are certainly striking, and all the more so when one recognises that the external threat to Scotland comes in both [Home's *Douglas* and Macpherson's *Fingal, An Ancient Epic Poem in Six Books* (1761)] from Scandinavia.' While there may be other sources in Gaelic culture for Macpherson's 'translations' from Ossian, the pre-eminence of *Douglas* itself may constitute a primary source.

As Hook says, Home wrote six tragedies, and five of them 'sunk without trace'. One of these, *The Fatal Discovery*, was directly based on 'Fragment IX' of Macpherson's *Fragments of Ancient Poetry*, but its relative failure was perhaps most effectively due to the fact that the public had already become familiar with Ossian and the Ossianic atmosphere that had above all been a radical novelty when it appeared. We are looking at the phenomena of fashion, vogue and novelty. To quote Hook once again:

> *Douglas*'s popularity coincides exactly with the popularity of *Ossian*. It has to be borne in mind that *Ossian* was not an instant success everywhere in the 1760s. It took time – almost a generation – for the Ossianic vogue to begin its sweep across the whole Western world. Like the Romantic movement it helped to create, *Ossian* was at the height of its fame and influence in the early 19th century. *Douglas*, I believe, was carried along on that Ossianic wave. The settings, the landscapes, the sentiments, the Scottish historical background, the emphasis on martial heroism and valour, and on the inevitability of human loss and suffering, all blend easily into the seductive world of *Ossian*. This is the explanation of *Douglas*'s enduring success.

All of which helps us to understand the play in its own time and why it has fallen out of the repertoire and is so little known in the 21st century, outside of literary and theatrical history. And yet that is no reason to say that it should not be given a revival, just for the fun of seeing and hearing it performed live today. Its very obscurity seems to invite such a theatrical production. After all, it provided one of the funniest, most arcane references in Hugh MacDiarmid's *A Drunk Man Looks at the Thistle* (1926). In the court scene that opens Act II of the play, Lord and Lady Randolph enter from one side, and servants and 'a Stranger' at the other. Lord Randolph asks who this stranger is, and is answered:

> A low born man, of parentage obscure,
> Who nought can boast but his desire to be
> A soldier, and to gain a name in arms.

Lord Randolph asks him to 'declare his birth' and the stranger replies:

> My name in Norval: on the Grampian hills
> My father feeds his flocks; a frugal swain,
> Whose constant cares were to increase his store,
> And keep his only son, myself, at home.
> For I had heard of battles, and I long'd
> To follow to the field some warlike Lord:
> And heaven soon granted what my Sire deny'd.

Almost 200 years later, lines 2188–2195 of MacDiarmid's poem shift references with slippery quickness from T.S. Eliot to John Home, and from macabre and sinister darkness to morbid, gloomy hilarity:

> The circles of our hungry thought
> Swing savagely from pole to pole.
> Death and the Raven drift above
> The graves of Sweeney's body and soul.
>
> My name is Norval. On the Grampian hills
> It is forgotten, and deserves to be.
> So are the Grampian Hills and all the people
> Who ever heard of either them or me.

If Home's play warranted such reference in 1926, perhaps it is worth resurrecting it in the 21st century, prompted by the intrinsic optimism of curiosity. Why not?

One answer is given by Edwin Morgan, in his essay 'Scottish Drama: An Overview' (cited above): the play is, he says 'A gloomy, almost static historical tragedy, with no comic relief of any kind, with long flashbacks which explain the plot but don't advance it, and even with a misleading title since the central character is not Douglas but his endlessly grieving mother who at last discovers her long-lost son just before he is killed and then kills herself: what was the attraction?' And it is 'written on a Scottish theme but not in Scots, and indeed in a monotonously heavy and unidiomatic, tonally inert English blank verse'.

Experimentation in production can only go so far. Morgan is cautious: 'Attempts to revive it may in fact be doomed – unless we could find some Mrs Siddons to play Lady Randolph, because it is a fact that she mesmerized her audiences with her portrayal of the part – all stops out, vast gestures, tears at command, ham acting if you like to call it that – so perhaps that is what it needs, turn it almost into an opera, add strong atmospheric music to cover up the fustian of the language. When it was played at the Edinburgh Festival in 1986 it was panned by even the most sympathetic critics, partly because this was a rather genteel production, in the Signet Library, by a company that obviously felt too timorous to risk anything more robust in case that would have had the audience rolling in laughter.' Perhaps some things truly earn their own oblivion. And yet, one wonders...

Morgan mentions one further play, or playlet, that we should note here: *The Hubble-Shue* by Christian Carstairs, who died in 1794. Its author was a governess in Fife, and, Morgan says,

> judging by her play the fortunate children she looked after must have had a whale of a time. Indeed, since there are children as well as adults in the cast, it's possible she wrote this piece in the first instance for a family in a big house, though that's only a guess.

This miniature play is a fresh breeze of anarchic comedy, linguistically various in tone, unsettling in suggestion, bizarre in essence, and as much fun to read as it must have been to watch – or be part of. It's a miniature example of the playwright's art, an almost-forgotten, almost ephemeral comedy whose bizarre humour suggests a Picasso-like cubism or even a Dalí-like surrealism hundreds of years in advance of these modernist artists. It's a brief work that evidently could be performed domestically, although it might warrant a professional production. We won't really know until we see one. It's an astonishment, perfectly capable of being given a performance in various amateur circumstances and almost short enough to be reproduced in its entirety here.

Morgan explains:

> The title, *Hubble-Shue*, is an old Scots word with a variety of meanings from 'uproar.', 'commotion', 'riot', to something like 'a milling crowd gathered together to watch an event'; it can be good or bad. I suspect that Ms Carstaires, being a well-educated governess, had probably come across William Dunbar's poem (at least it's attributed to him) 'The manere of the crying of ane playe' (crying = public proclamation), which begins 'Harry, harry, hobbillschowe, Se quha is cummyn nowe...'

There is a play within a play, and frequent confusion in the narrative, with stories hiding behind other stories. So, 'HUBBLE' rhymes with Shakespeare's witches, 'Double, double, toil and trouble; / Fire burn and cauldron bubble.' and 'SHUE' is 'Show' or 'Performance'. This is part of Scene 2, when the characters go into a drawing-room:

> FAT MINISTER: Come, Miss, give us your Italian –.
> MISS: Yes, Papa.
> Si li si ti o to

Ki li qui si o so
Fa la se scud
Qui a vi a vi a
Que a vi a ve a
Qui a vi a bo. &c.&c.
[Enter Mrs Consul and her Grandchild.]
MRS CONSUL: Madam, I beg you ten thousand pardons, it was not in my power to wait upon you at dinner; there is no separating my grandchild and the little black girl.
CHILD: O, Mamma, I'm frightened.
MRS CONSUL: Why are you frightened?
CHILD: The little girl says a great fish (a crocodile) came out of the water (the Ganges) and devoured her father – and a fine gentleman came running with a sword and stab'd the monster – and her father was all bloody, and she would have been killed; but the fine gentleman took her away, and they were carried by a black man with muslin on their head (turbans) – and the fine gentleman gave her to a great lady – All the fine things could not make her forget her poor father...
FAT MINISTER: Hold your tongue, my bonny dear, and you and the black girl shall go to the dancing school.
CHILD: No, Mamma. [Crys]... Take me home, Mamma...
MRS CONSUL: Come my dear – excuse me, Madam – my child is really not well – feel her hand – I am afraid she's feverish.
Apothecary: Madam, you had better give miss a little Senna and a puke, if it operates six times it will be sufficient.
[...A coach calls to take them all to the playhouse to see the play... the play is delayed for half an hour, the audience is restive – a girl sings a song on stage to fill in:]
When you hear a mournful tale
Laugh and hide your tears.
When you hear a mournful tale
Laugh and hide your tears.
La-a-a-a-laugh, &c.
This is poor entertainment (from one of the boxes.)
An orange from the footman's gallery hits the Irishman such a blow on the nose – He flies upon the stage, drawing his dagger – throws one of the players heels o'er head – wounds Mr Hallion – makes such a hubbub, the gentlemen from the pit are obliged to interfere.
The house is in great confusion – the company crowding to the door with great difficulty get to their coaches – a Nabob's carriage driving

like Jehu – the coachman being drunk overturns one of the hackneys – they shriek frightfully, and the Minister roars like a bull.
The old Ensign, chancing to walk on foot, comes up and helps to lug them out.

Morgan concludes:

All quite mad? – and yet not entirely so – the author mocks the current Scottish craze for importing Italian singers – and she uses the two little girls to make a sympathetic comment on the unhappiness of Indian children snatched from their families to become servants in Britain, even if they're well looked after as the black girl in the play evidently is... Altogether the playlet with its light touch makes a refreshing contrast to the stiff formalities of *Douglas*.

Consider what this presents us with in terms of power relations: between men and women, adults and children, churchmen, medical men and the laity, people of different racial or ethnic identities, the wealthy and the poor, cultural elitism, imperialism, colonialism, and conventions of performance culture. What might seem 'mad' is in fact a chaos of very edgy questions.

After Home's *Douglas* and Ramsay's *The Gentle Shepherd*, it's worthwhile pausing on *The Hubble-Shue* if only to demonstrate how much more there is to Scottish theatre or play history than is often suspected.

25

Tender strengths: Robert Fergusson

ROBERT BURNS FIRST read Robert Fergusson's poems in the early 1780s and in the 'Second Epistle to J. Lapraik' he damns the idle, callous rich whose wealth might have eased Fergusson's poverty:

> My curse upon your whunstane hearts,
> Ye Enbrugh Gentry!
> The tythe o' what ye waste at Cartes
> Wad stow'd his pantry!

Two hundred years later, in his book *Abhorrences: A Chronicle of the Eighties*, the American poet Edward Dorn offers a similar condemnation. Imagine the voice, whether 'Edinburgh Gentry' or London toff or Washington pontiff, it's the same old story: rich and poor, the widening gulf, and many of our best poets and artists have not been rich. Dorn's poem talks about a new name for an old disease: 'HELPS' for 'Heritable Long-range Endemic Poverty Syndrome' and asks: 'Do you think there would be much tea and sympathy for this affliction?' And answers: 'Neither do I.'

Burns recognised Fergusson's worth as a poet immediately and made sure his 'elder brother in misfortune / By far my elder brother in the muse' would be commemorated. At his own expense, Burns had a memorial stone inscribed in Edinburgh's Canongate Kirk cemetery, where now, outside the front gate, a life-size statue of Fergusson by David Annand can be seen, striding down the Royal Mile towards the Scottish Poetry Library in Crichton's Close. Tourists and visitors of all kinds stop and consider, take photographs beside him, wonder who this is, read the inscription.

Burns wasn't alone in affirming Fergusson's neglected genius. Robert Louis Stevenson, writing from Samoa in 1894, said: 'Now the injustice with which the one Robert is rewarded and the other left out in the cold sits heavy on me...'

Fergusson was born in Edinburgh in 1750, his parents from Aberdeenshire; he studied in Dundee and St Andrews. He returned to Edinburgh after the death of his father in 1767, supporting his mother and sister as a clerk, copying documents for the court. The work was dull and Fergusson was a flamboyant young man, had been a wild prankster as a student, enjoyed theatre and the company of actors. He mixed with artists, musicians, performers and bright conversationalists. He was highly strung and full of fun.

All his poems are the work of a young man with energy, quickness and flair. Many are filled with the exuberance of youth, quick velocity and healthily derisive laughter. Their range is surprising: fully-charged, vigorous, ironic, deprecating, satiric, enchanted, enraptured, lyrically sustained at perfect pitch, some half-serious, half-comic, some wholly scabrous, some elegiac, dark and grim. Poignant melancholy in familiar 18th-century poise is exercised but sometimes a deeper, darker sense of grief cuts through. His Edinburgh poems are a kaleidoscope of city pictures: 'Leith Races', 'The Ghaists' and the definitive cityscape, 'Auld Reekie'. Burns recognised the scene in Fergusson's 'The Farmer's Ingle' and used it as his model for 'The Cotter's Saturday Night'. His poems in English are an essential part of his work, especially his address to Dr Samuel Johnson. The world is a much better place for his unfazed, lashingly athletic brio. 'Then hie you home,' he advises Johnson at the end:

> And be a malcontent, that naked hinds,
> On lentils fed, could make your kingdom quake,
> And tremulate Old England libertized.

Johnson's championship of the English language has had its long-term legacy. For Fergusson, it was nothing but English imperialism at its most foetid. A related poem in Scots, 'Lines, to the Principal and Professors of the University of St Andrews, on their superb treat to Dr Johnson' castigates the officials of his old university for their obsequious prostration before the pompous southron. Both poems connect Fergusson to his Gaelic contemporary James Macintyre (1727–99), whose view of Johnson was equally scornful, as we've already noted. This is how Fergusson's poem 'To Dr Samuel Johnson: Food for a New Edition of His Dictionary' begins:

> Great Pedagogue! whose literarian lore,
> With syllable on syllable conjoined,
> To transmutate and varify, hast learned
> The whole revolving scientific names
> That in the alphabetic columns lie,
> Far from the knowledge of mortalic shapes;
> As we, who never can peroculate
> The miracles by thee miraculized,
> The Muse, silential long, with mouth apert,
> Would give vibration to stagnatic tongue,
> And loud encomiate thy puissant name,
> Eulogiated from the green decline
> Of Thames's banks to Scoticanian shores,
> Where Lochlomondian liquids undulize.

Fergusson can be iconoclastic but there is depth and deliberation to his thinking. He gives us a varied panorama of both his contemporary Edinburgh and rural life. Classical imitations from ancient authors prompt the Odes: to Pity, Horror, Disappointment, the Epigrams and the Pastoral poems. The world of theatres and public bars is evoked in 'To Sir John Fielding, on his attempt to suppress the Beggar's Opera'. 'The Rivers of Scotland' and 'Elegy on the Death of Scots Music' open up the whole country: he is, indeed, a national poet.

'Ode to the Gowdspink' (the goldfinch) begins as a beautiful vision but then is given a darker cast: Liberty is a 'bonny dame' round whose stream the birds rejoice in gratitude, and the goldfinch sings joyously but when freedom is taken away, the goldfinch, confined to 'some daurk chaumer's dowie nook' is cheerless and cursed. The final point is made with reference to the poet himself, and has its fearful application to his short life:

> For whan fair Freedom smiles nae mair,
> Care I for life? Shame fa' the hair;
> A field o'ergrown wi' rankest stubble,
> The essence o' a paltry bubble.

Fergusson began suffering bouts of depression, the horrors of melancholy, mental affliction, remorse and guilt. After a fall, he was taken to the Edinburgh madhouse in a sedan chair, his bearers pretending they were going to visit a friend. He died aged 24, in a bare stone cell, on straw, surrounded by lunatics, in October 1774.

In the 20th century, Robert Garioch recognised in Fergusson a poetic ancestor of his own, writing about Edinburgh in Scots, puncturing hypocrisy and sham. Given his characteristic scepticism, Garioch's reverence, in his sonnet 'At Robert Fergusson's Grave, October 1962', is all the more effective: 'Lichtlie this, gin ye daur: / Here Robert Burns knelt and kissed the mool.' ('Make light of this, if you dare / Here Robert Burns knelt and kissed the earth.')

In the 21st century, Douglas Dunn, Kathleen Jamie, Les Murray, Edwin Morgan, W.N. Herbert, Don Paterson and others have also paid poetic tribute to him.

There is a tradition in Scottish literature that goes right back to David Lyndsay and further, a distinctive theme in the whole story of Scotland, described by Marshall Walker in his book *Scottish Literature since 1707* (1996), as 'the democratic strain' or an 'egalitarian line'. This tradition includes

> the socialism of Lewis Grassic Gibbon in a 'world rolling fast to a hell of riches' and 'the dispensation of the poor' in the mind of Sorley MacLean' and 'his redefinition of Calvary in terms of 'a foul-smelling backland

in Glasgow' and 'a room in Edinburgh, / a room of poverty and pain" or 'Bill Bryden's sympathy for a moderate shop-steward in his 'Red Clydeside' play, *Willie Rough* (1972); the 7:84 Theatre Company's attack on capitalist exploitation of Scotland in John McGrath's *The Cheviot, the Stag and the Black, Black Oil* (1974); the television mini-series *Edge of Darkness* (1985), Troy Kennedy Martin's realistic and mythopoeic exposé of nuclear-age capitalist cynicism towards the well-being of the planet in Margaret Thatcher's visigothic Britain; the 'copies of the *Daily Worker*... dove of peace... poster of Paul Robeson' which a pregnant woman thinks she had better hide when a social worker calls to check her suitability for a housing waiting list in Jackie Kay's poem, 'Chapter 3: The Waiting Lists' [in *The Adoption Papers*]. A democratic manifesto is implicit in Ian Hamilton Finlay and Tom Leonard's use of Glasgow *patois* to cut through to the real lives of ordinary people and in doing so to protest, as Gaelic could never quite do, against the bending of a country's mind by 'a police regime of the signifier', to co-opt a phrase of Edward Said's, that is, by the undemocratic authority of a language whose insidious 'correctness' derives from the bullying power of a remote parliament and a chimerical throne.'

The key point here is that Fergusson, like Burns after and Ramsay before him, did not arise as a singular phenomenon. The lives of all three men overlapped: Ramsay (1686–1758), Fergusson (1750–74), Burns (1759–96). And as we have seen, Ramsay was a figure of immense importance in Scottish literary history.

So what does all this amount to?

The 18th century saw a retrieval and renewal of the Scots poetic tradition, particularly in the wake of Ramsay's anthology, *The Ever Green*. This was the world that Fergusson and Burns rose from: a regeneration of an understanding of what the history of Scottish poetry was. After the Union of 1707, after the violent suppression of the Jacobite rising in 1745, an entire historical tradition which had been obscured was made available once more to new generations. It was a resurrection of a kind, a rebirth of possibilities. It was to happen again in the 1920s. And in the 1980s. Sometimes such regeneration is demanded by the dead, of the living responsible to them. Ultimately, it's about how you understand what value really is.

26

The politics of song: Robert Burns

WILLIAM POWER WROTE in his book *Literature and Oatmeal* that, given 'the idolatry of a sand-papered Burns' and 'the genteel and touristic attitude to Scotland' fostered in the wake of Scott, 'one is almost tempted to wonder whether it would not have been better for Scotland had Burns and Scott never existed.' He rebukes himself and rejects the thought but seeing such iconic figures unencumbered by the history of their exploitation is an unlikely aspiration. It's as well to remember that there are still many parts of the world and generations born and unborn who have never heard of them and never read a word they wrote. How lucky and good it might be to make their acquaintance and get to know their work as if for the first time is our task.

THE CENTRALITY OF MUSIC

The story of the life of Robert Burns (1759–96) is familiar to many but unknown to many more: born in Alloway, Ayrshire, growing up mainly working on farms, he was considering emigration to the West Indies before the publication of his first book of poems in Kilmarnock caught the fashion of the day. He was not only popular among his contemporaries locally but also quite suddenly flavour-of-the-season among the literary fashionistas of Edinburgh. One of them, Henry Mackenzie, described him rather patronisingly as a heaven-taught ploughman, as if he was a living model of Rousseau's noble savage, when in fact he had been well educated, was highly literate and possessed an intellectual curiosity, verbal wit, shrewd judgement and a range of experience and knowledge that matched any of his contemporaries. Coming from the farming world of Ayrshire he had a richer knowledge and experience of what were once termed 'country matters' (the physicality of life, what human and animal bodies are made of, and do) than many of his city-bred, genteel contemporaries. But he was equally well-grounded in the sophistications of good manners and polite behaviour. In short, to quote Byron: 'What an antithetical mind! – tenderness, roughness – delicacy, coarseness – sentiment, sensuality – soaring and grovelling, dirt and deity – all mixed up in that one compound of inspired clay!'

Mackenzie (1745–1831) was the author of a bestselling novel, *The Man of Feeling* (1771), the quintessential literary text of the age of refined sensibility in which Burns's poems became an attractively spicy taste. It was the subject of Robert Fergusson's scorn in his poem 'The Sow of Feeling' but it was a favourite book of Burns himself, which indicates not only that Burns's expressivity in the Scots language could be animated by socially refined emotions, but also how Mackenzie's novel might be read as prototypical of a humanist impulse. It extolled with its own genteel politeness the common virtues of people of whatever race or nation, and was ostensibly opposed to commercial exploitation. Paradoxically, Mackenzie's pre-eminence in Enlightenment Edinburgh was conveyed through his expertise with Augustan forms of decorum in the English language, while Burns's poems employed the language of both his literate and non-literate country companions. Burns also wrote in Augustan English with precision, flair and sometimes arch pleasure, both in poems of delightful artifice and in prose, in journals and letters. When Burns visited Edinburgh he was popular, revered and lionised, but he obtained no secure wage-paying employment or even steady patronage until his appointment as an Exciseman, and his move to Dumfriesshire, where he died in his 30s, as his loyal, long-enduring wife Jean was giving birth to their ninth child, Maxwell.

Such a thumbnail sketch only indicates that there are more important things to say about Burns than the story of his life. Yet the life has become a fetish for generations and Mackenzie's version of an acceptable Burns was taken up by the Edinburgh middle-class literati and genteel fashionistas to lasting iconic effect. William Power comments that his 'strong vein of sentiment' was 'joined with the currents of pious respectability' and the result was a discrediting of the 'coarsely clever' old rustic genre and the creation of 'the lilting and facetiae of persons of poor temperament and inferior intellect.' The pity is in the exploitation.

There are at least three vital contexts in which we can best read Burns's work. His biography is the first and most obvious and the least important.

The second is the world he inhabited, among his contemporaries in Scotland and internationally, amidst the major revolutionary changes in that world in France and America, with the poets who preceded him and those who came after, like Wordsworth, trying to catch up. In the transition or mix of the Enlightenment and the Romantic eras, Burns is central. The political revolutions that characterised that whole period might allow us to describe it fairly as the major turning-point in the western world before the second decade of the 20th century, when once again it was possible to imagine what the world might be like if it were reorganised along completely different lines. After the revolutions in France and America, the world would be a different place and Burns understood this deeply.

The third is the broader spectrum of writers and artists whose commitment remained to a vision of a different social order, where, in William Dunbar's words, law might be delivered equally to ape and unicorn, eagle and wren. These would include Scottish poets from Henryson to MacDiarmid, and writers from all around the world, from Whitman and Tolstoy to Lorca, Neruda, Soyinka and

Joyce. Burns opens the door to all these writers, and back to the whole history of Scottish literature, and he points forward to the writers who came after him. It is so obvious that it is normally unsaid that in Scotland especially, attention devoted to Burns as an icon has been at the expense of critical attention to his predecessors, peers and successors, and any deep and broadening understanding of his vision.

Of course he should be read first through his collected poems and songs. The fact that he collected so many songs, rewriting or adjusting many of them and matching them to music is of equal consequence with his achievement as a poet. But he should also be read through his letters and journals, his accounts of his tours of the Highlands and Borders. He emerges as a writer continually in touch with other people, either in his verse-letters to fellow poets in Ayrshire (correspondence in verse by other poets might be read along with Burns's poems so that you can see the bagatelle taking place), or physically in the company of men and women of different economic strata. Burns may be a singular phenomenon but he is continually a social poet. He is rarely the isolated Romantic individualist himself, even if his persona in some ways projected that to the full-blown English Romantics who followed him. Of those poets, Keats came closest to seeing the vulnerability of Burns and the liability of Burns's legacy: both were young writers, with feverishly intense commitment to their poetry. Keats, visiting Alloway after Burns's death, foresaw the alpine avalanches of ignorant nonsense that would accumulate around Burns in centuries to come. So our task here must be to introduce Burns's poems as if to a reader who might never have read him before. And there is one essential way to do this.

Burns is impossible to read without a sense of music. And there is no morality in music. You can read Milton and Wordsworth silently, sounding their magnificent lines in your head. But Burns's words move differently. His book is not only a book, but the score of a performance in sound and physical movement. The familiar stanza of many of his poems, with its block of statement followed by a shorter line, a longer one, then a short and long line repeated, is primarily a musical structure, rather than a verbal, rhetorical, linguistic one. The movement of those last lines in what's called the 'Habbie Simpson' stanza is intrinsically musical. Habbie Simpson (1550–1620) was the town piper of Kilbarchan and possibly his music may have influenced Robert Sempill the Younger (c.1595–c.1663), whose poem, 'The Life and Death of Habbie Simpson' (written around 1640) made this verse form fashionable once again. Later, Allan Ramsay, Robert Fergusson and Burns himself were to use this form brilliantly. The poem was printed twice in broadside copies before 1700, and then in James Watson's *Collection of Poems* (1706–1710).

In the magniloquent verse of Wordsworth's *Prelude* or even Coleridge's ballad-stanzas in 'The Rime of the Ancient Mariner', the English poets move at walking pace, telling stories in a gentle and regular measure. With Burns, the verse is equally the construction of personae and visible occasion, but it is also intrinsically something to do with the assumption of common rhythmical possession, internal and external, in voice and bodily movement. Burns's poems seem to inhabit a space that occupies the reader both mentally and physically, and work most effectively when learned by heart and sung or recited in company.

Even when a song moves at walking pace, this internal and external occasion is characteristic. 'Song, composed in August' ('Now westlin winds') shows him out in the countryside walking in the evening with a girlfriend. Burns describes to his lover the places and pleasures of all the birds of field and woodland, lonely dells and riverbanks, ferns, bushes and mountains, and warns of the threatening intrusion men make upon nature's propriety and loving order, when they approach with guns. So, he compels us (and his lover), as the evening is clear and the swallow flies swiftly, let's take our 'gladsome way' and do what comes naturally. Who could resist? The seduction is in his voice as he sings to her, something every actual performance of the song reminds us of. As performed by Dick Gaughan on *Handful of Earth* (Topic Records TSCD419), it is unforgettable: intimate, gravelly and charming. It ends:

> Not vernal show'rs to budding flow'rs,
> Not Autumn to the Farmer,
> So dear can be, as thou to me,
> My fair, my lovely Charmer!

The imagery is of the sexual act, regeneration: showers, flowers, budding and harvest. The brute fact of copulation underlies this most delicate, beautiful, perennial and robust sequence of images. There is nothing lurid or explicit about it. Its suggestion has happened musically, before we have had time to analyze it.

The way Burns uses the Scots language is part of this. When he looks around the dance hall and sees so many lovely young women he could happily be with, he is saddened because not one of them is the woman he wants. This one is lovely, that one is fair, but, 'Ye are na Mary Morison!' And there is all the difference in the world between saying that, with its tenderness, acknowledgement of preference, its recognition of the beauty of the others and his own healthy lust, and on the other hand, saying, 'You are not Mary Morison!' with its categorical emphasis of distinction between Mary and all others.

The pathos of the distinction in the Scots line is brought about by a recognition of how much Mary might share with the attractiveness of the others. The English line emphasises only her difference from them. The music of the Scots line carries that meaning in a way the English does not.

And this is one reason why Burns is often placed at the centre of Scottish literature. Hugh MacDiarmid once growled that Burns was not a great poet but rather a great song-writer. He was wrong. Burns is a great poet precisely because he was a great song-writer. The virtues he possessed as the latter raise his role as the former to a place of unique distinction. MacDiarmid probably knew this, and wanted to prompt thinking about it, rather than have us take it for granted. Such thought might prompt the pleasures of contemplation – but better yet, it prompts recognition and action.

Such a range in matters of tone and form is immediately recognisable: tenderness and satiric scorn, nimble lyricism and the robust speed and skill at turn and counter-turn that characterise song, the slender solitary voice or the invitation a voice might give to be joined in a chorus, are all equally ready within Burns's repertoire. The sensitivity in his love poems is matched by the vigorous velocity of the ribaldry in *The Merry Muses of Caledonia*. Burns's physicality and sense of humour is at its most masculine in this bawdry, songs and poems which were to ignite the plot of Eric Linklater's riotously comic novel *The Merry Muse* (1959). In the novel, a clandestine publication of obscene verses is circulated among the hyper-genteel citizens of Edinburgh at the height of the era of Miss Jean Brodie-like primness and propriety, resulting in unstoppable bouts of profane sexual self-expression and fleshly indulgence of a Rabelaisian stamp. The comedy is in tune with Burns. Both Linklater (trained in medicine) and Burns (familiar with farms) knew that the unavoidable facts of animal life might be a joy to self-conscious, healthily self-indulgent people, especially when tempered by a shared sense of humour. In the pastoral worlds of Ayrshire and Orkney which, respectively, Burns and Linklater knew well, such facts were unavoidable, and both their ubiquity and the absurdities of those who would wish to avoid them generate rich humour. Common humanity and vulgar animality in physical fact and emotional directness is the heart of their unquenchable festivity.

And if Linklater's novel achieves this in his characteristically poised and merciless English and Burns lets loose in a Scots unimpeded by shame, hesitation of embarrassment, there is a Gaelic companion to note here. The anthology, *An Leabhar Liath / The Light Blue Book: 500 years of Gaelic Love and Transgressive Verse*, edited by Peter Mackay and Iain S. MacPherson (2016), complements Burns's bawdry by introducing us to five centuries of exuberant and explicit Gaelic poetry and song. Also, as Mackay and MacPherson say in their introduction, 'One of the strengths of the Gaelic tradition is how many poems (and songs) there are by women'. Burns opens the door to others, doors best kept open or at least unlocked, and that sometimes need to be taken off their hinges altogether.

REVOLUTIONARY HUMANITY

The latent power so palpable in almost all Burns's work is a sense of the revolutionary potential in all humanity: the idea, without irony or qualification, that the world can be a better place, and that people can make it so.

The Complete Songs of Robert Burns are available on a 12-volume CD set on LINN records (CKD). This same quality of musical intimacy inheres to Burns's poems. It is perhaps what has helped make him so popular. There is a sense of dignity in it: no matter how degraded a condition the individual might be brought to because of economic circumstance, Burns's sense of common value raises the currency of human worth and confers the capacity for dignity. A 90-year-old friend of one of my uncles once told me that when he was a wee boy, his father had given him the poem to read, 'On a Wounded Hare' and he had understood, there and then, that this was a poet of good heart – someone he could trust, someone he'd want to have with him, a companion for life. This sense is there in the early 'Epitaph on my own friend, and my father's friend, Wm Muir in Tarbolton Mill –'

> An honest man here lies at rest
> As e'er God with his image blest.
> The friend of man, the friend of truth;
> The friend of Age, the guide of Youth:
> Few hearts like his with virtue warm'd,
> Few heads with knowledge so inform'd:
> If there 's another world, he lives in bliss;
> If there is none, he made the best of this. –

Both tenderness and appetite are entwined in the same character. In 'A poet's welcome to his love-begotten Daughter', Burns's unhesitating approval of the newborn child stands in perennial defiance of social censure of the physical attraction that produced her. In 'O leave novels, ye Mauchline belles' he expresses that physicality in a context of reading contemporary fiction, demonstrating how vigorous sexual desires and intellectual appetite are not opposed to each other but concurrent, indeed competing, priorities of young and healthy men and women.

This balance of cerebral and physical activity is often neglected in the pieties and homilies of aspects of Burns that have become too familiar. 'The Cotter's Saturday Night' is a family portrait that reeks of what Nietzsche would have called 'slave-mentality', an acquiescence in the backbreaking labour and religious conformity that enclosed the minds and bodies of generations of working families, leaving little room or time to develop the questioning intellect or the lusty desires of the body to which young people are healthily inclined. The stoic picture of the working cotter, his obedient family and his daughter's respectful suitor, has been treasured by generations unwilling to question its securities.

Burns's more familiar poems also, such as 'To a Louse' or 'To a Mouse' are so tired-out by recitation that, for many people, their trembling sensitivity has been anaesthetised by generations of bad readings. Yet their sensitivities – to the presence and temptations of physical proximity and to the law-enforced gulfs of social hierarchy – are real and perennial questions in the 21st century. Burns at his most flamboyant joyously dispenses with rules altogether, enacting a gleeful gesture of anarchy in 'Love and Liberty':

> A fig for those by law protected!
> LIBERTY's a glorious feast!
> Courts for Cowards were erected,
> Churches built to please the PRIEST.

Burns's poems and songs are socially engaged, many addressed to specific people, his contemporaries, friends, young women, lovers, fellow-farmworkers. But this should not disguise their literary sophistication. 'Rattlin' Roarin Willie' describes the predicament of a poor fiddler who is thinking about selling his instrument. The different voices heard in the song create a company in which the dilemma of the fiddler is central. We hear the voice of someone looking in on the scene in a pub, where Willie is with his friends. We hear the voices of those friends, we hear Willie's words as he reflects on what his fiddle is worth, and we hear the voice of his wife or lover, welcoming him.

> As I cam by Crochallan
> I cannily keekit ben,
> Rattlin, roarin Willie
> Was sitting at yon boord-en',
> Sitting at yon boord-en',
> And amang guid companie;
> Rattlin, roarin Willie,
> Ye're welcome hame to me!

The meaning of shared conviviality, in drink, music, the company of others, is central. This is the opposite of an egocentric, first-person singular lyric: it is characteristically a work of communal identity, a masterwork in the art of participation.

Singular in Burns's works is the narrative poem 'Tam o' Shanter'. This tells the story of a farmer on a market-day, who, after a long session drinking with cronies in a pub in Ayr, sets out on horseback to return to his wife. In the pub, Tam is seated, comfortable, a central part of a warm world of welcome and support. But it doesn't last.

> Kings may be blest, but *Tam* was glorious –
> O'er a' the ills o' life victorious!

In an age when royal families and aristocrats were being scorned, repudiated and executed, Burns's approval of the common man's superior joy expresses a preference with revolutionary potential. Tam is in no hurry to leave, but he knows his pleasure has ending. Riding home, he pauses at a ruined church where he sees mysterious lights and hears bagpipes, and looking in, is mesmerised by a diabolical dance of witches and warlocks. Insanely attracted by a glamorous young witch, he cries out his praise of her sexually explicit gyrations: 'Weel done, Cutty-sark!' (the name, 'Cutty-sark' means 'Short Shirt' – she's wearing next to nothing, an enticingly brief upper garment that barely comes over her loins). This is the only direct utterance in the poem – all the other voices can be heard through the dexterous rhyming couplets of the narrator but only Tam is quoted using his voice. And it's a wild exclamation of praise and compliment. At this intoxicated cry, immediately, the devilish company rushes out of the ruined kirk to chase him, intending to claim him for the underworld. He frantically urges his horse onto the bridge across the river Doon (the original Brig o' Doon) and manages to clear the keystone, the central stone of the bridge, which the demons cannot pass because they cannot cross running water, being confined to their own local area. However, the young witch in her cutty sark is the most athletic of all and leaping forward, catches Tam's horse's tail and pulls it off, leaving the poor horse with a stump and the farmer with an embarrassing consequence he will have to explain to his wife, when he gets home to his farm.

The poem was first published as a footnote in a book about ruined buildings, with an illustration of the roofless old church that can still be visited in Alloway, Ayrshire, just uphill from the old stone Brig o' Doon. Yet it is a masterpiece of exhilarating and irreverent pleasures, reversing conventional pieties and moralistic homiletics to endorse the simple joys of sitting drinking with friends in an hours-long binge of excess, of the spectacle of sexual voyeurism, of the temptations of the flesh, the lures of enchantment, music and dance, and the breathlessness of the chase, escape, relief and homecoming. It is Calvinism's happiest nightmare.

Burns's authority as a national poet of Scotland is emphatic in 'Such a parcel of rogues in a nation' – an intensely bitter song of condemnation, reflecting on the Treaty of Union of 1707, which leaves Scots people 'bought and sold / For English gold' – and 'Robert Bruce's March to Bannockburn', or 'Scots, wha hae wi' Wallace bled…' which rises from the passion Burns felt for the story of

William Wallace, as he read it in William Hamilton of Gilbertfield's version of Blind Harry's *Wallace*. The force of these songs defies irony or disenchantment, carrying with it a sadness and lasting commitment to non-commercial value and fierce pride in the rights of people to national self-determination.

And Burns's love songs are also still with us, impossible to paraphrase, impervious to ironists. 'My luve is like a red, red rose' brings images of colour, delicacy and temporal presence into contact with those of geological time, the love of a singular couple measuring its value against the time it would take for rocks to melt and oceans to dry. Velvet is too solid a thing to compare with the softness and living vulnerability of those warm petals. The rocks and seas are as palpable and actual as they are abstract, metaphoric and imaginary. 'Ae fond kiss' holds the moment of parting without the indulgence of sentimentalising its singularity. In 'Tam o' Shanter' an image of the temporality of all things is given in 'the snow falls in the river, / A moment white – then melts forever': that word 'melts' is permanently present-tense. It is not 'gone', not 'gone forever'. Burns preserves the precise moment of melting, of vanishing, without letting go of the image of the snow's presence. Burns's writing is characteristically as strong, delicate and almost imperceptibly quick as that suggests. 'Oh wert thou in the cauld blast' is a gesture of compassion, a promise of protection, or at least the effort a good heart would make to be protective of things more vulnerable than itself. Such a principle of care confirms the authenticity of feeling in the secular hymn to kinship, 'A Man's a Man', in which social class and rank are scorned as measures of human value. What it is to be human is not to be measured by class, property or material wealth. Burns always keeps us in touch with the challenge inherent in such a principle of permanent revolution.

27

Poetry in English: from Thomson to Byron

ON EITHER SIDE of Robert Burns were two major Scottish poets writing predominantly in English: James Thomson and George Gordon, Lord Byron.

James Thomson (1700–48) was one of the most influential Scottish poets ever, effectively inventing the genre of landscape poetry and invigorating that of landscape painting in his epic sequence *The Seasons* (1726–30, revised 1744). Born in Ednam, Roxburghshire, he was taken as a baby to Southdean, near Carter Bar on the border, and went to Edinburgh University. He moved to London, where, as we noted above, he became well-known as a dramatist, most famously writing the lyrics of 'Rule Britannia' for Thomas Arne's music in the anti-Jacobite play he co-authored with David Mallet, *The Masque of Alfred* (1740). But as the poet of *The Seasons*, his influence grew. Written in London, it both processes boyhood memories and universalises the landscape it describes. But it arises from Scotland, most unmistakably in 'Winter':

> Then comes the father of the tempest forth,
> Wrapt in black glooms. First, joyless rains obscure
> Drive through the mingling skies with vapour foul,
> Dash on the mountain's brow, and shake the woods
> That grumbling wave below. The unsightly plain
> Lies a brown deluge; as the low-bent clouds
> Pour flood on flood, yet unexhausted still
> Combine, and, deepening into night, shut up
> The day's fair face.

This is exciting poetry: nature is a new subject. The poem's influence was extensive. Thomson started more than he knew. He describes Scotland explicitly in 'Autumn', naming the river Tweed and praising the 'patriot-hero' Wallace. Thomson's Wallace, however, is named with other heroes including Sir Francis Drake, opposing tyranny in a universal struggle. Any particularly Scottish character or landscape, like the poem as a whole, is sublimated into a general context. Joseph Haydn used a translation for the text of his three-hour oratorio.

The Anglocentric aspect of Thomson's work was characteristic of much Scottish writing of the time. James Beattie (1735–1803), professor of moral philosophy and an anti-slavery campaigner, was the author of the popular poem 'The Minstrel' (1771–72) and, anonymously, of a little book entitled *Scoticisms,*

Arranged in Alphabetical Order, Designed to Correct Improprieties of Speech and Writing (1787), itemising the idiomatic Scots aspects of writing that should be extracted from works addressing an English-language readership. Dr Johnson met him in London and liked him well enough.

In a world where British naval power was growing, Allan Cunningham (1784-1842), biographer of Burns and friend of Hogg, Scott and the English poet John Clare, wrote 'A Wet Sheet and a Flowing Sea', a classic anthology poem of sailing ships:

> There's tempest in yon horned moon,
> And lightning in yon cloud;
> And hark the music, mariners,
> The wind is piping loud;
> The wind is piping loud, my boys,
> The lightning flashing free –
> While the hollow oak our palace is,
> Our heritage the sea.

Such bravado in English however is matched by his lament from exile, written in Scots, 'The Sun Rises Bright in France':

> The sun rises bright in France,
> And fair sets he;
> But he has tint the blithe blink he had
> In my ain country.

We noted with reference to Gaelic poets of this era that it would be wrong to see literature in English, Scots and Gaelic as totally independent traditions in the 18th century: there were overlapping priorities, connections and continuities in these literatures, even when many of their readers came from different constituencies. For example, the vigour and vitality of humour and appetite, the unquenchable thirst for life in Burns at his best, or in Alasdair mac Mhaighstir Alasdair or Duncan Ban MacIntyre, equally characterise the works of George Gordon, Lord Byron (1788-1824).

It is worth reminding ourselves of Byron's praise of Burns quoted above, for it applies equally well to Byron: 'What an antithetical mind! – tenderness, roughness, delicacy, coarseness – sentiment, sensuality – soaring and grovelling, dirt and deity – all mixed up in that one compound of inspired clay!'

In *Don Juan*, Byron wrote: 'I am half a Scot by birth, and bred / A whole one…' An Aberdeen boy, he was sent to the English public school at Harrow and then Cambridge. With effortless ease, he took flamboyance to excess. Nobody was more highly spirited. In *Don Juan*, Byron's satiric edge runs sharp through thousands of stanzas, bridging a classic Enlightenment laconicism, a sense of being cool, over to the high passionate gestures of isolated Romantic individualism, in the role of the outcast sinner. He maintains a fierce critical disdain towards the religious subservience of approaching Victorianism. Byron sustained a huge contempt of bourgeois propriety, simpering moralism and the idea that usefulness could only be measured by money. As a poet, he worked hard but his laughter still shreds work ethic and piety.

If the ploughman Burns lived in a world where Holy Fairs and houghmagandie, public boxing, drinking sprees, music and dancing, were familiar enough in the yearly round, aristocratic Byron also exulted in such activities, and like Burns, Byron knew – albeit from a different perspective – how earthy values crossed social strata. But by Byron's time, polite society was even more thoroughly committed to grinding down public festivities in fairs, sports and open air gatherings. Byron was a shock for polite, well-educated readers. He horrified his public. However, his wide and deep popularity was not founded merely on literary fashion and sensationalism, but on a broad understanding of what he represented: ideas about defiance of oppression and the courage of self-determination. In Canto 12 of *Don Juan*, he says:

> I'm going to be immoral, now
> I mean to show things really as they are,
> Not as they ought to be...

Like Scott, Byron welcomed material improvements and new technology. He was privileged and comfortable enough to be able to dissent from the conventions of his class, but no-one could predict the intensity, energy and accuracy of his dissension, the lasting strength of the forms it took, in coruscating verse allied with the earthed values he recognised in Scott and Burns. The spirit of the ballad describing the outlaw Macpherson's rant below the gallows tree, his song, dance and defiance of his murderers and of death itself, was something Byron knew innately. In Canto 9 of *Don Juan* we read:

> Death laughs. Go ponder o'er the skeleton
> With which men image out the unknown thing
> That hides the past world, like to a set sun
> Which still elsewhere may rouse a brighter spring.
> Death laughs at all you weep for...

From 1813 to 1824, Byron was the best-selling living poet. The reading public was expanding, in Scotland and internationally, eager for newspapers, critical review journals, novels, long narrative poems published in books.

The single most piercingly beautiful Scottish song in Byron's *oeuvre* is 'Dark Lochnagar'. Here is the opening:

> Away, ye gay landscapes, ye gardens of roses!
> In you let the minions of luxury rove;
> Restore me the rocks where the snow-flake reposes,
> Though still they are sacred to freedom and love:
> Yet Caledonia, belov'd are thy mountains,
> Round their white summits though elements war,
> Though cataracts foam 'stead of smooth-flowing fountains,
> I sigh for the valley of dark Loch na Garr.
>
> Ah! there my young footsteps in infancy wander'd;
> My cap was the bonnet, my cloak was my plaid;
> On chieftains long perish'd my memory ponder'd,
> As daily I strode thro' the pine cover'd glade;
> I sought not my home till the day's dying glory
> Gave place to the rays of the bright Polar star;
> For fancy was cheer'd by traditional story,
> Disclos'd by the natives of dark Loch na Garr!

The song continues through two further verses, bright evocations of youthful vitality and high company, the pleasures of energy and the affirmation of his native place, then in the final verse, after all these recollections of childhood, youth, and the wild uncontrollable world of potential still to come, now comes the backward-looking poignancy of the adult acknowledging a love still unfulfilled, a wanting, an upward-looking turn of respectful, fearful, wondering recognition of the 'steep frowning glories' still unconquered:

> Years have roll'd on, Loch na Garr, since I left you,
> Years must elapse ere I tread you again:
> Nature of verdure and flow'rs has bereft you,
> Yet still are you dearer than Albion's plain.
> England! thy beauties are tame and domestic
> To one who has roamed o'er the mountains afar:
> Oh! for the crags that are wild and majestic!
> The steep frowning glories of dark Loch na Garr.

That mellifluous, rich, wordy yet fluent, irresistibly onrushing poem is a single coherent statement of love for a particular Scottish territory and affirmation of value in wilderness as opposed to the domesticated and aesthetically sophisticated but energy neutered values of polite and genteel civilisation. The classic tropes of Romanticism are flexed in full presence: the isolated individual, the lonely outcast's retrospective yearning, the mysterious potential for fulfilment beyond knowledge. Byron's brilliance is clear in it. But the rollercoaster, epic satire of *Don Juan*, the arch, poised and posturing narrative poems such as 'The Siege of Corinth' (1816), 'The Prisoner of Chillon' (1816) and 'Childe Harold's Pilgrimage' (1812–1818), all contributed to a distinct European sense of the Byronic personality. And it is notable that Byron, along with Macpherson's *Ossian* and Walter Scott, exerted a far greater extended international influence throughout Europe and further than any they have been accorded in English literature.

The Byronic personality remains iconic: essentially that of the stylish romantic sinner, ultimately doomed but defiant, both passionate and icy, calm and yet sweepingly gestural, overtly expressive, outspokenly opposed to convention, hypocrisy, 'cant' and servile self-abnegation, flawed but heroic.

Byron like Burns thrives on his youth, and, like Burns, died in his 30s.

28

The doctor's expeditions: Tobias Smollett

TOBIAS SMOLLETT (1721–71) was the first major Scottish novelist, a sharp, quirky, funny satirist, relishing the details of the lives of the underprivileged as much as Irvine Welsh in *Trainspotting* (1993). Grotesquerie, bodily functions, compulsions, addictions, corruptions, are depicted in detail in a social context of unstable movement, forces that can cut across desires, unpredictable friendships, inimical individuals: Smollett's world is close to Welsh in these regards also.

He was born in Renton, Dunbartonshire, was apprenticed to a doctor in Glasgow when he was 14, attended Glasgow University, and became a surgeon's mate in the navy, travelling to the Caribbean. In 1744, he settled in London, where Samuel Johnson was pontificating, George Handel was composing and David Garrick was managing theatres and acting in them. Smollett began his writing career with a play, *The Regicide* (1749), but when that was turned down by Garrick, he wrote political satire, trying his hand at whatever he could. But it is his series of picaresque novels that remain most fresh.

The first of these, *Roderick Random* (1748), is a riotous comedy about sailors on the British expedition to the West Indies in 1739–41 and distinguishes Smollett as both a great comic novelist and a great novelist of the sea.

Sample the humour. In Chapter 13, Roderick and his friend Strap reach an inn, sup, and retire, but their slumber is interrupted by 'a monstrous overgrown raven' with 'bells at its feet' which 'gave us several dabs with its beak through the blankets, hopped away, and vanished.' Soon after, an old man enters 'with a long white beard that reached to his middle' and 'a certain wild peculiarity in his eyes and countenance, that did not savour of this world'. He cries 'with a voice that did not seem to belong to a human creature, "Where is Ralph? Where is Ralpho?"' Hearing distant bells, he trips away, leaving our narrator 'almost petrified with fear.'

Strap speculates that the raven must have been the soul of someone damned ('his fears had magnified the creature to the bigness of a horse, and the sound of small morris bells to the clinking of massy chains') and the old man was the spirit of someone murdered long ago, whose assassin evidently was named Ralph. The old man must have been licenced to torture his murderer, appearing in raven-shape. In the morning of course they discover that the old man was the landlord's father who in his senility enjoyed the company of his pet, a tame raven. It's a momentary episode in an episodic novel, but it shows something of Smollett's disdain for gullibility and superstition.

Smollett could be bad-tempered, vigorously outspoken and offensive. He quarrelled with many influential people and fell foul of a senior navy man, Admiral Knowles, who prompted him to produce a fantastic piece of invective. Knowles, Smollett wrote, was

> an admiral without conduct, an engineer without knowledge, an officer without resolution, and a man without veracity... An ignorant, assuming, officious, fribbling pretender; conceited as a peacock, obstinate as a mule, and mischievous as a monkey.

The Admiral sued, Smollett was fined £100 and sentenced to three months in prison, but he had his revenge in *The Adventures of an Atom* (1769), in which a whole world of political authorities is satirised. He never admitted to being its author, for good reason. In it, an atom enters the brain of a citizen and records its impressions of politicians it has known. There's a Prime Minister who every day enjoys his 'posteriors' being kicked by the Emperor while having 'an orgasm of pleasure' as he has his 'perineum' licked by bishops and cabinet-members with bristly beards. Another politician, 'Quamba-cundono' is sent north to put down a rebellion by the Ximians. This is the Duke of Cumberland, the Butcher of Culloden and post-Culloden infamy. The Ximians, the Scots, are to be crucified, eviscerated, boiled in oil and have their livers eaten by southerners. The humour is brutal, rising from a depth of outrage barely controlled by the literary speed, fluent felicity and the hot swipe of Smollett's satire.

A musical play, *Alceste* (ostensibly a classical tragedy), was to have been set to music by Handel but when Smollett offended the manager of Covent Garden, it was rejected. Smollett's biographer, Jeremy Lewis, tells us that no text of the play survives, and that Handel is supposed to have said of Smollett: 'That Scotchman is ein tam fool; I vould have made his vork immortal!'

Works of more lasting value were to come, however: Smollett's translation of Miguel de Cervantes's *Don Quixote* helped establish the great Spanish novel in English-language literary consciousness, and his writing and editing of periodicals engaged him in the most explosive arguments and contentious issues of his time. His *Complete History of England* (1757–58) was revisionary and closely tuned into the moment, the word 'England' standing for the turn to 'Britishness' which Smollett's south-bound career acknowledged.

Anglocentric as that seems, however, Smollett's sympathies remained with Scotland. He was acutely aware of the anti-Scottish prejudices rife in the London where he lived, and spoke out and wrote in protest against the bloody cruelty of the Duke of Cumberland and his troops in the aftermath of the massacre of Culloden. In the *History*, he wrote that after Culloden, the Highlanders were 'either shot upon the mountains, like wild beasts, or put to death in cold blood, without form of trial; the women, after having seen their husbands and fathers murdered, were subjected to brutal violation, and then turned out naked with their children, to starve on the barren heaths'. The Hanoverian victory was 'the triumph of low, illiberal minds, untinctured by humanity' and prompted only 'grief and horror'. He scorned those who approved Cumberland, including the dons of St Andrews University, who elected him to be their Chancellor, and respected the Jacobites, old men facing their execution with noble disdain, or exiles in Europe, poignantly described in *The Adventures of Peregrine Pickle* (1751).

Smollett's most lasting poems are 'Ode to Leven Water', which recollects the arcadian terrain of his childhood, and 'The Tears of Scotland':

> While the warm blood bedews my veins,
> And unimpair'd remembrance reigns,
> Resentment of my country's fate
> Within my filial breast shall beat;
> And, spite of her insulting foe,
> No sympathising verse shall flow;
> 'Mourn, hapless Caledonia, mourn
> Thy banish'd peace, thy laurels torn.'

Various as his writings are, Smollett's novels remain most fresh. *The Adventures of Peregrine Pickle* was a satire on the grand European tour, taking in Paris, where the scoundrel hero fights a duel and is imprisoned in the Bastille, in the pursuit of his true love, Emily Gauntlet (for whom he has to run, as it were). Caricature and speed are the novel's methods, comedy its sustenance, and it offers a panoramic vision of 18th-century European politics and society. *Ferdinand Count Fathom* (1753) was such a success that he gave up surgery. His journal *Travels in France* and *Italy* (1766) is bitterly farcical, critical, shrewd and sharp, an account of a tour he made of the continent in search of better health. His last novel was written in Italy in the last two years of his life, *The Expedition of Humphry Clinker* (1771).

This is the major work, the tale of a family's journey through England and Scotland, with the subjects of sex, national characteristics, politics, religion, social convention and various forms of politesse, all looming into focus and lurching away again. Satire flourishes throughout. The novel takes the form of various letters from the different characters in the group, each with a different perspective on the same event and with differing literacy skills, and includes an encounter with a certain Dr Smollett in London. The method builds up a sophisticated, many-sided picture of human character typified by the commerce between the idiosyncrasies of people and their common needs.

It is a demonstration of what desires bring people together, and a celebration, quick, unexpected, of what constitutes differentiating aspects among individuals, men and women, old and young, their forms of language, social expectations and the economic strata of the nations they come from. Ostensibly an endorsement of the new British state it is arguably an exposé of its impossibility, a careful anatomisation of the incompatible components of the priorities of humanity and the burgeoning imperial ethos with which now-familiar Anglocentric British nationalism was burdening the citizens – or rather, the subjects – of the quite recently and abruptly United Kingdom. Moreover, it is very funny.

Smollett mixes the racy and rancid, the shocking and indignant, the socially committed and humanly sympathetic, the frenetic and the determined. Smollett's 'Ode to Independence' was published in Glasgow in 1773, two years after its author's death. This is how it begins:

> Thy spirit, Independence! let me share,
> Lord of the lion-heart and eagle-eye;
> Thy steps I follow with my bosom bare,
> Nor heed the storm that howls along the sky.
> Deep in the frozen regions of the north,
> A goddess violated brought thee forth,
> Immortal Liberty, whose look sublime,
> Hath bleach'd the tyrant's cheek in every varying clime.

After giving various examples of freedom's resistance to tyranny, this is how the poem ends:

> Nature I'll court in her sequester'd haunts,
> By mountain, meadow, streamlet, grove, or cell,
> Where the poised lark his evening ditty chaunts,
> And Health, and Peace, and Contemplation dwell.
> There Study shall with Solitude recline,
> And Friendship pledge me to his fellow swains,
> And Toil and Temperance sedately twine
> The slender cord that fluttering life sustains;
> And fearless Poverty shall guard the door,
> And Taste unspoil'd the frugal table spread,
> And Industry supply the humble store,
> And Sleep unbribed his dews refreshing shed;
> White-mantled Innocence, ethereal sprite!
> Shall chase far off the goblins of the night,
> And Independence o'er the day preside,
> Propitious power! my patron and my pride!

If Smollett was Scotland's first novelist, or at least first major novelist, he was also perhaps the last writer for whom the vision of an independent Scotland was an actuality, slipping out of living memory and almost beyond imagining. From Scott to Stevenson the idea would be unrealistic and unrealisable, a dream of the unreclaimable past. Byron's commitment to national liberation was pledged to Greece, not Scotland, and the nationality of Thomas Carlyle and John Davidson was not occupied with a desire for political intervention in the British state. But Smollett knew Scotland as the British Empire was only beginning its rule and had some measure of what that Empire was to overwhelm and attempt to destroy.

29

What can this thing be?: James Hogg

JAMES HOGG (1770–1835) seems a more modern writer than Walter Scott. Not to undervalue Scott, but Hogg's major work, *The Private Memoirs and Confessions of a Justified Sinner* (1824) is curiously darker, more terrifying and pessimistic than almost all of Scott's work and it stays with you, questioning, unresolved and hauntingly mysterious. Hogg is the first dark prophet of modernity.

Hogg was born in the Ettrick valley in the Borders. He was a boy when his father's sheep-farm became bankrupt. He grew up as a cowherd and shepherd, learning the ways of the country. When he went to work at Blackhouse Farm in Yarrow he had access to a collection of books which stirred his literary appetite. He worked throughout his life, both in farming and as a professional writer, travelling between the Borders and Edinburgh. A giant statue of Hogg, seated, overlooks St Mary's Loch and by the loch-side, Tibbie Shiel's Inn sits snugly, scene of many a long evening of music, song and storytelling for Hogg and his friends. Tibbie (Isabella) Shiel (1783–1878) was a fascinating character herself, who worked for Hogg's parents before marrying a molecatcher and later becoming an innkeeper. She lived to the age of 95. It's said that her ghost occasionally visits the old inn.

Hogg saw himself in a direct line of connection with Burns, claiming to share Burns's birthday. Certainly, his songs share with those of Burns a popular immediacy and rise from the foundations of an oral culture. His collection of them, *Jacobite Relics* (1819), includes items by Burns, some revised by Hogg himself, so his work as a song collector follows Burns and was followed by Scott. His longer poems, like Scott's, can sometimes be a bit wearying, demanding an effort of attention that is repaid, but comes at a cost. Some of them, however, remain extraordinarily memorable. Most haunting of all, 'Bonnie Kilmeny' tells the story of a young woman who goes missing, then, after a time, returns:

> When many a day had come and fled,
> When grief grew calm, and hope was dead,
> When mass for Kilmeny's soul had been sung,
> When the bedesman had pray'd and the dead bell rung,
> Late, late in gloamin' when all was still,
> When the fringe was red on the westlin hill,
> The wood was sere, the moon i' the wane,
> The reek o' the cot hung over the plain,

> Like a little wee cloud in the world its lane;
> When the ingle low'd wi' an eiry leme,
> Late, late in the gloamin' Kilmeny came hame!

She tells of her wandering through the world and across time in a series of verses that amount to a paradigm of the supernatural traveller's tale.

Hogg himself travelled widely in the Highlands and his accounts of these Highland tours are among the most vivid, humorous and perceptive of many similar works of the period. He is a wonderful storyteller. The oral and the written traditions do more than overlap in his life and work, they enrich and energise each other. Between them and the ghosts that haunt the memory, in the concurrence of songs, poems, short stories and novels, Hogg is a bridge from Burns to Scott. He also points forward to Robert Louis Stevenson, Muriel Spark and Iain Banks. Sinners and innocents, wanderers and locals, sophisticates and demons, unreliable narrators, fighters and wizards, honourable women, good men and bad, all richly populate his fiction. In contrast to Scott's narrative authority and lovely disposition to digression, notes, historical accounts and supplementary materials, many of Hogg's best works are characterised by dramatic intensity and might therefore be more immediately accessible to a 21st-century readership.

His first novel, *The Brownie of Bodsbeck* (1818) opens with one of the most dramatic sentences in fiction:

> 'It will be a bloody night in Gemsop this,' said Walter of Chapelhope, as he sat one evening by the side of his little parlour fire, and wrung the rim of his wet bonnet into the grate.

In that opening sentence, we are given so much: the fearful, good-hearted, reflective character, his foreboding, looking to the future with a sense of looming violence threatening domestic security, and the context of wet weather outside, the warmth of indoors, and their imminent collision. We are led into the historical context of the 17th-century 'Killing Times' of the Covenanters, who were in hiding from the King's army, and Walter finds himself caught between the persecutions of the soldiers and the devious needs of the puritans, and between forms of belief, in portent and superstition, material fact and historical change.

The Three Perils of Man: War, Women and Witchcraft (1822) combines a series of stories with an overarching epic work of fiction with a castle under siege in which characters tell tales to each other. It's a similar device as that used in the 14th century by Boccaccio in *The Decameron* and then by Chaucer in *The Canterbury Tales*, and Hogg cleverly allows the situation surrounding the storytellers to filter into the tensions that arise in the stories themselves. The compendium of short stories of various genres includes the wildly supernatural account of how the wizard Michael Scott split what was a single small mountain into the three Eildon Hills we can see today near Melrose. Scott (c.1175–c.1235) was himself an actual person but seems more of a legend when we meet him in Dante's *Inferno* (1320). The novel is a marvellous phantasmagoria, reaching a happy and buoyant resolution only after a series of massive digressions and interludes. If the earthly wisdom of Hogg has much in common with Boccaccio and Chaucer, his willingness to suspend disbelief in a good tale that stretches credibility gives him a character very much his own.

The Three Perils of Man was followed by *The Three Perils of Woman: Love, Leasing and Jealousy* (1823), a counterpoint in every respect. It begins as a domestic comedy of manners, subverting the proprieties of Jane Austen in a Scottish context, but it changes tack and moves into very different territory very quickly. This multi-layered novel ends with perhaps the most horrifying account of the massacre at Culloden, including lurid depictions of the frozen corpses of women and children. This is very grim writing indeed, a corrective to both the ebullient enthusiasms of *The Three Perils of Man* and to the dramatic poise of Scott's *Waverley* (1814). In *Waverley*, the principle characters, Jacobite and Hanoverian, move slowly then increasingly swiftly and inevitably towards the battle but the horrors of Culloden are not described. It takes place 'off-stage' and only the aftermath is described, leading to the execution of some of the most sympathetic characters and a fortunate outcome for Waverley himself. Dramatically effective as this is, with qualities of pathos and sympathy intensified and the ambiguous nature of the title-character disclosed as he lives on in well-heeled comfort, happily married yet haunted by his former familiarity with the Jacobites and their cause, Hogg must have felt that Scott had avoided the issue of brutality and violence. His novel is an act of redress.

The extremes of these works suggest Hogg's range. The narrative invention of which he was capable is best exemplified in the novel for which he is now most famous, *The Confessions of a Justified Sinner*. Here, two principal narrators present a single story in a way that leaves the reader with the unsettling understanding that no single story, no single point of view, can ever reveal reality. It's an extremely prescient text, predicting modernity.

The 'Editor' of the book presents the 'Confessions' in what we take at first to be an informed and reasonable perspective and style. He concludes:

> I have now the pleasure of presenting my readers with an original document of a most singular nature, and preserved for their perusal in a still more singular manner. I offer no remarks on it, and make as few additions to it, leaving everyone to judge for himself. We have heard much of the rage of fanaticism in former days, but nothing to this.

The 'Sinner' then tells his own story, beginning like this:

> My life has been a life of trouble and turmoil of change and vicissitude; of anger and exultation; of sorrow and of vengeance. My sorrows have all been for a slighted gospel, and my vengeance has been wreaked on its adversaries. Therefore, in the might of Heaven, I will sit down and write...
> I was born an outcast in the world...

Hogg's 'Sinner' discloses his horrible story in such a way that we realise as we turn the fatal page half-way through the book, that everything we have read up to this point simply cannot be trusted, and everything we are about to read must also be questioned. The memoir ends with the Sinner's suicide (or are we to infer murder by a devilish arrivant?):

> And thou, sun, bright emblem of a far brighter effulgence, I bid farewell to thee also! I do not now take my last look of thee, for to thy glorious orb shall a poor suicide's last earthly look be raised. But, ah! who is yon that I see approaching furiously, his stern face blackened with horrid despair! My hour is at hand. Almighty God, what is this that I am about to do! The hour of repentance is past, and now my fate is inevitable. Amen, for ever! I will now seal up my little book, and conceal it; and cursed be he who trieth to alter or amend.

But the novel hasn't finished yet. The 'Editor' returns with the question, 'What can this work be?' and goes on to tell how he acquired the manuscript. Having received a letter from a character named 'James Hogg' (and quoting from a letter that was actually published in the press at the time), he is prompted to travel to the Sinner's grave with some companions, dig up the corpse and find the manuscript of the Confessions. Material fact and fiction merge.

So, indeed, what can this work be? Are the Sinner's 'Confessions' to be accounted for as psychological aberrance or the intervention of supernatural forces? Does the novel subscribe to, or even initiate, the horror genre, or does it open the way to Freud, Jung and R.D. Laing?

The answer, of course, is that it does all these things. It was so far ahead of its time that it was scarcely recognised as a major literary achievement when it appeared. But it was reconsidered in five distinct ways in the 20th century. When the French novelist and memoirist André Gide read it in the 1920s, he saw in it a proto-modernist work of radical perception and narrative invention. Then, when it was republished with a translation of Gide's introduction into English in the 1940s, it was seen as a proto-postmodernist novel with close connections to existentialism, Jean-Paul Sartre and Albert Camus. Then it fully re-entered Scottish literature as both a major novel drawing on folk tradition and literary expertise to open the way towards Stevenson's *Jekyll and Hyde* and *The Master of Ballantrae* in the Scottish literary tradition. It became a direct influence on later writers, from Ian Rankin to Irvine Welsh. It's now also seen as a central text of British novels of the Romantic era.

Gide is often credited with early and prophetic recognition of the quality of the *Confessions*, but we should note that in 1925, in an essay, 'The Literature of Tweeddale', contributed to *A History of Peeblesshire*, edited by J.W. Buchan, John Buchan drew particular attention to the novel, saying that in it, Hogg

> showed an insight into the psychology of religious mania which would have done credit to a modern realist, as well as an unexpected reticence of style.

That observation is acute. The essay is reprinted in Buchan's *Homilies and Recreations* (1926).

The scene in which the Sinner confronts his dark nemesis Gil-Martin on Arthur's Seat in Edinburgh stays in the mind, an essential moment in Scottish literature. It covers that high, shouldering, rocky obtrusion rising over the capital in a dark and mysterious pall. It also indicates something essential about the character of Edinburgh, the city in which Walter Scott was born and lived for important parts of his life, the cradle of banal unionism, yet also, somehow, in Hugh MacDiarmid's phrase, 'a mad god's dream', whose doubleness and layered levels of history, current urgencies, wildness and conservatism are aspects of identity experienced so profoundly later by Stevenson, Spark, Rankin, Welsh and others.

There is much more to James Hogg than the *Confessions* and much more to the *Confessions* than I have been able to indicate here, but this is simply an introduction and recommendation. Like all great works of literature, the more you read it the better it gets. And it lodges its questions like fish hooks, very deep.

30

Divided loyalties, sympathies unbound: Walter Scott

D.H. LAWRENCE, IN *Studies in Classic American Literature* (1923), proposed the principle: 'Never trust the teller. Trust the tale.' Oceanic as his output was, Scott had his limitations. He was a conservative man and an ambitious landowner, a would-be aristocrat whose adult habitat was primarily polite, genteel, urban and urbane. His disposition was to invest in property. Common wisdom is that he approved of the Union of Scotland and England, imagining the prosperity it might bring. And yet his greatest novels measure its consequences and give some account of its terrible cost to the people of Scotland.

The sense of the vastness and dignity of diversity in human character in history and across geography is a lasting pleasure Scott gives us. It arises from the sensibility of a humane and tirelessly curious, hopeful, optimistic, sympathetic man. He was curious and cared about people, most closely his family, friends, colleagues, business partners and dependants. He valued nature and respected virtue. He recognised the worth in human character as much as the vileness of populist mob rule. The characters in *Woodstock* (1826) range from fanatic puritan materialist to credulous, superstitious believer: that range is comprehended by an author neither credulous nor fanatic but committed to remaining open to experience, with an understanding of extremes and the force called up by confrontation. The end of one social order and the decency by which people may try to live their lives in times of violent change are Scott's central subjects. Burns's dates (1759–96) overlap Scott's (1771–1832) in the aftermath of Culloden, in the time of the revolutions in America and France: both men were witnesses to the most violent revolutionary era of the western world before the second decade of the 20th century.

THE PROVISIONAL LIFE

Scott (1771–1832) was born in a flat in a narrow alley named College Wynd, in Edinburgh's Old Town, but his family soon moved to the cleaner, more refined George Square, where he grew up. In 1773 he contracted polio and walked with a limp in his right leg all his life. He visited England, London and the spa town of Bath in 1775–76 but the waters there gave him no cure. As a boy, he spent a lot of time in the wild landscape of the Borders with his grandfather at Sandyknowe farm next to Smailholm Tower, listening to stories and songs. He attended school in Edinburgh and in Kelso, again in the Borders, before going to Edinburgh University to follow his father's profession as a lawyer.

As a teenager in his father's service he travelled north of Glasgow in a company of soldiers whose captain claimed the friendship of Rob Roy. The purpose of the journey was to force eviction. Scott was seeing the Clearances take place at first hand, from the point of view of the law. His sympathies may have extended to the evicted but he was on the establishment side. David Richards, in his book *Masks of Difference: Cultural Representation in Literature, Anthropology and Art* (Cambridge: Cambridge University Press, 1994), says this:

> In the autumn of 1786, Walter Scott spent a working holiday with one of his father's numerous Highland clients. Scott was only 15 and already bored with his work as a clerk in his father's office. [Scott wrote] that he was so overcome by the scene that he had to convince himself that what he saw was real.

But the journey was not all sight-seeing; he was given the task of evicting a sept of the clan MacLaren from the lands of Stewart of Appin.' Richards quotes Scott's account, where he describes the company: 'a sergeant and six men... from a Highland regiment lying in Stirling' over whom Scott was

> invested with the superintendence of the expedition, with directions to see [...] that the gallant sergeant did not exceed his part by committing violence and plunder.

Thus, Scott tells us, he

> first entered the romantic scenery of Loch Katrine, of which he may perhaps say that he has extended the reputation, riding in all the dignity of danger, with a front and rear guard, and loaded arms. The sergeant was absolutely a Highland Sergeant Kite, full of stories of Rob Roy and of himself, and a very good companion.

They found the house deserted. The MacLarens had gone to America, and Scott, in his account, notes his hope that they prospered there.

The immediate economic incentive of the Clearances was to remove people who paid low rents and introduce sheep which provided large profits. The motive came from commercial calculation rather than human sympathy. Those who benefited usually lived somewhere else, in Edinburgh or indeed London. This was the law Scott witnessed and engaged in as a teenager. His pride in being in the company of soldiers, his engagement with the garrulous sergeant with direct (if possibly or partially apocryphal) experience of the companionship of Rob Roy, his relief that no confrontation took place, and his exhilaration at the 'scenery', the terrain and landscapes of the southern Highlands (Loch Katrine is not far north of Glasgow), all speak of Scott's developing character and have direct bearing on the ambiguities and dividedness that pervade and characterise many of his best novels.

In the winter of the same year, Scott met Robert Burns at a social gathering in the Edinburgh home of the Enlightenment philosopher Adam Ferguson. Burns, then aged 27, admiring a print of a painting hanging on a wall on which were quoted unidentified lines, asked for the name of the poet who apparently prompted the artist. Scott's biographer Edgar Johnson tells us that the picture was of a soldier dead in the snow, his dog by his side and his widow with a child in her arms. When all the learned men in the room were stumped, the wee boy Scott was able to answer the question. It was the English poet John Langhorne (1735–79). Scott treasured the memory of the meeting and later recollected Burns's presence. His eyes, he said, were 'large, and of a dark cast' and 'glowed (I say literally *glowed*) when he spoke'. Perhaps some kind of affinity sparked between the poet from Ayrshire visiting the city-folk and the teenager a guest among adults, as recorded in the iconic painting 'The Meeting of Burns and Scott' (1893) by Charles Martin Hardie (1858–1916). The encounter is loaded with portent: did Burns see something valuable to come in the young teenager's aptitude and appetite for knowledge and poetry? Did Scott recognise the self-possession, sensitivity and forthright curiosity of the adult poet, and beyond them a measuring judgement, an intrinsic honesty of character? Another painting, 'Burns in James Sibbald's Circulating Library' (1856) by William Borthwick Johnstone (1804–68) shows the young Scott seated, looking up as the poet enters the room, surrounded by such contemporary literary luminaries as Hugh Blair, David Allan, Lord Monboddo and Henry Mackenzie and others. Both paintings imply a hinterland of imagination and history, the different priorities of poetry, fiction and philosophy, the stratified languages and forms of speech, public and private, the encounter between country and city, the physical presence of these people and unseen literary, artistic and political assumptions and expectations. They convey multiple kinds of understanding and open many more questions than they define.

Scott's literary enquiry into the human fact of divided loyalties had its personal roots in these early experiences as well as in his grasp of the larger political world he was growing up to inhabit, and the bloody conflicts it had come from, not far in the past. For most of his life, Britain was at war with France: the context of international military conflict and the priorities of domestic comfort was the world in which he lived.

In 1790, Scott met and fell in love immediately with Williamina Belsches and although he qualified as a lawyer and practised as an Advocate from 1792 to 1796, Williamina (and her family) rejected him finally in 1797 and she married someone more financially reliable, William Forbes of Pitsligo. Scott, heartbroken, went on a trip to the Lake District, met a young Frenchwoman named Charlotte Carpentier and married her in Carlisle Cathedral on Christmas Eve of the same year.

In 1799 Scott became Sheriff-Deputy of Selkirkshire, a position he continued to hold throughout his life; he was deeply and increasingly connected with the Borders and the workings of the law. In 1805 he entered a secret business partnership with James Ballantyne, the publisher, and in 1809 he became half-owner of the company. Meanwhile, he had become Principal Clerk to the Court of Session, so he was able to earn a living from the law, both in Edinburgh and in Selkirk.

Throughout his youth, Scott was reading widely, translating poems and collecting Border ballads from oral sources and revising them in his own more polished style. He was taken by James Hogg to visit Hogg's mother, who, when she heard what Scott was doing, reprimanded him for taking the ballads out of their oral context and away from song, and placing them between the hard boards of a silent book, from which she thought they would never be sung any more. The ballads were published as *The Minstrelsy of the Scottish Border* (1802–03). He went on to write his own extended narrative poems, at that time the most popular literary genre: *The Lay of the Last Minstrel* (1805), *Marmion* (1808) and *The Lady of the Lake* (1810).

Scott was becoming prosperous. The Scott household in Edinburgh was the centre of a varied, lively, cultural, literary scene. In 1811 he bought Clarty Hole Farm near the banks of the Tweed outside Melrose and extended the four-room cottage into the mock-baronial mansion Abbotsford, where the family resided from 1812. His home life was socially selective but gregarious: he, his wife and family extended hospitality and generally enjoyed popular affection and respect as well as a growing international reputation and innumerable visitors.

The poems continued. *The Lord of the Isles* (1811–15) centres on Robert the Bruce but *The Field of Waterloo* (1815), capitalising on Wellington's victory over Napoleon, marked a downturn. The battle had been fought on 18 June and Scott sailed for Belgium in August. He was one of the first British civilian visitors to the battlefield, but authentic details and immediate observation guaranteed nothing. According to the *Critical Review*, this poem was 'absolutely' its author's 'poorest, dullest, least interesting composition' – though it did prompt a memorable, anonymous squib:

> On Waterloo's ensanguined plain
> Full many a gallant man was slain,
> But none, by sabre or by shot,
> Fell half so flat as Walter Scott.

The vogue for the long poem was finding its most popular proponent in Byron. Scott recognised Byron's genius and the speed and immediacy of his poetry. The best of Scott's poems were historical narratives but after he met Byron in 1813, Scott turned his attention to a different narrative form: the novel. He had started what became his first novel in 1805 but put the manuscript aside and only returned to it now. He was 43 years old, finishing *The Lord of the Isles* and *Waverley* had just been published when in the summer of 1814 he was given the chance to travel around the islands of Scotland, from Edinburgh to Glasgow via Shetland, Orkney, the Hebrides and the north coast of Ireland. He went with the Commissioners of the Northern Lights and their Surveyor-Viceroy Robert Stevenson, lighthouse-builder and future grandfather of Robert Louis Stevenson. Officially an inspection tour of Scotland's lighthouses, Scott kept a record in his journal for July-September and his observations were to inform his novel *The Pirate* (1821). He wrote at the end of his account:

> I have enjoyed so much pleasure as in any six weeks of my life. We had constant exertion, a succession of wild, uncommon scenery, good humour on board and objects of animation and interest when we went ashore –

Coming ashore from the voyage finally he was about to embark on another kind of epic journey, as the author of *Waverley*.

When *Waverley* was published in 1814, a shift in reading preference began to take place. The popularity of the novel was to rise but something more was going on. Something happens with *Waverley* that had never happened before. It marks a significant moment of change in terms of what literature might do. Its significance is essentially to do with the relation between literature and history, not only in the discernable textual interconnections, how writing operates, but in the multiple and often invisible ways in which popular understanding of the relation between history and fiction affects lived experience, the culture we inhabit. These include our understanding of the past, our constructions of the future and our habits of thought in the present.

The comprehensiveness Scott's vision in *Waverley* encompassed the possibilities of wildly contrasting and complementary characters, developing understanding through highly differentiated cultures and languages. It explores various ways in which the genre of the novel might explore moral complexities within the whole complex matter of Scottish national history. The country's immediate past century was still pressing in popular consciousness when the book was published. The novel culminates in the battle of Culloden, which it does not describe directly but presents as a crucial event affecting the lives of all the characters and Scottish, British and indeed European history. The battlefield itself retains an aura in the 21st century. It is a recognised site of war graves and atrocity.

Scott's fiction continued this exploration of the relation between fiction and history. In three novels over the course of his writing the Jacobite story is central. *Waverley* is the first. In *Rob Roy* (1817), published only a few years later, Scott goes back from 1745–46 to 1715 but his subject is really an extension of *Waverley*, deepening and qualifying the same vision of Scotland's history. And we shouldn't neglect the growing popularity of these novels. *Rob Roy* was first published in an edition of 10,000 copies and sold out within two weeks. Scott's readership extended quickly, east at least as far as Russia and west to the United States and beyond.

In 1818, Scott led a team to rediscover the hidden Crown Jewels of Scotland in Edinburgh Castle and was awarded a baronetcy. He was elected to the Presidency of the Royal Society of Edinburgh in 1820 and in 1822 he was central in organising the first visit of the Hanoverian monarch to Scotland. King George IV made a grand tour of Edinburgh in a spectacle of garish pageantry. In the aftermath of such successful public performance, Scott wrote his most poignant novel, *Redgauntlet* (1824). This extended his vision of Jacobite history forward from *Rob Roy*, set in 1715, and *Waverley*, set in 1745–46, to 1765. Perhaps it was an endorsement of his deepening commitment to the establishment, ending with the conclusion that 'the cause is lost forever!' Or perhaps it was a reclamation of what that cause might have been, and, by its vivid evocation, a reminder that the dream never really dies.

In 1826, the failure of Scott's publishers Constable and printers Ballantyne made him insolvent and he dedicated himself to an immense programme of writing to rescue the situation from disaster. His identity as a popular writer had been concealed from the wider public as his novels were known to be 'by the author of *Waverley*' rather than by Walter Scott but at a public dinner in 1827, he made the announcement of his authorship. It had been well-known by many but now he was lionised. In 1828 he began work on the annotated and newly-introduced edition of his collected works, the *Magnum Opus*.

The story of the last six years of Scott's life is told in his *Journal*, posthumously published and edited by W.E.K. Anderson in 1972, a day-by-day account of his life from 1825 through financial disaster, personal bereavement when his wife Charlotte died in 1826, and the experience of his own sickness and ageing. This is a uniquely valuable work about growing old while maintaining an even temper, a generous spirit, a strength of will and disposition to fairness. In his later fiction, in *Chronicles of the Canongate* (1827), the short stories 'The Highland Widow' and 'The Two Drovers' are outstanding examples of his art, succinct to the point of abruptness, yet emotionally devastating. It is as if he knew he simply did not have time to elaborate. These were stories he had to tell with as much intensity and urgency as possible. Other late, posthumously published works are more prolix yet all retain some aspect of his character, a fascination with everything always in evidence, from *The Siege of Malta* to *Reliquae Trotcosienses*, a self-consciously ironic ramble through the contents of his own Gothic home, Abbotsford, its library and artefacts, and therefore, an excursion through the fragments and facets of his own, vast, centripetal imagination.

In the late 1820s, Scott's health declined and in 1831, after a stroke, he travelled to Italy to try to recuperate, returning, still very ill, in 1832. As his carriage approached home, he seemed to be unconscious, but when the Eildon Hills appeared, he roused himself and according to his first biographer and son-in-law, John Gibson Lockhart, Scott became 'greatly excited' and when he saw Abbotsford, 'sprang up with a cry of delight.' In his *Memoirs of the Life of Sir Walter Scott*, first published in seven volumes (1836–38), Lockhart gave a version of the story of Scott's life the public wanted to hear. He was determined to present an idealised picture of the last days of Scott, to give the impression that his characteristic decency was rewarded with a tranquil passing. Doubts have been raised about this. Modern biographies have compromised and complicated Lockhart's idol, and critical approaches to Scott's work have revised his popularity, downvalued it and then extensively revalued his significance. But Lockhart's account is undeniably touching:

> About half-past one p.m. on the 21st of September, Sir Walter breathed his last, in the presence of all his children. It was a beautiful day – so warm, that every window was wide open – and so perfectly still, that the sound of all others most delicious to his ear, the gentle ripple of the Tweed over its pebbles, was distinctly audible as we knelt around the bed, and his eldest son kissed and closed his eyes.

At his funeral procession, from Abbotsford to Dryburgh Abbey, Lockhart tells us, the hearse and the horses halted on the summit of the hill overlooking the Tweed valley, Scott's favourite view: 'The day was dark and lowering, and the wind high.'

Scott's life was committed to provision, his giving – in words, money, love and the accommodation his property, profession and activities encompassed and afforded him – was prodigious. But in his writing the sense of provisionality is everywhere. It's what makes his main characters so often tense and tentative, frequently in circumstances where security is uncertain, hard won and costly. Confirmations are always partial, dependent on political power and time's mortal editing. All is provisional. In Scott's work, this generates a sensitivity to vulnerability, a belief in structures of social law, a resolution and commitment to production and the partial and provisional imbrication of both work and play. Maybe this is what underlies the wry, amiable, attractive wisdom in the phrase he seems to have acquired from Cervantes and used on more than one occasion, 'Patience, cousin, and shuffle the cards – until we have a stronger hand.'

DIVIDED LOYALTIES

Repeated readings deepen the pleasures of Scott's poems. The more familiar they become, the richer the colour and detail in the pictures they paint, and the quicker the movement of their characters. In literature, language has to be working both through movement as it progresses, and through form as it structures itself. The liability of Scott's poetry is felt when the structures dull the movement and freeze the frame. Until you get into the practice, it's a familiar feeling to find one's eyes drifting off to the side of the page and away from the printed words. You haul the gaze back and re-concentrate. Read them twice and the story and pictures sink in and the practice of reading itself becomes a self-conscious pleasure, not to be taken for granted. Reading is different with prose. In Scott's novels, the sentences unfold over long paragraphs and accumulate at their own pace, building vast, layered, labyrinthine narratives in which individual characters are closely described, both physically in their often exotic outward appearance, but also inwardly, as conflicts of sympathy, attraction, courage and fear rise within them. Further: giving the characters in his fiction different voices allowed Scott to write not only in standard English but also in an English that represented the Gaelic of his Highlanders, and in the broad Scots of the Lowlanders. In fact, his writing in Scots is one of the great attractions of his novels, the language itself carrying gestural and dramatic power.

The language Scott employed in his Scottish novels made their texture so much richer than the standard English of his poems. It also earthed the conflicts of political allegiance in an intimate sensing of linguistic disposition. Preference in terms of social justice is connected to the honesty characters have towards their own language. And the novels arise from a lifetime's marinading in the compromised politics of Scottish history and the political context of Scott's contemporary world.

Let's sample a few of them.

Waverley; or, 'Tis Sixty Years Since. That sub-title is crucial, dating from when Scott began writing the novel, in 1805 (as he notes in its first chapter). Scott is assuring his readers that it's 60 years since the Jacobite rising which ended so disastrously for Highland Scotland, and with the passing of time, we can look back on those events coolly, but with sympathy, to write and read a novel about them and try to come to terms with the complex loyalties and long grievances they bequeathed to Scotland and the United Kingdom. The central character, Edward Waverley, is a young Englishman who travels north and finds his loyalties divided between the people he has come from and the people he meets and lives with in Scotland.

The novel begins in England, then takes us north, over the border, and then into the Highlands, before returning south. It moves slowly to start with, so slowly you begin to wonder where it is taking you, but then you begin to meet characters and encounter Waverley in situations which follow each other, folding over each other, before he understands what they mean. He becomes involved in prompt actions and commitments, and is led into circumstances he could not have predicted, and dangers he could not have foreseen. It appears to be a story of an innocent abroad, seduced by novelty, exotic landscapes and the promise of adventure, to which he is susceptible because of an upbringing more indulgent of his sense of fantasy than reality. Yet it takes us into a hard world of politics with consequences, violent conflicts in which choices have fatal results. And when we get to the Highlands, the narrative moves with increasing and unstoppable velocity.

Waverley is officially an officer in the Hanoverian army, but unresistingly travels with friends, companions, a possible lover, in the company of the Jacobites, ultimately joining the Jacobite troops in battle, where, seeing his own Hanoverian battalion on the opposite side, he is driven in anguished self-consciousness to ask what he has done, what he has come to, how to deal with his own divided loyalties. Things are out of his control, as he marches with the Jacobites on London, then retreats with them back to the Highlands, is wounded and drops out, only returning to the story after Culloden has happened. He meets once again his former Jacobite comrades, now prisoners-of-war, witnesses their trial and sees them taken off to brutal execution.

Things end happily enough for him, married and secure in his own property, but the ambiguity of his moral dilemma is not easily or comfortably resolved. Questions still hang in the air. His ultimate good fortune is not a comprehensively assuring conclusion. Far more impressive than anything Waverley does, the behaviour of the Jacobite prisoners in their trial, resolute in the face of their sentence, is deeply moving. The complex oppositions of honour and law, comfort and hard choices, property and poverty, the differences of language, manners, belief-systems and priorities of humour, all build a world of ambiguities, threats and enactments of violence. Cliffs and forests, plunging waterfalls and imminent dangers characterise the landscapes of the Highlands. Waverley is seduced and lost among them. His guides are the natives. He trusts them. In the end, he finds security and home but cannot deny there is more than one truth, more than one story in the narrative he has been taken through and taken us through.

The whole series of Scott's Waverley novels unfolds a comprehensive vision of his nation, geographically from the Borders to Shetland, and historically through centuries. The most successful of his Scottish novels are set around the Borders, from Selkirk and the east coast to the Solway Firth in the west, in the central cities of Edinburgh and Glasgow, and in the Highlands north of Glasgow and around Perth, while his poems take us to the Western Isles, and *The Pirate* (1821) draws from the diary of his journey round the archipelagos of Shetland, Orkney and the Hebrides. But *Waverley* is where it all begins.

This is the confrontation of cultures and meaning in the trial of Evan Dhu, in Chapter 68 (or Book 3, Chapter 21). The climax of the trial is the proposition diffidently made by Evan Dhu Maccombich to find six of his clansmen to give their lives for their captured chief, Vich Ian Vohr:

> [R]ising up, [Evan] seemed anxious to speak, but the confusion of the court, and the perplexity arising from thinking in a language different from that in which he was to express himself, kept him silent. There was a murmur of compassion among the spectators, from the idea that the poor fellow intended to plead the influence of his superior as an excuse for his crime. The judge commanded silence, and encouraged Evan to proceed.
>
> 'I was only ganging to say, my lord,' said Evan, in what he meant to be an insinuating manner, 'that if your excellent honour, and the honourable court, would let Vich Ian Vohr go free just this once, and let him gae back to France, and no trouble King George's government again, that ony six o' the very best of his clan will be willing to be justified in his stead; and if you'll just let me gang down to Glennaquoich, I'll fetch them up to ye mysell, to head or hang, and you may begin wi' me the very first man.'
>
> Notwithstanding the solemnity of the occasion, a sort of laugh was heard in the court at the extraordinary nature of the proposal. The judge checked this indecency, and Evan, looking sternly around, when the murmur abated, 'If the Saxon gentlemen are laughing,' he said, 'because a poor man, such as me, thinks my life, or the life of six of my degree, is worth that of Vich Ian Vohr, it's like enough they may be very right; but if they laugh because they think I would not keep my word, I can tell them they ken neither the heart of a Hielandman, nor the honour of a gentleman.'
>
> There was no further inclination to laugh among the audience, and a dead silence ensued.
>
> The judge then pronounced upon both prisoners the sentence of the law of high treason, with all its horrible accompaniments.

Waverley asks questions about divided loyalties perennially pertinent in a Scotland oppressed by Anglocentric authority. The novel takes its time but *Old Mortality* (1816) is as fast, lean and violent as the best of modern thrillers, dealing in a series of battles, negotiations and further confrontations between fanatics of different extremes and moderates caught in the middle.

In the immediate aftermath of the French Revolution, the American War of Independence and violent rebellion in Ireland, Scott was writing in the period of peace following Waterloo, but the questions arising from extremes of religious beliefs finding expression in military conflict pressed upon him. The fear of revolution was in the air. The historian Angus Calder's insightful introduction to the Penguin edition of *Old Mortality* emphasises this. Scott sets the novel in 1679, when Scotland was divided into three parties: the Kirk Party of extreme Presbyterians (led by Argyll), absolute Loyalists (followers of Montrose), and moderate Presbyterians. Three characters represent these parties in the book: Burley, Claverhouse and Morton. One battle described in the book, at Loudoun Hill, was commemorated in 1815 – the year before the novel was published – by thousands of West-of-Scotland textile workers proclaiming democracy in a demonstration celebrating the escape of Napoleon from Elba. In this, Scott saw nothing of liberation but rather the proximate threat of the mob's decisive action. *Old Mortality* expresses his opposition to fanaticism and belief in moderation, expounded in a story full of tension, colour and urgency.

If intensity characterises *Old Mortality*, one of the delights of *Rob Roy* (1817) is its extraordinary structure. Part 1 (chapters 1–18) is set in England, chapters 1–4 in London and 5–18 in Northumberland, at Osbaldistone Hall: this is about half the length of the whole book. Then in Part 2 (chapters 19–26) we move to Glasgow. Part 3 (chapters 27–36) finally gets us into the Highlands north of Glasgow, with the final chapters 37–39 returning us via Glasgow to Osbaldistone Hall. Each of the three main sections gets faster, more unpredicted and action-packed, leading to the story's astonishingly swift climactic violence and resolution.

Layers of intrigue and conspiracy sweep around and over each other as you read into the book. When Rob Roy himself appears he's a strangely reassuring figure, even when we only suspect who he is because he's often in disguise, intervening in various crises to save or help the narrator, young Frank Osbaldistone, who is recounting his story in 1763 as an old man. We look back with Frank on the events of the tale, which take place in 1715, when he was 21, so there's a multi-faceted quality about the book, reaching back through time with a sense of different political priorities appropriate for different eras, and a personal sense of tragic loss in Frank's elderly state as a widower, still grieving over the loss of his wife, Diana Vernon. Iain Crichton Smith ended his poem, 'At the Scott Exhibition, Edinburgh Festival' from *Love Poems and Elegies* (1972), with these lines: 'I tremble in this factory of books. / What love he must have lost to write so much.' Something of that feeling attaches to Frank's narrative.

Diana Vernon alone would be reason enough to value the novel but she is only one of the two most vitalising women in all fiction presented in *Rob*

Roy. Die Vernon, dark, elusive, mysterious, decisive and self-determined, is complemented by Helen MacGregor, utterly self-possessed and immensely powerful, who commands her own agenda with ruthless authority. She is Rob Roy's wife. They are counterpoints of independent femininity and their actions are always impressively unpredicted and uncontrolled by the men who would match them. Thus the structure of counterpoints, these balanced characterisations and the narrative of the whole novel, as it unfolds, or rises, from bounce to bounce, to third bounce and return, increases tension and gathers suspense. At the centre of the book, the Highlander Rob Roy is balanced against his cousin, the Lowlander merchant unionist Bailie Nicol Jarvie.

Underneath the surface colour and action of the novel, the plot is slowly revealed as the villain Rashleigh is attempting to make possible a Jacobite rising to foil the Protestant ascendancy in the recently United Kingdom. The conflict is presented through characters who for all their vividness and presence are often unaware of the deeper motives and machinations at work. The economic context therefore is not only national, as in, Scotland and England, but rather UK-wide and historical, between progress as commercially class-based and community as familial and clan-based. Indeed, it goes further: Bailie Nicol Jarvie's good fortune comes out of slavery. The world of *Rob Roy* is a global exploitative economy intrinsically sterile, inevitably destructive and impossible to sustain. Over time, it kills native people, devastates cultures and extinguishes languages. At some deep, unspeakable level, perhaps, this was Scott's understanding of what the Union meant. Yet the focus on the hero of the novel's title presents us with the ambiguity of personal experience. Who was he? Who did he think he was? What were his motives and purpose? His character, resourceful, elusive and marvellously sympathetic, is summed up in the closing paragraph, and even there is reported in the words of another character:

> Old Andrew Fairservice used to say, that 'There were many things ower bad for blessing, and ower gude for banning, like Rob Roy.'

The Heart of Midlothian (1818) is Scott's greatest novel, with the widest range of characters and locations, the deepest insights into human motivation, and a compelling story. The novel overflows with characters, social and family situations, intrigues, plot twists, and conflicting national priorities.

It begins with the supposed murder of a child by his mother, and ends with the actual murder of his father by the same child, who returns and fails to recognise his own connectedness to a society which has abandoned him. The Whistler, illegitimate child of George Staunton and Effie Deans, escapes capture and heads west, crossing the Atlantic and taking up with a tribe of native American Indians in the last pages of the novel, never to be heard of again. His fate resembles that of Frankenstein's monster in Mary Shelley's novel, which Scott reviewed around the time he was writing his own novel, and referred to as his favourite book. The social stability affirmed for the major characters at the close of *The Heart of Midlothian* cannot accommodate The Whistler, or the wildness he represents. Scott's recognition of this is courageous. The novel centres on distinct individuals whose stories carry us through, but it also has the power to evoke the threatening growth of mob feeling, imminent civic unrest that rises to moments of violence. This was a social circumstance that Scott knew could be fuelled by political anger, an understandable sense of injustice and the desire to redress wrongs, even if it might lead directly to bloody violence and unknown outcomes. In Chapter 4, the sound of the voices of the Edinburgh protestors against the imposition of unjust law is described fearfully, as the people turn into a mob:

> the hitherto silent expectation of the people changed into that deep and agitating murmur, which is sent forth by the ocean before the tempest begins to howl.

The central drama of the novel is focused on the two sisters, Jeanie and Effie Deans. When Effie's baby (long before he comes back as The Whistler) is abducted she is imprisoned for child murder in the Tolbooth prison, known as the Heart of Midlothian, and Effie undertakes to walk to London to appeal for a royal pardon as she knows her sister is innocent. Here's the climactic dialogue between Jeanie and Queen Caroline in Chapter 37. Prior to this, the Edinburgh mob has killed the officer Porteous, hence the reference to the 'Porteous mob'. But the English and Scots languages in the voices of the characters energise this confrontation as much as the narrative context. Jeanie addresses the Queen:

> 'I would hae gaen to the end of the earth to save the life of John Porteous, or any other unhappy man in his condition; but... He is dead and gane tae his place, and they that have slain him must answer for their ain act. But my sister – my puir sister Effie, still lives, though her days and hours are numbered! – She still lives, and a word of the King's mouth might restore her tae a broken-hearted auld man [her father], that never, in his daily and nightly exercise, forgot to pray that his Majesty might be blessed with a long and prosperous reign, and that his throne, and the throne of his posterity, might be established in righteousness. O, madam, if ever ye kenned whit it was to sorrow for and with a sinning and a suffering creature, whose mind is sae tossed that she can neither be ca'd fit to live nor die, have some compassion on our misery! – Save an honest house from dishonour, and an unhappy girl, not eighteen years of age, from an early and dreadful death! Alas! it is not when we sleep saft and wake

merrily ourselves, that we think on other people's sufferings. Our hearts are waxed light within us then, and we are for righting our ain wrangs and fighting our ain battles. But when the hour of trouble comes to the mind or to the body – and seldom may it visit your Leddyship – and when the hour of death comes, that comes to high and low – lang and late may it be yours – O, my Leddy, then it isna what we hae dune for oursells, but what we hae dune for others, that we think on maist pleasantly. And the thought that ye hae intervened tae spare the puir thing's life will be sweeter in that hour, come when it may, than if a word of your mouth could hang the haill Porteous mob at the tail of ae tow.'

Tear followed tear down Jeanie's cheeks, as, her features glowing and quivering with emotion, she pleaded her sister's case with a pathos which was at once simple and solemn.

'This is eloquence,' said her Majesty to the Duke of Argyle.

The Bride of Lammermoor (1819) is Scott's darkest book, a gloom-enfolding tragedy in which a very black humour, prophetic of the God-bereft world of Samuel Beckett, infects the whole atmosphere. The exaggerations of grand guignol drama do not distract from the pathos of vulnerable individuals, helpless in the face of oncoming events that readers can sometimes see approaching, though the ending is stunningly abrupt. The English novelist Thomas Hardy described it as 'a perfect specimen of form' and Scott's biographer Edgar Johnson said it was 'the most perfectly constructed of all Scott's novels'. This is perhaps surprising, since Scott wrote it while suffering intense pain from gallstones, was drugged on opiates, and, physically unable to lift his pen, dictated most of it through groans and moans. Once recovered, reviewing the book before publication, he couldn't remember a single character or incident it contained.

The horrifying anti-climax of the novel is the culmination of an increasingly awful spiralling vortex of helplessness and confrontations that fail to resolve anything equably. Scott's recognition of tragedy arriving as a result of inflexible commitments and fanatic conviction, cruelty and vanity opposed to love, the pathos of affection torn apart by hostile priorities, the implication that there might have been a better way to resolve the conflicts, is delivered here with dramatic but understated force. Devious lawyer Ashton has impoverished Lord Ravenswood, but Ravenswood's son falls in love with Ashton's daughter, Lucy. Things don't go well. After Lucy's awful descent into madness and death, the two are set to confront each other.

Colonel Ashton, frantic for revenge, was already in the field, pacing the turf with eagerness, and looking with impatience towards the tower for the arrival of his antagonist. The sun had now risen, and shewed its broad disk above the eastern sea, so that he could easily discern the horseman who rode towards him with a speed which argued impatience equal to his own. At once the figure became invisible, as if he had melted into the air. He rubbed his eyes, as if he had witnessed an apparition, and then hastened to the spot, near which he was met by Balderstone, who came from the opposite direction. No trace whatever of horse or rider could be discerned; it only appeared, that the late winds and high tides had greatly extended the usual bounds of the quicksand, and that the unfortunate horseman, as appeared from the hoof-tracks, in his precipitate haste, had not attended to keep on the firm sands on the foot of the rock, but had taken the shortest and most dangerous course. One only vestige of his fate appeared. A large sable feather had been detached from his hat, and the rippling waves of the rising tide wafted it to Caleb's feet. The old man took it up, dried it, and placed it in his bosom.

The inhabitants of Wolfshope were now alarmed, and crowded to the place, some on shore, and some in boats, but their searches availed nothing. The tenacious depths of the quicksand, as is usual in such cases, retained their prey.

Donizetti's opera, *Lucia di Lammermoor* (1835), elaborates Scott's drama, especially in the famous 'mad scene' where Lucy's wedding night ends in her death. On 19 May 2007, I attended a Scottish Opera production in Glasgow where the leading singer slipped and fell on stage in the first act, but agreed to carry on if there was anyone in the audience who could lend her a wheelchair. The whole opera was intensified by this unexpected incident and the climax, with a flashing knife and Lucy's white nightgown lavishly spattered with crimson blood as she wheeled herself around in the chair, singing at the top of her voice, has always stayed in my memory. It seemed a crazily appropriate if unplanned adaptation, as if mixing Scott and Beckett in an Italian musical gorefest. The soprano, Sally Silver (1967–2018), managed to combine the vulnerable volatility of Lucia's psychological state with a brilliantly controlled expressiveness. The piercing flamboyance of the music and the terrible pathos of the story in such an intensely committed production brought the grotesque and agonising character of the story to the foreground. Perhaps this is a kind of confirmation of the resilience and flexibility of Scott's imagination, its openness to interpretation, even when that interpretation is forced upon you, as when dealing with an accident in a live on-stage performance. Like all great writers, Scott always needs to be read in new ways, and always repays your attention.

Just as *Rob Roy* is set at the time of the first Jacobite rising in 1715 and *Waverley* during the second rising in 1745, *Redgauntlet* takes place during a third, apparently entirely fictional approach to a rising that never happens, in 1765.

There are wild things going on in the dangerous borderlands around the Solway Firth, where the tidal estuary comes and goes with such speed that anyone caught on the sands at the wrong moment may drown in a matter of minutes. The specific geography stands for the general atmosphere of risk: quick movement is required, uncertainty is constant, and the novel unfolds through different narratives, letters, accounts that gradually come together in an anti-climactic denouement, the dissipation of romantic idealism. Embedded in the novel is 'Wandering Willie's Tale', a self-contained short story in Scots, an eerie representation of supernatural forces coming in contact with the necessary rectitudes of fiscal and economic authority.

In this story, rational, reasonable explanation covers up the unanswerable mysteries of the hellish world that lies beneath, but its legacies carry on through future generations. The sleep of reason produces monsters. But who wants reason all the time? Scott knew as surely as Shakespeare that monsters have their value.

BRINGING OUT THE BEST IN US

Scott's popularity was international. The later 19th century saw numerous adaptations of his novels for stage as plays, musical compositions and operas. Hector Berlioz composed his 'Rob Roy' overture in 1831 and it was first performed at the Paris Conservatoire in 1833, although Berlioz was not happy with it, considering it too long and rambling. The theatricality of Scott's fiction is acutely summarised by Cairns Craig in his book, *The Wealth of the Nation* (2019): 'the final act of George IV's visit to Edinburgh in 1822 was a performance of *Rob Roy* where the King was accompanied by the as-yet-unannounced author to behold the sources of his own kilted persona. Scott's works adapted for the stage were so important to Scottish national consciousness that Barbara Bell has described them as the backbone of a specifically National Drama that lasted until the late 19th century. Equally, of course, it was as much through theatre, whether dramatic or operatic, as through his novels that Scott helped shape European romantic nationalism.' Craig's observation is keen: 'Scott's characters are presented not as actors in history, but as actors upon the stage of history' compelled to deliver 'their best performance.' Thus on stage in performance and pageants, and in the imposing sculptures placed in various niches around the heights of the Scott monument towering above Princes Street, Scott and his characters have been part of the cultural condition of Scotland since the early 19th century. Like the image of his portrait on Bank of Scotland notes, his presence is ubiquitous and normally unremarked, an unexamined continuity of currency.

The Scottish composer Hamish MacCunn (1868–1916), in *Jeanie Deans* (1894), produced a rich, concentrated version of *The Heart of Midlothian*, packed with beautiful orchestration, intensifying individual characters and dramatic developments. Among numerous songs in the opera, especially notable are Effie's aria of longing for her home while she is locked up in prison awaiting trial on the charge of murdering her own child ('Oh! Would that I again could see / The little cot that sheltered me…'). She protests her innocence and the lyrical tenderness of the song is convincing testament to the quality of her feeling. But there are numerous examples of MacCunn's technical proficiency in the extracts from the opera and the other pieces collected on *Hamish MacCunn* (hyperion CDA66815), including the breathtaking setting of Scott's famous lines from *The Lay of the Last Minstrel*, where a solitary voice begins:

> Breathes there the man, with soul so dead,
> Who never to himself hath said,
> This is my own, my native land!

After which, the full orchestra and chorus comes in ravishingly with:

> O Caledonia! Stern and wild,
> Meet nurse for a poetic child!
> Land of brown heath and shaggy wood,
> Land of the mountain and the flood.

For MacCunn, in London, this would not have seemed merely patriotic self-glorification but rather an affirmation of his national identity in an atmosphere too often characterised by hostility, disdain or even contempt. In Scott's work, pride of this kind is almost always tender and vulnerable. When truly warranted, it's hard won. Yet gloriously affirmative as MacCunn's orchestral setting remains, it was part of a development of defining Scott which led to a reaction against the certainties and assurances he seemed to represent.

Scott remained widely read until three things lowered his status in the first half of the 20th century. Modernism, in its various formulations in the aftermath of the First World War, had no time for him. For T.S. Eliot, Ezra Pound and James Joyce, by far the preferred exemplar of prose fiction was Gustave Flaubert (1821–80), prioritising aesthetic precision in language over the extensive rambling narratives encompassing all they could reach. Also, the contemporary Scottish Renaissance writers of the 1920s rejected Scott for endorsing the Union, for prioritising money-making, and for what they thought of as his compromised class aspiration. For them, Scott was the main source of 'false' ideas of 'Scottishness', the 'Romance' of the Highlands, and generally, imagery made popular for tourists: 'Phoney Bonnie Scotland'. Finally, English literary criticism, defined in the title of F.R. Leavis's book *The Great*

Tradition (1948), undervalued Scott (and to a large extent Dickens), and favoured Jane Austen, George Eliot, Henry James and Joseph Conrad and later, D.H. Lawrence. Under all these assaults, Scott was discredited. However, increasingly in the second half of the 20th and into the 21st century, his work has been reappraised. This has become possible not least through the indefatigable work behind the new Edinburgh edition of the *Waverley* novels, whose editors have done an astonishing service to all who care for literature.

Most of Scott's novels have their inevitable longeurs. Allegedly, there is a copy of *Peveril of the Peak* (1823) in the Victoria & Albert Museum in London, opened to the page, surrounded by a black band, which shows the point at which, while Victoria was reading it out to him, Albert finally died. However, the almost interminable passages challenge the reader to a different kind of appreciation from that to which we have become accustomed since Flaubert, Joyce and Modernism. You have to immerse yourself in Scott's language to get a sense of its movement, its long rhythms and sometimes startling quicknesses.

Even the novels which seem wordy in prospect contain passages of vivid depiction. In *Kenilworth* (1821), a sunny, lavish occasion of Elizabethan pageantry covers over one of the most ghastly sudden murders in fiction (think of a version of *Kidnapped* in which Uncle Ebenezer is victorious and David Balfour goes over the edge at the top of the broken staircase). In *The Fortunes of Nigel* (1822), which is steeped in Scott's knowledge of Shakespeare, Jonson and the dramatists of Jacobean London, the city streets are sensually realised: noisy, smelly, colourful, ever-active, making themselves both refuge and threat.

Quick destruction also ends *St Ronan's Well* (1823), a novel which begins in a world very similar to that of Jane Austen, would-be high society, a domestic scene of characters in a provincial spa-town in the Scottish Borders (including an English Baronet, Sir Bingo Binks). But there are darker motives at work in the rivalry of two half-brothers, and a brilliant characterisation of the landlady of the guest-house (Meg Dods of the Cleikum Inn). A shockingly sudden violent duel concludes the book – not Austen terrain at all. It had tourists flocking to Innerleithen, near Peebles, where you can still visit the wells in summer.

In *The Surgeon's Daughter* (1827), set mainly in India, the villain meets his unexpected end by sudden execution in the form of an elephant obedient to its master, throwing the unsuspecting man on the ground and 'stamping his huge shapeless foot upon his breast' thus putting an end 'at once to his life and to his crimes.' Grand guignol indeed. In *Anne of Geierstein* (1829), though Scott never visited the Swiss Alps, there are unforgettable episodes in the high mountains, which counterpoint the underground trial of a central character at the sinister court of the 'Wehm' – hooded lawgivers delivering absolute judgement.

Not one of Scott's novels is without considerable pleasures, even *Count Robert of Paris* (1831), written when he was ill and near to death. This evidently shows Scott's conservatism in his endorsement of hierarchical social structure and preference for order: Normans and Saxons and women and men keep their appropriate places. But there's an unforgettable chapter in which Count Robert, awakening from a drugged sleep in a Byzantine dungeon, is set upon by a ferocious tiger, which he manages to kill by throwing a wooden footstool at its head. There is also a rather sad Orangutan, referred to as 'The Sylvan', who comes and goes more or less threateningly in the gardens of Constantinople, leaping from the undergrowth or lurking in basements, foreshadowing Edgar Allan Poe's killer ape in 'The Murders in the Rue Morgue'.

Scott's legacy is immense beyond literature, imagining Scotland through visual, musical and theatrical media, in paintings, symphonic music, plays and operas. From the early narrative poems through the great Scottish novels to the later disillusionment of the dark novel *Redgauntlet* and the story, 'The Two Drovers', Scott built up a picture of Scotland, its terrain and cities, its people, the way they spoke, the languages they used, their codes of culture and difference. The central theme of all Scott's work, in Donald Davie's words in *The Heyday of Sir Walter Scott* (1961), is 'the question of the rule of law in a society where loyalties are legitimately divided.' Acknowledge that and you see that Scott's novels explore both the costs and values of action and patience. This is what puts him beside Hugo and Tolstoy.

Reading Scott closely won't guarantee either a positive or a negative preference when you're alone in the ballot-box. He knew the needs, in his time, of practising a social commitment to repel misinformation and regulate blatantly effective forms of misleading mass persuasion. His repulsion from mob rule might be read as anti-democratic but it rests on an understanding of what violence fanaticism leads to, how a one-eyed perspective helps nothing sensitive. His writing itself is an endorsement of better and broader political self-knowledge among people, generally. He knew as deeply as we should that if you say certain things to certain people in certain ways, you'll bring out the worst in them. So the lasting question in all his work remains, how to bring out the best?

The epigraphs to individual chapters in his novels were frequently left unattributed and that to Chapter 13 of *Rob Roy* seems to have been composed by Scott himself. It suggests the fatal threat of a pervasive prioritisation of certain cultural values at the expense of others, and how the idea of 'progress' might be mistaken:

> Dire was his thought, who first in poison steep'd
> The weapon form'd for slaughter – direr his,
> And worthier of damnation, who instill'd
> The mortal venom in the social cup,
> To fill the veins with death instead of life.

It is almost as if Scott is indicating a silent, unnoticed, creeping mortality, a poison that might come to any mortal creature and to particular nations in time, through social historical change, enforced by law and arms, that might seek to extinguish a culture completely, and all its inhabitants. Scott's work witnessed and engaged such a conflict. How we interpret it is part of our engagement in the same struggle.

NOTE
The best place to start further exploration of the world of Walter Scott is the Edinburgh University Walter Scott Digital Archive: http://www.walterscott.lib.ed.ac.uk/home.html. Just about everything that encompasses Scott's life and works and leads out to almost everywhere else not included in the Archive itself, is here. It begins with a page on the life and work of James C. Corson and the Scott material he bequeathed to Edinburgh University Library. This is followed by pages devoted to each of Scott's novels, narrative poems and major prose works, with synopses, histories of composition and publishing and their original reception by public and critics. Then a full Scott biography is followed by a database of visual material relating to Scott and his work. There are further sections on events, new publications and various archived written and visual material and a collection of links to over 150 websites or pages devoted to aspects of Scott.

31

Domestic politics, fanatic extremes: John Galt

THE FICTION OF John Galt (1779–1839) is both geographically grounded and historically specific to the period from around 1760 to the 1820s, with the exception of *Ringan Gilhaize* (1823), a violent novel of action, religious extremism and the Covenanters, set mainly in the 1680s, a corrective both to Scott's *Old Mortality* (1816) and Hogg's *Brownie of Bodsbeck* (1818). Galt's self-righteous 'justified sinner' *Ringan Gilhaize* foreshadows Hogg's deluded fanatic in the *Confessions* (1824). Ringan, if he sees himself as an agent of God's justice, is powerfully motivated by desire for revenge on the murderers of his wife and children, the Royalist troops he dedicates himself to hunting down.

The story takes years and tests the hero's endurance and resourcefulness until, at the Battle of Killiecrankie (1689), he finally enters history by killing Claverhouse, leader of the Royalist forces. The moral ambiguities Galt explores in the novel, based on the question of religious conviction and human justice, are close to those at the forefront of post-Civil War American western films like John Ford's *The Searchers* (1956) or Clint Eastwood's *The Outlaw Josey Wales* (1976). In the former, racist prejudice against native Americans, and in the latter, the accident of political difference brutally defined in the American Civil War, are profoundly involved in the choices confronting the heroes. Similarly, it's the self-justification conferred by religious authority that helps Ringan in his blood-drenched quest, but his humanity is both humbling in reflective passages and exciting in the action scenes.

The Ayrshire Legatees (1820–21) and *The Provost* (1822) are very different works. The former recounts the journey to London of Dr Pringle, a minister of 'Garnock' in Scotland, and his family, to accept a legacy. The latter is set in 18th-century Scotland, a memoir of a small-town politics blending the precise detail of social description with a psychological portrayal of the central character with subtlety, sympathy and irony. It was a best-seller in its time. Both exemplify Galt's understanding of legal and social priorities and principles, the liabilities of human temptation and the virtues of a balanced appraisal of the necessary priorities of law and the inevitable contingencies of society.

In the later 1820s, Galt was a company manager in Canada, founding the city of Guelph, Ontario. *Lawrie Todd* (1830) and *Bogle Corbett* (1831) are both set in Canada, and like John Buchan's *Sick Heart River* (1941) might be read in the context of that country's literature. Galt's later works, *The Member* and *The Radical* (both 1832) are novels about the politics of parliamentary reform, the first novels to focus on the foibles and fumbles, the humour and waste, of people in local and domestic situations of political ambition. These people are idealistic or selfish, propelled by their own rhetoric or scrambled by self-generated confusions and ambitions that breed chaos. Galt's depiction of them is both satirical and sympathetic. The distinction of these novels lies partly in this balance of sympathy and irony in their presentation of the work of politicians. Galt acknowledges that political work has to be undertaken responsibly but he also has a sense of the absurdity, weaknesses and vulnerability of the people undertaking it.

In the long aftermath of the Union of 1707, Scots continued to look after their own institutions of religion, law and education. If national political control was exiled to London, local politics remained in towns and city councils. Galt's work was to restore the experience of local politics to the provenance of literature, through his intimate experience and knowledge of its workings. His most ambitious novel is *The Entail* (1823), crossing three generations, tracing the evolution of an inheritance (the 'entail') through an extended theatre of strong, colourful characters. It has moments of surreal humour and crazy absurdity, episodes and confrontations of grating Dostoevskian strangeness. The prioritisation of materialism sometimes cuts everything away except the worst aspects of greed and self-promotion. Characters stand out like grotesques on a shadowy stage, or figures in expressionist cinema. Madness seems near.

In an episode reminiscent of a Marx Brothers film, a funeral procession in Book I, Chapter 9, sets out to the graveyard so well-serviced with food and drink that the coffin is left behind; after returning for the corpse, a further generous service of food and drink is required, and 'with a degree of less decorum than in their former procession' the mourners set out again, a number of them encountering such severe weather that they 'either lay down of their own voluntary accord on the road, or were blown over by the wind.' Galt's long-faced style masks the drunkenness and opens the occasion to grotesque hilarity.

Yet in Book II, Chapter 10, there is a description of another funeral, that of Charles Walkinshaw, Claud's son and Walter's father, which conveys a very different feeling:

> When the regular in-door rites and ceremonies were performing, and the body had, in the meantime, been removed into the street, and placed on the shoulders of those who were to carry it to the grave, Claud took his grandson by the hand, and followed at the head, with a firmly knotted countenance, but with faltering steps.
>
> In the procession to the church-yard no particular expression of feeling took place; but when the first shovelful of earth rattled hollowly on the coffin, the little boy, who still held his grandfather by the finger, gave a

shriek, and ran to stop the grave-digger from covering it up. But the old man softly and composedly drew him back, telling him it was the will of God, and that the same thing must be done to every body in the world.

'And to me too?' said the child, inquiringly and fearfully.

'To a' that live,' replied his grandfather; and the earth being, by this time, half filled in, he took off his hat, and looking at the grave for a moment, gave a profound sigh, and again covering his head, led the child home.

When, in Book II, Chapter 32, one potential heir is advised that a quarrel with the patriarch may be prejudicial to his interests, he curses the word:

> Your father seems to think that human beings have nothing but interests; that the heart keeps a ledger, and values everything in pounds sterling. Our best affections, our dearest feelings, are with him only as tare [a weight of commercial value]...

He is countered with the question, what have affections to do with the counting-house: 'I thought you and he never spoke of any thing but rum puncheons and sugar cargoes.' The reference is explicit to the fortunes built on the West Indian slave trade plantations, and the novel is carefully contextualised in the wake of the Jacobite 'Rebellion' (the word is used in Book II, Chapter 23), in the era of the American and French revolutions and the post-Napoleonic peace in which the last chapter ends, in 1815.

In this world of fierce international commercial economic competition and war, familiar signals of Scottishness are treated with satirical disdain. When one character proposes to visit 'Glengael' the language becomes Ossianic, rhapsodic and unbelievable: 'The spirits of my fathers hover in the silence of those mountains, and dwell in the loneliness of the heath. A voice within has long told me, that my home is there, and I have been an exile since I left it.' (Book III, Chapter 9). When a group of the characters embark on a sailing excursion around the western isles to Orkney and Shetland, it all ends in disaster, shipwreck and death. These melodramatic parts of the last third of the novel seem to have been written hastily at the publisher's request, but Galt effectively contrasts their clichéd Romanticism with the commercial materialism of his main narrative.

The most powerfully Scottish quality here is evident in the language of his characters, especially 'the Leddy', the matriarch who develops in the first Book and becomes the central character, presiding over all the others till her death, at a ripe age, at the end of Book III. Her final confrontation with the self-serving lawyer Mr Pilledge is a moment of great dramatic satisfaction (Book III,

Chapter 14). After having been told with pedantic insistence and supercilious authority by the lawyer that her late husband had intended the estate to go to 'the heirs-male of his sons' or other men in the family line, it is gratifying to see this self-possessed and powerful woman round on him:

> '...As yet I hae had but ae law-suit, and I trow it was soon brought, by my own mediation, to a victory; but it winna be lang till I hae another; for if Milrookit does na consent, the morn's morning, to gie up the Kittlestonheugh, he'll soon fin' again what it is to plea wi' a woman o' my experience.'

Pilledge was petrified; he saw that he was in the hands of the Leddy, and that she had completely overreached him.

In Galt's novel, human worth needs to be tough to get what is rightfully its own, and the strength of the Leddy is impressive in contrast to the sympathy extended to Watty the daftie, whose set-piece scene is a court-trial to consider his mental capacity (again, humour and pathos are in careful counterpoint). Watty is a better person than his brother George, the eminently reasoning, judicious businessman. Galt's ability to see these people in the round, caught up in their interwoven trajectories, moving in a circumscribed geography in Ayrshire and south Glasgow, is sustained and impressive. His realism is hard-headed, his compassion is tough-minded, his humour contagious but tainted with the sense that chaos and catastrophe are never far away. The Leddy reminds one character of the value of self-righteous intervention that Ringan Gilhaize would have agreed with:

> For sure am I, had no I ta'en the case in hand, ye might hae continued singing Wally, wally, up yon bank, and wally, wally, down yon brae, a' the days o' your tarrying in the tabernacles o' men.
> (Book III, Chapter 29)

Galt was prolific, not only as a novelist but also a poet. 'The Selfish' is one of those poems that retains perennial relevance.

> There is a death, an apathy profound
> As that of those who in the churchyard lie,
> Although the sepulchres be above ground,
> Where rot these moral morts unconsciously.
> They rot with vermin, dead as clod of clay,
> And greedy sycophants, heart-eating worms,
> Forever gnaw on them, forever they

> To all that crawl or creep or coil or prey
> Remain insensible; not fear informs
> Their cold residuum, – if a man may call
> That thing a residue, which never knew
> One throb for others; wrapt in cerements all,
> In shrouds of selfishness they cannot rue
> The loathesomeness of their estate and hue.

This is the work of a writer who knows intimately the world of callous greed and vanity familiar among certain bankers, politicians, and senior managers of various institutional organisations, and whose compassion sees them so wanting in a world more human than that maintained behind their pillars and closed doors.

In the *Sunday Herald* of 9 June 2002, the journalist Ian Bell wrote this:

> Coleridge believed that Galt was 'second only to Sir W. Scott in technique'. Certainly they shared an ambivalence towards the disappearance of the old Scotland.

But in his exploration of local politics, perhaps Galt is more our contemporary: 'Sometimes he is hard going, a writer with important things to say and a leisurely way of saying them. Grant him the effort he deserves, however, and the Scotland he portrays with such assurance begins to seem very familiar indeed.' Galt has dropped from popular currency even more than Walter Scott but he is an important novelist and warrants reappraisal.

32
The Tavern Sages and
Ferrier, Baillie, Brunton, Oliphant, Cockburn and Reid

WALTER SCOTT AT his most genteel was the legacy taken up by his son-in-law, John Gibson Lockhart (1794–1854), who edited the influential (Tory) *Blackwood's Magazine* with John Wilson ('Christopher North', 1785–1854), caricaturing contemporary literary figures and establishing a popular series of critical reviews to counterpoint the politically-opposed (Whig) journal, the *Edinburgh Review*. Lockhart became embroiled in the Edinburgh literary establishment and together with Wilson, satirised various figures in the pages of the magazine, most centrally James Hogg. It's an unattractive story of literary exploitation. Hogg saw Wilson and Lockhart as friends and supporters but while they evidently enjoyed his company, they considered him a country buffoon. The satires published in *Blackwood's* demonstrate this and have a cruelty about them, yet the comedy of the 71 pieces collected as the *Noctes Ambrosianae* (1822–35) is riotous enough to confirm Hogg's willing participation.

The scene is Ambrose's tavern in Edinburgh, the characters include the Shepherd (Hogg), the English Opium-Eater (Thomas de Quincey), North (Wilson), Tommy Tickler (Wilson's uncle, Robert Sym) and others, and the contest between the genteel and the vulgar is the crux of the humour, demonstrated in Anglified language and the subject of food:

> SHEPHERD: Oh, sir! but I'm unco fond o' the English accent. It's like an instrument wi' a' the strings o' silver, – and though I canna help thinkin' that you speak a wee owre slow, yet there's sic music in your voice, that I'm perfectly enchanted wi' the soun', while a sense o' truth prevents me frae sayin' that I aye a'thegether comprehend the meaning, – for that's aye, written or oral alike, sae desperate metapheesical. – But what soup will you tak, sir? Let me recommend the hotch-potch.
> ENGLISH OPIUM-EATER: I prefer vermicelli.
> SHEPHERD: What? Worms! They gar me scunner, – the vera luk o' them. Sae, you're a worm-eater, sir, as weel's an Opium-eater?
> ENGLISH OPIUM-EATER: Mr Wordsworth, sir, I think it is, who says, speaking of the human being under the thraldom of the senses, –
> SHEPHERD: I beseech ye, my dear sir, no to be angry sae sune on in the afternoon. There's your worms – and I wuss you muckle gude o' them – only compare them – Thank, you Mr Tickler – wi' this bowl-deep

trencher o' hotch-potch – an emblem of the hail vegetable and animal creation.
TICKLER: Why, James, though now invisible to the naked eye, boiled down as they are in baser matter, that tureen on which your face has for some minutes been fixed as gloatingly as that of a Satyr on a sleeping Wood-nymph, or Pan himself on Matron Cybele, contains, as every naturalist knows, some scores of snails, a gowpen-full of gnats, countless caterpillars, of our smaller British insects numbers without number numberless as the sea-shore sands –
SHEPHERD: No at this time o' year, you gowk.

When the Opium-Eater pontificates about Robert Burns, the Shepherd interrupts him: 'Dinna abuse Burns, Mr De Quinshy. Neither you nor ony ither Englishman can thoroughly understaun three sentences o' his poems – ' The Opium-Eater protests: 'I grant that most of them are uncouth and barbarous, to English ears – even to those of the most accomplished and consummate scholars.' And the Shepherd interrupts again to ask pointedly: 'What's a gowpen o' glaur?' and he answers his own question: 'It's just tua neif-fu's o' clarts.' He concludes that

> kennin' something o' a language by bringin' to bear upon't a' the united efforts o' knowledge and understaunin' – baith first-rate – is ae thing, and feelin' every breath and every shadow that keeps playin' owre a' its syllables, as if by a natural and born instinct, is anither –

Hogg wins the argument but the prevailing sense remains of the superiorism of English and the Anglicised. Lockhart's Tory and Christian biases left a long legacy and were most powerfully scorned in the 20th century by D.H. Lawrence. When Lawrence heard in the 1920s that his friend the novelist Catherine Carswell was going to write a new biography of Burns, he wrote to her husband Donald and commended her, noting the need for a different view of the poet than the one commonly held:

> I read just now Lockhart's bit of a life of Burns. Made me spit! Those damned middle-class Lockharts grew lilies of the valley up their arses, to hear them talk... My word, you can't know Burns unless you hate the Lockharts and all the estimable *bourgeois* and upper classes as he really did – the narrow-gutted pigeons. Don't for God's sake, be mealy-mouthed like them – No, my boy, don't be on the side of the angels, it's too lowering.

Lockhart, alas, was all too determined to be on the side of the angels. A more complex writer was Susan Ferrier (1782–1854), whose novels *Marriage* (1818),

The Inheritance (1824) and *Destiny* (1831) were admired by Scott and evidently effected a bridge from his northern context to that of Jane Austen's southern one. Like Austen, Ferrier was genteel and never married. Scott described her as 'full of humour and exceedingly ready at repartee'. Later, though, she became a devout member of the Free Church, stopped writing fiction and repented of what she now considered her frivolous career as a novelist. The angels got her in the end.

Marriage is centred in the domestic and interior world inhabited by Juliana Glenfern, revealing the conditions of women in this patriarchal society. It is memorably funny and begins like this:

> 'Come hither, child,' said the old Earl of Courtland to his daughter, as, in obedience to his summons, she entered his study; 'come hither, I say; I wish to have some serious conversation with you: so dismiss your dogs, shut the door, and sit down here.'
>
> Lady Juliana rang for a footman to take Venus; bade Pluto be quiet, like a darling, under the sofa; and, taking Cupid in her arms, assured his lordship he need fear no disturbance from the sweet creatures, and that she would be all attention to his commands – kissing her cherished pug as she spoke.
>
> 'You are now, I think, seventeen, Juliana,' said his Lordship, in a solemn important tone.
>
> 'And a half, papa.'
>
> 'It is therefore time you should be thinking of establishing yourself in the world. Have you ever turned your thoughts that way?'
>
> Lady Juliana cast down her beautiful eyes, and was silent.

His Lordship having no fortune to bestow, Juliana is promised to be married to an 'odious Duke' but by the opening of Chapter Two, she is eloping with the dashing Captain Henry Douglas and travels to his Highland castle: 'Many were the dreary muirs, and rugged mountains, her Ladyship had to encounter, in her progress to Glenfern castle...' Her companion 'expatiated... on the wild but august scenery that surrounded his father's castle' but then the scene is revealed:

> a tall thin grey house... A small sullen looking lake... a few dingy turnip fields... A dreary stillness... 'What a scene!' at length Lady Juliana exclaimed, shuddering as she spoke; 'Good God, what a scene! How I pity the unhappy wretches who are doomed to dwell in such a place! And yonder hideous grim house; it makes me sick to look at it. For heaven's sake, bid him drive on... what is the name of that house?'

And the driver replies: 'Hoose!... ca' ye thon a hoose? Thon's Glenfern Castle!'

As Val McDermid says, in her book *My Scotland* (2019), Ferrier shares social satire and sharp observation with Jane Austen but she has a broader canvas: 'her servants had personalities and a role to play within the story.'

Ferrier's two later novels continue the vein of forthright satire and ironic comment. If the scenario in her novels resembles that of Austen, her robustness and clarity, her eye for wild and wayward angles of approach, also suggest the almost surreal humour of Smollett, and point forward to that of Eric Linklater. The irreverence of her humour is suggested by the bold and cheeky first line of *The Inheritance*, with its eyebrow raised over Austen's first novel, which had been published only five years earlier, in 1813: 'It is a truth, universally acknowledged, that there is no passion so deeply rooted in human nature as that of pride.'

In *Literature and Oatmeal*, William Power recognises Ferrier's virtues and limitations succinctly:

> Many of her characters, like Uncle Adam, Mrs Violet Macshake, the egregious Highland minister in *Destiny*, and the inimitable Miss Pratt, are masterpieces of humorously satirical portrayal, and her pungently realistic picture of Highland life in *Destiny* is a salutory corrective of romantic rubbish about chiefs and retainers. Yet her serious young ladies and gentlemen are spouters of moral sentimental platitudes, and in her own reflections and comments she indulges in the flattest kind of pietistic pulpiteering.

Compared to Jane Austen, Power notes, Ferrier is deficient in balance, perspective, essential wisdom and a sense of reality.

Contemporary with Ferrier were the Lanarkshire-born playwright Joanna Baillie (1762–1851) and the Orcadian Mary Brunton (1778–1818), the titles of whose novels *Self-Control* (1811) and *Discipline* (1814) suggest her chief co-ordinate points. For both, Christian morality leads the way but humour leavens the priorities of proto-feminism, the need to recognise and protest against the prevalent conditions of society. Indeed, there is a distinct tradition that runs forward from Ferrier, Baillie and Brunton to Margaret Oliphant, Catherine Carswell, Dot Allan, Nan Shepherd, Elspeth Davie, Joan Lingard, Janice Galloway and A.L. Kennedy.

Carolina Oliphant, Lady Nairne (1766–1845) came from a staunch Jacobite family. Her father and grandfather both were with Prince Charles Edward Stuart in the rising of 1745 and were consequently exiled from Scotland. Her songs were memorised and sung throughout the world, including 'The Land o' the Leal', 'Wi' a Hundred Pipers' and the Jacobite favourite 'Will ye no' come back again?' addressed to the Prince 'over the water'. After Walter Scott masterminded King George IV's 1822 visit to Edinburgh, some Jacobite properties and positions, which had been in forfeit after Culloden, were restored, and Lady Nairne's husband was instated to the family Barony.

Looking back over the whole complex period from the Enlightenment to the Romantic era, the memoirs of Lord Cockburn (1779–1854), published as *Memorials of His Time* (1856), and his *Journal* (1874), reflect on the Edinburgh of Scott and his contemporaries, its characters, contexts and contradictions, with forensic precision and infectious relish. They remain among the richest accounts of the era. Yet there was another growing movement in this period. The fiction, plays, poems and songs represent this to some extent, but it was taking explicit form in the world at large, through and beyond the literary works and playful shenanigans of the relatively well-off.

Marion Kirkland Reid (1815–1902) was one of the earliest explicitly feminist writers, whose book, *A Plea for Woman* (1843) was especially influential in America, where it was reprinted in 1847, 1848, 1851 and 1852 under the title *Woman, Her Education and Influence*. After her husband Hugo's death in 1872, she lived with their daughter in Hammersmith, London, where she had attended the World's Anti-Slavery Convention in 1840, outraged at the exclusion of female American delegates. This was what prompted the polemical *Plea for Woman*. The book argues for emancipation in the context of both patriarchal domesticity and conventional Christianity. Chapter Five begins with a quotation from Talleyrand: 'To see one half of the human race excluded by the other from all participation of government, is a political phenomenon which, according to abstract principles, it is impossible to explain.'

Reid says that the disadvantages under which women are currently suffering are threefold: (1) Want of equal civil rights. (2) Enforcement of unjust laws. And (3) Want of means for obtaining a good substantial education. She states her case:

> The ground on which equality is claimed for all men is of equal force for all women; for women share the common nature of humanity, and are possessed of all those noble faculties which constitute man a responsible being, and give him a claim to be his own ruler, so far as is consistent with order, and the possession of the like degree of sovereignty over himself by every other human being. It is the possession of the noble faculties of reason and conscience which elevates man above the brutes, and invests him with this right of exercising supreme authority over himself. It is more especially the possession of an inward rule of rectitude, a law written on the heart in indelible characters, which raises him to this high dignity, and renders him an accountable being, by impressing him with the conviction that there are certain duties which he owes to his fellow-creatures. Whoever possesses this consciousness, has also the belief that the same convictions of duty are implanted in the breast of each member

of the human family. He feels that he has a right to have all those duties exercised by others towards him, which his conscience tells him he ought to exercise towards others; hence the natural and equal rights of men.
We do not mean to enter into the question of the claim of all men to equal rights, but simply to state the foundation on which that claim rests, and to show that the first principles on which it does rest apply to all mankind, without distinction of sex.

Reid's book is not fiction but it is a masterpiece of controlled literary rhetoric and heartfelt passion and, as such, it warrants full notice in any literary account of the era.

33

Victorian Sages: from Thomas Carlyle to Margaret Oliphant

AMONG A NUMBER of intellectually influential writers of the 19th century, generally known as the Victorian Sages, J.S. Mill and John Ruskin both had important connections to Scotland, while beside them Matthew Arnold contributed to a burgeoning sense of British cultural identity. Central to this group was Thomas Carlyle (1795–1881), whose essay, 'Signs of the Times' (1829), is a major protest against Victorian utilitarianism:

> The truth is, men have lost their belief in the Invisible, and believe, and hope, and work only in the Visible... Only the material, the immediately practical, not the divine and spiritual, is important to us.

Virtue, Carlyle says, has become 'finite, conditional... a calculation of the Profitable': 'Our true Deity is Mechanism.' Carlyle opposes the rules of 'Profit and Loss' by asserting that greatness in mankind is never mechanical, always dynamic, and submission to the mechanical makes human beings inferior. This is how he ends the essay:

> On the whole, as this wondrous planet, Earth, is journeying with its fellows through infinite Space, so are the wondrous destinies embarked on it journeying through infinite Time, under a higher guidance than ours. For the present, our astronomy informs us, its path lies towards *Hercules*, the constellation of *Physical Power*; but that is not our most pressing concern. Go where it will, deep HEAVEN will be around it. Therein let us have hope and sure faith.

The moral authority of Carlyle's stance, the clotted densities of his style, his advocacy of hard work, deep belief and commitment, were instilled from his upbringing in the small border market town of Ecclefechan. Local schools, church and Edinburgh University encouraged his conviction and he devoted himself to opposing the mechanistic preferences of his era. However, he equally opposed free-thinking atheists and sceptics like Voltaire and Rousseau. If their questioning had helped undermine corrupt authoritarian hierarchy in France, all well and good, but Carlyle didn't believe that this had created a better society. By contrast, in Germany as it then was, before unification, Carlyle saw an extensive country of small, rural kingdoms and city-states, where independence of thought, self-sufficiency and neighbourliness were paramount.

His convictions were founded on extensive historical research. Through voluminous studies of the French Revolution, Oliver Cromwell and Frederick the Great, he built up a ground of knowledge upon which his speculative work was based.

Perhaps his most endearing book remains *Sartor Resartus* (1831) – the Latin title meaning 'The Tailor Reclothed' – an extended work beginning with the idea of metaphor, the relation between the Visible and the Invisible, things and signs, material goods and words in language. This strange, convoluted book introduces Herr Teufelsdrockh, Professor of Things in General at Weissnichtwo University (the German words mean, Professor Devil's dung of the University of Nobody-Knows-Where).

The French Revolution: A History (1837) is a panoramic, dramatic visualisation with hundreds of characters combining vital and vivid evocations with representations of social ideals and a cultural zeitgeist from which its author stands back at a dispassionate distance. Its violence and sweep are contagious and as William Power says, here and there you encounter 'the summary fashion in which kings and authors, soldiers and politicians, are haled for judgement before a court which rather suggests the kirk session of Ecclefechan'. Ironies, insights, sympathies and insights abound. This is the reductive idiom judiciously exercised on an epic canvas.

On Heroes, Hero-Worship and the Heroic in History (1841) called for the recognition of qualities of greatness in individuals, and is evidently related to the idea of the elect in Presbyterian theology. Yet where church teaching might indoctrinate the idea that people are either among the few who are 'saved' or the majority who are 'damned', Carlyle's heroes are heroes because they offer imperishable examples of greatness to all people, and so might help others to live. So far, the idea may be described as democratic. But there is a liability here also, and in later years, Carlyle's radicalism became increasingly authoritarian.

Carlyle's endorsement of human sympathy in his description of poor women preparing the family meal in small cottages and his conviction that his work should somehow be for them, demonstrate humility and faith. Yet he would come to approve slavery, militarism and dictatorship. His depiction of Cromwell as a liberator, prompted perhaps by Ralph Waldo Emerson, led to American readings of Cromwell as an ancestor of the American revolutionary spirit, a violent republican, inspiring John Brown and leading to the Civil War and the emancipation of slaves. Yet Carlyle himself wanted to justify slavery in the West Indies in 1850. George Orwell described him as sadistic. Maybe those terrifying components of his character in later life made him peculiarly insightful and prophetic of the worst tendencies in human nature that were still to find expression in the genocidal wars and mass destruction of the next century. According to Ian Brockie, in the entry for Hitler in *The Carlyle Encyclopedia* (2004) edited by Mark Cumming, Goebbels is recorded as having read Carlyle's *Frederick the Great* aloud to Hitler, as the defeat of Nazism grew more imminent. Herbert Grierson, in *Carlyle and Hitler* (first published in 1933, from a lecture delivered at the University of Manchester in 1930), described Carlyle's influence on Nietzsche and the adoption and distortions of the views of both philosophers by the Nazis.

But Carlyle's virtues elude such associations. One was the recommendation of Christian Isobel Johnstone (1781–1857) as 'the brave-hearted lady' whose epic novel *Clan-Albin: A National Tale* (1815) is one of those remarkable 19th-century works fallen from view until its republication by the Association for Scottish Literary Studies, edited by Andrew Monnickendam (2003). Written before Walter Scott's influence took hold, it follows the wanderings of the central character, orphan Norman Macalbin, through a deepening understanding of Scotland's relations with Ireland, Spain and Europe. The novel is propelled by the voices of strong women. Lady Augusta, Monimia, Flora and others form a chorus for Johnstone's lament for the destruction of Highland culture and her scorn for the priorities of money-makers. Published in the year of Waterloo, there is nothing triumphal and nothing to portend the later priorities of fascism in this humane, sympathetic, 'national tale'.

Hugh Miller (1802–56) was born in Cromarty. His father, a ship's captain, was lost at sea in 1807 and his mother was a major influence, telling him supernatural tales as he grew up, walking the shoreline and questioning authority, including his schoolmaster, with his own independent, tough-minded intellect. He became an apprentice stonemason and looking curiously around him, developed an interest in fossils and geology. As the heavy work affected his health, he became more devoted to writing, first poems then journalism in the *Inverness Courier*, and local lore collected in *Scenes and Legends of the North of Scotland* (1835). Miller characteristically joins sharp observation of hard facts with fictional or mythic episodes and stories.

The central debate in church-going Scottish society in the late 1830s and 1840s was whether landowners should have the right to appoint ministers to churches, above the choice of local congregations. The power of ministers to sway public opinion had been tested in the 18th century, when many had endorsed landowners' authority and complied with the Highland Clearances. Congregations saw it as their democratic right to choose their minister. Miller supported this right and moved to Edinburgh as editor of *The Witness*, a newspaper which opposed the landowners and the Patronage Act. The disruption of the church in 1843 saw Miller staunchly with the Free Church, opposing the landowners. Miller wrote hundreds of articles on social injustices and a major book of geology, *The Old Red Sandstone* (1841). His childhood and youth is described in *My Schools and*

Schoolmasters (1854) and he became one of the most widely-read figures in Victorian Britain, highly praised by Dickens, among others.

Of the next generation is George MacDonald (1824–1905). After university at Aberdeen, he began training as a minister but he resigned from the church and lived as a man of letters largely from the charity of friends. The preoccupying theme of all his work, an extended series of novels, many written specifically for children, is an exploration of the relation between material reality and the constructions of the imagination (Carlyle's 'Visible and 'Invisible' worlds). Francis Russell Hart, in *The Scottish Novel: A Critical Survey* (1978), sums up like this: 'His romances envision the transformation of stern natures by the providential agents of divine love and the assimilation of all hells on earth into a design for universal redemption.' This is offensive to neo-Calvinists for its sentimentalism, and to radical humanists for its conservatism, so MacDonald's 'theological romances' have limited appeal for some readers engaged in redefining Scottish literature. Yet their very quirkiness should draw us back to reconsideration. In his work, as Hart says, ' the fantastic and the normal, the ideal and the real, are separated only by semivisible and shifting boundaries.' And the central subject of both romantic and theological sensibilities is 'the mystery of inheritance'.

MacDonald's novels vividly depict characters in dramatic – sometimes melodramatic – stories. Unpredictable sequences of images and narrative twists and turns, present worlds packed with moral meaning and allegorical suggestion, which never yield too easily one-to-one symbolic significance. They always retain an edge of uncertainty, a feeling of proximate danger, a sense of otherness, of the sheer strangeness of existence, and of wonder. Concrete imagery and the interpenetration of immaterial realities are everywhere in evidence. In *Phantastes* (1858), the wandering hero seems hypersensitive to the inward sensibility of non-human living things such as a beech tree: 'A trembling went through the leaves; a few of the last drops of the night's rain fell from off them at my feet...' The particular materiality of the leaves and raindrops is matched by a sense of what the tree itself may be feeling. Libraries, tunnels, stars and strange landscapes are MacDonald's endlessly alienating territory. He also wrote over 20 novels intended for a popular readership, but the theme of redemption in the susceptible universe of human relationships increasingly occupied him, from *David Elginbrod* (1863) through *Malcolm* (1875) to *The Marquis of Lossie* (1877) and on.

His children's novels *At the Back of the North Wind* (1871) and *The Princess and the Goblin* (1872) and *The Princess and Curdie* (1882) are classics, perennially in print, but arguably his strongest work, along with *Phantastes*, is *Lilith* (1895). Mr Vane, an heir to an English country manor, is troubled by visions of an elderly man in his library; following him, Vane finds a dusty mirror that becomes the entranceway to a journey through inexplicable scenes, beautiful and hideous, life-enhancing or horribly threatening, questioning the value of reason and the presence of sanity in a world beset by pressing manifestations of the unknown. Sexuality is at the heart of the book: it is there in the physical presence of sexual identity in the title-character, and in the meaning of what children ('The Little Ones') are. They are living creatures who require protection and respect for their tenderness and vulnerability, and the initiations they will engage with. Their very existence has been brought about by the sheer animality of the act of procreation. Childlike simplicity and naturalness are essential to MacDonald's vision of redemption and the process whereby 'truth' is encompassed and elated by what Francis Russell Hart calls 'an emergent higher truth'.

MacDonald's contemporary Margaret Oliphant (1828–97) wrote over 90 novels, *The Chronicles of Carlingford* (1863) being a series similar in scope and design to Anthony Trollope's Barsetshire stories. But Oliphant's major achievements are much closer to MacDonald in her 'Tales of the Seen and Unseen' and her novel *Kirsteen* (1890) is prophetic of Catherine Carswell.

Kirsteen is a powerful work of protest against the social structures that make women subservient to male-dominated conventions. The villainous patriarch Mr Douglas of Drumcarro and the vain lover Lord John Campbell may border on stereotypes, but the character of Kirsteen herself is complex: victimised but independently-minded and ultimately convincing, sympathetic and attractive. If *Kirsteen* is a proto-feminist novel, Oliphant's short stories are even more subtle and subversive. That three of her children died young and she wrote to earn a living, maintained her Christian faith and was hypersensitive to the rising authority of science and materialism may provide a biographical explanation for some of the themes in her fiction, but these facts do not account for its lasting, haunting power. Her critique of a world given to venality, false ideals of economic 'progress' and technological expertise, might make her seem like Carlyle being weightily moralistic, but in her best fiction, the critique is poignant and memorable.

In the novella *A Beleaguered City* (1880), a small town in provincial France is overwhelmed by an inexplicable presence:

> There was in the air, in the night, a sensation the most strange I have ever experienced... This was the sensation that overwhelmed me here – a crowd: yet nothing to be seen but the darkness... We could not move for them, so close were they around us. What do I say? There was nobody – nothing.

The women of the town sense this presence while the men want a reasonable explanation. These are the spirits of the dead, returned. Finally, when the townsfolk understand what is happening, the spirits retreat, and everything seems to return to normal, but the story tells us that this sense of normality will always require the corrective of fully sensitised and intuitive understanding. The scientific, mechanistic, materialist and factual, is and always will be inadequate to any fully human life.

'The Land of Darkness' is a representation of industrialisation, and the crude rewards and costs that come with it. In 'The Library Window' an unnamed woman living in St Andrews sees a window in the wall of a house opposite her own, yet it is vague and indistinct. Looking at it over time, she makes out a man in the room behind it, seated at a desk, writing. Towards the end of the story he comes forward, waves, and acknowledges her. But when she visits the house, there is no window, no library and no man. A story that says so much by suggestion, that restrains itself from the obvious or blatant so carefully, and yet carries such a power of implication, is a major achievement. 'The Library Window' is close to Henry James's 'The Turn of the Screw' and predates it by two years. These stories (along with 'The Secret Chamber') are masterworks of supernatural suggestion, lasting reminders of demands the dead continue to visit upon us, immaterial realities that surround us all and permeate out lives. There are more than 'Victorian values' at work here.

34

Gaelic poetry of the 19th century

*JOHN MURDOCH, MÀIRI NIC A' PHEARSAIN / MARY MACPHERSON
(OR MÀIRI MHÒR NAN ÒRAN, BIG MARY OF THE SONGS) AND UILLEAM
MACDHUNLÈIBHE / WILLIAM LIVINGSTON,
WILLIAM SHARP OR FIONA MACLEOD*

WHEN WE ENTER the Gaelic world of the 19th century, our sense of what the dead demand of the living takes on new meaning, with Donald MacLeod's *Gloomy Memories*, or, to give it its full title: *Gloomy Memories in the Highlands of Scotland versus Mrs Harriet Beecher Stowe's Sunny Memories in (England) a Foreign Land: or a Faithful Picture of the Extirpation of the Celtic Race from the Highlands of Scotland* (Edinburgh, 1841; second edition Greenock, 1856; third edition, enlarged and improved, Toronto, Canada, 1857, reprinted Glasgow, Edinburgh, Inverness and Oban 1892 and reissued in the 1980s as *Highland Clearances: Donald MacLeod's Gloomy Memories*, Fort William: Nevisprint, no date).

Written entirely in English, this searing account of the Highland Clearances by a contemporary witness is a detailed indictment of the landowners ultimately responsible for the Sutherland Clearances and the people they authorised to carry out the evictions. It is prose non-fiction, but it's central to any understanding of 19th-century Scottish literature. It was first published as journalism, and read at the time by Karl Marx, then the London correspondent of the New York *Daily Tribune*. In 1853, Marx wrote in the London periodical *The People's Paper*: 'The history of the wealth of the Sutherland family is the history of the ruin and the expropriation of the Scotch-Gaelic population from their native soil.'

In the power of Marx's rhetoric, founded on MacLeod's first-hand accounts, the history and myth of the Highland Clearances were brought to a broader English-language readership. The significance of the Gaelic story crosses from the world defined by the language to an international context of politics, society, and human morality to which literature in the widest sense is a lasting testament.

Contrast *Gloomy Memories* with Queen Victoria's *Journals*, where rhapsodic intoxication with the unpeopled Highlands emphasises the picturesque and scenic: here is the empty wilderness, a spectacle for the delight of the viewer, as opposed to a lived-in landscape with a vulnerable economy. In the three opening paragraphs of her *Journal* for 8 September 1848, giving her 'First Impressions of Balmoral', the following words pile up on each other like so many unreliable cars in a bad road accident: 'pretty... picturesque... nice... pretty... charming... beautiful hills... beautiful wooded hills... calm... solitary... All seemed to breathe freedom and peace, and to make one forget the world and its sad turmoils... The view of the hills towards Invercauld is exceedingly fine.'

Despite such rapture, and unlike the Sutherlands, Victoria was to become a patron of the Gaelic arts, protecting and encouraging the language. She was not in the same category as the landowner evictors.

But even today, next time you travel to the far north of Scotland and visit the Smoo caves, which Walter Scott writes about in his journal of a tour of Scotland, take your time and go through Strathnaver. It's one of the most beautiful long valleys in all of Scotland. Yet you cannot miss the loneliness and emptiness of the place. In his book, *Invisible Country: A Journey through Scotland* (1984), James Campbell writes of the people he met there, and the legacy of the Clearances that persists over centuries. Over a hundred years earlier, another study of the landscape and economy of the edge of the Highlands, *A Journey from Edinburgh through Parts of North Britain* (1802; new edition 1811), by Alexander Campbell (1764-1824), a native Gaelic speaker and music tutor to Walter Scott, included trenchant comments on the evils being visited upon the Highlands. They became even more devastating as the century progressed. Campbell went on to publish *Albyn's Anthology* (1816-1818), collecting Scottish melodies and poems after extended travels throughout Scotland.

This work of reclamation and revalidation of the traditional was common throughout the work of native Gaelic poets distinguished by their attachment to particular places. In the 19th and 20th centuries, William Livingston (1808-70), Duncan Johnston (1881-1947), Charles MacNiven (1874-1944) and Duncan MacNiven (1880-1955) all had their roots in Islay and the island is at the core of their work. In the islands of Mull and Lismore, traditional bards included Lachlan Livingstone (1819-1901), John MacDonald (1883-1940), James MacDonald (1885-1970) and Lachlan MacDonald (1889-1956), whose work is collected in Maighread Dhòmhnallach Lobban's *Lachlan Livingstone and his Grandsons: Bards of Mull and Lismore* (2004). Traditions crossing centuries are described by Eric Cregeen and Donald W. Mackenzie in *Tiree Bards and Their Bardachd: The Poets in a Hebridean Community* (1978), while Timothy Neat and John MacInnes, in *The Voice of the Bard: Living Poets and Ancient Tradition in the Highlands and Islands of Scotland* (1999) track these traditions through the 20th century.

However, Gaelic poetry in the 19th century shows most characteristically a widening range, as the Gaelic-speaking people whom the poets represented were relocated throughout Scotland and the world. Many continued to live in their native territories, maintaining family traditions and clan loyalties, but many others were victims of British imperialism, just as there were many who did that Empire's work, both in British cities and in colonial and military positions overseas. John MacFadyen's 'Song on General Gordon' praises the martyr of Khartoum as a warrior laid low, 'a hero in time of need'.

In Bertolt Brecht's great play *Galileo*, the main character hears his apprentice sigh, 'Unhappy is the land with no heroes!'

His reply is salutary: 'No. Unhappy is the land that is in need of them.'

The essential collection of the poetry of the era is *Caran an t-Saoghail / The Wiles of the World: Anthology of 19th Century Scottish Gaelic Verse*, edited by Donald E. Meek (2003), in which the thematic grouping of poems indicates the range and diversity of perspectives from which the poets began. Poems in praise of the working economies of those territories in the Highlands and Islands where Gaelic people continued to live may be read in contrast with the poems and songs of leave-taking, those commemorating the Clearances and the evictions of people from their homelands. Some poems deal specifically with emigration, new worlds and new sights, and inspire new forms and metaphors. 'Eas Niagara' / 'Niagara Falls' by An t-Urr. Donnchadh Blàrach / Rev. Duncan Blair (1815–93) compares the vision with steamships, furnace bellows and the day of judgement. In other poems, the Greenock train becomes an iron horse: 'the deer could never catch him'. New experience of industrial cities presents Glasgow overwhelmingly 'shop-filled' with 'fashions' and cheeses of unprecedented size. Such wide-eyed wonder might seem naïve but it can also be edged with reductive irony. Meanwhile, local traditions continued in satires, commentaries, praise-songs, salutations and elegies.

There is a complex balance of motives at work in some aspects of 19th-century Gaelic poetry. Love poems continue to be written as formal, yet personal, expressions – but at the other end of the spectrum, war poems were increasingly written as Gaelic-speaking soldiers were engaged in Scottish regiments in the British Empire. Poems and songs commemorating the Crimean War, or a Gaelic poet's encountering Egypt, evoke a patriotic, militaristic ethos which is brutally realistic and ferociously committed, without a trace of the Celtic twilight. 'Cogadh a Chrimea' / 'The Crimean War' by Alasdair MacDhòmhnaill / Alexander MacDonald (fl. mid-19th century), begins: 'Buaidh le Breatann's an Fhraing! / Sgrios air Rusia thall!' / 'Victory to Britain and France! / Destruction on Russia yonder!' And later we read of the commander-in-chief, Sir Colin Campbell (1792–1863):

> Gun robh e mar sheabhag san speur
> Feadh ealtainn gan sgapadh bho cheil',
> Gearradh nan ceann dhiubh gu smearail,
> Le spionnadh a ghairdeannan treun.

> He was like a hawk in the sky
> causing the bird flock to scatter,
> in manly style lopping their heads off
> by the strength of his mighty shoulders.

At the same time, poems and songs of political protest directly engage with deprivations in Scotland and Ireland, by natural disasters or human design. Niall Moireasdan / Neil Morrison (1816–82) writes of the potato famine: 'a plague entered the soil' and the staple food became as sour as coal, 'bringing sickness to the stomach'. Others describe the evictions of the Gàidhealtachd, people forced to make way for sheep farms, large areas given over to absentee landowners' hunting estates, generations of young men conscripted as soldiers or 'encouraged' to emigrate. Uisdean Ròs / Eugene Rose (or Ross) (c.1805–c.1880s) has a 'Lament' in which the 'Great Factor' is depicted in Hell, the flames all around him forever, in revenge for the women and children oppressed, the people he drove from their homes.

The 19th century saw the development of an international readership eager for stories, songs and poems about the Gàidhealtachd and Scotland generally. Such popular, misty-eyed material fostered a vision of how things had been in a golden glow, 'once upon a time'. That vision might infuse supine nostalgia for a benevolent neverland of happy clans, but another, militant aspect was fuelled by the sense that the Gàidhealtachd was being broken down and its people dispersed, that the values of kinship, hospitality and familial support were being destroyed by rapacious mendacity. One popular song for generations extending well into the 20th century was Malcolm MacFarlane's Scots translation of 'The Thistle of Scotland' by Eòghann MacColla / Evan MacColl (1808–98):

> Its strength and its beauty the storm never harms;
> It stan's on its guard like a warrior in arms;
> Yet its down is as saft as the gull's on the sea.
> And its tassles as bricht as my Jeanie's blue e'e.

MacFarlane also translated the lastingly popular 'Isle of Mull' by Dhùgall MacPhàil / Dugald MacPhail:

> The Isle of Mull is of isles the fairest,
> Of ocean's gems 'tis the first and rarest;
> Green grassy island of sparkling fountains,
> Of waving woods and high towering mountains.

Paradoxically, the valorisation of the Highlands and Islands as a kind of utopian heaven-on-earth or lost Eden may have endorsed not sentimentalism but militant resistance to imperial oppression. A similar paradox can be observed in the religious Gaelic songs and hymns of the period. Ostensibly adhering to church convention that might approve the rule of law and establishment authority, they might also invoke a Biblical sense of justice and a religious conviction that could help people find the moral force to stand against unjust authority.

A sense of what justice means underlies the Gaelic world.

A body of religious and theological writing from the 18th and 19th centuries testifies to this but goes much further back. 'The Laws' or 'Laghan' is the term by which a number of manuscripts are known, many fragmentary, collectively significant, reaching through centuries, from 6th-century legal documents onwards. Arguably, they are among the oldest forms of Gaelic 'literature'. They describe responsibilities, obligations, forms of restitution, and the prices to be paid for legal transgressions. They confirm social status, including that of bards, jesters and musicians, embodying questions of property and possession, rightful ownership and legitimate actions. Irish law in the 21st century essentially derives from English law, but Scottish law inherits some aspects of the old Gaelic laws, such as the legal status of corroboration. The details are in Fergus Kelly's *A Guide to Early Irish Law* (Dublin: Dublin Institute for Advanced Studies, 1988; reprinted 1991), p. 203: 'The evidence of a single witness is usually regarded as invalid. The section on the law of evidence in *Berrad Airechta* states that "one man is not proper giving evidence, it is [necessary for there to be] two or three".'

Something of the sense of justice of which such laws are evidence, and the need for redress, must have empowered the people who acted in the Battle of the Braes in Skye in 1882, which led directly to the Crofters' Act of 1884 and the drive to establish better legal rights for Gaelic-speaking people. Life matters. The fight goes on.

35

Prophet of modernity: Robert Louis Stevenson

SCOTTISH TO THE marrow, Francophile, anti-Calvinist, international traveller, Robert Louis Stevenson (1850–94) crossed America and went into the South Pacific, breaking new ground and crossing new seas, developing the meaning of 'Scottish literature' with his prophetic visions of an approaching century of division and disaster. Yet the energy and delight of his writing is perennially infectious. Like no other writer, Stevenson conveys the pleasures of childhood's energy, appetite, movement, growing pains and growing strengths.

Yet his children encounter the viciousness of adulthood. Jim Hawkins comes to understand that Long John Silver is a murderer. The long journey of *Kidnapped* (1886), taking the reader by sea around and then on land across Scotland in a geographical exploration that has allowed generations of readers to follow the map to places we have never actually visited, even on our doorstep, is not only exhilarating but also discomforting. Friendship is at the heart of the book, but parting is its conclusion.

PROPHET OF MODERNITY

Stevenson is a major author whose concern with the relation between the worlds of child and adult is a central and prophetic theme of modernity. In the early 21st century, in the 'developed' world, largely through commercialism and advertising, mass media encourages a wide acceptance of the priorities of glamour and fashion, neon and glitz, stimulating appetites for self-indulgence and vanity. Sport, film and television 'celebrities' are highly prized and paid, and the priorities of childish gratification are almost unconsciously endorsed in western society, while the serious and adult matter of the arts is dangerously and generally trivialised. This is not to undervalue or ignore the extent to which the arts are supported by governments, educational and public institutions, but rather to note a gulf between the financial rewards of 'the entertainment industry' and the hard work demanded by great art. We live in dangerous times and Stevenson is their prophet.

He stands at a curious turning point in modern literature: in the tradition of fiction, he seems much more modern and contemporary than the major Scottish and English novelists of the 19th century, from Hogg, Scott and Galt to Dickens and George Eliot. He is an eloquent essayist and man of letters, a travel writer, a letter writer, a writer of children's fiction and genre fiction, a writer for the periodicals, popular mass media journals in which fiction was serialised for international consumption, most notably trading skilfully in techniques of mystery and suspense. In Stevenson's moment, children's fiction, adventure fiction, Gothic fiction, exotic romance, literal accounts of travel, essays and belles lettres, were flourishing. He can be as meticulous as Henry James when it comes to the artifice of writing and as direct as Jack London in dealing with personal experience and action. He was an aesthetic stylist who wrote thrillingly. His work repudiates the developing presumption of separating 'high' art from 'mere' entertainment which Modernism was to confirm.

For Stevenson, the art of the writer was balanced against the experience of society in different social classes as well as different geographical, cultural and religious locations. He explored the idea of cultural relativism, beginning in Scotland's capital city, where he became intimately familiar and at home in the spacious, light-filled streets and buildings of the new town, and the dark wynds and alleys of the old town. Yet such a simple dichotomy was not merely a polar opposition, but rather a double focus in a longer perspective: Stevenson was young in an Edinburgh where everything was old, from the prehistoric volcanic plug on which the castle sits to the 18th-century new town, one design for which literally laid out a street-plan in the form of the Union Jack flag.

The long sea voyage and overland journey made by David Balfour in *Kidnapped* traverses Scotland geographically, historically and linguistically, delivering an account that works into itself conflicting points of view and commitments. The novel embraces a comprehensive, multi-faceted nation in a kaleidoscope of identities, and is driven by the hero's uncomfortable, flawed, always sympathetic purpose and his evolving friendship with his companion Alan Breck Stewart. Again, the story is of a complex association of childhood, innocence and ignorance with adulthood, knowledge, experience, skill and worldly wisdom, where foolishness is liable to intrude upon the adult's as well as the child's sensibility.

Stevenson's poems might also be read in this way, the most famous collection, *A Child's Garden of Verses* (1885) evoking not only the delights of being young and small but also the fearful vulnerability of childhood. The poems as a whole explore dark, ambiguous, complex areas, as well as the pleasures of hope and the optimism of youth.

A line can be drawn from Scott through Hogg to Stevenson pointing forwards to the modern revitalisation of Scottish writing in the 1920s and 1930s, pre-eminently in MacDiarmid, Gibbon and Gunn. In that line, Stevenson's position is fixed at the confluence of so many disparate and overlapping areas that it has sometimes been difficult to acknowledge his greatness.

Think of him in the company of other literary prophets of modernity, Oscar Wilde and Joseph Conrad. He was a good friend of Henry James, and used his names for the doubled 'heroes' of *The Master of Ballantrae* (1889), Henry and James Durie. James thought highly of Stevenson's work and read it not as light fiction, but as serious, adult, morally profound enquiry. And in Scottish fiction, he is immediately contemporary with the novelists of the Kailyard, S.R. Crockett and Ian Maclaren, and their opponents, the anti-Kailyard novelists George Douglas Brown and John Macdougall Hay, and poets such as James Thomson ('B.V.') of *The City of Dreadful Night* and John Davidson with his testaments of lonely outcasts. But Stevenson is his own singular self. It was to S.R. Crockett that Stevenson wrote in a letter of Spring 1888 from Saranac Lake, taking exception to Crockett's self-styled address:

> Don't put 'N.B.' in your paper: put 'Scotland' and be done with it. Alas, that I should be thus stabbed in the home of my friends! The name of my native land is not *North Britain*, whatever may be the name of yours!

No Scottish writer understands more deeply the relativity of cultural identity, how different people are, in different parts of the world, travelling as he did from Scotland to England and France, to America and across America, and finally into the Pacific to Samoa, where he died at the age of 44 and is buried, still revered by Samoan people as 'Our writer – our writer in eternal residence.'

His writing in the South Seas marks a further development. It's most evident in the story 'The Beach of Falesá' and the novel, *The Ebb-Tide* (1894), and in a number of other stories, letters, historical and topographical accounts, anecdotes of the people of the Pacific islands. He came to know the priorities and ways of life of three kinds of people: the indigenous people of the islands, the people who lived on the beach (neither wholly indigenous nor wholly incomers but familiar transients in a commerce of exchange and compromise), and the administrative, colonial authorities. Stevenson himself was an outsider to each one of these three groups but he knew them all closely, and was intensely aware of the cultural checks and balances of the situation. His forensic detachment and intense sympathies in this circumstance are prophetic of early 20th-century Modernism. Stevenson might be seen in a constellation with Herman Melville and others whose central themes of empire, innocence and guilt were forged through the experience of the Pacific world, far beyond anything familiar in Scottish literature of earlier generations. Yet it is a coherent *oeuvre*, reflecting back on his Scottish experience just as his Samoan home Vailima invites us to read back and see Scott's Abbotsford in a new light. His life was cut short but it was filled with achievement.

Stevenson's commitment to writing was declared when he was 21. He decided with conviction. His family was austere – his father a lighthouse engineer – and in childhood, he was often unwell. His imagination was a major resource that ran counter to the practicalities of his family's professional work. Accounts of travel in Belgium and France were followed by fiction. *Treasure Island* was first serialised in 1882 before book publication in 1883. Three years later, *Kidnapped* was well received by critics and *Dr Jekyll and Mr Hyde* (also 1886) became an international best-seller.

Already the core of his achievement was clear: the boy's adventure-story *Treasure Island* is a revelation, as childhood encounters the duplicity and murderous ambiguities of the adult world. *Jekyll and Hyde* was to take that revelation to its darkest depths. This murderous tale foreshadows the extremes of childish appetite and adult power so terribly familiar in the 21st century.

MASTERPIECES

Stevenson has sometimes been dismissed as 'merely' a writer for children but *Strange Case of Dr Jekyll and Mr Hyde* is a moral fable of an entirely adult character. For all its sensational success and longstanding popularity in multiple versions in a variety of media, it is in Henry James's words, 'the most serious of the author's tales' – a story whose seriousness resonates with ever more sinister conviction. The work is made up of different written accounts by various characters: an unnamed narrator, Mr Utterson the lawyer, Mr Enfield the man-about-town, Dr Lanyon and Dr Jekyll himself. Each partial perspective casts a different light on events.

A mysterious, dark and evil-looking figure is seen in London. This person is tracked to Dr Jekyll's home, confronted by Utterson, but his identity not disclosed. He is seen assaulting a young girl, trampling her brutally; a maid glimpses him; the mystery gathers. Everything builds to the final section, 'Henry Jekyll's Full Statement of the Case' where the proposition from which the whole story has developed is revealed: Dr Jekyll says that he began with the conviction 'that man is not truly one, but truly two' and that later, others may go even further, and discover 'that man will be ultimately known for a mere polity of multifarious, incongruent and independent denizens.' But meantime, his own 'two natures' were bound together 'in the agonised womb of consciousness' and that these 'polar twins' were condemned to be 'continually struggling.'

Here, Dr Jekyll considers the fatal question of what follows the dissociation of his 'two selves' from each other with a scientific potion that engenders his transformation into his horrendous evil self:

> [H]e thought of Hyde, for all his energy of life, as of something not only hellish but inorganic. This was the shocking thing; that the slime of the pit seemed to utter cries and voices; that the amorphous dust gesticulated and sinned; that what was dead, and had no shape, should usurp the offices of life. And this again, that that insurgent horror was knit to him closer than

a wife, closer than an eye; lay caged in his flesh, where he heard it mutter and felt it struggle to be born; and at every hour of weakness, and in the confidence of slumber, prevailed against him, and deposed him out of life.

Hyde hates Jekyll. Driven by fear of the gallows, he returns to his 'subordinate station of a part instead of a person' to occupy the body that once was wholly his own. He loathes this necessity and resents it. When Jekyll writes his final account, he knows that the chemical potion he has taken to keep Hyde at bay, within himself, will lose its effect. Hyde will return. His only solution is suicide:

> this is my true hour of death, and what is to follow concerns another than myself. Here, then, as I lay down the pen, and proceed to seal up my confession, I bring the life of that unhappy Henry Jekyll to an end.

The seriousness of the argument that runs so urgently through the whole work increases in intensity and pathos, and grows with each new reading. The argument is that duality, even multiplicity, of identities, in a singular human self, is not to be tolerated by the priorities of science. Science wants things neat and fixed in categories. You are a sole commodity, a unit to be dealt with. Yet every human being knows the complex, shifting selves that make the self, make any one of us who and what we are. Many make one. And one among many creates the polity of selves called society. Alienation from separate selves and isolation in the city, make the choice of London as location frighteningly apt.

Stevenson's work is shocking, indeed, but it prophesies major trends in the history that followed it: the exaggerations of violence in the service of childish appetites, the indulgence of vanity at the expense of good reason, the centring upon the self, the legitimisation of greed, self-righteousness and physical might, at the expense of social contact, admission of complexity, openness to difference and change. Stevenson knew bad weather was ahead.

The quality of conflict between inflexible power and the necessary forces of change informs the fragment of the novel he was working on at the time of his death, *Weir of Hermiston* (1896), an exploration of the relation between an authoritarian patriarch and his free-spirited son. Here, the language of many of the most vivid characters is a rich vernacular Scots and the characters themselves – women and men – are among the most memorable Stevenson ever created.

Stevenson's most famous travel books, novels, short stories, poems and his letters also show the range, insight and quality of his writing. His fiction is linked in one specific way to the Scottish tradition, back to James Hogg and Walter Scott (and further back, to Robert Henryson's *Fables*) and forward to Muriel Spark, James Kelman and Irvine Welsh (and thinking of Hawthorne and Melville, to American literature as well): this is the literary device of the 'unreliable narrator'. Iain Banks began his novel *Transition* (2009) with the sentence, 'Apparently I am what is known as an Unreliable Narrator, though of course if you believe everything you're told you deserve whatever you get.' When we consider Stevenson's stories, however, there is a specific historical moment that must be taken into account. Hogg, Scott and Stevenson all grew up in a Scotland where oral storytelling was a common currency. Hogg and Scott were pioneers in the work of recording and writing oral stories, songs and ballads. Something very particular in written narrative is happening in this transitional overlap between the literary artifice of these writers and the oral traditions they experienced, and Stevenson's experience of oral storytelling culture was expanded in the South Pacific islands and especially Samoa.

We have already written of the essay that opens up questions about this, Walter Benjamin's 'The Storyteller' (1936), easily available in the collection *Illuminations*. In Hogg's novel *The Confessions of a Justified Sinner*, the ambivalence of either a rational or a supernatural explanation of events sustains tension, as the narratives – plural – of the novel reveal themselves. In *Jekyll and Hyde*, the multiple narrative perspectives delivered in different forms of written address help create an equally effective tension. Something similar happens in *The Master of Ballantrae* (1889). What seems certain becomes increasingly questionable. The principal narrator, the factor Mackellar, seems to be a reasonable and reliable witness, but Stevenson is assiduous in indicating that there is more to it than that, and if the sinister figure of Secundra Dass takes the role of the familiar companion to the ostensibly 'evil' James, Mackellar stands in the same relation to the ostensibly 'good' Henry. So the tale of the two brothers Durie is far from unambiguous. This is conveyed in the imagery when Stevenson depicts Mackellar's view of the Master in Chapter 9, bringing out the ambivalence of the figure, literally ascending and descending in a constantly shifting perspective. They are both on board the ship aptly named *Nonesuch*, crossing the Atlantic, and the sea is rising and falling:

> Now his head would be in the zenith and his shadow fall quite beyond the *Nonesuch* on the further side; and now he would swing down till he was underneath my feet, and the line of the sea leaped high above him like the ceiling of a room. I looked upon this with a growing fascination, as birds are said to look on snakes... [The Master's] tale, told in a high key in the midst of so great a tumult, and by a narrator who was one moment looking down at me from the skies and the next peering up from under the soles of my feet – this particular tale, I say, took hold upon me in a degree quite singular...

In his shorter fiction, the matter of ambiguity presents itself most forcefully both in the way the narratives are disclosed and in the palpable physicality of the language – or languages – in which they are written.

'Thrawn Janet' (from *The Merry Men & Other Tales*) is a good example. The basic trope of the story is that a minister who thinks he knows what's what, is confronted with inexplicable realities. The story begins in the minister's English language, suggesting a formal, logical, ecclesiastic or legal mind at work. By the end of the opening section, though, we are in 'an atmosphere of terror' and the story now immerses the reader in the Scots language, close enough to English to be easily readable but different enough to make the experience strange. The unknown, violent, distorted and devilish parts of the world wreak revenge upon the Minister's self-righteous sense of order and the justness of things in what he believes is God's universe.

Other stories of immediate appeal include 'Markheim', a Dostoevskian vignette on the meaning of good and evil, 'A Lodging for the Night: A Story of Francis Villon' (from *New Arabian Nights*), depicting medieval winter in Paris, 'The Bottle Imp' (from *Island Nights' Entertainment*), a version of the Faust story with a happy ending, and 'A Fable: The Persons of the Tale', an 'interruption' to *Treasure Island*, ostensibly taking place between chapters 32 and 33, where Captain Trelawney and Long John Silver have a conversation, Silver confidently asserting, 'If there is a Author, by thunder, but he's on my side…'

Stevenson was keenly attuned to the dynamics of the late 19th century that were to generate what was to follow, but in the 1920s, they had to be rediscovered. The biologist, town-planner and social visionary Patrick Geddes had heralded what he called an approaching 'Scottish Renascence' in the 1890s but it took a while to arrive. The First World War of 1914–18, the Easter Rising in Ireland in 1916, the Russian Revolution in 1917, all blew apart the imperial certainties and authority of British monarchical rule upon which the 19th-century empire had been built.

Stevenson, hypersensitive to the attractions and compulsions of evil, keenly aware of the vulnerabilities of virtue, already knew exactly what humanity was capable of.

36

Stevenson's contemporaries: from Charles Mackay to Florence Dixie

STEVENSON IS ONE of Scotland's best-known and most-loved authors, but some of his less familiar immediate contemporaries are worth our attention. Among them, the lasting value of Charles Mackay (1814–1889) is probably as an essayist. It's salutary to look at the Preface to the 1852 edition of his curious works, *Extraordinary Popular Delusions* (1841) and *The Madness of Crowds* (1852), especially in the context of the mass media and political priorities of early 21st-century Britain:

> In reading the history of nations, we find that, like individuals, they have their whims and peculiarities; their seasons of excitement and recklessness, when they care not what they do. We find that whole communities suddenly fix their minds upon one object, and go mad in its pursuit; that millions of people become simultaneously impressed with one delusion, and run after it, till their attention is caught by some new folly more captivating than the first.

Such follies seem 'to defy the progress of knowledge to eradicate them entirely from the popular mind.' Mackay concludes:

> Men [and, we should add, women too], it has been said, think in herds; it will be seen that they go mad in herds, while they only recover their senses slowly, and one by one.

Mackay was a lexicographer, a man simply fascinated by words, who compiled *The Poetry and Humour of the Scotch Language* (1882) and *A Dictionary of Lowland Scotch* (1888) and he edited anthologies of Jacobite and Cavalier songs, but of his poetry, a few titles are indicative: 'Cheer, Boys, Cheer!', 'To the West! To the West!', and 'England Over All'. He was clearly not immune to delusion himself.

Another man of letters and a good friend of Stevenson was Andrew Lang (1844–1912), an antiquarian, translator of Homer, literary archaeologist, critic, essayist, poet, editor of the Waverley novels, and, most extensively, a folklorist. Lang was small-c conservative and backed off from Stevenson at his most flamboyant, sharp-eyed and adventurous. Not for Lang was Stevenson's velvet jacket, bright shirts, 'every impulse of his heart and mind flashing out in the play of eye, feature and gesture,' as Sidney Colvin put it. But their affection grew. After Stevenson's death, Lang wrote in an elegy:

> Once we were kindest, he said, when leagues of the limitless sea
> Flowed between us, but now that no wash of the wandering tides
> Sunders us from each, yet nearer we seem to be,
> Whom only the unbridged stream of the river of death divides

Lang himself is not easily categorised: he never wrote extensively in fiction, his poetry is neglected and his prose style is often pedantic, yet his 'Fairy Books' (there were 12, each given a different colour in their title, *The Blue Fairy Book*, *The Red Fairy Book*, and so on), published from 1889 to 1910 (*The Lilac Fairy Book*), were popular retellings of traditional stories from international sources, some literary, some based on folk-tales. Lang was an enthusiastic friend of Henry Rider Haggard and co-wrote an affectionate parody of Haggard's famous novel *She* (1886), entitled *He* (1887), but he was a gentle critic, as his biographer Roger Lancelyn Green puts it:

> For the lesser writers of adventure stories Lang made no exaggerated claims, and was among the first to remonstrate with the uncritical admirers of S.R. Crockett who were placing that worthy on a level with Scott. But Crockett, as well as Doyle [...] owed much to Lang for the praise and encouragement which he bestowed on them.

As an essayist, anthropologist and travel-writer, *Letters to Dead Authors* (1886), *Myth, Ritual and Religion* (1887), *How to Fail in Literature* (1890) are enjoyable rambles, and the tales about Casanova, Prince Charlie after Culloden, Rorke's Drift, Cervantes, Cortes, Montezuma and the Aztecs included in *The True Story Book* (1893), and the discussions of Alan Breck Stewart, Kaspar Hauser and the history of the Kirks in Scotland in *Historical Mysteries* (1904) are fascinating excursions. Like these, *Adventures Among Books* (1905) takes us on further curious paths of the imagination while *Highways and Byways on the Border* (written with John Lang, 1913) follows cartographically similarly less-explored routes.

Lang's introduction to *Prophecies of the Brahan Seer* (1899) by Alexander Mackenzie (1838–98) introduces the Seer, Kenneth Mackenzie or Coinneach Odhar of Uig on the Isle of Lewis, supposedly born in the early 1600s, and Mackenzie, author of the influential *The History of the Highland Clearances* (1883, revised 1914). Mackenzie's account of the Seer's prophecies gripped the popular imagination and comparisons were made with Nostradamus. Mackenzie himself was born on a croft in Gairloch, earned his living as a labourer and ploughman before becoming an apprentice in the clothes trade, setting up a clothes shop in Inverness in 1869. He became an editor and publisher of the *Celtic Magazine* and became known as a historian, author of various clan histories, a fellow of the Society of Antiquaries of Scotland and a founder member of the Gaelic Society of Inverness. His account of the Clearances stayed in print and impressed John Prebble (1915–2001), whose own book, *The Highland Clearances* (1963) superseded Mackenzie's in popularity. He was also active in the issue of land ownership in the Highlands, campaigning for crofters' secure tenure, befriending Màiri Mhòr nan Òran (Big Mary of the Songs), or Mary MacPherson (1821–98), the great Gaelic poet of the era. We shall return to her.

Lang was a distinctive kind of writer, a phenomenon of his time, perhaps similar to George Eyre-Todd (1862–1937), travel-writer, literary historian, critic and editor, and general populariser of early Scottish literature, author of *Byeways of Scottish Story* (1900), *Scotland for the Holidays* (1910) and *Through Scotland by the Caledonian Railway* (1906).

These were contemporaries who might be ranged on Stevenson's more conservative flank. The herald of a very different disposition and philosophy was Thomas Common (1850–1919), the first translator of Friedrich Nietzsche into English. He lived near Corstorphine, just outside Edinburgh, and in the mid-1890s, was involved in a project to publish Nietzsche's collected works, translating *Thus Spake Zarathustra* (1909). This was the version Hugh MacDiarmid read, which informed his thinking when he was writing *A Drunk Man Looks at the Thistle* (1926). Common's study *Nietzsche as Critic, Philosopher, Poet and Prophet* (1901) was praised by George Bernard Shaw and apparently read by W.B. Yeats, who, like MacDiarmid, responded eagerly. From 1903 to 1916 Common attempted to spread Nietzsche's ideas through the production of a quarterly periodical, *Notes for Good Europeans* (later titled *The Good European Point of View*).

Also widely influential was J.G. Frazer (1854–1941), author of *The Golden Bough* (1890). He was a social anthropologist and authority on folklore and comparative religion, but might fairly be considered alongside Thomas Carlyle, Hugh Miller, Charles Mackay and others, in the rapidly changing Victorian era as it moved inexorably towards modernity. His conviction that human belief systems were progressive, evolving through stages from primitive magic towards organised religion, which in turn would ultimately be replaced by science, had the effect of instating the recognition that all three stages had a contemporaneous existence in a world of cultural relativism. A major influence behind the paradigm of modernist poems, T.S. Eliot's *The Waste Land* (1922), Frazer's work is also related to the imaginative travels of George MacDonald and the literal world-travelling of Stevenson himself.

In the realm of the imagination, Frazer's understanding also links back to the writings of Charles Mackay's daughter, Mary Mackay (1855–1924), who was born in London and whose mother, Elizabeth Mills, was Mackay's servant.

Mary was sent to a convent in Paris in 1866, returned to Britain in 1870, and started working as a musician giving piano recitals under the name by which she became famous, Marie Corelli. Her novels include *A Romance of Two Worlds* (1886), which weaves together supernatural and science fiction themes as a young woman suffering from illness and suicidal thoughts is given an addictive potion by the mysterious 'Raffell Cellini': she has hallucinatory visions and awakens to meet a guardian angel, who guides her through unknown solar systems and questions the nature of religion and human destiny. She decides that she must not be under the tutelage of an angel but take charge of her own life and retreats to a monastery to seek further spiritual exploration.

Ideas about biological evolution and the priorities of the immaterial spirit confront each other in the novel. It was clearly attuned to its era and it became a bestseller. Marie Corelli was the most popular author of her day, collected by Winston Churchill, the royal family, and innumerable 'common readers' while literary critics scorned her. The theatre critic James Agate described her as combining Edgar Allan Poe's imagination with 'the mentality of a nursemaid'. Her companion of 40 years was Bertha Vyver and she seems to have been bisexual. In later life she moved to Stratford, where she campaigned to preserve the 17th-century buildings and their timber-framed façades. Mark Twain, who had been sceptical, visited her there and found her more sympathetic than he'd imagined.

William Archer (1856–1924) was born and grew up in Perth, spending some of his youth with relatives in Norway, learning the language and becoming a strong advocate of Henrik Ibsen and, later, George Bernard Shaw. Archer studied at Edinburgh University, wrote for the press, and after a year visiting his family in Australia, where they had emigrated, went to London and became a prominent and influential theatre critic. He translated Ibsen's plays, including *Peer Gynt* and *A Doll's House*. His critical writings include *Masks or Faces? A Study in the Psychology of Acting* (1888), *A National Theatre: Schemes and Estimates* (1907), *India and the Future* (1917) and *The Old Drama and the New* (1923). Archer is worth studying in his own right but he is most remembered because on 23 April 1900 he wrote to James Joyce passing on Ibsen's compliments about the review Joyce had written for the *Fortnightly Review* of Ibsen's *When We Dead Awaken*. Joyce was 18 and this was his first published work. The play was to be Ibsen's last: he was now in his 70s. Ibsen had written to Archer about Joyce's review, appreciating its kindness and describing it as 'velvellig' (benevolent). Joyce replied to Archer thanking him for his kindness and promising to treasure Ibsen's words. When Joyce visited London in May 1900 he and Archer dined together (on wild duck) at the Royal Services Club. Joyce sent Archer his first play, *A Brilliant Career*, and the Scot replied firmly but gently criticising; Joyce then sent him some poems, which received similar careful criticism. When *Ulysses* was published in 1922, Joyce was grateful enough for Archer's guidance and kindness to have a copy sent to him.

Charles Mackay, Andrew Lang, Alexander Mackenzie, Màiri Mhòr nan Òran or Mary MacPherson, George Eyre-Todd, Thomas Common, J.G. Frazer, Mary Mackay or Marie Corelli and William Archer: nine contemporaries of Robert Louis Stevenson who remain under-researched but whose lives and works tell us a great deal about the era Stevenson lived through and pointed forward from. They take us from the late Victorian era to the early modern world.

One of the authors Andrew Lang thought highly of, the half-Scot Rudyard Kipling, became Lord Rector of St Andrews University in the same year the name Hugh MacDiarmid was first seen in print, the same year as the publication of *Ulysses* and *The Waste Land*, the same year that a British colonial court sentenced Gandhi to six years' imprisonment for sedition after a protest march led to violence in Bombay. These facts overlap Modernism with the legacy of the British Empire and colonial struggles for independence in a chronology that disrupts the security of firm divisions.

And the drive towards another form of emancipation is paramount in the fiction of Lady Florence Caroline Dixie (née Douglas, 1855–1905), novelist, war correspondent and feminist. *The Young Castaways, or, The Child Hunters of Patagonia* and *Aniwee, or, The Warrior Queen* (both 1890) are exotic travel adventures for children while her astonishing political science fantasies *Gloriana, or the Revolution of 1900* (1890) and *Isola, or the Disinherited: A Revolt for Women* (1902) are lively adventures with feminist priorities and a lucid style close to Conan Doyle, H.G. Wells or Jack London. The fluency and facility of the writing quickens the narratives and the characterisation is light, rather than psychologically complex, but the ideas in these novels, their imagining of revolution in society, their critique of class structures, and their affirmation of women's rights are refreshing, invigorating and fun to read. *Gloriana* takes us from London's industrial heartland and its seething mob to the lonely Hebrides where the central character, a woman adept at male disguise, with redress in her sights, gathers her energies for the final push for social change. Dixie was an independent international traveller. She had the means to be so but also the courage and resourcefulness to make her expeditions into wild territories intellectually profitable. She learned from other cultures and wrote well of them for English-language readers, in *Across Patagonia* (1880) and *In the Land of Misfortune* (1882), where she reports on her trip to South Africa. A child of the British Empire, she sympathised with the Boers of South Africa as well as the Zulus and supported Home Rule in both Scotland and Ireland. As a writer, her sympathies and imagination were greater than specific political strategic allegiances. Her life's work remains in need of revaluation.

The influences of these writers and the world they inhabited continue to extend in subterranean ways or in dream-like imaginations, for better and worse, well into the 20th and 21st centuries.

37

Writers of the Industrial Revolution: from Thomas Campbell to Arthur Conan Doyle

INDUSTRIALISATION MEANT INCREASING the concentration of the population of Scotland in the cities throughout the 19th century, particularly in Glasgow and Dundee. This had a deep and lasting legacy in terms of modern national self-representation. The rate of urbanisation in Scotland, the rising number of emigrants leaving the country early in the century, and consequently the growing international readership yearning for images and icons of Scotland delivering consoling images of the country, were crucial to how the literature of Scotland changed in this period. Industrialising Scotland changed the nation's character.

Thomas Campbell (1777–1844) was one of the most popular poets of his era, particularly with the unlikely 'Gertrude of Wyoming' (1809), a long narrative poem set in wilderness America. In 'Lines on Revisiting a Scottish River', he laments so-called progress as industrial effluvia have turned the rippling beauty of the Clyde into a seething, polluted mess. Campbell's Clyde is now a place where 'Nature's face is banish'd and estranged' and the riverbanks are 'With sooty exhalations cover'd o'er'. 'Unsightly brick-lanes smoke, and clanking engines gleam' in the effort 'To gorge a few with Trade's precarious prize…': 'And call they this Improvement?'

Similar abhorrence of industrialisation is present in the poetry of Elizabeth Hamilton (1756/58–1816) and William Thom (1788–1848). In 'Glasgow: A Poem' by John Mayne (1759–1836), the merchants at Glasgow Cross 'shine like Nabobs' and 'Commerce engages a' their care', while in 'Glasgow' (1857) by Alexander Smith (1829–1867) the city is depicted in vivid images of haunting ferocity and spectacle. Yet there's a feeling of dark belonging in this poem which takes pride in the scale of industrialisation and identification of the poet with a world of 'Black Labour' and 'secret-moaning caves': 'City! I am true son of thine.'

Tom Leonard's ground-breaking anthology *Radical Renfrew* (1990), drew attention to the neglected poetry of 19th-century industrial Scotland and new ways of reading it. It included consideration of emigrant poets like John Barr (1809–89), who went from Paisley to Otago, New Zealand, in 1852 to sing the praises of a non-industrialised social order in which capitalist economics might be practised without tyranny and the agonies of class discrimination. Other poets, particularly women writing between 1850 and 1900, reflect and protest about the social conditions of industrialised Scotland. Much work is still to be done to revalue these poems. Janet Hamilton (1795–1873) writes in 'Oor Location' of 'the whisky-shop and pawn' and the 'ruination' characteristic of cities of 'ragged laddies... enginemen, and Paddies... colliers... fechtin', drinkin', while Jessie Russell (1850–1881) in 'Woman's Rights versus Woman's Wrongs' is unforgiving in her feminist priorities. Many wives are beaten by husbands who never suffer due punishment: 'a life for a life, and the murderer's hung, and we think not the law inhuman, / Then why not the lash for the man who kicks or strikes a defenceless woman?'

Like that of Alexander Smith, the poetry of James Young Geddes (1850–1913) also presents the sense that industry might have a strange, terrible beauty of its own but it is charged with moral force at the civic hypocrisies evident in industrial Dundee. 'Glendale & Co. (After Walt Whitman)' begins with the American poet's sense of social justice and democratic constitution and employs Whitman's long line and free verse, chanting a litany of bitter indignation as he describes the firm of Glendale & Co., 'grown from small beginnings' to something now hellish that 'dominates the town': 'Lit up at night, the discs flare like angry eyes in watchful supervision, impressing on the minds of the workers the necessity of improving the hours and minutes purchased by Glendale & Co.' The bitterness of the poem escalates in indignation, as that of the English poet William Blake does in his poem, 'London' (from his *Songs of Experience*, 1794). Other important works include 'The New Jerusalem' ('Machineries / Are there whose vast pulsations tear and thrash / the groaning air'), 'The New Inferno' (full of 'harsh dissonance') and 'The Spectre Clock of Alyth'. Geddes is Scotland's most radical social poet between Burns and MacDiarmid.

Both John Davidson and James ('B.V.') Thomson (1834–1882) were influences on T.S. Eliot and Hugh MacDiarmid. Thomson's visionary poem, *The City of Dreadful Night* (1880) is a phantasmagorical nocturnal journey through a nightmare city of enervated, alienated sleepwalking individuals. Deeply read in Dante and Leopardi (whose work he translated), Thomson's vision belongs in their company as well as that of early modern Scottish poetry. It is not, like that of James Young Geddes, one of an actual industrialised city, nor like Davidson's, one of moral turpitude firmly based in historic fact. It is rather a metaphoric, illuminated nocturnal city, like Dante's subterranean Inferno, whose inhabitants are doomed by something more inescapably human than alterable social conditions. Thomson's injustice is not curable in economic terms though the moral authority of his poem might charge us to address social and remediable economic causes of alienation. Perhaps all cities bleed into one emblematic 'dreadful' city in a vision where industrialism has brought about a dark spiritual uniformity. Thomson was also the author of extraordinarily perceptive essays, collected as *Biographical and Critical Studies* (1896), and of *Walt Whitman: The Man and the Poet* (1910).

For John Davidson (1857–1909), the Nietzschean character rises most strongly in the pessimistic Testaments. 'The Testament of a Vivisector' is perhaps the most repulsive poem ever written, a coldly objective description of the flaying and anatomisation of a horse: 'I study pain, measure it' and the proof is in the surgery:

> ...I fixed
> The creature, impotent and moribund,
> With gag and fetter; sheared its filthy mane;
> Cut a foot's length, tissue and tendon...
> And made this faithful, dying, loathsome drudge,
> One diapason of intensest pain

The conclusion is the discovery that 'Matter in itself is pain... being evermore / Self-knowledge.' Scientific chill runs all through 'Snow': a Dickensian phenomenon of feeling is examined through the lens of a cold crystallographer.

Davidson turns the objective gaze upon himself in 'The Testament of a Man Forbid'. This is how it begins:

> Mankind has cast me out. When I became
> So close a comrade of the day and night,
> Of earth and of the seasons of the year,
> And so submissive in my love of life
> And study of the world that I unknew
> The past and names renowned, religion, art,
> Inventions, thoughts, and deeds, as men unknow
> What good and evil fate befell their souls
> Before their bodies gave them residence...

Even when Davidson writes in the working-class voice of the wage-slave in 'Thirty Bob a Week', sympathetic compassion and class solidarity bring no alleviation to the human waste enacted by the industrial world:

> It's a naked child against a hungry wolf;
>   It's playing bowls upon a splitting wreck;
> It's walking on a string across a gulf
>   With millstones fore-and-aft about your neck;
> But the thing is daily done by many and many a one;
>   And we fall, face forward, fighting, on the deck.

The metre here connects with traditional ballads and this is even more evident in Davidson's 'Thomas the Rhymer' and 'A Runnable Stag' yet he is also one culmination of the tradition of Romantic sinners, from Milton's Satan to Melville's Ahab and on. For Davidson, 'Greenock' is 'this grey town / That pipes the morning up before the lark / With shrieking steam... where hammers clang / On iron hulls' and 'men sweat gold that others hoard or spend, / And lurk like vermin in their narrow streets.'

While Davidson's vision is clearly of an industrial city, the fantastic vision of a metaphoric city of darkness informs it. Darkness also characterises many of the poems of Robert Buchanan (1841–1901), who wrote Robert Browning-like dramatic monologues such as 'Fra Giacomo', memorably set to music in 1914 by Cecil Coles (1888–1918). Here, an Italian Renaissance aristocrat addresses a priest and gives him a glass of wine, while his wife lies dead in the bedroom upstairs, only to reveal in the course of the poem that he has discovered that the priest was his wife's secret lover. He then reveals that the wine is poisoned, and just in case, he stabs the priest repeatedly and has his corpse thrown into the canal below. A grotesque poem of grand guignol, it skilfully indicts the fickleness of upper-class men and women and the hypocrisies of the church.

Buchanan's city-poems 'London' and 'Vanity Fair' and his portrait-poem, 'The Ballad of Judas Iscariot', teem with people and make an immediate formal appeal to a popular readership, but their subject is alienation. Desolation, loneliness and elemental, inhuman nature are most powerfully present in 'Sonnets written by Loch Coruisk, Isle of Skye'. 'We Are Fatherless' ends with Nietszchean finality:

> There is no God – in vain we plead and call,
> In vain with weary eyes we search and guess –
> Like children in an empty house...

Fiction in Scots of the time occupied a much more populated context. The work of William Alexander (1826–1894), in *Johnnie Gibb of Gushetneuk* (1869–71) and *The Laird of Drammochdyle* (1865), rediscovered by William Donaldson along with a great deal of 19th-century popular fiction, often in Scots and frequently published serially in newspapers, charts closely the relation between the rural world of Aberdeenshire and the urban, industrialised world with its hard commercial imperatives. An eel-like intelligence and humour is at work in W.E. Aytoun (1813–1865), whose story 'How we got up the Glenmutchkin railway and how we got out of it' (1845) is reminiscent of Mark Twain in its wry engagement with the priorities of the new commercialism flourishing in industrial society. Alexander Anderson, known as 'Surfaceman' (a railway worker) in a well-known poem of the 1890s, 'Nottman', tells the story of an engine-driver who one day sees a small dim object ahead and recognises a child asleep on the track, climbs forward from the cab and positions himself outside at the front of the engine as it rushes forward, and manages, a micro-second ahead of the train, to gently kick the child to one side and off the rails, recognising as he does so his own son.

Another popular writer of the period whose fame has been sustained throughout the following century and into our own connects the ambitions of serious literary work and the pleasures of light entertainment: Arthur Conan Doyle (1859–1930). Beside his extended historical novels, among his most enjoyable stories are perhaps the *Adventures* and *Exploits of Brigadier Gerard* (1894–1903), set in the Napoleonic wars. Doyle saw himself primarily as a historical novelist but his most enduring works concern Sherlock Holmes and Professor Challenger, two archetypal characters, the professional detective and the adventuring speculative scientist. Their influence is evident in innumerable later manifestations but the originals retain a perennial charm and value.

Both are men of science in an age of industrialisation and materialism, when orthodox religion was increasingly marginalised. Holmes offers the reassurance of material and rational explanation in a world from which God has departed. Challenger, while offering the same sense of scientific certainty, is an eccentric who keeps an open mind in an age when his colleagues and newspaper reporters are increasingly cynical. Challenger leads us to the Lost World, where prehistoric time and its monsters are present-tense. Holmes, confronting villains from the furthest reaches of Empire, maintains the virtues of imperial centrality, the core of urban life, but his opposite number is the fearful Moriarty, the secret at the centre of the web of urban evil.

Morality is important in Doyle's fiction but the work of the imagination, the unpredictable development of stories in a world on the brink of profound and permanent, violent change, is what gives them a resonance that points forward from R.L. Stevenson to John Buchan and Ian Fleming, a continuity of adventure surfing the high curling waves of the long declining empire, and heading for the rocky shore.

38

Gaelic poetry: from the 19th to the 20th centuries

FROM JOHN MURDOCH, MÀIRI NIC A' PHEARSAIN / MARY MACPHERSON
(OR MÀIRI MHÒR NAN ÒRAN, BIG MARY OF THE SONGS)
AND UILLEAM MACDHUNLÈIBHE / WILLIAM LIVINGSTON
TO WILLIAM SHARP OR FIONA MACLEOD

DUNCAN BAN MACINTYRE'S last visit to Ben Dorain on 19 September 1802 prompted the following day his composition 'Last Leave-taking of the Bens', a moving farewell to the mountains, especially Ben Dorain, which his 18th-century poetry sang of so piercingly. It's an old man's elegy recollecting the energies of youth, the chase of the greyhound quickening as its owner's breath becomes more laboured. Donald E. Meek, in his anthology *Caran an t-Saoghail / The Wiles of the World* (2003), notes that George Calder in 1912 tells how Duncan Ban made the song 'sitting on a stone opposite Annat, less than a mile upstream from the Railway Viaduct in Auch Glen' and that the bard could not finish it 'owing to the extreme agitation he experienced on beholding the scenes of his youth and early manhood, and that he was assisted to complete it by his brother Malcolm.' The environment of the mountains he had known was being devastated by the new economy of sheep.

This is one of the most immediate legacies of 18th-century Gaelic poetry and portends what followed. Personal pathos and social conflict are entwined in poems evoking 'the faithful native people' who were 'being displaced' by landowners, landlords, overseers and accountants – named and disgraced in some of the verses. The conflicts involved in a Gaelic sensibility profoundly committed to loyalty to clan and kinship, confronted with the insults of absentee landlords, remote and ignorant political power and ruthless economic exploitation, found expression in poems of different genres and perspectives.

One key figure in the story of the 19th-century Gaelic world is John Murdoch (1818–1903), one of Scotland's great radicals, leader of the Crofters' Revolt and the movement for the recognition and revival of Gaelic culture in Scotland. He was an associate of the Irish leader Charles Stuart Parnell, Professor John Stuart Blackie, major propagandist, translator and advocate of Gaelic literature, and Keir Hardie, founder and leader of the Labour movement. Selections from his work are collected in *For the People's Cause*, edited by James Hunter (1986).

In *The Company I've Kept* (1966) Hugh MacDiarmid places Murdoch alongside John MacLean, Thomas Muir and John Swinton: 'Scots who are relatively far too little known and yet, in our opinion, of far more consequence than most of those who figure prominently either in our history books or in contemporary life'. MacDiarmid describes Murdoch as 'MacLean's agrarian counterpart.' James Kelman, in an interview in the *Scottish Review of Books* (vol.8, no.3) observed: 'Heroes who are radical heroes, like John MacLean, John Murdoch and Donald Macrae, James Connolly or Arthur McManus, Helen Crawfurd, Agnes Dollan, they're not really known. In other countries they would be heroes, but they're not known in their own country, they're radical figures politically.'

And they remain unfamiliar to most of us. It's a long legacy, from the 18th century through the 19th and 20th, to now. The conflicts involved when people profoundly loyal to clan and kinship are confronted with the insults and abuses of absentee landlords, remote and ruthless political power and economic exploitation are still among us. Misplaced loyalties are nothing new.

One of the most memorable poets of the 19th century was Màiri Nic a' Phearsain / Mary MacPherson (1821–98), known as Màiri Mhòr nan Òran (Big Mary of the Songs) partly because of the magnitude of her outspokenness and partly because of her girth. She was energised by the agitation for land reform in the 1880s on the Isle of Skye, where she was born, though later she lived in Inverness and Glasgow. Her songs combine elements of yearning for the isle of her youth and overt commitment to political reform. Love of homeland and political outrage formed a dynamite mix.

Imprisoned on a charge of theft, she wrote 'The Oppression I Suffered' and stated that injustice was what drove her to verse. 'When I was young' is a characteristic song of nostalgic longing made bitter by factual reference to the Clearances. In 'Song of Ben Lee' she lists the heroes of the land reform movement and in 'Incitement of the Gaels' pledges loyalty to the reform candidates in the 1885 elections and describes the boatloads of soldiers and policemen sent to put down the protestors.

MacPherson was the subject of a play, *Màiri Mhòr – The Woman from Skye* (1987) by John McGrath and the 7:84 Theatre Company, a filmed version of which was broadcast on television (1993). Her presence is also intensely felt in the brilliant short film *An Ceasnachadh / Interrogation of a Highland Lass* (2000, broadcast on BBC Alba in 2020). This centres on the police interrogation of Kay Matheson, one of the small group who brought the Stone of Destiny from Westminster Abbey back to Scotland in 1950. The performance of Kathleen MacInnes in the film is stunning, most piercingly when she remembers Mary MacPherson's example and sings one of her songs, vividly connecting the 19th, 20th and 21st centuries in an unfinished history of dispossession and reclamation. Mary Macpherson stays with us, not in history but in living memory, and her example is vital. Produced by Douglas Eadie from his own scripts with Gaelic translation by Dolina MacLennan and directed by Mike Alexander, *An Ceasnachadh / Interrogation of a Highland Lass* is one of those rare films throughout which, for the duration of every one of its 55 minutes, you cannot take your eyes off the screen.

Mary MacPherson brings us to the threshold of the 20th century. The Clearances, the land raids, the question of who owns the land, what it is and is not used for, and how the Gaelic language is treated were among the most pressing urgencies of her world. They have not gone away. In the anthology, *100 Favourite Gaelic Poems* (2020), Mary is represented by an extract from the poignant and perennially beautiful song, 'Nuair bha mi Og' / 'When I Was Young' and the asportation of the stone is commemorated in 'Òran na Cloiche' / 'The Song of the Stone' by Dòmnhall Ruadh Mac An t-Saoir / Donald MacIntyre. These songs define two aspects of the tradition: one of immediate historical reference, the other of lasting human significance. Poetry and song and all the arts enact this complementarity. We measure one against the other.

When we see how badly misreported and misleading are contemporary accounts of events in the news we should step back and remember how utterly disregarded the whole historical understanding of contemporary politics has been over centuries. Not only misreported, but simply not reported at all. The most dangerous policy of all is the slow infiltration of consciousness to gently persuade people generally that this is how it is, how it always was, and how it should forever be.

This is wrong. It is morally repugnant. It is the work of liars and villainy. Some things we must never get accustomed to. Some things must always be resisted. Reading Duncan Ban MacIntyre, John Murdoch and Mary MacPherson is a perpetual reminder and renewal of this truth.

By some accounts, 19th-century Gaelic poetry is less impressive than that of the preceding century, yet on the evidence of Donald E. Meek's anthology of poems from that era, it is rich, and intricately connected with the processes of industrialisation, colonialism and imperial expansion, and thus also with what was happening in contemporary Scottish literature in English and Scots. Gaelic is essential to the national story.

Uilleam MacDhunlèibhe / William Livingston (1808–70), in 'Fios chun a' Bhàird' / 'A Message for the Poet', sees townships wasted by the imported economy of sheep, islanders scattered over the oceans. No-one will answer a call to military service: their homelands have been made desolate. In this landscape, there is neither shelter for the poor nor voices to be heard in song.

> Tha Ilse 'n diugh gun daoine;
> Chuir a' chaor' a bailtean fàs;
> Mar a fhuair 's a chunnaic mise,

> Thoir am fios seo chun a' Bhàird.

('Islay is today devoid of people; / the sheep has laid its townships waste; / just as I found and as I saw, / take this message to the Poet.') In 'Ireland Weeping' the beauty of the landscape, linking Ireland and the west of Scotland, becomes itself a protest against its own emptiness.

> Eilein iomallaich na- Eòrp',
> A thir as bòidhach' fo cheann-bhrat speur,
> Bu tric a chunnaic mi mhòr nam beuc.
>
> Nuair a shèideadh gaoth chiùin on iar-dheas,
> 'S an iarmailt gun cheathach, guin neul,
> Bhiodh na Gàidheil san Roinn Ilish
> Ag innse da chèile do sgèimh...

('Distant island on Europe's edge, / loveliest country under canopy of skies,/ often did I see your coast / across the great channel of the cries. // When a gentle, south-west wind would blow / and the sky was cloudless and clean, / the Gaels in the Rhinns of Islay / would tell each other of your sheen...')

This is part of the strange process by which real things turn into symbols – and in this case, symbols of themselves. The legacy of the later 18th century saw the prohibition (legal or by emphatic enforcement) of weaponry, forms of clothing and the Gaelic language itself. The land too in its deliberately depopulated emptiness becomes a symbol of itself. And the legacy of this stays with us. There's a gulf between material conditions of actuality and fantasy visions uncoupled from history, imported and imposed. But across that gulf negotiations of one kind or another are always taking place.

While the Gaelic-language poets and storytellers of the 19th century were producing extraordinary work like that of Mary MacPherson, another phenomenon was occurring in the English-language tradition. Most readers of modern literature will be familiar with the notion of the 'Celtic Twilight' and its significance for the early work of W.B. Yeats, especially in *The Wanderings of Oisin* (1889), a dialogue between Saint Patrick and Oisin or Ossian, and 'Cuchulain's Fight with the Sea' from *The Rose* (1893). The foundations of Celtic identity and the extent to which writers of the Irish revival drew upon them is well-known, not only in Yeats's work but also in that of Lady Gregory's versions of the Celtic stories in *Cuchulain of Muirthemne* (1902) and *Gods and Fighting Men* (1904), following retellings by Standish O'Grady, in *Early Bardic Literature, Ireland* (1879) and *The Coming of Cuchulain* (1894).

For Yeats, these foundations gave substance to his troubled writing on contemporary political events in Ireland in the early decades of the 20th century. They informed the writing of J.M. Synge and numerous plays performed in Dublin's Abbey Theatre. But they're best understood in a deeper historical context, keeping both Ireland and Scotland in mind, with reference to Macpherson's 18th-century versions of the Ossian stories for a Scottish Enlightenment, English-language readership, and all that followed from that.

Writing on Celtic identity in the 19th century, Matthew Arnold (1822–88) in *On the Study of Celtic Literature* (1867) promoted the idea of the Celts as dreamers, complementing the hard-headed practical-minded Anglo-Saxons, thus fostering the fiction of such priorities in the development of a global British empire. This connected to the work of Ernest Renan (1823–92) in France, writing on the Celtic 'character' in *The Poetry of the Celtic Races* (1896): 'at once proud and timid, strong in feeling and feeble in action, at home free and unreserved, to the outside world awkward and embarrassed.' But as always, there's more to it.

At the least, the 'Celtic Twilight' connected the idea of Gaelic-language literature with English-language readers. Among the most fascinating Scottish writers in this respect was William Sharp (1855–1905), who created an alternative identity for himself in Fiona MacLeod, the fictional author of his neo-Celtic stories, plays and essays. Sharp himself had grown up learning Celtic stories from his nurse, then travelled to Australia in the 1880s and married his cousin, Elizabeth Sharp, editor of the collection *Lyra Celtica: An Anthology of Representative Celtic Poetry* (1896), who had her own fascination with 'Celtic' identity.

They were childless. 'Fiona MacLeod' may have fulfilled the role of a surrogate daughter. Visiting Rome, Sharp identified an affinity between the heroic women of the ancient Roman, Greek and Celtic worlds. His first work as Fiona MacLeod, *Pharais* (1894), evokes 'the Hidden Fire' of the 'soul's desire'. Such predilections are evident even in the titles of his – or her – books of stories and essays, *The Winged Destiny* and *Studies in the Spiritual History of the Gael* (both 1904).

The writing of Sharp, or MacLeod, need not be rejected as mere fabrication. As with Macpherson's *Ossian*, it drew attention to a world of lived experience which later, more analytic writers would examine on its own terms. If it obscured that lived experience in its time, it also helped a broad readership begin to ask questions about what lay behind such obscurity. For example, as Ian Brown has discussed in his book, *Scottish Theatre: Diversity, Language, Continuity* (2013), Sharp's plays are akin to those of the expressionist Belgian Maurice Maeterlinck (1862–1949). Sharp's first play, *The House of Usna* (1900) once shared the bill with two plays by Maeterlinck, *The Death of Tintageles* (1894) and *Interior* (1895). As Brown says, with regard to theatre MacLeod was 'located in an intersection of the Celtic revival and European Symbolism.'

And there are further connections. In the first performance of Debussy's opera *Pelléas et Mélisande* (1902), for which Maeterlinck wrote the libretto, Mélisande was played by the famous Scottish soprano Mary Garden, who is noted in the opening pages of Hugh MacDiarmid's long poem of 1926, *A Drunk Man Looks at the Thistle*. And before all these was the first Celtic opera by a Scottish composer, Hamish MacCunn's *Diarmid* (1897).

MacDiarmid once called for a move 'out of the Celtic twilight – and into the Gaelic sun!' but what all these associations and connections suggest are much richer diversities and far more complex networks of connection than have yet been fully explored.

39

Beyond the Kailyard

VIRTUES AND LIABILITIES: FROM R.M. BALLANTYNE, S.R. CROCKETT, IAN MACLAREN, J.M. BARRIE AND NEIL MUNRO TO MARION ANGUS AND CHARLES MURRAY

KAIL IS A GREEN vegetable like cabbage and the word kailyard means cabbage-patch or vegetable garden, an essential in self-sustenance in late 19th- and early 20th-century Scottish small-town or village life. The implication is that in the communities of Scotland, people grow their own and look after themselves quite happily; domestic virtues prevail in little societies presided over by minister and schoolteacher. In this world, sentimentalism and small-mindedness go alongside anti-intellectualism and evade the difficult questions. Political matters of national and international import are the provenance of Westminster. Novels, stories and poems of the 'Kailyard School' might be especially exemplified in the fiction of the ministers Ian Maclaren and S.R. Crockett and the poems collected in the 'Whistlebinkie' anthologies, whose contents have been described ungenerously as 'the art of sinking in poetry'. The Kailyard at its worst is characterised by respect for community values, social conservativism, political unionism and subservience to the authorities of church, state and education. The most excoriating assessment of these writers is by the novelist George Blake (1893–1961) in his *Barrie and the Kailyard School* (1951). As a realist novelist dealing primarily with life in industrial Glasgow, Blake found the rural homilies of the Kailyard abhorrent but he is sensitive to discern between the excesses of Maclaren and Crockett at his most egregious and the achievements of Crockett and, in more complex ways, of Barrie. He points out that in an era when most of Scotland's people were 'confined to slums of the foulest order', these writers for three decades 'held up their fellow-countymen as comic characters for the amusement of the foreigner.' Their popularity is attested by their sales: Maclaren's *Beside the Bonnie Brier Bush*, Blake tells us, sold a quarter of a million copies in Britain, half a million in the United States. The comforts and reassurances these writers offered were presented

> in an age of great prosperity and self-satisfaction. The British industrial effort was near its peak. Income tax was still at a few pence in the pound; Britannia ruled the waves; and if the bulk of the working population were still condemned to low wages and grim working conditions, the

middle classes, constituting the reading public, were still strong and safe and in no mood to consider the long-range political and economic implications of their prosperity.

These qualities are crossed by the critical discontent that the end of the Victorian era and the rise of the modern world came to embody, as we'll see in the writing of R.B. Cunninghame Graham and others. And yet there is more to be said about these Kailyard writers. Their virtues were genuine to many, and the their writing proved extremely commercially successful to some. And some retained charm for generations. Many children over generations encountered the mysterious twilight twinkling rhymes of 'Wee Willie Winkie' by William Miller (1810–72):

> Wee Willie Winkie rinnin' through the toon,
> Upstairs, doonstairs in his nicht-goun,
> Knockin' at the window, cryin' at the lock,
> 'Are a' the weans in their beds? It's past ten o'clock!'

The virtues embodied in the Kailyard writers were not limited to pastoral locations but also prevailed in the industrial cities. In 1879 the American evangelists Moody and Sankey visited Scotland and their campaign of soliciting sympathy – rather than better wages and radically improved living conditions – for the impoverished working class had a tidal effect. Many middle-class people of these decades sang their hymns with lusty lungs on Sundays while the profits rolled in. The pieties of Kailyard fiction and poetry escalated in the wake of such hypocrisy. Yet this is a caricature. The spirit of reform was also generated and practical social improvememts were underway too. George Mills (1808–81) exposed the darker and more brutal aspects of industrial working-class life in his novel *The Beggar's Benison* (1866). Mills was partner in a shipbuilding company before becoming a journalist, literary critic and novelist. He wrote from experience. The most extensive revaluation of the work published in the anthologies and regularly in national and local newspapers throughout the country is Kirstie Blair's *Working Verse in Victorian Scotland* (2019), which gives a valuable account of the immense extent and popularity of these rhymes by people in all sorts of professional, skilled occupations.

In Scotland and more generally, children's literature of the late 19th and early 20th centuries inevitably sought to inculcate imperial certainty, to confirm that being patriotically Scottish is a good component part of British identity, if you keep your attention diverted from mad desires and unpredicted wildness. Thus is the status quo maintained, as children become adults. In this respect, the children's novels by R.M. Ballantyne (1825–94), most lastingly *The*

Coral Island (1858) and *The Gorilla Hunters* (1861), were part of a unionist, conservative ideology. In the former, boys marooned on a desert island adapt themselves nobly, resourcefully and with common purpose, making the best of things; in the latter, intrepid big-game hunters penetrate darkest Africa, with the main purpose of shooting gorillas and taking back corpses, or bits of corpses, as trophies. The courage of both groups, boys and men, in each novel, their integrity and unwavering self-confidence, are appalling to most modern readers, as we understand the extent to which they are driven by imperial self-righteousness, extreme racism, and unrestrained self-gratifying destructiveness. The profound liabilities in their behaviour are indicated by the extent to which William Golding's *Lord of the Flies* (1954) is a reimagining of *The Coral Island*, but they also suggest the reason why so many major Scottish writers of the early 20th century found the Kailyard as a defining idea so abominable. The implicit assumptions of these fictions have their foundations in unquestioned imperialist priorities, and these have direct political consequences.

Yet there is more in the Kailyard writers than such absolute condemnation allows, whether in the jocularity and ironic humour of poems such as 'The Pawky Duke' by David Rorie (1867–1946), or in the fiction of those writers most closely associated with the term, S.R. Crockett and Ian Maclaren. J.M. Barrie and Neil Munro, often linked to the Kailyard, are not at all contained by what the label implies.

The novels of S.R. Crockett (1859–1914) are varied. *The Raiders* (1894) and *The Grey Man* (1896) are adventure stories set in Galloway, the latter with the 18th-century cannibal family of Sawney Bean as central villains. *The Lilac Sunbonnet* (1894) and *The Stickit Minister* (1893) are rural romances and gently satirical sketches of the church in small-town Scotland, where melodrama and moral fortitude prevail. Lavishly over-written in places, they surely reveal more of the author's – and his readers' – psychological liabilities than was intended. Urban Edinburgh is the setting for *Cleg Kelly, Arab of the City* (1896), which begins with Kelly's astonishing exclamation that throws his entire Sunday-school congregation into astonished silence: 'It's all a dumb lie! – God's dead!' The words repudiate the Sunday-school teacher's comment that God sees all, punishes the bad and rewards the good. On this assumption, the Kailyard school of benevolent fiction, boy's own adventures or small-town homiletics, rested. But clearly, even Crockett (a minister himself and paragon of Kailyard sensibility) seems to have encountered Nietzsche.

Francis Russell Hart, in *The Scottish Novel* (1978), sketches the rich liabilities that inhabit Crockett's world. In *The Lilac Sunbonnet*, he tells us, 'Crockett's lovers are young adults whose innocence is inseparable from their fleshliness.' The girls in the story are 'physically very present' and the heroine, disinguousnly named Winsome, possesses 'excessive curls', shocks us with her 'bare limbs trampling blankets' and is 'as ready for a midnight tryst as Jess Kessock is to substitute herself; and the kiss of Ralph, the mistaken lover, is genuine and lengthy.' Winsome's sinlessness allows Crockett to give her happy marriage and prosperity and Hart comments that 'her "first full kiss of full surrender" has few analogues in Victorian fiction', oddly anticipating Alan Sharp's descriptions of 'sinless sexuality' in the 1960s. We'll return to this theme when we come to J.M. Barrie.

Ian Maclaren (1850–1907) was the pen-name of John Watson. Educated at Edinburgh University and ordained as a Free Church of Scotland minister, he worked in Logiealmond, Perthshire and Glasgow, before a long residence in Liverpool. He published religious works under his own name but his first fiction collection, *Beside the Bonnie Brier Bush* (1894) established him at the centre of the Kailyard school. The book is a series of interconnected stories, set in the village of Drumtochty, where Church affairs and piety are the focus of attention. Any bright young man aspiring to an education may win out to university, and any elderly member of the community may stay resident and gain a wealth of local wisdom, but both will end up on their deathbeds, either taken off too early or passing on in the fullness of time, presided over by a weeping mother or devoted descendants, under the minister's spiritual guidance.

Between the extremes of Kailyard and anti-Kailyard stands J.M. Barrie (1860–1937). Barrie was born in Kirriemuir, the small town in the north-east of central Scotland which he fictionalised as Thrums. He was the son of a handloom weaver and went to school in Glasgow, Forfar and Dumfries, took an MA from Edinburgh University and worked as a journalist in Nottingham before basing himself in London from 1885, at the age of 25. He began writing stories and novels, then turned to plays, including *The Admirable Crichton* (1892) and *Quality Street* (1901), and probably the most famous children's play ever written, *Peter Pan* (1904). The poignancy of the idea of the boy who would never grow up resonates throughout his career.

Barrie's fiction and plays make up a complex body of work, a greater achievement than many critics have allowed until recently. His early books, including *Auld Licht Idylls* (1888) and *A Window in Thrums* (1889), gather stories and sketches evidently defining Kailyard conventions: a benign world of small-town Scotland presided over by the local minister and wise schoolteacher or dominie. Summers are warm and sunny, winters cosy by the fireside. But his novel *Sentimental Tommy* (1896) and its sequel *Tommy and Grizel* (1900) take the conventions and wilfully destroy them. Tommy, the bright young man of the small town, goes to London to make his fortune, but fails to realise his ambitions, either socially or in love, and at the end of *Tommy and Grizel*, hangs himself accidentally in a horrifying moment of futility. This desperately pitying aspect of Barrie's work is less well-known.

His late ghost story *Farewell, Miss Julie Logan* (1931) is the most haunting and powerful of all his works. A small-town minister, Adam Yestreen (his name boldly declares that he is from and of the past),in an extended first-person narrative, reveals his growing awareness of the ambiguous and tempting world that surrounds him. The community of people he finds himself among prompts his disclosures, revelations of his own unstated desires for the sensual, the sexual, the world of art and shapely forms. Austerity is not enough. Liberated habits displayed by the annual English tourists bring out the contrasts: Adam is envious, at first seeming disdainful, claiming moral superiority, but he begins to see the flaw and lack in himself. He comes to full recognition when he meets the beautiful Julie Logan. He feels an actual, physical need and a new sense of spiritual longing. These play against each other in the elusive, palpable energies of the novella, reminiscent of the ambiguities of *The Confessions of a Justified Sinner*. Yet where Hogg is dark and his novel is ultimately tragic, Barrie is poignant and poised on the edge of comic absurdity. The novella retains a sense of tempered wonder and the good purpose of human imagination. Yet that good purpose is a liability. The climactic revelation at which Adam loses his hold on Julie both literally and imaginatively is a moment of supreme bathos. Its weirdness is probably even more palpable now than it must have seemed in 1931. But the sudden, unpredicted thrust of what feels inappropriate repulsion has a lasting effect. The bathos delivers an instant, intrinsic shock. As in the Border Ballads, the comic and the cruel combine. Adam's instantaneous action leaves him with Julie gone and only his own haunted loneliness to live with.

Julie Logan herself is one of Scottish literature's mythical figurations of a lost, unattainable past, a figure of youth, childhood and arcadia. Her sexual allure is in itself a dangerous ambiguity. She is a symbol of how much potential is wasted by adults, yet she also possesses an immediate physical presence and leaves a lasting sense of yearning. She makes imagination hungry. She is Scotland's Lolita. This is Barrie at his ambivalent best.

In *The Scottish Novel*, Francis Russell Hart neatly summarises: 'Kailyard fiction is chiefly Victorian pastoral, sometimes neopagan (Crockett), sometimes elegiac (Maclaren), and sometimes ironic (Barrie).' As we've seen, there's more to it, as always, but that's a good way to begin.

Neil Munro (1863–1930) was the illegitimate son of a kitchen-maid and it's been suggested that his father was an aristocrat from the house of Argyll. He was born and schooled in Inveraray and went to work in the office of the Sheriff-clerk of Argyll. Writing was his trade and he moved to Glasgow and embarked upon a career in journalism, becoming the assistant-editor of the Glasgow *Evening News*. He retired from full-time journalism around 1902 but continued to write a weekly column for the *News* in which his most famous creations appeared in a series of short stories: his 'droll friend' Archie, the commercial traveller Jimmy Swan and the best-loved Para Handy, irascible skipper of the *Vital Spark*, a puffer – a small boat – chortling through the waters of the Clyde estuary and the inner Hebridean seas, a merchant vessel for hire, whose nautical inadequacies call for special reserves of humour and resources of intelligence that bourgeois employers or admiralty officials might not suspect. Para Handy and his crew were loved companions for generations who read the stories and saw the television versions in more than one series, and recognised the big-screen version in the carefully-poised film *The Maggie* (1954). The stories are less easily given to sentimental coherence than the television series and the film, though they present reliable figures and structures as any genre series must. All Munro's stories have a good journalist's eye for light but serious social comment on events of the day.

Munro's fiction has often been grouped with Maclaren and Crockett as a Highland version of the Kailyard priorities of the pieties of small-town Scotland, but, as with Crockett and Barrie, close reading opens up greater depths and complexities. *The Lost Pibroch* (1896) collected his short stories and *John Splendid* (1898) began a series of novels describing the Highlands at the precise turning point of a Gaelic world being lost to compromised modernity. Munro's Highlanders are often vain, self-serving, mean-minded and desperately fallible. In *Gilian the Dreamer* (1899), a memorable episode recounts Gilian's failure to act at a moment of crisis due to his imaginative disposition. His dreaminess and hesitancy spring the trap of misapprehension that closes on him through the book in a way very similar to the ambiguous action that haunts the title character of Joseph Conrad's novel *Lord Jim* (1900) from its very beginning, and is finally his mortal undoing. Munro and Conrad were friends; that they had discussed this proposition may not be accidental.

Munro's central theme is change in the Highlands. Instead of the placatory nostalgia often found in Maclaren and Crockett, there is a subdued anger and sometimes bitter resignation in Munro. *The New Road* (1914) has a fine portrait of malevolent intent in the villain, Simon Fraser of Lovat. Building the new road through the Highlands in 1733, between the Jacobite risings of 1715 and 1745, will establish southern control of the indigenous people and, it is threatened, subdue any independent spirit. But Munro knows that the new road will become an old road in time, with its own ghosts and hauntings.

Munro's son was killed during the First World War and although he continued in journalism through the war years, his later output diminished. Hugh MacDiarmid included his poems in the anthologies *Northern Numbers* in the early 1920s and by that time he was recognised as a senior figure in Scottish letters. He died in 1930 and is buried in Kilmalieu Cemetery, Inveraray and there's a fine monument on the hill overlooking the town. It's worth the climb.

The quiet life story of Marion Angus (1865–1946) belies the linguistic and narrative complexity of her poems. Her father was a Presbyterian minister and her mother came from the Borders. Born in Aberdeen, she spent her childhood in Arbroath but after her father's death, she returned to Aberdeen and lived there with her mother and sister for the rest of her life. Her poems, collected in various books through the 1920s and 1930s, arise from traditional ballads, observing regular metre, narrative development, characterisation and tension, but they show a modern woman's sensibility at work in their deployment of hidden or oblique stories, a rich and unpretentious fluency with the Scots language, a strength of character and independence of mind that seems self-sufficient without recourse to abstraction, philosophy or the intrusions of ego. She refers to particular places and familiar characters of the north-east but she refutes conventional expectations. In 'The Turn of the Day' the arrival of spring does not deliver hopeful renewal. Grief, loss and loneliness are poignantly expressed through understatement, in voices that tell their own stories without embellishment. Angus was also a fine writer of poems in English. Her portrait of Mary Queen of Scots, 'Alas! Poor Queen' is beautifully poised, catching the vulnerability and graceful cultural resonance of a woman often crudely caricatured in popular perception. Angus's poems evoke unfinished stories, mysterious encounters, tales of lives unfulfilled: their restraint is part of their pathos.

And that deliberately unsentimental pathos is essential to all these writers at their best. They knew their world was coming to its end.

Another poet of the period takes us from the comforting securities of the Kailyard at its worst to the dark judgements of the 'anti-Kailyard' writers. *Hamewith* (1900) by Charles Murray (1864–1941) was one of the most popular books of poetry for generations, culminating the long tradition of 19th-century poetry of exile (the title means, 'Homewards'). Sentimental as much of his verse might be, Murray sometimes hits a universal note with absolute accuracy. 'Dockens Afore His Peers' is a desperately moving monologue spoken by a soldier at an exemption tribunal. The Scots voice registers a sense of helplessness, human resilience and utter vulnerability. In 'A Green Yule', the sense of imminent mortality is shocking:

> Dibble them doon, the laird, the loon,
> King an' the cadgin' caird,
> The lady fine beside the queyn,
> A' in the same kirkyaird.
>
> The warst, the best, they a' get rest;
> Ane 'neath a headstane braw,
> Wi' deep-cut text, while owre the next
> The wavin' grass is a'.

This connects him in the Scottish tradition to Dunbar's 'Lament for the Makars' but also internationally and across time to the major poet of 15th-century France, Villon, translated here by Basil Bunting (1900–85):

> Remember, imbeciles and wits
> sots and ascetics, fair and foul,
> young girls with little tender tits
> that DEATH is written over all.

The same sentiment is perhaps more sympathetic in the Scots verse than in the nasty jingling rhythm and rhyme of the English version of the French original, but both are making the same, black, absolute and irrefutable point. They are as far from Kailyard conventions as you can go.

THE DEVASTATORS: GEORGE DOUGLAS BROWN AND J. MACDOUGALL HAY

But even these do not go far enough. There are two classic 'anti-Kailyard' novels, both full-blown works of imaginative horror.

The short life George Douglas Brown is a tragic chronicle. The illegitimate son of a farmer and a woman of Irish descent, he excelled at school, went on to study classics at Glasgow University and from there to Balliol College, Oxford. What looked like high promise and good prospects crashed when, after returning to Ayrshire to nurse his dying mother, he only scraped through his final exams and found work as a journalist in London, writing articles for *Blackwood's* and other periodicals. He published an adventure story, *Love and a Sword* under the pseudonym Kennedy King, before *The House with the Green Shutters* gained him serious recognition and he intended another novel, *The Incompatibles*, but died of pneumonia before it got very far. He is buried in the cemetery in Ayr.

If you stand outside the house where George Douglas Brown (1869–1902) was born, in the long main street of the little Ayrshire town of Ochiltree, you can look downhill and out for miles over the widening farm landscapes to the north and east. On the tall, sloping street, his birthplace is commemorated by a plaque but while the street and prospect are pleasant and broadening, any reader of Brown's masterpiece, *The House with the Green Shutters* (1901), must feel a sense of small-town social oppression, the weight of malicious gossip, the fierce contestation in a capitalist economy at the moment when (even in Ayrshire!) the agricultural world was about to give way to the priorities of industrialisation. The novel hinges on the period when the small-town patriarch, Gourlay, dominating family, workers and town, is matched and outdone by the younger merchant James Wilson, who knows better how to exploit the coming changed world in which trains have taken over from horse-drawn wagons. Barbie – the fictional small-town – is a foetid nest of horrible people, brutalised by the economy in which they are embroiled, taking cruel pleasure by inflicting nastiness upon each other, and commented on by the local men who foregather every day to talk about the latest miserable occurrences and developments. By the end of the book, even they seem stunned by the violence. Gourlay's son has returned from university, his gifts squandered in alcoholism and inadequacy. His temper flares and he murders his father. Coming upon the scene, his mother despairs:

> Mrs Gourlay raised her arms, like a gaunt sibyl, and spoke to her Maker quietly, as if He were a man before her in the room. 'Ruin and murder,' she said slowly, 'and madness; and death at my nipple like a child! When will Ye be satisfied?'

No answer arriving, the son poisons himself. His mother and sister, discovering some poison left in the bottle, kill themselves too. What would be melodrama is held down to believable and horrifying reality by a precision of language and stylistic restraint which delivers clear, understated descriptions and a gathering strength in the story's development. Conspicuous by their absence in the novel are any depictions of the community of the Christian Kirk. There is no saviour and no redemption. All the characters are caught in an intensifying vortex of forces that destroys them, as devastating as Dostoevsky. No other novel ends in such an utterly comprehensive vision of death, disease and disaster.

Gillespie (1914), by John MacDougall Hay (1881–1919), tells a similar story on a larger scale. The location for this apocalyptic vision of small-town Scotland is Brieston, based on Tarbert, Loch Fyne, a fishing village with its own small-town rivalries, hostilities and nastinesses to rival that of Brown's rural Barbie. Hay grew up in Tarbert and, like Brown, went to Glasgow University, becoming a headmaster in Lewis in the Outer Hebrides, then moving back to the mainland to teach in Ullapool before returning to Glasgow to study divinity. He became a church minister in 1909 and in the same year married Catherine Campbell. They had two children, Sheena and George Campbell Hay, who was to become a fine poet. Hay had been writing journalism for various magazines and newspapers such as *The Glasgow Herald* and when *Gillespie* appeared he wondered about leaving the ministry to take up writing full-time. A second novel appeared, *Barnacles* (1916), and a memorable poem, 'Their Dead Sons' (1918), but *Gillespie* has sustained his reputation.

The central character, Gillespie Strang, combines the qualities of Brown's Gourlay and Gourlay's nemesis, Wilson: he is both brutally domineering and commercially astute, but in the moral and social world he is shown to be completely bereft of decency. He is almost literally monstrous. The novel is deliberately extended and epic in scale, both in its social vision and its thundering denunciation of the evils it displays. As in Brown's novel, there's a tortured, self-doubting son, and a cataclysmic ending in which all the principal characters meet their demise. Francis Russell Hart, in *The Scottish Novel*, comments that the conclusion of *Gillespie* 'makes the end of Brown's *The House with the Green Shutters* austerely tame by contrast'. He gives details: 'The final horrors – the son with his throat cut, the guilty mother with her head smashed, and Gillespie [...] dying in slow agony of lockjaw' are presented as proof that 'a terrible law has worked itself out' and that 'Nature for Hay is violent, erratic, in collusion with the amoral force of Gillespie.'

There are some passages of heavily-written prose reminiscent of Herman Melville at his least buoyant, yet the book stands the comparison. There are two lastingly memorable sections, one describing the effect of plague decimating the town, at which point the doctor, rather than the minister, offers real help; the other describes the burning of the fishing fleet in Brieston harbour, the whole town illuminated by the hellish blaze on the water. This is one of the most spectacular scenes in modern Scottish fiction and suggests the book's filmic potential while it drives home a bitter lesson in the novel's moral universe: 'Those who set fire to Gillespie's fishing fleet must discover that their vengeance simply allows Gillespie to sell them new boats.' This reverses a central theme of *The House with the Green Shutters*, in which, as Hart notes, the 'bodies' help bring about the downfall of the idolator. By contrast, 'Gillespie is so brilliant and unscrupulous in his entrepreneurial tricks that he exploits each new resistance.' Until everything ends in domestic apocalypse.

Like Brown, Hay's health failed him too young. When he died in 1919 at the age of 39, his funeral was held at Paisley Abbey.

JOHN BUCHAN, ANNA BUCHAN (O. DOUGLAS), PATRICK MACGILL, GEORGE BLAKE, JAMES BARKE, DOT ALLAN, A.J. CRONIN AND OTHER NOVELISTS

The novels of John Buchan (1875–1940) often vividly describe Scottish landscapes and characters. *Prester John* (1910) begins with a boy on the shore at evening, witnessing the amazing dance of the tall black man John Laputa around a blazing bonfire. This prefigures a fascination with the power of his nemesis that develops when they meet again in South Africa. John has become the charismatic leader of a black African rebellion to overthrow white imperialism, while the boy has become an adult who will have numerous adventures and hair-breadth escapes before the rebellion is defeated and the noble savage meets his end. Structurally, the novel is a revision of Scott's *Waverley*, with the main character seduced and enthralled by the villain – except that in Scott's novel loyalties are culturally entwined and progress is diminishment. For Buchan, imperial authority is paternal, good and strong. Racism and the sexuality of power relations are flagrantly evident but Buchan's prose is so clear, the narrative so fast and well-balanced, that the tension between the 'virtues' of Empire and the justified energy of self-determination rising against it is vibrant throughout.

Buchan is a terrific storyteller. It's only by reading against the grain of his prose that his allegiances can be questioned. The tension in his writing derives from the way his literary skill is applied to the edge of the historical moment in which he was living. Joseph Conrad's *Heart of Darkness* (first published in Edinburgh in *Blackwood's Magazine* in 1899) and the stories of R.B. Cunninghame Graham also come out of this moment. Buchan exploits the context for adventure, while Conrad and Cunninghame Graham expose its deepest horrors for literary and moral judgement, but they all come out of the same late 19th, early 20th-century, transitional world.

Born in Perth, Buchan grew up partly in the Borders, took his first degree at Glasgow then went to Oxford. His love of Scotland was compromised – or complemented – by his commitment to Anglocentric political authority. In his worldview, England afforded civilised security, Scotland meant wildness and adventure. He loved the Scots language, poetry, and the fiction of Scott and Stevenson, but his career was firmly embedded in the British establishment, and he became Baron Tweedsmuir, Governor-General of Canada, where he died. The pathos of his position is partly what engendered his fine last novel, *Sick Heart River* (1941) in which the main character, Sir Edward Leithen, sacrifices himself in Canada to save a tribe of indigenous people from extinction. The descriptions of the Canadian wilderness, the moral dedication of Leithen and the principle that the native people have a right not to be treated as mere subjects by a distant imperialist authority are all strongly depicted. It's as if, in the relation between indigenous people and the authority of imperial power, there is an unspoken allegory of the relation of all native peoples, including those of Scotland, to Westminster.

Buchan was the author of many novels of lasting value, as well as entertaining 'shockers' as he dismissively called them, of which *The Thirty-Nine Steps* (1915) is the best-known. The first film version was directed by Alfred Hitchcock in 1935, with others following in 1959 and 1978, and adaptations for theatre in 1995, revised in 2005 and for television in 2008. The novel contains the most loving descriptions of Scotland when Richard Hannay is on the run in the Borders. In literary terms, it has the most fascinating final confrontation. The villains are exposed by the hero only when he recognises them through their disguises – disguises which are not supplied by make-up or false moustaches, but by essential ways of presenting themselves in behaviour, body-language, mannerisms and attitudes. In other words, Buchan recognised how visual appearance informed politically persuasive propaganda well before the rise of mass media. Buchan's writing in this part of the book is intensely well-judged and adroit, and, it would seem, completely untranslatable to screen media. No screen version has ever tried to present the book's actual climax. It presents something only writing can do.

Mr Standfast (1919) includes colourful and politically-determined descriptions of Glasgow and the (allegedly) Irish- and Communist-controlled political revolutionaries of Red Clydeside, with a portrait of a character who seems to be modelled on John Maclean, the revolutionary appointed by Lenin as the Communist Soviet government's Glasgow consul. *Huntingtower* (1922) gives us a group of Glasgow boys from the slums, the Gorbals Die-Hards, taken into the Scottish Highlands by the benevolent retired grocer Dickson MacCunn, where they become embroiled in anti-Tsarist Bolshevik plots. Buchan's imperialist ideal is clear enough but the representation of slum-children in this sympathetic context suggests his benevolent, paternal attitude to improvement for the working-class, and if that seems uncomfortably patrician, we should remember that the fictionalising of the characters gives them a life beyond the limitations of their author's intentions. Wee Jakey, for example, beyond sentimentalism, is a master of his own self-determination who might come to scare any aristocrat when he grows up. Imagine what the Gorbals Die-Hards could have done if John Maclean had been leading them instead of Dickson MacCunn.

Witch Wood (1927) is a historical novel in the line of Scott and Stevenson, in which the central character is torn by religious doubt and ambiguous social allegiances: politics and sexuality are drawn into the mix. And *A Prince of the Captivity* (1933) is an important anti-Nazi novel, possibly the first popular novel to affirm Jewish integrity in the face of rising Fascism. Its date, like that of the other novels, suggests the proximity of Buchan's writing to the major political events of his time. Its closest companion in fiction is Hemingway's *For Whom the Bell Tolls* (1940).

Anna Buchan (1877–1948), John's sister, published many novels under the name O. Douglas, the best of which is perhaps *The Setons* (1917). Her fiction is in the same sphere of close observation of domestic life as that of the Findlater sisters, Mary (1865–1963) and Jane (1866–1946), who wrote individually and in collaboration, notably in their novel-of-manners *Crossriggs* (1908). While never profoundly exploring social and sexual potency, as Susan Ferrier, Catherine Carswell, Nan Shepherd, Willa Muir, Janice Galloway or A.L. Kennedy have done, their novels open up domestic Scottish life in more unsettling, comic and ironic ways than their male contemporaries of the Kailyard school, Crockett and Maclaren, and deserve more extensive revaluation.

Another kind of outsider, Patrick MacGill (1889–1963), born in Donegal,

Ireland, left school at 12 and headed for Scotland at 14 as a 'tattie-howker' (an itinerant potato-picker) and a labourer working on the Caledonian Railway before publishing poems, novels and autobiographical accounts of working-class life, stylistically similar to his American contemporary Jack London. *Children of the Dead End* (1914) and *The Rat Pit* (1915) are works of grim brilliance.

At least four other novelists of the period are worth revisiting. George Blake (1893–1961), born in Greenock and wounded at Gallipoli in World War 1, became a journalist on the Glasgow *Evening News* when Neil Munro was editor and a familiar figure in the literary world of the 1920s and 1930s. His literary reputation rests on a series of novels depicting industrial Glasgow and the development of shipbuilding on the river Clyde, such as *The Shipbuilders* (1935) and the 'Garvel' series (set in Greenock), including *The Westering Sun* and *The Constant Star* (both 1946). Blake was also a fierce critic of the Kailyard novelists, partly because his fiction embodied a social realism from which the Kailyarders insulated themselves. His work is close to that of Dot Allan (1892–1964), in her classic of the Depression, *Hunger March* (1934), and points forward to that of Edward Gaitens, William McIlvanney and James Kelman.

By contrast, although James Barke (1905–58) did write of industrial Glasgow in *Major Operation* (1936), his most lasting book is *The Land of the Leal* (1939), a Tolstoyan vision of the lives of farmers' workers in the south-west of Scotland, in the Rhinns of Galloway. His most popular books are a series of novels on the life of Robert Burns, *The Wind that Shakes the Barley* (1946), *The Song in the Greenthorn Tree* (1947), *The Wonder of All the Gay World* (1949), *The Crest of the Broken Wave* (1953), *The Well of the Silent Harp* (1954) and the posthumously published sequel, *Bonnie Jean* (1959). The writing is lucid and the narrative fast in all these novels, in the style of Russian socialist realism.

A.J. Cronin (1896–1981), on the other hand, apparently died a millionaire, a tax exile in Switzerland, the richest writer Scotland produced till J.K. Rowling. A writer of international popularity, his fame rests on the invention of Dr Finlay, whose stories were adapted for television (1962–71 and 1993–96), variations on the Kailyard ethos of small-town domestic dilemmas. His most commercially successful novel was *The Citadel* (1937), an exposé of the British medical world which, it's been suggested, prompted the foundation of the National Health Service. Cronin's popularity might have arisen from the formula of his narrative structure(s): a solitary-hero figure is engaged under pressure and in conditions of critical isolation, to address a situation of social hypocrisy and to redress the wrongs of an establishment's moral self-righteousness. It's a David versus Goliath scenario designed to be popular (especially if David wins). This scenario itself contributes to the perhaps mythical sense that The Citadel and Cronin himself were to some degree responsible for the founding of the NHS. That is, we might like to think so, despite there being no way to prove it conclusively.

His most notorious work was his first novel, *Hatter's Castle* (1931), about a monstrous patriarch, a kind of anti-Kailyard novel akin to *The House with the Green Shutters* or *Gillespie*. Cronin's commercial skill, therefore, rested on a keen sense of topicality and a determined exploitation of both Kailyard and anti-Kailyard positions.

The writers we've looked at in this chapter 'Beyond the Kailyard' range across almost the entire political spectrum, from Conservative, imperialist and reactionary to revolutionary socialist, from the deeply committed to orthodoxy in religion and piety in convention, to the anarchic, apocalyptic visionaries of social devastation. Only in some works and in a few of the writers can the familiar clichés of 'Kailyard' writing be described as predominant. Many of them, in fact, explode the conventional idea that the era of the 'Kailyard' was typified by mere sentimentalism, but A.J. Cronin's success, like that of Crockett and Maclaren before him, and of other 'neo-Kailyard' writers in the 21st century, is also a warning. Commercial exploitation of human feeling was inevitable in the world these writers inhabited, and has become even more ingrained in modern culture since then. But not all writers were enthralled by commercial success. Some set their sights on more important things.

NOTE
Kailyard writing preceded, and its popularity continued through and extended into the aftermath of the First World War. Further explorations of the different ways in which Scottish authors responded to the First World War are in *Scottish Literature and World War I*, edited by David A. Rennie (Edinburgh: Edinburgh University Press, 2020).

40

The internationalists:
from R.B. Cunninghame Graham to Violet Jacob

R.B. CUNNINGHAME GRAHAM (1852–1936) was born in London but travelled throughout Europe, Morocco and North Africa, the United States and South America, gathering a vast resource of experience and a reputation as an aristocratic adventurer. He was a highly cultivated literary man of action, a professional amateur, a flamboyant optimist whose belief in socialism, Scottish independence and cultural authority made him friends even of people who totally disagreed with him. In Morocco, it's said that he was once confronted by armed tribesmen who challenged him with the question, 'Are you a Christian?' He replied with self-righteous indignation and hauteur, 'I am of the Church of Scotland!' and was told to pass freely. One good friend, the novelist Joseph Conrad, wrote to him sternly in a letter dated 31 January 1898: 'There is no morality, no knowledge and no hope...' But Cunninghame Graham, with ironic humour, deep understanding and Quixotic idealism, maintained a fatalistic belief in all three. And in a letter of 3 February 1905, Conrad acknowledged that his 'artistic assent' to 'the intellectual and moral satisfaction with the truth and force of your thought living in your prose' was 'unbounded'. High praise from one master to another. William Power in 1935 called him 'perhaps the finest literary artist alive in Europe today' and living proof that 'national feeling is strongest in the cultured and travelled internationalist.' Power specifies the 'cynical humanism' that characterises Cunninghame Graham's writing: the cynicism comes out of the humanism, the sympathy gives rise to the irony and wry humour.

This quality of shrewd measurement, the ability to administer uttermost disdain, when and where it is due, to the sharpest effect, is as Power says, 'as different as possible from the cosily insular sentiment of the Kailyarders.' His Scottish essays and sketches depict 'a twilight Scotland, ennobled by tragedy and defeat' and yet the dream of a new Scotland, 'nobly self-reliant and bravely idealistic, worthy of her own finest social and cultural traditions' is not to be consigned to fantasy or nostalgia. It is something Cunninghame Graham 'is valiantly helpng to create' – not *trying* to create but literally making, helping to make actual, with 'self-sacrificing devotion to her interests and prestige'. This too distinguishes his writing from that of almost all his contemporaries.

And it connects his writing and his political career and confirms the courage he brought to both. If, through the end of the 19th century and the beginning of the 20th, Ireland had become an increasingly fervid national idea for which young men and women were prepared to die, then Scotland had become more familiar as what William Power calls 'a bagpipe obligato to "Rule Britannia!"' Throughout the history of the British Empire, almost the only country in the world to which Scots had not devoted their skills of construction was Scotland itself. It saw an extending social class, wherever on the scale from poverty to wealth, disdainful of rustic life and language, pious in religion, ruled by law, led by exclusively Anglophone and Anglocentric educational priorities, and devoted to 'reading nothing save for trivial entertainment and superficial comfort'. These poeple inhabited a world of 'imaginative nullity'. Into this world Cunninghame Graham rode as a knight without armour.

And yet he was a practical man and a realist. In 1886–87, he was an MP in the House of Commons in London. Famously, condemning the hypocrisy of the London parliament, he was told to withdraw. He replied, 'I never withdraw!' Unintimidated by the priorities of civil disobedience, he was truncheoned to the ground on 'Bloody Sunday', at the protest in Trafalgar Square in 1887.

Along with Keir Hardie, he was a founder member of the Scottish Labour Party (1888), which joined the Independent Labour Party (1895) and later the Labour Party (1906), and he was also a founder member of the National Party of Scotland (1928), evolving into the Scottish National Party (1934). Hugh MacDiarmid said that he was introduced to Cunninghame Graham in the early 1920s: 'My decision to make the Scottish Cause, cultural and political, my life-work dates from that moment.'

Cunninghame Graham's conviction was that principles of universal socialism and Scottish independence were intrinsically aligned, both in need of each other, and neither ultimately able to deliver without the support of the other. His priorities were to nationalise land, mines and other industries, to abolish the House of Lords and the Church of England, and to establish an eight-hour day for working people, free school meals, universal suffrage and Scottish Home Rule. He was ahead of his time.

Conrad was a pivotal figure for him, as for Neil Munro and Hugh MacDiarmid (Cunninghame Graham and Munro were Conrad's friends and MacDiarmid met him in London in the early 1920s). Cunninghame Graham never attempted a novel but his range is as wide as Conrad's: travel writing, astute political accounts of the grandeur and squalor of the British Empire, perfectly poised short stories, sharp, ironic, compassionate vignettes of Scottish life. Various pieces are gathered in substantial collections crossing different genres, made up of sketches of landscapes and the lore and characters of particular places (in South America, North Africa, Scotland and elsewhere), evocations of scenes of high tension, stories distilled to pointed, if sometimes oblique, resonance, speculative studies arising from actual events, and they all reflect upon a central theme: the transition from imperial to post-imperial or postcolonial worlds.

'A Memory of Parnell', from *His People* (1906), and 'Inveni Portum', from *Redeemed* (1927) are accounts, respectively, of the Irish leader Charles Stewart Parnell (1846–91), and Conrad's funeral in 1924, factual but with narrative structure, a personal tone, shrewd, passionate, wry, committed, ambiguous. 'Might, Majesty and Dominion', from *Success* (1902), is a depiction of the funeral of Queen Victoria in 1901. It opens with a sense of optimism:

> Full sixty years of progress; wages at least thrice higher than, when a girl, she mounted on her throne; England's dominions more than thrice extended; arts, sciences, and everything that tends to bridge space over, a thousand times advanced, and a new era brought about by steam and electricity...

However, by the end of the piece, the tone has changed. The crowd disperses,

> leaving upon the grass of the down-trodden park its scum of sandwich-papers, which, like the foam of some great ocean, clung to the railings, round the roots of trees, was driven fitfully before the wind over the boot-stained grass, or trodden deep into the mud, or else swayed rhythmically to and fro as seaweed sways and moans in the slack water of a beach.

A dog or two roams around, sniffing the rejected scraps of food, an old man stumbles about, slipping on the grass, devours from the scraps of paper whatever food the dogs have left, and disappears in the gloom. It is not a happy ending, and it unsettles any sense of the glory and wealth of an empire that might have been, momentarily, present.

Cunninghame Graham's finest work is in *Thirteen Stories* (1900) and *Scottish Stories* (1914) but he is best read in his entirety, preferably in the sequence in which his books were first published. *Thirteen Stories* includes a variety of locations: South America, North Africa, Scotland, New Caledonia, New Zealand, a German tramp steamer. This geographical range belies the links between the stories, which often deal with common human activities driven to extremes by circumstance. 'The Gold Fish' is a classic tale of commitment and futility where the absurdity of the proposition and the realism of the depiction generate tension as the story develops. An Arab messenger is entrusted to carry a bowl of goldfish across the Sahara desert and dies in the attempt. It's an account of desperately misplaced loyalty but its pathos disallows superficial judgement. Like many of the stories, this was based on an actual meeting in Morocco, when Cunninghame Graham encountered a man on exactly such a mission, who told him that his failure would be his death. 'Cruz Alta' offers exoticism in its subject of buying, riding and selling horses in South America, but the commercial transactions driving the narrative bear a moral weight that tempers the action. This is not escapist adventure.

Norman Douglas (1868–1952) set his first novel, *South Wind* (1917), in the sun-drenched island of Capri, which he calls Nepenthe, intending that it should describe a set of circumstances which would make the murder of a bishop excusable. Douglas was born in Austria, grew up speaking German and rejected both the Calvinist ethos of his Aberdeenshire family background and the north European oppressiveness of his childhood, settling in the south of Italy and indulging himself apparently guiltlessly in the company of adolescent boys, paganism and sunshine. Equally outré is John Henry Mackay (1864–1933), a committed anarchist who wrote novels and poetry in German, including a novel of homosexual sub-culture in Berlin, *The Hustler* (1926) and the poem 'Morgen' ('Morning') which was set by the great composer Richard Strauss (1864–1949) and became one of his most widely-known and best-loved orchestral songs.

A contemporary international traveller of a very different stripe, Violet Jacob (1863–1946) was long resident in India and journeyed elsewhere, painting, writing diaries and novels as well as poems in rich vernacular Scots. She was born into the Kennedy-Erskine family, near Montrose at the ancestral home, the House of Dun. She married the British Army soldier Arthur Jacob, an Irishman, in 1894, travelled with him and his regiment to India and Egypt, then lived in England. Her mother was Welsh and her first novel was set in the Welsh borders, *The Sheepstealers* (1902). *The Interloper* (1904) was set in Scotland, many characters speaking Scots, and she wrote other books for children and popular romance fiction, but her finest novel is *Flemington* (1911), a spy story set in Jacobite times, an exploration of divided loyalties (Balnillo House in the novel is modelled on the House of Dun). Themes of mistaken or disguised identity had been prominent in *The Interloper*, but here they are put to intensely dramatic effect, linking with Scott's *Waverley* and Stevenson's *The Master of Ballantrae*. Landscape as metaphoric expression of unreliable co-ordinate points, human motivation as mysterious and flawed, loyalty and hope as compromised, tragically broken by circumstance and the politics of the time, are all clearly focused themes in the novel. There are good short stories in *Tales of My Own Country* (1922) and of her poems, 'Tam i' the Kirk' and 'The Wild Geese' have a piercing vernacular pathos and poignant authority. The latter, performed by Jim Reid or Jean Redpath, is heartbreaking and strong.

There's an immediate, factual tangibility and mysteriousness about Jacob's poems that draw upon ballad tradition but carefully and poignantly leave questions unanswered. In 'The Jaud', the life of a respectable woman may seem unfulfilled compared to that of someone less 'virtuous' or morally strict, but the question is: Whose experience is more valuable? A child whose father has drowned at sea has a ghostly premonition on his way to the shore to meet him, when another question arises: What has really happened? Like Marion Angus, Jacob has the virtue of leaving ego, philosophy and politics out of her poems: there are spare, lean strokes and sharp, suggestive lines, packed with implication and understatement. Her only son was killed at the Battle of the Somme in 1916 and her husband died in 1937. She returned to her native Angus, where she lived till 1946. Her diaries, novels, paintings and stories are varied, curious, and have an international provenance, but haunting, longing, loyalty and home are keynotes in her later work. They are contemporary with the Kailyard writers. While Douglas Brown and MacDougall Hay responded violently to the couthy sentimentalism of the worst of them, Jacob maintained an independently-minded subtlety and emotionally poised style. In her writing, tragedy is understated but no less powerful for that.

41

Gaelic Poetry of the early 20th century

ALEXANDER CARMICHAEL, DÒMHNALL RUADH CHORÙNA / DONALD MACDONALD, DONNCHADH MACDHUNLÉIBHE / DUNCAN LIVINGSTONE, CIORSTAI NICLEÒID / CHRISTINA MACLEOD, DÒMHNALL MAC NA CEÀRDAICH / DONALD SINCLAIR

IN THE 20TH century there were four major tides of poetry in the Gaelic tradition, rising alongside and washing into the provenances of poetry in English and Scots. They form a corrective complement to the legacy of more familiar Scottish writers extending from the 18th and 19th centuries.

Perhaps two defining images from that time are encapsulated in verses from two poems which suggest two deep, pervasive priorities as influences upon the developing myth of 'Scottishness' as a unionist fiction: patriotic self-assertion and respectful piety. We've already encountered this verse from Walter Scott's 'Land of the Mountain and the Flood' from *The Lay of the Last Minstrel* (1805):

> O Caledonia! stern and wild,
> Meet nurse for a poetic child!
> Land of brown heath and shaggy wood,
> Land of the mountain and the flood...

This might read today in the context of British nationalism, a militant, demonstrative prioritisation of 'Caledonia' as a supplement of imperialism. It might be the sort of thing exclaimed by proud Scots who are also proud Brits: Scotland as holiday camp. At the other end of the spectrum, the domestic, conservative stability of the humble family gathered around for a communal reading of the Bible, as depicted in Burns's 'The Cotter's Saturday Night' (1786), summarises a pastoral, reactionary, nuclear humility.

> 'And O! be sure to fear the Lord alway,
> And mind your duty, duly, morn and night;
> Lest in temptation's path ye gang astray,
> Implore His counsel and assisting might:
> They never sought in vain that sought the Lord aright.'

Not even the biological urgencies of youthful lust can shake the securities of hierarchy depicted here. When a young neighbour lad arrives to visit the daughter of the house, 'The wily mother sees the conscious flame / Sparkle in Jenny's e'e, and flush her cheek' but the youth is identified as 'nae wild, worthless rake' so the family welcomes him, an appropriate suitor behaving impeccably.

To an unsympathetic eye, sceptical laughter might be prompted by such an idealised pastoral scene but there isn't much evidence of that in the poem. It would be inappropriate: piety rules.

These two examples set up two images of priority whose legacies might lead on to endorse unionist militarism and homely subservience. In this context, Gaelic poetry is a corrective. Priorities of locality and communal responsibility, inhabited landscapes, not visited but lived in, an understanding of the immaterial world, revulsion from the pathos of war, not only human liabilities but unembarrassed virtues too.

The most marvellously comprehensive modern collection is *An Tuil: Duanaire Gàidhlig an 20mh Ceud / Anthology of 20th Century Scottish Gaelic Verse* (1999) edited by Ronald Black, who introduces the book by saying that each quarter of the century offers variations on the related themes of tradition and innovation.

The first begins with *Carmina Gadelica*, a collection of poems and songs of religious and folk significance, translated by Alexander Carmichael (1832–1912) in the second half of the 19th century. Two volumes were published in 1900, a further four through the 20th century. With extensive notes and stories added to the songs and poems, Carmichael's book was an impressive gathering of Gaelic culture. (It should be read alongside the folklore of superstitions, second sight and witchcraft, collected by John Gregorson Campbell (1834–91) in *The Gaelic Otherworld* (2008; new edition, 2019) also edited by Ronald Black, which we looked at earlier.) The devastations of World War One, when so much of Gaelic-speaking Scotland was disproportionately depopulated, broke across Carmichael's accumulated achievement. The war is the subject of poems by Dòmhnall Ruadh Chorùna / Donald MacDonald (1887–1967), 'Òran Arras' / 'The Song of Arras', 'Air an Somme' / 'On the Somme', 'Dh' fhalbh na gillean grinn' / 'Off went the handsome lads' and 'Òran a' Phuinnsein' / 'The Song of the Poison':

> 'Fhearaibh, a bheil cuimhn' agaibh
> An là thàinig am puinnsean oirnn
> 'Nar seasamh anns na truinnsichean
> 'S gun nì ann gus ar còmhdach?
>
> Lads, do you remember
> The day the poison came
> As we stood in the trenches
> With nothing to protect us?

The second major period is centred on World War Two and when Donald MacDonald returns to his earlier subject of war, the threat has escalated with new technology in 'Òran an H-Bomb' / 'The Song of the H-Bomb': the lightning from the enemy will come without bias: 'Théid gach duine 's bruid a thàrradh / 'S théid gach càil a smàladh còmhla...' / 'Each man and beast will be caught / And everything snuffed out together...'

Gaelic poetry of the Second World War and its aftermath was centred in the work of Sorley MacLean and George Campbell Hay. Their poetry arose from that war and comes forward well in to the second half of the 20th century, both men facing and addressing the matter of tragedy which that century – and ours – makes unavoidable, inescapable. No matter how misleading the priorities of a particular culture over a specific historical period might be, some poets and artists will not permit us to live in denial. The most courageous and insightful of them present us with permanent truths, even when these can be terrifying.

The third major period in 20th-century Gaelic poetry is characterised by new beginnings in the poetry of Derick Thomson and Iain Crichton Smith.

The fourth is led by poets such as Aonghas MacNeacail, Meg Bateman, Angus Peter Campbell, Fearghas MacFhionnlaigh, Rody Gorman and Anne Frater.

Throughout this story there is a growing distinction between the 'traditional' forms and subjects of Gaelic poems, songs and stories, and those distinctly 'modern'. So much traditional work was composed either as songs to be sung or stories to be told, designed for oral performance. Increasingly, Gaelic work was being written to be read on the page. Unrhymed, open or free verse superseded regular stanza structures although the oral tradition continued alongside the written one. As with the contemporaneity of oral and print-based forms in the 18th and 19th centuries in the works of Burns, Hogg and Scott, in Gaelic there is a difference as well as an overlap. Four decades after the first publication of his poems, Sorley MacLean became eagerly sought to give public readings, at many of which his delivery, including the introductions he gave to each poem, created an immediate atmosphere of intensity, attentiveness and respect for the passion the poems themselves possess. Public poetry readings brought the written texts into an air where the sounds of the words could be heard. This is a very different practice from the commercial priorities of celebrity festivals.

However modern the subjects (explicit treatment of sexual passion, modern warfare, technological developments, mass media) or however traditional (love, anguish, personal commitment, political liberation from oppression), all poems are made out of language, images, tones and structures. And however different the Gaelic poems of the 20th century might be from conventional structures of metrical regularity, there is no diminishment of value.

There's more than one way to read those poems of Burns and Scott that we began with but jingoistic, superficial patriotism and reactionary, domestic pieties are the wrong priorities when opposition to the absolutes of nuclear threat and the authority of Empire is essential and urgent.

The four 'high tides' of modern Gaelic poetry form a helpful metaphor but they're not closed-off categories. Many poets move across them and their experiences of war, of the international conflicts of the century and the conditions of cultures within imperial conflicts are not neatly contained and form a long threnody.

Donnchadh MacDhunléibhe / Duncan Livingstone (1877–1964) of Mull left for South Africa in 1903 and settled in Pretoria. While earlier poems include festive celebration, later work reflects on, and protests against, racism and imperialism. For example, from 'Feasgar an Duine Ghil' / 'The Evening of the White Man':

Fhuair an duine geal a chumhachd, is thugar ceanna dha le Dia;
Innleachd chum an t-saoghail a chumadh air a bhuileachadh air gu fial.
Ach bhrath e Dia agus an tàlann a fhuair e chum math an t-saoghail gu léir;
Is rinn e an cinne-daonna a thràilleadh; 's an toradh uile ghléidh e fhéin...

The white man got his power from God, who gave him his authority;
A strategy to shape the world that was generously granted him.
But he betrayed God and the talent that he got for the sake of all the world;
And he enslaved mankind; and he kept all the proceeds for himself...

In 'Bean Dubh a' Caoidh a Fir a Chaidh a Mharbhadh leis a' Phoileas' / 'A Black Woman Mourns her Husband Killed by the Police' we read:

> Am fear bòidheach laigh ri m' thaobh-sa
> An-sin 's a mhionach ás a' slaodadh.
> Baba Inkòsi Sikelele, Baba Inkòsi Sikelele.
> Aichbheil, aichbheil, sgrios is léireadh
> Air an luchd a rinn mo cheausadh.
> Baba Inkòsi Sikele, Baba Inkòsi Sikelele.
>
> The handsome man who lay beside me
> There with his intestines trailing loose.
> Baba Inkòsi Sikelele, Baba Inkòsi Sikelele.
> Vengeance, vengeance, grief, destruction
> On the people who've had me crucified.
> Baba Inkòsi Sikelele, Baba Inkòsi Sikelele.

The familiarity of this is a signal of our own condition today. This is a poetry about racist South Africa but its pertinence here and now is inescapable, and contrasts with earlier poems, celebrating the company of Gaelic and Scots folk in Pretoria. After the death of his wife in 1951, Livingstone's poems were passionately engaged with politics and society: no longer benevolent confirmations but anguished resistance to immediate injustice. Yet in form and mode of address, they draw directly from the Gaelic tradition. After all, extremes of prejudice and violent oppression in early 20th-century South Africa were hardly unknown in the Gaelic world of the 18th, 19th and 20th centuries.

The two priorities which characterise 20th-century Gaelic poetry and song, the adherence to tradition and the development of print-based modernist poetry intended for silent reading and contemplation rather than oral performance, are both evident in Livingstone's work, arguably, in the subjects rather than the forms of his poetry. Poems of this period cannot ignore the impositions of violence. Ciorstai NicLeòid / Christina MacLeod (1880–1954), ends her poem 'Cuimhneachan 1914–1918' / 'In Memory of 1914–1918' like this:

> Nuair hoinnicheas sinn càch aig clachan no tràigh
> Bidh luaidh air gach sàr bhios 'àite falamh;
> Is togaidh sinn càrn mar chuimhneachan gràidh,
> An euchdan air clàr don àl a leanas.

> When we meet others at township or ebb
> There'll be talk of each hero whose place is empty;
> And we'll raise a cairn as a monument of love,
> Their deeds on a tablet for the next generation.

And Dòmhnall Mac na Ceàrdacich / Donald Sinclair (1885–1932), in 'Slighe nan Seann Seun' / 'The Way of the Old Spells' provides one of the most concentrated poems of lament and commemoration of an era rich in the genre. Here is its conclusion:

> Cha neònach cill mo shluaigh an cois nan cuan bhith balbh,
> Chan iongnadh uchd nan tuam bhith 'n tòic le luach na dh'fhalbh,
> O shaoghail, s truagh nach till aon uair a shearg.
> 'S nach tàrr mo dheòin, ge buan, aon fhios á suain nam marbh!

> It's not strange that my people's graves at ocean's edge are dumb,
> It's no surprise for the tombs' outsides to swell with the worth of
>   what's gone,
> O world, alas that that which withered once will not come back.
> And that my will, though lasting, will evoke no word from dead
>   men's slumbers!

At the end of the First World War, over 200 soldiers returning to the Isle of Lewis were drowned when the steamship *Iolaire* went down within sight of Stornoway harbour. Horrific in itself simply as historical fact, the event has entered myth as a potent evocation of irrecoverable loss. In a census of 1891, the Gaelic-speaking population of Scotland was recorded as 210,000. In 1991, it was 65,000. In 2011 it was c.58,000. After the First World War, the role of village bards or local poets diminished, as did the publishing of Gaelic books. Songs might be heard among the Gaelic communities, scholars might continue to research and recover ancient texts, but a lively commerce of literary interest was becoming sparse and thin.

The formation of the Gaelic society An Comunn Gàidhealach in 1891 and its annual festival, the Mod, helped sustain verse-recitation, dance and music and other forms of Gaelic culture. Stories were published in the monthly magazine *An Gaidheal* but the intellectual rigours and austerities of international modernist literature were not a priority for a movement essentially preoccupied with retrieving and protecting an ancient culture.

And this is an essential point to understand about modern Scotland.

If Modernism was an intervention and fragmentation of imperial cultural certainties, that fragmentation had *already happened* in Scotland. The imperialist certainties that underscore and give regulation and authority to the English laureates such as Alfred Lord Tennyson were exactly what radical modernists like Ezra Pound and T.S. Eliot were blasting into fragments. But Scotland as a cultural identity, especially in the Gaelic and Scots languages, in the nation's cultural diversity and its political dividedness, had already suffered that destruction. It had been delivered in the enforced disintegrations of cultural life enacted throughout centuries of Empire. Imperial financial wealth benefits only a few and comes at great cost to many. Scotland was already a proto-modernist culture of broken narratives and fragments before Modernism happened. So modern Scottish writing was an attempt to reconnect with an ancient constitution, to retrieve and renew. To break the pentameter meant to reclaim a wounded inheritance.

If this was true of Hugh MacDiarmid's poems in Scots, it was even more so in Gaelic culture. Traditional songs in the early decades of the century were not reactionary so much as recuperative.

From such foundations, a greater freedom of literary expression might arise. And with Sorley MacLean and George Campbell Hay, through and after the Second World War, we can see that beginning to happen.

42

Playwrights and plays: from Joanna Baillie to John Brandane

THE HISTORY OF 19th-century Scottish drama is conventionally thought of as derelict area but from Joanna Baillie to J.M. Barrie, there are surprises awaiting reappraisal, with difficult themes and questions about jealousy, neglect and stifled potential.

Joanna Baillie (1762–1851) started writing plays in the 1790s. *De Montfort* was produced in London in 1800 and 1821, a large-scale tragedy in which the title character fights a duel with his old school rival, Rezenvelt, and loses, but when his life is spared, his hatred and resentment festers over time, and when he hears a rumour that Rezenfelt and his saintly sister Jane are secret lovers, intense and jealous hatred drives him to murder. After this came another tragic love story *Count Basil* and then *The Tryal*, a comedy in which the hero is less important than the heroine. Baillie is trying out the skills of the playwright in various capacities, drawing on different traditions.

De Montfort has plenty of brass and extravagance but many of Baillie's plays were domestic in setting, to be read or performed in small-scale locations. Not all of them were primarily designed for professional theatrical performance. They are psychologically acute and lyrically poised, intimate in detail and often low-key, undemonstrative, drawing more on nuanced expression and verbal dexterity, rather than brassy performance.

In this respect they have some things in common with *The Hubble-Shue*: a small-scale 'playlet' designed for domestic performance in a big house, with children and adults all taking part, as we've seen. Baillie's plays are more serious, adult and sometimes sombre but they are always curious and attractive. They counterpoint the more spectacular large-scale productions in the big city theatres which were coming into contemporary vogue.

Baillie was a correspondent of Walter Scott, and throughout the 19th century and into the 20th, there were numerous stage adaptations of Scott's novels, primarily associated with the Theatre Royal, Edinburgh, as well as a dramatic version by Charles Bass of Burns's poem, 'Tam o' Shanter'. These proved much more successful than Scott's own plays and formed part of the 19th-century appetite for 'national drama'.

We should also note here Burns's 'cantata' *The Jolly Beggars*, a series of songs and poems 'set' in a rural hostelry, presenting a company of fairly disreputable 18th-century characters gathered for some revelry and self-administered pleasures. Read as a play, this brings brilliant song-writing and seemingly improvised theatricality together through flamboyant gesture and verbal and musical precision. The pleasures of Burns's cantata are local and intimate but also gestural and expressive, and they depend neither on internalised emotion nor on externalised spectacle. If *The Jolly Beggars* is a play, it's a play you'd like to be in, as well as watch.

The conventions of 'staging' and 'performance' in this work are intrinsically different from those of Joanna Baillie, as they are from the big theatre adaptations of Scott, and the large-scale spectacles of operas based on Scott's novels that were popular internationally. Scott's work was staged 'operatically' with musical choruses and lavish sets all the way into the 20th century, before the First World War changed all priorities. And public 'performance' of Scott extended beyond theatres to advertising for 'jams and jellies'.

More thoughtful theatre experience was to be found in the plays of Robert Louis Stevenson. These are arguably best performed in intimate theatres and were certainly written with theatrical production in mind. *Deacon Brodie or The Double Life* (1884), *The Hanging Judge* (1887) and *Admiral Guinea* (first performed 1897) are suspenseful and curious, each with its own intensities, redolent with issues central to Stevenson's major fiction.

Stevenson's success was not in the theatre, but unquestionably popular as a playwright as well as a novelist was J.M. Barrie (1860–1937). His dramatic apprenticeship was completed in 1900 with the Ibsen-like *The Wedding Guest* (1900), before he negotiated the modes of light comedy with serious intent in such plays as *Walker, London* (1892), *Quality Street* (1902), *The Admirable Crichton* (1902), *Peter Pan* (1904), *What Every Woman Knows* (1908), *Dear Brutus* (1917), *Mary Rose* (1920) and *The Boy David* (1936).

We've noted Barrie's fiction already, but by far his most famous work is *Peter Pan, or The Boy Who Wouldn't Grow Up*. The play is perennially rejuvenated, on stage and in film. Later versions have sanitised and sentimentalised it, but Barrie's original has its sinister and fearful aspects, not to be lightly dismissed.

The paradox of 'the boy who wouldn't grow up' is intrinsic to its emotional knot. This is not simply about childish appetite and adventure but rather about the relation between thwarted potential and lively aptitude. If Stevenson's fiction for children – pre-eminently *Treasure Island* and *Kidnapped* – presents young men who see what adults are capable of, Barrie's works deal with similar difficulties but with the sense that childhood's potential can be stopped in its tracks by adult rule.

The results are sometimes much more disturbing than reassuring. His plays were emphatically written for theatrical performance, rather than only to be read, yet his career as a novelist is vital for understanding his career as a playwright. The tragic arc of the story told in the novels *Sentimental Tommy*

(1896) and T*ommy and Grizel* (1900) comes to a deeply unsettling resolution, as noted above. The up-and-coming young Scotsman from the rural village, kailyard Scotland, goes to London but meets a grim end: accident or suicide? We just don't know. Conventional and dated as he may seem, Barrie was considered radical in his time: why? The answer once again is partly that since his time he has been too often misread and too easily undervalued.

Dublin's Abbey Theatre was the model for the Glasgow Repertory Company, established in 1909 and suspended in 1914. Their early productions included work by Bernard Shaw and Ibsen and two Scottish plays of lasting value: Donald Colquhoun's *Jean* (1914) and J.A. Ferguson's *Campbell of Kilmohr* (1915). The former is a realistic portrayal of the life of a farming family in hard times, with strong Scots dialogue and powerful characters from different generations, a proto-*Sunset Song*. The latter is set after the Jacobite rising of 1745 and portrays the predicament of a Highlander confronted with the sly duplicity of a Lowlander's military interests. It would have some resonance after the First World War in its treatment of loyalty and betrayal. In the 21st century, in the context of the international popularity of the TV series *Outlander*, it warrants reappraisal.

These intensely literary plays and others were written just before the First World War in the national context of commercial theatres, traditions of music hall and pantomime, and a lively tradition of amateur and touring companies, visiting towns and villages throughout the country. We'll return to these, but the whole trajectory just covered, from Baillie to Barrie, encompasses a vast range of theatrical practices. No dismissal of the theatrical tradition as merely a 'minor strand' in Scottish literary history is adequate. There are simply so many Scottish plays neglected and underperformed that we're in a continual state of trying to find out more. There's a pleasure in that prospect but there are also reasons for the neglect it demonstrates, and those reasons are neither neutral nor innocent.

Beyond the theatres, there were some strange practices of Scottish theatrical performance, some things weird and wonderful, leading forward towards a National Theatre for Scotland.

A long tradition attaches to 'The Galoshins' – travelling people who would come to local communities and stage productions performed by themselves and sometimes locals as well. The word is from Galatians – the people from Galatia, after whom a New Testament book is named, implying that for centuries, these players had travelled across all Europe, performing folk versions of the Christ story, and continued to do so in different parts of Scotland.

Walter Scott, when he was a wee boy, maybe played Judas in an early 1780s Edinburgh version. This is mentioned in Brian Hayward's *Galoshins: The Scottish Folk Play* (1992) and comes from Scott's notes to his poem *Marmion*:

It seems certain, that [...] the Guisards of Scotland, not yet in total disuse, present, in some indistinct degree, a shadow of the old mysteries, which were the origin of the English drama. In Scotland, (me ipso teste,) we were wont, during my boyhood, to take the characters of the apostles, at least of Peter, Paul, and Judas Iscariot; the first had the keys, the second carried a sword, and the last the bag, in which the dole of our neighbours' plum-cake was deposited.

I have personal experience of this tradition. Talking with my grandmother in the 1970s, I remember her recollecting the 'Galoshins' from her own childhood, in Salsburgh and Shotts, in Lanarkshire. They toured the places of her youth before the First World War and 60 years later she was remembering their performances vividly and with great fondness. My grandmother never went to a professional theatre production in her life until I took her to the National Theatre in London in December 1986 to see Anthony Hopkins in Shakespeare's *King Lear* and Hopkins again with Judi Dench in *Antony and Cleopatra*. One of my most pleasing memories of my grandmother is the sheer joy and edge-of-her-seat engagement and thrill she effused sitting beside me in the theatre on the South Bank in London, that winter.

The 'Galoshins' overlap or connect with the tradition of 'guisers' performing stories or recitations in costume that disguised the wearer, for customary gifts, normally associated with Hallowe'en.

And 'Guisin' was common practice among my uncles at family parties when I was a boy. At big family gatherings – and it was a big family, and everyone would make a point of being present at Hogmanay for the ringing of the bells at midnight – two or three of my uncles out of a company of maybe 16 or 18 people (uncles, aunts, cousins as well as grandparents and parents) – would disappear. After 20 minutes or so some of us might notice they weren't in the room anymore but before anything was said the doorbell would ring and these bizarre-looking people in strange costumes, fur coats, scarves, big hats pinned to their hair, men in women's clothing with handbags and walking sticks, utterly unrecognisable, would be standing at the door, speaking in the strangest voices, almost incoherent words but in a very self-assured tone. These people were invited into my grandparents' house to tell their stories, and they did, and the game was to see how long they could keep up the disguise. These were my uncles but you couldn't tell who was who under the disguise, and the stories they told were fabulous and fantastic. It was a tradition of domestic performance I suspect now completely extinct.

These personal anecdotes alert us to three complementary theatrical traditions that have existed in parallel for centuries, that of the popular touring companies or groups like the Galoshins, that of domestic performance, and that of the repertory companies and established theatres whose most culturally canonical manifestation is a National Theatre.

Immediately after the First World War, the push to establish a National Theatre of Scotland was one of the strands in the literary movement led by Hugh MacDiarmid. In an essay of 1924, 'R.F. Pollock and the Art of Theatre', collected in *Contemporary Scottish Studies* (1926; new edition 1995), MacDiarmid noted that an authentic Scottish drama must represent 'the profound differences in psychology between Scots and English'.

Musical comedy, London-based touring productions, Scots comedians and comic storytellers and singers all had a huge following but when the Scottish National Players gave their first performance in 1921, and the Scottish National Theatre Society was formed in 1922, the emphasis was on productions of literary impact and national character, such as *Gruach* (1921) by Gordon Bottomley (1874–1948) and *The Glen is Mine* (1925) by John Brandane (Dr John McIntyre, 1869–1947).

Gruach is about the future of the Highlands, and whether depopulated land should be the resource of wilderness or industrial mineral mining. The father and son who take opposing sides are compromised by their best and worst intentions (nostalgia and reverence for nature, as against greed and recognition of the need for progress). The problem of employment is as pressing in the Highlands as in any of the cities. Similar questions surface in *The Inn of Adventure* (1925), set in 1829 (Scott and Byron are referred to as popular contemporary authors), and *Heather Gentry* (1927), set in the then 'present day'. Conventions of misapprehensions of inheritance, family and love-commitments are worked out in both plays to comic effect. George Reston Malloch (1875–1953) had five one-act plays and two full-length works performed by the Players, the most impressive being *Soutarness Water* (1926), a fluent Scots-language play addressing the Calvinist doctrine of predestination, concluding with incestuous marriage and suicide. This was hot stuff for its era and like so many plays in the history of Scottish drama, ripe for rediscovery.

MacDiarmid and Neil Gunn both wrote short plays and R.F. Pollock, following Stanislavski, speculated that a drama attentive to distinct aspects of Scots' psychology should begin by acknowledging that one characteristic of many Scots was a terse, restrained, succinct use of language: more goes on below the surface than is ever seen.

This might seem opposed to an art of verbal expressiveness, but it could empower a theatre of intensified action and implication, more like Beckett than Boucicault. In Liz Lochhead's version of Euripides's *Medea* (2000), you can see exactly how effective this is, and how powerfully it conveys the meaning of tragedy. In the more sedate Penguin translation by Philip Vellacott, the chorus brings the play to an end with these lines:

> Many are the Fates which Zeus in Olympus dispenses;
> Many matters the gods bring to surprising ends.
> The things we thought would happen do not happen;
> The unexpected God makes possible;
> And such is the conclusion of our story.

Lochhead's version has dramatic authority exactly in concurrence with Pollock's and MacDiarmid's perceptions:

> the Gods look down
> expect the unexpected
> what we wish for work for plan for hope for
> think is bound to happen won't
> what is fated will
>
> end of story

Brevity risks bathos, but tone gives depth, and restraint supplies a bitter power. But that was more than 70 years after MacDiarmid and Pollock were writing. In the 1920s and 1930s, new forms of Scottish theatrical production were still taking shape. How the different traditions were brought together as available possibilities for effective deployment is a long story, still without ending.

43

Renaissance: Hugh MacDiarmid

IMMEDIATELY AFTER THE First World War, Hugh MacDiarmid (C.M. Grieve, 1892–1978) edited a series of three anthologies called *Northern Numbers*, placing the young war poets alongside older, more conservative, establishment writers. Evocations of a Romantic, pastoral Scotland were exposed as outdated sentimental fantasies when read beside poems that evoked the horrors of war and the degradations of post-war industrial Scotland. At the same time, women were writing from the home front of their own experience of broken promises and loss. MacDiarmid published work by Marion Angus and Violet Jacob in these anthologies, and the third book in the series was made up of poems by ten men and ten women: an equal representation.

The revolutionary breakthrough into modernity came in 1922, with a handful of MacDiarmid's short poems. He had written poems in English but when he began writing in dense, difficult Scots he created work of intense, compact power, little sticks of gelignite that exploded all expectations. In form, they drew on the ballad tradition but injected it with philosophical questions, egocentric assertion, a sense of cosmic mystery and potent sexuality, everywhere drawing on Freud, Marx and Nietzsche as much as on the Scottish tradition.

THE REVOLUTIONARY

When MacDiarmid began writing, it was precisely this sense of a new dispensation, an urgent need to write Scotland into the new century, that motivated him and many of his contemporaries – in music, painting, sculpture and literary and cultural criticism. This was the period MacDiarmid named 'The Scottish Literary Renaissance'. Social and political vision informed literary production in the works of novelists such as Lewis Grassic Gibbon, Neil Gunn, Naomi Mitchison, Catherine Carswell, Willa Muir and Nan Shepherd; poets such as William Soutar, Edwin Muir; playwrights such as James Bridie, Ewan MacColl, Joe Corrie, Ena Lamont Stewart. In the same era, there was a flourishing of work by composers F.G. Scott and Erik Chisholm, artists William McCance, William Crozier, William Johnstone and Edward Baird, sculptors William Lamb and James Pittendrigh MacGillivray. All the writers addressed political issues directly and their poetry, fiction and drama had to find new forms in which to develop their ideas of what Scotland – and Scottish literature – might be. We will return to them in more detail later, but it is important to register the surge of creative energy which was rising through the 1920s and 1930s.

That imaginative revolution involved both reawakened national purpose and a commitment to egalitarian socialism. The word 'Renaissance' in this context signifies a regeneration of both cultural and political purpose. It might be considered alongside other contexts which were also political and artistic: not only the Irish revival, but the Harlem Renaissance in New York, roughly contemporary, asserting and demonstrating the cultural authority of black writers, artists, musicians, photographers, poets, and scholars, in a world of white political and cultural predominance; or the Bengal Renaissance, which began in the 19th and continued well into the 20th centuries, an anti-British imperialist political and cultural rejuvenation of Indian self-determination. In every instance, as with the 16th-century Italian Renaissance, the defining characteristic of the movement was a rediscovery and reapplication of the past, and a new sense of purpose for the future. But where the Scottish aspect of that European efflorescence is rightly described as 'the Renaissance in Scotland', calling MacDiarmid's modern movement the 'Scottish Renaissance' is equally apt.

Try to imagine MacDiarmid's short lyrics published in the early 1920s hitting your consciousness as if for the first time.

'The Bonnie Broukit Bairn': The human earth turns in the night sky, a small globe among the spectacle of the inhuman planets and stars in their orbits around it and in a sudden shift of understanding, the images change: the earth is an orphan child standing outside in tears, looking in through a window at a group of supercilious, chattering, upper class nobodies opening their mouths and emitting sounds like 'yah-yah' at an evening's swanky party and paying no attention to the face at the window: 'Their starry talk's a wheen o' blethers, / Nane for thee a thochtie sparin', / Earth, thou bonnie broukit bairn !' The tears become rain. The night sky is obscured in the storm. Poverty is made by the rich. Pathos and energy enact a redress. The parade of the excessive wealth and vacuous blether of the young man in the red suit, the young woman in green silk and the rich old widow with her feather boa, is worthless before the human value of the neglected child: *'greet, an' in your tears ye'll droun / The haill clanjamfrie!'*

The Scots language creates a curious obscurity the reader works hard to see through, until the vision reveals itself in a startling, intense clarity. In 'Empty Vessel', a young woman who has lost her baby sings of her grief and almost inexpressible sorrow as the sunlight bends over her and the winds curve out across the earth's surface: again, humanity is central in the elemental universe.

In 'The Watergaw' three points in time are threaded together: the moment of the poet's father's death, the moment of seeing a broken shaft of rainbow in the stormy sky, and the moment of writing (and reading) the poem itself. Standing in the downpour, seeing the promise of colour and light in the fragment of rainbow storm, and then looking back, the poet records his memory: 'An' I thocht o' the last wild look ye gied / Afore ye deed!' And years later, tentatively, 'I think that mebbe at last I ken / What your look meant then.'

In 'The Eemis Stane', the midnight earth in the cosmos is rich with human stories and truths that cannot be read from a distance; they are like words on a gravestone, covered by moss, lichen and snowdrifts of time and false rumour.

'Ex Vermibus': A mother bird tells its chicks to open their mouths so that she can feed them a worm, telling them that the nourishment they will get by eating these slimy creatures of earth, will give them the power to fly from dawn till dusk, and light up the sky with their songs.

> Gape, gape, gorlin',
> For I ha'e a worm
> That'll gi'e ye a slee and sliggy sang
> Wi' mony a whuram.

A 'whuram' is a musical note, the word's two syllables already enacting a vocal performance suggesting speed, breath, a grounded, rolling 'r' and impact ('-am'). The suggestiveness of the musicality intrinsic to the language is part of the poem's meaning. The poem itself is the worm. Read it, digest it and let the nourishment work. The reader will sing her or his own song and set the sky on fire.

In 'The Sauchs in the Reuch Heuch Hauch' (was there ever a more delightfully challenging rebarbative velar fricative-rich poem-title?) a group of willow trees grow twisted and mis-shaped by prevailing winds.

> O we come doon frae oor stormiest moods,
> And licht like a bird i' the haun',
> But the teuch sauchs there i' the Reuch Heuch Hauch
> As the deil's ain hert are thrawn.

Human beings may be wild, drunk, intoxicated with passion, fired up with indignation, but we can calm down and settle as snug and hushed and cosy as a bird in the palm of the hand, but these trees are not like that. They are 'thrawn' (twisted) as the devil's heart. They might seem comic distortions and stand in wayward, oblique, diagonal shapes, at the opposite end of the spectrum from the magnificent, tall, strong oak trees of the English artist John Constable. They are ugly, perhaps, yet beauty is in the eye of the beholder, and these knotty and intractable things are permanent living symbols of stubborn resistance to all authority, sunshine, Rome, England, or even God himself.

MacDiarmid's short lyrics in Scots – these are brief summaries of five of them published in his first two books, *Sangschaw* (1925) and *Penny Wheep* (1926)

– and then *A Drunk Man Looks at the Thistle* (1926), a book-length bagatelle or 'gallimaufry' of lyrics, philosophical meditations, comic, satiric, digressive, festive, tragic verse-explorations of a Scottish national male psychology, were explosions in the cultural scene. Fully adult concerns of sexuality, moral choice, war and the priorities of peace and domesticity, the sometimes bitter business of what men and women are, the riotous or anarchic energy of nerves in astounding powers of delight, run through all these poems vitally. Their language is as intensely alive as anything in English or Scottish literature since the late 16th or early 17th centuries. These are lines 2108–2116 of *A Drunk Man Looks at the Thistle*:

> – Darkness comes closer to us than the licht,
> And is oor natural element. We peer oot frae't
> Like cats' een bleezin' in a goustrous nicht
> (Whaur there is nocht to find but stars
> That look like ither cats' een),
> Like cats' een, and there is nocht to find
> Savin' we turn them in upon oorsels;
> Cats canna.

Almost every one of MacDiarmid's best early poems is structured through an enactment of dramatic tension, beginning with a moment of piercing personal isolation, revealing human vulnerability, loss, grief, risk taken, cost demanded, price paid, followed by a greater vision of what this signifies in the global or cosmic totality, the worth of such risk, its consequence of tragedy or gain, its delivery of fulfilment of potential or devastation of possibility. We have seen this at work in the lyrics of *Sangschaw* and *Penny Wheep*. The structure recurs in *A Drunk Man Looks at the Thistle* repeatedly, in *To Circumjack Cencrastus* (1930) and throughout his career.

Lenin is crucial for MacDiarmid in the 1930s, as he delivers the moment of liberation that at the same time opens and closes possibility. MacDiarmid demands that we think about what the moment might lead to, if it succeeds, which is all the more difficult in the 21st century, knowing how badly it failed. 'The Dead Leibknecht' gives us the argument in miniature: working people liberated from factory regimentation (for industrial dehumanisation, we might substitute military uniformity of mind, mass media, the deadened imagination, religious fanaticism, capitalist indifference or numbness to history) – but is the result of the revolution freedom to build better lives or is it destruction of all that might be? The skull lies smiling under the earth. The memento mori is sinister, mocking, or maybe rather a permanent reminder of the value mortality places on each one of us, insists that we recognise and act upon. This is at the heart of

MacDiarmid's greatest later works, 'On a Raised Beach', 'Lament for the Great Music', *The Golden Treasury of Scottish Poetry* (which he edited in 1940), the wild and wayward 'autobiography' *Lucky Poet* (1943), *In Memoriam James Joyce* (1955), *The Kind of Poetry I Want* (1961) and *Direadh I–III* (1974).

At the centre of MacDiarmid's poems is a political, politicised vision. To balance the freedom people need for self-expression with the ways and means to bring that human expressiveness about, we're going to need the help of forms and structures. To ensure freedom, we need regulation – so, MacDiarmid's poetry always seems edgily to ask, what sort of regulations would you like?

MacDiarmid's essential argument was that the nation-state is a political identity both small enough to work as a self-determined economy and big enough to confirm diversity of identities within itself. In company with other nations, world-wide, the priorities this structure can endorse might oppose or subvert those of bigger, uber-nations or empires, which seek to dominate others, exploiting natural resources and repressing human expression. These fundamental beliefs fostered his commitment to Scotland's independence in the co-operating context of world communism. The vision was aggressively idealist but MacDiarmid was not a dreamer: he was embroiled in political meetings, elections, publications, standing as a party candidate on various occasions.

MacDiarmid's nationalism was an act of resistance. Without social revolution, he argued, nationalism was useless. Before the First World War, he was a member of Keir Hardie's Independent Labour Party and later of the Communist Party of Great Britain, convinced that an international socialist solidarity could be brought about.

So here we have a major poet who stands beside the other major politicised artists of the 20th century: Picasso, Stravinsky, Joyce, confirming their belief in both common humanity and the most wildly experimental formal artistic, musical and literary innovations to break from the conventions of the 19th century and enter modernity on their own terms.

MacDiarmid's early work triggered what he called the Scottish Renaissance in literature, the arts and political ideas. He set about doing this in three ways. He wrote the poems, he edited anthologies and periodicals, and he produced innumerable essays on all sorts of subjects – on literature, history, the arts, education, politics, on particular Scottish writers and international Modernism – in newspapers and periodicals, throughout Scotland, in London and elsewhere. The most famous series of these essays was collected as *Contemporary Scottish Studies* (1926). He was the most wide-ranging, intellectually demanding, infectiously curious and profoundly optimistic of the Scottish writers of his generation and of the great modernists.

MacDiarmid was the single most important Scottish writer of the 20th century. His work was the reinvigoration of the poetic, political and intellectual world. He was a founding member of the National Party of Scotland, demanding reinstated independence, and he was a member of the Communist Party, aligning himself with Vladimir Mayakovsky, Nazim Hikmet, Pablo Neruda, and in later years translating Eugenio Montale, Giuseppe Ungaretti and Salvatore Quasimodo. His internationalism matched his conviction in the ideal of national self-determination and these political beliefs informed his poetry.

By the 1930s, however, he had made so many enemies as a cultural provocateur that he was unemployable, isolated, living on an island in the Shetland archipelago far in the North Sea, scorned and spurned by the establishment. Here he wrote the central poem of his career, a philosophical enquiry into human value in artistic and political terms, measured against the scale of geological time: 'On a Raised Beach'. Difficult and austere, the poem is finally triumphant and points a way through, forward towards the future. It begins with the first person singular and ends in the first person plural. This was a time of extreme isolation – he suffered physical and nervous breakdown and was near to death – and yet he survived, and his poetry is a record of the survival of human value through the most difficult circumstances of the 20th century.

MacDiarmid was notorious, speaking his mind, welcoming younger writers who were dealing directly with contemporary reality and its ugly facts, blasting the establishment at every opportunity. Scottish literature had been submerged in British identity, had become a minor part of English literature, both in the way it was read and evaluated and in the aspirations of most of its working writers. The result, in MacDiarmid's opinion, was the creation of an uncritical, sentimental and anodyne culture, politically supine and generating what Nietzsche would have called generations of people fully possessed by a 'slave-mentality' not just in literary terms, but generally. MacDiarmid set out to destroy that complacency forever.

THE CONSEQUENCES

The two places most closely revealed in MacDiarmid's writing are his native town of Langholm in Dumfriesshire and Shetland (he lived on the island of Whalsay): the former on the southernmost edge of Scotland, and the latter among the northernmost archipelago of islands in the North Sea. This geographical range indicates the comprehensiveness of MacDiarmid's vision of Scotland and his sensitivity to the different components of the national identity. Neither in terrain nor language are the Borders and Shetland close, yet both are parts of Scotland.

His very early poems are in English, formal sonnets in which rain-beaten stones in the Highlands see-saw the weather, conjuring images of 'oblivion and eternity together'; or a free verse portrait of a Roman soldier at Christ's crucifixion, obliterating his guilt in wine and the flesh of prostitutes; or a surreal image of

Time as a broken column, the end of linear chronology brought about by the unprecedented destruction of 'order' and the slaughter of the First World War.

When he returned to Scotland, two other epoch-making events had broken the old idea of Time as an imperial certainty, with its centre legitimised at Greenwich, near London: the Easter Rising in Ireland in 1916 and the Russian Revolution in 1917. With the former, a Celtic nation asserting its independence from British rule set one example; with the latter, an ideal of communist egalitarianism asserting the overthrow of class and social hierarchy set another. MacDiarmid wanted Scotland to act politically on both.

His most immediate literary models came from W.B. Yeats (1865–1939) in Ireland and, later, Saunders Lewis (1893–1985) in Wales. By the early 1930s, the establishment saw him as a cultural public enemy. His first wife had had enough, took their children and left him. Drinking in despair, he met in London Valda Trevlyn, the woman who became his second wife and with her and their son, found haven on the island of Whalsay in Shetland. Here, in 'On a Raised Beach', austerity and value become his subjects:

> It is reality that is at stake.
> Being and non-being with equal weapons here
> Confront each other for it, non-being unseen
> But always on the point, it seems, of showing clear...

The echo here is of Hamlet: 'To be or not to be...' But the question is asked in a way that dissolves its familiarity and reinforces its depth, seriousness, and immediate threat. MacDiarmid goes on:

> What happens to us
> Is irrelevant to the world's geology
> But what happens to the world's geology
> Is not irrelevant to us.
> We must reconcile ourselves to the stones,
> Not the stones to us.
> Here a man must shed the encumbrances that muffle
> Contact with elemental things, the subtleties
> That seem inseparable from a humane life, and go apart
> Into a simple and sterner, more beautiful and more oppressive world,
> Austerely intoxicating; the first draught is overpowering;
> Few survive it.

His later, book-length poems, *In Memoriam James Joyce* (1955) and *The Kind of Poetry I Want* (1961) are vast – and exhausting – celebrations of the variety of languages, artistic forms of expression, scientific developments, cultural differences and senses of humour as far as it is possible to know them and throughout history, going back, as he says at one point, to the conversation between the Norse god Thor and the All-Wise Dwarf, which exists in a manuscript dating from over five centuries before Shakespeare. Cheekily, he asks, 'You remember it?'

MacDiarmid's gambit here is to invite the reader to imagine what the extent of knowledge might be, the pleasures of aesthetic and intellectual engagement, and to value the contents of libraries, museums, archaeologies of human life, not as acquisitions, property or prestige, but as things that help us to live more fully. When he writes, 'Poetry is human existence come to life', he's indicating a kind of quickening. It's a common metaphor. When a footballer starts to run with the ball in a certain way, co-ordinating purpose, speed, direction, then kicks and scores, you'll still hear people say, 'Pure poetry!' MacDiarmid's later poems are an invitation to recognise that quality in world history and all forms of cultural expression.

On 9 September 1978, in the evening, at the very end, in Chalmers Hospital, Edinburgh, Chris Grieve, then in his 87th year, turned for a last look over the Edinburgh skyline, and closed his eyes and passed away. Looking over that Edinburgh skyline today, what would he make of our brave new Scotland? And the literary and cultural life of the nation he fought so hard and so long to revitalise?

In the 1920s, national self-determination became a cultural priority. In 1926, MacDiarmid declared that the Scottish Renaissance was 'a propaganda of ideas'. The ideas involved immediate experience of the modern movement in the arts internationally and how that experience might flourish in Scottish terms. He declared that it would be 'utterly wrong to make the term "Scottish" synonymous with any fixed literary forms or to attempt to confine it'. In other words, he wanted a distinctive national culture of non-prescriptive self-expression, free but not directionless. He set out 'to increase the number of Scots who are vitally interested in literature and cultural issues; to counter the academic or merely professional tendencies which fossilise the intellectual interests of most well-educated people even; and, above all, to stimulate actual art-production to a maximum.'

So, did he succeed?

The Nobel laureate Seamus Heaney believed so. 'There is a demonstrable link' Heaney wrote, 'between MacDiarmid's act of cultural resistance in the 1920s and the literary self-possession of writers such as Alasdair Gray, Tom Leonard, Liz Lochhead and James Kelman in the 1980s and 1990s. He prepared the ground for a Scottish literature that would be self-critical and experimental in relation to its own inherited forms and idioms, but one that would also be stimulated by developments elsewhere in world literature.'

In the years since his death it has become more possible to see how this happened but there remains, of course, a homely distrust of MacDiarmid's greatness. Lazy critics and reactionary snipers are easy to find. Many Scots have the bad habit of self-belittlement. MacDiarmid can look after himself. When access to a major artist's finest work is foreclosed, however, it's the people who suffer from ignorance and obfuscation. Most literate Irish persons might take it for granted that James Joyce and W.B. Yeats are great and important writers. Why can Scots not find the easy strength to carry the weight of our major Scottish artists as confidently?

Perhaps MacDiarmid, looking out over Edinburgh today, would ask questions designed to discomfort. If the arts are Scotland's greatest asset, how are they enjoyed and experienced? He would have scorned the reverse-snobbery in self-righteous anti-elitism: fudge and obfuscation. He had, and still would have, no time for any politician (or anyone at all) who failed to see that the arts are not leisure pursuits but the most vital forms of self-expression people have. He had, and still would have, unquenchable indignation at the commercialisation of health and education, and only contempt for the tyrants of greed and exploitation as common today as they were in the 1930s, and more visible. And what would he have said of our 'national' broadcasters?

The consequences therefore are at least twofold. MacDiarmid succeeded in helping so much to be more possible now than before he came on the scene. At the same time, so much of that possibility only remains as no more than potential.

Partly as a result of the re-imagining of Scotland by MacDiarmid and other writers, artists, composers, critics and historians, the 20th century saw the irreversible development and re-establishment of cultural and political self-consciousness and ideals of self-determination in Scotland. The cultural lesson is also and always the political lesson. And the cultural argument is the only one that finally counts.

THE AFFIRMATION

Many readers have an immediate personal memory of encountering MacDiarmid's poetry for the first time. This is mine.

I remember finding a copy of *A Drunk Man Looks at the Thistle* (1926) in the beautiful little pocket-sized 200 Burns Club blue dust-jacketed edition of 1962 in John Smith's bookshop in Glasgow's St Vincent Street in the summer of 1976. I took it from the shelf, opened it, read a few pages in the shop, and was stunned. Here was a modern poem in immediate, accessible Scots, the language of my cousins, uncles, aunts and grandparents, friends and family. I was 18 years old and I had never seen anything like this in print before, dealing with adult matters of sexuality and politics, psychology, Scotland. It raised unanswerable questions, jealousies, hates, loves, making enquiries and restlessly moving in a lyrical, energised way across a range of poetic forms: ballad metre, free verse, translation, speculation, satire, scabrous denunciation and tender affection, and here and there a shaft of piercing humour, an irony, a wry, sly insertion of an unsuspected tone of voice, both utterly strange and deeply familiar.

Then later in the winter of that year, I found the address of the publisher William MacLellan in Glasgow, on Garnethill, near the School of Art. I went to the tenement, climbed the stairs, rang the doorbell unannounced and was taken into a high-ceilinged flat where a few white Scottie dogs were bounding around, and Bill MacLellan in kilt and tie was sitting in his armchair and beside him on the floor was a high pile of copies of the second edition of *In Memoriam James Joyce*. I asked if I might buy a copy, and did, for £4.95. I took it home to my grandparents' and the next day sat down and read it all, cover to cover, my mind reeling increasingly, literally dizzy by the end of the day, overwhelmed by the almost unending wealth of references, quotations, allusions to all sorts of things and so many writers I had never heard of. It would take a thousand libraries and more lifetimes than anyone could have to become familiar with them all. This strange work was firing new shots in every verse paragraph:

> Even as we know how
> Costa i Llobera's *Pi de Formentor*
> Is not Catalan but Majorcan,
> Not Majorcan but of Pollensa,
> Not Pollensan but a specific pine-tree
> Hanging in verdure over the rocks by the sea...

What is going on here? What but a directive to look in more detail, with a greater sense of particularity, a stronger sense of identity being multiple and different according to ways of seeing and places from which the seeing operates? The whole poem is an unfolding of particularities that challenge, exhaust and stimulate, provoke, direct and sometimes misdirect. Take this for another example:

> Even as we know that in B.C. 500
> The Chinese symbol for 'moon' was pronounced 'ngiwpt'
> But in Peiping today is read 'yueh', 'ut' in Canton,
> 'Ngwok' in Foochow, and 'yo' in Shanghai,
> And it is called 'saran' in Mongolia
> And 'biya' in Manchuria,
> While in Tibet, Korea, Annam, and other places
> Still other sounds are attached to it
> But in each case the meaning is perfectly clear
> And its uses through many centuries by the literate sections

> Of so many linguistically different peoples
> Surely proves there must be something in it,
> Quite aside from its sound,
> That is universally accessible...

Indeed, 'there must be something in it' even while the reader is asking, who exactly is 'we' here? Or take this example:

> Even as we delight in the letter of Aristeas
> Which contains less than 2000 words
> (All listed in Wendland's *Index Verborum*)
> Of which more than 500 are various forms
> Of twenty-eight words only;
> – Apart from the interest of its contents
> This short treatise is of unique value to men like us
> Because it contains no fewer than thirty-two hapax legomena
> And thirty-seven other words which can be described as rare.
> We who have sat with Kurds in their appalling cellars,
> With Kazaks in their round igloo-like huts,
> With Persians in their earth-floored hovels,
> And talked with Uzbeks, Tadjiks, Tartars,
> We, who know intimately *meddah*, *karagöz*, and, above all,
> *Orta oyunu*, that imitation of peasants and of all
> The various nationalities composing the Ottoman Empire,
> Are coming now to the *orta oyunu* of all mankind.
>
> And even as we know Shelta, Hispanic Latin, and Béarlagair na Sāer,
> (Knowing them as a farmer surveying his fields
> Can distinguish between one kind of crop and another
> At a stage when that is a mystery to the unskilled eye
> – Knowing that wheat has a deeper green,
> Barley a twisting blade that gives it a hazy look,
> Oats a blue, broad blade.
> The beans blossom, and the cloverfields also,
> Now the valley becomes clothed as with diverse carpets
> – Red clover, white clover,
> The silver blue of beans,
> And occasionally
> The wine-glow of a field of trefolium).

And then we get to this:

> And rejoicing in all those intranational differences which
> Each like a flower's scent by its peculiarity sharpens
> Appreciation of others as well as bringing
> Appreciation of itself, as experiences of gardenia or zinnia
> Refine our experience of rose or sweet pea.

And then on to all the words in the Shetland Islands for 'the restless movements of the sea' and we haven't even got past page 41 yet. But what was that about the scents of flowers? Pause on that.

Is there not a truth worth dwelling on here, something about difference and variety and the fostering and savouring of identities in a world ever-changing through time, made of diversities across continents, across nations, a world of so many languages and so many cultural forms of creation, all inviting, all to be experienced. In the little book, *The Revolutionary Art of the Future* (2003), a collection of MacDiarmid's poems gathered from the archives of the National Library of Scotland mainly by the independent scholar John Manson and edited by Manson, Dorian Grieve and myself, there is this little poem:

> How glorious to live! Even in one thought
> The wisdom of past times to fit together
> And from the luminous minds of many men
> Catch a reflected truth: as, in one eye,
> Light, from unnumbered worlds and farthest planets
> Of the star-crowded universe, is gathered
> Into one ray.

Sometimes such a feeling comes to you, you have that sense of gratitude, simply for the gift of life itself, and an opening out to all that it has held and holds and gives, and continues to offer. This is the great invitation of *In Memoriam James Joyce*. T.S. Eliot was right to praise it: 'It is a very fine monument to Joyce...'

But that word 'monument' needs qualification. John Purser, in an essay on J.D. Fergusson ('Bringing legend to life: John Purser on J.D. Fergusson and the Celtic Revival', *The National*, 7 January 2019) said this:

> We think of pattern as static, but that was never the case in Celtic art. We are subject to a dynamic environment and that dynamism is found throughout the formal structures incorporated into early Celtic design.

This understanding is at the heart of *In Memoriam James Joyce* and this kinetic quality is what underlies Eliot's description of the work as 'a very fine monument to Joyce.' Monuments are normally thought of as solid, enduring, emphatically static. This is the opposite of that: counter-intuitive, it requires a heavy push and an acrobatic leap of the mind to understand the essential point but once arrived at, the perception clears the air instantaneously.

And I think that this is what is at the heart of MacDiarmid's declared opposition to what he called 'the English ethos'. On page xii of the 1972 'Author's Note' to his 'autobiography', *Lucky Poet* (1943), MacDiarmid wrote: 'The principal theme of *Lucky Poet*, and of all my other books, has been my unqualified opposition to the English ethos.' He goes on:

> I agreed fully with my friend the late Professor Denis Saurat, when he wrote that unless the Second World War was to have been fought in vain there must be a profound change in English mentality (and he did not mean that availability of Yankee trash-culture which has since developed apace)...

For MacDiarmid 'the English ethos' meant something which assumes superiority by virtue of imperial strength and domination, boasting of its 'stability'. It is essentially an imposition of power and an exploitation of the world's wealth, as opposed to an engagement with all its living cultures and languages. That is why Saurat's reference to what the Second World War was fought *against* and *for* is so important. It is easy to caricature and reject MacDiarmid's position. His notorious entry under 'Recreations' in *Who's Who* was 'Anglophobia' and his writings about various forms of extreme politics have been eagerly quoted by lazy commentators, superficial critics and faux historians. And yet there is an intractable truth in his argument.

On the one hand, there are the exhilarations and delights, the forms of knowledge and kinds of wisdom and humility and the risk of love, the hard understanding of difficult and painful things, that may be experienced and gained by the long, deep work of reading such books as *A Drunk Man Looks at the Thistle* and *In Memoriam James Joyce*, while savouring their humour, being humbled by their reach and challenge and responding to that challenge in your own distinctive way. On the other hand, there is acquisition, taking all that this world offers only as property, captured hedge funds, pillaged wealth, stolen goods, and dismissing all else and all others. The 'English ethos' in MacDiarmid's formulation is essentially superiorism, xenophobia and exploitation of resources writ large.

Of course these qualities are not reserved only to English people but as a short-phrase provocation it does its job. It is not to deny the virtues of millions of people nor such exceptional writers, artists and composers as Shakespeare, Blake, George Eliot, J.M.W. Turner and Ralph Vaughan Williams, but it is to identify a capacity of human potential at its worst. Not Shakespeare but his Iago, his Tybalt, signify this. Not George Eliot but Grandcourt, in *Daniel Deronda*. And how are the virtues to be measured against the despicable foreclosures of what Ezra Pound called Empire, 'an old bitch gone in the teeth'?

Mortality is what MacDiarmid returns us to. In 'On a Raised Beach', he tells us that 'In death, unlike life, we lose nothing that is truly ours.' In other words, life has its brutes, thieves and charlatans but mortality insists and ensures that we seek out and savour what is really worthwhile.

And this is what *In Memoriam James Joyce* is: a great long poem, one of the greatest artistic creations of the 20th century. A book of 150 large format pages, a single poem defined perhaps only by its covers, in six sections: the first bears the book's title, 'In Memoriam James Joyce'; the second emphasises its subject material: 'The World of Words'; the third evokes the nets the world throws at us in its attempts to entrap: 'The Snares of Varuna' (in Hindu culture, Varuna is the god of oceans, his vehicle is part fish, part sea creature and his weapon is a Pasha, a noose); the fourth brings the world's two ends together: 'The Meeting of the East and the West'; the fifth declares its unfaltering opposition: 'England is Our Enemy'; and the sixth takes us into the realm of music: 'Plaited like the Generations of Men'.

The last line of *In Memoriam James Joyce* is this: '*Sab thik chha.*'

For years I had no idea how to pronounce this until my father once heard me and asked me to let him see the words written down so I showed him the book, page 145, and he chuckled and said, 'Aye, it's pronounced "Sa'ab [as in Sahib], teek hai [as in, high]" – it means, "Boss, everything is really all right."' My father said he had heard it, it was a familiar phrase in sailors' and dockers' bazaar-bat in all the ports of India he had sailed into as a master mariner in the Merchant Navy. When the derrick gets buggered up or the cargo falls in the water or some disaster or another crashes down upon you, 'T'ik hai, Saab, t'ik hai!'.

Or as MacDiarmid himself glosses it:

> The final (Gurkhali) sentence means 'Everything's O.K.' This indicates that the author shares Werner Bergengruen's conviction of what the German writer calls 'the rightness of the world,' despite all that may seem to enforce the opposite conclusion.

Affirmation is what the struggle is for.

44

Questions of language: William Soutar and Edwin Muir

IMPORTANT AS IT is to emphasise the scale of MacDiarmid's achievement, it's equally important to see it in context and value the writing of his contemporaries. For MacDiarmid and for many others, a crucial figure in the first half of the century was the composer Francis George Scott (1880–1958). Scott's correspondence with MacDiarmid, Edwin Muir and other major figures of the Renaissance is an essential, centralising body of work only partly collected to date. One of the most vital poets whose work Scott set to music was William Soutar (1898–1943), whose *Diaries of a Dying Man* (1954) and extensive journals and 'Dream Books' record his dreams and daily experiences after he became confined to bed with the disease of spondylitis, from 1930 till his death in 1943.

Born in Perth, Soutar joined the navy, later graduating from Edinburgh University in 1923, by which time his first book of poems had appeared. His poems in English retain a spare, poised, limpid quality, most powerful in compressed expressions of pathos and compassion. 'The Children' (1937) is about the effect of the bombing of Guernica during the Spanish Civil War, and might be read with Picasso's great painting of the subject in mind. The endless expression of horror in the painting and the restraint of Soutar's poem, working together, create an uncanny effect: 'A wound which everywhere corrupts the hearts of men'.

Many of Soutar's English poems keep this poise between specificity and universality. Their constant point of reference is children, the next generations. 'To the Future' begins:

> He, the unborn, shall bring
> From blood and brain
> Songs that a child can sing
> And common men...

And it ends its three verses in praise of 'sure simpleness': 'Sunlight upon the grass: / The curve of the wave.' In 'Autobiography', Soutar describes the expanding, then increasingly limited perspectives to which his life confined him: from womb, to bed, a room, then travelling up and down the earth, then back to a garden, a room, a tomb, and 'the world's womb.' The effect is not morbid but a solemn and unswerving recognition of a common life, built on unknown ancestors, promising unknowable future generations.

His poems in Scots include marvellous 'Bairnrhymes' – poems for children to memorise and recite, playful, linguistic fun, full of eldritch humour and turns of dramatic expression, like the piano pieces, the earliest of Bartók's sequence 'Mikrokosmos' (1926–39), Erik Chisholm's 'Scottish Airs for Children' (from the 1940s), or Ronald Stevenson's 'A Wheen Tunes for Bairns tae Spiel' (1963). These are all available for purchase, so if you're thinking of learning to play the piano, why not start here?

Soutar's riddles and 'Whigmaleeries' like 'Coorie in the Corner' and 'Bawsy Broon' are loaded with charm, energy and fascination. His finest work in Scots, though, is unmistakably adult. 'Birthday' is a ballad-like allegory describing three mysterious 'men o' Scotland' who ride into the night through a dark, unspecified landscape, and suddenly see a unicorn, a promise of life renewed, a glimpse of what might be. They ride on, now transformed into a company, looking squarely at each other, living for the future this new vision might deliver. 'Ballad' ('O! shairly ye hae seen my love…') captures a shuddering moment of terrible understanding of the lover's mortality. Maybe the most unforgettable of all his poems is 'The Tryst' (1935). It evokes an inexplicable visitation from a beautiful woman, who arrives and departs without words ('luely' just means 'softly' and 'caller' means 'cool'):

> O luely, luely cam she in
> And luely she laid doun:
> I kent her by her caller lips
> And her breists sae sma' and roon'.
>
> A' thru the nicht we spak nae word
> Nor sinder'd bane frae bane:
> A' thru the nicht I heard her hert
> Gang soundin' wi' my ain.

When she leaves, she takes with her, finally, 'a' my simmer [summer] days / Like they had never been.' It has been set (more than once) to music, with one particularly beautifully nuanced and accented version by James MacMillan.

MacDiarmid included 'The Tryst' in *The Golden Treasury of Scottish Poetry* (1940) and dedicated his poem, 'Tam o' the Wilds and the Many-Faced Mystery' to Soutar, marking his respect and liking for Soutar's commitment, imagination and firm grasp of material reality. They both understood the Scots language as essential in the regeneration of Scottish literature and the validation of the speech of Scots children, in all its different forms throughout the country. F.G. Scott endorsed this emphatically in the Scots idiom of his musical settings of their poems, alongside those of Dunbar, Burns and others. But an argument was coming. In 1936, Edwin Muir (1887–1959) published a book entitled *Scott and Scotland: The Predicament of the Scottish Writer*, in which he asserted that the only possible way forward for Scottish literature was for Scottish writers to write exclusively in English. Only by doing so could an international readership be addressed, he said, and thereby Scottish writers could be valued alongside their Irish contemporaries, Joyce and Yeats.

MacDiarmid's response to this was violent opposition, for he himself had written major work in Scots, and he insisted on revaluing the traditions in Gaelic and indeed Scottish literature in French and Latin. He insisted that Scotland's literature was written in more languages than English and that English was not adequate to encompass the experiences of these other languages. When he edited *The Golden Treasury of Scottish Poetry*, he included work in Scots, English and translated from Gaelic and Latin – but nothing by Muir. There are surprises. One of the most striking poems in the anthology is 'The Path of the Old Spells', translated from the Gaelic of Donald Sinclair (1886–1932), a still undervalued playwright and poet. Time has proven that MacDiarmid won this argument. The value of the diversity of languages is acknowledged as a fact in the 21st century in a way that was less widely accepted by Anglophone readers in 1936. But it was already understood by some, profoundly. In the same year as *Scott and Scotland*, W.B. Yeats edited and published the *Oxford Book of Modern Verse 1892–1935*, which included a selection of MacDiarmid's poems, two in Scots: 'Parley of Beasts' from *Penny Wheep* and 'O Wha's been here afore me, Lass' from *A Drunk Man Looks at the Thistle*, followed by two in English, 'Cattle Show' and 'The Skeleton of the Future'. Yeats, though he never wrote in a vernacular idiom, consistently writing in Irish-inflected English, knew and appreciated MacDiarmid's Scots language poems and those of others, from Robert Burns to the Ulster-Scots poets of Northern Ireland. Yeats's evaluation of MacDiarmid outweighed Muir's and MacDiarmid appreciated that keenly. When Sorley MacLean wrote to him on 26 December criticising Yeats's selection as 'misleading and not at all representative of your best work', MacDiarmid replied on 15 January 1937 that he did not agree:

> He could of course have made a more representative selection of my stuff – and that of most of the poets he includes – but that would not have suited his special purpose – to give a very shrewd thrust from an unexpected quarter at the 'English-English' view of poetry in the English language. And his thrust has been telling enough – witness the bad press the book has had from all the stuffy little English Ascendancy reviews.

The letters are collected in *The Correspondence Between Hugh MacDiarmid and Sorley MacLean: An Annotated Edition*, edited by Susan R. Wilson (2010). In a letter to MacDiarmid of 1 September 1936, collected in *Dear Grieve:*

Letters to Hugh MacDiarmid, edited by John Manson (2011), the composer F.G. Scott describes his confrontation with Edwin and Willa Muir decrying *Scott and Scotland* and everything in it, challenging Muir with the fact that Burns was a major poet especially in Scots, and that his own musical compositions were in a distinctively Scots idiom, and reports that Edwin could not refute him and Willa 'turned extremely grave and *silent*'.

But Muir had a point. Anglophone literature has had an international acceptance denied to most writing in Scots and Gaelic. And Muir's work itself still stands. Born in the Orkney island of Wyre, his childhood on his father's farm, the Bu, was idyllic, made more so by his later experience of the squalor of industrial Glasgow, where close members of his family – both parents and two of his five siblings – died, and later still by his travelling through Cold War Europe. In the 1920s, his aphoristic and critical writing in *We Moderns* (1918), *Latitudes* (1924), and *Transition* (1926) established him as a driving force in critical revaluation in the Scottish Literary Renaissance. His autobiographical writing, *Scottish Journey* (1935), *The Story and the Fable* (1940; later revised as *An Autobiography*, 1954), and his three novels (*The Marionette*, 1927; *The Three Brothers*, 1931; *Poor Tom*, 1932), extended his range and developed his mythical sense of the parallel worlds of 'the story' (the material biographies of human lives) and 'the fable' (the universal allegory in which all lives take part).

The theory might seem simple yet it was appropriate for its era. The human story is a vital corrective, delivering a sense of common vulnerability, in the particular contexts of Cold War alienation and anxiety. Muir's translations – or rather, the translations by his wife Willa Anderson, which Edwin helped with and gave his name to – of Hermann Broch's *The Sleepwalkers*, and Kafka's *The Trial*, *The Castle*, *America* and *Metamorphosis*, marked the moment when existential, alienated, pessimistic European literature irrevocably entered Anglophone sensibility.

Following T.S. Eliot's notion of the dissociation of sensibility in emotion and language, Muir's poems were of a different character to either Eliot or MacDiarmid, utilising neither the modernist forms of fragmented narrative, nor revitalised Scots ballad-like depiction and introspection, or explicit political command. Muir's poems are always clear syntactic structures, using sentences, verse-paragraphs and logic that seem both internal (dreamlike) and external (depicting scenes, unspecified places, conflicts), but deliver moral judgements with terrible pathos. 'The Good Town', from his book *The Labyrinth* (1949), like C.P. Taylor's play *Good* (1981) or Len Deighton's novel *Winter* (1987), shows closely how an entire society is overcome by evil disposition and ultimately, a social practice of cruelty and murderous discrimination:

'…once the good men swayed our lives, and those
Who copied them took a while the hue of goodness,

> A passing loan; while now the bad are up,
> And we, poor ordinary neutral stuff,
> Not good nor bad, must ape them as we can,
> In sullen rage or vile obsequiousness...'

Perhaps this is something only Muir could have described so accurately, in such neutral language, giving an unstressed pathos to the conclusion:

> 'Our peace betrayed us; we betrayed our peace
> Look at it well. This was the good town once.'
>
> These thoughts we have, walking among our ruins.

The European context and the English language allowed Muir this distanced, cool, melancholy objectivity. Closer to home, 'Scotland 1941', from *The Narrow Place* (1943), gives a panoramic national history that culminates in utter despondency, in which Burns and Scott are 'sham bards of a sham nation' and yet, at the end, Muir has told a story that still might 'melt to pity' the 'iron tongue' of the historian. Change may come, but Muir is not hopeful. 'Scotland's Winter' and 'The Horses', both from *One Foot in Eden* (1956), are the anthology favourites. In 'Scotland's Winter', everything is stilled into bias and all hope is thwarted:

> Now the ice lays its smooth claws on the sill,
> The sun looks from the hill
> Helmed in his winter casket,
> And sweeps his Arctic sword across the sky.

In this world, mere people, neither good nor bad, are ignorant and exiled from their history and human potential, yet 'content' (the word itself is a condemnation) with their 'frozen life and shallow banishment.' In 'The Horses' the pastoral imagery of the farm – the Orcadian Eden of childhood – remains, or arises once again, in the aftermath of nuclear winter and the obliteration of modern technology, and into this recuperating world, 'the strange horses' arrive, coming 'from their own Eden': 'Our life is changed: their coming our beginning.'

There is hope in Muir's poems, and it counters the characteristic despair and fearfulness of the Cold War. And yet the emblematic authority of the imagery, the poems' symbolism and understated emotions – frustrations, angers, trepidations – are carried by an oblique and dispassionate language, a steadiness of diction, grammatically secure and safely balanced, in which the urgencies of feeling are pressing at the limits.

> One foot in Eden still, I stand
> And look across the other land.
> The world's great day is growing late,
> Yet strange these fields that we have planted
> So long with crops of love and hate.
> Time's handiworks by time are haunted...

The grim sorrow of many of these poems is entirely just. The effects brought about by Muir in his sustained vision and syntactic balance are unlike anything else in contemporary Scottish poetry. MacDiarmid was right when he said that poetry in Scots could gain effects impossible to poetry in English, but the opposite is also true: poetry in the English language could do things poetry in Scots couldn't do, and at his best, Muir proves it.

Considering the era of warfare that MacDiarmid, Soutar and Muir lived through, world wars and Cold War, one musical legacy that sets itself against the prevailing ethos of violence should be noted here. Settings by the pacifist composer, Ronald Stevenson (1928–2015) are collected on the CD *A'e Gowden Lyric: Songs by Ronald Stevenson* (Delphian DCD34006). The title song – 'A'e Gowden Lyric' – takes a few lines from a longer poem by MacDiarmid, itself a small part of the book, *To Circumjack Cencrastus* (1930), and makes an intense and piercingly beautiful assertion of the eternal value of a 'golden lyric' and how it can surpass all the military might and political power of any castle's soaring walls, transmitting human quality across all such barriers that separate the peoples of the earth. It is one of the most adult, prayerful, secular, heartfelt songs:

> Better a'e gowden lyric
> Than the castle's soaring waa
> Better a'e gowden lyric
> Than onythin' else avaa!

All militarist authority, all imperial power, is worth nothing compared to the piercing beauty of this, what Wordsworth called 'the still, sad music of humanity'. When heard, even without the words, played on a fiddle with piano accompaniment, it is (like the tune of the second movement of Sibelius's third symphony) one of those things that everyone should give themselves a present of, and keep in their heads – and hearts – forever.

45

Thin ice and voluminous works: Compton Mackenzie and Naomi Mitchison

MODERN SCOTTISH FICTION follows a different trajectory from poetry and plays, though they overlap and some novelists were also poets and playwrights. The best writing of Compton Mackenzie (1883–1972) and Naomi Mitchison (1897–1999) arises from their literary priorities and personal and political dispositions. These are of far greater interest and variety than is conventionally assumed. They were two of the most prolific multi-faceted writers to emerge from the 19th century, both political activists, both authors in many more than one genre. It is difficult to get a clearly focused overview of their very different achievements and a firm grip on why they are still worth reading today.

Compton Mackenzie is best known for what might be called Scottish 'comedies of manners' such as *The Monarch of the Glen* (1941) and *Whisky Galore!* (1947) but the film and television versions of these novels fail to represent the utterly dry, extended humour, the unfailingly patient ironies, the strange mix of droll, laconic tone and farcical circumstance by which they are characterised. The tartan comedy which is their caricature belies the fact that Mackenzie was deeply politicised, not only as a British government agent at the beginning of the century, but as one of the founding members, alongside Hugh MacDiarmid and R.B. Cunninghame Graham, of the National Party of Scotland in 1928. The NPS became a component of the Scottish National Party when it was formed in 1936.

Moreover, the Scottish comedies are a small part of Mackenzie's achievement. His earliest major novels were *Carnival* (1912) and the autobiographical *Sinister Street* (1913–14) and its sequels *Guy and Pauline* (1915), *The Early Life and Adventures of Sylvia Scarlett* (1918) and *Sylvia and Michael* (1919). These long novels, set in polite London society and packed with social detail, elegant behaviour and characters loaded with human liabilities and vulnerabilities poured forth throughout the 1920s: *The Altar Steps* (1922), *The Parson's Progress* (1923) and *The Heavenly Ladder* (1924), along with *Coral* (1925), a sequel to *Carnival*. They are kin to John Galsworthy's *The Forsyte Saga* (1922) but richer, with a more varied cast of characters and social dilemmas. *Vestal Fire* (1927) and *Extraordinary Women* (1928) extend Mackenzie's tragi-comic provenance to gay society on the Isle of Capri.

There was a new departure with *Water on the Brain* (1933), which initiated the parodic genre of the absurd spy novel and prompted Mackenzie to open his writing up fully to comedy in *The Red Tapeworm* (1941), *The Monarch of the Glen* (1941) and *Keep the Home Guard Turning* (1943). Then in *Whisky Galore!* (1947) he produced one of the archetypal images of post-Second World War Scotland in the presentation of sly and crafty islanders cunningly outwitting the establishment authorities in maintaining access to the water of life in an age of oppressive bureaucracy.

There's a lasting pleasure in this scenario, beyond the overfamiliarity of the archetype. Mackenzie understood this as deeply as Shakespeare. In Michael Long's words, in *The Unnatural Scene: A Study in Shakespearean Tragedy* (1976):

> When the Lords of Navarre vow [in *Love's Labours Lost*], with 'statutes', 'oaths' and 'strict observances', to shut themselves off from life and wage their war against 'the huge army of the world's desires', we sit back and wait for the 'brave conquerors' to be humbled and defeated.

Similarly, when Captain Waggett decides that the islanders of Little Todday have no right to the 50,000 cases of shipwrecked whisky, we know that the natural virtues belonging to those who understand how to make best use of the treasures of life will prevail over the assertions of social power, and relax into the arch deliberations of Mackenzie's prose as it explores the conundrum of the conflict that yields comedy as surely as it otherwise might bring about tragedy.

Mackenzie continued the comedy with effortless endeavour and seemingly endless ink supplies in *Hunting the Fairies* (1949), *The Rival Monster* (1952) and *Ben Nevis Goes East* (1954). But a little earlier, throughout the Second World War, he had published in six volumes *The Four Winds of Love* (1937–45), in which the central character John Ogilvie takes us through the first 40 years of the 20th century.

Then came *Thin Ice* (1956), his most impressive work, an edgy, tense, dramatic and singular short novel about honesty, deceit and betrayal in the political world, centring on a good man whose homosexuality has to be concealed because of social prejudice and stigma. Edwin Morgan thought highly enough of this to include it in his list of *Twentieth-Century Scottish Classics* (Glasgow: Book Trust Scotland, 1987), describing it as 'short, well-crafted, movingly restrained', written 'in a masterly way to convey a mixture of suspense, bafflement, and sympathy.' Surprising as it may seem, I would say this is the one to start with.

Still, the comedy continued with another sequel: *Rockets Galore* (1957), then *The Lunatic Republic* (1959), *Mezzotint* (1961), *The Stolen Soprano* (1965) and *Paper Lives* (1966), a sequel to *The Red Tapeworm*.

Mackenzie published plays and poems as well as books of history and biography, including *Gallipoli Memories* (1929), *First Athenian Memories*

(1931) and its continuation, *Greek Memories* (1932), *Prince Charlie* (1932), *Catholicism and Scotland* (1935), *Aegean Memories* (1940), *I Took a Journey... A Tour of the National Trust Properties* (1951) and *The Queen's House. A History of Buckingham Palace* (1953).

Musical and literary criticism gathered in *My Record of Music* (1955), *Literature in My Time* (1933) and *Echoes* (1954), is very much of its time but still acute: both historically and critically revealing. Mackenzie was well-known to a wide public through his broadcasting and the periodical *Gramophone*, which he founded in 1923 and is ongoing in the 21st century. His massive autobiography *My Life and Times*, published in ten volumes, each covering eight years (1963–1971), is complemented by the shorter but comprehensive and lucid biography, *Compton Mackenzie: A Life* by Andro Linklater (1987).

Naomi Mitchison began writing fiction with *The Conquered* (1923), *Black Sparta* (1928) and *The Corn King and the Spring Queen* (1931), in which ancient Greece and the classical world, and the world of pagan myth explored by J.G. Frazer in *The Golden Bough* (1890), promise historical verisimilitude but are also effectively allegories for political questions in contemporary Ireland and Scotland. Mitchison's unflagging, endlessly inquisitive mind seemed compelled to look deeply into history but also to bring in, by inescapable implication, current concerns and applications.

She was her own singular person, self-determined, quirky, uniquely quizzical, judgemental and sensitive, and she kept a healthy scepticism about the cultural ambitions being fermented by MacDiarmid in the 1920s and 1930s. Nevertheless, in a poem entitled 'The Scottish Renaissance in Glasgow: 1935' she emphatically acknowledged and praised the movement he was leading:

> Somewhere up grim stairs, steep streets of fog-greased cobbles,
> In harsh, empty closes with only a dog or a child sobbing,
> Somewhere among unrhythmic, shattering noises of tram-ways
> Or by cranes and dock-yards, steel clanging and slamming,
> Somewhere without colour, without beauty, without sunlight,
> Amongst this cautious people, some unhappy and some hungry,
> There is a thing being born as it was born once in Florence:
> So that a man, fearful, may find his mind fixed on tomorrow.

Her autobiographical and non-fiction books are in sequence *Vienna Diary* (1934); *Small Talk: Memories of an Edwardian Childhood* (1973; reprinted with an introductory essay by Ali Smith, 2009), *All Change Here: Girlhood and Marriage* (1975), *You May Well Ask: A Memoir 1920–1940* (1979), *Mucking Around* (1981) and *Among You Taking Notes* (1985). The alignment of her personal story and her commitment to social conditions is evident in *The*

Wartime Diary of Naomi Mitchison (1986), *Rising Public Voice: Women in Politics Worldwide* (1995) and a posthumously-published collection *Essays and Journalism* (2009), while the earlier *Lobsters on the Agenda* (1952) describes in quasi-fictional form her work in post-war regeneration in the Highlands. Her changing entries under 'recreations' in *Who's Who*, over the years, include: walking delicately, untying knots, learning new skills, being somewhere else, accelerating the wheels of God, a little danger, forwarding mutual enjoyment when possible, and crossing barriers.

Her most important later fiction continued to astonish in its variety, including *The Delicate Fire* (1933); *Beyond this Limit* (1935); *We Have Been Warned* (1935); *The Fourth Pig* (1936) and *The Blood of the Martyrs* (1939). *The Bull Calves* (1947) is a family drama ostensibly set in the aftermath of the 1745 Jacobite rising but imaginatively driven by her experiences of the Second World War. This was Edwin Morgan's favourite of her works, 'the most solidly enjoyable of her novels':

> The calves of the title are the Haldanes, her own ancestors, and the book mingles real and imagined characters gathered in Perthshire for a couple of days in 1947.

This novel set a precedent for the internationally popular television series *Outlander*.

She was active in feminist, socialist and peace movements, and in the late 1950s became 'mother' to the Bakgatla people of Botswana, at their request, and was treasured by them. *When We Become Men* (1965), set in Africa, might be read alongside Chinua Achebe and Wole Soyinka, as they were establishing the traditions of postcolonial writing in English at about the same time. Mitchison's *A Life for Africa: The Story of Bram Fischer* (1973) tells the story of the anti-apartheid Afrikaner of the governing class imprisoned for his beliefs. *Images of Africa* (1980) draws on her experiences with the Bakgatla. It is said that on one occasion, flying home from Africa, she landed in London and discovered that a strike had stopped all transport that could get her home to Carradale, on the Mull of Kintyre. Undaunted, in her 80s, she hitchhiked all the way.

The unexpected was her mode of transport. *Memoirs of a Spacewoman* (1962) is feminist science fiction, which she followed up with *Solution Three* (1975). Nobody could have predicted *When We Become Men* (1965) or *Cleopatra's People* (1972) and among her last works, *Early in Orcadia* (1987) was a beautiful and surprising depiction of prehistoric people in that island archipelago, freshly imagined.

Her poems are collected in *The Cleansing of the Knife* (1978) and there's an excellent biography by Jenni Calder, *The Nine Lives of Naomi Mitchison*

(1997), republished as *The Burning Glass: The Life of Naomi Mitchison* (Inverness: Sandstone Press, 2019), which contains an anecdote illustrating Mitchison's occasional propensity to express her idealism in blunt terms:

> J.A. Ford, Scottish Office assessor, remembers a meeting in Stornoway in which Naomi was getting carried away with ideas for expanding agriculture and forestry. He pointed out there was a limited amount of money in the till. 'Fuck the till,' was Naomi's rejoinder.

That spontaneous rejection of contemporary limitations counterpoints the pondered consideration in her writings of recognisable human struggles through the depths of history and across continents. Her sharp immediacies arose from deep and long thoughtfulness.

46

The morning star: Lewis Grassic Gibbon

THE MAJOR ACHIEVEMENT of Lewis Grassic Gibbon (James Leslie Mitchell, 1901–35) is the trilogy of novels *Sunset Song* (1932), *Cloud Howe* (1933) and *Grey Granite* (1934), first published in a collected edition as *A Scots Quair* in 1946, in the immediate aftermath of the Second World War and 11 years after his death. He was born at the beginning of the 20th century and grew up in the Mearns of Kincardineshire, where the vast rolling farmlands stretch towards the North Sea and the cycle of the seasons and the conservative rhythms of farm work grounded his sense of the earth as the final source of elemental value, an inhuman authority against which humanity aspires. It will always claim us in the end. It will never really let us leave. And yet, human purpose drives imagination towards a better world, despite all oppressions.

Faced with the human waste of the First World War, Wilfred Owen asked the question: 'Was it for this the clay grew tall?' Its echo seems endless and maybe has no deeper literary resonance than in Gibbon's trilogy. *Sunset Song* takes us from the beginning of the 20th century to the end of that war, in the farming country he knew intimately. By the end of the novel, all the main male characters have been killed, and the minister's elegiac sermon concludes the book with the eternal judgement all wars ask us to make, again and again: '*They died for a world that is past, these men, but they did not die for this, that we seem to inherit.*' In other words, the value of their lives, if we remember them, preserves a critical edge, cutting across the value of the lives we lead now, in the present.

Gibbon insisted that the music of the traditional song 'The Flowers of the Forest' should be printed in the closing pages of his book. The characters at the standing stone listen to it played on the pipes, and it is worth dwelling on its role here. It is an elegy for the dead, an old pipe tune that exists in more than one version. A traditional song is associated with it. An early version is on *Whip My Towdie: Popular Music from Renaissance Scotland* (CD CMF 005) and the more familiar tune on *O Lustie May* (CMF 003), both performed by Coronach. In the 18th century, Jean Elliot (1727–1805) wrote verses for it which remain with us. The melody is sometimes still played at funerals as a lament. In fact, it is only rarely that the tune can be heard performed live, outwith actual occasions of mourning, for it is not to be given as entertainment and pipers generally shy away or refuse outright to play it except on such occasions. It was carefully and appropriately adapted into the closing movement of a fine string quartet by the distinguished composer John Blackwood McEwan (1868–1948), his Quartet

No.7, written during the First World War, entitled 'Threnody' and dated 1916 (available on CD from Chandos, CHAN 9926). When Gibbon describes the end of an entire way of life and the consequences of the horrors of the First World War at the close of his novel, he is calling up a spirit of lament and mourning that runs through history. This is why he insisted that the words and music of the song be printed in the novel itself. Both McEwen and Gibbon were thinking of the Great War, but the moment the song refers to is the slaughter at Flodden in 1513. The 500th anniversary double-CD, *The Flooers o' the Forest: Songs and Music of Flodden* (CDTRAX1513) includes a stunning performance of the song by Dick Gaughan.

Sunset Song was planned as the first part of a trilogy and it is essential to understand it within this structure. The central character, Chris Guthrie, survives to move to a small town in *Cloud Howe* and then to the city, in *Grey Granite*, but she is increasingly decentred from the narrative and her son, Ewan, materialist, socialist, ruthlessly dedicated to making a better world and breaking the class system forever, begins to take centre-stage. But he is not made heroic, and his utterly callous behaviour to the young woman we think he will marry leaves us disenchanted with him, but also, more seriously, challenged to ask ourselves questions about wishful expectations in a world of cruelty and injustice. Gibbon offers hope in the struggle for a better world and that hope is commemorated in the words on his tombstone in Arbuthnott Kirkyard: 'For I will give you the morning star...' Yet if this hope returns with each day's dawn, it can never be trusted as having been achieved: it always demands further participation, regenerated effort, the pathos of the epic effort, engagement in a world that remains elemental, inhuman, and gathers us all back to it in the end.

Gibbon's design in the trilogy was self-consciously to take his readers through Scottish life, first in the rural countryside, then into the world of a small town, and then to an industrial city, and to move through history, from mythical times at the beginning, and then through the first 30 years of the 20th century as the trilogy progresses. The ending of *Grey Granite*, in the early 1930s, is left open: readers, it insists, must now take the story forward.

The three novels comprising *A Scots Quair* amount to an immensely artful achievement. *Sunset Song* especially has been loved by generations internationally since its first publication. Over-familiarity (*Sunset Song* has been voted the favourite Scottish novel in readers' polls in newspapers) blunts the point of its political force, but that force remains. Going forward from *Sunset Song* to the greater human dilemmas and complexities of society and religious belief in *Cloud Howe* (Sorley MacLean once told me this was his favourite novel of the three) and to the apparently more doctrinaire Marxist oppositions of *Grey Granite*, the trilogy continues to ask unanswered questions, still urgent in the 21st century.

Like the trilogy, the three short stories 'Clay', 'Smeddum' and 'Greenden', are all written in a Scots linguistic idiom, both in dialogue and narrative. In *Sunset Song*, Chris has to choose between her 'English' self and her 'Scots' self, the former wanting education, university, a life of her own, away from the yoke of the farm and its locality, the latter loving the land and the people who work it. Chris marries and stays on the land in that novel. In the short story 'Clay', Rachel Galt faces a similar dilemma but has no hesitation in the end: she will leave, as Gibbon did.

These are the last two paragraphs of 'Clay', in which Rachel Galt recognises the power and attraction of the land, but decides to abandon it and go to university, for 'the life that was hers', leaving behind forever the farm-world of her father and his ancestors across millennia.

All life – just clay that awoke and strove to return again to its mother's breast. And she thought of the men who had made these rigs and the windy days of their toil and years. The daftness of toil that had been Rob Galt's, that had been that of many men long on the land, though seldom seen now, was it good, was it bad? What power had that been that woke once on this brae and was gone at last from the parks of Pittaulds?

For she knew in that moment that no other would come to tend the ill rigs in the north wind's blow. This was finished and ended, a thing put by, and the whins and the broom creep down once again, and only the peesies wheep and be still when she'd gone to the life that was hers, that was different, and the earth turn sleeping, unquieted no longer, her hungry bairns in her hungry breast where sleep and death and the earth were one.

Other novels were written under his name James Leslie Mitchell, with narrative and dialogue predominantly in English. The major works are *Spartacus* (1933), the large-scale heroic story of the revolt of slaves against the Roman Empire; *Stained Radiance* (1930), an astonishing first novel set mainly in contemporary 1920s London, with the experience of a young woman at its centre; and *Gay Hunter* (1934), a startlingly fresh science fiction novel, named after its main character, another woman. In almost all his major works, women are the central characters.

He lived under pressure and died young. After leaving school in Scotland, he tried journalism but joined the army, travelled in Egypt and the Middle East, married his childhood sweetheart Rhea and settled in the new town of Welwyn Garden City in England, far from his ancestral home. In the last years of his life, his literary production was immense. His first published book was *Hanno: or, the Future of Exploration* (1928) and he maintained a fascination for science fiction, speculation on the future and social organisation, and on cultural relativism as discovered by explorers of the past. His biography *Niger: The Life of Mungo Park* (1934) achieves the uncanny effect of not allowing the reader foreknowledge of Park's career: you never really know when death will cut in. Events in Mungo's life arrive without prediction, and when he meets Walter Scott the vignette is unexpectedly poignant and surprising: 'They rode the Peebles hills together, and talked with great affection [...] Mungo seems to have done most of the talking – talk that returned again and again to his quest of the Niger.' Scott interrupts him to ask, 'And you want to go back there again?' At which point, 'Mungo's mask went down for a moment. He would rather brave Africa and all its horrors than spend his life in toilsome rides amidst the hills...'

The same conflicted sense of loyalties and questing is possessed by Thea Mayven, in *Stained Radiance*: 'Scots, she had never ceased to feel foreign in London, and intrigued by it.' Gibbon elaborates:

> In Scotland, on the little farm where she had been born, she had hated the peasant life. In London she remembered it with gladness and with tears, a thing of sunrises and rains and evening scents and the lowing of lone herds across the wine-red moors. Yearly she went to Scotland for a holiday, seeking the sunset and the peewit's cry. Then she would find her days obsessed with talk of cattle disease and the smells of uncleaned byres and earwigs crawling down her back when she lay in a field [...] She came back from her holiday and her heritage of the earth, homing to London like a lost bird.

But 'Then the old songs of the winds and skies of the grey northland would go whispering through her heart again...'

The urgency of his writing sharpened his vision. Collaborating with his friend Hugh MacDiarmid on *Scottish Scene: or The Intelligent Man's Guide to Albyn* (1934), a collection of essays, stories, poems, and 'newsreels' (assembled quotations from contemporary newspapers), he produced some of his most searing depictions of city life, heartbreakingly perceptive descriptions of the north-east Scottish farming country, and the classic short stories. Essays ('Literary Lights', on contemporary Scottish writers; 'The Wrecker', on the first Labour Prime Minister, Ramsay MacDonald; and polemical depictions of the cities of Glasgow and Aberdeen) are coruscating.

In language, the revolution Gibbon effected in the Scottish novel has been permanent. The hierarchy of authority had been effectively established in the Enlightenment, writers pruning Scots-language words and phrases, writing in English as far as they could. Scott's characters speak Scots, or register their

Gaelic in English forms, but the language of the narrative is authoritatively English. The ambiguity of authority and reliability in narration, in Scots or English, is central to Hogg, Galt, Stevenson, many others, but in Gibbon's trilogy it is utterly deconstructed. The narrative itself is delivered in the voices of the characters he is writing about, so the reader enters the streams of their consciousness and steps out again, often in the same sentence, to see the characters pictorially, as in a film, and then again, following their linguistic, conscious perceptions in their own tongue, what he called 'the speak of the Mearns'. The vocabulary is predominantly English, posing no problem for an international English-language readership, but the idiom is unmistakably Scots. Gibbon is being true to his readers throughout the world, trying to convey his stories without interference, honestly, artfully, but at the same time he is being true to the experience of his characters, felt and understood through their own language and idiom.

After Gibbon, and after the Second World War, the authority of English continued to dominate most popular novels in which characters speak Scots, but to writers who understood Gibbon's achievement (consciously or not), a new authority was taken up. This is what gives the writing of James Kelman such distinction and is carried on by others. The degree of self-confidence demonstrated by our contemporaries was partly made possible by Grassic Gibbon's pioneering explorations of what the future might make not only possible but actual – which in his time must have seemed almost impossible. In literature, this was his great gift, his 'stained radiance': the morning star.

47

Matters of spirit: Neil Gunn

NEIL MILLER GUNN (1891–1973) was born in Dunbeath, Caithness, his father a fisherman and his mother a domestic servant. The fishing industry was declining and at the age of 12 he went to stay with his married sister in St John's Town of Dalry, Kirkcudbrightshire, and at 15 went to London. He became a Customs and Excise officer and returned in this profession to the Highlands. In the First World War, he was employed with shipping and based in Kinlochleven. He was married in 1921 to Dallas Frew, or Daisy, and after a year in Wigan, where he was involved with the coalminers' claims against the mine-owners, which confirmed his socialist ideals, they returned north and settled in Inverness.

Gunn was writing stories through the 1920s and his first novels, *The Grey Coast* (1926) and *Morning Tide* (1931) are inwardly-focused, psychologically perceptive presentations of Highland life. From the start, Gunn demonstrated an uncanny ability to describe the relation between spirit and matter. These are subtle, slow and marvellously patient novels about characters of depth and tenacity, insight and common feeling, who find themselves on the edge of economic survival. Old age and childhood are presented tenderly but robust adults, their frustrations, hopes and resourcefulness in difficult conditions, are central. Hugh MacDiarmid saw immediately that Gunn's writing was capable of developing modernist tendencies in depth, precision and – crucially – with a distinctive Scottish focus and character. Gunn was positive about MacDiarmid's aims for a Scottish Renaissance in the arts and they corresponded encouragingly, often humorously. Gunn was also in touch with novelists and poets Nan Shepherd, Edwin Muir and Willa Muir. In the 1930s, he was increasingly committed to Scottish independence and engaged in various social commissions and reviews of the conditions of life in the Highlands, pushing for improvements. The success of *Highland River* (1937) convinced him he should resign his job and take up writing full-time.

Highland River is Gunn's most accessible novel, with one of the greatest opening chapters of any book, as the young boy Kenn chases a salmon upriver and finally catches it, carrying it home in triumph. A fine statue in Dunbeath by Alex Main (1940–2010) commemorates this, with the big, weighty salmon hoisted on the spindly little boy's shoulder. The brilliance of both statue and chapter is in their demonstration of Kenn's determination to carry the fish home. In Celtic lore, the salmon represents knowledge, so of course it's far bigger than the child and it takes huge effort to get the nourishment from it. But the novel goes further, dealing with the lives of Kenn and his brother through the First World War and the mature commitment to political progress that comes with the surviving brother's return to Scotland. In its carefully crafted structure, the stories the novel tells are placed in juxtaposition, so that a modernist estrangement from linear narrative generates both tension and pathos. Gunn retains the best qualities of humanist sympathy by engaging this progressive literary technique.

His greatest novel is *The Silver Darlings* (1941). The title refers to the herring, the fish the fleets go out for and the men spend their lives harvesting. The novel is the story of a fishing community created in the aftermath of the Highland Clearances, a small group of people among whom the boy Finn grows up after his father, Tormad, is press-ganged, in the opening chapters. Finn's grandfather, asking about Tormad's abduction, approaches the men who witnessed it and asks how long he might be kept away: 'What is the longest time you have known of anyone?'

'Oh, I have known men nearly twenty years in it, but they came out at the end well and strong and with a pension. Some men like it. It agrees with them. It has got that side to it. There's no need to worry in that way. Many men on the south side have joined the Navy of their own free will…'
'Twenty years,' repeated Tormad's father, looking beyond his own death. 'Ah, well,' he added quietly, 'I'll be getting back. It's hard on them at home. He has a young wife.' Then he thanked Murray and departed.

The understated power of this writing is extraordinary. Something of that sense of human vision seeing beyond the time of its own life's duration surely appealed to T.S. Eliot, who published *The Silver Darlings* and more of Gunn's novels with his company Faber and Faber in London.

The Silver Darlings is strongly but unobtrusively structured, Part One (chapters 1–13) centred in the Land and Woman; Part Two (chapters 14–18) centred in the Sea and Man, and Part Three (chapters 19–26) representing Land and Sea, Woman and Man, the 'circle' reconnected, bringing the whole world of the novel together. However schematic this seems, in the detailed descriptions of characters and places, the gradual development of the story, which is carefully paced, full of tension and terrific, with sweeping, highly dramatic but never melodramatic, episodes, Gunn is always convincing. He knows these people. The constrictions of identity imposed by social custom, economic priorities, biology and bigotry, are all patiently explored in Gunn's pacifically sympathetic and consistently poised writing. He shows how the limitations of human identity are made liveable by a sense of the pleasure involved in their habitation. Yet this never allows for complacency.

The novel is the third of a trilogy, again, unobtrusively structured: *Sun Circle* (1933), which deals with the Highlands and Islands at the time of the Viking raids, and *Butcher's Broom* (1934), which deals directly with the Clearances, leading up to the world of *The Silver Darlings*. But in fact, all Gunn's novels might be read as a grand, unfolding vision of Scotland as a whole, including vivid depictions of Glasgow, in *Wild Geese Overhead* (1939) and Edinburgh, in *The Drinking Well* (1946). Cities, Highlands and Islands all come into his panorama. The closest similarity in the arts I know is the series of symphonies of Anton Bruckner, each one distinct but building and developing upon the preceding one, or ones, until they can all be held in the mind as a single, comprehensive vision. In this respect, like Scott before him and MacDiarmid and Lewis Grassic Gibbon in his own time, Gunn presents a comprehensive vision of Scotland. His achievement is of that scale.

Gunn pretty much stopped writing in the 1960s and died in 1973. His later works explore aspects of Zen Buddhism, bringing the quality of spiritual serenity to balance the recognition of the need for material improvement. His *Whisky and Scotland* (1935) is a beautiful exposition of the many virtues and varieties of Scotland's national drink. It endorses qualities of distinctiveness and discernment. With infinite care and authority, Gunn extends the argument from different whiskies to distinctive national identities, in the chapter entitled 'The International Cup'. The same qualities apply to the islands of Scotland in *Off in a Boat* (1938), a celebration of sailing in Hebridean waters which describes a trip made with his wife Daisy immediately after resigning from his job as an excise man. It breathes a bright, refreshing air of first-hand experience of the sea and the island communities of the west. One important legacy of this is two books by Ian Mitchell, which examine the politics and economics of these parts of the world and their potential: *Isles of the West* (1999) and *Isles of the North* (2004). Both Gunn's book, and Mitchell's books, prompt considerations of the question of what might yet be made of Scotland's archipelagos.

In *Young Art and Old Hector* (1942) and its sequel, the parable-like *The Green Isle of the Great Deep* (1944), Gunn looks closely at what young and old can teach each other, and how learning, knowledge and ultimately wisdom are increasingly threatened by totalitarianism, fascism, and war, authorities of power and violence. These novels are of the same era and as important as Aldous Huxley's *Brave New World* (1932) and George Orwell's *Nineteen Eighty-four* (1949) but are better than either, for Gunn works through to actual possibilities of regeneration beyond despair, in full acknowledgement of the difficulties and the almost impossible odds of the time. *The Green Isle of the Great Deep* was written as news was coming to Gunn of the horrors of the Holocaust and the Nazi death camps, and this news enters the novel with a quiet horror, connecting the moment of the novel's composition and the universal understanding of what human potential at its worst might be. What rises in resistance to the facts of this history is evoked with hushed determination. What we think of as immaterial 'spirit' is determined in Gunn's writing through depictions of matter and movement, physicality. And as British imperialism fails, these senses of spirit, community, well-being and social purpose redefine themselves through our sense of nationality. Co-ordinate points of good temper and understanding are always required. Gunn supplies them.

His presentation of what we might call, for want of a better term, 'the spiritual' is most vividly delivered through physical descriptions of startling immediacy, both in their intimate physicality and their visual presence, in images evocative of transparencies and opacities. Normally he disdains metaphor and employs nuanced depictions of immediate creatural relations that embody a sense of individual and communal life without explaining, categorising, numbering or codifying it. Wonder is its key, but in the balance of mystery, experience and knowledge, horror and repulsion may also be present. The relationship between the physical and the spiritual is dramatised in his novels in tensions and harmonies discovered and enacted between individual bodies and the society or community they live in.

Let's look at one example: his second novel, *Morning Tide* (1931). Its structure is clear but again, unimposing. Spaced through half a year, each of its three parts takes place over a 24-hour period.

In Part One, it's January, and we move from dusk till dawn. We begin outdoors, at evening. Hugh is on the beach picking bait. He meets Sandy Sutherland, and walking home, he encounters other boys and there is a fight. We follow Hugh home, where his Mother is preparing dinner, his Father threading bait for the fishing. The meal of steak and onions is relished, described with a strong sense of the physical experiencing of taste, what nourishment is: the mastication and swallowing of food and the drinking of water is of vital importance.

Also present are Hugh's sisters Grace, home for now but working as a maid to a rich woman in London, and Kirsty, a dairymaid at the Home Farm nearby, and his brother Alan, who's going out to the fishing that night. Later that night, the storm rises and Hugh and the three women are down on the beach with the other villagers, anxious. The boats come back in as dawn arrives. Hugh is exalted in the return, first of Alan and his boat, then of his Father, and exclaims: 'O red ecstasy of the dawn!'

In Part Two, it's March. We begin in the morning as Hugh goes to school, is set to learn Walter Scott's poem *The Lady of the Lake* but doesn't get very far. Meanwhile, on the pier, there's the 'dividing of the fish', allocating quantities of the new catch. Hugh's Father is described as someone who 'sees': 'but not with my eyes'. He works and behaves intuitively but with absolute precision. We spend the day at the school under the rule of the cruel schoolmaster and at evening, we return home, and after dinner, we accompany Alan and Hugh to a ceilidh at Hector's house. That might seem the end of the night but there's more to come: the nocturnal poaching of a salmon. Finally, Hugh returns home to bed. Then it's morning and we witness the leave-taking of Alan, bound for North America, as Grace heads off to London. After the goodbyes, the characters return home. Hugh's sorrow is replaced by a return of confidence: 'He started running.'

Part Three takes place in July, moving from a summer afternoon to the following dawn. There's another salmon-poaching expedition to the pool in the forest. Returning home, Hugh is met by Elsie, who tells him that his Mother is 'worse' and asks for Kirsty. Kirsty returns and keeps vigil as Hugh runs for the doctor, who advises that things look bad: their Mother seems to be declining. Kirsty and Hugh sit up with their Mother, Kirsty reading from the Bible. Finally Hugh gets some sleep and is awakened by Kirsty, who tells him 'Mother is better': she 'had been given up for dead but was alive'. The novel ends in exhilaration, Hugh running once again, 'across the fields of the dawn.'

Such a bald outline gives no sense at all of the pace and poise of the writing, the energies that build and ebb, the pressures and relationships, the suspense and satisfactions you experience in the book. The novel carries enormous evocative power. Few writers present concentrations of spiritual energy so well. They're present in the quality of watching: even in the first pages, with Hugh looking at the seashore and the boulders upon it, seeing the approaching man, Sandy, and then in the way the writing turns and it's as if the seashore itself is watching Hugh and Sandy as they leave it. The sea is figured as horse or deer, moving, turning, a living creature of motion and power. The elemental forces of sky-air-storm-wind are figured vividly. Each living thing and every inanimate thing too, possesses its own identity and dwells within its own world of relations, distinctively, in dignity and diversity.

48

Tragedy and comedy: Fionn Mac Colla and Eric Linklater

COMPLEMENTARY TO NEIL GUNN'S vision of the Highlands is that of Fionn Mac Colla (Tom MacDonald, 1906–75), whose novel *The Albannach* (1932), dealing with contemporary Gaelic Scotland, was followed by *And the Cock Crew* (1945), reading back into history and exploring the Highland Clearances from a position of passionate commitment to the modern regeneration of Highland life.

Mac Colla was born in Montrose, trained as a teacher in Aberdeen and taught in Wester Ross before going to the Scots College at Safed in Palestine. He returned to Scotland in 1929, although he had already joined the National Party of Scotland in 1928, the year it was formed. He and his wife lived in Montrose near Hugh MacDiarmid and his first family in the 1920s and they encouraged each other in their commitment to writing and art. Mac Colla was appointed to a teaching position in Benbecula in the Outer Hebrides in 1940 and lived in the Western Isles, mainly in Barra, till he retired in 1967. He died in Edinburgh in 1975.

His autobiography, *Too Long in This Condition* (1975) includes an angry story from his teaching days in Aberdeen, when he was called in to witness an interview between the headmaster of an approved school and a delinquent boy who had been referred there by the courts. The boy stammered and stumbled trying to read from an English reading-book but when Mac Colla asked him to read 'Tam o' Shanter' his voice 'became strong and resonant, his stammer disappeared, he read with fluency, expression and obvious pleasure and satisfaction.' The headmaster dismissed this with a snort, saying the boy had probably read it before. Mac Colla's point was this: 'He was not a legal or social problem, he was a linguistic warning... He should have been allowed to speak his native tongue.'

Mac Colla's essays, *At the Sign of the Clenched Fist* (1967), constitute a politico-religious condemnation of post-Reformation Scotland, presenting it as the development of a negative ethos which 'snuffed out' what he said must otherwise have developed into the greatest culture in Christendom. Wayward and wild as such claims might seem, in the context of Mac Colla's writing, much of it unpublished in his lifetime, the bitterness and rage they express are not easy to dismiss. The novels are intense and strong, dramatising the arguments in characters and confrontations, with scenes of great pathos and power. *The Albannach* bears comparison with James Joyce's *A Portrait of the Artist as a Young Man* (1916). The novel is set mainly in the Highlands but takes in a nightmare sojourn in Glasgow as well. For Murdo Anderson, the spirit and economy of contemporary Scotland lead to constriction and negativity. The repression of Calvinist church teaching and the subversive, sly resilience of common people are fundamentally opposed. Murdo goes through disastrous experiences before coming to an acceptance of possibility that resides in humour, patience, sympathy and understanding. Towards the end of Joyce's *Portrait*, Stephen Dedalus imagines an old man one of his friends has met in the west of Ireland: 'Old man had red eyes and short pipe. Old man spoke Irish.' Stephen's first response is repulsion but then he corrects himself: 'I fear him. I fear his redrimmed horny eyes. It is with him I must struggle all through this night till day come, till he or I lie dead, gripping him by the sinewy throat till... Till what? Till he yield to me? No. I mean him no harm.'

Stephen's animosity gives way to a recognition of the value of native Irish identity which his own allegiance to a European world ultimately respects. Similarly, Murdo recognises a depth he needs in the Highlanders who play the pipes, tell stories and sing. One of them closes the novel with a last laugh: 'In the depths of his beard, the old dotard chuckled.'

That patient, quizzical laughter is restorative in *The Albannach*. In *And the Cock Crew* there is no such redemption. The central confrontation is an extended dialogue between Fearcher, the old poet, and Maighster Zachairi, the minister who, effectively working for the Hanoverian establishment, is advising his parishioners to allow themselves to be cleared out of their own homes quietly and passively. It is a central conversation in the whole of modern Scottish literature, placing pagan and prehistoric values of art, poetry and song against the work of administration, political and economic exploitation and authoritative rule by violence. That conflict is as vital today as it ever was. Mac Colla understands the opposition but he shows the minister's complicity sympathetically, as Zachairi is increasingly aware of the destruction his commitments are leading to, and Fearcher's sympathies are not sentimentalised. He is shown to be increasingly aware of his own helplessness in the face of what bears down upon him and his people with the weight of an inevitable outcome. Yet Mac Colla's skill as a writer is to show in this confrontation how permanently relevant this conflict is.

It rests on the myth of Ossian after the Fianna, returning after the world of heroes has disappeared, to tell his stories to the enquiring St Patrick in the new dispensation of Christianity. Ossian's world is gone. But St Patrick's questions prompt the telling of the stories and the songs that will continue to commemorate it, and make of it a living imagery for the future. The power of literature is always subversively at work like this. Even when the absolute commitment of writers like Mac Colla might grind into despair, the novels teach through the drama they enact.

This is evident in the novel-fragment, or extended short story, *Scottish Noël* (1958), a chilling midwinter tale of the 16th century, where, to quote Sydney Goodsir Smith, 'A lance sticking in the snow becomes portentous, a stricken horse, screaming, bleeding, the moonlight, the cold, the impersonality of the action as if the gods of death were playing chess with living men.' It's as if Wyndham Lewis were translating a Gaelic heroic ballad.

The novel, *The Ministers* (posthumously published in 1979) begins unforgettably, as if from a godlike distance: 'The sidereal universe: existent, in energy: this moment of time. The planetary order: in motion: the earth tilting over. The northern hemisphere: Europe facing sunwards: the British islands. To their west, at the ocean's edge, the north-west coast of Scotland, rockful, splashed and sun-splintered standing over the waters of the Minch.' And then we're with the main character, 'a consciousness at a window there... looking on those fickle waters...' Mac Colla's distinction, ultimately, was to predicate all his best writing from such a position of disinterested distance, but to engage the human story with a fearfully passionate commitment and seriousness.

Although Eric Linklater (1899–1974) was born in Wales, his family connections with Orkney drew his own inclinations to the northern archipelago and he was committed to the Orkney Islands as his favoured place. He studied medicine at Aberdeen University and something of the clinical detachment, compassionate yet distanced, sometimes ironic stance of the surgeon is a characteristic of his writing which connects him to the forensic anti-sentimentalism of Modernism. After service in the First World War as a sniper with the Black Watch, he completed a degree in English and became a newspaper reporter, working as assistant Editor of *The Times* of India and travelling through America before returning to Scotland. He wrote 23 novels, each very different. The first, *White-Maa's Saga* (1929), is a fictionalised autobiography with a dramatic resolution, while *Juan in America* (1931), his greatest popular success, breathlessly follows the adventures of a descendant of Byron's Don Juan in the United States, with vivid, fresh encounters with new cities, independent women, radically un-British attitudes, prohibition, gangsters and rising new world optimism. Its follow-up, *Juan in China* (1937), includes its hero's lovemaking with beautiful Siamese twins and a military attack with tanks made of cardboard. The shock and satire remain challenging, forceful and sometimes outrageous. In an utterly different tone, Linklater also wrote *The Men of Ness* (1932), an eerily self-conscious story based on the Icelandic sagas, *A Spell for Old Bones* (1949), set in the Cold War period, and numerous short stories, the most memorable in *God Likes Them Plain* (1935) and *Sealskin Trousers* (1947).

Magnus Merriman (1934) is a comic tour-de-force, again beginning in fictionalised autobiography with Magnus in the trenches of the First World

War (Linklater himself was badly wounded when a bullet ploughed through his helmet and head, leaving a furrow in his skull in which, I have been told, at dinner parties, he would occasionally rest his pen). Magnus returns to Scotland for the rising tide of political and literary national reawakening of the 1920s. There is a hilarious portrait of Hugh MacDiarmid as the poet 'Hugh Skene' (which MacDiarmid relished!) but at the heart of the book there is Magnus's wavering commitment to the idealistic vision of a revitalised Scotland and his more hedonistic indulgences in the pleasures of flesh and high adventure. As the novel progresses, these oscillate convincingly. Rich comedy is sustained through touching pathos and sympathy. The ending is a perfectly judged balance: rhapsodic wish-fulfilment gives way to realism that presents its own consolations and forward-pointing (arguably, perhaps, feminist) strengths.

Roderick Watson, in the second edition of *The Literature of Scotland* (2007) describes Magnus as

> a sexual and political adventurer who moves from the ambitious social circles of London to end up as an inefficient crofter on his native Orkney, where he is trapped in marriage by the shy guiles of a young, beautiful and pragmatically unimaginative farm girl. She may represent his punishment or the making of him, but it is difficult to tell, for he is a romantic chameleon who changes his stripes to suit his situation whatever it may be – city sophisticate or island poet.

As such, Watson speculates, *Magnus Merriman* may disclose Linklater's personal feeling about his own position in Scotland, his careless brush with politics, his satirical depiction of nationalists and his deep love of Orkney, yet the ambiguities do not rest upon cynicism. Rather, they arise from the divided loyalties of someone exceptionally capable of imagining reality different – and maybe better – than it is. Compassion overrules scepticism, in the end. The future is as full of unknown possibilities as it is of inevitable certainties. Presenting these ambiguities and loyalties in a sharp, fast narrative which pauses long enough in episodes to allow you to enjoy speculation of what might yet be brought about is Linklater's forte.

His post-war fiction includes *Private Angelo* (1946), in which the title character is a good Italian man caught up in war, whose life and suffering is described with a care both detached and sympathetic. It remains one of the finest novels to emerge from the Second World War. It reaches forward beyond its date of publication to imagine life in the years of peace, and the human potential for comedy and understanding that might dissolve the legacy of war's brutalities. Linklater's wartime 'conversations' such as *The Cornerstones* (1941) and *The Raft & Socrates Asks Why* (1942) exercise his talent for dramatic dialogue and his autobiographies, including *A Year of Space* (1953) and *Fanfare for a Tin Hat* (1970) are compelling.

Laxdale Hall (1951) is a Highland comedy of manners with a social realist edge, sometimes almost farce-like and riotous, but good-hearted rather than cruel, celebrative as well as satiric, refreshingly puncturing the pomposities and relishing the absurdities and natural degradations of being human. *The Merry Muse* (1959) is a comic satire of douce, pretentious Edinburgh subverted by a newly-rediscovered, surreptitiously circulated copy of Burns's 18th-century erotica. Clandestine glee breaks the surface of prim, dour, dismal Scottish convention. Sexual liberation on the eve of the 1960s is the promise, with the city's denizens inspired to unimagined abandon. Pastoral themes prevail in the Orcadian setting of *A Spell for Old Bones* (1949) while wry objectivity and Biblical drama and import informs *Husband of Delilah* (1962).

His last and most mysterious novel, *A Terrible Freedom* (1966), is a tense, dialectical work counterpointing the forensic realism he had learned as a medical student with a deepening sense of the authority of the imagination, a proto-postmodern *nouveau roman* with the undecided, ambiguous nature of reality at its core and conclusion. The central character alternates accounts of his life, traumatised in the First World War, with descriptions of his dreams, sexually risky, wildly unpredictable, at times absurdly comic, in a deepening understanding of tragedy, loss and despair, culminating in heartfelt praise of taking dreams – for which we might read, imagination and the arts – seriously.

Linklater's recommendation for a happy and contented life comes in *The Merry Muse*: 'a bad memory and a good digestion'. But his own memory was packed and his writing is always lucid, balanced, dramatic, surprisingly unpredictable and consistently a pleasure to read. His grave and that of his wife Marjorie are in the kirkyard near Harray Loch in Orkney, not far from the house that was their home for many years.

49

Self-determinations:
Catherine Carswell, Nan Shepherd and Willa Muir

THESE THREE WRITERS prompt revision of any sense that the Scottish Renaissance spearheaded by Hugh MacDiarmid was a men-only affair. But we need to be discriminating in our understanding of the term, for it was not a unitary or coherent club that members took out subscriptions to join. In fact, the 'Scottish Renaissance' might be thought of in at least three different ways.

MacDiarmid, drawing on the vision of Patrick Geddes in the 1890s, used the word then attributed it to the French scholar and literary critic Denis Saurat, who called the movement 'la Renaissance Écossaise'. In 1923 MacDiarmid said that the Scottish Renaissance was over, it had happened: it had been principally 'a propaganda of ideas' and now that the ideas were out, all that remained was to let them ferment and fructify, and we would see what would happen. Still, if we were to name a few writers, composers and artists immediately associated with MacDiarmid as the 'core' of the Scottish Renaissance we would have to note the writers William Soutar, Edwin Muir, Lewis Grassic Gibbon, Neil Gunn, the composer Francis George Scott, and the artists William Johnstone and William Crozier. All men. And we would date the movement closely to the 1920s and 1930s.

But then there are others who were not directly inspired by MacDiarmid's lead but who were working earlier, at the same time, and later, who might be described as contributing to the enormous upsurge and outpouring of artistic and creative works energised in the immediate aftermath of the First World War. Playwright James Bridie would be an obvious name but there are many others, including Violet Jacob, Marion Angus, Helen Burness Cruickshank and Catherine Carswell. They all had different degrees of contact, friendly or otherwise, with MacDiarmid and his closer associates. So we might describe the Scottish Renaissance as inclusive of a wider range of writers and artists, including the great modernist composer Erik Chisholm.

Then thirdly, we might identify further waves or a successive series of cultural proliferations, some in a continuity and progression from MacDiarmid's initial movement, some responding to it critically, some with no direct relation to it but simply taking its achievements for granted (or rejecting them) and moving forward in different ways, revitalising energies in the wake of the Second World War, and on into the 21st century. A 'second wave' might be that generation of poets, pre-eminently men, depicted in Alexander Moffat's painting 'Poets' Pub'

(1980), and a 'third wave' might be the writers of prose fiction who became most conspicuous and widely-appreciated in the later 1980s, while yet another 'wave' might be the poets and playwrights who span the 20th and 21st centuries, pre-eminently women. But of course, women were there all along.

Catherine Carswell (1879–1946) was born in Glasgow, read English at the university there then studied music in Germany. Married in 1904, her marriage was annulled in a famous court-case because of her husband's mental illness, and she had a long relationship with the artist Maurice Greiffenhagen, head of life drawing at Glasgow School of Art.

Catherine worked as a professional reviewer for *The Glasgow Herald*, moved to London in 1912 and married Donald Carswell in 1915. She was a long-standing friend of D.H. Lawrence, and was sacked from *The Glasgow Herald* when she reviewed Lawrence's novel *The Rainbow* (1915) there. Lawrence encouraged her writing and closely supported her work on her own novel *Open the Door!* (1920). The development of self-determination, independent thought and the understanding of sexuality in the novel's heroine, Joanna Bannerman, makes her one of the great women characters in modern fiction: vulnerable, tough, bright and strong. Like Willa Muir's Elizabeth Shand in her novel *Imagined Corners*, the Scottish world is not enough for Joanna, and Italy and Europe must be experienced before she can fully inhabit her own potential. Carswell's distinction was to see this and to balance the cultural richness described in the novel against the individual strength and sensitivity of the heroine.

Her second, equally unique novel, *The Camomile* (1922), is a portrait of a woman who begins as a student of music but turns to writing as her chosen art. Written in oblique, psychologically penetrating, epistolary form, the novel is modernist in both subject and technique.

Her next major work was a biography, *Robert Burns* (1930), which reads more like a novel than a historical reconstruction and, appearing when it did, caused a furore. Carswell's presentation of the man was offensive to pious or even idolatrous devotees who held Burns in high reverence. One apparently sent her a bullet in the post, advising her to desist from such defamation of the icon, but the book changed the way Burns was perceived forever.

Further biographies followed: *The Savage Pilgrimage*, a life of D.H. Lawrence (1932), and *The Tranquil Heart* (1937), a life of Boccaccio. A posthumous autobiography *Lying Awake* (1950) was edited by her son and a biography by Jan Pilditch was published in 2007. Carswell was of a slightly older generation than Hugh MacDiarmid and kept her distance from the Scottish Renaissance movement he led, but, after initial suspicions were overcome, MacDiarmid and Carswell became good friends and they thought highly of each other's work.

Two further volumes have appeared which invite reconsideration of her achievement, both edited by Jan Pilditch and published in 2016: *Selected Letters* covers the period 1900–46, and *Catherine Carswell's War Letters* concentrates on 1939–46. Organising the material in this way was a bold editorial decision. The books provide an overview of Carswell's story in one, while the letters of the war years, given most fully in the other, give a deeper and more nuanced understanding of her experience of that period. Both are rich and complex.

Nan Shepherd (1893–1981) was a perceptive critic of MacDiarmid's writings and endorsed his ambitions for a Scottish Renaissance but pursued her own vision without compromise. Her three finely-written, carefully balanced novels, *The Quarry Wood* (1928), *The Weatherhouse* (1930) and *A Pass in the Grampians* (1933), combine the priorities of feminism – her central characters are women, especially young and elderly women – with a rigorous attention to aesthetic precision and the exploration of philosophic ideas about identity and freedom, landscape and spirituality, responsibility and choice. Her fiction – and the meditation on feeling and fact, spirit and matter, in *The Living Mountain* (1977) – amount to an irreducible achievement, modernist in its calculation and intensity of focus, feminist in its commitment to liberation from the ideology of patriarchy.

The Quarry Wood is the story of Martha Ironside, from farm croft to university to the point of assertion of total independence from subservience to men. Complementing the strength of the novel's thesis (which never seems merely programmatic), there is a detailed picture of pre-World War One Aberdeen University life. *The Weatherhouse* is set during the war, but concerns characters, motivation and morality in a small Scottish town, ultimately delivering a sense of the intimacy between the doctrinaire, morally unambiguous world of fact, and the flawed, frail, compromised world of people. The novel deals equally and squarely with each of its main characters, their outward actions and internal motivations, rejecting simple polarities of moral authority and infusing the social context with a measurement of value drawn from landscape, weather, the visual world and a sense of geological depth. Her work is made more enjoyably accessible by the publication of a thorough biography, *Into the Mountain: A Life of Nan Shepherd* (2017) by Charlotte Peacock and a selection of her writings, *Wild Geese* (2018), edited by Peacock. If Carswell's world is characterised by social engagement in the worlds of Glasgow and Europe, Shepherd's is much more centred in her own individual relation to the natural world in the Grampians.

An early work by Willa Muir (1890–1970), *Women: An Enquiry* (1925), is a sharply-focused study of the extent to which women were discouraged from fulfilling their potential. It was later developed into *Mrs Grundy in Scotland* (1936). Her two novels are lastingly impressive: *Imagined Corners* (1931) and *Mrs Ritchie* (1933). The first is craftily constructed, even-handedly showing the repressions at work on men as well as women in small-town Scotland. In the town of Calderwick, modelled on Montrose, Elizabeth Shand follows the prompt of her desire and marries Hector, only to discover the inadequacies of her husband, though Muir never simply caricatures or dismisses him. Muir realises the pressures that have led to his failings as much as those that have prompted Elizabeth. The complex picture of their social and family context is deftly built and convincing. The book then takes an unexpected turn with the arrival of Elizabeth's namesake and widowed sister-in-law from Europe, bringing self-confidence and a wide range of experience and knowledge to this oppressive world. It is as if the two Elizabeths are mirrors of each other, and the small-town mind begins to open hungrily towards the possibilities indicated by her well-travelled relation. Finally, they set off together for France.

Mrs Ritchie is also set in Calderwick, and seems more extreme and exaggerated as the protagonist Annie Rattray develops into a domestic monster, close to the dominating patriarchs in *The House with the Green Shutters* and *Gillespie*. *Imagined Corners* is the more balanced novel, and optimistic in its sense of what women might make of themselves, but the power of *Mrs Ritchie* should not be underestimated and it can stand comparison with the more famous anti-Kailyard novels of George Douglas Brown and John MacDougall Hay. The Shands offer the promise of how Scotland might benefit from reconnecting with European culture, while *Mrs Ritchie* presents, arguably, the fulfilment of a Scotswoman's potential at its worst.

Muir's non-fiction, in her autobiographical and critical accounts *Living with Ballads* (1965) and *Belonging* (1968) are also memorable, describing with self-confidence and discrimination her life with Scottish literature, with her husband Edwin, and with other men and women in the cultural milieux they moved in. *Belonging* includes a revealing portrait of MacDiarmid – Chris Grieve – and his first wife Peggy, when they and the Muirs were living near each other in Montrose in the 1920s. While never merely following MacDiarmid's 'leadership' the achievement of Edwin (who had been one of MacDiarmid's strongest allies) and even more, the achievement of Willa, is singular, lasting, and not to be undervalued. More than simply offering portraits of individuals in an autobiography, though, *Belonging* reveals the imposition of gender roles, the pleasures and liabilities of social and personal expectations, in Willa's story. Aileen Christianson's critical study, *Moving in Circles: Willa Muir's Writings* (2007) is an excellent introduction to her work and a revealing exploration of her life and times.

50

Playwrights and plays:
Joe Corrie, James Bridie, Joan Littlewood and Ewan MacColl

FROM THE 1920S to the 1940s, the work of a number of Scottish playwrights spans through times of strife, class division and loyalties betrayed or confirmed.

Joe Corrie (1894–1968) was a working miner who became a playwright, poet, journalist and short-story writer. In the same decade as Sean O'Casey's great socialist, Irish nationalist and humanist plays were being first performed in Dublin, Corrie was writing his poems and plays. One-act plays performed by the amateur Bowhill Players led to his first full-length play, *In Time o' Strife* (1927) and his collection of poems *The Image o' God* (1928). The play is a modern classic, depicting the aftermath of the General Strike in a mining community in Fife, and revived to new acclaim in 1982. At its climax, the matriarch Jenny cries out to the men singing 'The Red Flag' off-stage: 'Sing! tho' they ha'e ye chained to the wheels and the darkness. Sing! tho' they ha'e ye crushed in the mire. Keep up your he'rts, my laddies, you'll win through yet, for there's nae power on earth can crush the men that can sing on a day like this.' The defiance of the spirit in the face of such oppression remains exemplary, while there are today no fewer hearts of lead.

Before, during and after the Second World War, James Bridie (Osborne Henry Mavor, 1888–1951) worked to embed professional theatre in Scotland. The Glasgow Citizens' Theatre was founded in 1943. Bridie, a founder member of the Arts Council, chair of its first Scottish Committee in 1948, and adviser to the Edinburgh Festival, also helped establish the College of Drama in Glasgow, attached to the older Music College, which became the Royal Scottish Academy of Music and Drama and then Royal Conservatoire of Scotland. His original plays combine deft stagecraft, delight in the energies of words and ideas, characters and conflicts, immediately engaging seriousness and high-spirited fun.

The Prologue of *The Sunlight Sonata or To Meet the Seven Deadly Sins* (first performed 1928) sets out themes that recur in later works. Beelzebub appears among great, dark, cold, grim mountains, the Bens, asking: 'What are the Bens to me? / Give me the bonny wee glens with the quick brown whispering water...' Then his thoughts turn to 'the living heart of a man':

> Man. Man. Man.
> You're feart o' me, you're feart o' me,
> Droll wee slug wi' the shifty e'e!

> Raise your praise to the Ancient of Days.
> I prevent you in all your ways.

The Scots voice, the sharp versification, the Deadly Sins who then appear and the human dilemma enacted, all indicate essential aspects of Bridie's style and concerns. These overlap with those of John Brandane (Dr John McIntyre, 1891–1947), who helped him with the text. In Bridie's *Tobias and the Angel* (1930), *Jonah and the Whale* (1932) and *Susannah and the Elders* (1937), Biblical themes explore perennial dilemmas with contemporary references. These are plays that remain pertinent and can be studied both as historical texts and as lastingly appropriate explorations of ideas.

They all address questions that never really go away. Does anyone know how far their selflessness may be trusted in the ideal of helping humanity at large? Who would be a traitor to their own comfort? Do good things emerge from ruthlessness? Can cruel means justify beneficent ends? Can people ever really work for the benefit of others when self-destruction and vanity are components of the human character?

In *Daphne Laureola* (1949), a young man becomes obsessed with an older woman in upper class society. Social limitations encroach on people of different stations and a sense of human worth adheres to some people of no social privilege whatsoever. Human value is not measured by class distinction. Egalitarianism is at the heart of this vision, but idealism may be just a liability.

The Anatomist (1930) is based on the story of the body-snatchers Burke and Hare, and the moral dilemma of the anatomy teacher Dr Knox, who needs corpses to dissect to teach his students and advance the benefits of medical understanding: but at what cost? *A Sleeping Clergyman* (1933) tells the story of a family across generations, from the 19th century till after World War II, in the conflict of social morality and natural desires. At the centre of *Mr Bolfry* (1943) is a question about the nature of Presbyterian belief. It is set in a Highland manse during the Second World War. Raging good and evil are pitched against each other in the dialogue. How can anything be good when it denies the happiness, energy and decency of life? And if a religion configures itself in such a way, how can we accept it, especially in the context of international warfare? In the play, two soldiers from London, Cohen and Cully, are staying in the manse of the self-righteous Free Church minister Mr McCrimmon. His niece Jean is with him, also from London, in Scotland to recuperate after a bomb incident. Jean and Cully are radical thinkers, tired of McCrimmon's moral certainty. For them, his religion itself contains demonic elements, so opening a book of old spells, they conjure up a devil: Mr Bolfry. A long night follows: morality, war and peace, society and the individual, come into the discussion of the question of self-justified hypocrisy, as McCrimmon sees the spirit world he has spoken of so readily come to life in front of him.

Holy Isle (1942) is set in the islands, about to be invaded: colonial domination is the theme. *The Queen's Comedy* (1950) is set in the Trojan Wars, questioning the authority of the gods and asking questions about human suffering and endurance. *The Baikie Charivari* (1952) is a challenging, pessimistic, disorientating work representing various kinds of dislocation in the post-war world, with the Devil making comment on contemporary society.

Bridie's plays were commercially successful in London but they show again and again familiar themes from Scottish literature. His medical training served him well as a writer whose forensic attention to unanswerable questions was tempered by a constant sympathy and understanding of the human. He has been criticised for sometimes failing to resolve his plays in satisfying conclusions but the point of the open-ended questions is Brechtian: the audience is invited to carry on asking these questions, not to feel smug with reassuring answers. His autobiography, *One Way of Living* (1939) is beautifully written, an eloquent testament to his ideals and vision.

It would be as facile to caricature Bridie's plays as no more than 'middle-class' as to dismiss Corrie's as merely 'working-class'. Both are perennially provocative and will always warrant new productions. There is an essential question: In the 21st century, many Scottish plays from earlier periods have fallen entirely out of the repertoire – why? Is modern culture so shy of reconsidering our inherited file of theatrical history? This is not to be merely dismissed with a shrug and acceptance of the proverbial 'Scottish Cringe'. What does that phrase mean anyway? Nothing less than a vast psychological trap of conditioning into massive cultural self-suppression. Well, pilgrims, if we're going to be avalanched by a stupendous vomitorium of 'British' cultural priorities, with fools, horses, grandads' armies, carry on empires and Great Brutes of Britishness, we'll need to do a lot more than we have done so far. The examples have been set.

Some are found in the plays of Unity Theatre, Theatre Workshop and Ewan MacColl from the 1930s through to the nuclear age, most arising from what we would call the Labour Movement. Joe Corrie and James Bridie respectively might represent 'working-class' and 'middle-class' theatrical conventions and audiences, but in Scotland's theatre history the complex totality is more important. But the story of specifically working-class experience being represented in plays needs further exposition. Two companies and an extraordinary writer are central.

Unity Theatre was established in 1940, drawing on various left-wing theatre groups in the 1930s, in America and internationally. It worked throughout Britain, a radical initiative generated at first by amateur companies, two of which became fully professional after the Second World War, in London and Glasgow. Glasgow Unity helped found the Edinburgh Fringe with productions such as their Scots version of Maxim Gorky's *The Lower Depths* (1947) and plays by Joe Corrie, Robert McLeish with *The Gorbals Story* (1946) and Ena Lamont Stewart (1912–2006) with *Men Should Weep* (1947). James Bridie's criticism of them perhaps prompted some of the later antipathy to his own work. From our perspective, it's more valuable to see these different aspects of Scottish theatre as complementary. An alternative to the international, commercial, subsidised, official Edinburgh Festival, which frequently neglected Scottish work, was the People's Festival (originally 1951–54, and revived in 2002).

Theatre Workshop, founded in Manchester by Joan Littlewood (1914–2002) and Ewan MacColl (1915–89), was similarly committed. After the war, Littlewood moved to London's Theatre Royal, Stratford East, and developed the company's most famous production, *Oh! What a Lovely War* (1963). The Scottish branch of Theatre Workshop produced MacColl's *Johnny Noble* (1945), a documentary ballad-opera. In his introduction to the anthology *Agit-Prop to Theatre Workshop: Political Playscripts 1930–50* (1986), MacColl recollected his early playwriting in the 1930s: at first he and his comrades had no sense that they were involved in art, but were rather 'guerillas using the theatre as a weapon against the capitalist system'. Only when working on a script containing a passage by Gorky did he become aware that there was 'art' in this.

Later, in *Last Edition*, written with Littlewood, MacColl presented 'Extracts from a Living Newspaper': news stories enacted on stage.

Imagine it: instead of rolling soundbites delivered in clichés by overpaid idiot-board eyelash-flapping newsreaders on a TV screen, you have living actors on a proximate stage presenting the human facts of the news stories, people made unemployed, caught up in a pit disaster, or the Spanish Civil War, or the results of the Munich Pact.

Immediately after the Second World War, MacColl wrote *Uranium 235* (1946), asking what atomic energy threatened for the future. It set a precedent for the television serial *Edge of Darkness* (1985) by the Scottish screenwriter Troy Kennedy Martin (1932–2009), in which the conflict between moral justice, commercial priorities, political authority and the nuclear industry is laid bare in a devastating dramatic narrative. Both works raise further unresolved questions.

Uranium 235 was published in 1948 with an introduction by Hugh MacDiarmid where he identified its affinity with David Lyndsay's 16th-century *Satyre of the Thrie Estaitis*. There too, people were 'subjecting their rulers to the wholesome test of ridicule'. The *Satyre* was produced at the Edinburgh Festival in the same year, so MacDiarmid was timely. Inevitably, he said, Lyndsay's play would be 'abridged, bowdlerised, and modified' and it remains doubtful 'whether anything like the same freedom is accorded to the arts in Scotland today as was enjoyed' in Lyndsay's era. Nevertheless, he assures us, *Uranium 235* takes its place in 'a many-sided movement to create a Scottish National Drama'.

Uranium 235 begins with the Scientist:

We have, if I may say so, in the course of the last few years, brought about considerable changes in what may be called the map of human knowledge...We can change the face of the earth in two generations.

Meanwhile the Crooner sings:

> Enjoy yourself, it's later than you think,
> Enjoy yourself while you're still in the pink.

And a voice comes over a microphone telling of Hiroshima, Nagasaki, the Cold War, the British in Malaya and Greece, the French in Indo-China, the Dutch in Indonesia, the Americans in Korea, and on. The play was updated over the years following its first publication. Its argument is undiminished: 'Men, women and children dying in countless millions because we couldn't be bothered to think.' If we don't eat, we starve and if we don't think, we die.

The play takes us from Athens, 470 BC, where, as now, businessmen and bankers define what life requires: 'War is necessary to the economy, it's inevitable.' But since Democritus has disclosed that atoms are what everything is made of, parity becomes defensible: a slave is as good as a senator. That's not philosophy, the Businessman tells us, that's treason. What next? A wife might challenge her husband, a soldier the general's right to give orders.

And so to 1300 AD, then 1450, then 1550, and then the 19th century, with the scientific discoveries leading to the play's present day, the mid-20th century. After the interval, a new character, the Puppet Master, appears, noting, 'all the world's a stage'. The Scientist replies, 'Yes, but we haven't booked the world for our production.' And laughingly the Puppet Master replies, 'No, but I have.'

And the final fugue of descent comes to its shuddering end: 'Act One, 1914. Rehearsal for Act Two, 1936. Act Two, 1939. Act Three...' Winsdscale, 1957; Kyshtym, USSR, 1958; Detroit, USA, 1966; West Germany, France, Switzerland, Japan, and Three Mile Island, 1979. And in Britain, as the play concludes, we note the Magnox reactors at Windscale and Hunterston, Chapel Cross and Dungeness, Hinkley Point, Dounreay, time-bombs in the nursery. They'll deal with all our problems. After them, there are no problems. They make more than electricity. They generate a poison that breeds cancers in the bones and flesh, we kill ourselves, our children, families and friends.

A Woman speaks:

> You don't seem to understand what is at stake... Plutonium has a half-life of 24,000 years and it takes about ten half-lives for radioactive material

to become harmless. That means plutonium has to be kept out of the environment for a quarter of a million to half a million years. If at any time during that period it is released into the environment, land and water are poisoned forever.

The Puppet Master comments, 'We can stop them, you know!' It will not be easy, but 'Do you think we might give it some thought? It's worth thinking about.'

And the Woman adds: 'But don't take too long.'

MacColl's work is essential to the story of working-class theatre in Scotland, to the folk-song revival, Hamish Henderson recording traditional singers literally out in the field, the scholarly reappraisal of folk culture at the School of Scottish Studies in Edinburgh, and the literary significance of both oral and text-based culture, the anti-nuclear popular songs of the 1950s and 1960s. All are related to this nexus of politicized literary and scholarly activity, plays, songs, poems and demonstrations. And to what once was the Labour Movement.

In the 21st century, we might ask, where is that nexus now?

One answer is, with the poets. I'll end this chapter with a poem by Pàdraig MacAoidh / Peter Mackay, published here by permission of the author.

Mèirlean

Slat à coille, bradan à linne, fiadh à fireach –
trì 'mèirlean' às nach do ghabh Gàidheal riamh nàire

Chan eil e gu leòr a-nis nach bi nàir' oirnn
slat a gheàrradh às a choille a mhàireas fad bheatha,
's a chleachdas sinn air na mìltean, a' cur duircean-dàireach
a thigeas gu bàrr agus sinn nan dust.

Fanaidh iad seo bèo nas fhàide dhuinn' cuideachd:
an tiona brot a' meargadh sa mhòine, an fhleodrainn
orainns a' dubadaich am measg nan creagan,
an sgudal niùclasach a' cunntadh sìos, gach dìog air dìog.

Tha tìde air ar cùlaibh leis an teanga fala;
tha tìde a' sgaoileadh romhainn mar fhàsach.

Cha bhi càil air fhàgail dhuinn ach ar mearachdan,
na tuill loma a sgiùrr sinn san domhainn,
gearraidhean air grunnd na mara

an samchair de dh'fhaclan, ìomhaighean, làraich bàn.

Neo: cha bhi càil air fhàgail dhuinn ach ar leirsinn,
an obair chruaidh ud de chàradh 's cur, de dh'àrach 's gleidheadh,
talamh far am bi fàs ann an ath-bhliadhna,
cladach nach tèid a chaitheamh leis an stoirm.

Chan e nàire a th'ann a bhith ri 'meirle' cùmhachd
o ghaoth is grian is tìde,
a' cur air ais nas motha na chleachdas sinn,
a' cuimhnicheadh ainm gach lus.

Bidh sinn beò ann gach roinn de thìde
eòlach gur iad plastaig is meatailt a th' unnainn
coille agus fireadh agus linne
agus a' ghaoth, is na clachan air bleith.

Thefts

*A rod from a wood, a salmon from a pool, a deer from rough
    ground*
three 'thefts' no Gael was ever ashamed of

No longer enough not to be ashamed
of taking a stick from a wood
to last a lifetime of planting acorns
that will bud when we are all dust.

For these things will outlive us too:
the soup tin rusting in the moorland, the orange
float bobbing among rocks,
atoms counting down tick by tick.

Time is behind us with its bloodied tongue.
It stretches before us like a desert.

We will become our mistakes,
the caverns emptied out of the bedrock,
the scores dug in the sea bed,
the silence of empty ruins, images, words.

Or else we'll become our vision,
the work to mend, plant, tend and keep,
a land where – a miracle – crops grow each year,
a shore not eaten away by the storms.

There is no shame in taking power
from wind and sun and tide
of giving back more than we use
of remembering the many names of each plant.

We cannot but live in split worlds of time,
we are now made up of plastic and metal
wood, rough ground and pool,
and the wind, and the cliffs we wear down.

51

Edinburgh and Lochinver: Robert Garioch and Norman MacCaig

WHEN DONNY O'ROURKE edited the first edition of the anthology *Dream State: The New Scottish Poets* (1994; second edition 2002), the presiding spirits of older generations were still around to inform the book. Indeed, Edwin Morgan and Iain Crichton Smith were still writing when the first edition appeared. Norman MacCaig was to renew his currency posthumously with a generous selection of hitherto uncollected poems when they appeared in the new collected edition, *The Poems* (2005). MacDiarmid, when his rediscovered poems from manuscript sources mainly in the National Library of Scotland were published in *The Revolutionary Art of the Future* (2003), a quarter of a century after his death, caused front-page controversy in the newspapers. (On 11 April 2003, *The Herald*'s misleading headline ran: 'Why MacDiarmid welcomed the London Blitz' and on 20 April, Angus Calder in *The Times* discussed 'Verse that hit like a bombshell'.) Differences between each poet are marked, but continuities, affinities and connections across generations were, and continue to be, active.

Robert Garioch (1909–81) was an unassertive, shy-seeming Edinburgh man, very much in the tradition of Dunbar and Fergusson as a poet of the old city, the characters, encounters and events taking place in the capital. He went to school and university in Edinburgh, joined the army and went to North Africa during the Second World War, was captured and spent the years from 1942 to 1945 as a prisoner-of-war in Italy and Germany, later writing a memoir of this experience, *Two Men and a Blanket* (1975). He was a schoolteacher in Edinburgh, London and Kent before retiring in 1964 and working as an assistant on the *Dictionary of the Older Scottish Tongue*, describing himself as a 'lexicographer's orra body'.

His teaching career afforded him targets for some of his best satiric poems, such as 'Garioch's Repone til George Buchanan' and the Edinburgh Sonnet, 'Elegy' which begins, with reference to his elders in the profession: 'They are lang deid, folk that I used to ken, / their firm-set lips aa mowdert and agley...' Those 'firm-set lips' give the clue: self-righteousness, visible rectitude, stiff and solemn, now gone into the good Scots earth as depicted in the words that mean 'rotted and out-of-shape', that latter sense given in the word 'agley' which already evokes one of Burns's proverbial phrases and 'best-laid plans' going twisted and awry. With incomparably sly precision, Garioch undercuts these senior teachers' self-importance. He describes them: one was 'beld-heidit, wi a kyte' (bald, with a pot-belly) and another 'sneerit... and sniftert in his spite'. Then comes the cutting judgement: 'Weill, gin the arena deid, it's time they were.' This gives some sense of Garioch's ability to make use of words and phrases drawn from colloquial speech but also from literary sources, utilising tones and timbres that appear immediately accessible in poems that are structured with great literary sophistication (he is one of the finest modern authors of sonnets) and flawless ease of allusion.

Garioch was writer-in-residence at Edinburgh University and on Radio Forth, composing poems on events of the day, making use of a range of registers of speech. The most serious, humble, rueful tone imbues the salutation in 'At Robert Fergusson's Grave'. The most wry, reductive and hilarious tone is in 'Heard in the Cougate', where a local Edinburgh resident is overheard stammering and spitting in disgust when disparaging the pompous flags and fountains in Princes Street Gardens, put up and turned on to mark the visit of the Queen and the King of Norway: 'Ah ddae-ken whu' the pplace is comin tae / wi aw thae, hechyuch! fforeign potentates.'

His *Complete Poetical Works* (1983) collects a number of slim, small-press publications but amounts to a substantial achievement, both for the sharp perception and humour of the occasional poems, the seriousness and sober reasonableness of tragic enquiry into human destructiveness and waste in 'The Bog', 'The Wire' and 'The Muir' and for the impressive translations of the Roman poet Giuseppe Belli, whose sonnets of Rome Garioch felt might be transposed effectively to Edinburgh. This is nowhere felt more movingly than in 'The Puir Faimly', the unsentimental, heartbreaking monologue of a helpless mother attempting to comfort her starving children. Garioch's 'Edinburgh Sonnets' are another masterly sequence and, like his translations of the Roman sonnets are full of elemental sympathy, urban grace and quiet, insinuating humour.

He is poet of masterly vernacular wit and compassion: poems such as 'Brother Worm', 'Perfect' and 'Doctor Faust in Rose Street' are effortlessly local and universal alike. There is far more than mere whimsy in his humour. A whole series of remarkable translations complements those he made from Belli. Garioch's Scots language versions of poems by Pindar, Hesiod, the Anglo-Saxon poem 'The Wanderer', 'The Swan' from the *Carmina Burana*, Goethe's 'Prometheus', and 'A Fisher's Apology' from the Latin of Arthur Johnstone, 'Ferlie of the Weir' and 'A Phantom of Haar' from the French of Apollinaire, from the Gaelic sequence *Dàin do Eimhir* of Sorley MacLean and above all, perhaps, 'The Humanist's Trauchles in Paris' from the Latin of George Buchanan are serious achievements.

The collected poems of Norman MacCaig (1910–96) are an enormous thesaurus of similes and metaphors: a sheepdog rushes through a fence 'like a piece of black wind', a thorn bush is 'an encyclopedia of angles' and a hen 'stares at nothing with one eye, then picks it up'. Overtly descriptive of animals, reptiles, birds, creatures of the natural world, particular people, specific places in the north of Scotland around Lochinver and in Edinburgh, his poems are also quizzical about the inadequacy, uncertainty, inefficiency, unreliability and the limits of language itself, the borders of what language permits us to understand. Writing exclusively in a clear, unaffected English, the tone is usually conversational and wry. He did not typically use capitals at the beginning of lines or even (after the first letter) in titles of poems. In 'A man in my position', MacCaig writes: 'Hear my words carefully. / Some are spoken not by me, but / by a man in my position.' And in 'Limits', we are told that 'our knowledge goes, / so far as we know, only / so far as we know'. Yet the limits to our knowledge do not excuse us from certain understanding:

> when molecules jump
> from one figuration to another
> they may not go hallelujahing into heaven
> or howling into hell,
> but
> water becomes ice.

MacCaig began with two slim volumes in the 1940s which he later disowned, claiming that their avalanching language and obscurity were too much of their time, part of a quasi-surrealist movement in poetry called the 'New Apocalypse' that had been prompted by Dylan Thomas, asserting the value of imagination over that of social realism. After a pause of a decade, MacCaig returned with *Riding Lights* (1955). While his poems up to the 1960s were usually metrical and regularly rhymed and, after the 1960s, normally in free verse, the absolute precision of his unmistakable tones of voice was maintained throughout his writing. All his poems, even when they seem slight, are the work of a mature intelligence.

He is characteristically ironic and, at times, wildly and wittily funny, yet both MacCaig and Garioch share a sense of the pathos of the epic effort. The predominant ethos of the Cold War, the existential anxieties of the era, have specific correlatives in MacCaig's work, in his sensitivity to the provisional and sometimes duplicitous nature of language itself. Like other poets of his generation, he was an educationalist, a primary school teacher and, undemonstratively, an exponent of Scotland's cultural and literary history.

He is also one of the funniest poets, ever. His extraordinarily dry, ironic humour delivers from unsuspected corners a shrewd sense of value. This can be both withering and comforting. Consider how precise observation and meticulous annotation of trivial things seen in 'Five minutes at the window' implies a profound understanding of people, and about what political idealism always neglects at its peril. Its message is urgent but the poem gives no sign of anxiety. We are invited to note that 'a tree with lights for flowers' says 'it's Christmas' and a 'seagull tries over and over again / to pick up something on the road' while 'a white cat sits halfway up a tree.' Each observation invites the question, 'Why?' and then another: 'What are trivia?'

>They've blown away my black mood.
>I smile at the glass of freesias on the table.
>My shelves of books say nothing
>but I know what they mean.

He is suddenly 'back in the world again / and happy' even though he acknowledges 'its disasters, its horrors, its griefs.'

In the middle of the poem is a single line, 'Oh, the motorcars.' No other poet could have written that line. It is imbued with a precise inflection, a sigh of recognition and an invisible shaking of the head at the vanity of people spuriously rushing to unnecessary appointments, instead of simply pausing to take pleasure in the virtues and values of trivia in a world of fortunate and vulnerable peace. A master of tone, humour and irony, MacCaig is a great love poet of the natural world and a great elegist in the sequence, 'Poems for Angus'.

These poets are high mountains in Scottish literature's modern history. Good people pay attention to them. Fools look away and wait for them to crumble.

52

Love and war: Somhairle MacGill-Eain / Sorley MacLean and Sydney Goodsir Smith

WHEN SOMHAIRLE MACGILL-EAIN / Sorley MacLean (1911–96) went to Edinburgh University in 1929, he read English and was taught by H.J.C. Grierson, champion of the Metaphysical poets so important to T.S. Eliot. MacLean's connecting of his own traditional Gaelic cultural hinterland with English-language Modernism, his early reading of Yeats and his discovery of Hugh MacDiarmid's Scots-language poems all fuelled his unique combustible creativity. Vatic bardic authority, the courage to deal directly with intense and intimate personal experience, war, love and loss, overt political commitment to revolutionary socialism and Scottish independence from British imperialism, were all braided together.

His first publication was a pamphlet, *17 Poems for 6d* [sixpence] (1939), where a small number of his poems appeared alongside a selection by Robert Garioch, who printed the pamphlet himself on his own hand-press, presenting the Gaelic and Scots languages side-by-side. But MacLean's first major work was *Dàin do Eimhir agus Dàin Eile / Songs to Eimhir and Other Poems* (1943), with surrealist illustrations by William Crosbie. This was a turning-point for modern Gaelic literature, yet for decades MacLean's work was difficult to find. An English-language version by Iain Crichton Smith of *Poems to Eimhir* had been published in 1971 but I remember the eagerness we felt when *Reothairt is Contraigh / Spring Tide and Neap Tide: Selected Poems 1932–72* was published in 1977. A collected poems, *O Choille gu Bearradh / From Wood to Ridge* followed in 1989 and then after the scholarly, annotated editions of *Dàin do Eimhir / Poems to Eimhir* (2002and *The Cuillin* (2011), the fully annotated collected edition appeared as *Caoir Gheal Leumraich / White Leaping Flame* in 2011. MacLean's critical essays in Gaelic and English were published as *Ris a' Bhruthaich* (1985). What is remarkable about his publishing career is how few books he published in his lifetime. Yet his reputation and growing respect for his work was immense, from the 1940s on.

His distinctiveness was to bring to the forefront of attention a poetry in Gaelic that was everywhere, evidently, 'modern' in its psychological intensity, its unflinching address to matters of modern warfare and brutal conflict, and its understanding and sympathy with the common cause of anti-fascism. This reached from the 1930s and his concern with people caught up in the Spanish Civil War, and drove him towards his own physical commitment to enlisting and fighting Nazism. But it reached further back into his own history as a Gael, opposed to the authority of the landowners who exploited and sent into exile the people of the crofting communities from which his family had come.

Yet his poetry was also distinct because of its psychological individuality and self-torturing anguish with regard to his love and loyalties to women, his own family, his language and his cultural history. This was a poetry to be read silently, as opposed to most traditional Gaelic verse, created to be held in memory and performed as song. MacLean had read and been influenced, in terms of sensibility rather than style, by W.B. Yeats and T.S. Eliot, and had seen what the early lyrical poems of Hugh MacDiarmid could achieve in their mix of traditional Scots language, ballad form and radically modern perspectives, in politics and sexual understanding. Part of MacLean's impact is due to the depth from which his poems drew upon these experiences.

In 1943, *Dàin do Eimhir agus Dàin Eile / Songs to Eimhir and Other Poems*, was recognised as a major turning-point for modern Gaelic literature. It was widely read immediately after the war and had an immense impact on Gaelic-speaking readers of poetry, and others. Hugh MacDiarmid, who had been in correspondence with MacLean and first met him in the 1930s, welcomed his poetry and that of George Campbell Hay and other contemporaries of a new generation with deep and lasting enthusiasm.

Even before the *Poems to Eimhir* were published, MacLean's work was understood to be a herald and catalyst of new ways forward in Gaelic and Scottish poetry. In a 1942 collection entitled *The New Scotland: 17 Chapters on Scottish Reconstruction*, MacDiarmid warmly hailed the appearance of MacLean, George Campbell Hay, W.S. Graham and others. At the end of his essay, 'Scottish Arts and Letters: The Present Position and Post-War Prospects' MacDiarmid says this (and the bold at the end is in the original text):

> The [Second World] war may thus have acted as a forcing-bed, bringing to somewhat speedier development what was already securely rooted in the circumstances of our nation; and in this sense it may, perhaps, be said later that: **'The Scottish renaissance was conceived in the First World War, and sprang into lusty life in the Second World War.'**

A major poet of love and war, the range of MacLean's poems include the politically passionate, lyrically personal epic sequence 'The Cuillin' (1939) in which the mountain range on the island of Skye stands as a living symbol of heroic opposition to those forces that would foreclose life's potential. The great anti-fascist poems, including the war poems from North Africa in the 1940s, are contemporary with the most self-lacerating of the love poems, and include 'Reason and Love', 'The Choice', 'Dogs and Wolves', 'The Bolshevik',

'Going Westward', 'Heroes', 'Death Valley' and 'An Autumn Day'. In 'Dogs and Wolves', the eternal savage hunt 'without halt, without respite' races over hills and mountains, both an eternal nightmare and an absolute dedication.

Perhaps the central poem of his career is 'Hallaig', a haunting elegy for a cleared township on his native island of Raasay, where the ruined homes of his ancestors can still be seen in a beautiful location redolent with its own tragedy. MacLean's poem is likened to a bullet that will kill the deer of time and preserve the memory of his people and his place forever: 'The dead have been seen alive.' His later elegy for his brother Calum and his passionate denunciation of the authorities and priorities behind the submarines in Hebridean waters with their nuclear-powered weaponry in 'Screapadal' are also required reading. Later poems reflect on the relations of language, power and violence in the legacies that reconnect Scotland and Ireland, especially in 'The National Museum of Ireland' and 'At Yeats's Grave'.

MacLean's significance within the Gaelic context is pre-eminently both as a poet delivering intensely forceful, emotionally determined and personal work and in his equally determined commitment to revitalising the Gaelic language in educational, literary and social contexts.

Friend to MacLean, Garioch and MacDiarmid and a catalyst for enjoyment in any good company, Sydney Goodsir Smith (1915–75) was a flamboyant figure and in his writing and in his person, a lavish verbal profligate. Born in New Zealand, Smith adopted Edinburgh and the Scots language to produce vivid evocations of the old city and its raucous, sensitive, loving and drinking inhabitants in his poems and plays. If Robert Garioch's urban Edinburgh Scots is authentically vernacular, Goodsir Smith's is rhetorically charged and gestural, yet, like Pablo Neruda, Goodsir Smith also carries a humility and compassionate grace that are instantly recognisable:

> There is a tide in luve's affair
> Nae poem ere was made
> The saul hings like a gull in air
> For aa the words are said.
>
> Nou in this saagin-tide we swey
> While the warld wags and empires faa
> But we that burned high Ilium
> What can we rack, that ken it aa?

While he is a fine lyric love poet he also developed a fluent, conversational Scots-language idiom in long-lined free verse, portraying characters and situations, in poems such as 'The Grace of God and the Meth-Drinker' and his masterpiece, the fabulous book-length sequence of love poems, *Under the Eildon Tree* (1948). This gathers the stories of the great lovers of world literature into a Rabelaisian company where he finds himself in an affinity of comic and tragic realisation.

Deirdre and Helen are here beside Naoise and Paris, but alongside them equal in importance and as pungently present is the 'bonny cou' (a prostitute) from the Black Bull o' Norroway, an Edinburgh pub. The dark bars and dingy alleyways and wynds of the historical old town are as populous with lusty lovers as the realms of myth and fiction. Grandiose gestures and declarations of love rub shoulders with massively reductive and deflating gutter-low perspectives. Elation is there, but so is the pox. His version of the Orpheus story might be read alongside that of Robert Henryson, for contrast more than comparison.

Goodsir Smith also wrote the riotous 'novel' of extended wordplay, caricature and anti-narrative bagatelle, *Carotid Cornucopius* (1947), in which many of the major characters of the Scottish literary and artistic scene are described, almost as if in code, obliquely, drinking heavily and roaming through adventures of various Rabelaisian sorts in the bye-ways, alleys and wynds of old Edinburgh. You have to squint to see them. The central character is Carotid, SGS, the great auk or auk-tor, depicted in various stages of self-indulgence with his friends, poets Chris Grieve (Hugh MacDiarmid), Sorley MacLean, and the artist Denis Peploe. In the first 'fitt' (or chapter), Carotid is introduced at home, with his library, drinking vessels and the places they have come from, his friends ('cronies') and his predilection for drinking. Then in the second fitt his friends are introduced, the 'least Drouk of Hardbile' and his estranged wife (and Carotid's lover) Colickie Meg. In the third fit the Auk loses his characters. In the fourth, we have a prologue, and in the fifth, there is the birth of Rorie, whose bride Biddie is born in the sixth while he's away at the wars. He returns in the seventh fitt and goes to school and plays games with Biddie, mainly of a sexual nature. In the eighth, Rorie and Biddie have a birthday party. There is, as that summary demonstrates, not much plot and almost no narrative. The book is a spouting cataract of bawdy puns and mock-epic lists through which Edinburgh can be sensed, smelled and tasted as much as seen, and in which an exuberance and appetite is sustained by ingenious invention and a mighty yoking together of the contradictory impulses of a prodigious forward drive and an utterly self-determined immobility. The language moves irrepressibly and unstoppably but at the same time, like Tam o' Shanter in the first part of Burns's poem, it is 'planted unco' right'. You can feel the alcoholic pulsing of the brain at work here, its heat, its expressive delightedness, and its propulsive, self-caressing pleasures.

Goodsir Smith was art critic for *The Scotsman* and had a wide range of friends in all sorts of social strata. His *A Short Introduction to Scottish Literature* (1951) was an important publication in its timely attempt to provide a comprehensive overview in accessible language and a small number of pages. It remains contagiously enthusiastic. His chronicle history-play *The Wallace* (1960) was an enormous success at the Edinburgh International Festival and his *Collected Poems* (1975) appeared posthumously and included translations (including a brilliant version of Alexander Blok's 'The Twelve'). A dedicated drinker, it is said that he once rolled up to a bar and asked for a beer and whisky chaser, only to discover that he was leaning on the counter of a branch of the Royal Bank of Scotland. Personally vivacious, he was by all accounts an enhancer of character, one of those people who could walk into a room and almost helplessly turn everything on, and Whitman-like, spread, and liberally squander his own beneficence, and celebrate that of all around him.

Sorley MacLean and Sydney Goodsir Smith are complementary figures and were good friends: one delivering a compellingly serious tragic vision, the other raucous, comic, sharply poignant, both masters of linguistic intensity with the courage of unquenchable conviction.

NOTE
Valuable explorations of aspects of MacLean's life and work are in *Ainmeil thar Cheudan: Presentations to the 2011 Sorley MacLean Conference*, edited by Ronald W. Renton and Ian MacDonald (Skye: Clò Ostaig, 2016), and *Sorley MacLean* by Peter Mackay (Aberdeen: AHRC Centre for Irish and Scottish Studies 2010). An extraordinarily valuable collection of essays covering the many different aspects of Sydney Goodsir Smith's achievement is *Sydney Goodsir Smith: Essays on His Life and Work*, edited by Richie McCaffery (Leiden / Boston: Brill Rodopi, 2020).

53
Scouts of the limits:
W.S. Graham and Deòrsa mac Iain Dheòrsa / George Campbell Hay

ALTHOUGH HE COULD be thoroughly convivial, sing and tell stories (like Sydney Goodsir Smith) and bring cheer to good company, in his poems W.S. Graham (1918–86) is at the other end of the spectrum. He spent most of his adult life in Cornwall and developed an intensely solitary poetic persona. Graham's poems are close to the plays of Samuel Beckett in their exploration of existential loneliness and searchingly poignant appraisal of the use and uselessness of language. In every one of his poems, you feel the immense pressure of the silence that surrounds it.

In 'The Nightfishing' and 'What is the language using us for?' the delicacy of his ear and the sensitivity of his judgement is at its best. It is worth emphasising that 'The Nightfishing' was recognised the moment it appeared in 1955 as a work of breakthrough quality. Norman MacCaig, who, like Graham, had been published in the company of the poets of the 'New Apocalypse' movement, once told me that he had read Graham's early work with interest, but with the same suspicion he felt about his own first two books.

> But then it all changed: you opened 'The Nightfishing' and on the first page the poem began with the words: 'Very gently struck / The quay night bell.' And you knew that something different had begun to happen in Graham's poetry.

And Graham's work has this strange restraint and steely tenacity, unlike anything else in modern Scottish poetry. And not only Scottish poetry. The poem entitled 'Loch Thom' is one of the essential poems of the 20th century, a magnificent epiphany describing the 'lonely, freshwater loch' up in the hollow of hills above Graham's native town, industrial Greenock, west of Glasgow, to which he said he would walk as a wee boy. As an adult, his return visit is chilly, restrained, solitary, heart-wrenching. This is the third and final section of 'Loch Thom'. The last words in capital letters are like the chilliest whisper you've ever heard:

> I drop my crumbs into the shallow
> Weed for the minnows and pinheads.
> You see that I will have to rise

> And turn round and get back where
> My running age will slow for a moment
> To let me on. It is a colder
> Stretch of water than I remember.
>
> The curlew's cry travelling still
> Kills me fairly. In front of me
> The grouse flurry and settle. GOBACK
> GOBACK GOBACK FAREWELL LOCH THOM.

The style is inimitable. After a period in which his work had fallen out of circulation, he was asked if he was still writing and replied that indeed he was, and was still beginning each line with a capital letter. In other words, his tough determination extended from his commitment to the practice of writing to the definitive presence of each line of a poem as a made thing and the final poem as a carefully secured, constructed utterance. He would never permit his writing to relax into a merely conversational idiom, although some poems have the hushed tones of the most intimate, whispered conversations. Each of them carries the fierce, emphatic and measured authority of a work of art, yet none are merely monumental. Each one is alive as a fish on the line, and strong.

The essential theme in Graham's poems is the relation of companionship and solitude. Again and again, his poems evoke distance and intimacy, loneliness and proximity. Concrete autobiographical data and abstract implications of language and silence are central to everything he wrote. The primary consideration is language. The titles of poems clearly indicate the attention: 'I Leave This at Your Ear', 'The Dark Dialogues', 'Language Ah Now You Have Me', 'Five Verses Beginning with the Word Language'.

The intensity of the contrast between Graham's poems and the white noise, the silent page, the illimitable darkness that surrounds us all, is negotiated specifically by the reader, addressed as he or she might be in the future of their composition; or in their own time, in particular poems, by their specific addressee, such as the poet's wife or the recipients of the poem-letters. The poems are sometimes addressed to particular people, either the historic persons of the biography or figures constructed by the text. In this regard today it is almost as though readers overhear the poems. They create a hush and a sense of respect and wonder.

The contrast with MacDiarmid's later poetry is evident: *In Memoriam James Joyce* (1955) is subtitled, 'From a Vision of World Language' and that 'Vision' may be described as a plenitude of languages – plural – evolving in different times in all the different places of the world. No single person could comprehensively understand all these languages, but MacDiarmid proposes that such an understanding might be imagined, and this work of the imagination vitalises particular engagements. This generates wonder, yes, but also prompts curiosity about the wide world, engagement with others – other people, languages, art forms, countries. It challenges you to exercise the optimism of curiosity.

For MacDiarmid, languages – in the broadest sense – and the forms they take – in artistic constructions of all sorts, paintings, ballet, sculpture, symphonies and quartets, bagpipes and flutes – from the dancing of Fred Astaire to the Eddic manuscripts of five centuries before Shakespeare – all offer a wealth of cultural identities in endless correspondence. For Graham, the English language is fraught with ambivalence. Yet its solitary authority yields a wealth of sensitive appreciation, coming through in poems freighted with subtleties of 'accent', hard logic, great strength and wonderful tenderness. Read aloud, they offer a tensile, singular occupation of the air. In silence, their lines are steel on the page.

Deòrsa mac Iain Dheòrsa / George Campbell Hay (1915–84) grew up familiar with Gaelic, Scots and English, becoming a brilliant linguist and translator from Welsh, Irish, French, Greek, Italian and Arabic. His poetry is written primarily in English, Scots and Gaelic and his long poem *Mokhtàr is Dùghall*, begun during the Second World War and never completed, approaches questions of cultural difference and identity with the profound understanding of the languages of its characters. Growing up in Tarbert, on the shore of Loch Fyne, with the fishing industry present as a fact of his society's economics, the materiality of salt, air, sea and the struggle of elemental realities were ingrained in the spoken language of the people around him. His father, the novelist J. Macdougall Hay, set a literary precedent, but if the elder Hay's novel *Gillespie* (1914) is a dark and violent picture of a 19th-century Dostoevskian Scotland, set in a fishing village much resembling Tarbert, George Campbell Hay's poetry would be intrinsically modern and forward-looking.

As a boy, Hay went out with the fishermen and spent time wandering in the woods and hills around the village. He was intimately knowledgeable and precise in his descriptions of the natural world, animals, birds, flowers and trees. His literary and linguistic expertise was tempered by a social understanding of people in the community he belonged to. The fishermen grew to be close friends and their working economy became deeply familiar. In October 1940, in his 20s, Hay went into the hills of Argyll, avoiding conscription. He was stopped in Arrochar on 3 May 1941, imprisoned until reporting for service in June in the Royal Army Ordnance Corps. At Catterick, he met Sorley MacLean and according to MacLean, they 'had two splendid afternoons and evenings when we talked Gaelic poetry the whole time.'

In early November 1942, Hay sailed from the Clyde on a week-long voyage to Algiers, one of the many soldiers taking part in Operation Torch, the American-British advance against Rommel's desert army. While MacLean was seriously wounded at El Alamein, Hay's company ventured further east, crossing the North African desert into Tunisia, where the fighting continued through to May 1943. Hay encountered civilians in Tunis and Bizerta and witnessed how they were caught in the crossfire and bombing.

He became an unofficial interpreter for his unit in French, Italian and Arabic, having picked up the last two languages since arriving in North Africa. His expertise was undervalued and his status as a private soldier may have been because of his history of avoiding conscription and his continuing concern with conditions in Scotland. He'd heard that Scottish women were being forcibly removed to armaments factories in England and was bitterly anxious: 'I think that the maiming or extinction of the Scots as a nation is intended...I think of her as a nation against whom a white war, biological and economic, is being waged under this bloody war against Germany.'

'Why did the poets go to the desert?' The question is the opening of Edwin Morgan's poem 'North Africa' in his sequence *Sonnets from Scotland* (1984). He goes on to list Hay, MacLean, Hamish Henderson, Robert Garioch, G.S. Fraser alongside himself, all moving through the North African theatre of war. Hay, MacLean and all these Scottish poets crossed each other's trails in the desert but their lives took different directions thereafter.

War polarises. It works by defining otherness. But for Hay, North Africa yielded a particular sense of how all cultures live across their differences. This doesn't polarise or neutralise anything so much as partialise it. It is not simply that death levels all, but that languages deepen and extend humanity. In this perception, Gaelic, English, Scots, Italian, French and Arabic, the African language-worlds he encountered, bring other dispensations, different from the arbitrary absolutes and polarities of war. For Hay, no language could have absolute power. Writing his own poetry in Gaelic, Scots, English and other languages, Hay knew viscerally that any one language was only a partial realisation of humanity's potential. When he witnessed the destruction of Bizerta he had heard the voices of people there, their languages silenced in the bombs exploding in city streets and bringing the buildings down. This is the force of the vision of devastation in 'Bizerta', one of the key war poems of the 20th century: destruction, irreparable loss, the literal burning away of life, are all present. It is an incandescent *Götterdämmerung*, anti-heroic, concerned with common human purpose and a human need far beyond political, national, or any specific particularities. This is how it begins:

> C'ainm a-nochd a th'orra,
> na sràidean bochda anns an sgeith gach uinneag
> a lasraichean 's a deatach,
> a sradagan is sgreadail a luchd thuinidh,
> is taigh air thaigh ga reubadh

> am brionn a chèile am brùchdadh toit' a' tuiteam?
> Is cò a-nochd tha 'g attach
> am Bàs a theachd gu grad 'nan cainntibh uile,
> no a' spàirn measg chlach is shailthean
> air bhàinidh a' gairm air cobhair, is nach cluinnear?
> Cò a-nochd a phàigheas
> seann chìs àbhaisteach na fala cumant?
>
> What is their name tonight,
> the poor streets where every window spews
> its flame and smoke,
> its sparks and the screaming of its inmates,
> while house upon house is rent
> and collapses in a gust of smoke?
> And who tonight are beseeching
> Death to come quickly in all their tongues,
> or are struggling among stones and beams,
> crying in frenzy for help, and are not heard?

It is a vision of the ultimate consequence of war. The banal devastation, the destruction of human fact and human potential, is expressed in a poem that stands comparison and has an effect as lasting, deep and terrible as any war poem ever written. Hay's vision of Bizerta is a parallel to blitzed Clydebank, near Glasgow. His war is universal.

In Africa, Hay saw the Arab world as a balance to that of his native Gaelic Scotland. But the devastation of the war left him shattered, living reclusively and sometimes in conditions of mental disturbance, in Edinburgh. Only after meeting Derick Thomson in 1978 did he reveal the long poem he had begun decades before, allowing Thomson to publish what there was of it in 1982. His collected works, now thoroughly edited with scholarly annotation by Michel Byrne, are a major body of work, still not fully assimilated into the history of modern poetry. For Hay the human drive to power was as characteristic of British as of German imperialism, and the military tradition of Gaeldom held no appeal. Hay's father was a novelist and a Church of Scotland minister but Calvinism, with its notions of the elect and the damned, was not part of Hay's sensibility. Yet his poetry stays with us, an eternal opposition to barbarity.

When he returned from the war, Hay recaptured in his poetry the youthful qualities of speed and engagement, in the living terrain of Tarbert and Argyll, its forests and seas. Energy is exuberant, enthusiasm everywhere in 'Seeker, Reaper', a poem in praise of a boat at sea, full of a hard, muscular music, evocative not only of the resilience, grace and strength of the boat and her crewmen but also of the contending forces of sea and weather. Even contemplating an end to its own life, the boat speaks for itself, quick and brilliant, in a breathtaking celebration of physicality and constant action:

> When my gunnel's worn wi raspin' nets,
>   and my sides are white wi salt,
> when my ropes unlay wi haulin'
>   and my steerin's aa at fault;
> when my seams are chinked and strakes are crushed,
>   and the decks are tramped tie spales,
> when the length o me is sterted
>   wi hammerin' intae gales;
> when my motor scarce can drive me
>   from off some loud lee-shore,
> then anchor me in Tarbert,
>   gie me chain. And no' afore.
>
> Aa the points o Scotland
>   wi their wheelin' lights in turn
> I've raised them bright aheid,
>   and I've sunk them faint astern,
> scourin' by tie heidlands
>   where new lights burn.

Hay is a great poet not only of war but of boats and the sea and the men who work at sea. The determining fact of his life was an unwavering dedication to Scotland's independence. His knowledge of languages speaks of the extent of his conviction and authority. But the war left him in a state of what we would call post-traumatic stress disorder.

For Hay, heroic aspects are found in elemental things – conflicts of weather and language, difficult decisions, consequent pain – but there is also a binding force in the light that never falters, the voices moving unendingly like water, at times harsh, straining or mellifluous, coloured by humility or regret. This is what underlies his unfinished epic, 'Mokhtar is Dougall' – a poem about different voices, different cultures in dialogue with each other, one from the Gaelic world, one from the world of Islam. This sense of plurality and value is in evidence in the multi-linguistic dimensions of Hay's writing, in Gaelic, Scots and English.

Hay's English-language poetry is related to that of W.B. Yeats and the tradition of the long-lined verse of Anglo-Irish poetry, a tradition inherited by Yeats predominantly from translations from the Gaelic. There is also an inherited tradition of the bardic voice, because at the heart of Hay's poetry is an incremental tension between confidence and certainty, on the one hand, and anguish and doubt on the other. Implicitly, the first-person singular of the poems is thinking about his audience or readership. The bardic voice without listeners is a paradigm underpinning almost all the visionary poets of the 20th century. Some of Hay's Scots poetry has its roots in the Ballad tradition: structuring principles are metrical and a narrative drive propels the movement.

His poems develop over four chronological periods: (1) 1932–44, where poems of the sea and seafaring predominate, including such wonderful works as 'The Old Fisherman' and 'The Kerry Shore', which have been set to piano accompaniment by F.G. Scott; (2) 1944–61, which includes the war poems, especially 'Mokhtar is Dougall', and a deepening of strength in the vision of the Gaelic world in poems such as 'The Walls of Balclutha' (confirming 'the old, sure ground on which our fathers stood...'), 'The Fisherman', 'The Smoky Smirr o Rain' and 'Seeker, Reaper'; (3) 1964–79, where nationalist politics are emphatically endorsed in 'Nationalist Sang', 'Orion over Bute' ('Scotland will wake with the waking dawn / and step out from two centuries gone...'), 'Howes an' Knowes' ('The yird's a hoose for aa oor race'); and finally (4) 1980–83, with more occasional verse: 'Sunday Howffs o Morningside' may offer temporary release and relief when their doors open on an otherwise sober Sunday, but the Muse of Scotland, 'Musa Caledoniae' continues forever: 'In wind and rain the screes she trudges. / Hear but her voice! It nivar ages'.

Hay's significance lies not only in his evocation of the Gaelic community of Tarbert and Argyll but also in his exceptional comprehensive understanding of language – and different languages among which Gaelic has an essential place – as a vital human capacity. It is this multi-faceted tragic sense of the loss brought about by the devastations of the Second World War that distinguishes his work. While buoyancy, velocity and energy sustain some of his most popular songs and fast-moving evocations, the dreadful weight of grief and loss in the aftermath of that war are a testament that has both universal application and specific reference to the condition of Gaelic in the modern world. In 'We Abide Forever', the Highland Clearances are seen as both particular history and as permanent symbol. Scotland's specific history has a symbolic, mythic power in Hay's poems.

The works of these poets form two contrasting worlds of discovery, one centred in the liminal space between self and utterance, the other engaged in a diversity of languages and experiences of conflict and confrontation, both in a fierce relationship with the tyrannies of silence, both Scottish to the marrow in different ways, both giving voices to experience we all can learn from.

54

Folk song and the dance of the intellect:
Hamish Henderson and Edwin Morgan

HAMISH HENDERSON (1919–2002) was a unique figure among his contemporaries. He emerged from World War Two with a political commitment that strengthened and deepened as the second half of the 20th century wore on. His writing is varied: he composed not only the memorable songs that entered popular consciousness without reference to their author, such as the 'John MacLean March' and 'Freedom Come All Ye':

> So come all ye at hame wi' Freedom,
>   Never heed whit the hoodies croak for doom.
> In your hoose a' the bairns o' Adam
>   Can find breid, barley-bree and painted room.
> When MacLean meets wi's freens in Springburn
>   A' the roses and geans will turn tae bloom,
> And a black boy frae yont Nyanga
>   Dings the fell gallows o' the burghers doon.

But Henderson was also the author of the aesthetically refined, emotionally loaded *Elegies for the Dead in Cyrenaica* (1948), probably the finest sequence of poems to emerge from World War Two.

Moreover, his translation of the *Prison Notebooks (1929–1935)* of Antonio Gramsci was pioneering work. Gramsci was a key figure in modern political thought, a Marxist intellectual incarcerated in Mussolini's fascist Italy, writing up his ideas about the relations between politics, cultural distinction and popular culture in the modern world. In introducing Gramsci to English-language readers, especially in Scotland, Henderson was working out and strengthening the connections between the folk, oral and literary and intellectual traditions. Henderson's collected writings, including essays and public letters, amount to a major achievement. But his significance goes further.

The *Elegies* are a lasting poetic testament, but what he learned from Gramsci he was to transform and apply in Scotland. This was a lifelong drive to review national potential not only in realms of high poetic distinction but also in popular culture: literally, what people do, what we make, how we act and what we choose. Henderson's democratic conviction in education, knowledge, experience and conversation among people, the exchange of ideas and information, is at the heart of this. He was a convivial man but that was not merely personality. It was an embodiment of his vision of what people might make of their lives and what Scotland might be in the world.

Henderson's championship of the traditional singer Jeannie Robertson, his engagement with the folk tradition and then the folk music revival, arising from specific locations and recorded for the archive of Edinburgh University's School of Scottish Studies, remain signal achievements. Like MacDiarmid, he was a brave man to be as open as he was to public statement and demonstration in Scotland. His commitment to people – most marvellously to the travellers whose stories and songs he recorded in the 1950s – takes us to various parts of Scotland and removes the carapace of cliché to bring us encounters with lives of enormous diversity and quality.

His own songs have entered the popular folk repertoire almost anonymously. 'The 51st Highland Division's Farewell to Sicily' was written during the Second World War, literally as he witnessed the soldiers leaving Sicily during the Italian campaign, but it has passed into popular memory and many, many people, soldiers and pacifists alike, have sung it without knowledge of its author. Another song, 'Rivonia', with its refrain of 'Free Mandela, free Mandela, free Mandela!' is said to have been sung by fishermen working in the waters around Robben Island when Nelson Mandela was imprisoned there, so that he could hear the words.

However, very little of Henderson's achievement was taken up by mass media and given air time on radio or television in Scotland. In his song, 'The Flyting o' Life and Daith', each force makes its claim with fighting energy. The synthesis of the song, of course, is its own energy, which, whenever you hear it or read it, conveys its declaration of faith in the energy of life, victorious. Similarly, it is the triumphs of his long life that shine on. There were many.

His biography in two volumes by Timothy Neat gives the sense that Henderson was constantly engaged in changing history. The process of change is not engendered by any single person, of course, but Henderson is seen at crucial moments, acting, picking up a telephone, writing a letter, talking to someone, delivering a song, taking part in something he believed in. The lesson of his example is not heroic. It is not singularly Henderson's achievement. It is rather that every single one of us takes part in the story, one way or another. Or, you might say, on one side or another. A thorough, carefully nuanced and comprehensive study of his work is Corey Gibson's *The Voice of the People: Hamish Henderson and Scottish Cultural Politics* (Edinburgh University Press, 2015).

Edwin Morgan (1920–2010) was the most voluminous and varied of all Scottish poets since MacDiarmid. A professor of English at Glasgow University, he drew (but not uncritically) on the American poets of the 1950s and 60s, especially the Beats and Black Mountain poets, and on poets from the Eastern

Bloc countries, translating their work, including Soviet Russia's Mayakovsky, to balance the emergence of his own vast florilegium of voices. Like Garioch, MacLean, Campbell Hay and Henderson, Morgan was a soldier in North Africa during the Second World War, though not a combatant. He thought about registering as a conscientious objector (as Norman MacCaig did, on the grounds that he simply would not kill people) but decided to join the Royal Army Medical Corps, which meant he worked mainly as a secretary and a medical orderly, assisting medical staff, doctors and officers. He saw death at first hand, and out of this early experience of war in the international arena, and the homosocial world of the soldier, Morgan returned to Scotland and a university career with a sensibility deepened and tempered.

The first product of his war years was a translation of the Old English poem, *Beowulf*, which was first published by the Hand and Flower Press and then by the University of California and became a standard teaching text. It may be read in terms of his personal history as a representation of the violence, frustrations and thwarted potential inherent to the decades of war and the idea of creativity in the grey 1950s. He called it 'my war poem' but not until *The New Divan* (1977) would he write directly of his war experiences. *The Vision of Cathkin Braes* (1952) appeared in the same year as *Beowulf*, a 'vision' but of a literal hillside overlooking Glasgow, bringing together specific locality and the play of imagination.

But a far more colourful, effervescent, blossoming character was biding its time and growing in Morgan's subterranean self, which broke into publication with the astonishing first fully expressive volume of his own poems, *The Second Life* (1968), boldly entering into the new generation, heralding a long career. It introduced him as a poet opening the doors of possibility, a poet at play, putting his imagination to work, hard, clever and fast. The 'local habitation' of his work was the city of Glasgow and he was recognised as an urban poet, distinct from his contemporaries, many of whom were from rural, country, small town or village backgrounds. Morgan was the only major Scottish poet of his time to be completely at home in the city. He was different also because his work embodied an international provenance, he could write about space travel, engage new technologies, reimagine the past not only as past but also as part of contemporary reality, opening out to both East and West, and giving voices to voiceless things, animals, birds and other beings. *The Second Life* was a new beginning. In *Glasgow Sonnets* (1972) he applied the European high cultural poetic form to the brutalities of the city. *Instamatic Poems* (1972) assembled verses like camera snapshots of international and local moments of revelation. In *From Glasgow to Saturn* (1973) and *The New Divan* (1977) he consolidated all these themes. *Poems of Thirty Years* (1982) was his first major retrospective gathering, retrieving and renewing.

Also distinctively, both in poems and criticism, he was foremost in championing MacDiarmid's later poetry, which celebrated the variety of languages and forms of creativity throughout the world. Morgan's festive poems like 'Trio' (a snapshot of three people with a chihuahua and a guitar, walking at night in Glasgow 'under the Christmas lights') rubbed shoulders with lyrical, autobiographical poems like 'In the snack-bar' (about the difficult human work of helping a disabled man to a public toilet) and concrete or sound poems, like 'The Loch Ness Monster's Song' which begins with the question, 'Sssnnnwhuffffll?' and ends with the monster descending back into the loch:

Gombl mbl bl –
blm plm,
blm plm,
blm plm,
blp.

These curious, playful, seriously determined yet inherently unpredictable, often funny poems of the 1960s and 70s gave way in the 80s to a more evident commitment to the matter of Scotland. In 1984 he published *Sonnets from Scotland*, a sequence giving a panoramic view as if it were an account by space- and time-travellers, of Scotland from before the beginning through real and imaginary aspects of the nation, into what the future might hold for us: nuclear destruction or liberating prosperity and independence, with a beautiful man-made canal running along the border with England. This was the central work of his writing life, his own personal favourite of all his books, where Scotland is real but the imagination encompasses the liberations of comedy and the real potential of tragedy. In *From the Video Box* (1986), the international world of screen technology is shown to be illuminating, dangerous and hilarious. After the fall of the Berlin Wall and the dissolution of the USSR, *Hold Hands Among the Atoms* (1991) is a reconsideration of the relation between the personal and the European context. *Virtual and Other Realities* (1997) presents another new world of internet technology, artificial intelligence, information access, and how these things begin to pervade material reality.

In the late sequence entitled 'Demon' (1999), Morgan describes an irrepressible character, or aspect of character, who seems to be available to disconcert and trouble any sense of fixed and settled security. When serenity becomes complacency and threatens to turn you smug, in comes the Demon. It is almost an extended credo for the outlaw status that all poetry demands. In *A.D.: A Trilogy of Plays on the Life of Jesus Christ* (2000), Christ is presented as a young man in his specific historical time, and the plays amount to an epic parable of his life and death.

He continued to write well into the 21st century. *Cathures* (2002) returns him to Glasgow in all its multi-facetedness and *Love and a Life* (2003) is a candid autobiography with love at its centre, collected in *A Book of Lives* (2007). *The Play of Gilgamesh* (2005) is a dramatic revision of the oldest 'written' story in the world. Like his reimagining of Christ, his portrait of Gilgamesh, the lawgiver and king, and his companion Enkidu, the green man of the forest, effects a revision into a contemporary ethos of characters and stories so ancient they had become fossilised in religious orthodoxy or archaeological scholarship. The quality of intimacy and the investment of directly personal understanding went along with the outward-facing, public aspect of his late poems. The sequence collected in *Beyond the Sun* (2007), written to accompany a list of Scotland's 'favourite paintings' published after a readers' poll in *The Herald* newspaper, is by turns witty, clever, deflationary, sharp, moving and valedictory. And Morgan's dedication to Scotland's independence is nowhere more strongly expressed than in his commissioned poem 'For the Opening of the Scottish Parliament, 9 October 2004':

What do the people want of the place? They want it to be filled with thinking
    persons as open and adventurous as its architecture.
A nest of fearties is what they do not want.
A symposium of procrastinators is what they do not want.
A phalanx of forelock-tuggers is what they do not want.
And perhaps above all the droopy mantra of 'it wizny me' is what they do
    not want.
Dear friends, dear lawgivers, dear parliamentarians, you are picking up a
    thread of
 pride and self-esteem that has been almost but not quite, oh no not quite,
    not ever broken or forgotten.
When you convene you will be reconvening, with a sense of not wholly the power,
    not yet wholly the power, but a good sense of what was once in the
    honour of your grasp.

That 'thread' that has 'not quite, not ever' been broken or forgotten leads back through the labyrinth of Empire to independence, and its challenge, placed so carefully and delicately and with such authority and determination in this poem, is clear. The power that 'was once in the honour' of the possession of the representatives of Scotland's people must be resumed. If the date of the occasion named in the poem's title, 9 October 2004, is, like all dates, transient, it is a mark on the way towards that full resumption of self-determination.

In his essays, Morgan was also a major critic of modern Scottish literature and, after MacDiarmid, modern Scotland's foremost man of letters. His biography by James McGonigal, *Beyond the Last Dragon* (2010) and *The Midnight Letterbox: Selected Correspondence* (1950–2010), are essential reading. As Marshall Walker puts it in his *Scottish Literature since 1707*, 'Morgan's work offers the hope that comes from the intrinsic optimism of curiosity'.

55

Deadliness and grace: Robin Jenkins and Muriel Spark

HIGH AMONG THE major novelists of postwar Scotland, in the quantity as well as quality of their output and dedication to their art, are Robin Jenkins (1912–2005) and Muriel Spark (1918–2006).

Jenkins's earlier novels are set in Scotland, and *The Changeling* (1958) is a connection between the Romantic patriotism declared so boldly by Walter Scott in the Sixth Canto of *The Lay of the Last Minstrel* (1805) to the utter depths of cynicism uttered by Renton, the main character in Irvine Welsh's *Trainspotting* (1993). In Scott's poem, the spectacle of the Scottish landscape is the subject of rhapsody: 'Breathes there the man with soul so dead / Who never to himself hath said, / This is my own, my native land!' In his poem 'Retrieving and Renewing', written in 2004 for the Association for Scottish Literary Studies, Edwin Morgan quotes this:

> Breathes there the man
> With soul so dead—? Probably! But a scan
> Would show his fault was ignorance:
> Don't follow him. Cosmic circumstance
> Hides in nearest, most ordinary things.
> Find Scotland – find inalienable springs.

This is encouraging. Morgan urges us to 'Find Scotland' in 'ordinary things' and 'inalienable springs'. But there's a more pessimistic, darker response to Scott's enthusiasm in the film version of *Trainspotting*'s most famous scene, when Renton refuses to walk into the Scottish landscape. In answer to the question, 'Doesn't it make you feel proud to be Scottish?' he protests with stunning invective that he hates being Scottish because the Scots are 'the scum of the earth, the most wretched, servile, miserable, pathetic trash [...] we can't even pick a decent culture to be colonised by' – and all the fresh air, brown heaths, shaggy woods, stern and wild mountains, he says or implies, won't make any difference.

Between these extremes, in *The Changeling*, Jenkins has a middle-class schoolteacher in the 1950s take one of his pupils from the working-class slums on a family holiday to a Scottish island. The teacher is all too proud, extolling the virtues of Scotland's natural beauty, but the boy is overwhelmed by a world he cannot comprehend or engage with. Lacking the strength of cynicism animating Welsh's characters, and unpersuaded by his teacher's elation following Scott's exhortations to praise, the boy is caught in the current of dislocation and Jenkins's novel ends in tragedy.

In 1957, Jenkins left Scotland, teaching in Afghanistan, Spain and Morocco. His novels set in such locations and later in Borneo, many populated by Scottish characters, can be read in the context of the development of Commonwealth or Postcolonial writing, particularly that of Chinua Achebe and other African novelists whose work was being published in the 1960s. His later work returns to Scotland, revisiting his favoured west coast locations and reviewing the whole history of Scotland in the 20th century, most effectively in *Fergus Lamont* (1979). From industrial Glasgow in *Just Duffy* (1988) to faded aristocracy in *Poverty Castle* (1991), Jenkins's vision maintained its scepticism and sympathy. One of his most risky novels, *Willie Hogg* (1993), begins in Glasgow but finds a kind of redemption in what is discovered in America, in a visit to a mission for Navajo Indians in Arizona. There is 'some kind of grace' discovered in humanity but it comes through a constant apprehension of fallibility. People are vulnerable and sympathetic, presented with a full complement of failings and foibles, greeds, self-justifications and vanities.

For Jenkins, the dichotomy of location is between Scotland and elsewhere, and that 'elsewhere' is what we might call 'postcolonial' nations, including the USA. In Muriel Spark's fiction, there is a similar 'Scotland and elsewhere' dialectic at work, but the 'elsewhere' for her is not postcolonial countries but more frequently Europe, Italy or most often the centre of colonial authority and of Empire itself, London. The first poem in her collected poems is 'A Tour of London'.

Spark described herself as a poet with her literary roots in Scotland's Border Ballads, with their sinister humour, supernatural overtones, human relationships, intense states of unexpected and unreliable influence, and strongly-defined characters. The last poem in *All the Poems* (2004) is a ballad, or a neo-ballad, a 'literary' ballad, 'The Ballad of Fanfarlo'. At 20 pages, it's a long, mysterious, unfolding story that combines traditional styles and stances, oblique references and sly, knowing tones with familiar Spark figures, performative, arch. They act inexplicably, both threateningly and attractively. You can't take your eyes off them even as you know they portend violence. It ends with a dialogue with death.

Spark's most famous Scottish novel, *The Prime of Miss Jean Brodie* (1961) is a classic, both frighteningly serious and inescapably comic, and even in its title, *The Ballad of Peckham Rye* (1960) acknowledges a Scottish allegiance. Both novels are about dislocation, different Scottish identities in an unstable, international or cosmopolitan world, and both tap into qualities of humour, horror and wry understanding recognisable from the ballads. As in the traditional ballads, her novels are rich in oblique ironies, razor-sharp tones acknowledging the cutting indifference of the world to piety, hope and idealism. The connection to the ballads is palpable but there is also a different aspect to her work: modern, urban, delivering a sense of alienation or exile or distance from community, security and any familiar idea of home, hearth and family. The haunted memory is an essential element in her work, yet whatever it is that is past and lost remains elusive and ungraspable, whether the novel's setting is London, Israel and Jordan, Rome, Geneva or New York. This makes the territorial imperative inherent in the adjective 'Scottish' a questionable designation. That sly questioning is the priority of her writing. It takes reassurance away. Her capacity for unsettling the reader, disturbing any comfortable complacency in writing, is the evidence.

Most crucially and consistently, Spark deploys a quality of dark humour. It is possible to imagine Spark's novels and stories being written by someone else with equal stylistic precision and narrative compulsion but it is impossible to imagine anyone else doing this and sustaining her quality of humour. It is neither committedly, reassuringly satiric and disdainful (as in Evelyn Waugh) nor consistently sustained by compassion (as in William Boyd). Cruelty is part of its merriment, as in the sound of bagpipes.

It's worth emphasising those distinctively Scottish aspects of her work, like the character of Dougal Douglas in *The Ballad of Peckham Rye*: charming, poisonous, bringing out the worst in people who cannot see past his charismatic fluency. He's a seductive, merciless character familiar from ballads of false or demon lovers in the worlds of Burns, Hogg, Byron and Scott. In *The Prime of Miss Jean Brodie*, the satiric exposure of propriety in the context of an Edinburgh school is clear enough, but more deeply shocking is the deliberation with which Spark manoeuvres the reader's knowledge and expectations through disjunctions of narrative. Informing readers of later events that will befall her characters, including their deaths, alters the way in which readers relate to the characters in their linear histories. The conventions of linear narrative are distorted and turned against you. The sense of an omniscient narrator no longer offers reassurance (as in Scott or George Eliot) but takes on a threatening, smiling, villainous distance. Yet the humour connects.

It is when Brodie and others act most self-centredly that authorial distance delivers tonal balance and ironies to be savoured. In *Symposium* (1990), Margaret Damien (or Murchie) appears in London, fashion-conscious, newly married, cosmopolitan, yet the subterranean implication that she may be a witch and murderess sets the tone. Absolute moral judgements on acts of good and evil are embroiled in Spark's fiction in a social world of unreliable witnesses, foreknown consequences, and ignorance that can never claim to be innocent. As with Jenkins, people are sympathetically vulnerable and ridiculously fallible. Grace is momentary: is there any promise of redemption? In the act of writing itself, there is the trust to exposition, engagement, exploration: it may be that art supplies a reprieve from confusion. But the physicality of being, the pleasures of sexuality, the gravity compelled by age, all insist on fleeting apprehension. Nothing abides. And that prompts speed, not slowness. One might have expected the realisation of mortal vulnerability to slow the characters down but with Spark, the narrative usually quickens in this understanding, and mortality comes closer at an alarming rate.

Spark's writing is complementary to the great novels of Lewis Grassic Gibbon and Neil Gunn. It's a post-Second World War revision or rebuttal of the post-First World War effort of rebuilding the nation to which Gibbon and Gunn were committed. Spark's work anatomises the limitations of people and the inevitability of failure and futility. And she brings the reader into a position of complicity with this.

The most striking example occurs in the first paragraph of Chapter Two of *The Prime of Miss Jean Brodie*. The focus is on Mary Macgregor, one of Jean Brodie's girls whose future life is disclosed with insidious speed, so that almost before the reader understands what's going on we're caught up in an unwelcome comprehension of the character's death. The opening sentence runs like this: 'Mary Macgregor, although she lived into her 24th year, never quite realised that Jean Brodie's confidences were not shared with the rest of the staff and that her love-story was given out only to her pupils.' The first time you read this, you're well into the second half of the sentence before you realise you've just been informed that Mary will die at 24. That word 'although' is a brilliant decoy. A bit later in the same paragraph, we're told that Mary thought of her first years with Brodie as the happiest time of her life, then this sentence occurs: 'She thought of this briefly, and never again referred to Miss Brodie, but had got over her misery, and had relapsed into her habitual slow bewilderment, before she died while on leave in Cumberland in a fire in the hotel.' All those commas, the phrases they separate and connect, structure that sentence for maximum effect. And the next sentence gives you a hideously immediate sense of her death: 'Back and forth along the corridors ran Mary Macgregor, through the thickening smoke.' Spark's forward-projection in the narrative here abandons linear exposition to discomfort the reader, to place us in a state of extreme unease. We have suddenly been given a God-like foreknowledge that we cannot shake off when we go on to read what happens to Mary during her time with Brodie, when the narrative goes back to an earlier period. The foreknowledge is a foreclosure. Just as there's no escape for Mary in Spark's novel, there's no way back from what Spark has delivered to the reader with such icy precision.

There's a contrast to be noted between this and the narrative structure of Lewis Grassic Gibbon's *Sunset Song*. Each section of that novel begins by combining the end of the preceding section with the end of the new one. So, at the beginning of Part II, Chris is pictured running uphill to the standing stones and lying down to gather her thoughts, remembering the last time she was there, which we've just read at the end of Part I. The second section then recounts the narrative of events that has taken her from the end of Part I to the beginning of Part II, to which we return at the end of the section. The effect is the opposite of Spark's foreclosure. What Gibbon gives us again and again is a sense that the narrative cannot be predicted. What happens in consequence of our actions involves a multitude of choices and possibilities. Nothing is inevitable, and therefore the struggle is worthwhile because a better outcome might be made. Spark offers no such hope or consolation of possibility. In contrast to Gibbon, her vision is brutal and bleak. But it is funny. And its humour is constant, sustaining and thoroughly black.

Most of her work addresses an international readership but her knowledge of the Scottish literary tradition – however implicit, deeply-processed and unspecified – informs everything, in aspects of humour, grotesquerie, the juxtaposition of polite society and gory violence, the mysterious stranger and the presumptions of class distinction, the supernatural and the materialistic, the ambiguities of writing and oral storytelling, objectivity and seduction, intention and subversion, the quest to reach beyond the self and the human surrender to the desire for self-fulfilment. These major themes are at the heart of all her work, from early novels like *The Comforters* (1957) and *Memento Mori* (1959) through *The Mandelbaum Gate* (1965) and *The Driver's Seat* (1970) to *The Takeover* (1976) and *A Far Cry from Kensington* (1988).

She was a convert to Catholicism but no orthodox structures dim her sceptical intelligence and needling suggestiveness. She is destabilising, constantly insisting on the unfinished nature of the world and all the people in it. Neither nationality nor religion offer ultimate security for Spark. Like that of Robin Jenkins, her art is never naïve and sometimes shocking. We need them both.

NOTE
Two collections of critical essays are particularly insightful and offer in-depth readings of the work of these two major writers: *The Edinburgh Companion to Muriel Spark*, edited by Michael Gardiner and Willy Maley (Edinburgh University Press, 2010) and *The Fiction of Robin Jenkins: Some Kind of Grace*, edited by Douglas Gifford and Linden Bicket (Leiden and Boston: Brill Rodopi, 2017).

56

Lords of the Isles: George Mackay Brown and Iain Mac a' Ghobhainn / Iain Crichton Smith

A POET OF the islands, George Mackay Brown (1921–96) was centred in the Orkney archipelago off the north coast of Scotland, his poems exploring, with patience and bright imagery, his favoured territory, seascapes, history and legends, celebrating the generations of his parents and grandparents and Orkney's richly textured past. His central themes are of the essential rhythms of the everyday, the rites and rituals that help keep things sacred. The theme of sacrifice enacted in the particular martyrdom of St Magnus on the island of Egilsay was something he returned to repeatedly.

He lived almost all of his life in Orkney, a poet, novelist, short story writer, dramatist and local newspaper columnist writing for the people of the islands. References in his poems might be religious, esoteric, sometimes obscure, and themes in his novels and stories might draw from less familiar aspects of history and myth, but his address was not primarily to a specialised readership. His affirmations frequently returned to a common humanity, an open sense of vulnerability, the pleasures and illuminations brought by literature and the arts, and a sense of value and safekeeping, unsentimentally treasuring qualities that a more ruthless world dispenses with too quickly and too easily. A Roman Catholic convert, his personal self-sufficiency – he never married though he had many friends, affectionate and close – his dedication to the modest, regulated practice of the writing life, and his loyalty to pastoral ideals (like that of his mentor Edwin Muir) seem at first very different from the more spontaneously engaging contemporaneity of his peers. His beliefs in the proper relation between individuals and society were deeply conservative. Yet his poetry has important things to say about the ecological and political crises of the 20th century, the value of sacrament and the sacral world and the social obligations of the individual and the community.

His output is varied, ranging from writing of crystalline brilliance to the virtually twee, and sometimes he adapts the formula of simply going through rites quite mechanically: the days of the week, the seasons of the year, the stations of the cross. For example, these are opening lines of 'Beachcomber':

> Monday I found a boot –
> Rust and salt leather.
> I gave it back to the sea, to dance in.

> Tuesday a spar of timber worth thirty bob.
> Next winter
> It will be a chair, a coffin, a bed.

And proceeding through further discoveries on Wednesday, then Thursday, each one presented in bright, surprising imagery, we come to:

> Friday I held a seaman's skull,
> Sand spilling from it
> The way time is told on kirkyard stones.

And at the end of the poem, a question – and answer: 'What's heaven? A sea chest with a thousand gold coins.'

Part of Brown's singularity and distinction lies in the fact that he was a self-conscious celebrant of art and a deft portraitist in verse as well as prose. He commemorates the islanders, going back to the great Norse sagas, developing a poetry written in sparkling, precise English, wonderfully cadenced (his student research centred on Gerard Manley Hopkins), capable of engaging profound matters with a delicate touch, and finding qualities of permanence in the acts of ordinary days. In 'Hamnavoe' and 'Hamnavoe Market' he paints an inimitable portrait of Stromness, the town he lived in most of his life. In 'The Funeral of Ally Flett' and 'Old Fisherman with Guitar' he presents local characters both in their essential, almost universal identities, and yet also utterly differentiated and unique. In 'The Five Voyages of Arnor', 'Tinkers' and 'Dead Fires', he ranges through history, moving out from and returning back to Orkney. 'Stations of the Cross' goes through the series of designated moments in the journey to Christ's crucifixion with due observance, yet sharply felt immediacy. 'Uranium' – in its first version, published in the book *Seven Poets* (1981), edited by Christopher Carrell, and not in its subsequently revised and weaker version, remains among the most memorable poems of a world in the context of nuclear power. The poem is terrifying in its restraint and implication.

Brown was pre-eminently a poet but he was also a playwright with *A Spell for Green Corn* (1970) and *Three Plays: The Loom of Light, The Well and The Voyage of Saint Brandon* (1984). But more impressive than his plays are his short stories and novels. The best stories are collected in *A Calendar of Love* (1967), which notes in its Foreword that 'Orkney is a small green world in itself', *A Time to Keep* (1969), *Hawkfall* (1974), *The Sun's Net* (1976), *Andrina and Other Stories* (1983) – in which the title story is one of the most haunting, economic in style and emotional restraint – *The Masked Fisherman* (1989), *The Sea-King's Daughter* (1991), *Winter Tales* (1995) and, published posthumously, *The Island of the Women* (1998).

Both *A Calendar of Love* and *A Time to Keep* establish and return to his favoured themes and questions: archetypes (tramps, ministers, lairds, shopkeepers), Christian rituals (nativity, transfiguration, passion, death and resurrection), worrying matters of technology, progress and commercial exploitation. All these tropes are set against the perennial virtues of the stories, songs and traditions people bear. 'Bear' is the appropriate word: these things form a people's culture and are carried, a cargo, a valuable weight that demands effort but also delivers real nourishment for present and future, drawn from the past. They require both respect and good use.

Travel and residence are his characters' polar determinants: the urge felt by some, to travel and return, and the role of those who do not roam, but whose residence might also hold a yearning to leave and see the world. Time, mortality, violence and sacrifice are cradled in a distinctive archipelago where everyday acts of kindness and support are valued, treasured, performed gratefully.

All Brown's work presents a shifting, kaleidoscopic reimagining of Orkney, from its ancient past to late in the 20th century. The single best place to begin is *An Orkney Tapestry* (1969), a collection of stories, poems, short plays, essays and drawings which introduces not only his style and preferred subjects and themes, but also quickly draws you into Orkney itself, delivering both reverence for, and engagement with, the life of the islands and the lives of the islanders, through time and across the various islands of the archipelago. But this is not to underestimate the deepening meditations on sanctity and the value of sacredness in the modern world, especially in his essays from *The Orcadian* newspaper, collected in *Letters from Hamnavoe* (1975), *Under Brinkie's Brae* (1979), *Rockpools and Daffodils: An Orcadian Diary, 1979–91* (1992) and *The First Wash of Spring* (2006), and his autobiographical writing in *For the Islands I Sing* (1997) and *Northern Lights* (1999).

His most lastingly impressive novels are *Greenvoe* (1972) and *Magnus* (1973) but there are others. The grim cycles of warfare happening all through history, all over the world, encountered in *Time in a Red Coat* (1984), are cautionary but the graceful lucidity of his last novels, *Vinland* (1992) and *Beside the Ocean of Time* (1994), is deeply refreshing and heartfelt.

Edwin Morgan declared a preference for his first novel, *Greenvoe*. It has a multi-layered structure: 'On one level, we follow the gossipy, ingrown, and not very edifying lives of a small community in the imaginary island of Hellya. A historical extension is provided by the Skarf, who writes up the island's past in an old cash-book.' There is 'a quasi-futuristic element towards the end' when 'the military-industrial Dark Star project first quickens and then kills the village. A less persuasive mythical cult of The Horsemen promises resurrection.' Morgan summarises judiciously, judging that the book is 'striking' and there is 'precision' in the writing: it is 'a poet's novel'.

But I would argue that Brown's strongest novel is *Magnus*, which dramatically retells the story of the martyr and his place in Orkney history, and startlingly connects it to political violence and human bloodshed throughout history, specifically in the Second World War. Nazism is not demonised but rather seen as an understandable human evil, the realisation of the worst of human potential. It is presented in Brechtian terms as the exaggeration and aberration of recognisably human motives and it shows their horrific results. It is the toughest of his books, gathering the deepest questions his writing addresses, the value of locality, character and community, the human worth of art and sacrifice, the tension between the natural world and the end of all things, the threat of apocalypse.

Historical evocation of the 12th-century Magnus, the seemingly perennial cast of peasants, tinkers, crofters, businessmen, courtiers, landowners and aristocracy, and figures from a Nazi concentration camp, the cook and butcher, the officers, the helpless and obedient, the resistant, the powerful, all come into a configuration of social conflict and power which is never easy to accept and disallows complacency completely. It is unsettling reading and its value as a permanent challenge to orthodox assurances is profound.

Iain Mac a' Ghobhainn / Iain Crichton Smith (1928–98) is associated with the Isle of Lewis in the Outer Hebrides, where religious austerity and bleak landscapes confirmed the self-questioning character of his childhood imagination. Gaelic was his first language and he never abandoned it, but the tensions of different tongues were always with him. Between Gaelic and English, Smith was determined to find a point of balance and a kind of continuity. This determination charged him with urgency in a quest to see beyond the enclosures of any language to the elemental world. The silent stare of the 'Deer on the High Hills' is eerie and eloquent beyond words:

> A deer looks through you to the other side
> and what it is and sees is an inhuman pride.

The central tension in Smith's work is between the inhuman world and the desired ideal of a humane community, between absolute dogma and diffident actuality. He feels the weasel's teeth in the rabbit's neck, observes an owl in a nocturnal landscape, where 'All seems immortal but for the dangling mouse.' The deer sees past the human to the real and metaphysical landscapes surrounding it, but human words are all we have to come to terms with either.

In the Isle of Lewis, austere religion permeated social convention, forming a hard stratum of judgement which the poet turned to his own advantage. His poems celebrate the colourful and transient things extreme Calvinism considers frivolous, but he also reckons the human cost, the raging alongside the grace. He can be a very funny poet, but the comedy and joy in his work always works to abet a serious argument. In 'Poem of Lewis' the austerity is paramount:

> Here they have no time for the fine graces
> of poetry, unless it freely grows
> in deep compulsion, like water in the well,
> woven into the texture of the soil
> in a strong pattern.

Even 'the early daffodil, purer than a soul' will, the poem promises, be 'gathered into the terrible mouth of the gale.' Beginning in such austerity, Crichton Smith developed a fluent, exploratory poetic style which sometimes seems careless but in fact is invigorating, risky and immediately accessible, arising linguistically from his own Gaelic foundations. The darkness of depression gripped him in the 1980s but in the *Murdo* stories he developed a quizzical, comic aspect, particularly in the sometimes absurd juxtapositions brought to the world by modernity. In 'An TV' / 'The TV', a series of laconic, three-line stanzas offer miniature snapshot observations on the impact of small-screen media on traditional culture:

> Tha e nas fhaisge air Humphrey Bogart
> na tha e air Tormod Mór –
> on fhuair e an TV.

> He's closer to Humphrey Bogart
> than he is to Tormad Mór –
> since he got the TV.

And in a miniature lament for traditional love poetry, he writes with reference to the black-and-white television:

> Thainig nighean a-steach do rum
> gun bholtrach gun fhiamh –
> ás an TV.

> A girl came into the room
> without scent or colour –
> out of the TV.

Crichton Smith's sharpness, humour and openness to contemporary influences helped make him an example many poets of succeeding generations would gain from. His serious portent is carried in his light quizzicality. The apparent carelessness and prolific output are themselves a repudiation of notions of

Calvinist predestination and economic austerity.

The austerity experienced in his childhood is vivid in 'Lewis, where we have 'the smell of seaweed...the wind on the Atlantic, / a seagull lying dead on a bare headland', 'the sea breaking whitely on the long sand' and 'flowers among the stones'. The poem ends like this:

> The wind is beating against the headlands
> with its lonely song,
> the moor yellow with flowers,
> the small elegant lochs
> like blue rings, there they used to walk
> when they were children.
> The loom of the wind on the headlands
> with its eternal whine.

Exile is a central theme, both from place and from language. While cripplingly serious at times, it evolves in his work towards a wry, chuckling, quizzical humour. His novels, stories, radio plays, and his personality at literary gatherings in his last 20 years, were often full of boyish laughter and warm modesty. His imagination seemed endlessly playful.

Pathos characterises 'The Departing Island': 'It's the island that goes away, not us who leave it...' The island is real, but it is also childhood, and the language of our childhood: a loss any adult might feel. And yet, even in his earliest collection, *The Long River* (1955) there is the exhilaration of childhood:

> Some days were running legs and joy
> and old men telling tomorrow would be
> a fine day surely...

The worlds of books and other media often mingled in his poems: Hamlet, Homer, Orpheus, Chaplin, *Shane*, *The Sound of Music*, *Alien*, spangles of neon in wet Oban nights. For Smith, Scotland was both 'the land God gave to Andy Stewart' – a dismal caricature of a country, a tartan cliché-corner, a monstrous, malignant deformity – and yet it was also the country where the mountains rage in dignity:

> The Cuillins stand and will forever stand.
> Their streams scream in the moonlight.

Crichton Smith was a distinguished novelist, short story writer and playwright (not least for radio, and in Gaelic). In the short novel *Consider the Lilies* (1968), he produced the most lucid, spare and moving account of the Highland Clearances in fiction. It might be read alongside Neil Gunn's *Butcher's Broom* (1934) and Fionn Mac Colla's *And the Cock Crew* (1945) as the three great modern Scottish novels of the Clearances, but Crichton Smith went on to produce numerous collections of stories and novels which amount to a substantial *oeuvre*, complementing his poems, plays and other writings.

Consider the Lilies is written with dream-like restraint, almost as if the gentleness of Crichton Smith's prose is a counterpoint to the dramatic, violent and emotionally charged events it describes. The larger context for the story is the social upheaval which followed in the aftermath of the Jacobite risings of 1715 and 1745 and Culloden in 1746, the relentless and remorseless devastation of the clans and families throughout the Highlands and islands of Scotland, and the assertion of Anglocentric military authority on the Gaelic-speaking people of the north and west; but the novel centres on one old woman, at first baffled and bewildered by her notice of approaching eviction, then gradually comprehending her place in the world of Sutherland, Scotland, Britain, and the moral universe being viciously assaulted by the priorities of monarchy, government and power. When the minister gives her no help or solace but an atheistic neighbourly stonemason does, she realises her own capability and capacity for change at the same time as she comes to understand the atrocities of oppression of which some people are capable.

The depth of human meaning demonstrated in this novel is a lasting and prevailing opposition to the depravities of monstrous regimes, and Crichton Smith's writing supplies a timeless, floating, shrewd quality to the storytelling. We know, by the end of the book, how the judges themselves will be judged, and this is not only a consolation but a continuing source of strength in resistance, an endorsement of sensitivity and profundity of sympathy, affection and indeed love. The book is unsentimental and deftly avoids emotional excess and it is all the more effective for that.

Among his later story collections and novels there are *The Last Summer* (1969), *Survival Without Error* (1970), *My Last Duchess* (1971), which records the breakdown of a marriage, *Goodbye Mr Dixon* (1974), a tentative love story with a happy ending, *The Hermit and Other Stories* (1977), *On the Island* (1979), with its idyllic elaborations of a young boy growing up; *A Field Full of Folk* (1982), which presents the lives of a number of characters in a small village, most centrally a minister struggling as he loses his faith, and *The Search* (1983). There are vivid depictions of Lewis school life in *Mr Trill in Hades, and Other Stories* (1984) and interrelated stories set in different apartments in *The Tenement* (1985).

In the Middle of the Wood (1987) is a frightening account of paranoia and breakdown. The central character is a writer, a married man, who, without warning, falls victim to paranoia, like Shakespeare's Leontes in *The Winter's*

Tale. He convinces himself that his wife is having an affair and that he is being spied on and monitored. He loses touch with reality and is driven to contemplate murder and suicide. He spends time in a mental hospital and then, suddenly and unexpectedly, recovers. He returns to his wife and the book ends in repair and stability. It's a strange novel, both threatening and ultimately reassuring, delivering a sense that the inexplicable can bring both bad and good things to any human life. Similarly tentative resolutions occur in *The Dream* (1990), in which the relationship between Jean, dreaming of sunny islands far away from her troubled childhood and her husband Martin, a university lecturer in Gaelic dreaming of the western isles of Scotland, negotiates its difficulties.

Smith's last novel is a tragedy. *An Honourable Death* (1992) tells the story of Major-General Sir Hector Macdonald, a boy from the Black Isle who rose through the ranks of the army and was renowned for his courage, admired and loved, yet whose reputation was ruined by accounts of his homosexuality and encounters with young men in Ceylon. He shot himself in a Paris hotel, avoiding a court-martial. The story is moving, loaded with pathos and oblique judgement on social prejudice and personal fallibility. Human liabilities are its central concern and the limpid, neutral style counterpoints the sensational subject matter.

Smith's quasi-autobiographical character Murdo first appeared in funny, satiric stories in 1981 then reappeared in longer, more personal and moving novellae. Edwin Morgan describes him like this: 'Murdo is mad, but harmless. He shatters the complacent surface of life wherever he goes. He casts some doubts on the supremacy of reason. Like MacGonagall, he is perfectly serious, and that is what makes him so funny'. Here's a sample:

> One day Murdo visited the local library and he said to the thin bespectacled woman who was standing at the counter:
> 'I want the novel *War and Peace* written by Hugh Macleod.'
> 'Hugh Macleod?' she said.
> 'Yes,' he said, 'but if you don't happen to have *War and Peace* I'll take any other book by the same author, such as *The Brothers Karamazov*.'
> 'I thought,' she said doubtfully, 'I mean are you sure that...'
> 'I'm quite sure that the book is by Hugh Macleod,' said Murdo, 'and I often wonder why there aren't more of his books in the libraries.'
> 'Well,' she said, 'I think we have *War and Peace* but surely it was written by Tolstoy.'
> 'What's it about?' said Murdo, 'Is it about a family growing up in Harris at the time of Napoleon?'

'I thought,' she said, 'that the story is set in Russia,' looking at him keenly through her glasses.

'Bloody hell,' said Murdo under his breath and then aloud,

'Oh well I don't think we can be talking about the same Hugh Macleod. This man was never in Russia as far as I know. Is it a long book, about a thousand pages?'

'I think that's right,' said the woman, who was beginning to look rather wary.

'Uh huh,' said Murdo. 'This is a long book as well. It's about Napoleon in Harris in the eighteenth century. Hugh Macleod was an extraordinary man, you know. He had a long beard and he used to make his own shoes. A strange man. I don't really know much about his life except that he became a bit religious in his old age.'

Although in fact born in Glasgow, Smith began with the austerities of his favoured place, the Isle of Lewis in the Outer Hebrides with its pressures of religious disposition, confronting his own abundant imagination with priorities he struggled to transform into strengths in his writing. Through his own breakdown and recovery, he gradually permitted a kind of quizzical intelligence to emerge supreme, confident and strengthened. Murdo came out of this process and remains a brilliant creation, tough and resistant but also spontaneous and at times hilarious.

Edwin Morgan comments:

Murdo is not the only character in Smith's short stories to have been brushed by the wing of insanity. One of the best of these stories is 'Napoleon and I', about an old married couple where the husband has gone mad and thinks he is Napoleon, leaving messages for the milkman to deliver five divisions of troops tomorrow, calling his wife Josephine, and dressing in a Napoleonic coat and hat. The story is told by his wife, who is at her wits' end knowing what to do with him; she thinks a hospital would be cruel; she simply has to look after him, though they are both in their eighties. Like the Murdo stories, it is extremely funny – even the wife finds her husband comical at times. But the comedy is very deceptive; it is really a tragedy where no-one is at fault. The wife remembers that she once loved him – where is that love now? They cannot even talk to each other. The contrast between what might have been and what is now is very moving.

If Smith's vision is ultimately accommodating and comic, it is also riddled with intensities, passions, and anger. The tyranny of puritanism levers pressure upon him and the absurdities of everyday life are also potentially the pitfalls of the unhinged or unattached imagination. He can be a poet of domestic aridity ('what room was Mr Bleaney in? It's like / going to any tenement and finding / any name you can think of on the door...'), a poet of forgotten bricabrac ('Old beds, old chairs, old mattresses, old books... // How much goes out of fashion and how soon!'), but he is also a poet of realistic hope. In a world of small 'Scottish towns with Town Halls and with courts, / with tidy flowering squares and small squat towers,' 'Stout fleshy matrons send their pekinese / on wolfish expeditions' and 'The butcher's hairy hand raises an axe' while 'distant Belsen smokes in the calm air'. And yet this world of 'Milk jugs, cups, / pastries with pink ice' is also a world of 'Waitresses with frilly aprons' who might be transformed out of their jobs and costumes, into the 'Two Girls Singing' on the upper deck of a city bus at night, 'for miles and miles together':

> And it wasn't the words or the tune. It was the singing.
> It was the human sweetness in that yellow,
> the unpredicted voices of our kind.

Iain Crichton Smith was well-known, loved and liked, through his English-language writing and equally as Iain Mac a' Ghobhainn in his Gaelic writing, as well as personally, in both Gaelic and Anglophone communities. That component of his work overlaps with but is not the same as the English writing and we shall return to it with reference to his place in the distinctive story of modern Gaelic fiction. But comprehensively, the great virtue of Crichton Smith's vision of Scotland is that it is a country not only occupied by the 'voices of our kind' – Gaelic and English and Scots, as well as others – but also that those voices are 'unpredicted'. George Mackay Brown would have understood that too.

57

Gaelic poetry of the later 20th century

FROM RUARAIDH MACTHÒMAIS / DERICK THOMSON AND DÒMHNALL
MACAMHLAIGH / DONALD MACAULAY TO ANNA FRATER / ANNE FRATER AND
PÀDRAIG MACAOIDH / PETER MACKAY

RUARAIDH MACTHÒMAIS / DERICK THOMSON (1921–2012) was Professor of Celtic at Glasgow University and publisher and editor of the periodical *Gairm* (*Call*, or *Cry*), author of a number of reference books on Gaelic, including *An Introduction to Gaelic Poetry* (1974) and *The Companion to Gaelic Scotland* (1983), as well as a poet of depth, commitment and sharp, poignant evocation. A native of Lewis, his poetry arises from his experience of that place, while international travels and commentary on the changes of the later 20th century inform his wry humour. His life's work was therefore multi-faceted: a champion of younger writers, publishing new work, encouraging others through extending critical awareness of the Gaelic world; a public figure, in scholarly research and teaching; an introspective poet enriching depictions of landscape and place with reflections on the people who inhabit them. The poems ring true because he is of the people about whom he writes, often with personal detail, warm or satirical. The poems might deliver strong political judgements but their humanity is characteristically generous.

'Clann-Nighean An Sgadain' / 'The Herring Girls' begins: 'An gàire mar chraiteachan salainn / ga fhroiseadh bho 'm beul...' / 'Their laughter like a sprinkling of salt / showered from their lips...' and complements this: 'Ach bha craiteachan uaille air an cridhe, / ga chumail fallain...' / 'But there was a sprinkling of pride on their hearts, / keeping them sound...' and their tongues are sharp as gutting-knives. References to television programmes of the 1970s and 1980s contrast with abiding care for the old, the infirm, the diminishing public presence of Gaelic and the cultural distinction of Scotland. A vision of apocalypse in Glasgow has its horrors and its humour in 'Deireadh an t-Saoghail' / 'The End of the World':

> [...] tuitidh an t-adhar 'na chnap
> air Sràid Earra-Ghaidheal
> a' cur Boots is Lewis's 'nam màl,
> le ìsbeanan is clòimh-cotain is cloimh-cotain
> an amhaichan a-chèile,
> is peant dearg air an talc,

> 'a bidh na diathan-brèige'bromadaich
> anns a' BhBC 's aig STV,
> 's gun facal a' tighinn ás am beul.
>
> [...] the sky will fall suddenly
> on Argyle Street
> throwing Boots and Lewis's into confusion,
> with sausages getting all mixed up
> with cotton-wool,
> red paint spilt on the talcum,
> and the false gods farting
> in the BBC and STV,
> speechless.

Thomson can be moralistic, self-disciplined and strict but equally comic, quick and compassionate. The tidal, rocky landscape of his childhood, the austerities of religious orthodoxy, the warmth of family, the diktats of economy, are keynotes in his work.

Dòmhnall MacAmhlaigh / Donald MacAulay (1930–2017), like Derick Thomson a university professor, was particularly open to formal innovations in affinity with the American poets of the 1950s and 1960s, bringing to Gaelic verse an intellectual aptitude unwilling to be compromised by prioritising formal accessibility. In a literary context so deeply protective of traditions, this was determined and courageous. To some degree it was undertaken by all the major Gaelic poets of the century from MacLean onwards, but MacAulay's poems have a formal integrity with which Aonghas MacNeacail (b.1942), Fearghas MacFhionnlaigh (b.1948), Angus Peter Campbell (b.1952) and Rody Gorman (b.1960) were also to engage.

Instead of the grim cliché of the Gael being looked upon by the Sassenach as an outsider, MacAulay's sensitive depiction of a holiday market in Turkey presents himself as the visitor observing the locals:

> Thig iad a-nuas às na cnuic
> Dimàirt 's Dihaoine
> tuathanach air asal
> 's triùir nighean
> crùibte
> fo chliabh is iaismac.
>
> From the hills they come down,
> Tuesdays and Fridays,

> a farmer on a donkey,
> and his three daughters
> bowed down
> with creels, and the double veil on their faces.

And although the poet is 'counted among the foreigners' he can see 'an ancient story' so the recognition of difference confirms an affinity of understanding. This is an old tale of class, empire, power and survival and MacAulay's evocation is also a judgement, tender but firm, a tale…

> that neatly in its folds encloses
> the Queen of England
> and Ankara
> and the town, a fortress –
> that has stood there almost as long as the hills –

Familiarity with the international world and the circumstances of domesticity, an unpretentious simplicity of diction and tone, all inform Rody Gorman's short poem, 'Deich Bliadhna' / 'Ten Years', where he presents himself and his wife celebrating their tenth wedding anniversary:

> 's tha a' chlann
> san lobhta-làir fodhainn 'nan laighe
> 's gun de dh'fhuaim air feadh an taighe
> ach an dithis againn a' gabhail ar biadh.
>
> – Tha seo math fhéin –
> arsa mise – Se goulash a th' ann, nach e?
>
> and the kids
> are all asleep on the ground floor below us
> and there isn't a noise about the house
> but the two of us eating.
>
> – This is really good –
> I said – It's goulash, isn't it?

Gorman's collection *Beartan Briste agus dàin Ghàidhlig eile / Burstbroken Judgementshroudloomdeeds and other Gaelic poems* (2011) takes the practice of translating his own work to extraordinary lengths. As is evident in the title, he presents not only a 'primary' translation of the Gaelic but explores associations and implications in English arising from the Gaelic words. The result is a phantasmagoria of possibilities governed by the poised disclosures of multiple meanings. Gorman begins by telling us that in Dwelly's great Gaelic dictionary, we're told that 'one of the words used for moon / Means a greyhound or paunch, a loin and kidney also.' So, he says, if he describes 'the very pupils of your eyes' as being like 'landed mackerel' he's simply trying to 'describe you just so'. The playfulness belies the seriousness as the poems question relations of language and understanding and how understanding arrives through different structures of language.

As with poetry in English and Scots, the voices of women writing in Gaelic became more widely heard in the latter decades of the century: Catriona Montgomery (b.1947), Morag Montgomery (b.1950), Meg Bateman (b.1959) and Anne Frater (b.1967), very different poets in themselves, occupy a range of authoritative positions in the early 21st century. Anne Frater's 'Question' asks about the priorities of communication beyond all writing, in a language that cannot be scripted:

> A bheil do cheann cho làn
>   de dh'fhacail Ghallda
> 's de litreachas
>   nan cànanan caillte
> nach urrain dhut
>   teachdaireachd mo shùilean
> a thuigsinn?
>
> Is your head so full
>   of foreign words
> and of the literature
>   of lost languages
> that you're unable
>   to understand
> the message of my eyes?

This speaks of universal themes. The 'foreign words' and 'the literature / of lost languages' are counterbalanced by love's signals, crossing all differences. Against that is the whole history of the British Empire's violent impositions, from the repressions and extensive evictions enforced since the 18th century, through the removals to industrial cities in the 19th century, to the further emigrations of the 20th century and to the continuing – if resisted – depopulations of communities and language deprivations of the 21st century. Pàdraig MacAoidh / Peter Mackay (b.1979), in his books *Gu Leor / Galore* (2015) and *Nàdar De*,

(2020) balances sharp commentary on immediate history while maintaining wry observational irony. In the anthology *An Ubhal as Àirde / The Highest Apple: An Anthology of Scottish Gaelic Literature* (2019), he has a poem entitled 'Tiotalan Diereannach' / 'End Credits' where this is the central paragraph:

> Tha mi gus bruidhinn air Raidió na Gaeltachta,
> gus 'eólas' a thoirt seachad ann an nàdar-de-Ghaeilge,
> agus beagan saorsa agam dè chanas mi: tha gach
> taobh aca mar-thà o BPA no seann-Bh-PA
> (Làbarach agus Nàiseantach); tha fear-naidheachd
> a' BhBC ann airson neo-chlaonachd. Obair freelance,
> beachd le saorsa na lannsa. Ach dè tha ri ràdh?
> Cuin' a bhios reifreann eile ann? Chan eil ann ach a bhith
> ri gàire. 'Och, rim o linn-sa. Chan eil aon dhiubh gu lèor
> airson beatha sam bith,' Air an t-slighe dhachasigh,
> a' dol seachad air baidean beaga fhathast ann an teis-
> meadhan deasbaid, air an suaineadh ann am iomadh bratach,
> seacchad air Teàrlach II, Smith, Ferguson,
> Alexander, Hume, chan eil mi idir cho earbsach.
>
> I'm here to talk on Raidió na Gaeltachta,
> to give expert opinion sort of as-Gaeilge,
> and have some freedom to what I can say:
> both sides are covered by MSPs or ex-MSPs
> (Labour and SNP); there is a BBC journalist
> for impartiality. A strictly freelance basis,
> freedom like a lanza. But what is there to say?
> When will there be another referendum?
> There's nothing for it but to laugh. 'Och,
> in my lifetime. One is never enough for any lifetime.'
> Walking home, I overhear conversations
> deep in huddles, still wrapped in various flags;
> I pass Charles II, Ferguson, Smith, Alexander,
> Hume on my way, and I'm not so sure.

The ironies and sadness in these words are multi-layered and deep – but so is the strength. Such uncertainty might slowly form into even greater resolution. Gaelic poetry of the 20th century and now well into the 21st century is one of the richest yields in modern Scottish literature and part of a greater story whose end is not foretold and – for better and worse – not inevitable either.

58

Playwrights and plays: from Robert McLellan to John McGrath

ROBERT MCLELLAN (1907–1985) was born at Kirkfieldbank, Lanarkshire, and spent many happy boyhood summers on his grandparents' farm in the Clyde valley, an area abundant in orchards and gardens. *Linmill Stories*, written initially for radio between 1960 and 1965, in fluent, unstressed Scots, are flavoured with the scents and tastes of the outdoors from the early decades of the 20th century, evocatively describing the characters and terrains of the fruit farms around Lanark. You can feel the sinew and pith of the characters, see the sunlight on the hills and river, touch the fruit, leaves and bark of the trees and bushes. These are stories based on a young boy's perception of a benevolent world. Brutality is present but so is the dream of fairness and justice.

In 1938 McLellan moved to Arran, where his poems 'Sweet Largie Bay' and 'Arran Burn' are set. His comprehensive study of the island's history, lore and geology, *The Isle of Arran*, was published in 1970. And as well as these achievements, McLellan was a ground-breaking playwright.

Jamie the Saxt (1937) is a major work in Scottish play literature presenting the character of the Scots King up to the moment when he is about to embark for England and assume the crown of the United Kingdom on the death of Elizabeth I. James ends the play looking forward to his new position and thinking of the moles in the earth, that will soon be approaching Queen Elizabeth's buried corpse. The Lord Chancellor Maitland reminds him, 'But the auld bitch isna deid yet.' And the King responds: 'Jock, here's to the day. May the mowdies sune tickle her taes!' While the play shows James's personal strengths and ambitions, fears and overriding self-interest, the deeper, stronger, implicit questions are about the relation between personal ability and statehood. Its essential subject is not the King, but Scotland, and the personal ambition, pride and power as the King assumes political centrality, and the effects such things have upon a whole nation's people and their future. Its pertinence not only in Scotland but also in England is immediately clear.

The Flouers o' Edinburgh (1948) is a comedy centred on the conflict between the Scots and English languages in the 18th century, a comprehensive exposition of politics enacted in forms of speech. Premiered by Unity after James Bridie had rejected production at the Citizens' Theatre, it's an extraordinary play where drama and theatricality rises as much from language as from its characters and actions. Anyone who doubts its lasting relevance might consider the prejudice against Irish Gaelic in Northern Ireland and the dire political consequences that have followed from that, and the prejudice against Scottish Gaelic and Scots in Scotland. Linguistic imperialism is at the dark heart of all this and has been the preference of fools and monsters throughout history. And still is. McLellan's play is a comedy, but its concerns are deadly serious.

In his book, *History as Theatrical Metaphor* (2016), Ian Brown argues that there are two distinct arcs in McLellan's work, the earlier one patriarchal, not to say sexist, focused on a nostalgic vision of the Borders and its conflicts, the later more profound, concerned with matters of cultural identity and freedom of spirit. The first arc follows the sentimental strain in the work of the Scottish National Players, the second develops the legacy of Unity Theatre. McLellan wrote nine full-length and four one-act plays. All of them employ incisive humour as they make serious points about language, nationality, politics and social justice.

That legacy drew from such Unity productions as George Munro's *Gold in His Boots* (1947) and Benedick Scott's *The Lambs of God* (1948) and was followed by Unity actor Roddy McMillan's *All in Good Faith* (1954) and *The Bevellers* (1973). All point forward to later plays which draw on working-class life in contexts of international, mass media culture, most famously in John Byrne's *The Slab Boys* (1978) and the television dramas *Tutti Frutti* (1987) and *Your Cheatin' Heart* (1990). Byrne (b.1940) based his small-scale play *Colquhoun and MacBryde* (1992) on the lives of the two Scottish artists known as 'The Two Roberts' in London in the 1940s.

Many plays in this constellation by authors such as Donald Campbell, R.S. Silver, Robert Kemp, Stewart Conn, Hector MacMillan, Bill Bryden, through to Liz Lochhead and James Kelman, address flashpoints of historical significance using various forms of confident, powerful and eloquent Scots.

Problematic as 18th-century plays such as *The Gentle Shepherd* and *Douglas* may seem to a modern audience, as discussed earlier, reading them in their own history and through their own codes allows us to understand their subtle complexities. Many of the plays of the mid- to late-20th century draw on historical locations. The representation of historical periods in drama adds an explicit layer of distancing for any audience, insisting upon attention to the artifice not only of the production, the playhouse, and the conventions of theatre, but to the language the characters speak. And this applies not only across history and territory but also across class.

At some distance from the working-class drama of Unity and Theatre Workshop, there was the growth of repertory theatres: the Byre Theatre in St Andrews opened in 1933, becoming professional during the Second World War. Repertory theatre in Perth began in 1935, and in Dundee in 1940, and in Glasgow, the Citizens opened in 1943, and the Gateway in Edinburgh in 1953, turning into the Royal Lyceum in 1965. Pitlochry was founded in 1951. In 1963 the tiny, 60-seat Traverse Theatre opened in James Court off Edinburgh's Royal

Mile. Its opening decade presented mainly standard repertory fare alongside some experimental drama, but from the mid-1970s it focused on new writing, earning it the title 'Scotland's National New Writing Theatre'. It moved in 1969 to a larger 100–seat theatre in the Grassmarket and in 1992 to a new, two-auditoria venue near the Lyceum.

The smallest theatre in Scotland, perhaps the smallest in the world, smaller than the original Traverse, was established in 1966 on the Isle of Mull by Barrie Hesketh (1930–2021) and Marianne Hesketh (who died in 1984): Mull Little Theatre, built in a converted byre. In 2008, it moved to a larger site at Druimfin, near the island's main town of Tobermory. In its great decades of the 1970s and 1980s, Mull Little Theatre was a signal attraction on the island, with productions of plays by Chekhov, Cocteau, Shakespeare, Strindberg, Shaw and Wilde, as well as new work by Scottish writers such as Iain Crichton Smith, Lorn Macintyre and the Heskeths themselves.

I have a particular memory of the Heskeths' *Mull Little Theatre Cookery Book*. This was produced to supplement their theatre work, but it has its own sense of dramatic flourish. The unlikeliness of the success of so many of the 'achieve-the-impossible' ventures we've been describing in this book might be summed up in their recipe for a lettuce sandwich. It was very short: 'There's only one way,' it read. 'Use a whole lettuce.'

In these chapters on Scottish plays, theatres and dramatic literature, one area we haven't discussed yet, with the exception of *The Hubble-Shue*, is playwriting for children. Since at least the late 20th century, there has been a significant rise in theatrical writing specifically for children. This movement has been led by fine playwrights like Stuart Paterson who, besides writing for adults, has written scripts for children that bear no trace of patronising or 'talking down'. Moreover, specialist companies like Catherine Wheels led by Gill Robertson and Wee Stories led by Andy Cannon and Iain Johnstone, have produced and presented plays for all age ranges of children. This upsurge was encouraged by the development since 1990 of the Edinburgh International Children's Festival, retitled Imaginate, under the long-term inspiring leadership of Tony Reekie who stood down from that role to go to work with Catherine Wheels in 2019.

Also noteworthy is Bertha Waddell's Children's Theatre which was influential for generations of children in the mid-20th century, having achieved a tremendous reach by the 1950s. Ian Brown personally recollected primary schools from all over Clackmannanshire coming to see their annual shows in Alloa Town Hall. They toured in Lanarkshire and Central Scotland, were noticed and invited to perform in local schools and before royalty in the 1930s and the next generation of royal children in the 1950s. Their shows would begin with a sound effect and Bertha's head appearing through the curtains, announcing 'Item Number One'. As Ian Brown writes in *The Biographical*

Dictionary of Scottish Women (2006), 'Each performance comprised some dozen or more individually introduced scenes, usually based on folk tales or nursery rhymes. Some used mime or puppets, and music and song were central to the aesthetic. Design was simple, suited to touring constraints.'

As children, Bertha Waddell (1907–63) and Jenny Waddell (1907–80) learned dance, singing and piano, and attended drama and speech classes in Glasgow, later joining local amateur companies and then the Scottish National Players. They launched the first professional company specifically for children in 1927 in the McLellan Galleries, Glasgow, as the Scottish Children's Theatre (later called variously The Children's Theatre and Bertha Waddell's Children's Theatre). The company and their productions might not be described as 'primarily literary' but they were important in developing through the mid-20th century lively and memorable theatre performances designed for children that amounted to much more than an annual Christmas pantomime.

Not that one should ever disdain the pleasures of panto. In 1972, Tom Buchan and Billy Connolly wrote *The Great Northern Welly Boot Show*, satirising the heroic ship-building industry with a humour that was both reductive and explosive, as the characters were depicted building Wellington boots, singing, joking and telling tall tales all the way. Connolly went on to become perhaps Scotland's most internationally famous storyteller in mass media, achieving popularity through LP records and TV appearances as well as stage shows and working-class men's club gigs. The precedent set of immediate humour, sharp wit, remorseless disregard of genteel sensibilities and sheer contagious brio was a key component of the best theatre of the era. And aspects of children's theatre, pantomime and popular theatre conventions in music hall and comedy were also drawn upon in the most revolutionary moment in modern Scottish theatre, in 1973.

This was when the 7:84 (Scotland) Theatre Company and John McGrath (1935–2002) took *The Cheviot, the Stag and the Black, Black Oil* (1973) on tour, performing in town and village halls, to audiences most of whom had possibly never previously been to a city theatre, telling a story about Scotland's history and natural resources – land, sheep, deer, oil, and above all, people – being exploited by commercial interests utterly at odds with the health and priorities of most of the folk who lived in this nation.

It was a 'ceilidh-play', a performance punctuated and driven by songs, recitations, re-enacted historical episodes and comic routines that had no pretension to literary elitism and every intention to communicate without condescension, directly, both seriously and through satire and comedy, with local audiences made up of all kinds of people.

The play took its audiences from the Jacobite rising of the 1740s and the period of the Clearances and the introduction of large-scale sheep farming, through the 19th century, when vast tracts of depopulated land were (as they still are) used for stag-hunting by absentee landlords, high fee-paying guests and royalty, to the period when the discovery of oil in the North Sea meant a new wave of exploitation of Scotland's natural resources and people (a tide that has risen even higher in the 21st century). Famously, the company's name, and that of its separate English counterpart, founded by McGrath in 1971, was taken from a statistic: 7 per cent of the population own 84 per cent of the country's wealth. The gulf has become even greater since then.

The play was a watershed in modern theatre, expressly socialist and deeply traditional in its carefully structured polemic and use of folksong and cèilidh techniques and yet drawing daringly on agitprop, music hall and stand-up comedy methods to revitalise its theatrical impact. It also had – and continues to have – international resonance. When I was teaching in New Zealand in the late 1980s, after screening the play, Maori students would come to me to point out in recognition, 'But that's our story! That's our story too!' It has been revived to considerable acclaim more than once in the early 21st century.

McGrath and the 7:84 company were keenly aware that in performance, conventions from the commercial theatre might be used in non-commercial plays, sometimes to overturn the ideology they arose from. Theatrical techniques used to present jokes that relied on stereotypes, racism, sexism and pantomimes of violence, might be put to use in plays deliberately intended to oppose such things. Populist techniques can carry a progressive message. Pleasure can serve more than one political purpose.

7:84 carried on with a series of engaged political plays, including *The Game's a Bogey* (1974) about the Glasgow Communist teacher John Maclean, Bolshevik representative for Scotland appointed by Lenin. McGrath's writings on theatre are collected in *A Good Night Out: Popular Theatre: Audience, Class and Form* (1981), *The Bone Won't Break: On Theatre and Hope in Hard Times* (1990) and *Naked Thoughts that Roam About* (2002). The offshoot from 7:84 was Wildcat, a company which also addressed political issues of the day directly and combined original songs commenting on, or evocative of, the action. Their plays were events that rose to specific occasions, most fiercely and poignantly in *Dead Liberty* (1984), centred on the miners' strike of the time, in which traditional trade union-organised working-class miners found themselves opposed by the Conservative Thatcher government and the police authorities of the day.

In 1982, 7:84 revived a number of plays from the repertoire of Unity, including Ena Lamont Stewart's *Men Should Weep*. This was in the aftermath of the torpedoed referendum on Scottish devolution and the triumph of Margaret Thatcher and the Conservative Party through the preponderance of voters in England in 1979. The appetite for the Clydebuilt season of plays in Scotland was keen. Both working-class cultural conviction and the priorities of feminism were joined in opposition to Thatcher's ascendancy, and there was a deeply held national self-awareness that people in Scotland had not voted for the same things as people in England. All these concerns came together. Internationally, *Men Should Weep* was recognised as a classic of both Scottish and feminist literature, and the production directed by Giles Havergal demonstrated its theatrical effectiveness.

In short, the 1970s and early 1980s saw a radical revitalisation of and broadening access to Scottish drama. The impact was immense.

59

Literary fiction: from George Friel to Jessie Kesson

THE TERM 'LITERARY' has its ambiguities: what does it mean? Maybe the quickest understanding is to define what it's not. It is not driven by money. Its priority is not commercial.

That's not to say that money can't be made from it. Walter Scott was paid by the word. Serialising Dickens's fiction brought financial rewards. The work of George Friel, Fred Urquhart, Jessie Kesson and Ian Niall, like that of Scott and Dickens, arises from a crafted mix of lived experience and imaginative understanding. It invites readers to engage patiently, not to seek instant gratification but to take time to understand human desires and motivations, conflicts and resolutions, failures and triumphs, and to enter worlds with character and ethos different from those of the more familiar fictional genres.

The urban contexts in Friel, the personal relations in Urquhart, the contradictions and oppressions of class, gender and propriety in Kesson and the necessities of farming and country life and how human beings are creatures inhabiting a natural world with all its tenderness and violence in Niall, all these themes and concerns are written about with deliberation and care, rather than exploitative immediacy.

George Friel (1910–75) published only a handful of books. *The Bank of Time* (1959), *The Boy Who Wanted Peace* (1964) and *Grace and Miss Partridge* (1969) are lucid, even-toned, carefully balanced works, but then, just before his final novel, *An Empty House* (1975), we come to we come to *Mr Alfred M.A.* (1972). Here Friel brings realism and nightmare into conjunction, the former gradually giving way to the latter in a horrifying vortex of inadequacy, evil, despair and tragedy. The pathos of a hopeful, optimistic but vulnerable, very limited teacher catches the reader's sympathy from the start, but when we see him confronted by a satanic figure of inflexible opposition, the trap closes inexorably. Both the descriptions of school-life and the anguish of the novel's conclusion are utterly convincing, visually and metaphorically emphatic. It begins in a realism reminiscent of the 19th century and ends in a world as terrifying and unredeemable as anything in Kafka. Edwin Morgan, in his booklet *Twentieth-Century Classics* describes the novel as a 'study of the decline of a pedantic, old-fashioned, alcoholic and totally inadequate middle-class teacher' gripping the reader with its 'specific detail, whether grim or funny'. He goes on: 'The background of Glasgow's young gangs and their graffiti runs a thread through the book which leads to Mr Alfred's final mugging by some ex-pupils, and his subsequent mental crack-up, signalled by an interior dialogue with a mysterious youth who is in fact Satan, architect of anarchy.' Morgan appropriately sums it up as 'not a "social problem" novel, but a vigorous, grotesque, bitter piece of imaginative writing.'

The novels and stories of Fred Urquhart (1912–95) are constantly impressive and diverse in tone, setting, mood, irony, compassion and range of characters. Edwin Morgan singled out his first novel, *Time Will Knit* (1938) as his best, but noted: 'it is in the short story that his touch is surest'. The stories are various 'in settings and moods, contemporary and historical, racy and deliberative' but a central and recurring characteristic is his placing of women as pivotal figures:

> the Rabelaisianly slatternly but irrepressible heroine of 'Dirty Minnie', the brilliant squabbling of the women washing in the steamie in 'Dirty Linen', the jilted TB girl in the hospital in 'We Never Died in Winter'.

He also drew attention to 'the sombre study of a bachelor farmer and an Italian prisoner in "English in Three Months".' Urquhart's short stories are collected in *I Fell for a Sailor* (1940), *Selected Stories* (1946), *The Clouds are Big with Mercy* (1946), *The Last GI Bride Wore Tartan* (1947), *The Year of the Short Corn and Other Stories* (1949), *The Last Sister* (1950), *The Laundry Girl and the Pole* (1955), *The Dying Stallion* (1967), *The Ploughing Match* (1968), *Proud Lady in a Cage* (1980) and *Seven Ghosts in Search* (1983). His novels also include *The Ferret was Abraham's Daughter* (1949), *Jezebel's Dust* (1951), *Palace of Green Days* (1979) and *A Diver in China Seas* (1980).

Jessie Kesson (1916–94), in her unique novels *The White Bird Passes* (1958), *Glitter of Mica* (1963), *Another Time, Another Place* (1983), and the stories collected in *Where the Apple Ripens* (1985) fictionalises aspects of her own life, growing up an illegitimate child in north-east Scotland. She also wrote more than 90 plays for radio and television. Isobel Murray's biography of Kesson is carefully judged and her selection of Kesson's early stories, poems, radio work and autobiographical reflections was published as *Somewhere Beyond* (2000). Edwin Morgan said of *The White Bird Passes*:

> The heroine, Janie, is brought up in the slum tenements and wynds of a north-eastern Scottish town in the 1920s, and from there goes to an orphanage, triumphantly surviving these environments in her determination to make something of her life.

Norman MacCaig, poetic master of lucidity and brevity, gave his praise succinctly: 'Beg, borrow or steal this book.' Compton Mackenzie was equally enthusiastic: 'She can make the printed page alive.' Notably absent are tones of miserabilism, whining or complaint, as the liveliness and energy of the central character lifts and sustains the narrative and invests vitality, gusto and smeddum in the prose.

Glitter of Mica describes a tough, lonely farming community, exploring its characters, concentrating on the Riddel family, a dairyman, his wife and their college-educated daughter, their humour and animosities, loyalties and jealousies, evolving over 30 years. It's a story of hardship and struggle but also of the indomitable spirit that was the essential character of its author.

The novels, autobiographies and 'nature writings' of Ian Niall or John McNeillie (1916–2002) maintain sharp focus on rural life, unsentimental encounters with animals, women and men. He grew up in Galloway and moved to North Wales in the 1940s and from there to England, but the landscapes and lives of southwest Scotland inhabit some of his best writing.

His first novel, *Wigtown Ploughman* (1939) introduces us to Andy Walker, son of an abusive father who goes off to the First World War and is never seen again. Andy finds work on a farm but his temper is short, he's eager to pick fights and his attitude to women is brutal and blunt. He is forced to move on from one place to another, always a victim of his own character and making victims of others, remorseless and increasingly ugly in his moral turpitude. The book was serialised in the Glasgow *Sunday Mail* and caused a scandal. As a portrayal of the lives of agricultural labourers and the homes they inhabited, it prompted a public enquiry into the living conditions of farmworkers and prompted reform through the Rural Workers Housing Act, the matter being raised in the House of Commons. McNeillie admired Émile Zola and John Steinbeck, and a reviewer noted that *Wigtown Ploughman* was 'a vigorous counterblast' to Burns's pious poem 'The Cottar's Saturday Night'. The author's son, Andrew McNeillie, has written of the novel: 'Its plotting is minimal, its trajectory sweeping and full of dark and light, earth and sky.' Published in the same year as James Barke's Tolstoyan epic of farm life in the same territory, *The Land of the Leal*, as McNeillie notes,

> The two books might not share scale but they occupy neighbouring and related terrains and have much in common as to the depiction of agricultural life and its associated hardships.

It is also in the literary company of Lewis Grassic Gibbon, J. MacDougall Hay, George Douglas Brown and Neil Gunn, as well as Thomas Hardy, Patrick Kavanagh, Seamus Heaney and R.S. Thomas.

Using different names for different works, John McNeillie / Ian Niall went on to publish over 20 books, including the novels *Glasgow Keelie* (1940) and *Morryharn Farm* (1941) and as Ian Niall, *No Resting Place* (1948), *Foxhollow*

(1949), *The Deluge* (1950). Niall's 'nature writings' are among the best of that genre, from *The Poacher's Handbook* (1950) to *Fresh Woods* (1951) and *Pastures New* (1952). The latter two were republished in one volume in 2012, where Andrew McNeillie notes in his introduction that their titles derive from the great English poet John Milton's 'Lycidas' (1637):

> And now the sun had stretched out all the hills,
> And now was dropped into the western bay;
> At last he rose, and twitched his mantle blue:
> Tomorrow to fresh woods, and pastures new.

There are also warm, affectionate autobiographies: *A Galloway Childhood* (1967), *The Galloway Shepherd: A Story of the Hills* (1970) and the posthumously published *My Childhood* (2004). All are worth finding and yield treasures, as does the biography by Andrew McNeillie, *Ian Niall: Part of His Life* (2007).

George Friel, Fred Urquhart, Jessie Kesson and Ian Niall: four authors whose works, like all great literature, improve the more you reread them.

60

Scotland and America: Alexander Trocchi and Gordon Williams

WHAT WE MIGHT describe as Alexander Trocchi's rejection of the orthodox was sensational and infamous. Alexander Trocchi (1925–84) may seem to have more in common with the American Beat writers Allen Ginsberg and Jack Kerouac, or the European contemporaries he published, Samuel Beckett and Eugene Ionesco, than with Scottish writing, but he re-entered the commercially fashionable literary world of Scotland's 1990s partly through the enthusiasm of that inescapably Scottish enfant terrible, Irvine Welsh. He had never really been away since his famous confrontation with Hugh MacDiarmid at the Edinburgh Festival in 1964. MacDiarmid was seen by some at that time as an outdated, outmoded nationalist parody figure in clichéd kilt, a champion of reactionary extremist politics, while Trocchi represented a new cosmopolitanism, disregarding national Scottish priorities in favour of internationally fashionable weariness and opposition to anything to do with 'the state'. Yet as their correspondence at the time suggests, Trocchi saw MacDiarmid as a true revolutionary whose example he recognised, and did not scorn or dismiss. Deeper reading of his own two novels show his investments of sympathy, self-consciousness and writerly skills.

Trocchi's first novel, *Young Adam* (1954), is an existential murder mystery mainly set in the liminal space on the barges along the Forth and Clyde canal. The moral ambiguities at its heart are definitive aspects of post-war Scotland. In its film version (2003), erstwhile *Star Wars* and *Trainspotting* actor Ewan McGregor plays Joe, the central figure. From the moment when Joe witnesses, and is perhaps responsible for, the death of his girlfriend, at the beginning of the novel, a whole world of unease opens up: questions of guilt and responsibility, to oneself and society, to others, remain unanswered. Is it cowardice to turn away, or is there courage in refusing the traps of social morality? No easy answers come, and in the end, with horrible, haunting uncertainty, everything begins 'to dissolve'.

Young Adam's successor, *Cain's Book* (1960), while ostensibly set on the Manhattan waterfront in New York, includes the central character's recollections of humorous, touching scenes of his family life back in Glasgow. It is an equally intense study of character, motive, the individual, relationships and the morals of society typical of its era. It is the first novel to introduce the word 'cool' into Scottish literature, in its opening paragraphs, referring to a state of mind which Trocchi says may be experienced through the use of heroin, but it is also referring to a style of writing: level, restrained, continuously edged with unspoken personal passion and social judgement, dangerous (always on the point of violence) and accented by an omnipresent sense of threat. It's an unmistakably Scottish take on what the French critic and cultural theorist Roland Barthes called 'writing degree zero'.

On a scow in New York harbour, Joe Necchi drifts on the waters and his writing and consciousness drifts from one heroin fix to the next, from one expedition into the city to another, to meet friends, to score, and to enter the labyrinth from which he will return to continue his work on the typewriter in the cabin of his boat, hammering out the novel we're reading. Joe is one of the essential existential outsiders of the 1950s and his ghost haunts the ethos of the more colourful 1960s. Identity is a lost cause and unspoken yearning sustains a plaintive but not self-pitying tone, beautifully poised as he draws tenderly on memories of the Glasgow and Scotland he has determined to leave behind.

Trocchi's courage is in his sustained representation of the life of someone removed from any access to such a community as that evoked time and again by such writers as George Mackay Brown and Iain Crichton Smith, someone who, perhaps, would not want it, but who dreams of what it might be, remembers something of it, and whose very act of expression, the writing itself, registers a need for some kind of recognition, or in other words, for readers: that is to say, for others.

For Alexander Trocchi as much as for George Mackay Brown or Iain Crichton Smith, the world is always in need.

The most famous novel by Gordon Williams (1934–2017) is probably *The Siege of Trencher's Farm* (1969), notoriously filmed by Sam Peckinpah as *Straw Dogs* (1971), yet the novel bears little resemblance to the film. It is a masterpiece of suspense writing and is best read without reference to the film. By contrast, later in the same decade, Williams wrote *The Duellists* (1977), an adaptation of a Ridley Scott film based on a screenplay by Gerald Vaughan-Hughes, from a story, 'The Duel' by Joseph Conrad.

With Terry Venables, under the name P.B. Yuill, Williams wrote three novels about a London-based Cockney private eye named Hazell: *Hazell Plays Solomon* (1974), *Hazell and the Three Card Trick* (1975) and *Hazell and the Menacing Jester* (1976), which triggered a successful TV series. His last novel was *Pomeroy, an American Diplomat* (1983).

Williams's other novels include *The Last Day of Lincoln Charles* (1965) and *The Camp* (1966), a grainy, grim and gravel-toned account of life in RAF Zeedorf in post-war Germany. Sex, drink, fighting, crudity and some of the least attractive aspects of masculinity tip over into worse yet: outright sadism and brutality. More seductive, equally insidious temptations suffuse *The Man Who Had Power Over Women* (1967). The duplicities and desperations of masculinity are Williams's recurrent subject and in much evidence here. *The*

Hard Case (as Jack Lang, 1968) was followed by *From Scenes Like These* (1968). This is based in Ayrshire and presents a number of boys and young men at crucial turning points in their lives. Again, the potential and squandered energies of masculinity, along with sharp records of time and place, are central.

After *The Upper Pleasure Garden* (1970), Williams wrote *Walk Don't Walk* (1972), an extraordinary novel, an updated version of Eric Linklater's classic *Juan in America* (1931), a fast-moving, verbal avalanche recounting a Scottish novelist's publicity promotion tour of the United States. Almost without plot, the book carries you through encounters and adventures, throwing out self-deprecation to accompany the self-indulgence, unapologetic lusts for booze, starlets and sheer appetite for what was then the novelty of flights, hotels and television publicity. Finally the narrator returns to the heavy conformities of home, wife and babies' nappies, in a Scotland 'where nobody had a name like Jelly Roll Morton'. Tam o' Shanter gets back to his wife Kate. The drunk man returns to Jean. And a Calvinist is always waiting for you, telling you it's time to sober up and to never be so hungry for the big wide world again. The book's humour is acid, its velocity unstoppable and its aftertaste sour. It is depressing and exhilarating in equal measure: an American nightmare.

If Trocchi and Williams both demonstrate different ways of realigning Scottish backgrounds, histories, and social contexts, with new ways of living being brought to international acceptance from the United States, both are critical, sharp, and restless enough to engage with these new perceptions with a characteristic irony. They bring restraint and exuberance, measurement and recklessness together in startling ways.

61

Bestsellers: from Annie S. Swan to Nigel Tranter

THE CHANGING FASHIONS and appetites for different kinds of 'bestseller' are perennial. In Scotland, if we open the term 'literature' to include such works of commercially popular fiction, perhaps the three most famous authors in the second half of the 20th century were Ian Fleming, Alistair MacLean and Nigel Tranter. And there is every reason to give further consideration to romance genre fiction. Two of the most popular novelists of their time were Annie S. Swan (1859–1943) and D.E. Stevenson (1892–1973). Stevenson published three books of poems and sold over seven million copies of her more than 40 'light romance' novels, from 1915 till 1969, many inter-linked by recurring characters, some semi-autobiographical, such as *Mrs Tim of the Regiment* (1932), the first of a 'Mrs Tim' series: Stevenson was married to James Reid Peploe, a captain in the 6th Gurkha Rifles. There were other 'series' with central characters such as Miss Buncle, Vittoria Cottage, Bel Lamington, Katherine Wentworth, and 'Gerald and Elizabeth'. Many of her works were translated into different languages yet in the 21st century, she is hardly remembered at all, despite the fact that her father, a lighthouse engineer, was first cousin to Robert Louis Stevenson.

Annie S. Swan published more than 200 novels and short story collections, starting with *Wrongs Righted* (1881), serialised in *The People's Friend* magazine. Her most famous novel was *Aldersyde* (1883), a romance of the Scottish Borders, approved by Poet Laureate Tennyson and Prime Minister Gladstone. D.H. Lawrence noted her popularity among female readers in *Women in Love* (1913). Her fellow novelist Margaret Oliphant, however, dismissed her writing as presenting 'an entirely distorted view of Scottish life' and she was bracketed with the 'Kailyard' writers of the time, stigmatised for sentimental portraits of small-town life. Yet if the prevailing ethos of Kailyard writing was conservative and unionist, Swan was an exception. She was politically active throughout her life, a suffragist, standing unsuccessfully for a Glasgow constituency in the general election of 1922, only four years after women had been given the vote, a Liberal activist and a founding member and vice-president of the Scottish National Party.

The fact that the works of D.E. Stevenson, Annie S. Swan, Alistair Maclean and Nigel Tranter have fallen so far from sight, and those of Ian Fleming are kept in print by the strategic financial regenerations of an international film industry, reminds us that anything we have to say about commercially 'popular' work has a long time in which to be tested. Yet there are a few lasting curiosities about these authors worth pausing on.

The poet George MacBeth brought Ian Fleming (1908–64) and Raymond Chandler (1888–1959) together in 1958 for an interview recorded for the BBC. Twenty-five years later, in fragment 13 of his book *My Scotland* (1973), MacBeth succinctly notes the genealogy of Fleming's character, linking his author to John Buchan (Lord Tweedsmuir):

> As in Raeburn's portrait of The Two Archers, enigmatic, half-intrinsic to the arc suspended between the bow-string and the bent yews, they leap out, smiling, the two faces. Buchan's. Fleming's. If one is to drive, surmounting the other, into a frail lead, as horses, racing against the current of blocking air, towards fame, money, it might be Tweedsmuir's. Neck ahead by the edge of appropriate honours, anchoring the English empire as securely as Kipling. Later it flails, tail fluke in the squirm of dependent vassals, into the beached vortex of Southern Florida, the playfields of Bond, emergent over the shirred eggs and the waffles. Half-Scotsmen, androgynous heroes of mid-cult, they amaze, worry, and flicker, ghostly candles over the vault of fiction. Close behind them in the waxed air, I hear Byron chuckle, the cracked knuckles of the bad Lord.

Fleming's Bond is the commercialisation of Buchan's Richard Hannay. Fleming was moving into a market much expanded from the one to which Buchan appealed, and feeding appetites Buchan would have considered vulgar. Although his national identity has not always been acknowledged, James Bond is surely the most famous Scottish character in post-war Scottish fiction. According to his obituary, as published in *The Times* at the end of *You Only Live Twice*, 'James Bond was born of a Scottish father, Andrew Bond of Glencoe, and a Swiss mother, Monique Delacroix...'

Fleming's Scots background is well documented. His grandfather's and his father's financial successes chart the movement of the Flemings into English 'society' circles, and Ian's introduction to Eton and Oxford was the result of their aspirations. His experience of Scotland, though, was antipathetic. Fleming's biographer John Pearson says:

> He had a horror of family gatherings, especially at Christmas, and would do almost anything to avoid having to go near Scotland – 'all those wet rhododendrons and people with hair on their cheeks sitting around peat fires wrapped in plaid blankets'.

Despite this, of course, James Bond does have May, his treasured Scottish housekeeper (first introduced in *From Russia With Love*) and in Chapter 9 of *On Her Majesty's Secret Service*, when Irma Bunt (May's opposite number) asks him if he likes the Alps, Bond (acting the part of Sir Hilary Bray) replies 'I love them...Just like Scotland.' But there are no Scottish locations in the Bond adventures as there are in John Buchan's works.

The villains in the Bond books are usually based on racial stereotypes. Three of the most memorable are red-haired (a traditionally Scottish characteristic since long before Rob Roy): Red Grant, Hugo Drax and Goldfinger. (And Red Grant, like Medina in Buchan's *The Three Hostages*, is associated with the idea of Irish independence.) These villains are in a direct line of descent from the criminal masterminds who oppose Richard Hannay and Sherlock Holmes: almost all of them are opponents of the British Empire. There is no need to elaborate on the importance of repression – or self-suppression – in the formation of 'others': it is characteristic not only of the great fictional hero of Empire and the villains he faces, not to mention Fleming himself. (Or Buchan. Or Conan Doyle.) Hugh MacDiarmid's dedicated quest to uncover the reasons for 'Scotland's self-suppression' surely applies.

Fleming referred to Bond as a 'cardboard booby' and in the BBC archive interview between Fleming and Chandler, described him as 'on the whole a rather unattractive man'. Subsequently, critics have seen him as either a template for fantasy or a stooge of Empire. But he is more than merely pathetic. Fleming's Bond is tragic.

The sexism of the films is certainly there in the fiction but the arc of Bond's story is not one of happy male superiority. The death of Vesper Lynd, at the end of the first novel, *Casino Royale* (1953), haunts Bond. Ten years later, at the beginning of *On Her Majesty's Secret Service* (1963), he has been revisiting her grave near Royale-les-Eaux, when he meets Tracy, who will become his wife. In the aftermath of Tracy's death, at the opening of *You Only Live Twice* (1964), Bond is broken, neurotic. When the villain is revealed as Tracy's murderer, Blofeld, the success of Bond's mission dissolves his character's purpose. The obituary towards the end of the book is well-placed.

Kingsley Amis suggested that the death of Tracy would turn Bond into the apotheosis of the Byronic hero: a man with a 'secret sorrow over a woman, aggravated by self-reproach'. Fleming recognised the appropriateness of the Bond family motto: 'The world is not enough.' It certainly suggests the final, cancelled stanza of Byron's *Don Juan*:

> The world is full of orphans: firstly, those
> Who are so in the strict sense of the phrase
> (But many a lonely tree the loftier grows
> Than others crowded in the forest's maze);
> The next are such as are not doomed to lose
> Their tender parents in their budding days,

But merely their parental tenderness,
Which leaves them orphans of the heart no less.

It is wrong to describe him as 'an English hero'. Only a Scot could confirm imperial identity so thoroughly, because, in the history of the Scottish nation within the British Empire, loyalty is the key. Bond's only function is service. His identity depends on his willingness to risk self-sacrifice. His failure, despite the elephantine extensions of the industry he generated, is tragically shaped, from *Casino Royale* to *O.H.M.S.S.* and its aftermath, and it is complete.

Fleming's work points forwards to the even more prolific war, espionage and adventure stories of Alistair MacLean (1922–87): *HMS Ulysses* (1955), *The Guns of Navarone* (1957), *South by Java Head* (1958), *The Satan Bug* (1962), *Ice Station Zebra* (1963), *When Eight Bells Toll* (1966), *Where Eagles Dare* (1967), *Puppet on a Chain* (1969), *Breakheart Pass* (1974) and further novels continuing well into the 1980s. Of them all, *When Eight Bells Toll* is set extensively in Scotland and its locations on the Isle of Mull and its main town, Tobermory, were faithfully used in the film version (1971), starring a young Anthony Hopkins as the James Bond-like secret agent hero.

MacLean himself was a native Gaelic-speaker from a Gaelic-speaking family, born in Glasgow, but growing up near Inverness. He was in the Royal Navy during the Second World War and his first book, *HMS Ulysses* (written after completing a degree in English at Glasgow University in 1953), was based on his own experiences. During the war, he had seen action in the Atlantic, then in the Mediterranean, and then in the Far East, around Burma, Sumatra and Singapore. These locations inform some of his novels but he wrote of Scotland with most affection, even while increasingly prioritising the commercial imperatives of best-seller fiction.

Each of Maclean's books balances the two necessary components of commercial fiction: novelty and familiarity. Each offers new characters and scenarios on the one hand, and reliable structures and plots on the other. It's a formula that cannot be endlessly repeated and there is no overarching trajectory to the novels as there is with the Bond stories. Densely written, they speak of an era in which reading itself was a different a kind of activity from those familiar in the early 21st century or in the 1920s and 30s. Their style itself is now part of history.

This is also true of Nigel Tranter (1909–2000), but a different kind of popularity pertained with him. Tranter was the pre-eminent historical novelist of his time. One reason for this is that his popular novels were, arguably, the main source of historical information for thousands, perhaps millions, of Scots for generations, because Scottish history was not taught in Scottish schools. There was a deep, long-lasting appetite for stories and information about

Scottish history, accessible, written with a sense of dramatic urgency. And, as with John Prebble, the drama in Tranter's writing is in the historical stories themselves, rather than in style or plotting.

His best works include his quasi-fictionalised tales of the lives of Saint Columba, William Wallace, Robert the Bruce, James IV, James V, Andrew Fletcher of Saltoun, and the Marquis of Montrose. Sometimes these historical figures are seen in different novels from different perspectives, almost as different people, yet the vast panorama of Tranter's national saga takes them all in, from *Druid Sacrifice* (1993), set c.518–543 AD, through *True Thomas* (1981), based on life of King Alexander III and Thomas of Ercildoun or Thomas the Rhymer, set c.1265–1292, to the James kings (I, II, III, IV, V and VI), taking the reader from the Wars of Independence to Mary Queen of Scots and the Union of the Crowns. *The Wisest Fool* (1974) tells the story of James VI as he became James I of the abruptly United Kingdom, and is set 1603–1611; the Montrose trilogy is set during the Wars of the Three Kingdoms; *Honours Even* (1995) tells of Cromwell's bloody invasion of Scotland; and *The Patriot* (1982) leads up to the Union of the Parliaments in 1707, with Andrew Fletcher of Saltoun as the central character. The MacGregor trilogy (1957–62) describes the first half of the 18th century and there are a number of other novels set in later historical periods, including the 19th-century Clearances.

Tranter was prolific: children's books, westerns, contemporary adventure novels and many non-fiction books, histories, topographical studies, architectural guides to castles and fortified houses. When he died at the age of 90 at the beginning of the 21st century, he had probably done more to bring the history of Scotland to generations of readers than any other single person.

The virtues of popularity should never be too swiftly dismissed. In some respects Tranter was attempting a cure for what MacDiarmid called 'Scotland's self-suppression'. That it has taken so long to establish Scottish history and literature as an entitlement in Scottish schools is itself a historical tragedy but that these areas of enquiry are now embedded is progress, and Tranter would have been glad of that.

62

Resisting repression: James Kennaway, Agnes Owens, Archie Hind and Alasdair Gray

THE WORKING CLASS characters in the fiction of Agnes Owens and Archie Hind contrast sharply with the military officers in James Kennaway's most famous novel, *Tunes of Glory*, but all are, in different ways, trapped. Comedy and tragedy are interconnected in the work of these novelists, and the idea of the family is central to each of them. When we come to Alasdair Gray, the conflict is also between materiality and the imagination and the result is a triumph and breakthrough.

Tunes of Glory (1956), the first novel by James Kennaway (1928–68) was an immediate success and the film adaptation of it (1960) ensured its wider appreciation. Its impact comes from lucidity, intensity, brevity and dramatic structure. Its claustrophobic atmosphere in a Highland regiment's army barracks builds towards a violent conclusion. Two opposed main characters, a colonel from Eton and Sandhurst and another who has worked his way through the ranks, increasingly develop their rage against each other. The latent chaos and suppressed emotions bulge beneath the clean prose, suggesting the farcical, but distorting human potential until its tragic ending.

Kennaway's later work is more experimental. *Household Ghosts* (1961) is a suspenseful exposition of neurotic family relations in a claustrophobic country house, haunted by the past. It was followed by *The Mindbenders* (1963), *The Bells of Shoreditch* (1963), *Some Gorgeous Accident* (1967), *The Cost of Living like This* (1969) and *Silence* (1972), published posthumously and set in America, centring on the relation between a white man and a black woman in another kind of threatening atmosphere of sexual tension and social hostility. Essentially, these works anatomise power and prejudice, and show them for what they are, acted out in human relationships.

Agnes Owens (1926–2014), in her first work, *Gentlemen of the West* (1984) and with continuing humour, pathos, curiosity and determination in later novels and stories, explores and extends the perspectives and enquiries of working-class families. Her depictions of mothers are in themselves a singular achievement. She continued with contributions to *Lean Tales* (1985), a collection shared with James Kelman and Alasdair Gray, then with *Like Birds in the Wilderness* (1987), *A Working Mother* (1994), *People Like That* (1996), *For the Love of Willie* (1998), *Bad Attitudes* (2003) and *The Complete Short Stories* (2008). Class conflict acted out in a different social stratum from that depicted by Kennaway is her forte but the redemptive self-sacrifices sometimes brought forth in her characters heighten both the pathos and the comedy of her stories. Indeed, the comedy itself sharpens the tragic sense of human potential lost in the social circumstances imposed upon her characters. Her work is a register of sympathy depicting unrequited need.

The realism of these stories testifies to their conviction, yet realism is also its own constriction. Archie Hind (1928–2008), in *The Dear Green Place* (1966) delivered one version of a definitive 'Glasgow novel' as a young man struggles to complete a novel while working in a slaughterhouse. The symbolism is understated. Mat Craig fails to fulfil his artistic ambitions but in the determination of its realism Hind's writing pointed forward to the counterpoint that would be delivered by Alasdair Gray's equally determined depiction of Glasgow in *Lanark* (1981), yoking together realism and fantasy. Hind left unfinished one further novel, *Fur Sadie*, which was published posthumously in 2008 in an edition with an essay, 'The Men of the Clyde' and an introduction by Gray himself.

Alasdair Gray (1934–2019) takes things further. He is the author of novels, stories, plays, poems, and a visual artist of major distinction. Consider a mere selection of his books: *Unlikely Stories, Mostly* (1983), in which the Erratum slip reads: 'This slip has been inserted by mistake'; *1982, Janine* (1984), the quintessential vision of abject despair and reawakening with its searing introspective portrait of a character working through his own worst aspects to emerge on the other side of degradation; *The Fall of Kelvin Walker* (1985), a provocative parable in which a young Scotsman travels to London to find his career and confront his nemesis: patriarchal authority (it is, in a sense, a version of Conrad's *Heart of Darkness*: an expedition into the 'interior' that is funnier, but turns out to be no less fearful); *Something Leather* (1990); *Poor Things* (1992), a neo-Gothic-quasi-Victorian-satiric-pastiche self-discovery mystery story that also manages to deliver Carlylean moral authority in its presentation of the social, political and personal constructions of identity, our relations with others and with ourselves; *A History Maker* (1994); *Mavis Belfrage* (1996); *Old Men in Love* (2007), a compendium of stories crossing European history, from an ancient civilisation to modern Glasgow (both built on slavery). The stories are connected by the perhaps fictional executor of the author's estate and brought into existence by Alasdair himself, with the assistance of various mysterious interventions and fortunate local assistance. And in 2010, the long-awaited collection of his drawings and paintings, *A Life in Pictures*.

But the key work is *Lanark: A Life in Four Books* (1981), a major landmark in modern Scottish fiction. Gray had been working on it for years and parts had been published in tantalising tastes of what was to come. The completed work did not disappoint but it baffled some readers because of its structure: we begin like the central character in a state of bewilderment, are taken back through time into a different world and a different literary convention, from fantasy to realism, then returned to the world of imaginative fiction to begin to see how the two worlds interconnect.

This structure deliberately achieved two things: first, it revised the convention of linear sequence; second, it demonstrated conclusively that realism without imagination, or, life without the arts, is hopelessly inadequate. The Moebius-strip-like rewinding of the narrative and the difference between the two literary modes took the sense of possibility in modern Scottish fiction into a new dispensation. In this respect, its cognate works from the same decade were Liz Lochhead's play, *Mary Queen of Scots Got Her Head Chopped Off* (1987) and Edwin Morgan's sequence of poems, *Sonnets from Scotland* (1984).

In *Lanark*, the aspiring artist Duncan Thaw sets out to draw the Blackhill locks on the canal near Glasgow:

> He knew how the two great water staircases curved round and down the hill, but from any one level the rest were invisible. Moreover, the weight of the architecture was best seen from the base, the spaciousness from on top; yet he wanted to show both equally so that eyes would climb his landscape as freely as a good athlete exploring the place. He invented a perspective showing the locks from below when looked at from left to right and from above when seen from right to left; he painted them as they would appear to a giant lying on his side, with eyes more than a hundred feet apart and tilted at an angle of 45 degrees. Working from maps, photographs, sketches and memory his favourite views had nearly all been combined into one when a new problem arose.

The 'new problem' is how to depict people in this landscape. Realism is a term bound up with the matter of perspective, and it is a key term in the transition from 19th-century to modernist fiction. *Lanark* takes you through two narratives, one pretty much strictly realist and the other fantastical, mysterious, dream-like. The constraints of realism and the violence it enacts upon not only the main character (who seems to be almost suicidal by the end of the second book), but also upon the other characters (by insisting upon their limitations, personal, social, national and imaginative) – these constraints and tensions are generated by realist narrative. Yet they are also viscerally connected to the dynamics and pressures in the fantasy-story. Thus, it is not that one story precedes the other or predicates it, but rather that the work of the imagination liberates itself from the imprisonment of realism.

Another crucial aspect of *Lanark* is the long story of its composition over decades, which many people in Scotland's literary world were well aware of. And crucial to that is the novel's connection with Archie Hind's *The Dear Green Place*. Hind's main character abandons and destroys the novel he's writing, yet

Hind's novel itself is a refutation of that defeat, while, doggedly, its resolution acknowledges the authority of realism. Gray is different. In *Lanark*, when we read that Glasgow, like most modern cities, is the place where many people live but few imagine living, we have one of the essential assertions of the value of imagination in modern literature. In *The Dear Green Place*, Mat Craig attempts to live up to that intuitive assertion of value and Hind courageously records his struggle and his failure. Hind's success in the novel resides in that courage. He gives us an artist, a writer, struggling with his own imagination, ultimately failing to complete the novel he so dearly, desperately wants to realise. Gray takes one incredibly transforming step further: he breaks through the confinements of realism and demonstrates with absolute certainty how reality and the imaginative life interpenetrate, how one helps change the other, and the former fuels the latter, in a kind of eternal recharging. What had blocked Mat Craig in Hind's novel, Gray blasts away, forever. To quote Marshall Walker's words, 'a narrow material world, unlit by imagination, is inadequate to human experience.'

There is an optimistic purpose here. At the end of the novel, Lanark is given the knowledge that he will die soon and a sense of his own mortality is strong in his mind, yet three unobtrusive things indicate continuing life, life that Lanark has been and remains part of, and by which he is comforted and the value of his life confirmed. There is the life of Lanark's son, Alexander, who evidently survives the end of the novel and goes on to live and work in a future Lanark himself will not see. Then the panoramic ending of the novel itself describes a tidal wave engulfing the city, washing away the familiar buildings and landmarks in violent demolition. It seems like an apocalyptic vision, but yet the tide begins to recede in the last pages of the book:

> Drunk with spaciousness he turned every way, gazing with wide-open mouth and eyes as light created colours, clouds, distances and solid, graspable things seemed close at hand. Among all this light the flaming buildings seemed small blazes which would soon burn out. With only mild disappointment he saw the flood ebbing back down the slope of the road.

After this devastation, something will rebuild itself. And finally, there is the last sentence itself, which depicts the title character: 'He was a slightly worried, ordinary old man but glad to see the light in the sky.'

The novel ends with a simple act of seeing and an affirmation of appreciation. Which is where we all need to begin.

63

An awkward squad: from David Lindsay to Andrew O'Hagan

IF GRAY'S *LANARK* is a singular engagement of the imagination with reality, it has precedents from science fiction, old and new, through fictional representations of the Second World War, to novels impossible to categorise. These works describe different ways of combining destruction, renewal and regeneration.

One of the classics of science fiction (or 'speculative fiction') is *A Voyage to Arcturus* (1920) by David Lindsay (1876–1945), noted by the American critic Harold Bloom as one of the only 17 Scottish books that make it into his list of major works in the 'Canon' of Western Literature. It's warranted. The novel begins with an interstellar space exploration leaving earth and Scotland far behind but as soon as Muspel, Crystalman and Krag get us to the planet of Tormance, orbiting Arcturus, we're into a wildly unpredictable, compelling spiritual quest. It's as if all the bleak austerities of post-Reformation Scotland, quests and yearnings, frustrations and thwarted desires, are transposed to a world of tropical, hallucinatory colour and shifting forms. Ultimately, however, the rules of human mortality prevail. The search for order and the quest beyond the self are brilliant motivations, driving the narrative forward, and the characters are all highly realised, so in the end, there's a sense that material reality may be real, but it's never enough. The world is always in need, and imagination is the most essential weapon in the armoury.

Eighty years on, Matthew Fitt (b.1968), in *But n Ben A-Go-Go* (2000) returns us to earth but in a horrifying future where Scotland has been almost entirely drowned by another great flood and a supervirus is raging. There's a quest of another kind here, and the novel is entirely written in Scots, which presents readers with a different mix of alienation and intimate infection. You start in bewilderment and unknowing but very quickly get taken up into the urgency of the 'rescue mission' at the core of the story. What's to be rescued? A character, a culture, the language itself.

Between these two stands Ian Macpherson (1905–44), whose first novel, *Shepherds' Calendar* (1931), foregrounds love of country and a yearning for education, as, growing through the seasonal regenerations, young John Grant finally sets out to leave his domineering family for university in Aberdeen. The novel is similar in some respects to Lewis Grassic Gibbon's *Sunset Song* (1932) and his short story, 'Clay' but it has its own lonely distinction. This is even more tragically realised in Macpherson's *Wild Harbour* (1936). Here is science fiction at its most despairing, a Scotland of war, malignant bacteria, poison gas, bombs exploding far off, coming closer. The couple – Hugh, the narrator, and his lover Terry – want nothing to do with the approaching conflict and take to the hills to avoid the violence. The first sentence reads: 'This morning I said to Terry, "I thought I heard guns through the night."' Indeed he has, and they're getting near. The novel tells of the outbreak of the Second World War three years before it happened, and how feelings of hopelessness and horror spread among the people who care most about the landscape so tenderly evoked in *Shepherds' Calendar*. As John Burns writes in his introduction to the 1989 Canongate edition, the novel is 'imbued with a deep and haunting apprehension of man's precarious position in the universe'.

Other forms of domestic and universal hope and despair across Scotland's geographical diversity are found in *The Gowk Storm* (1933) by N. Brysson Morrison (c.1906–86): three daughters growing up in a manse in the Highlands are set to find love or tragedy. The novel is written with emotional authority in its characterisation and immediacy in its depiction of landscape and weather. And in *The Land of the Leal* (1939) by James Barke (1905–58), a farming couple, David and Jean Ramsay, move from Galloway to Fife and then Glasgow; fascist and socialist politics battle each other while creatural mortality is measured in the scales of contested politics and seasonal regeneration.

These books are fiction but closely based on the life experiences of their authors. More specifically memoirs, similarly charming at times, yet realistic, tough, convincing and beautifully written, are the collections of Finlay J. Macdonald (1925–87), *Crowdie and Cream* (1982), *Crotal and White* (1983) and *The Corncrake and the Lysander* (1985), all set in the Outer Hebrides on the Isle of Harris. A counterpoint to this collection is *The Leper's Bell: The Autobiography of a Changeling* (2009) by the Gaelic poet, novelist, comedian and singer Norman Maclean (1936–2017), which is as mercilessly self-lacerating about the author's alcoholism as it is infectious in his lust for life. And a third counterpoint is the Gorbals trilogy by Ralph Glasser (1916–2002), *Growing Up in the Gorbals* (1986), *Gorbals Boy at Oxford* (1988) and *Gorbals Voices, Siren Songs* (1990). These different aspects of Scotland, archipelagic and urban, are complementary and suggest the multi-facetedness of the nation.

And there are many works of fiction that don't fit into any categories in particular. Bruce Marshall (1899–1987), in *Yellow Tapers for Paris: A Dirge* (1943), gives us a portrait of the capital city of a France about to be overrun and occupied by the Nazis, not only facing military defeat and occupation, but already suffering moral desolation and urban ennui. That feeling of self-indulged vulnerability is the object of Marshall's sorrowful but caustic satire, his scornful yet humane compassion. We meet the main character, Bigou, an accountant in an industrial firm, his desultory wife Marie and sulky daughter Odette, his uninspiring friends and fellow-workers, and the general inclination towards money and pleasure as goals without purpose, in a country given over to despondency and helplessness. It presents a fearful picture of the tragic reduction of national aspiration, pointing towards inanition and beyond that, violence. It's an extraordinary novel, having more in common with *Berlin Alexanderplatz* (1929) by Alfred Döblin (1878–1957) or *The Sleepwalkers* (1932) by Hermann Broch (1886–1951) than with better-known novels set in Scotland. In 1948, for a new edition of the book published in 1949, Marshall wrote:

> While I am not prepared to pretend that *Yellow Tapers for Paris* is as good a novel as I should have liked it to be, I am still convinced that it contains a more accurate picture of life in that city from 1934 till 1940 than my no doubt well-intentioned critics imagined. This conviction has been strengthened by a recent residence of 14 months in Paris, where I found the same yellow tapers still burning, only slightly lower in their sconces.

The tapers were the candles used in the Catholic Church for funeral and remembrance services.

Marshall himself was long-lived and prolific, saw service in both World Wars and retired to France, dying in his 87th year. He remains a neglected Scottish novelist well deserving reassessment.

Neil Paterson (1915–1995), in his short novel *The China Run* (1948), tells the story of a Victorian woman who becomes a ship's captain after the death of her husband, enduring storms around Cape Horn, and taking bizarre cargoes (dead bodies, nitrate, umbrellas) to unfriendly harbours. And Dorothy K. Haynes (1918–1987), collects her astonishing short stories in *Thou Shalt Not Suffer a Witch* (1949), each one infused with inexplicable, mysterious atmospheres, focusing on such subjects as a Polish woman refugee or the mechanics of medieval punishment. The art world is the context of *Creating a Scene* (1971) by Elspeth Davie (1918–1995), with the teacher, Foley, and his pupils Joe and Nicola, working on an ill-fated mural at an old swimming-pool about which local people have mixed feelings. And in *A Truth Lover* (1973), a finely-edged, sympathetic, stylishly self-conscious comedy, by John Herdman (b.1941), a wide-eyed student travels through Paris, Zurich, prison, and a Speyside hotel, slowly coming to realise his potential, and insignificance, in the world. Herdman takes the Candide-like idea further in *Pagan's Pilgrimage* (1978).

Christian Miller (1920–2012), in *A Childhood in Scotland* (1981), recalls her life in an ostensibly aristocratic family home in 1920s Scotland, where her resilient humour has to endure and contest the disciplinary rule of her father and the attempt to maintain the priorities of decayed feudalism. Another vision of 'aristocracy' is presented by Elspeth Barker (b.1940), in her weird short novel *O Caledonia* (1991), taking us into the domestic mysteries of certain members of an upper-class family in the Gothic Highlands. Desires and nightmares are uneasily set against oppressive priorities of reason and righteousness. The opening of Miller's novel suggests the atmosphere of both these books:

> When I was a little girl, the ghosts were more real to me than the people. The people were despotic and changeable, governing my world with a confusing and alarming inconsistency. The ghosts, on the other hand, could be relied on to go about their haunting in a calm and orderly manner.

A more immediately humane sensibility rises in the writing of Bernard MacLaverty (b.1942), not only in his early novels *Lamb* (1980) and *Cal* (1983) but perhaps most hauntingly in *Grace Notes* (1997), where a composer, Catherine Anne McKenna, introduces us to her family conflicts and resolutions in Glasgow and the Hebrides, and also her art and practice in the composing of music, unemphatically demonstrating the counterpoints of art and life, how they help and enhance each other. *Midwinter Break* (2017) follows a retired couple to Amsterdam, where they are taking a holiday and recollecting their earlier lives in a troubled Ireland. Again, the gentler virtues are set against our human potential for self-destruction, and the tension generated is held taut in personal, but also in political and European-wide contexts.

An even larger canvas is painted by William Boyd (b.1952) in *The New Confessions* (1987), which takes John James Todd from genteel Edinburgh through the historical panorama of the First World War, and in *Any Human Heart* (2002), where Logan Mountstuart emerges from the Second World War to New York's 1960s art industry. In *Ordinary Thunderstorms* (2009), a John Buchan-like premise catapults the symbolically-named Adam Kindred from his comfortable social zone into an existential quest through London's unreliable fogs of competing powers and strange identities.

Across society's strata and geographical diversities, Andrew O'Hagan (b.1968), in his first novel, *Our Fathers* (1999), centres once again on Glasgow. The novel's focus is the housing in which people live, from the tenement slums to the high rise flats, and what follows after them. Its deeper concern, however, is what the term 'living conditions' really means, from one generation to another, as the grandson of one pioneering architect tries to understand and move forward into an architecture of his own. The novel ends with a scribble on a board, a quotation from Hugh MacDiarmid: 'There are ruined buildings in the world,' it said, 'but no ruined stones.'

64

Gaelic prose fiction: from the 16th to the 20th centuries

WHEN I WAS at school, getting ready to go to university, I bought a copy of *A Short History of English Literature* (1940) by B. Ifor Evans, in a 1970s blue Pelican paperback edition. I had what seems now like a completely ridiculous idea that if I read everything it told me about, I'd have a good grasp of the whole field of the subject. But you don't really understand anything by knocking off the big names, though it helps. You don't understand mountains by bagging Munros, although that can help too. But you certainly can't make art through doing things only by numbers. You can't develop a sensitised knowledge of the extent of a literature by thinking only of those authors deemed to be 'canonical'.

Many years later, I was visiting the Kolkata Book Fair in India and this was brought home to me more powerfully than ever before. Numbers bring their own wisdom. There were far more books and authors to think of than could ever be encountered – or numbered, let alone read – by a single person. And the same is true once you get past the 'canon' of English literature, or indeed of Scottish literature. And even within our subject, the literature that has come from the Gaelic world, composed, written or sung in that language, remains ungraspable, even unimaginable, to many even of the best-intentioned readers, and especially those of us who don't know the language sufficiently well to read confidently the poetry, plays and novels written in it.

These novels have been published in large numbers only since the latter part of the 20th century and amount to a major literary achievement in themselves. We might become familiar enough with the trajectory of Gaelic poetry and song through the inevitably inadequate but eminently practical medium of translation, but to understand the novels, you need to have the language. And yet, we can approach them. We can get a scent, a trace of what's there, a sense of the shape of the outline.

Moray Watson's invaluable book, *An Introduction to Gaelic Fiction* (2011) gives an account of the story and allows us to attempt to introduce it. To a non-Gaelic reader, it's like describing a room full of things, some palpably fine, some entirely unknowable, but with your eyes shut and the light off and only your hands and nose at work. My chapters on Gaelic fiction in this book are the result of this attempt. Their sole purpose is to bring to attention the fact that the room is there and there are such things in it. The liabilities are obvious enough and if all I achieve is a stumbling try at an indication, perhaps that in itself will have some value. As Alasdair Gray once noted had been said by John Buchan, as quoted by Hugh MacDiarmid (though I can find no source for it): 'Even maps that are wrong are better than no maps at all. At least they show that the land is there.'

Although most literary work in Gaelic is poems or songs, there is a wealth of prose fiction in Gaelic. There are various early sources, as traditional myths became folk tales, recounted orally and transcribed to manuscript. Narratives in church sermons and secular poetry frequently included recounted dialogue or conversations. Narrative tension, recurring themes and multi-vocal encounters were all familiar in the repertoire, and all found their way into written prose texts, and then into print.

The first Gaelic printed book appeared in 1567, a Gaelic version by John Carswell (c.1522–72) of the *Book of Common Order*, setting a model for publishing the language, and a form: translations of religious works. Fiction, as generally understood in European terms, is a rather different thing, and translation, both into and out of Gaelic, is an essential component of the story. And timing is crucial. The influence exercised by fiction translated across languages is variable. Few works are contemporaneously accommodated between different cultures. Cervantes's *Don Quixote* first appeared in two parts in 1605 and 1615, and Shakespeare seems to have been well aware of it, but it did not exert any great influence on English-language fiction until the 18th century, when the English novel was becoming a more established genre. George Orwell's *Animal Farm* was published in 1945 and most Gaelic-speaking readers will probably have encountered it in English, but translated into Gaelic as *Tuathanas Nan Creutairea*n by Angus Peter Campbell in 2021, it now has a new life in the Gaelic world. How might its lessons have bearing upon the ethos of linguistic totalitarianism? We might paraphrase: 'All languages are equal but some languages are more equal than others.' The relative power of the languages in which most Scottish literature has been created, Gaelic, Scots and English, is thrown into a new light via Orwell's vivid perception. And now its Gaelic application can be read – in that language.

The Rev. Dr Norman MacLeod's periodical *An Teachdaire Gaelach* (1829–31) presented dialogue and conversation as a literary form, and in the last quarter of the 19th century, as Donald Meek puts it, 'the ceilidh-house moved into print', partly because many Gaels of the Highlands and Islands were moving into cities like Glasgow and Inverness, and heading south, so their stories and songs could be shared, as in a ceilidh, in transportable printed texts. Among the earliest collections of this kind was Henry Whyte's *The Celtic Garland* (1895). In the early 20th century, periodicals such as *Guth na Bliadhna / The Voice of the Year*, edited by the enthusiastic and politically-charged Ruaraidh Erskine of Marr, self-consciously offered a platform for printed prose fiction.

The first Gaelic novels include *Dùn-àluinn no An t-Oighre 'na Dhìobarach / Dunaline or the Banished Heir* (1912), by Iain MacCormaic / John MacCormack, an adventure set during the 19th century, with a Gaelic inheritance in jeopardy and a central character travelling to the New Zealand gold rush before returning to Scotland only in the nick of time to reclaim his legacy. Then there is *An t-Ogha Mór / The Great Grandchild* (1913) by Aonghas MacDhonnchaidh / Angus Robertson, set in Skye and London between the 1715 and 1745 Jacobite risings, with a feud raging between clan chieftains Iarlom Mac Coinnich and Goiridh Mac Fhraing. There are rivals in love, properties burnt and child abduction propelling the action. Taking us from Skye to Edinburgh, to London, then back to Skye, the novel is carried by its narrative rather than its dialogue. Specific locations characterise Gaelic identity in contrast to that of the southerner, or specifically, the English. That contrast itself is palpable in the voices of the characters: the young woman Mairearad's Gaelic song is described as sweet sound, but English as the noise a hound would make, not to be spoken by 'a proper man'. As Watson says, 'it is difficult to identify any decent or good-hearted characters in the novel who are not Gaels'. The Gaelic scholar Ronald Black tells me the novel's vocabulary is 'weird and wonderful', presenting words that were becoming redundant, but that the plot is perfunctory and the characterisation wooden.

Cailin Sgiathanach: no Faodalach na h-Abaid / Skye Girl: or Foundling of the Abbey (1923) by Seumas Macleòid, set in 18th- and early 19th-century Skye, is a love story where a young woman, Mórag, faces various challenges, but like the earlier novels, it's also redolent with commentary on the conditions and identity of the Gaels. We can't blame the English for all the ills of the Gael, but the emphasis falls on how foreknowledge of heritage, family and identity affects a person's life and the choices they make. The happy ending reunites parted lovers and family. Macleòid was an uncle of the poet Norman MacCaig.

Short stories drawing upon humorous anecdotes, folk tales and traditional sources, from the 1950s through the second half of the century, found a home in the pages of the periodical *Gairm*. Particularly in the 1960s, aspects of fantasy and science fiction moved a conservative narrative style towards more experimental techniques. Humour frequently arose either from domestic situations or by placing Gaels in unfamiliar surroundings, juxtaposing conventions and expectations of country and city. Some works of fiction incorporated magical or supernatural experience. As the century went on, writers began to take more risks.

Watson notes some individual stories of lasting import. Tormod Dòmhnallach's 'Làraich' / 'Ruins' dwells on the symbolic imagery of fracture and breakage; Donald Meek's 'Cuairt do'n Launderette' / 'A Trip to the Launderette' is a comic portrayal of a naïve young man leaving the islands and coming to terms with the demands of self-sufficiency in the absence of matriarchal provision. Meek is unsentimentally clear-eyed yet gentle in his observation of the collapse of patriarchal expectations.

Emotional intensity prevails in Iain MacLeòid's 'Dealbhannan' / 'Pictures', where a man takes a photograph of his lover, accidentally discovering that she is in the arms of someone else. 'Ketilsdair' is a violent story of Picts and Vikings. And 'Aisling Otis' / 'Otis's Dream' is a comic story about an American who decides to move to an island and become a Gael, discovering that this is not as straightforward as he thought it might be. In a number of the stories of Dòmhnall Iain MacÌomhair the central conflict is in the meeting of different cultures, Gael and German after the Second World War, Gael and Arab at university. The risks and exhilarations of transition, of daring to enter that space where change is possible, recur. In 'Facail Sheumais ris an Psychiatrist', the psychiatrist tells us: 'although you can tell a person what a table is by showing him a table, you can't do that with love'.

Modern technology invading traditional society is a key theme. Rob Shirley's 'An Duine Ur' / 'The New Man' (1961) is a science fiction story where surgeons have developed the skill to reanimate corpses, using different parts of the dead to create superbeings. Rarlon Seixias / Rev. Donald N. MacDonald, in 'An Starsach' / 'The Threshold', takes religion as an expression of the enduring strength of the human spirit, as seen by a young boy witnessing increasing hardships befall his family. In 'A' Phrosbaig' / 'The Telescope' people are observed through a telescope: neighbours and family are suddenly distanced yet remain sympathetic in a world of increasing alienation. Aonghas MacBhàtair takes a similar idea further in 'Am Fòn' / 'The Phone', where the central character must deliver the news to their children that her husband of 50 years has died, and then she must organise the funeral, all through the mechanism of the telephone, without the traditional personal contact that would have humanised the trauma. It's a paradigm of the imposition of progress upon the personal.

In these stories, the realistic takes on the presence of the fantastic. These things are literally a telephone and a telescope, but the social and psychological worlds of the characters insist that we see them without conventional familiarity. This is a kind 'alienation technique' whose foundation is social fact brought about by political history, and it generates a literary fascination of its own.

Such recurring themes as the juxtaposition of new technologies and rural traditions involving immediate human contact, transitions between myth, magic and science fiction, cultural alienation and individual psychological strengths and vulnerabilities, reach across languages. To be aware of them as central in early modern Gaelic fiction suggests how much there is for us still to discover, as more collections of stories and novels appeared in Gaelic in the late 20th and early 21st century than ever before. Even without access to Gaelic, we should be aware not simply of their existence but of their phenomenal success, developing genres and possibilities in fiction that indicate a growing achievement and unprecedented prospect in Gaelic literature. The appetite of Gaelic readers is evidently keen. Fostering that is understandably a higher priority than translating the works for readers who still have to acquire the language.

65

Gaelic prose fiction in English and the Ùr-sgeul initiative

IN *Oirthir Tim / The Edge of Time* (1969), *Mar Sgeul a Dh'Innseas Neach / Like a Tale a Person Tells* (1971) and *Nach Neònach Sin / Isn't That Strange* (1973) Cailein T. MacCoinnich / Colin MacKenzie draws on conventions of 1950s and 60s genre fiction, with time travel, detectives, supernatural elements and Highland folk traditions. 'Am Prìosan Sàile' / 'The Sea Prison' features a rebellious outlaw who claims he can escape from anywhere but when he's marooned on an island, finds that his value to the community there persuades him to help them – before escaping once again. MacKenzie is pre-eminently the pioneer of Gaelic science fiction but Ronald Black described his novel *A' Leth Eile / The Other Half* to me as 'a solid old-fashioned piece of work (not science fiction)' which 'can be said to mark the end of the first wave' of modern Gaelic fiction writing. The main character is a young man, Daibhidh, who, having graduated with an LLD., sets off Candide-like to see the world and experience the arbitrary encounters it provides. He meets a tinker on the road and gets on well with him, and then a strong young man who attacks him without provocation, and he continues his journey.

Moray Watson suggests that the best story in the collection by Iain Moireach / John Murray, *An Aghaidh Choimheach / The Mask* (or, *The Strange Face*) (1973) is 'Am Partaidh' / 'The Party', in which Ailean, at a party in a student city flat, thinking of the Gaelic poet Uilleam Ros / William Ross and the English poet Shelley, is troubled by his own divided loyalties and love for his late father, while Mairi-Ann, attempting to get close to him, cannot understand him as deeply as readers are invited to, through his emotional memories. But 'The Party' is not the only memorable tale in the collection. In Ronald Black's words: '*An Aghaidh Choimheach* is a wonderful and ground-breaking collection of stories. Everyone I have met has a different favourite.' And 'Until John Murray came along, Iain Crichton Smith had held the field practically on his own. Smith's terse, deeply psychological style, symbolised by a perpetually ticking clock, dominated his work. Murray's style is so much less pervasive that in his hands every story could have been written by a different person. The book was a huge achievement, and the tragedy is that he never really followed it up, he branched out into broadcasting and writing plays.' He died in 2017.

What Moray Watson describes as the 'second wave' of Gaelic novels begins with *An t-Aonaran / The Hermit* (1976) by Iain Mac a' Ghobhainn / Iain Crichton Smith. This is a miniature masterpiece, a novella rather than a novel. Its English-language version was published in *The Hermit and Other Stories*

(1979). A solitary figure settles on the outskirts of a small Gaelic-speaking village; the local people find his presence disturbing, troubling in various ways. Their lives unfold to the reader according to their own differences and while the isolated individual is recognisably humanized in the social context, there is nevertheless an existential loneliness about the tale which is haunting, psychologically convincing and socially accurate. The problem of characters not speaking the same language to each other is familiar but here it has a universal resonance. The physical, moral and metaphysical problems echo in the silence surrounding the central character and the spare, lean brevity of the text enhances this haunted feeling.

Iain Mac a' Ghobhainn returned to the Gaelic novel with *Na Speuclairean Dubha / The Dark Glasses* (1989), another short novel, blending aspects of detective fiction with existential enquiry into solitude and investigation, recognisably set in Taynuilt. Crichton Smith was a schoolteacher for many years in Oban; after his retirement, he and his wife Donalda lived in Taynuilt, where he became a full-time writer. Before *The Dark Glasses*, though, he had been writing a series of short stories which collectively form a kind of episodic novel. In English these were published under the main character's name, *Murdo and Other Stories*; in Gaelic, as *Murchadh*, the stories were published in *Gairm*, comprising what Watson calls 'almost a random collection of musings about the crazy character' himself. The Murchadh / Murdo stories are, by turns, wildly funny and poignantly painful, generating a sense of psychological extremity through the character's isolation and frustration. His experience of life's oppressive absurdity finds release only rarely, if at all, in the company of others, and in his own sometimes flamboyant but usually futile gestures and exclamations. Watson notes that Crichton Smith's later emphasis falls on the comedy rather than the tragic side of the Murchadh saga, but it is the latter 'which makes it such an under-rated masterpiece'.

We've noted already how Crichton Smith's seriously dark times of depression dogged him, but that somehow the development of a quality of quizzicality helped rescue him from what might have been its worst consequences. Especially in the 1980s, when he was gaining popularity as a reader of his work in public gatherings, the recognition his audiences gave him, and the laughter he prompted by his readings of some of these stories, must have encouraged him out of that sense of isolation and implosive frustration. Crichton Smith described himself as a 'double agent' or a 'double man'. Trying to understand the significance of this not only in his work as a poet but also as a storyteller, novelist and through his presence as a radio playwright and reader, working in the Gaelic language as well as in the English, for different but overlapping readerships, emphasizes the particularities of the language worlds he inhabited. Those worlds move at different speeds, in different orbits and constellations. Their dimensions interpenetrate but are not identical. Any adequate understanding of Scottish literature requires that understanding of difference.

Questions about assumptions of superiority, colonialism and feminine self-determination, are raised, emphasised, and then left unresolved rather than neatly concluded in *Gainmheach an Fhàsaich / The Desert Sand* (1971) by Màiri NicGill-Eathain / Mary MacLean. Sìne, the main character, living at home after the death of her mother, is hardly capable of looking after herself. With her boyfriend, the alcoholic waster Ruaraidh, she ends up in Africa, assuming superiority over not only the native people there but also the English colonials in power. Ruaraidh's death leaves Sìne free to marry. The exploration of ideas and assumptions that the narrative and characters prompt is compelling.

The very lack of such compulsion affords ironic humour in *Deireadh an Fhoghair / The End of Autumn* (1979) by Tormod Caimbeul. In this work, in Moray Watson's words, 'almost nothing happens'. The three characters are growing old and infirm, as if representing in their personal condition the Gaelic world and language, facing the approach of a real and metaphoric winter. The satire of conventions is both despairing and comic: 'Thuirt athair ris gun duirt a sheanair gun duirt athair gur e athair e athair-san a thuirt gur e athair-fhéin a fhuair i...' / 'His father said to him that his grandfather said that his father said that it was his father who said that it was his own father who got it...' And so on.

The title of Pòl MacAonghais's collected stories, *An Guth Aoibhneach / The Joyful Voice* (1993), seems ironic, since their grim, meditative character, leavened by a playwright's quick sense of dialogue, prevails. The internal monologue of 'Cur As an t-Solais' / 'Putting Out the Light' carries the reader along with the main character's thoughts as death approaches.

There are numerous works of fiction written in English presenting a distinctively Gaelic world. The first novel by Anne MacLeod, *The Dark Ship* (2001), takes the sinking of the *Iolaire* as a key point of reference but gives a full picture of the lives of families of different generations for whom it was a devastating event of lasting importance. Also centred in the experience of people in the islands, the writing of Norman Malcolm Macdonald (1927–2000) in plays, in the connected stories of *Calum Tod* (1976) and in the novel *Portrona* (2000) connects history and modernity. *Portrona* links two events which had particular bearing on the people of Lewis: the mutiny on *The Bounty* in 1789 and, again, the sinking of the *Iolaire*. Yet the novel moves across time, charting the herring-fishing industry, the economy of landlords, fishermen and the women of Lewis, in a panoramic sweep.

The poet Angus Peter Campbell, in *Invisible Islands* (2006) delivers a fantasy of almost-imaginary places, owing as much to Italo Calvino, Jorge Luis Borges or Gabriel Garcia Márquez as to the experience of Scottish island life. Twenty-one chapters, stories, vignettes, present 21 islands of the mind, where history draws on the real and traditional but is dreamt into memory, taken from myth and turned into fabulation. His novel, *Memory and Straw* (2017) carries these themes and questions further and deeper, bringing 'the glass and steel of our increasingly controlled algorithmic world' to the judgement of the world of the ancestors, governed by 'traditions and taboos, the seasons and the elements.' It is both realistic and optimistic, in defiance of all the odds. The same might be said of two further writers whose work in English opens our understanding of and sensitivity to the Gaelic world.

Donald S. Murray (b.1956), from Ness, in Lewis, long a resident of Shetland, in novels, stories, poems, journalism and historical accounts, has covered an extraordinary range of subjects. *The Guga Hunters* (2008) and *Herring Tales* (2015) are vivid evocations of encounters between human beings and the birds and fish of the northen islands and seas; novels include *As the Women Lay Dreaming* (2018), centred on the wreck of the *Iolaire*, and *In a Veil of Mist* (2021), about the biological weapons test perpetrated by the British government off the coast of Lewis. *The Guga Stone* (2013) is a collection of 'lies, legends and lunacies' from St Kilda (anecdotes, poems and stories, shockingly realistic or crazily surreal), *SY Story* (2015) is a portrait of Stornoway from various unpredicted angles and *The Man Who Talks to Birds* (2020) collects poems from the period of the COVID pandemic.

Another Lewis man, Ian Stephen (b.1955), poet, writer, artist and storyteller, began with the poems of *Varying States of Grace* (1989), in which free verse forms and tonal subtleties were imbued with a rich conviction of emotional determination evidently drawing on a wealth of experience of island life and familiarity with the sea. Further books of poems and artworks carry these qualities on, culminating in the achievements of *Maritime: New and Selected Poems* (2016) and the major work, *A Book of Fish and Death* (2014). This is an epic novel made up of very short chapters, stories, observations, accounts of characters, episodes, encounters and meditations, centred on the narrator Peter MacAulay. Growing up in the islands, travelling to Glasgow, experiencing the joys and disjunctions, the bizarreness and warmths of family, friends, school, work and the exercise of the imagination in an increasingly complex, sometimes inimical, sometimes generous world, MacAulay provides a panoramic vision of modern Scotland and the world more broadly from the perspective of an old islander, re-inhabiting his youth at different stages and in various locations. The singularity of his life and the places and times he has inhabited opens new ways of seeing the familiar, deep challenges to expectations and assumptions, and profoundly refreshing affirmations of qualities it's all too easy to pass over. It is one of the major novels of modern Scottish literature.

These works in English are accessible to those of us limited to that language but the escalation in the number of stories, novels and plays in Gaelic since the early 20th century (not least by authors who have learned the language) demands full recognition in itself.

66

Modern Gaelic prose fiction: a flood of new novels

THE MAJOR PLATFORM for Gaelic short stories was the periodical *Gairm*, edited by Derick Thomson and published usually four times a year from 1951–2002, an astonishing rate of production. Eilidh Watt, who contributed many articles to *Gairm*, published the collections *A' Bhratach Dheàlrach / The Shining Banner* (1972) and *Gun Fhois* (1987). The title story of the former hinges on the startling simile of a woman whose attention to detail in her garden makes her like an old warship resisting surrender and flying its flags to demonstrate her resistance. The latter centres on the theme of second sight and the burdens, as well as the privileges, the gift brings. As Ronald Black says, she was 'pre-eminently the Gaelic writer who occupied the boundary between psychology and the supernatural, a very Gaelic place to be.'

Am Fear Meadhanach / The Middle Man (1992) by Alasdair Caimbeul centres on the middle brother of three, Murchadh – there is also a sister who plays a much smaller role – who has been a teacher in Glasgow and has now returned to Lewis as he approaches his own death. Looking back over his own life and those of his siblings, he reflects on what has made them such individual characters, and he reconsiders the choices he has made. There's a fine balance between the morbidity and seriousness of the subject and the bright evocations of the natural world, the unforeseen opportunities life brings, the vividness of transient experience.

In *Cò Rinn E? / Who Did It?* (1993), Dòmhnall Iain MacÌomhair (Donald John MacIver) produced the first Gaelic whodunnit. And in Ronald Black's judgement, 'a good one'. It might seem aimed at younger readers but is perfectly suitable for secondary-school children as well as adults. MacIver worked to provide reading matter for Gaelic teaching in Western Isles schools.

Ciorstaidh is the central character of *Clann Iseabail / Ishbel's Children* (1993) by Màiri NicGumaraid / Mary Montgomery. As she works in Glasgow, thinking of her island upbringing, her beliefs and assumptions are sensitively explored. Opposed to the British Army's presence in Northern Ireland and committedly anti-imperialist, her conviction is at odds with her people at home on the island, who are loyalist, royalist and conservative, Anglocentric British subjects. This positions Ciorstaidh politically and personally in an awkward, painful place, and the novel negotiates her dilemma in the contexts of both the psychological realities of her situation and the political and ideological questions with which it is permeated. The depth of the novel's engagement is sustained through the seriousness of its sustained enquiry and its presentation of character, social circumstance and political and religious history.

An Sgàineadh / The Schism (1993) by Tormod Calum Dòmhnallach / Norman MacDonald is experimental in structure, as the first-person narrator struggles with alcoholism in New Zealand in the first part of the book, moves to London and begins work as a writer in the second part, and in the third and fourth parts, deepens and develops his sense of the meaning and value inherent in exile and homesickness. His identities – Scottish, Gaelic, Celtic – and the stereotyping they are subject to, he realizes intuitively, are themselves ways of keeping a distance from reality. Alienated identities are foregrounded in the very artifice of the novel's structure.

In 2003, the Gaelic Books Council initiated the publishing venture Ùr-sgeul, devoted to prose fiction and developing an increasingly impressive list of new titles: short stories and anthologies but mainly single-author novels. (The term itself might mean a novel, a story or romance.)

Ath-aithne (2003), a collection of stories by Màrtainn Mac an t-Saoir, was the first book to appear under the Ùr-sgeul series, each one characterised by questions of social conscience and urban realities. It was followed by novels *Gymnippers Diciadain / Gymnippers Wednesday* (2005) and *An Latha as Fhaide / The Longest Day* (2008) and a further short novel, *Tuath air a' Bhealach* (2014).

An Oidhche Mus Do Sheòl Sinn / The Night Before We Sailed (2003) by Aonghas Pàdraig Caimbeul / Angus Peter Campbell (whose fiction in English we noted above) was the first novel to be published in the Ùr-sgeul series, an epic of nearly 400 pages, following the lives of members of a South Uist family from 1913 to 2003, and the various fortunes of the island, its people, their language and religion. It was followed by *La a' Deànamh Sgèil do Là / A Day Spent Making Tales Till Dawn* (2004), in which Seòras Stubbs, an Englishman settled on Skye, falls in love with and marries Catriona as she escapes from a previous abusive relationship. The personal story is weighted by concerns of religion and ideology, and the ways in which the characters carry and bear the burdens of conviction and commitment. *An Taigh-Samhraidh* (2006) centres on questions of ownership and possession, land rights and legalities, imagination and obsession. *Tilleadh Dhachaigh / Returning Home* (2009) takes place on a train journey from Aberdeen to Kyle of Lochalsh, as the narrator heads towards Skye, each chapter named for stops on the line, prompting reflections, memories and judgements.

All these works raise fundamental human questions of cultural value that can be recognised even when they cannot be experienced. There are recurring themes, subjects, and forms of address in the work of all these authors: the difficulties or failures of communication, confusions arising in the interface between Gaelic and English, psychological danger and violence, threats of transition and liminality, family tensions, social morality, lovers separated and the quest to rediscover inheritance, belonging, personal independence and integrity, and the priority of caring for others. The stories cover different historical periods, and there is a considerable body of writing for children and teenagers.

Yet as John Storey puts it, in his essay 'Contemporary Gaelic fiction: development, challenge and opportunity', in *Lainnir a' Bhùirn – The Gleaming Water: Essays on Modern Gaelic Literature* (2011), edited by Emma Dymock and Wilson McLeod, 'For many Gaelic writers, the economic reality is harsh.' And while the work of the Gaelic Books Council has been major, and the success of the Ùr-sgeul series has been a welcome catalyst for new Gaelic fiction, resources are seriously underfunded.

Tormod Caimbeul's second novel, *Shrapnel* (2006), centres on retired Edinburgh detective Walter Watson, whose past returns to haunt him. By contrast with his first, this draws on the speed, violence and underworld atmosphere of both Irvine Welsh's *Trainspotting* and classic crime fiction, propelled by fast dialogue and black, ironic humour.

John Storey quotes Aonghas MacNeacail talking about Aonghas Phàdraig Caimbeul / Angus Peter Campbell and Màrtainn Mac an t-Saoir:

> What they do seem to have gained from their background, as have writers from other Catholic cultures, such as Latin America, is an ability to introduce elements of magic realism in ways that seem integral, even matter-of-fact. Things that were driven underground by a more austere theology, being accommodated by Catholicism, have retained an energy such writers can access.

Yet access to things 'driven underground' is never only the provenance of any single group. There is no monopoly on the imagination.

67

Possible dancers: Irvine Welsh, Carl MacDougall and A.L. Kennedy

WHEN IRVINE WELSH (B.1958) published *Trainspotting* (1993) one of the shocks delivered was that the reputation of Scotland's most violent city had been shifted from Glasgow to Edinburgh. The hitherto genteel, polite, pretentious world of Jean Brodie and her 'set' was exposed as the habitat of drug-addicted young men and women, lacking neither intelligence nor inventiveness but cynical to the point of nihilism in the legacy of high Thatcherism. When Welsh entitled a chapter 'Scotland takes drugs in psychic defence' he was making a gesture of scornful opposition to the Anglocentric British Conservative status quo. Continuing into the 21st century, Welsh's journalism and other writings contributed enormously to the rejection of the political assumptions and conventions of class-based Anglocentric conservative 'superiorism' so brutally endorsed by the era he emerged from.

The linguistic energy of Welsh's writing and the flagrant yet cunning structure of *Trainspotting* (a series of short stories, sketches and jokes increasingly intricately interconnecting to deliver the impact of a novel in the extended narrative of the second half of the book), both contributed to Welsh's popularity and lasting status. *Trainspotting* set a challenge to readers to engage sympathetically with characters who might seem overwhelmingly repugnant, people in whose company you would never wish to be.

Welsh followed it quickly with *Marabou Stork Nightmares* (1995), a blunt morality tale of lurid immediacy which revises the colonial world of John Buchan in a hellish nightmare portrayal of social, colonial and misogynist violence. Then *Filth* (1998) centred on the exploits of a corrupt policeman, cruel, self-serving and malicious to the point of perversity. The central character is appalling but his story is compelling and, at times, bizarrely, discomfortingly sympathetic. *Glue* (2001) and *Porno* (2002) brought the characters from *Trainspotting* back and as Welsh's books proliferated it became clear that almost all of them were connected in an epic vision of Thatcherland and its aftermaths. *The Bedroom Secrets of the Master Chefs* (2006), *Crime* (2008), *Skagboys* (2012), *The Sex Lives of Siamese Twins* (2014), *A Decent Ride* (2015), *The Blade Artist* (2016) and *Dead Men's Trousers* (2018) unfold a panorama in which even Iain Banks's Frank from *The Wasp Factory* would feel uneasy. Welsh's short stories, collected in *The Acid House* (1994), *Ecstasy* (1996), *If You Liked School You'll Love Work* (2007) and *Reheated Cabbage* (2009), are hit-or-miss, unflappable, unflagging in energy and appetite.

Welsh's writing in fiction is complemented by plays, films and journalism, and while it is, to say the least, uneven, it demonstrates a deepening engagement with social morality and political culture: undeniably left-wing, democratic, socialist or egalitarian in a broad sense, and in the approach to the 2014 referendum, out-and-out in favour of independence.

In a television interview from 20 April 2012, Welsh was introduced by the English TV *Newsnight* presenter Jeremy Paxman, well-known at the time for various Scotophobic asides (describing Burns in *The Telegraph*, August 14, 2008, as 'no more than a king of sentimental doggerel'). Paxman's opening question, trying and failing to be provocative, was: 'Now, are you surprised to find yourself a nationalist?' Welsh replied:

> Yeah, I don't really see myself as a nationalist, I see much more the Union as being in a kind of secular decline. The Union was very much conceived to facilitate British imperial expansion, British industrial expansion, sustained by a kind of welfare state and the *ésprit de corps* of two world wars. All these things no longer exist. They've gone. So I just don't actually see what's driving the Union, what's holding it together.

Challenged by the Labour MP Tristram Hunt, Welsh continued:

> People feel in Scotland now that it's not so much Britishness that they're against but it's the actual concept of the UK and the actual Union. The two political cultures have become very divergent... Scotland [...] is a very different society that's developed in a very different political culture. I just don't see any kind of connection there.

When Hunt says that one of the strengths of the Union is the stature of the United Kingdom on the world stage, Welsh responds:

> When you look at some of the decisions we've made in foreign policy, if you look at Afghanistan, where so many people were against that war, I don't think you can pick these things as being plusses.

Hunt admits that English people themselves need space to consider the complexities of Englishness. Welsh responds by emphasising the difference within the political construct of the United Kingdom: 'People have moved on from that in Scotland. I just sense that people have rejected that model.'

Welsh's commitment to independence was salutary but even more telling was the sense that people need time to move on from the definitions that constrain them. In that respect, the velocity and sensationalism of his fiction has been complemented by a more enduring understanding of the value of patience.

With the work of Carl MacDougall (b.1941), that quality of patient understanding is an essential element. In the novel *The Lights Below* (1993), MacDougall places at the heart of a vivid Glasgow cityscape a sensitive and resilient central character in a grim tale culminating in an entirely credible sense of redemption. Andy Paterson, an innocent man imprisoned on drugs charges, is released and sets out to discover who framed him. It's a classic 'noir' structure, brilliantly handled.

MacDougall is also a master of the short story, often drawing on traditional sources, and in both his stories and novels, fabular fiction and retellings of traditional tales in modern contexts, familiar tropes are transformed with sharp, fresh edges. Underlying designs, like the returning prodigal, the need of the wronged to be justified, survival in a world of preying and exploiting powers, are revitalised and burnished by his writing.

Stone over Water (1989) tells of Angus MacPhail, conforming to work while his adoptive brother attempts to rescue Scotland by robbing banks. Lightly written, it gently deepens a sense of family and social responsibilities, the tensions and balances of comfort and risk. *A Cuckoo's Nest* (1974) and *A Scent of Water* (1975) are charmed and eloquent collections of stories for children built on traditional tales. The short stories in *Elvis is Dead* (1986) centre on Glasgow life in its variety of strange capacities. *The Casanova Papers* (1996) begins in Glasgow with a widower taking stock of his situation after the death of his wife, his own sense of life's worth and his own mortality, his children, their lives, and his relationships with them, then he moves to Paris where he discovers a set of manuscripts relating to Casanova, which takes the narrative in entirely unexpected directions. *The One Legged Tap Dancer* (1981) is both funny and serious, presenting the efforts of a working-class man simply to earn a living.

Of the stories collected in *Someone Always Robs the Poor* (2017), style is the key. This is not to say style overtakes substance, characters, relationships or situations but rather that the form of address in each story is perfectly matched to its subject. The stories require the reader's patience but offer ample reward. The words work quietly, unobtrusively, because the drama and tension (and there's plenty) come from what's being written about. When things go beyond the power of adequate exclamation, you have to make good use of persistence. In 'Is this the place you now call home?' the plot twists and develops, taking you somewhere different from where you thought you were going, yet delivering the perfect conclusion. As Marshall Kutuzov says to Prince Andrei in Tolstoy's *War and Peace* (Book Three, Part Two, Chapter 16, translated by Rosemary Edmonds): '"Believe me, my dear boy, the two most powerful warriors are *patience and time*: they will do everything."'

Novels and short story collections by A.L. Kennedy (b.1965) include *Night Geometry and the Garscadden Trains* (1990), *Looking for the Possible Dance* (1993), *Now That You're Back* (1994), *So I Am Glad* (1995), *Original Bliss* (1997), *Everything You Need* (1999), *Paradise* (2004), *Day* (2007), *The Blue Book* (2011), *Serious Sweet* (2016), *The Little Snake* (2018) and her non-fiction includes *The Life & Death of Colonel Blimp* (1997), *On Bullfighting* (1999) and *On Writing* (2013). The latter is a rich exposition of matters of writerly craft and imagination, borne out by her own work.

Imagination bagatelles from each of Kennedy's books to the next, never predictable, always intense. *So I Am Glad* (1995) begins as a realist account of a young, dissatisfied woman working in radio but takes on another dimension as Cyrano de Bergerac appears in her life: a fictional dream-figure, he breaks the parameters of the character's expectations and of the possibilities of the novel itself, bringing a magic realist component to a feminist scenario in modern Glasgow. In *Paradise* (2004), the delusional self-justification of an alcoholic bleeds into the unreliable narrative itself: terror and compassion are woven together. It is a study of alcoholism, almost expressionist in its narrative structure and frightening in its representation of the liabilities of rationalisation. *Day* (2007) is the story of an air force bomber machine-gunner who returns to his wartime experiences in later years.

The judgement Kennedy delivers at the end of the title story of her first collection, *Night Geometry and the Garscadden Trains* (1990), might stand for everything she has written since. She describes people, women and men, in so many situations and through so many different forms of desire and vulnerability, that it is easy to miss the underlying connective tissue where compassion and indignation are grafted together. Here she spells it out. The sense given arises perhaps from the similar intimation of human value George Eliot described in the closing words of *Middlemarch* (1871):

> for the growing good of the world is partly dependent on unhistoric acts; and that things are not so ill with you and me as they might have been, is half owing to the number who lived faithfully a hidden life, and rest in unvisited tombs.

Kennedy's world is recognisably that of the late 20th and early 21st century but the same compassion is here:

> contrary to popular belief, people, many people, almost all the people, live their lives in the best way they can with generally good intentions and still leave nothing behind.

There is only one thing I want more than proof that I existed and that's some proof, while I'm here, that I exist. Not being an Olympic skier, or a chat show host, I won't get my wish. There are too many people alive today for us to notice every single one.

But the silent majority and I do have one memorial, at least. The Disaster. We have small lives, easily lost in foreign droughts, or famines; the occasional incendiary incident, or a wall of pale faces, crushed against grillwork, one Saturday afternoon in Spring. This is not enough.

As the priorities of mass media, celebrity culture and political posturing continue to enact their distortions, Kennedy's quiet opposition to that which numbs and silences is one of the steeliest instruments on the tray.

68

Risky desires and natural needs: Iain Banks and Janice Galloway

BOTH IAIN BANKS and Janice Galloway made a huge impact with their first novels and carried on from there in richly varied and unpredicted ways. John Berger once wrote that the great virtue of art is that it teaches us not to want more but to want better. Taking up the challenge of acknowledging the 'risky desires' all of us have and combining them with a sympathetic understanding of what we might call our 'natural needs' (both masculine and feminine), Banks and Galloway each take us along very different roads and in various directions. Do they have anything in common? Let's see.

The shocking literary debut of Iain Banks (1954–2013) came with *The Wasp Factory* (1984), starting his career with one of the biggest bangs in modern literature. His publishers were astute to open the paperback edition of 1985 with three pages of extracts from both good and bad reviews. *The Sunday Express* described it as 'A silly, gloatingly sadistic and grisly yarn of a family of Scots lunatics' and the *Evening Standard* said it was 'A repulsive piece of work' yet *The Financial Times* called it 'A Gothic horror story of quite exceptional quality'. *The Mail on Sunday* hedged its bets: 'If a nastier, more vicious or distasteful novel appears this spring, I shall be surprised. But there is unlikely to be a better one either.'

After that, what next?

Each of Banks's 'mainstream' novels is distinct and different, commenting obliquely on traditional genre fiction. Science fantasy is folded into *Walking On Glass* (1985); in *The Bridge* (1986), one of his best novels, a comatose young man reviews his life up to the point of his disastrous car crash, while struggling to get out of his terrifying dream world. It's Kafkaesque, and also reminiscent of William Golding's *Pincher Martin* (1956), but primarily it's an adventure, a kind of 'great escape' story. The happy ending twists the sense of despair into a welcome, triumphant yet also ironic tone ('Lie back and think of Scotland'). The relation between dream and actuality becomes the source of the book's tension. *Espedair Street* (1987) focuses on the world of rock music and a reclusive musician in Glasgow: urban realist comedy collides with the biography of a rock star at the end of his career, and at the start of another kind of life. *Canal Dreams* (1989) is an eerie mixture of exotic espionage thriller and hallucinatory horror fiction.

His most ambitious novel is *The Crow Road* (1992), a family saga of national identity, exploring issues of social class, individual psychology and sexuality.

A broad range of eccentric characters over two generations of the McHoan family centres on Prentice, a Glasgow University student whose investigations into his family's past lead him to the solution of one of its darkest secrets. *The Crow Road* is a murder mystery, a black comedy, an infuriating love story, a tale of a young man growing up, a dynastic family saga and an exploration of the relations between dream and actuality. (It also has one of the most unforgettable first sentences of any novel: 'It was the day my grandmother exploded.') It was made into a wonderful four-part television mini-series broadcast on BBC Scotland in 1996.

Complicity (1993) brings the brutally competitive aspect of modern Britain into focus with an apparently ruthless main character obsessed with fashionable drugs, high speed cars, and sado-masochistic sex. Banks's world comes from the era of Margaret Thatcher and John Major: another awful episode of Conservative Party UK rule. Later novels include *Whit* (1995), an 'innocent abroad' fable; the unrelievedly grim war story, *A Song of Stone* (1997); satires on criminality and commerce such as *The Business* (1999) and *Dead Air* (2002); and further family sagas, *The Steep Approach to Garbadale* (2007), *Stonemouth* (2012), and *The Quarry* (2013). Other works include *Against a Dark Background* (1993), *Feersum Endjinn* (1994), *The Algebraist* (2004) and non-fiction: *Raw Spirit* (2003) and *Poems* (with Ken MacLeod) (2015).

Banks developed a series of vast science fiction novels, which he described in a 1990 interview as 'space operas': *Consider Phlebas* (1987), *The Player of Games* (1988), *Use of Weapons* (1990), *Against A Dark Background* (1993), *Excession* (1996), *Inversions* (1998), *Look to Windward* (2000), *Matter* (2008), *Surface Detail* (2010) and *The Hydrogen Sonata* (2012). Banks noted:

> Space opera works on a broad canvas, it gives an impression of the operatic where some science fiction might feel like a small ensemble... Yet in a way I am just trying to tell a yarn. There's all this space paraphernalia, but you can paraphrase the story as just being about a ship-wrecked sailor who falls in with a gang of pirates and goes off in search of buried treasure...

Or in other words: Robert Louis Stevenson 'somewhere out there'.

Let's go back to *The Wasp Factory* for a moment. It's an anti-pastoral of island life. The main character, the adolescent Frank, presents us with an inverted idyll. He takes us on a number of lurid childhood adventures, including encouraging his baby brother to beat an unexploded mine with a wooden stick (effectively murdering him), and sending a young cousin on a fatal flight across the North Sea attached to a home-made kite (effectively murdering her). Frank behaves like a cool-minded hooligan but retains the appeal of a gentleman murderer (think of Dennis Price in the marvellous 1949 film, *Kind Hearts and Coronets*).

He tells us in Chapter 7:

> All our lives are symbols. Everything we do is part of a pattern we have at least some say in. The strong make their own patterns and influence other people's, the weak have their courses mapped out for them. The weak and the unlucky, and the stupid. The Wasp Factory is part of the pattern...

So what is the Wasp Factory?

Over half the novel is spent working up to the moment when it is put into action. When it comes, it might seem an anti-climax but it has a quietly potent symbolic significance. The Wasp Factory is an enormous clock-face, placed flat in the attic of Frank's house and redesigned as a maze for live wasps. Once introduced, a wasp has to follow any one of a series of options, all of which lead to its death (by drowning, electrocution, a carnivorous plant, or other means). Each death is variable and open to the creature's momentary choice. Symbolically, it's a platform upon which mortality plays itself out. But the clock-face itself comes from an old Royal Bank of Scotland building. Frank discovered it in the town dump. It is, you might say, malevolent time – but it also suggests the idea of Scotland itself as a maze, as a discarded unit, a lapsed state, a mortality trap.

And both Banks and Janice Galloway are enablers of reclamation from such lapsed trap-states.

Five years after *The Wasp Factory*, *The Trick is to Keep Breathing* (1989), the first novel by Janice Galloway (b.1955), made an equally impressive but very different kind of impact. In the novel, various careful experiments with typography and narrative structure at first appear flamboyant but in fact deepen the reader's understanding of the central character, Joy Stone, and her predicament. Her anguish, breakdown and recovery constitute both a detailed account of a personal crisis and a radical critique of the social conventions that have overtaken us all. The immediacy of the typographic devices have their effect. The conventions and conditions they alert us to have saturated our society even more thoroughly since the 1980s. The compassion and growing strength of resolution of Joy and of Galloway's writing itself continues to develop, enduringly impressive. She teaches us how to want better.

In *Clara* (2002), Galloway portrayed Clara Schumann, composer and pianist, her relation with her husband the better-known composer Robert Schumann, and the pressures exerted upon her. Again, the intimacy of personal detail as the portrait builds up is weighted and deepened by a sense of the stifling social conventions she lived under. *Clara* remains Galloway's most ambitious novel and a major achievement. It might be read literally, in terms of the biography and history of the Schumanns, but any particular story has its universal resonances and any work of literary art has metaphoric significance. The novel is not only bristling with feminist priorities but assured in its grasp of complex social and musical contexts. With no overtly Scottish components, *Clara* is arguably Galloway's most profoundly Scottish novel, as, unencumbered by literal Scottish locations or characters, the metaphor of oppression and the struggle for meaningful artistic creation is intricate, subtle, and immensely powerful in the Scottish context of its time of publication and place of continuing circulation and readership.

The centrality of creativity, both in composition and performance and simply in the daily life of the imagination, is at the heart of these and all Galloway's works, the short stories in *Blood* (1991) and especially through the novel *Foreign Parts* (1994), in which two women, Rona and Cassie, explore questions of identity, humour and culture while on a driving holiday in France. The writing is equally lucid and compelling in Galloway's family portraits of domestic tensions, hurt and survival arts in her 'memoirs', *This Is Not About Me* (2008) and *All Made Up* (2011). Further stories are collected in *Where You Find It* (1996) and *Jellyfish* (2015).

Both of these writers bring characters whose lives are blighted and oppressed into our understanding and prompt us to give of our sympathy. Sometimes, more than sympathy: imaginative support. The remarkable thing is not only that the appeal succeeds so much but that they help us understand more deeply the need to exercise such sympathy and give such support. It's a natural need. Yet there are also these 'risky desires' depicted in the writings of both Banks and Galloway, yearnings and hopes for, frustrations and oppressions of, and sometimes assertions and violent insistence upon those things that would make our lives more fulfilled: ultimately qualities of self-determination. These are what make us human after all. Their writing describes the consequences of retreat from a world in which touching and understanding are necessities. Withdrawal and repression drives us to divisions and despair. The truth of their visions has become even more horribly familiar since their first novels were published. These writers, each in his and her own way, are liberators.

69

Scotland and further: James Robertson, Ali Smith and Alan Warner

THE NOVELS OF James Robertson (b.1958) include *The Fanatic* (2000), *Joseph Knight* (2003), *The Testament of Gideon Mack* (2006), *And the Land Lay Still* (2010), *The Professor of Truth* (2013), *To Be Continued...* (2016) and *News of the Dead* (2021). His short stories are collected in *Close* (1991), *The Ragged Man's Complaint* (1993), *Republics of the Mind* (2012) and *365: Stories* (2014). And his poetry shouldn't be neglected: *Sound-Shadow* (1995), *I Dream of Alfred Hitchcock* (1999), *Stirling Sonnets* (2001), *Voyage of Intent: Sonnets and Essays from the Scottish Parliament* (2005) and *Hem and Heid* (2009).

Start with *Joseph Knight* (2004): a determined exploration of Scots complicity in the slave trade and the West Indian plantations. Joseph is one of the most original creations of modern fiction. Arriving in Scotland and suing for freedom from slavery, he confronts the property-owning racists who command commercial Scotland's financial authority. This is a novel of epic geographical scale, confronting ethical, political and social issues that continue to bear upon us in the 21st century.

The Testament of Gideon Mack (2006) revises James Hogg's *Confessions of a Justified Sinner* (1824) in a complex parable of belief and delusion in modern Scotland. A minister whose faith appears to have disappeared attempts to rescue a dog as it slips on a cliff-edge, and finds himself in a cavern, saved by, and opening a dialogue with, the Devil himself.

In *The Professor of Truth* (2013), Robertson takes a number of stories associated with the Lockerbie airplane bombing of 1988 and creates a fiction set in snow-bound Scotland for its first half, then in sun-beaten, ultimately fire-consumed Australia for its second. A structure that looks broken-backed delivers a profound sense of the drive to discover the truth, from one side of the earth to its polar opposite, across all weathers and against all odds.

But Robertson's most ambitious work is a multi-faceted chronicle fiction of modern Scotland, travelling from 1950 to the beginning of the 21st century, *And the Land Lay Still* (2010). This panoramic exploration of the modern nation takes us through major political changes and growing cultural self-confidence with a cast of memorable characters, including portraits of historical figures like Hugh MacDiarmid. It culminates in an overwhelming sense of awareness, determination and political commitment to the unfinished business of Scotland, the universal value of the arts, from poetry to photography, and the common virtues and failings of individual men and women.

Realism and fantasy combine in *To Be Continued...* (2016). The central character, Douglas, confronts a telepathic toad, Mungo Forth Mungo. They have various dialogues as the novel progresses. Early on, Douglas is impressed by Mungo's knowledge of historical Scottish explorers, such as Mungo Park, after whom he has taken his name. 'With respect,' Douglas asks the toad, 'what possible use to you, a toad, or to your survival, is knowledge of long-dead Scottish explorers?' Mungo replies that the phrase 'with respect' normally signifies its opposite and that Douglas's question endorses this general rule, and furthermore, asks his human interlocutor whether his supposed knowledge of the so-called 'common' toad is relevant to his own existence or survival. Douglas is about to reply, hesitantly, when Mungo interrupts with one of those crucial little speeches that sticks in the mind forever:

> 'Do you or do you not subscribe to the view that all knowledge is potentially valuable, and that its value, potential or realised, cannot be determined by the superficial assessment of its perceived utility at any given moment?'
> 'I'll have to think about that,' Douglas said. It seemed too grand and complex a proposition to be unscrambled so late in the garden of October darkness, especially after the best part of a bottle of red wine.
> 'Do so,' Mungo said. 'I already have.' And in one untoad-like leap he left the table and landed somewhere in the night.

This might stand as a motto for enlightened thought about literature, the arts, and the world, a maxim that carries proverbial wisdom and bears repetition:

> All knowledge is potentially valuable, and its value, potential or realised, cannot be determined by the superficial assessment of its perceived utility at any given moment.

Ali Smith (b.1962) would acknowledge the truth in this, I think. She has won high acclaim for her novels and stories, and their distinction lies primarily in their demonstration of understanding of human values beyond 'perceived utility'. Her novels, including *Like* (1997), *Hotel World* (2001), *The Accidental* (2005), *Girl Meets Boy* (2007) *There But For The* (2011) and *How to Be Both* (2014), all deploy original formulations of narrative and character, juxtapositions of time and place. Her story collections, *Free Love* (1995), *Other Stories and Other Stories* (1999), *The Whole Story* (2003), *The First Person* (2008) and *Public Library* (2015) employ similar technical virtuosities. And in *Autumn* (2016), *Winter* (2017), *Spring* (2019) and *Summer* (2020), she addresses the continuing condition of Britain since the referendum on membership of the European Union.

Spring begins like this: 'Now what we don't want is Facts. What we want is bewilderment. What we want is repetition. What we want is repetition. What we want is people in power saying the truth is not the truth'. And goes on:

> We want the people we call foreign to feel foreign we need to make it clear they can't have rights unless we say so. [...] We need emotion we want righteousness we want anger. We need all that patriotic stuff. What we want is [...] fury we want outrage we want words at their most emotive antisemite is good nazi is great paedo will really do it perverted foreigner illegal we want gut reaction we want [...] We need words to mean what we say they mean. We need to deny what we're saying while we're saying it. We need it not to matter what words mean. [...] We're what this country's needed all along we're what you need we're what you want.

Smith's passionate satiric indignation is compelling. The novel begins as political commentary but moves into a fictional exploration of the human capacities for survival, of fallibilities, vulnerabilities, frailties, and susceptibilities to temptation. She presents human potential at its worst, as well as its best.

The Book Lover (2008) is a collection of her favourite writing by others, including Muriel Spark, Margaret Atwood and Joseph Roth, an eclectic, unpredicted and illuminating selection. *Shire* (2013) is part autobiography, part biographical tribute to the great pioneering medievalist scholar of Scottish literature, Helena Mennie Shire. And *Artful* (2012), based on four lectures on European Comparative Literature given at Saint Anne's College, Oxford, combines the scholarly enquiring mind with the storyteller's art of singular focus, as it builds into a quasi-novel with characters, lovers, narratives and encounters. Ultimately, it's a meditation, serious and playful, erudite and humble, on life and presence, death and absence, memory and revitalisation, and the arts, pre-eminently writing, painting and film.

Each 'Chapter' has a title that combines thesis, provocation and pun: 'On Time', 'On Form', 'On Edge' and 'On offer and reflection'. It is partly critical enquiry but it is also a personal account and testament about the capabilities of the arts, and proof of why they're so vital. It might be read alongside her 2017 Goldsmith's lecture, 'The novel in the age of Trump': 'When politics is built on fictions, it's fiction that can help us get to truth.'

Alan Warner (b.1964), in his debut novel *Morvern Callar* (1995), described the west coast ferry port of Oban as no-one had before, and presented a new fictional character, whose self-serving ambition is understandable, sympathetic and unsettling. The town, and the landscape around it, are not immediately recognisable. Morvern herself is a young woman living there but more familiar with the working-class areas, pubs, supermarkets and the day-to-day lives of people than with the picturesque seafront and the ferries to the islands best known to tourists. *These Demented Lands* (1997) and *The Man Who Walks* (2002) are surreal, visionary: dream landscapes shift into nightmares, pastoral fields, coastlines, seas and islands are momentarily idyllic, then ragingly infernal. The bodily properties of individual characters and the terrain they move through are permeable, tough, vulnerable, wounded and bleeding, pregnant and regenerative. Nothing is inevitable.

More conventionally realist are *The Sopranos* (1998) and *The Stars in the Bright Sky* (2010). These novels follow Morvern's contemporaries, both at home and away. In *The Sopranos*, Orla, Kylah, (Ra)Chell, Manda and Fionnula (the Cooler) are on an excursion from Our Lady of Perpetual Succour School and go pub crawling, shoplifting and body-piercing, as they make their way to a singing competition in 'the city'. The Sopranos are a brazen antidote to Muriel Spark's schoolgirl set in *The Prime of Miss Jean Brodie*. *The Stars in the Bright Sky* reunites them, out of school now, meeting in Gatwick, set for an economy-flight holiday. Published in 2010, it is set in 2001 and concludes with the twin towers of the World Trade Centre in New York brought down by suicidal terrorists flying two planes into them. The Sopranos are sobered, for once: 'Why would people do that?' one of them asks. And the final sentence leaves us in suspense: 'They all waited to see what would happen next.'

Set in London, *Their Lips Talk of Mischief* (2014) takes place in 1984. Date and place make a cradle for the uncertainties of Douglas Cunningham (Scots), Llewellyn Smith (Welsh), and Aoife McCrissican (Irish), each caught in the metropolitan capital of imperial legacy. In *The Worms Can Carry Me to Heaven* (2006), though Spain is never named, the story centres closely on its first-person narrator, Manolo Follana, and builds a deep historical background, a history of fascism and its relation to media: the questions here apply anywhere, regardless of nationality.

The Deadman's Pedal (2012) returns to Oban, a coming-of-age story centred on a young man encountering divisions of class, gender, social employment and expectation. Set mainly in the 1970s and 1980s, the novel moves with its main character, leaving school to find work as an apprentice on the unionised trains while his father runs a lorry company. The book delivers a strange sense of dignity in its portrayal of every character, avoiding any tendency to caricature or satirise. It describes childhood dens and adult homes, private worlds and public lives, motives rising from selfishness and senses of responsibility, modes of commercial transport, lorries and trains, social structures of class. Questions of tradition and change in the political system and the economy are implicit throughout. The cultural moment sees the rise of punk rock, opposing the unctuous friendliness of mass media and the rise of celebrity culture and mediocrity.

In all Warner's fiction, as in Robertson's and Smith's, what seems final is always only partial. There are still and always will be folk out there wanting to rule over you. Imperialism never goes away forever. These writers show us the arts of resistance.

70

Forms of revival: Allan Massie, James Kelman and Alan Spence

ALLAN MASSIE (B.1938) is well-known for a series of novels set in ancient Rome, but his Scottish novels, including *The Hanging Tree* (1990), depicting the Scotland of the Border Reivers and *The Ragged Lion* (1994), a fictionalised biography of Walter Scott, are equally vivid. His satires of manners set in rural Perthshire *The Last Peacock* (1980) and *These Enchanted Woods* (1993) are low-key acidic comedies, while his novels set during and after the Second World War explore the theme of divided loyalties central to the experience of being both Scottish and British, especially in the final years of the British Empire.

Massie's fiction begins with *Change and Decay in All Around I See* (1978) and *The Last Peacock* (1980). With *The Death of Men* (1981) it became evident that this was a novelist capable of deeply impressive work. Edwin Morgan noted this novel particularly in his *Twentieth-Century Scottish Classics*: more than a fictional account of the kidnapping and death of the Italian politician Aldo Moro in 1978, it is

> an exploration, through fictional characters, of the complex issues of political change and political stability in modern society. The brutal fact of abduction, especially when as in this case the most probable end is assassination, is shown in a penetrating way in its impact on friends, on Americans, on an English journalist, and on members of the family, among whom is one involved in the kidnapping.

Impressions of Rome colour the background but the main focus is on the extremes to which compromised commitments and faltering faiths can take people.

Later memorable works include *One Night in Winter* (1984), *Augustus* (1986), *A Question of Loyalties* (1989), *Tiberius* (1991), *The Sins of the Father* (1991), *Caesar* (1993), *King David* (1995), *Shadows of Empire* (1997), *Antony* (1997), *Nero's Heirs* (1999), *The Evening of the World* (2001), *Caligula* (2003), *Arthur the King* (2004), *Charlemagne and Roland* (2007), *Surviving* (2009), *Klaus and other stories* (2010), and a series of crime novels set in occupied France, where divided loyalties once again are set against the sense of moral justice in a deeply compromised society, *Death in Bordeaux* (2010), *Dark Summer in Bordeaux* (2012), *Cold Winter in Bordeaux* (2014), *End Games in Bordeaux* (2015).

James Kelman (b.1946), from the very first novel, *The Busconductor Hines* (1984) – with its descriptions of family life in a tenement flat, the main character's attempt to organise protest at work, to hold his family together and teach his son as best he can – focuses on the experience of working people (not all of them 'working class'). His writing carries a moral force, insisting that we must not evade the central matter of social injustice, economic division and the need people have for better lives than most of us are likely ever to get. The central character of *The Busconductor Hines* is conscientious, concerned and committed to doing his best for his family and workmates. He lives with his wife and small son in a small tenement flat, feeling the threat of losing both his family and his job. He worries about his own well-being too, and yet he wants to keep his family together, he wants the best for his son and to improve the working conditions of his life. His language is attractively inventive and he has a quirky sense of humour, and these are conveyed through rich, extended monologues. The novel curiously and uniquely blends a sense of honesty, aspiration and care. Kelman's second novel, *A Chancer* (1985) is less complex but equally compelling.

His work after these novels became even more complex and restless. His commitment and earnestness has not restrained him from trying new things. His Booker Prize winner, *How Late It Was, How Late* (1994), explores the world of a blind man, victimised and bullied, trying to find a way through experience as he struggles to make sense of himself and the impositions placed upon him. It's a tour-de-force of the writer's art, and his later work extends his range, most searchingly in his exploration of childhood, *Kieron Smith, Boy* (2008), which dwells within the boy's point of view, with untiring verbal invention and tightly-controlled qualities of humour and sympathy. Further works of fiction are written as if from the point-of-view and through voices of women, and he inhabits characters very different from his own experience.

His short stories are collected in *An Old Pub Near The Angel* (1973); *Three Glasgow Writers* (1976, with Alex Hamilton and Tom Leonard); *Short Tales from the Night Shift* (1978); *Not Not While The Giro* (1983); *Lean Tales* (1985, with Alasdair Gray and Agnes Owens); *Greyhound for Breakfast* (1987); *The Burn* (1991); *The Good Times* (1998); *If It Is Your Life* (2010); *A Lean Third* (2014); *That Was a Shiver* (2017).

His third novel, *A Disaffection* (1989), takes as its central character a school teacher and explores his world with a tight time-frame and forensic understanding, thereby allowing sympathy to grow without any excessive linguistic indulgence. Later works such as *Translated Accounts* (2001), *You Have to Be Careful in the Land of the Free* (2004), *Mo Said She Was Quirky* (2012) and *Dirt Road* (2016) deploy his experience of America and his imaginative projections into the minds and feelings of characters very different from himself.

It is this intensely professional writing that takes him beyond anything that might be described as simple exploitation of sensationalised working-class experience. Kelman's fiction is fundamentally contemplative, and resists the pressures of conformity brought to bear by middle-class conventions.

Alan Spence (b.1947) similarly made an impressive impact with his first book, *Its Colours They Are Fine* (1977), a collection of 13 interwoven stories comprising a panorama of Glasgow life through the 1950s and 1960s. A child's-eye view of Glasgow life opens with optimism and hope and comes to terms with disappointment in the resilient world of fallible but supportive family and friends. Childhood, adolescence and old age are treated equally with direct and careful attentiveness. Truths arise without dramatic gesture, poised and strong. A six-year-old boy in a Glasgow tenement awakens to the vulnerability and emotional sensitivity of his parents, dazzled and attracted by the tinsel of Christmas decorations. A teenager finds himself on the edge of becoming a Glasgow 'hard man', reaching into his pocket, 'feeling the steel comb with the long pointed handle'. Religious bigotry and public festivity combine in an Orange march and a Catholic wedding. Two old codgers chew over the past in the warm sanctuary of the Botanic Gardens. There is no nostalgia but rather a balanced, poignant, sustained and gentle sense of the temporary and transient nature of even the most vivid experience.

This was followed by *The Magic Flute* (1990), a kind of sequel to *Its Colours They Are Fine*. Further novels and story collections include *Stone Garden* (1995) and *Way to Go* (1998), which takes the profession of funeral directing and confronts the gloom and darkness of traditional Scottish enactments of burial and entombment with an international range of attitudes to death and the removal of the body. Like all Spence's works, this takes great risks with the balance of seriousness and humour – it could be farcically flamboyant or meditative to the point of being almost humourless – but it manages, sometimes necessarily unsteadily, to bring these together. It leaves you with a feeling of hope in the sense of possibility, and that old things that have always 'been done that way' might not be done in the same way, but better, somehow, differently, in the future.

The next two novels take you into Spence's favoured territory beyond Scotland: Japan, its challenges, wisdoms and histories. *The Pure Land* (2006) ambitiously tells the story of Thomas Glover, the 19th-century trader, travelling from Aberdeen to Japan. He develops his own businesses, including arms-dealing, leading to the overthrow of the Shogun. A global political canvas depicting industrial-scale capitalism and imperial power is focused on the pathos, limitations, aspirations and humanity of one man, his relations with native women, friends and family, addressing questions of loyalty, value and loss. Glover (a historical character) helped found Mitsubishi, and the industrial centre that Nagasaki thereafter became was one reason why it was the target for atomic holocaust at the end of the Second World War.

Spence's next novel *Night Boat* (2013), set entirely in 18th-century Japan, was another fictionalised biography. It tells of Hakuin, the man who became the world's most famous teacher of Zen Buddhism. In light, pellucid prose, in short chapters paused by bright, sharp-edged poems, Hakuin's human story unfolds from his childhood family, through meetings with teachers, confrontations and solitude, to temples and wanderings, writings and conversations, through history, into old age. The pathos of the novel is deeply personal but also takes place on an epic scale.

The essence of that pathos might be sensed in Spence's poem 'Un Bel Di (One Fine Day)', which is a register of feeling, watching Puccini's opera *Madame Butterfly*: 'This time I tell myself I will not cry / I will not let Puccini rip the heart / right out of me...' In the poem, Spence is sitting 'in this gilded circle / right up in the gods': 'But then she sings.' And at that point, everything surrenders to the music and its meaning:

> We all wait for the night to pass, the dawn
> to break, we all stand watching on some shore,
> looking for that ship on the horizon,
> the plume of smoke that signals hope once more.
> She sings, Un bel di... And it's no use –
> I weep for everything I love and lose.

Spence is a fine playwright, not least in *Sailmaker* (1982) and *No Nothing* (2015), in which the ghosts of the Clydeside working-class leader Jimmy Reid and the poet Edwin Morgan meet each other in the afterlife and discuss the lasting priorities of their lives. He's also a fine poet. In his book, *morning glory: haiku and tanka*, with illustrations by Elizabeth Blackadder (2010), there is this little poem:

> it was *this* big!
> the child tells her mother
> on the phone

Reading this, you can see the invisible, hear the unspoken, understand what intuition is, feel that family connection reaching beyond the data, and grasp afresh how language and imagination work together, and what sympathy actually is. It carries affection and prompts liking. It comes from a happy working marriage of both skill and care.

71

Scotlands (plural): from Janet Paisley to Kirstin Innes

IN HER NOVELS, Janet Paisley (1948–2018) presents Scotland at two different crucial moments in history. First, *White Rose Rebel* (2007), set during the Jacobite rising of 1745, takes a perspective that immediately stretches our understanding not only of a woman's position but of a woman's potential and capabilities. Furthermore, it fluently foregrounds qualities of Scottish identity that contrast fiercely with those of the ascendant authority of the Hanoverian, English, and assertively British power. Then in *Warrior Daughter* (2009), Paisley takes us back to the ancient Celtic world of Skaaha, the woman who went on to teach the great Celtic hero Cuchulain the arts of war on the Isle of Skye. The novel recounts the ferocious contest between men and women vying for dominance in a pagan Scotland, where human priorities are seen in stark immediacy, undisguised by religious or mediated obfuscations. Violent, sexually explicit and vigorously paced, both her novels are also passionate revaluations of conventional historical priorities.

As she explains in an 'Author's Note', to write *Warrior Daughter* realistically

> meant avoiding post-Roman and Christian influence, additions or opinions, though I often used what came next to determine what went before. Archaeology and classical histories provided evidence and information. Anthropology filled the gaps. Britain was tribal, its land called Alba (Scotland) or Albion (England). Since Skaaha lived on the margin between native Picts and Irish Gaels, I gave her lineage from both. Myths and archaeology indicate a settled society of artisans, food producers, warriors and priests, trading with Europe and beyond. Skaaha's culture is often described as Celtic, its people known for beauty, strength and ferocity. She was a warrior queen who preceded Cartimandua, queen of the Brigantes, and the Icenian, Boudicca.

Reclaiming Skaaha in fiction in this way nudges Boudicca to one side and allows Scotland – Skye and the Western Isles especially – to take their place as the territory of an ancient history and a world of imaginative truths we need to acknowledge. Both novels act in this way, reclaiming history and ways of imagining not only 'what went before' but also what we might make of the future.

Paisley's collection of short stories, *Not For Glory* (2001) is written in a distinctive Scots, the idiom and language of the narrative matching the speech and voices of the characters described. This is a different kind of reclamation, presenting contemporary society with a vivid presence, sympathy and a sense of moral questioning that vitalises the characters and the stories told. It's also very funny. The setting is a village in central Scotland, where a multitude of characters, at all stages and roles of family life, in various professions and sometimes none that could be easily categorised, come and go. As James Robertson puts it, this is writing that thoroughly refuses to concede Edwin Muir's assertion that Scots 'think in one language and feel in another': this is writing that both feels and thinks at the same time, where thinking is done with the heart and feeling with the head, and the two are connected viscerally as well as intellectually. The division itself is shown as false, fabricated and inappropriate, as we see characters in situations of utter despondency and uproarious friendship, and hear them and feel for them, as well.

Paisley's life and work is commemorated in *Janet Paisley: Growing and Dying*, edited by Linda Jackson (Glasgow: Seahorse Publications, 2019).

Frank Kuppner (b.1951) draws as much from surrealism as from Scottish literature, his poetry and prose writing a perfect blend of the keen witnessing of unexpected juxtapositions and the intimate investment of personal experience. Perhaps the most deeply engaging of his works of fiction (what can we call them? – 'quasi-novels'?) is *A Very Quiet Street* (1989), which combines elements of murder-mystery, autobiography, scholarly reconstruction and almost endless wandering through Glasgow streets and the city's dark history. It begins:

> This book, an investigation of some aspects of the Oscar Slater case by someone with an accidental but close interest in the matter, is written in such a free manner that anyone who did not already know the outlines of the story would have extreme difficulty in following it.

Kuppner's introduction then gives the story's outlines and the book takes us through the author's observations of the streets and buildings he inhabits and those where Slater lived decades before. It's a murder mystery of a kind, a portrait of a part of changing Glasgow, and employs Kuppner's personal engagement and self-distancing on every page. It is not quite like anything else.

Kuppner's second 'novel of another sort' was called *A Concussed History of Scotland* (1990) and is also not quite like anything else. Its premise is: 'Scotland's appalling history sits on its back like an incubus. What it needs is a new one.' But Kuppner isn't writing history:

> There is not a single major historical figure in unequivocal sight in this work – although we do glimpse the author from time to time. Instead we

have refracted from the broken crystal shards of a sequence of intense personal experiences, dazzling, witty, lyrical moments, episodes and interchanges which defy reductive and neat pigeon-holing.

Something Very Like Murder (1994) followed the method of *A Very Quiet Street*, extending the provenance from Glasgow to Eastern Europe, looking into family origins, roots and motives. In *Life on a Dead Planet* (1996), 'an unnamed and irresponsible narrator' walks through a city in the twilight, 'looking into lit windows and imagining the life within', picking up strange objects, meeting odd people and imagining their lives, and imagining what the world would be without his presence in it. One short paragraph of speech gives the essential flavour of the book's tone:

'You like doubt, don't you? You sound very keen on it sometimes.'
'I had never thought of it that way. I suppose I do. I prefer health to illness too, by a fairly wide margin, and I suppose that, things being as they actually are, doubt is often something very like mental health.'

In the Beginning There Was Physics (1999) collects short stories, or rather, 'brilliantly observed set pieces' addressing all sorts of odd things, from 'life's little follies to world religions, characters let loose in unnamed cities and the slow termination of the human species.' It is packed with deadpan humour and deadly anecdotes, even-toned and often very funny.

Kuppner's fiction presents an urban, maze-like, mysterious, recognisable but confusing Glasgow – and other bits and pieces of the world – all mapped with forensic accuracy but explored in a fog which makes every co-ordinate point not quite reliable, subtly shifting, sometimes dangerous, occasionally reassuring, sometimes strangely dazzling. Can an obscuring thing dazzle? Reading Kuppner, the answer is very peculiarly affirmative.

Christopher Whyte (b.1952) introduces religious and sexual questions and affirmations which are almost unique in modern Scottish fiction. He began with a wilful subversion of Catholic assumptions in *Euphemia MacFarrigle and the Laughing Virgin* (1995). Set in Glasgow, we have three pregnant virgins in a West End convent, rumours about the extraordinary size of an Episcopalian clergyman's penis, an archbishop beset by a virus that prompts excessive flatulence, a group of respectable middle-class housewives collecting condoms. All these and other phenomena are mysteriously perhaps caused by the eponymous Euphemia. The novel risks outrageous humour not everyone will share – even readers sympathetic to the satiric intent and the indictment of misery brought about by religious and sexual bigotry.

The revisions of expectations of character and location in *The Warlock of*

Strathearn (1997) are less risky as the novel centres on a familiar figure: the shapeshifter, a character who can converse with animals and dead people, heal wounds and impose curses. In an assuring convention, the novel seems to be a translation of an obscure manuscript describing events of the 1640s, but we come to understand the perennial force of prejudice and questions of identity, disposition and choice that can never be fully consigned to history.

Whyte's most original work perhaps is the compendium of different kinds of fiction centred on various experiences of homosexuality, sometimes reticent, sometimes forceful short stories covering a panorama of interlinked experiences in *The Gay Decameron* (1998). The premise is in the title: ten gay men arrive for a dinner party in Edinburgh's New Town. Each has a different story but one becomes immersed in an Oriental tale which appears and reappears at different places in the book, linking the whole narrative effectively as a novel, and giving permission for each man's story to be differentiated. Loss and fear exert their human pressures but the AIDS epidemic forms a pressing historical context where the physical threat of disease is exacerbated by a social world of prejudice and misunderstanding. All these contribute to a consistent dramatic tension in the book and give conviction to the affirmation of hope in its conclusion, when two of the men calmly denounce the lack of imagination blinding so many in Scotland as elsewhere to the fact of difference among people. It is, to so many, 'as if we were immigrants, and could be deported' and the dream would be a 'world without homosexuals' or a 'denellified Scotland' – then the questions come: 'If only they had eyes to see. Who do they think sold them the newspaper they are reading? Did they look at the man who punched their ticket on the train?'

The fear that, as in Hitler's Germany, murderous violence could enforce prejudice to the point of an extinction of knowledge or visibility is answered by the affirmation, rejecting that prospect: 'We'll never go underground again. We're here to stay.'

Whyte's fourth novel, *The Cloud Machinery* (2000), is set in early 18th-century Venice, where a disused theatre is about to be reopened and put on a programme of operas and comedies. However, everyone involved must deal with the aftereffects of what happened when the theatre closed down, a decade earlier. Magical occurrences and detailed descriptions interweave in a rich evocation of the work of theatrical and musical performance in the 18th century and the relation between objective physicality and life's inexplicable pleasures and visions. Machinery, in a theatre, might make clouds move. Yet magic, after all, is what cannot be explained.

There is something of that sense of magic at work in different ways in each of these three novelists. And an abundance of equally unpredicted qualities may be found in a range of their contemporaries. Kirsty Gunn (b.1960), in her novel *The Big Music* (2012), takes a profoundly local contemporary Scottish

Highland family and focusing on the senior male figure and the youngest child circles around their priorities, past and potential, in an elaborate sequence of interwoven chapters dealing with geography, history and the music of the Highland bagpipe, pibroch, or to be accurate, piobaireachd, the big music of the title. The novel is as tense as a short story and as packed with information as an epic. Suhayl Saadi (b.1961), in *Psychoraag* (2004), starts with a Glasgow radio DJ playing the Beatles, the Stranglers and film soundtracks from old, romantic Indian films, then extends the kaleidoscope of music to a shifting panorama of memories ranging from Lahore to Scotland, crossing continents, cultures, languages and personal dispositions and cultural preferences. Aminatta Forna (b.1964), has published a memoir, *The Devil that Danced on the Water* (2002), dealing with her father's execution in the context of the interconnected wars in Sierra Leone, Liberia and Guinea, in the 1990s. In this, like her novels, *Ancestor Stones* (2006), set in West Africa, *The Memory of Love* (2010), set in Sierra Leone, *The Hired Man* (2013), set in Croatia, and *Happiness* (2018), reference to Scotland seems unimportant but born as she was in Bellshill, Lanarkshire, her Scottish ancestry on her mother's side is not to be denied. The first two novels by Luke Sutherland (b.1971), *Jelly Roll* (1998) and *Sweetmeat* (2002) were followed by the novella *Venus as a Boy* (2004), which drew on his experience growing up in the Orkney archipelago as the only Scots-African boy on the islands. He and his sister had been adopted by white parents. It is set on Orkney and in Soho, London, bringing these disparate locations into a continuity based on the unpredicted discoveries and revelations in his own life: magic of another kind.

Alan Bissett (b.1975), gained wide acclaim not only for his novels, *Boyracers* (2001), *The Incredible Adam Spark* (2005), *Death of a Ladies' Man* (2009) and *Pack Men* (2011), and for his hilarious, barbed, affectionate, steely dramatic writing in *The Moira Monologues* (2009, and since revived), but also for his exuberant and persuasive political engagement in the extended satiric poem 'My Contribution to the Debate on Scottish Independence 2014', which he recorded as a straight-to-camera monologue and has gathered thousands of viewers on YouTube. It remains a vigorous, refreshingly unambivalent declaration of love and intention.

The first novel of Kirstin Innes (b.1960), *Fishnet* (2018), focused on the lives of sex workers and her second, *Scabby Queen* (2020) takes as a central character a young, unlikeable woman whose life extends through the first two decades of Scotland in the 2000s. Both novels are demanding, skilfully realigning expectations of sympathetic characterisation and narrative satisfaction, both effectively and memorably challenging not only literary but social conventions.

72

Gaelic fiction in the 21st century: satires, vexations and vicissitudes

TOCASAID 'AIN TUIRC / *The Hogshead of Iain Son of the Boar* (2004) by Donnchadh MacGillìosa / Duncan Gillies is a cycle of stories with recurring characters accumulating the impact of a novel. Its whimsical humour mixes Gaelic and English in unpredicted ways, drawing on both traditional tales and modern idioms and attitudes: comic, rebarbative, celebratory and exhilarating. Gillies followed it with similarly lively material, including *An Còta Dathach agus Deich Sgeulachdan Eile* (2018).

Iain F. MacLeòid's *Na Klondykers / The Klondykers* (2005) opens with the Piper Alpha oil rig disaster, a violent description in which time speeds up or slows down as the narrator-survivor gives his impression of what happened. Then the novel moves to a love story, but the power of the opening stays vivid in memory. *Am Bounty* (2008) is based on the famous historical mutiny in the South Seas, with the main character awaiting execution for his part in it. The novel takes us through the voyage to Tahiti, to the mutiny and its consequences, with a twist in the ending. And MacLeod's *An Sgoil Dhubh* (2014) moves genres from history to science fiction.

Tormod MacGill-Eain / Norman Maclean (1936–2017) was a famous figure in Gaelic life, in Scotland and internationally, through his presence on TV and radio, in his writing and his public performances, and as the translator of Ian Rankin's Rebus novels. He was the only person to be awarded both the Bardic Crown and Gold Medal at the same Royal National Mòd. His written works include *Cùmhnantan / Contracts* (1996; English version 2011), a comic satire on the cut-throat manouevres and interpersonal shenanigans in the 'new world' of Gaelic television and the broadcasting 'business' in the early 1990s. The novel plays seriously with the contrast between a social ethos where legal contracts (or 'promises') are up for unreliable negotiation, and the condition of reliable trust and community associated with a 'home' now left behind. Urban Gaels negotiate a world of greed, lust and crooked deals. Slippery movements between one language and another exemplify the nimble and sometimes inimical actions in which some characters are more adept than others. *Keino* (1998) centres on Eachann MacPhàil, psychologically disturbed, a serial womaniser, helplessly attracted to a married woman, Ealasaid, and fired by the memory of seeing his father having sex years earlier. Descriptions are graphic. The immediacy and speed with which physical encounters take place counterpoint the novel's growing concerns with Eachann's guilt, and his unanswered questions about the need and desire for love. 'Keino' is a betting game which is central in the second half of the novel, a confrontation between Ailidh, Ealasaid's husband, and Eachann. The developing story is an affirmation of the development of strength that comes through the confrontation and endurance of hardship, but the structure of the novel doesn't allow this to arrive in any easy or predictable way.

These were followed by *Dacha Mo Ghaoil / Dearest Dacha* (2005; English version, 2011) and *Slaightearan / Tricksters* (2007; English version, 2011). The former involves three aspiring criminals getting up to various more or less dubious money-making schemes and an overwhelming woman lawyer who sets out to clear the island of crooked practices before HM the Queen comes on a visit. The latter centres on Murdo and Rachel, hopeful actors on a journey around Skye, confronting obstacles like the attractions of alcohol and wastefulness, a manipulative TV director and an unreliable sculptor. These picaresque novellae are a strange, zany blend of comedy and potential grief, moving quickly over dangerous territory while never losing a sense of the comic absurdity of all the actions and characters they describe. Maclean's frank autobiography (in English), *The Leper's Bell: Autobiography of a Changeling* (2009) is a stunning testament to his tendency to self-destruction and innate resilience.

Wild comedy, hard and keen-eyed satire and an acceptance of the prospect of tragic destruction are recurring elements in modern Gaelic fiction. For example, Màiri Anna NicDhòmhnaill's *Cleas Sgàthain* (2008) focuses on identical twin sisters, one in London, one in Uist, who decide to swap places. The potential for comedy and satire is rich. That potential is similarly exploited in Fionnlagh MacLeòid's *Dìomhanas* (2008), which collects 24 short stories, including 'An Cluaisean' / 'The One who Hears', dating from the 1960s. Drawing on its author's interest in psychology and language, it centres on a boy who, after an operation, is able to hear, understand, and respond to Gaelic and English only with different parts of his brain and body. The reactions to this – that it might be a blessing or a curse – are held in play, the writing sensitive to the ambivalence of both comic and tragic potential. In 'Tiop' / 'Chip', the protagonist learns Gaelic by virtue of a chip implanted in his brain. 'An Dachaigh' / 'The Home' and 'Dùsgadh' / 'Awakening' explore the relation between culture, history and location, the latter taking us to New Zealand and exploring the extent to which religious difference might drive individuals so far away from a sense of belonging. Moray Watson describes MacLeòid as a 'virtuoso of the short story'.

Norma NicLeòid's *Dìleas Donn* (2006), takes three characters: Bellann, an islander who left Scotland for Canada, widowed young, returns to Scotland and is now a nurse in Aberdeen, Ailig Iain, father of Bellann's aborted child, and Muriel, his new wife. Ailig and Bellann separated because of their differences in religious faith but when they meet again in Edinburgh their love rekindles.

Bellann becomes pregnant, has the baby, Melanie, and when Muriel learns of the relationship, she suggests that Ailig and Bellann should go on and have another child. It's a complex saga of interpersonal relationships leaving unanswered the question of what might become of Melanie. In the sequel, *Taingeil Toilichte* (2008), set 20 years later, Melanie is taking a degree from Aberdeen University and has a brother, Dòmhnall. She intends to work for a PhD to study the psychological effects of religion in her home community in Lewis, so the personal, domestic, familial stories that unfold open out to social, and indeed political, contexts, suggesting a long, multi-faceted continuity of concerns, extending over generations. The trilogy of which these novels are the first parts was completed with *Suthainn Sìor* (2011).

Catrìona Lexy Chaimbeul's *Samhraidhean Dìomhair / Secret Summers* (2009) has five principal characters, young adults whose lives had been altered at the end of their schooldays some years before the novel takes place, and who are reunited in a journey back to Skye, suspensefully revisiting their earlier lives and finally trying to resolve their unanswered questions.

Alison Lang's stories in *Cainnt na Caileage Caillte / The Lost Girl's Language* (2009) accommodate themes both dark and light. 'Oidhche gun Urnaigh' / 'A Night without a Prayer' in which Gaels attending prayer meetings in Edinburgh, confront questions of sin and guilt, while 'Beul gun Phutan' / 'A Mouth without a Button' presents a family cooking a meal together. Promiscuous sexual relationships, friendships, loyalties and the perennial questions of human potential, are also central themes in other stories.

Am Balach Beag a dh'Èisteadh aig Dorsan / The Little Boy Who Listened at Doors (2018) is a beautifully poised, sensitively pitched novel made up of a series of stories absorbed by the boy of the title, Tormad or, in English, Norrie. It begins:

> 'Every flow must have its ebb,' said the old woman. Each breath caught on the croak in her throat and her aged voice was dry and tuneless, but if it made her companions uncomfortable to hear it they didn't say so.

That opening sentence is a wise motto for the structure of the book, as different stories begin and rise to flow in various chapters, moving at different speeds, sometimes connecting with each other, either engendering the shock of recognition or the puzzlement of something unfinished. Then they ebb away. The power of the story as a genre, how stories are told, how they are understood, is in one sense the central theme of the book.

There's the story of the young girl whose face is disfigured by smallpox but who finds love and happiness with a travelling blind musician whose sensitivity of hearing allows him to appreciate the sweetness of her voice and her singing, bypassing the visual repulsion common among others; there's the story of Iain, pressganged into naval service, whose eventual success as a merchant ship's captain comes at the cost of his wife marrying and having a family with someone else; there's the story of the last woman to engage in waulking the tweed and what became of the cloth and the spell she put upon it, when it returns via different owners, via Cambridge, back to the island; and there's the story of the boy's own family background, and what his father might have become, and where he might have been.

At the end of the book, the 'old woman' at its beginning, Marjory, is ill and not likely to recover. Tormad / Norrie, looking from the garden towards her house, sees a man walking on the road but when he looks again the man has gone. The man is too far away to make out clearly but echoes the mysterious presence of his own father, who appears, and disappears, at odd points in the narrative. His story is not fully told. Norrie and his mother live on their own and the boy visits an old man, Ruaraidh, who tells him a range of stories, all disclosing more or less reliable aspects of truth and wisdom, and who turns out to be his grandfather. The mystery of the boy's family history is disclosed gradually, and the whole book is rich with complementary, contradictory, fantastic or mundane tales of recent or distant history, conveyed with the delicate, vulnerable optimism that animates the boy's curiosity. The cusp of childhood and adult understanding is gently evoked, the characters deftly individuated, the small town community with its networks of support and traps of gossip and petty jealousy is delivered with assurance. A sense of disclosing just the right amount of information in each chapter is sustained throughout.

In the opening, Marjory, the old woman, goes on to say this: 'There's a skerry just beyond the shore that's only visible at very low tide.' This prompts the reflection:

> This was not how Norrie had expected the story to continue, but it had been going round in circles as it was – something old women often did, coming back to an earlier point in the tale and going over the same thing again. It was a quirk that annoyed Norrie.

But it's a technique that the novel employs to great effect.

The child, the adult, folk in old age, isolated individuals and close-knit communities, local realities and the wide world beyond horizons, all come into play, and the novel might stand as a signal of the potential achieved as well as the potential still latent in modern Gaelic fiction. I don't mean to suggest that potential is unfulfilled, only that there are always more stories to be told. There is more than one way forward for modern Gaelic literature. Its place and unpredictable movement continue to be essential in the weave and weft of the whole fabric of Scotland.

All I've been able to do in these chapters on Gaelic fiction is to introduce some of the work I have come to learn about, including work I have had access to only through the essays and critical accounts of others far more familiar than I am with the language in which the fiction is written. I should also note Alison Lang's *An Aisling*, which is an account of contemporary Scottish young middle-class society, and Seonag Monk's *Mil san Ti?* which is a novel whose characters are almost all female and takes the reader deep into differences of personality and psychology. I must thank Alison Lang, who allowed me to read her English translation of *Am Balach Beag a dh'Èisteadh aig Dorsan* and I should also note those extracts from some of the novels and stories in the anthology *The Highest Apple*. Of course, if I knew the language well enough and had full access to all the material, the account I've given in these chapters would have been very different. But that must wait until I know the language better. All I hope I've done is show that there's a plenitude of material there most English-language readers might not have suspected.

If – as one hopes – Gaelic increases its provenance, and more people speak and read it, and inhabit the world of its language, there will be less need to provide translations. Already for some people it is unfashionable and in fact objectionable to do so. If what I've written is no more than a prompt and reminder, I hope my readers who know better than I will forgive my transgressions.

73

Playwrights and plays: from Robert Kemp to Liz Lochhead

FROM THE 1950s to the 1970s, from Robert Kemp to C.P. Taylor and Liz Lochhead, Scottish plays encompassed a staggering range of themes, ideas, locations and characters.

A little while after James Bridie was establishing the Citizens' Theatre in Glasgow, in 1953, in Edinburgh, the Gateway Theatre – a property which had been gifted to the Church of Scotland in 1946 and became home to a range of professional and community theatre groups – was let by the Kirk to a professional independent theatre company led by the actor and writer Tom Fleming, the playwright and novelist Robert Kemp, and Lennox Milne, one of Scotland's leading women actors of the period. Times had changed from the opposition of some in the Kirk to Home's *Douglas*, nearly two centuries earlier.

The Gateway Company produced plays by contemporary Scottish dramatists as well as international classics, performed by some of Scotland's finest actors. When the Edinburgh corporation acquired the Royal Lyceum and established a civic theatre in 1965, the company unselfishly resolved to wind itself up so that available Arts Council support for professional theatre in Edinburgh would not be spread too thin. In effect the Gateway Company morphed into the Royal Lyceum Theatre Company. Tom Fleming became the first artistic director of the new Lyceum company. The Kirk retained the theatre for around two more years before selling it to Scottish Television to be its Edinburgh studios and using the proceeds to establish the Netherbow Theatre in the High Street, virtually next door to where Allan Ramsay's Carrubber's Close Theatre had been before it was suppressed in 1737.

In the 1950s, Orcadian Robert Kemp (1908–67), chair of the Gateway, wrote a number of plays with Scottish historical settings (three are focused on John Knox, Robert the Bruce and Robert Burns) as well as a wonderful version of Molière in Scots: *Let Wives Tak Tent* (1947). This free translation of *L'école des femmes* (1662) (*The School for Wives*) was performed by the Compagnie Jouvet of Paris at the Edinburgh International Festival in 1947. Kemp followed this with *The Laird o' Grippy* (1955), based on *L'Avare* (1668) (*The Miser*). Meanwhile Douglas Young (1913–73) produced Scots-language versions of Aristophanes in *The Puddocks* (1957) and *The Burdies* (1959). Alexander Reid (1914–82) based *The Lass wi' the Muckle Mou* on the story of Thomas the Rhymer and *The Warld's Wonder* on the wizard Michael Scott, both plays set in the Borders. Sydney Goodsir Smith (1915–75) produced an immensely popular, unambiguous, unsubtle and unashamedly partisan historical pageant in *The Wallace* (1960). Alexander Scott (1920–89), distinguished poet and first Head of the Department of Scottish Literature at Glasgow University, produced in *Right Royal* (1954) a flamboyant work centred on the rascally King Dod of Fife. Stanley Eveling (1925–2008), based in Edinburgh, flourished in the 1960s with sometimes absurd, quasi-surrealist or politically speculative plays such as *The Balachites* (1963), *The Strange Case of Martin Richter* (1967), *The Lunatic* (1968), *Vibrations* (1969), *Better Days, Better Knights* (1971) and *Union Jack (and Bonzo)* (1973).

To a greater or lesser degree, all these playwrights were engaged by Scottish history, translating from other cultures, languages and historical eras, employing naturalist conventions or surrealist innovations, and applying their imaginations rigorously to contemporary assumptions and conditions in Scotland.

Scottish history also informed Hector MacMillan (1929–2018) in *The Rising* (1973), about the insurrection of 1820 and *The Royal Visit* (1974), about King George IV in Edinburgh in 1822 but contemporary issues are at the heart of *The Sash* (1973), about religious sectarianism, and *The Gay Gorbals* (1976), which addresses then-current attitudes to homosexuality in Scotland. Stewart Conn (b.1936), in *I Didn't Always Live Here* (1967) and *Play Donkey* (1977), presented contemporary settings, while *The Burning* (1971), enacts the intense power struggle between King James VI and the Earl of Bothwell; *Thistlewood* (1975) centres on the Cato Street Conspiracy of 1820; *Herman* (1981) sees the author of *Moby-Dick* pursued by his own tormentors as the whale was by its, and *Hugh Miller* (1988) is a one-man play about the 19th-century stonemason and writer beset by self-doubt in the Godless universe. Donald Campbell (1940–2019) in *The Jesuit* (1976) wrote searchingly about religious conviction, goodness, persecution and martyrdom, while his *The Widows of Clyth* (1979) movingly explored the lives and bereavements of fishermen's wives in his ancestral Caithness. Tom McGrath (1940–2009) in *The Hardman* (1977) focused on the life of convicted murderer Jimmy Boyle, looking at what drives such a man to violence and what might promise redemption. Bill Bryden (1942–2022) explored the ideals and disappointments of Red Clydeside in *Willie Rough* (1972).

Though of an older generation, C.P. Taylor (1929–81), in *Good* (1981; film version 2008), describes the corruption of a German university teacher as he unwittingly rationalises his complicity in Nazism and ultimately finds himself caught up in 'the final solution' of genocidal murder. It is a terrifying play but he wrote around 70 others, again testifying to the abundant quantity of under-researched work in Scottish theatrical literature.

Taylor's *Good* and Tom Gallacher's *Mr Joyce is Leaving Paris* (1970) – to take only two examples – show conclusively how effectively Scottish playwrights could write without reference to Scotland. Tony Roper (b.1941), in *The Steamie*

(1987) shows the other side of this coin. Here is a very specific location and historical moment in Scotland, where the dialogue of Scotswomen busy at the regular communal washing in the industrial city opens up an entire society, its prejudices, loves and social structures of support and humour, but without over-sentimentalising working-class experience. It is a fond play, and the emotions it evokes are generally warm, but these women are credible, sometimes nasty, and their limitations are always evident. And yet there is a common factor of decency at work and a quality of resilience in the humour. For a contrasting vision of the women of the steamies, Ralph Glasser's memoir *Growing Up in the Gorbals* is a sobering corrective.

The sheer range of these plays – historical, contemporary, set in specific Scottish locations or internationally, translated from classical French or ancient Greek, nationalist by declaration, anti-Fascist by commitment and expressiveness – testifies to the wealth of Scottish theatrical history and the bulging file of plays that should be immediately available for revival and new performance and study, research and reconsideration. These plays amount to a sizeable steely gauntlet thrown down on the marble floor of common cultural indifference – or even hostility – to Scotland's literary history and vibrant potential. The question is, where does that indifference or hostility come from? And the next question is not how to oppose it, but how to end it, once and for all.

Throughout the 20th and 21st centuries, Scottish drama entwines revaluations, adaptations and new productions in a process of rediscovery and reassessment. *The Cheviot, the Stag and the Black, Black Oil* was as much of its moment in the early 1970s as *Ane Satyre of the Thrie Estaitis* was of its, in the 1550s. Revivals of both these plays have had to balance recognition of historical locations on the clock with the renewing value of contemporary application: how do we tell the stories about what really matters to new generations?

That question became especially pressing in the 1970s and increasingly since the 1980s. After the Second World War, the *Satyre* was freshly produced in 1948, revised by Robert Kemp and directed by Tyrone Guthrie, then in the 1980s a new production by the Scottish Theatre Company directed by Tom Fleming addressed a new generation. In 1996, a completely different play prompted by Lyndsay and satirising (among other things) the corruption of the popular press, was written by John McGrath and performed by Wildcat as *The Satire of the Four Estates*. In 2002, Alan Spence revised it as *The 3 Estaites: the Millennium Version*. An interdisciplinary research project led by scholars from Edinburgh and Brunel Universities staged a full-length production employing many of the finest of the Scottish acting community in 2013, the record of which can be visited on the website at: stagingthescottishcourt.brunel.ac.uk. *The Cheviot* was revived in 2015 by Dundee Rep, directed by Joe Douglas, also receiving high critical praise and achieving popular appeal, more than 40 years since its first production. In *The Herald* newspaper (8 September 2015), Douglas commented: 'I think the play is totally right for now and feels brand new.'

Revival is a form of translation through time. The long tradition of plays in translation from other languages and different cultures always has close pertinence in a Scotland where people are questioning their own lack of statehood and the status of their languages. There are many examples in major works by Liz Lochhead, Edwin Morgan, Hector MacMillan, David Harrower, John Byrne, Robert David MacDonald, Peter Arnott, Ian Brown, David Greig and Rona Munro, translating plays by Molière, Racine, Gogol, Brecht, Genet, Lorca and versions of ancient Greek tragedies.

While these Scottish playwrights worked over decades after the Second World War, the playwrights whose works they have translated come from various European languages and across centuries. Meantime, Bill Findlay, a Scot, and Martin Bowman, a Canadian of Scottish descent, translated eight plays by the Canadian playwright Michel Tremblay from Joual, the Quebec dialect of French, into a vibrant contemporary Scots, thus translating not only from one language to another, but from one political culture to a sister culture, both facing comparable dilemmas.

Liz Lochhead (b.1947) began publishing poems and dramatic monologues, portraits in voices, in the 1970s and 1980s. She was to write a series of plays drawing on feminist, Gothic, Scottish historical and contemporary linguistic resources, with *Blood and Ice* (1982), *Dracula* (1985), *Tartuffe* (translated into Scots, 1985) and most emphatically in *Mary Queen of Scots Got Her Head Chopped Off* (1987). Here, La Corbie, the chorus-like commentator on the action, a 'ragged ambiguous creature', introduces the main subject of the play, not simply Mary herself, but the nation:

LA CORBIE: Country: Scotland.
Whit like is it?
It's a peatbog, it's a daurk forest.
It's a cauldron o' lye, a saltpan or a coal mine.
If you're gey lucky it's a bricht bere meadow or a park o' kye.
Or mibbe... it's a field o' stanes.
It's a tenement hoose or a humble cot. Princes Street or Paddy's Merkit.
It's a fistfu' o' fish or a pickle o' oatmeal.
It's a queen's banquet o' roast meat and junketts.
It depends. It depends... Ah dinna ken whit your Scotland is. Here's mines.
National flower: the thistle.
National pastime: nostalgia.
National weather: smirr, haar, drizzle, snow.
National bird: the crow, the corbie, le corbeau, moi!

If we imagine the play 'set' in Mary's time of late 16th-century Scotland, references in that speech to the peatbog and forest draw on prehistory and the coal mine and tenements are prophecies of an industrial future. This opening monologue is a panorama of eras, revolving around the perspective of the carrion crow, a hideous dancer, nourished on roadkill, part scavenger, part parish priest, a minister skating on very thin ice. Youthful energy and childish glee are mixed with adult cruelty and consequence. The whole play keeps these connected. The play's title is the name of a children's game, with the actors representing the major historical characters both as adults and as children in a contemporary school playground. Playful? Yes, but ultimately, it's a deadly pageant of political entrapment and encroaching power.

The play asks us to consider how history is passed on to younger generations, through icons of divisiveness, religions of hatred and a politics of competing powers. In one memorable production, the climax was a dance of the characters around a maypole, long red ribbons stretching down from the top of the pole into the characters' hands. As they danced in devious rings, the ribbons encircled Mary's neck, until there was no way out. The children at play had become adults at the execution. The final image of Mary, the crimson bands around her throat, her pale hands raised, in silence, holds us – and then blackout!

Lochhead has gone further in *Medea* (2000) and *Thebans* (2003), adapting ancient Greek plays by Euripides and Sophocles with immediate impact. Her translations of these plays show her deep and intuitive grasp of the full sense of tragedy, addressing issues of feminism, self-destructiveness, social positioning and the extremes of passionate response. She brings these issues into Scotland with crafty, subtle and immensely powerful effect, enhancing cultural self-confidence and endorsing a political ideal of self-determination the establishment will always want to suppress.

Lochhead's sophisticated retellings of the Greek plays in 21st-century Scotland went hand-in-hand with her work in small theatre venues, such as *Piece of My Heart* (2007), a three-hander set in a kitchen with two students, Susie and Nick, and their landlady, Aggie. Love, sexuality, caring, death and old age are all there, lightly, movingly, unpretentiously delineated. It was written for Òran Mór, a converted church in Glasgow's west end, which established an annual lunchtime series, 'A Play, a Pie and a Pint', where folk could come in, buy a ticket, a drink and a bite to eat, and be entertained for an hour by a short play. Some of the best contemporary writers as well as newcomers writing first plays contributed to the Òran Mór seasons. In *Educating Agnes* (2008), Lochhead revised Molière's *School for Wives* (1662) and referred to Robert Kemp's Scots language version of 1948, *Let Wives Tak Tent*. Kemp's version is a lasting masterpiece of writing in Scots for theatrical performance. Lochhead's version does not supersede it but demonstrates how a play, as a work of literature, is not an unassailable, immaculate text, but engaged in contemporary dialogue with its audience, a crafted articulation in an immediate space. This sense of plays as practice, as opposed to immutable, individual masterworks, is carried forward in early 21st-century work by, for example, Anthony Neilson, Henry Adam and Douglas Maxwell.

To quote David Hutchison, 'the essence of the theatrical experience' is, always, 'Liveness'. That plays are 'live' rather than fixed artefacts is the key.

74

Plays: future prospects and past performance

THE COMPLEMENTARITY OF studious close reading with performativity and theatrical effect is continual but, as we have seen, it is not constant. In the history of performance, theatricality and drama in Scotland – and all these words have distinctive, if related, meanings – different kinds of plays are abundantly evident. And since so many plays await revival, much remains to be done.

A multitude of plays are stored in the archive, awaiting new productions. They constitute a silent, profound, multi-faceted, under-researched resource. For example, the plays by Joan Ure (Elizabeth Clark Thomson, 1918–78) have languished unperformed for a long time and reconsideration of their value is long overdue. Her first play, *Cendrillon*, was written in French for a fourth-year school class performance, and might be entirely of its place and moment, but she worked with Ian Hamilton Finlay at the Falcon Theatre in 1962, and her two short plays *Something in it for Cordelia* and *Something in it for Ophelia* centre on Shakespearian questions of sexuality and potential unfulfilled. Their concerns are as pertinent as ever.

Many of the collected poems of Scotland's first Scots Makar, or National Poet, Edwin Morgan, are characteristically theatrical. They enable different voices. 'The Apple's Song' or 'Hyena' or 'The Loch Ness Monster's Song' are effectively dramatic monologues, ideal for performance. This is surely the sexiest apple you've ever encountered:

> hold me, sniff me, peel me
> curling round and round
> till I burst out white and cold
> from my tight red coat
> and tingle in your palm

And the hyena is so much more than an African scavenger – his power is metaphoric, and deadly:

> I am waiting
> for the foot to slide,
> for the heart to seize,
> for the leaping sinews to go slack,
> for the fight to the death to be fought to the death...

> My place is to pick you clean
> and leave your bones to the wind.

Morgan developed this performative capacity in his dialogue or multi-vocal poems such as 'The First Men on Mercury' or the horrific 'Stobhill', in which various characters reflect on the reported incident of a still-alive newly aborted foetus being taken away to be incinerated. We hear the voices and understand the points of view of the doctor, the boilerman, the mother, the father and the porter, with an increasing sense of horror and sympathy. One of Morgan's earliest poems, 'The Whittrick' (1961, but not published until 1971), is a series of eight dialogues between famous characters – James Joyce and Hugh MacDiarmid, Hieronymus Bosch and Johann Faust, Queen Shahrazad and King Shahriyar, Charlotte and Emily Brontë, Marilyn Monroe and Galina Ulanova, The Brahan Seer and Lady Seaforth, Hakuin (the founder of modern Zen) and Chikamitsu (the 'Japanese Shakespeare'), Dr Grey Walter of the Burden Neurological Institute, author of *The Living Brain* (1953) and Jean Cocteau. Coruscating verbal wit, a sense of the speed of good repartee, and Morgan's ventriloquist's expertise all fuel the poem's lively theatricality. Teachers looking for Scottish plays might start here: not only dramatic dialogues but fascinating characters engaged in them.

Morgan's early plays in translation, *The Apple-Tree* (1982, from a medieval Dutch play) and *Master Peter Pathelin* (1983, from an anonymous 15th-century French farce) were followed by his magnificent 1992 translation of Edmond de Rostand's *Cyrano de Bergerac* (1897) and in 2000 by Racine's *Phaedre* (1677). These last two plays radically revise the language and formal proprieties of the originals, transferring their impact by use of Scots and contemporary references. In production, their popular success and literary brilliance are dazzling, exhilarating, bringing de Rostand and Racine to new Scottish audiences with an unpredicted immediacy.

In A.D.: *A Trilogy of Plays on the Life of Christ* (2000), Morgan treated the Bible story on the premise that Christ was a historical man who actually lived, reimagining his life for a modern audience. Temptations were actual, on stage, not locked within an orthodoxy of moral certainty. The plays offended leading members of various parts of the Christian church but remain triumphant achievements in Morgan's ouevre. Essential aspects of Morgan's personal credo are given voice when Jesus says: 'Take a crossbow to the bloated belly of convention' and explains, 'The kingdom of heaven is not a thing. / Nor is it a place, it is alive, it grows.' For 'in the midst of life I find myself in art. / In the midst of art I find myself in life.' Morgan's last major work for theatre was *The Play of Gilgamesh* (2005), deriving from a 5,000-year-old story recorded in one of the earliest known works of literature from ancient Sumer. In December 2021, an original 3,500-year-old clay tablet bearing a portion of the words of the epic poem was returned by the USA, to its place of origin, Iraq, from which it had been looted from a museum in the 1991 Gulf War. Morgan's play spans the western world's entire literary history and addresses the most profound and perennial questions.

Just as Morgan in his plays of Christ and Gilgamesh goes back in time to find contemporary questions of power and sexuality, in the fraught political and religious context of late 20th- and 21st-century Scotland, Jackie Kay brought keen perspectives to conventional representations of sexual identities, from *Chiaroscuro* (1986) to *The Maw Broon Dialogues* (2009). Sue Glover in *Bondagers* (1991), set in the rural landscape of the Borders in the 19th century, where women were exploited as labourers in the fields, Chris Hannan in *Shining Souls* (1996) and *Elizabeth Gordon Quinn* (1985; revised 2006), set in the Glasgow rent strike of 1915 with one of the strongest, most complex women characters in modern Scottish drama, and Rona Munro in *The Last Witch* (2009) and *The James Plays* (2014), an epic trilogy taking us across three generations of Scottish kings in the 15th century, have all written work drawing on history, demanding detailed study, and delivering the pleasures of live immediacy in performance. Indeed, a 'school of women playwrights' has been noted in this constellation: not only Sue Glover and Rona Munro but also Ann Marie Di Mambro, whose *Tally's Blood* (1990) addresses the fact of immigration, in this case of Italians living in the west of Scotland before, through, and after the Second World War, Sharman Macdonald, Marcella Evaristi, Catherine Lucy Czerkawska, Aileen Ritchie, Linda McLean and others. However, they cannot be easily grouped in any other way, since their work is intrinsically so diverse.

We've already noted the novelist, short story writer and poet Alan Spence, who, as a playwright, produced in *Sailmaker* (1982) a play of eminent practical use in schools, while in *No Nothing* (2015), a two-actor play imagining the politician Jimmy Reid and the poet Edwin Morgan meeting after death in an ante-room to who-knows-where, Spence presented an adult, but undeniably gamesome and sometimes very funny work in which the lives of two of the most significant public figures in modern Scotland introduce themselves to each other and to new generations of audiences with unpretentious immediacy. The pathos is deep, the humour comforting, but the serious and unresolved political questions stay sharp.

Playwrights such as Peter Arnott, David Greig, David Harrower, Ian Brown, Gregory Burke, Nicola McCartney, Rona Munro, Chris Dolan and others have demonstrated again and again, writing in both Scots and English, how historical characters and stories may be trans-historically pertinent in their themes and language, in plays closely focused on contemporary events, not least the question of the state of Scotland's national political identity. They have also written plays set in a Scotland more-or-less 'contemporary' with the time of their first productions. The pertinence of history in the exercise of national identity is crucial. And here's the lesson: Nationality cannot ever be only contemporary.

This applies closely to the plays of Peter Arnott, whose experimental epic *Thomas Muir's Voyage to Australia* (1986), about the Scottish radical reformer at the time of the French Revolution, was a powerful reminder of Muir's importance at a period when was underappreciated.

Arnott, with *White Rose* at the Traverse, Edinburgh, in 1985 (centred on Lily Litvak, also known as Lydia or Lilya, the only woman Russian fighter-pilot at the siege of Stalingrad in the Second World War), and *Thomas Muir's Voyage to Australia* in the Tron Theatre, Glasgow, in 1986, produced respectively one of the most intense plays and one of the most epic and expansive plays, both addressing themes of love, struggle, justice and the ideals of democratic socialism under oppression. The first production of *White Rose* at the Traverse, on a small, intimately lit stage, with a young Tilda Swinton in the main role, supported by a young Ken Stott, was unforgettable. It was 1985, with Margaret Thatcher's Conservative Government in its second term, miners throughout Britain on strike, and women setting a determined example of protest against nuclear weaponry at Greenham Common. The political atmosphere was packed with pressure.

Thomas Muir's Voyage to Australia was put on at the Tron Theatre in three substantial, text-rich acts, with trial scene, flogging, the sea journey to Australia and the revolutionary prospect of the future. *The Tom Muir Transportation Show* (also 1986) was a short version of the same story performed by young actors from the back of a lorry parked in the streets of Glasgow. The 'liveness' of both productions was vivid.

In the previous decade, Ian Brown, in *Carnegie* (1973), exposed the famous Scottish philanthropist as a brutal exploiter of his workers and partners in a way controversial at the time. Similarly, Brown's *Mary* (1977) defamiliarised the conventional characterisation of Mary Queen of Scots by presenting her career in different theatrical forms.

Other plays by Arnott and Brown exemplify this theme of 'the pertinence of history': for example, Arnott's *The Boxer Benny Lynch* (1985), set in Glasgow in the 1930s and 1940s, and his adaptations of Neil Gunn's *The Silver Darlings*, set in the early 19th century, and of Robin Jenkins's *The Cone-Gatherers*, set during the Second World War. Brown's *The Scotch Play* (1991), is a five-scene play in blank verse based on *Macbeth* and set in a contemporary football club, while in *A Great Reckonin'* (2000), the Royal Company of Guisers, imagined as King James I's own court theatre company, reconstructs the life of the king after his assassination, and *An Act o Love* (2011), is written in Scots and based on Le Roy Ladurie's study of a 14th-century French village, *Montaillou*. The key critical text considering the pre-eminence of historical subjects in modern Scottish plays and the pertinence of history in contemporary times is Brown's

History as Theatrical Metaphor: History, Myth and National Identities in Modern Scottish Drama (2016).

One of the most internationally renowned plays of the early 21st century was Gregory Burke's *Black Watch* (first performed at the Edinburgh Festival in 2006, embarking on a world tour in 2007). The play catches the language, strengths, suspicions and cares of a group of young Scottish soldiers in Iraq, their sense of where they are, what their best resources lie in, and whose power they are under. It brought onto the stage the language and lives of the individuals in the context of western ideological priorities in the 'war against terror', and difficult enquiries into specific Scottish conditions, such as the relation between unemployment and army recruitment, Scottish military history in both pro-Union and Scottish national causes and non-national issues like loyalty, state control of young lives, cynicism, idealism, sexism, racism, destructive energies and the function of performance in speech, action and theatrical representation, both on stage and in the so-called 'theatre' of war. Its contemporaneity was fierce, drawing deep questions up from the history of Scotland. Script and choreography utilised both playwriting traditions and the history of military spectacle enshrined in the annual Military Tattoo at Edinburgh Castle, one of the most bankable events of the International Festivals. (Technically, the Tattoo is separate from the 'official' Edinburgh International Festival but part of the joint organisation supporting all the Festivals.)

In performance, *Black Watch* is also an astonishing piece of choreographed action, depicting horrors in spectacular visual motion, sometimes ballet-like, ostensibly to bring about a Brechtian distancing from any ideas of easy commitment or simple solution. Arguably, however, it stresses an emotionally sympathetic response to the main characters as opposed to a more coldly objective understanding of their position and is therefore less Brechtian in effect than it seems. Had the work of the Black Watch in Northern Ireland been depicted our sympathies might be more compromised.

Trish Reid, in *Theatre & Scotland* (2013), notes that Anthony Neilson, in his play *Relocated* (2008), makes it 'difficult for audiences to distinguish between fantasy and reality or indeed develop a clear sense of the basis on which its characters are drawn'. This connects the play to an essential characteristic of modern Scottish literature more generally: the move beyond realism. It is most clearly seen in three works in three literary genres of the 1980s: Alasdair Gray's novel *Lanark* (1981), Edwin Morgan's sequence of poems, *Sonnets from Scotland* (1984) and Liz Lochhead's play *Mary Queen of Scots Got Her Head Chopped Off* (1987).

Each of these works radically destabilises what would normally be called 'realism'. In *Lanark*, a dark fantasy of socially thwarted people counterpoints a realist account of an artist growing up in Glasgow; in *Sonnets from Scotland*, the nation is conjured up before prehistory, through actual and imagined events – historical visitors to Scotland like Edgar Allan Poe and Gerard Manley Hopkins, a nuclear explosion, a newly-established Republic of Scotland which itself passes away in time – to a future as yet unrealised (for example, a broad canal stretching along the border with England). Lochhead's play weaves historical characters into their descendants, children in a school playground, imagining what horrible belief systems are maintained across generations and taken to murderous extremes. The work of the imagination in these literary texts is as vital as the accurate understanding of history and human character. And this is the irreplaceable value of the arts in the prospect and construction of an independent Scotland.

In her book, Trish Reid is led to a crucial conclusion:

> [Modern Scottish playwrights,] by engaging with a wide range of discourses of identity, including class, gender, ethnicity and multiculturalism, have insisted that if the notion of an inclusive and heterogeneous Scotland is to be taken seriously, the country must carefully consider how such positive ambitions are to be culturally animated and not simply take them for granted.

This is the core argument which has been running throughout my account of the history of Scottish plays and performances and it extends to all the arts. How can an independent Scotland encompass our own cultural plurality and animate the character and quality of our arts internationally, self-confidently, without pretensions of superiority but in the full knowledge of our inherited file of cultural achievement?

Learning about what our writers, artists and composers have done is the only secure foundation for independence. Without them, we are nothing but what Ezra Pound once called 'a mere barbarian dung-heap'.

The work of revaluing and revising that inherited file goes on within education, as much as I and my colleagues can help to make it happen, but it is also the provenance of the writers and artists themselves. For example, David Greig's *The Strange Undoing of Prudencia Hart* (2011) makes immediate use of music hall and variety traditions as well as older literary forms, particularly drawing from Walter Scott's *Minstrelsy of the Scottish Border* (1802). The world of medieval border ballads, with their rhyme, meter and supernatural themes and questions about the authority and vulnerability of women in society are central in *Prudencia Hart*. The play is designed for performance by a small group of actor-musicians in pubs or common rooms rather than traditional theatres.

All Greig's plays demonstrate the liveliness of an engaged and enquiring imagination healthily exploring ideas and willing to risk failure in the attempt.

His earlier work, *Europe* (1994), set in a railway station waiting room with refugees about to move between different countries, is redolent with both existential questions and immediately effective political point, all the more pertinent in the 2020s. *Dunsinane* (2010) centres on the historical figure of Gruach (aka Lady Macbeth), picking up where Shakespeare's play ends, but with the Queen still alive and in charge of bringing the next generation through and seeing off the occupying army. Matters of feminine and national empowerment and self-determination in the face of military intervention and political oppression are all here and applicable to more than one circumstance. Their relevance – metaphoric or otherwise – to contemporary Scotland is unmistakeable.

The key here is that sense of 'liveness' and risk that we've noted before. Fixed and unchangeable definitions of 'Scottishness', to quote Trish Reid once again, 'work to freeze the culture rather than allowing scope for variation and development.' If this is true of theatrical practice, and must be avoided, it is as true in the real, quotidian political world. Neither plays nor governments can afford to be fixed, formed and unchanging. The result of that is stasis, stagnation and sterility: a world of bias and thwart, fear and frustration.

Numerous playwrights working in the late 20th and early 21st centuries have taken up the challenge of 'variation and development': for example, John, later Jo, Clifford, in *Losing Venice* (1985), a tense parable about military occupation which toured internationally in the wake of the Falklands war; John McKay in *Dead Dad Dog* (1988), where the ghost of a father dogs the heels of the would-be trendy son; Stephen Greenhorn, in *Passing Places* (1997), in which two young men from small town post-industrial Lanarkshire flee away on a road trip through Scotland, heading through the Highlands to John o' Groats, confronting urban and rural identities, threatened violence and promised civility, delivering comic effect and serious questions as Scotland is introduced to its various 'selves'. Another example of exploring varieties of identity from the 1990s was the company Suspect Culture, actor/director Graham Eatough, playwright David Greig, composer/musician Nick Powell and designer Ian Scott, who, in a series of works crossing the conventional boundaries of various art forms, collaborated with artists in Scotland and throughout Europe, to become established as one of Scotland's leading companies.

New Scottish plays, the revival of older ones, and the replenishment of theatrical culture through encounters with new or neglected national and changing international contexts, are all of essential value.

One essential for the reappraisal that might lead to revival is fluent understanding of the languages of Scotland – Gaelic and Scots, as well as English – in which Scottish literature has been predominantly produced. Another is the collaboration between professionals in theatre and professional scholars and literary historians, to identify and help select work of both literary and theatrical vitality. That vitality becomes thin and irrelevant the further it is removed from literary substance. Literary drama becomes stodgy and dull the further it is removed from theatrical performance, presence and movement. Plays, performances and theatres of all kinds, have proven this through centuries. If anything worthwhile has come from the 'lockdowns' during the COVID pandemic of the early 2020s, it's surely the value of living presence.

What I've said about plays and theatre history applies to all the arts of Scotland. The arts are the genius of your country. Without them, you have nothing. And education is the key. That's the only way we unlock the door to independence.

75

Plays in Gaelic: on the page and on the stage

IN THE COURSE of this book, we've considered the history of Scottish plays, performances and theatres across centuries, introducing many works in Scots and English – but now we need to shift our thinking. The Gaelic world is different.

Start with the role of the seanchaidh, the storyteller, in traditional Gaelic society, a role that could be compared to that of both dramatist and actor, not just telling, but performing stories to an audience. And further: the storyteller and the bard could also be a genealogist and historian, and may have played music as part of the production, so could have been a composer as well. And consider folk drama, sometimes involving an element of dance, and the Gaelic-language tradition of the cèilidh, a celebratory gathering with communal performance, including song and monologue as well as storytelling. These performance forms were widespread in Gaelic culture, and after the Clearances, they travelled and settled themselves in industrial Scottish cities. Michelle Macleod alerts us to these components of Gaelic theatricality in her essay 'Gaelic drama: the forgotten genre in Gaelic literary studies', in *Lainnair a' Bhùirn – The Gleaming Water: Essays on Modern Gaelic Literature*, edited by Emma Dymock and Wilson McLeod (2011). And Adrienne Scullion has suggested that such songs and performances contributed importantly to the development of a specifically Scottish form of popular music hall performance. In the literary tradition, there were the còmhraidhean, or written dialogues, popularised by the Rev. Norman MacLeod ('Caraid nan Gàidheal', 1783–1862), published in Gaelic periodicals and collected in anthologies. MacLeod might be considered the first author of Gaelic plays as performed in the theatre tradition, which, of course, usually arises in an urbanised economy from which, for many centuries, the Gàidhealtachd was free.

Michelle Macleod identifies two ways of exploring the origins of drama in general: one is the concept of 'performance' and the other the development of the dramatic 'text'. Performativity is and always has been a key component in civic, social, political, even intellectual life. The courtroom is an intrinsically theatrical scenario. Its counterpoint is passivity, contemplation, resignation or resolution. Performance requires action. Friedrich Nietzsche summarized this most memorably in Part 4 of *Beyond Good and Evil* (1886): 'What? A great man? I always see only the actor of his own ideal.' Macleod's proposition suggests two ways of understanding drama: one, a capacity of engagement with others through acting, through gesture, in performance, and the other a literary text to be used in productions, a basis for performance, which mediates between the social world of day-to-day actuality and the political, domestic, human events from which an audience of civilians is normally drawn to witness, attend to, and learn from the production of this 'text'.

The play, Hamlet says, is where he'll catch the guilty conscience of the King. Plays are traps for the unwary, exhibitions, exercises for the speculating mind, tests for experimentation, staged constructions for trying out ideas, alternative prospects, interpretations of past events, thoughts about what might happen next, prompts for further understanding.

In the 'Drama' section of the essay by Michelle Macleod and Moray Watson, 'In the Shadow of the Bard: The Gaelic Short Story, Novel and Drama since the Early Twentieth Century', in *The Edinburgh History of Scottish Literature, volume 3: Modern Transformations: New Identities (from 1918)*, edited by Ian Brown, co-edited by Thomas Owen Clancy, Susan Manning and Murray Pittock (2007), we're told that Archibald Maclaren's *The Humours of Greenock Fair* (1789) and *The Highland Drover* (1790), include dialogue in Gaelic, in the latter case without any translation being implied in the English-speaking characters' responses. These were apparently performed in Inverness, Aberdeen, Perth, Dundee and Greenock. These towns are all on the borders of then Gaelic-speaking areas, Greenock being a major fishing port with a large seasonal population of fishermen from all over the West Coast, so audiences for these plays were quite probably bilingual in Gaelic and English. Audience records from the late 1700s are scarce, but these plays were successful enough to be toured around theatres close to the Gàidhealtachd.

Of all the literary arts, drama, with its need to employ actors and technical staff, is the most immediately dependent upon financial support. This usually comes through the box-office. Managers don't tour plays that aren't making money around five theatres, let alone ones as relatively far apart as these were. Clearly Maclaren's plays incorporating dialogue in Gaelic were successful in their time.

The seminal modern play about multilingual identity and its political and social contexts is Brian Friel's *Translations* (1980), set in Donegal in 1833. Irish, Latin and Greek are familiar in the local village school but when Irish and English characters speak to each other they are mutually incomprehensible, although the words of the Irish characters are 'translated' into English for the audience. The play presents map-making and the translation of Irish place names into English as part of a larger political, colonial struggle that has personal consequences, as lovers seek to cross linguistic and national divides with deadly results. Maclaren's 18th-century Scottish multilingual plays suggest that language apprehension and fluency in Scotland were much better than what is demonstrated by the conventions of English-language plays in 21st-century Britain and America.

There seems to have been a play performed entirely in Gaelic by Edinburgh University Celtic Society in 1902, but title and author are unknown. Earlier, Macleod and Watson tell us that plays were published in Gaelic periodicals like *An Gaidheal / The Highlander* and *An Teachdaire Gaelach / The Highland Messenger*, but the earliest sign of broader encouragement came from Ruaraidh Erskine of Marr, who published plays in his periodical *Guth na Bliadhna* in 1912. More details are in the splendid biography by Gerard Cairns, *No Language! No Nation! The Life and Times of The Honourable Ruaraidh Erskine of Marr* (Perth: Rymour Books, 2021). Meanwhile drama was also becoming popular in Highlands and Islands communities away from large urban centres and professional theatres. The tradition of the cèilidh combined with a developing amateur ethos and, after the Clearances, was influenced by the more urbanised experience of new generations. This helped develop the existing culture of performance towards something more recognisably theatrical and prompts a question about the relation between performativity and playwriting which remains healthily unanswerable.

If some early plays were often light-hearted and comic, Erskine of Marr insisted on the priorities of political engagement and education. Individual authors and plays might be noted: *Fearann a Shinnsear / Land of His Ancestors* (1913) and *Crois Tara / Cross of Tara* (1914) by Dòmhnall Mac na Ceàrdaich / Donald Sinclair, which focus on Gaelic history, the Clearances and the 1745 Jacobite rising, endorsing the virtues of the Highlanders and scorning the vicissitudes of the Lowlands, while *Domhnaull nan Trioblaid* (1912, 1936) and *Suridhe Raoghail Mhaoil* (1929) are comedies about the lives of crofters.

Both Gilleasbh MacCuillaich / Archibald McCulloch and Iain MacCormaic / John MacCormick wrote plays leavened with songs, endorsing Gaelic identity but hardly opening it up to questioning the ambiguities and liabilities that become more urgent in situations of cultural oppression.

Playwrights would often produce work for local drama groups. For example, Iain Mac a' Ghobhainn / Iain Crichton Smith wrote for the Oban Gaelic drama group. The principal characters and conflict, concerned with the impact of the Clearances on a Highland widow, in his classic English-language novel, *Consider the Lilies*, return in the play-version, *A' Chùirt* (1966).

A strong advocate for Gaelic drama was Tormod Calum Dòmhnallach, whose plays sometimes begin with a song or a poem, from which the action elaborates and unfolds. The play *Anna Chaimbeul* arises from the song 'Ailean Duinn' and *A' Bhean Iadach* from the song of the same name, while *Cnoc Chùsbaig or Na Seòid a th' oirre sealg* is based on the life of the poet Uilleam MacCoinneach (1857–1907), whose poetry was prompted by the death of his wife and his departure from the Isle of Lewis. *Aimhreit Aignis* (1888) deals with the land rights movement and *Bathach Chaluim* with religious evangelicalism in Lewis.

In 1977 the first professional Gaelic theatre company was established, Fir Chlis, though it closed in 1981; one successor, Tosg, was established in 1996, although it didn't last either, closing after a decade. Its brilliant founder, playwright, actor and director Simon Mackenzie, died in 2008. But generally, in Michelle Macleod's words, 'Gaelic drama has prospered in the environment of festivals and competitions'.

In the early 21st century, recognition and appreciation of Gaelic drama in the broader context of Scotland and internationally was growing. In the Preface to her edition of eight plays in Gaelic from the start of the 20th to the early 21st century, *Dràma na Gàidhlig: ceud bliadhna air an àrd-ùrlar: A Century of Gaelic Drama* (Glasgow: Association for Scottish Literary Studies, 2020), Michelle Macleod says this:

> Gaelic drama although popular with audiences from its beginning has not enjoyed a similar readership success and until fairly recently has not been the subject of scholarly criticism.

Her introduction summarises the essential story:

> Gaelic society has always enjoyed the spoken word and performance culture. In medieval Scotland and Ireland one of the most honourable professions was that of the poet who, like the harpist, could enjoy an enviable position in the employment of nobility. Performance of verse was equally valued in ordinary society as the rich body of Gaelic vernacular poetry and song demonstrates. Storytelling and storytellers have likewise been an important part of Gaelic tradition: folktales demonstrate the oral performance skill of the narrator as he winds his way along complex alliterative runs, used as a mnemonic and as a device to please the audience. Elements of performance can also be found in other aspects of Gaelic culture for example in preaching, prayer and rituals

but the 'staged play' was not a secure aspect of Gaelic culture until the early 20th century. Macleod notes that the development of Gaelic drama in a modern form is connected with the influx of Gaels into Scottish cities, especially Glasgow and Inverness.

The range of modern Gaelic drama can be noted in a brief list of plays, starting in the 1960s. Iain Moireach's *Sniomh nan Dual* contains six plays, from *Feumaidh Sinne Bhith Gàireachdainn* (1967) to *An Treas* Fàd (2007). *An Ceistear, Am Bàrd's Na Boirionnach / The Catechist, the Poet and the Women* (1974) draws on the dramatic performance traditions of the Gàidhealtachd, utilising historical stories and songs. And *Anna Chaimbeul / Ann Campbell*

(1977), while presenting traditional song, also makes use of the Japanese Noh theatre as transmitted by Yeats. *Rèiteach* (2007) presents the developing relationship between Ealasaid, a young Gaelic woman from Canada, and Uisdean, a middle-aged islander living with his mother.

Two posthumously published collections should be noted: *Eist: Sia Dealbh-chluichean* (2005) by Donaidh Mac'ill'eathain and *Solas na Gealaich: Deich Deilbh-chluich* (2001) by Pòl MacAonghais. Anxiety about the future of Gaelic is a recurring theme, as in *An Sgoil Dhubh / The Dark School* (1974). In Mac'ill'eathain's *An Dall*, the central character becomes so obsessed by watching television that he loses all connection to the world around; the onset of blindness comes as both curse and blessing. *Sgoil-Dubh* deals with the threat to traditional culture by splitting the stage into two halves, one in darkness with a son and his mother, the other brightly illuminated, a modern family home: the son moves from one side to the other. And this surreal, absurdist element is there too in MacAonghais's *An t-Aiseag* (2000), where what seems like a Caledonian MacBrayne ferries waiting room takes on the semblance of an existential vestibule in the context of an indifferent eternity. (Perhaps it's not too far removed from reality at that!)

Michelle Macleod's anthology begins with *Rèiteach Mòraig / Morag's Betrothal* (1911) by Iain M. MacLeòid / John Macleod, which centres on Gaelic traditions of betrothal and marriage. In *Am Fear a Chaill a Ghàidhlig* by Iain MacCormaig / *The Man Who Lost His Gaelic* by John MacCormick, the Gael leaves his native territory for Glasgow and begins to understand the disintegration of his own language, allowing both tragic and comic elements to come into play. *Ceann Cropic*, (1967) by Fionnlagh MacLeòid / Finlay Macleod (sometimes referred to as 'the play where nothing happens'), presents a Beckett-like dialogue between two people prioritising dilemmas of language and communication that have urgent, practical application as well as delivering the aesthetic pleasures of a bizarre, absurdist tragi-comedy, or comic tragedy. As in *Waiting for Godot*, the isolated arena of the stage heightens the utterance of the characters: banalities become heavy with implication. There is no reason why Gaelic plays should be any less experimental, radical and leavened with existential humour, than any in Scots or English, or for that matter, any other language

In *Tog Orm Mo Speal / Give Me My Scythe* by Iain Mac a' Ghobhainn / Iain Crichton Smith, the central character is the same Murdo from its author's short stories, whose actions and words again carry that double burden of innocence and incredulity which makes him both a clown and a victim obstinately resisting what seems to be inevitable. Macleod tells us: 'Smith used bilingualism both as a symbol of a broken self and as opportunity for humour; he wrote about his use of the jester figure to show just that.' For example, when the psychiatrist tries word association to help him understand Murchadh's problems:

PSYCHIATRIST: Facal eile. 'Gorm'.
MURCHADH: Feur.
PSYCHIATRIST: Feur? Feur? 'S ann a tha am feur uaine.
MURCHADH: Chan ann ann an Gàidhlig. 'S ann a tha feur gorm ann an Gàidhlig.
PSYCHIATRIST: Cò chunnaic a riamh feur gorm?
MURCHADH: Chunnaic muinntir na Gàidhlig feur gorm...

PSYCHIATRIST: Another word. 'Blue'.
MURCHADH: Grass.
PSYCHIATRIST: Grass? Grass? The grass is green.
MURCHADH: Not in Gaelic. The grass is blue in Gaelic.
PSYCHIATRIST: Who ever saw blue grass?
MURCHADH: Gaelic speakers saw blue grass...

'The psychiatrist cannot comprehend that the Gaelic colour spectrum is different to English [...] and even when Murchadh cites the famous Gaelic lexicographer Dwelly, the psychiatrist remains unconvinced. At the end of the play it is simple companionship with his friend Tormod which lifts Murchadh's spirits and persuades him to get back to work, although there is a degree of giving in to the futility when he utters at the end "tog orm mo speal" (*give me my scythe*) as prepares to get back to reaping on the croft.'

This play is followed by *Òrdugh na Saorsa / Order of Release* (1991) by Tormod Calum Dòmhnallach / Norman MacDonald, one of the most underrated modern Scottish writers, partly because so much of his best work in Gaelic drama has not reached wider audiences or readerships – or rather because so many of his potential readers and audiences remain ignorant of Gaelic. But within his own community and among Gaels it was deeply appreciated. His sense of the value of the human lives that constitute such a community is profoundly engaged in this play, set in the aftermath of Culloden. A revival should court appreciation, and in the era of the television popularity and commercial success of the *Outlander* series, might provide an attractive corrective. *Sequamur* by Donald S. Murray, translated into Gaelic by Catriona Dunn, is set in Lewis at the time of the First World War, its themes universal and timeless. *Scotties* by Muireann Kelly and Francis Poet, utilises Gaelic alongside Irish, English and Scots, foregrounding the mix and diversity of linguistic identities that form the speech of the characters, both a modern family living in Glasgow and a group of Irish farm labourers of the early 20th century, with the central character slipping between time-periods as he carries out a research project to discover what became of the labourers. Finally, *Bana-Ghaisgich / Heroines* by Màiri Nic'IlleMhoire / Mairi Morrison also opens a door into history, focusing on the sinking of the *Iolaire* off the coast of Lewis, when 201 service men returning from the First World War on 1 January 1919 drowned within sight of their homes.

Along with their individual excellences, these plays offer an overview of the history of a genre in one of the major languages of Scottish literature. Macleod's anthology delivers an invitation to see more deeply into what she describes as a 'domain of creativity in which so much innovative and emotive practice has taken place and which has been enjoyed by relatively large audiences for a minority community'. With her lucid and illuminating introduction and a substantial, rich bibliography, the book is indispensable for anyone interested in modern drama, Scottish literature and whatever we might mean by cultural identity. It is a threshold to riches.

76

Plays, theatres and drama: a good night out

TWO ESSENTIAL QUESTIONS arise from our reading of the history of Scottish plays, drama, and performance. What might it mean, in the 21st century, to have 'A Good Night Out'? And what might a National Theatre of Scotland be expected to provide?

Given the necessary flexibility and unfixed nature of theatre, and the political world which is the context of all literature, unanswered questions about the future of plays in Scotland stay live. The establishment of The National Theatre of Scotland in 2006 made a reality of something many people for more than a half a century had been pushing towards. It was argued that the distinction of the NTS was that it would be a theatre 'without walls' – that is, without an actual building. Its space would be 'a place of imagination, learning and play'. For some, the question remained: Is this a lasting, real achievement or a castle in the air? The situation was deeply unsatisfying to those who had campaigned for a substantial actual theatre, perhaps to be situated in the capital city, which would be recognised internationally as a cultural statement of self-possession and political self-determination. However, the argument for a theatre committed to productions that would be visible in different parts of Scotland, across the variety of the nation's terrain, addressing different audiences, was also recognised as valid and freshening. A number of NTS productions delivered impressive work and gained appropriate praise. And in 2017, the NTS found a permanent home along with Scottish Opera, the Royal Conservatoire of Scotland and other organisations in Rockvilla, near Cowcaddens in north Glasgow, affording three rehearsal rooms, meeting rooms and space for storage and production workshops.

Yet questions still remain. The big one is simply: What is a National Theatre for?

A National Theatre, given that title, might be expected to fulfil five essential functions. Resourced to the full extent it should be able: (1) to review, reappraise and perform new productions of plays from the entire history of Scottish literature (and considering how much I've written on the subject in this book, there can be no doubt that there are plenty of them); (2) to have an experimental space, where new plays, especially by Scottish authors, might be tried out, and encouragement directed explicitly to bring such work into the public arena; (3) to mount productions of professional international companies from anywhere in the world; (4) to present plays from the international history of drama on a contemporary stage to Scottish audiences; and (5) to make certain all these productions are publicly affordable, and known about, broadcast, nationally and internationally, according to the quality of their achievement.

If such desiderata remain poised with potential, then perhaps, rather than criticise what has not yet been achieved, it is worth recognising clearly what still remains in prospect, and what we have every right to demand.

In his book, *A Good Night Out: Popular Theatre: Audience, Class and Form* (1981), John McGrath says that there are 'different kinds of audiences, with different theatrical values and expectations' and the distinction might be made polemically: 'the two main kinds of theatre audience [are] the "educated" middle-class audience, and the "philistine" working-class audience.

However, McGrath reminds us, this will not do.

> For when we discuss theatre, we are discussing a social event, and a very complex social event, with a long history and many elements, each element also having a long and independent history.

Those elements, all of which contribute to this 'social event' have their own provenances, languages and idioms, and in Scotland, as in Britain and Europe more generally, class identity is a crucial factor in understanding them. Thus,

> The tradition created among the European bourgeoisie by Ibsen, Strindberg, Chekhov, Shaw, Galsworthy, Anouilh, Cocteau, Giraudoux, Pirandello became a strong and self-confident tradition. It declared, without too much bother, that the best theatre is about the problems and the achievements of articulate middle-class men and sometimes women, is performed in comfortable theatres, in large cities, at a time that will suit the eating habits of the middle class at a price that only the most determined of the lower orders could afford, and will generally have an air of intellectuality about it – something to exercise the vestiges of one's education on and to scare off the great Unwashed. There will be critics to make it more important and learned books written about it to prove that it really is 'art'.

By contrast, 'In the late [19]40s, Joan Littlewood, Gerry Raffles, Ewan MacColl and a few other socialists had formed various companies to tour with socialist plays before working-class audiences, in Scotland, around Manchester and eventually in the Theatre Royal, Stratford, in east London. There were several Unity theatres, which were closely connected with the Communist Party, and which put on agitational and other socialist plays to working-class audiences. In other words, another, different story was being told. Reality was being mediated in several very different ways.'

The polemical picture McGrath draws here perhaps oversimplifies the story but the central point holds good. In his book, McGrath describes sensitively the risks that were run in addressing working-class audiences in urban industrial centres, where the values of 'entertainment' had emerged from conditions that had been part of the life there since the Industrial Revolution, where 'the brutality, the violence, the drunkenness, the sexism, the authoritarianism' were pervasive. And yet, by identifying the liabilities here, he is able also to specify clearly the strengths that can be built upon in a progressive, rather than a reactionary, theatre.

McGrath identifies some 'fairly generalised differences between the demands and tastes of bourgeois and working-class audiences'. These would include:

1. Directness. As opposed to obliqueness or innuendo, what's needed are direct explorations of economic conditions, exploitation and working conditions and the history from which these arose.
2. Comedy. Laughter is welcome, and comedy has to be sharp, perceptive, critical and fast. If it is formulaic, mechanical or predictable, it fails.
3. Music. Lively, popular, melodic, performed by good musicians and singers, the presence of music and song can act to dramatically highlight a performance, and does not detract from a play's seriousness.
4. Emotion. The open expression of emotion by characters on stage may be vital to a play's effect, rather than emphasising the restraint or suffering silence characters might maintain in bourgeois drama.
5. Variety. Theatrical performances might draw on popular forms and switch rapidly from a singer, to a comedian, a juggler, a band, a chorus number, a comedian and a 'come-all-ye' finale. The public nature of all such performances is openly engaged.
6. Effect. If the performance is effective, it will be appreciated. There is no reason for restraint or endurance among members of the audience. The work of attending has to be rewarded.
7. Immediacy. There is room for improvisation, or topical reference. And this leads to:
8. Localism of place. Which is to say, some productions will have greater or lesser effect depending upon their application to specific localities. This applies most evidently in McGrath and 7:84's productions of *The Cheviot, the Stag and the Black, Black Oil* (1973) in the tours of the Highlands of Scotland, where the stories being told related so closely to the history of the people of those places, the audiences who attended the performances. But it applies equally to the same company's *The Game's*

a Bogey: 7:84's John Maclean Show (1975), which was performed in Glasgow and other industrial cities where Maclean's story had close local relevance. And finally:

9. Localism of performer. Particular effect can be achieved by a performer local to the audience in a specific area. Familiarity in this case breeds not contempt but recognition of affinity: this person is speaking on behalf of people in the audience who trust him or her.

So there are nine itemised qualities of live theatre that might be kept in mind in any application of value. And their priorities stand them in stark contrast to the essential characteristics of television, as McGrath described them in his follow-up book of essays, *The Bone Won't Break: On Theatre and Hope in Hard Times* (1990). As I list these, we might consider, what's changed since then? Have there been any improvements?

McGrath asks, what are the values represented on TV in 'the money-oriented society we live in'? And with the warning that 'we are in the hands of people with no concern for cultural well being', he gives six: (1) TV 'sells America, hour by hour, day by day, year by year'. Murderers, cops, tycoons, the rich and charming, the powerful. And British TV emulates this. (2) 'TV sells sport' of all kinds, cruel, dangerous, ruthless: competition is the only law and winning the only victory. (3) TV 'sells sentiment and nostalgia'. The emotional range explored on television is extremely narrow. (4) TV endorses the role of women as predominantly in the home, domesticated, disempowered, or else sexualised, even in seemingly self-determined action; in any role, they are presented as exploitable commodities and the objects of spectacle. Or more simply, TV sells patriarchy and misogyny. (5) TV 'sells news as a commodity, a set of tricks or disasters adding up to a fictional construct of the world'. And the built-in values endorsed are always profoundly conservative. Finally, (6) TV 'is advertising'. Not 'sells' but 'is'. And that's the final difference to note. Advertising exists to take stuff from you. Art exists to give. It is the work of minds that help keep other minds alive. Since governments know full well that an ignorant electorate is easier to guide, their interest by and large is not to educate anyone, and certainly not to invest in the arts.

Am I over-generalising? Are these judgements too sweeping and crude? Prove me wrong. Show me the government that invests in the arts as a priority and educates people to think for themselves and articulate clear criticism of any governments and the media representing them. Show me a government anywhere demonstrably committed to generating a culture of critical thinking.

So those are the options: a good night out or a bad night in?

What's changed since 1990? Perhaps predominantly only the sense that to find TV of palpable value you need to know what to look for and where to look for it. As far as the context of terrestrial society is concerned, forget it. Everything itemised there in 1990 has only become exaggerated since.

For McGrath, the theatre is or can be

> the most public, the most clearly political of the art forms. Theatre is the place where the life of a society is shown in public to that society, where that society's assumptions are exhibited and tested, its values are scrutinised, its myths are validated and its traumas become emblems of its reality. Theatre is not about the reaction of one sensibility to events external to itself, as poetry tends to be; or the private consumption of fantasy or a mediated slice of social reality, as most novels tend to be. It is a public event, and it is about matters of public concern.

That remains a judgement of lasting value, and one that any National Theatre must never neglect.

77

Lowlander and Gael: Stewart Conn and Aonghas MacNeacail

STEWART CONN (B.1936) was born in Glasgow and brought up in Ayrshire, then moved between Glasgow and Edinburgh, while regularly visiting the Western Isles. These locations figure throughout his poetry as natural contexts for evocation and curiosity. Many poems are prompted to consider questions raised by occasional encounters with works of art, paintings in galleries or music in concert performances. These are occasional poems set in places typical of middle-class cultural encounter, in Edinburgh, France, Italy and elsewhere. Such work risks the liabilities of privilege but these are dissolved by the virtues Conn invites us to savour and value. The sensitivities at work are refreshing in their indifference to the conventions of partisan politics. Nor are they exclusive or condescending in the manner of an elitist dilettante. Conn's attention to nuance, balance, subtlety and evenness of tone risks a lack of strong colour but it would be wrong to suggest that his poems are more watercolour than oil, though they are certainly more Renoir than Van Gogh.

His early books include *Stoats in the Sunlight* (1968), *An Ear to the Ground* (1972) and *Under the Ice* (1978). In each of them, the country world is a strong presence, often not the source of easy comfort but rather reminding human beings that self-importance stands to fall in nature's pre-eminence. Deftly, with assurance and light gestures, the poems evoke the bloody business of predators, the fact that under the earth are worms as well as roots, echoes of approaching armies as well as sounds of spring rising. From them we infer the dark threat of psychological depths unplumbed by reason, unconquered and not exploitable. These qualities never go away but are leavened by light and other arts, entering the poems as subjects in such collections as *In the Kibble Palace* (1987), *The Luncheon of the Boating Party* (1992) and *In the Blood* (1995). *Ghosts at Cockcrow* (2005) includes the moving sequence, 'Roull of Corstorphin', an exploration of the life and character of a poet named in William Dunbar's 'Lament for the Makars', but of whom almost nothing is known. Conn imagines him slipping out of the Court of James IV, where Dunbar is about to embark on a lurid flyting with Andrew Kennedy, and slipping back to Corstorphin, 'where in the shade of a seeding sycamore / he will sit penning his tender love poetry.'

Conn was head of radio drama for BBC Scotland from 1977–92, writing his own plays for broadcasting as well as theatre performance. We've already noted his plays, including *The Burning* (1971), about Bothwell, James I, and innocent people caught up in political and religious power-struggles, *The Aquarium*

(1973), an intense domestic family drama, *Play Donkey* (1977), about morality and family loyalty as a mercenary soldier is locked up in an African jail, and the biographical plays *Herman* (1981), about Herman Melville, and *Hugh Miller* (1988). He adapted Neil Gunn's novel *Blood Hunt* (1952) for BBC television (broadcast 1986) and produced John Purser's award-winning radio play *Carver* (1992) before taking up writing full-time. He was the first to hold the post of Makar or poet laureate of Edinburgh, 2002–05, taking forward his sense of the value of a public presence for poetry and literature. *The Touch of Time: New & Selected Poems* (2014) demonstrates a fine craftsman's care for structure and poise with a countryman's understanding of the hard realities of the farming world.

The emotional authority of Conn's poems resides in a gentle but steely sense of humour, an understated irony and an unaffected compassion. In his poems, the creatural character of being human is a dark presence alongside precise and unvaunted celebrations of humanity's cultural sophistication at its finest, and the tenderness and vulnerabilities of folk at every age and strata of their lives. His prose collection *Distances* (2001) collects memories of George Mackay Brown and Iain Crichton Smith, notes on Alasdair Maclean and W.S. Graham and recollections of Ayrshire.

Aonghas MacNeacail (b.1942) was born in Uig, on the Isle of Skye, and grew up with Gaelic as his first language. At school, he has written, the work priority of the first teacher he encountered was to teach 'her tearful new charges a foreign language [English], which most of us would soon learn to speak better than our own'. This gives his poetry in English a distinct sense of both fluency and strangeness, judgement and pronouncement on matters of politics and history but at the same time an introspective character, both engaged and meditative. He is a lyric love poet and a poet of explicit social engagement, a journalist prompt to comment and correct the still too frequent crass pontifications of public figures uttering their opinions about the Gaelic language. He is also a scriptwriter and filmmaker, librettist, songwriter and broadcaster.

His commitment to free verse, formally influenced by the American Black Mountain poets, and therefore evidently different from the more traditional forms to be found in earlier Gaelic poetry by Sorley MacLean and George Campbell Hay, is another distinction. In this respect, there are affinities with another fine Gaelic poet, Donald MacAulay (1930–2017). Like MacLean, MacNeacail began writing 'literary' poems in the context of a long and rich tradition of Gaelic song. His book *imaginary wounds* (1980) contained poems in English in which matters of Gaelic history, memory and identity were suggestively brought into the texts with quiet and powerful pathos. In 'interval', the evocation of a school playground vividly gives us children taking sides: not cowboys and Indians but 'campbells and mackenzies' – so far, it might seem, so innocent, until we get to the last lines: 'it was later we learned / about glencoe'.

The lack of punctuation and lower case letters are characteristic, from this early book, all the way through MacNeacail's writing. His name is given as 'aonghas macneacail' in his early publications.

His first major collection was *An Seachnadh / The Avoiding* (1986), poems set out in Gaelic and English on facing pages, and then poems in English were collected in *Rock and Water* (1990). In 'jock the shop's odyssey' reductive humour and formal layout on the page delivers a humour that is both sympathetic and critical, aware of a social and economic history, as well as a human vulnerability and danger:

> the
> > old
> > blue
> > > bedford
> >
> > does
> > > not
> >
> > follow
> > > a straight line
> >
> > when
> > jock
>
> is
> > steering
> > > homeward, heavy
>
> with provisions, the cattle will
> winter, the village eat, but
>
> first, jock's mother.   Her tongue will scorch
> the ears of her (once monthly) wayward son

Scottish poetry in Gaelic and Scots, and even in English, that makes such self-confident use of open forms like this was rare when MacNeacail began writing and he was aware of his originality in this regard. He presents himself in his poetry sometimes as 'the holy fool / the bard' but history is essential to his vision and the thrust of his political ideas comes through most forcefully in its personal application. His good humour and generous disposition is not a disguise, nor an evasion, when it comes to the seriousness of the questions which his poetry raises about cultural history and malign political priorities.

In *A Proper Schooling / Oideachadh Ceart* (1996), he writes: 'when i was young / it wasn't history but memory'. In 'air soitheach nam peann gu baile nan slige' / 'on the ship of pens to the city of shells', from the book, *laoidh an donais oig / hymn to a young demon* (2007), literary metaphor and historical references combine dramatically: 'destruction's an impartial judge, as measured by the gentle / level voice of the language professor, on the level deck of this / voyage to the red city of histories, of blows and deaths / where the sun would shine on us'.

MacNeacail lived for many years in the Scottish Borders. As well as writing in Gaelic and translating his own work into English, he has also written effectively in Scots, bridging Highlands and Lowlands as well as the old and the new, especially in the booklet *ayont the dyke* (2012) and in his contribution to the anthology *The Smeddum Test* (2013). A larger collection was published as *deanamh gaire ris a' chloc / laughing at the clock: new and selected poems* in 2012.

It's difficult to imagine two poets of such contrast and complementarity, but both are equally essential in modern Scotland.

78

Three kinds of poet:
Douglas Dunn, Tom Leonard and Liz Lochhead

DOUGLAS DUNN (B.1942) grew up in Renfrewshire and went to university in Hull, where he became a librarian, colleague and associate of Philip Larkin, then a fellow in Creative Writing there in the 1970s and at the University of Dundee in the 1980s. His early poems are sharply-honed accounts of aspects of this era of his experience, collected in *Terry Street* (1969). They bear little trace of the significance Scotland would have for him later, and yet 'A Poem in Praise of the British' discloses a hard irony that has been a characteristic of all his work:

> Heavy rain everywhere washes up the bones of the British.
> Where did all that power come from, the wish
> To be inert, but rich and strong, to have too much?

The politicised quality of the question is disillusioned and wry, distanced but impassioned.

In 'Ships', Dunn specifies 'restless boys' in Ayrshire, looking out at the Clyde estuary as a ship goes by, thinking that they too might have gone away, as they sit in their futility, 'in the glass cafés, / Over their American soft drinks'. His earlier poetry arises from such everyday objects, moments, people and places around him, plangently annotating tones and occasions of loss, regret, survival and qualities of social redundancy in the world around him, but he broke new ground with *Elegies* (1985). He was recognised for the work in this book as a poet whose self-constraint held depths of sorrow, understanding and a fundamental sense of human decency and he has maintained and developed these strengths throughout his later poetry.

He gives his account in *Northlight* (1988) of his transition back into Scotland from previous residence in England, a major reconfiguration of his own life story, as he experienced it through the work of chance and will, sometimes through terrible, unpredictable occasions of loss, sometimes through wilfully decisive moments in which choices were made. In 'Here and There', Dunn talks about his commitment to 'a regenerate // Country in which to reconstruct a self / From local water, timber, light and earth' and observes, 'fidelity directs / Love to this place, the eye to what it sees'. As he settles into residence on the east coast of Scotland, in Fife, the poetry tries out its habitation and grows into the place. 'Going to Aberlemno' begins:

> By archaeologies of air,

> Folkways of kirks and parishes
> Revised by salty haar,
> You reach the previous
> Country, the picturesque
> And the essential east

And he finds that 'A Pictish dialect, / Above a bridged Forth, cries / For lyric nationhood'. Another chapter was beginning.

Dunn became Professor of English at the University of St Andrews in 1991. His work developed its qualities of scrupulous critical attention to detail and meticulous appetite for everyday realities. Linguistically as much as socially, his attention to political questions has always been keen, and not afraid to be sometimes unfashionable. His achievement as a stylist in the English language is matched by his unfazed seriousness and uneasy acumen. As editor of *The Faber Book of Twentieth-Century Scottish Poetry* (1992) he had some influence on how modern Scottish poetry was read, and his introduction to that book is a strong-minded enquiry into the particularities and limitations of its subject, both historically across the century and as a means of categorising a body of work by national identity, in the knowledge that poetry does not march to a flag.

In *The Year's Afternoon* (2000), the everyday comes into alignment with professional expertise in such poems as 'A Theory of Literary Criticism' (with its commemoration of Pablo Neruda in Chile). In 'Three Poets', his elegy for Norman MacCaig, Sorley MacLean and George Mackay Brown, who all died in the same year, Dunn locates himself in that transitional generation between theirs, and before them, MacDiarmid's, and that which followed:

> Come, friends, it is time now to drink
> To three poets. It is time to sit quietly and read,
> Hearing them speak their lines, those whom we succeed.

Few poets could have said that with such understated intensity, gravitas and inclusiveness. *The Noise of a Fly* (2017) takes the sense of solitary fortitude into a world of acknowledged vulnerability and ageing, without the futilities of self-pity or arrogance, Dunn keeps that steely irony and human sympathy central and stronger than ever.

Tom Leonard (1944–2018), whose poems in *Intimate Voices* (1984) and prose works collected in *Reports from the Present* (1995) made a major, singular eruption in general literary sensibility, insists upon the validity of working-class experience and language, and demonstrates that validity in poems and essays of untiring moral ferocity and sometimes wild humour. The prospect of comedy in the phonetic representation of speech in 'Unrelated Incidents' belies the deadly seriousness of the point being made about speech, language, class and power. This is most evident in the second poem of the sequence, where the difference between 'yir eyes / n / yir ears' is elaborated on the page, as the reader is advised to think 'aboot thi dif- / frince tween / sound / n object n / symbol' and assured that, 'as god said ti / adam' he didn't care if the 'apple' was to be called 'an aippl' so long as his orders to leave it alone were dutifully obeyed.

Few poets (Jeremy Prynne might be one other) have been so committed to small press publications and timely interventions, in booklets, pamphlets and ephemeral publications to which the entire Scottish literary and cultural community responded immediately: *Six Glasgow Poems* (1967), *a priest came on at merkland street* (1970), *ghostie men* (1980), *if only bunty was here* (1979), *Satires & Profanities* (1982), *Glasgow, My Big Bridie* (1983), *situations theoretical and contemporary* (1986), *Two Members' Monologues* (1989), *nora's place* (1990), and *On the Mass Bombing of Iraq and Kuwait, Commonly Known as 'the Gulf War'* (1991).

Leonard's major contributions to literary scholarship are in two books, *Radical Renfrew: Poetry from the French Revolution to the First World War* (1990), which he edited, and which opened a whole world of poets based in urban Scotland, writing about conditions of squalor and deprivation in explicit literary resistance to oppression, and in stark contrast to conventional 19th-century Scottish pastoral poems; and in the biography, *James Thomson ('B.V.'): Places of the Mind* (1993), which reviewed and revised the understanding of the poet of *The City of Dreadful Night* (1880) and demonstrated the value and place of Thomson (1834–82) in the account of modern English-language poetry generally, and modern Scottish poetry in particular. After Leonard's scholarly work, literary histories had to be rewritten. His own work has been collected in *access to the silence* (2004), *outside the narrative* (2009) and *Definite Articles: Selected Prose 1975–2012* (2013).

With Edwin Morgan's example and encouragement a new generation of Scottish poets began publishing in the 1970s, pre-eminently Liz Lochhead (b.1947), whose first book, *Memo for Spring* (1972) was welcomed as heralding a new voice in Scottish poetry. Here was work by a young woman, dealing with domestic and intimate relationships, in a style that combined in a new way seriousness and humour. The poems are sharp, cutting, and deliver the priorities of feminism while maintaining an openness to a non-exclusive readership. They are convincing by virtue of tone and angle of approach rather than by polemic or exclamation. This is a lyric poetry whose political intent and effect was sly, subtle, subversive and unshakeably good-humoured.

Lochhead's second book, *islands* (1978), was a record of her encounters with the Inner and then the Outer Hebrides, so while there was a central gravitational authority in her upbringing in Lanarkshire and Glasgow, where she attended the School of Art and worked as a schoolteacher, there was an increasing openness not only to geographical distance but to the voices and experiences of others.

From the 1970s on, Lochhead broke open the way for a number of Scottish women poets to be more widely heard and read and appreciated, beginning with poems exploring her own experience as a young woman in Lanarkshire in the 1960s and 1970s and developing her skills in creating personae and characters through writing dramatic monologues and original plays. Her attention to interpersonal relationships, domestic situations, gestures and emotions in local or intimate contexts, is not an evasion of 'the big questions' but a different approach to them. This was most evident in her work as adaptor of traditional fairy or folk tales, in *The Grimm Sisters* (1979) and *Dreaming Frankenstein and Collected Poems* (1984), in her development of dramatic monologues, in *True Confessions and New Clichés* (1985) and then in her work as a playwright in *Mary Queen of Scots Got Her Head Chopped Off* (1987) and her versions of classic plays such as Molière's *Tartuffe* (1985) and Euripides' *Medea* (2000)

She was appointed Scots Makar, or National Poet of Scotland, on 19 January 2011, succeeding Edwin Morgan (who was the first to hold the post, from 16 April 2004 till his death in 2010). When the Scottish Parliament building was opened at Holyrood on 9 October 2004, Lochhead was invited to read Edwin Morgan's magnificent inaugural poem for the occasion.

Characteristic of the generational change that took place in the 1970s and 1980s, Liz Lochhead's 'Mirror's Song' begins with the command to the reader and the poet's persona and the mirror of the poem's title:

> Smash me looking-glass glass
> coffin, the one
> that keeps your best black self on ice.
> Smash me, she'll smash back –

The energy called upon by the poem, the agency of 'she' and the principle of self-determination enacted and unleashed in the words is specific to history, details and places, and the driving liberations of feminism. It is also a universal fact: a freedom-fighter is good for everyone who really believes in freedom. And if liberty is called for here, it liberates all. The references burst out from Kali to Kleenex, from lipstick to Lycra:

> Smash me for your daughters and dead
> mothers, for the widowed
> spinsters of the first and every war
> let her
> rip up the appointment cards for the
> terrible clinics,

> the Greenham summonses, that date
> they've handed us. Let her rip.

The poem ends by demolishing all the impositions of fashion, advertising and patriarchal oppression, breaking things up 'in the cave she will claw out of – / a woman giving birth to herself.' It's a key poem in Lochhead's career and pivotal in the story of modern Scottish poetry.

It is an act of self-generation, regeneration and active literary participation in the struggle in which all the poets we've been discussing are engaged. That is, the arduous work of cultural production in a world where culture itself is not only undervalued but the object of direct or implicit denigration and in a country whose cultural history is in continual need of defence, reassessment and reinstatement. If a nation still in the process of giving birth to itself is to be worth living in for all, it will always be in need of such freedoms as those Liz Lochhead's work delivers.

Lochhead's work marks another regeneration in the story of modern Scottish poetry. Looking over the whole terrain, that trajectory could be characterised like this. In the 1920s, in the aftermath of the First World War, the Russian Revolution and the Easter Rising in Ireland, Hugh MacDiarmid galvanised the Scottish Literary Renaissance in poetry, literature, all the arts and politics, opening the possibilities of a multi-faceted, multi-vocal nation, distinct from the unitary imperial story of the British Empire. And in the aftermath of the Second World War, another rising tide of poets, predominantly men, produced a major body of poetry favouring particular locations: Norman MacCaig in Edinburgh and Lochinver, Sorley MacLean in Raasay and Skye, Iain Crichton Smith in Lewis, George Mackay Brown in Orkney, Robert Garioch and Sydney Goodsir Smith in Edinburgh, Edwin Morgan in Glasgow.

Since the 1970s, another generation, pre-eminently women, beginning most emphatically with Lochhead and opening to include another diversity of voices, has changed the scene once again. Meg Bateman, Jackie Kay, Kathleen Jamie, Gerda Stevenson, Bashabi Fraser, Gerrie Fellows, Elizabeth Burns, all established not only the voices, perspectives and experiences of women as central to the story of Scottish poetry but also the fact that the judgements of women are of equal value to those of men. The priorities of the preceding generations were complemented and corrected by their successors.

And since the 1990s, the world of online technology has multiplied electronic publishing platforms alongside a vertical decline in literary criticism and public intellectual engagement. Since 2000 a prevailing priority of ecological self-awareness has affected poets' work to a further degree, in poems by men as much as women, with poets diverse in their sense of belonging, whether settlers or natives, ancestrally connected to a specified geography or of multiple national histories and identities.

79

Nothing in uniform: from Veronica Forrest-Thomson to Jackie Kay

VERONICA FORREST-THOMSON (1947–75) grew up in Glasgow, going on to university in Liverpool then Cambridge, where she was intensely engaged by the poetry of Jeremy Prynne. She published her poems with small presses in the 1960s and 1970s, including *Identi-Kit* (1967), *Language-Games* (1971) and, posthumously, *On the Periphery* (1976). Her critical and theoretical writing also appeared posthumously as *Poetic Artifice: A Theory of Twentieth-Century Poetry* (1978). She was championed by Edwin Morgan, who wrote a moving elegiac sequence in her memory, 'Unfinished Poems' in his collection *The New Divan* (1977). Morgan noted that her poems are 'shot through with a raw, moving, almost ballad strain' and in that brief comment insightfully connects her precisely-worded, intellectually acute, self-consciously literary poems with the deep tradition in which impersonal facts and immediacy of personal implication are in close, and sometimes dangerous, connection.

Forrest-Thomson's *Collected Poems and Translations* (1990) brings together her fierce intellectual passion with refreshingly clinical engagement in the sharpest of focal concentrations on the purpose, dynamics and artifice of language in poetry. For example, in 'Alka-Seltzer Poem', witty, comic, everyday things and events acquire an acute poignancy when connected to literary tradition, as with the quotation from Keats in the opening line, and to the sense that something personal is at stake here: 'With beaded bubbles winking at the brim / the effervescence is subsiding.' Her elegy, 'In Memoriam Ezra Pound', manages to evoke the authority of Pound's imperial and vatic pronouncements, undercut it with sharp personal feeling, and qualify it with allusions to other modern poets and barely-remembered references.

The ballad-like poems, 'I have a little hour-glass' and 'I have a little nut-tree', might seem whimsical in their lightness, but they are packed with understated qualities of pain. The nut-tree bears only anguish and a tear, which is all the fruit she can promise to give in return for a kiss. These poems are immediately touching and effective. 'Cordelia or "A Poem Should Not Mean, But Be"' is equally moving but manages also to be almost a scholarly essay on Shakespeare, literature, literary study, and the fact of mortality. It is essentially focused on what permanence might mean when embodied in words whose velocity is so fleeting. Forrest-Thomson's poems are of a rare kind: highly intellectual, emotionally piercing, fully-charged and direct yet often allusive and sometimes obscure. Their challenge is lasting.

Andrew Greig (b.1951) established his reputation as an iconoclastic but highly sensitised poet with *Men On Ice* (1977), in which three climbers are found on a mountain's ice-face: Grimpeur (meditative philosopher), Axe-man (down-to-earth rock musician), and Poet (recording the journey and its speculative interludes). Each of them is aware of a fourth presence accompanying their trek in the high altitudes. This is a mock-epic, drawing stylistically and tonally from American Beat and Black Mountain poets of the 1960s and 1970s, especially Edward Dorn, whose long poem *Gunslinger* (1968) is an important precedent and from which Greig quotes. An index acknowledges other quotations or echoes from Chuck Berry and Bob Dylan but cheekily notes that there is 'positively no mention of' Zola, Freud, Marx, Stalin or Hugh MacDiarmid.

Like Liz Lochhead and Forrest-Thomson, Greig took his primary bearings from English-language American poets rather than Scots-language ballads or Scottish poetry in traditional metres. In a note written for a National Book League pamphlet, Greig said that he saw himself 'as much a child of the 60s' international culture as of Scotland'. He consolidated his reputation in further volumes such as *Surviving Passages* (1982) and *The Order of the Day* (1990), in which lyrical or discursive poems elaborate the themes of climbing, the challenge and the arduous journey, which, while taking their premise from actual mountaineering expeditions, make use of appropriate imagery in depictions of domestic or romantic circumstance.

Western Swing (1994) returns to the characters, style and tones of *Men On Ice*, but moves the ethos on from the mid-1970s to the 1990s: we travel from Glencoe and East Fife to Katmandu and Marrakech but matters of judgement impose themselves on local and domestic references. After serious illness, *Into You* (2001) marked a recovery, an affirmation, and a greater reliance upon specific locations in Scotland, named and commemorated, unsentimentally, tentatively and with an increasingly fragile sense of mortality. An important gathering of Greig's work appeared in *This Life, This Life: Selected Poems 1970–2006* (2006), and *As Though We Were Flying* (2011) saw a maturity of recognition in poems of loss and resilience, celebrations and elegies. It was followed by another almost-narrative poem set in and around the Orkney Islands, *Found at Sea: The Expanded Log of the 'Arctic Whaler'* (2013), which was adapted into a play by David Greig.

Meg Bateman (b.1959), writing in Gaelic and translating her poems into English, published memorable work in *Aotromachd agus Dàin Eile / Lightness and other Poems* (1997), *Soirbheas / Fair Wind* (2007) and *Transparencies* (2013). Bateman's poetry returns again and again to the central theme of love, the exhilarations and deep delights that come with its presence, the despair and hard recognitions that come with its loss.

As a scholar of the Gaelic tradition, she is highly self-conscious of her location in the company of Gaelic poets – emphatically, women as much as men – who have addressed the same theme but this has never inhibited the spontaneity, immediacy and effectiveness of her writing. Its qualities of emotional speed, deft structuring, gentle but sharp implication and understatement are uniquely balanced and sustained. Perhaps because Gaelic was not her first language, and she learned it both as a poet and a scholar (she has taught at the University of the Highlands and Islands at Sabhal Mòr Ostaig, the Gaelic College in Skye, and co-edited and annotated major anthologies of traditional Gaelic poetry), she is particularly attentive to the linguistic energies at work in her English-language translations of her own Gaelic poems. These have a musicality of their own, partly delivered through restraint and poise, partly through techniques like refrain and repetition.

The four-stanza poem 'Because I was so fond of him' uses the title as a recurring last line in each of its three-line stanzas to haunting effect, as fondness and closeness give way to loneliness and hard recognition. Bateman draws on the song tradition in a literary way, engaging in the artifice of literary art while carefully evoking song's lyrical lightness of touch. The first collection, *Lightness*, is characterised by these qualities of intimacy and openness, surrender and self-contained self-determination. With *Fair Wind*, there are different kinds of paradox in the forms of the poems, some metrically regular, some in free verse, balancing the physical sense of the pleasures of the life of the body with a darker understanding of their ephemerality, especially when measured against the more lasting but less immediately fulfilling qualities of art, whether in literature or song. *Transparencies* takes in an expanding range of reference, from Japan, Estonia and singers and dancers from far beyond Scotland, but it remains centred in personal understandings and sympathies enacted in the Gaelic world, over generations and with a convincing, patient, tough, self-confident but humble maturity everywhere evident.

In 2016, the Scottish government appointed Jackie Kay (b.1961) as Scots Makar or national poet laureate following Edwin Morgan and Liz Lochhead. Her first book, *The Adoption Papers* (1991), was an autobiographical sequence depicting the child of a Scotswoman and a Nigerian man being adopted and welcomed into the home of a kindly, loving, staunchly communist and pacifist couple living near Glasgow. Different voices and a range of characters – the daughter, the adoptive mother and the birth mother – speak of their experience. Tough as it is at times, the humanity of the story never palls or falters.

Kay grew up in Glasgow, discovering her own gay sexuality and later travelling to Africa to meet her birth father. In her writing, she speculates on such ostensibly problematic yet liberating aspects of identity as belonging, love and political desire. The themes of family, local, national and ancestral identity and questions of sexuality and social prejudice run through all her work. All this might seem serious and maybe even sensational, outwardly-focused and explicit, and in her poems and plays, in her writing for children, in her short stories and the novel, *Trumpet* (1998), she can be exactly that. 'The Maw Broon Monologues' were a comedy blast, loaded with satiric intent. Yet the subtlety of her versification, the nuanced deployment of individual voices and tones, the tensions and sympathies between characters realised through speech recorded in verse, are all carried along on a sustaining sense of good humour, humanistic sympathy and sheer eloquence. The understanding invested in her 1997 'poet's biography' of the Blues singer Bessie Smith suggests that all her writing is attuned to an intrinsic sensitivity to the musicality of the voice.

Her further books – *Other Lovers* (1993), *Off Colour* (1998), *Life Mask* (2005), *Darling* (2007), *Fiere* (2011), *Reality, Reality* (2012) and *Bantam* (2017) – take her in all sorts of directions: public and personal, exploring politics and language, different generations, geography and history, motherhood, falling in love, racism, prejudice, pride, popular culture and Shakespeare, Scotland and Africa.

As Hugh MacDiarmid once said, 'If there is ocht in Scotland that's worth hae'in' / There is nae distance to which it's unattached.'

80

Worlds of difference: from Tom Buchan to Kathleen Jamie

PRE-EMINENT POETS OF the 1960s include Tom Buchan (1931–95) and Alan Jackson (b.1938), whose best books, respectively, *Dolphins at Cochin* and *The Grim Wayfarer* (both 1969) remain among the iconic *livres de cachet* of that era. Kenneth White (b.1936) also began in that era with *The Cold Wind of Dawn* (1966). In his longer poems, in *The Bird Path* (1989), and shorter poems in *Handbook for the Diamond Country* (1990) and in many subsequent collections of poems and essays, White's idea of 'geopoetics' brings together landscape, geology and intellectual nomadism. The relation between territory and cultural articulation was more locally and visibly demonstrated by Ian Hamilton Finlay (1925–2006), whose poetry was most literally realised in the residential garden of Little Sparta at Stonypath, his home in the Lanarkshire hills, which is open and can be visited and explored every summer.

For over half a century, since the Heretics group of the 1970s, the poetry-reading scene has grown to include festivals and regular events all over Scotland, such as St Mungo's Mirrorball in Glasgow, run by Jim Carruth, appointed poet laureate of Glasgow in 2014, whose own work is grounded in the farming world he grew up in, with its working men and women, animals, cultivated terrain and uncontrollable weather, and all that connects them in conflicts and compromises. Carruth is as deft in his poems as he is self-effacing in his depictions and narratives of this territory. *The Herald*'s 'Poem of the Day' curated by and sometimes featuring the poetry of Lesley Duncan complemented the live reading groups almost every day for decades until it became 'Poem of the Week' in 2022.

Many individuals have their own growing oeuvres: John Purser (b.1942), writing with incomparable immediacy of life as a crofter on Skye, and out of extensive knowledge of Scotland's composers and music; Ron Butlin (b.1949), Edinburgh Makar, 2008–14; Tom Pow (b.1950), who, besides his distinctively engaging, conversational poems, and as well as his children's books, has written accounts of his travels through the Caribbean to Peru and across Europe in encounters with village communities in decline, and whose commitment to Scotland is complemented by his explorations of what he calls 'elsewheres' – in history, geography, or otherness of various kinds; Bashabi Fraser (b.1954), drawing on the cultural traditions of her native West Bengal and India more broadly, and braiding them with those of her adopted home, Scotland, in works like *Tartan & Turban* (2004), *From the Ganga to the Tay* (2009), *Raga & Reels*

(2012) and *Letters to My Mother and Other Mothers* (2015); John Burnside (b.1955) who began with *The Hoop* (1988) and has published memorable collections including *Common Knowledge* (1991) and *Black Cat Bone* (2011).

From his first book, *The Apple Ghost* (1989), John Glenday (b.1952) presents a quality of determined attentiveness, moving around familiar objects to define or describe them almost as if by sculpting the air their shapes occupy. His second collection, *Undark* (1995) takes its name from the paint which turned out to be poisonous to the factory workers who used it. Such sensing of almost invisible forces affecting mortality, whether to evil consequence or for good, seems characteristic. Absence, presence, and the hard realities of both matter and spirit pervade his poems but what might be solemn is leavened by humour and the ironic yet appreciative application of oblique data. Probably nobody else could make a love poem from the information that the tin can had to wait 48 years before the invention of the tin opener. Nature, rivers, leaves and rain carry the detritus of modern human life and suffer its impositions, but Glenday's poems alleviate and sometimes maybe remedy that suffering.

W.N. Herbert (b.1961) begins his poem, 'Dingle Dell' with the line: There is no passport to this country, / it exists as a quality of the language.' The singularity of that last word belies its indicating not one but a plurality of languages, voices, and forms of articulation. Born in Dundee, Herbert went to Oxford University and published his research on Hugh MacDiarmid and a number of poetry collections which uniquely balance and exhilaratingly lift and tumble through a range of themes and ideas: *Forked Tongue* (1994), *Cabaret McGonagall* (1996), *The Laurelude* (1998) and *Bad Shaman Blues* (2006) engage with questions of language (Dundonian Scots, English, and other vocal forms), political preference, obscure or forgotten films, historical characters, writers, objects, places and moments, with unpredictable enthusiasm and unstoppable effervescence. Herbert, Richard Price (b.1966), David Kinloch (b.1959), Robert Crawford (b.1959) and Peter McCarey (b.1956) and I myself, were loosely grouped as 'The Informationists' in the anthology, *Contraflow on the Superhighway* (1994), co-edited by Herbert and Price. Yet they are highly individuated, with Price's inimitable evocation of domesticity and parenthood, Crawford's ranging applications to subjects in science, politics and biography, and Kinloch's explorations of the ekphrastic relations between visual art and poetic meaning. It was Price who applied the designation 'Informationists' to us collectively, perceiving our shared concerns with language, facts and data, persuasiveness and political power, personal conviction and the value of knowledge, and we have been professionally committed to education in one form or another.

In the 1990s, online technology changed people's lives generally. For poets, the transformation was immediately felt in available platforms for publication. These were increased yet also taken out of a general currency. You had to know where to look to find what you were after. Yet the conditions of Scotland's history, geography and politics have their own impositions, through and beyond new technologies. Every poet publishing in the first decade of the 21st century shows them at work. The early poems of Peter McCarey (b.1956) are in *Collected Contraptions* (2011). His vast project *The Syllabary* (online at: http://www.thesyllabary.com/) has generated an epic for the age of information technology. Price noted that the poetry of the contemporaries of the original group of 'Informationists', including Iain Bamforth (b.1959) and Alison Kermack or Alison Flett (b.1965), shared similar concerns and priorities, though our association was and remains unconstrained by definition. In a broad sense, each of us prioritises not only matters of language and education, but increasingly also questions of social engagement and self-conscious relations between creatural nature in the wilderness and the politics of social civilisation. We work in a time pervaded by immeasurable quantities of 'information' – much of which, they show or imply, is a decoy. 'Fake news' is what all poetry deconstructs by its very nature.

For Carol Ann Duffy (b.1955), appointed British Poet Laureate in 2009, otherness is a constant presence: born in Scotland, she moved to England as a child, recollecting not only places and people from childhood but much more intimately a language, idiom and music foreign to the environment which her mature choices and adulthood grew into.

Duffy and others have written poems specifically on the theme of linguistic dislocation. The women who published increasingly from the 1970s made use of the achievements of their predecessors in the development of their own distinctive work. Meg Bateman learned from, respected, honoured and made creative use of the example of MacLean, as Liz Lochhead made of Morgan, or any younger poet made of that generation of men in Alexander Moffat's painting, 'Poets' Pub', much as those men did of MacDiarmid. But none of them emulated anyone.

The sustained strength of character of Liz Lochhead, the clever turns and challenges of Duffy, the self-assurance and poise of Jackie Kay, the balance of self-centredness and vulnerability of Meg Bateman, the personal, historical and universal themes of Janet Paisley, the gingery decisions and tentative annotations of experience of Kathleen Jamie (b.1962), constitute a range of new poetic voices, techniques and approaches to experience. One of the most accomplished poets of this generation, Elizabeth Burns (1957–2015), from her first collection *Ophelia* (1991), and most effectively in *Held* (2010), quietly but with immense assurance, established an inimitable tone and timbre.

Plurality is evident in the range of poets working in the early 21st century: Thomas A. Clark (b.1944), emphasising the values of taking your time and walking in landscapes experienced not as possessions but visceral daily experiences; Robert Alan Jamieson (b.1958), Christine De Luca (b.1947), Jen Hadfield (b.1978) and Roseanne Watt (b.1991) drawing different strengths from their favoured place, the Shetland archipelago; Ian Stephen (b.1955) in relation to Lewis and the wild places around it; Angus Peter Campbell (b.1952) and Rody Gorman (b.1960), carrying forward Gaelic priorities; Don Paterson (b.1963), turning domesticity into zircon-hard realisations of tenderness and relativity; Gerda Stevenson (b.1956), also prioritising domesticity but equally in a fully politicised world, most forcefully in her 2018 collection *Quines*; Graham Fulton (b.1959), bristlingly satiric in social contexts, often Paisley-based; Rab Wilson (b.1960), serious or flamboyant in Ayrshire Scots; George Gunn (b.1956), who has taken on the bardic role in Caithness, not only in his poems, but also in his political essays for the online periodical *Bella Caledonia*, his writings about his native territory in the *The Province of the Cat* (2015), his novel *The Great Edge* (2017), and his plays, especially *Atomic City* (2010); multiple prize-winning Andrew Jackson (b.1965); Gerrie Fellows (b.1954), exploring senses of displacement and belonging from her own experience, both as a New Zealander adopting Scotland and as a mother writing about in vitro fertilisation and the virtues of family, art and medicine; Robin Robertson (b.1955), poet and publisher; Roddy Lumsden (1966–2020); Mick Imlah (1956–2009), poet and editor, whose last book, *The Lost Leader* (2008), carried strength and poignancy in equal measure; Peter Manson (b.1969), innovative, experimental poet and translator; Kathrine Sowerby, who, in these lines from 'Coastline Disturbance', might be writing for generations yet unborn: 'We emerge after midnight filling the darkness with living. / Disappointments seem further across the ice'.

These are only a sample of early 21st-century Scottish poets. There are many more. The archive of the Scottish Poetry Library is an essential resource, easily accessible online, with examples of poems from a growing number of writers from all over the country.

If MacDiarmid proposed a multi-faceted national identity, and the 'seven poets' generation of poets rising after the Second World War created their work from the geographical territories each one distinctively favoured, then the gendered, class-conscious, linguistically politicised world of the following generations has made our national identity an even more complex home to different diversities, accommodating – not always easily – nature and domesticity, chaos and order, cynicism and wonder, states and movements, selves and others, internationality and self-determined nationality.

And just as MacDiarmid evokes a constant process of change and unending renewal, a redisposition of things in a world that takes the risks of regeneration, so Kathleen Jamie, following Edwin Morgan, Liz Lochhead and Jackie Kay as Scots Makar, keeps us in mind of what that means. 'Crossing the Loch' from *Jizzen* (1999) begins with a quiet, conversational question, asking the reader if she or he might remember 'how we rowed toward the cottage' across a bay, after a night drinking in a pub. The poet says she cannot remember who rowed, only how the jokes and voices went quiet and the sound of the oars in the water 'reached long into the night'. The crossing is scary, the breeze is cold, the hills 'hunched' around the loch and the water itself seems to conceal nuclear submarines, nightmares lurking below, real and metaphorical.

Yet the water is phosphorescent and beautiful, shining on fingers and oars, and the passengers are like pilgrim saints making a crossing to another place, a destination from which they will enter their futures, recollecting

> the glimmering anklets
> we wore in the shallows
> as we shipped oars and jumped,
> to draw the boat safe, high at the cottage shore.

The boat may be safe, the travellers ashore, but the wild is still there, and the autonomous region is always in need of new creation. This is what poetry does.

My own poem, 'Drawn back by magic' is perhaps an appropriate summary of what the work of the artist or writer, and especially that of the poet, is all about.

> Whatever the hand holds: camera, paintbrush, pencil, pen,
> The fingertips upon the laptop's keys, the paper, screen or canvas
> And the air the senses carry in – make traces, tracks, a patterning
> That moves out from the place and its location on the clock,
> To be caught, glimpsed, held on, whatever may be,
> And at whatever time, but never trapped. That is what work we do,
> What help it might be, crosses then to now;
> But it is not only that. It also brings you back. Something unplanned,
> Intuitive, relaxed, working in the bones and muscle,
> Way below the memory of things: abstraction, yet as real
> As that salt spray that hit you like a shower switched on
> When the ferry smashed the cross-wave and a blast
> Of blue and green turned white as frost and drenched
> You in a sudden cold – as if all resolution, steel and ice
> Were sensitised. To see, and then, to see again
> What has changed and what remains, and by whatever
> Chance and will should be, what's drawn back by magic.

PART FIVE

Divagations

I

Languages, literature, humanity and tragedy

WHEN EDWIN MORGAN was invited to contribute to a commemorative anthology of poems and paintings, *The Wallace Muse* (2005), he was at first reluctant, but after a few days, he said, he felt a deep compulsion, a desire to write in tribute to Wallace that he had not expected. The poem begins: 'Surely it is better to forget?' then the next line gives the answer: 'It is better not to forget.'

Wallace stands for an embodiment of the commonality of all people in his resistance to tyranny and oppression: an essential virtue. If we put forward the notion that egalitarianism is a recurrent theme in Scottish literature, Wallace must be a central figure. The story goes – and here I'm not dwelling on historically verifiable data, but rather a myth with moral purpose – that the aristocrats of Scotland were in an awkward position when Wallace demonstrated his capacity for leadership: they had to give him a knighthood and title – the Guardian of Scotland – to allow him to circulate freely in the higher echelons of society.

Egalitarianism is the message of Burns's anthem 'A Man's a Man' and the revolutionary potential in the sentiment is explicit in the lines from 'Tam o' Shanter' which find Tam planted in the pub: 'Kings may be blest, but Tam was glorious / Owre a' the ills o' life, victorious' – in other words, this Ayrshire farmer drinking with cronies in a small town bar one market day evening is as good a man, with as valid and fortunate a life, as any of the crowned heads of Europe. In the era of the French Revolution and the American Declaration of Independence from Royalist Britain, Burns's throwaway couplet in praise of common humanity was a dangerous and potent gesture.

This is one of the central myths of distinctive Scottish identity – though the word 'myth' doesn't mean that it has no basis in reality. Myth has more potency than documented history and that can work in more than one way. From the Columban Celtic church with its principle of the missionary working as 'first among equals' (as opposed to imperial coloniser reporting back to central authority), through to the Reformation of the 1560s, with Knox's insistence on a school in every parish, the democratic idea of education as a birthright or entitlement rather than a privilege of class or economic strata is deeply embedded and even today has resonance in real conditions and prevailing ideals, distinctively, in Scotland. It's emphatic in the very title of the philosopher George Davie's study of 19th-century Scottish university education, *The Democratic Intellect* (1961).

The egalitarian ideal – equality of opportunity – is represented both in terms of education, generally, and in terms of social organisation even more generally.

However stratified in social structure Scotland was and remains, this ideal is profoundly different from that of the hierarchical structures embodied in feudalism or class division. Arguably, it's a conservative ideal, endorsed by the idea of community associated with small-town Scotland, as opposed to the industrialised cities.

At its worst it can be debilitating, as in Alexander Scott's two-line poem, 'Scotch Equality': 'Kaa the feet / Frae thon big bastard!' At its best, it can fuel connective sympathy and social support. The radical intervention of the voice of the 'common man' – John the Commonweal – is heard most clearly in the satiric attack on church, civil and royal abuses of power, David Lyndsay's *Satyre of the Thrie Estaitis* (performed in Scotland in the 1550s, published in London in 1602); it is also heard in the literature of the Court, as when Dunbar, in 'The Thistle and the Rose' (1503), has Dame Nature remind the Lion, the King, to 'do law alike to apes and unicorns' – to look after the poor as well as his courtiers. Walter Scott's ballad, 'Jock o' Hazeldean' theatrically enacts the story of a young woman rejecting the aristocratic husband promised to her by his father, the local Northumbrian landowner. Her preference is for Jock, the name suggesting a Scottish peasant, and in the end they escape: 'She's owre the border and awa' / Wi' Jock o' Hazeldean!' In other words, romantic love triumphs and validates the worth of the common man or woman, dismissing the attractions and splendours of propertied families.

There is a specific political bias to this idea: the King doesn't give audiences (or 'surgeries') – he goes out anonymously among his people and learns for himself what their conditions are like. This is the Gaberlunzie Man, the king as wandering beggar. It appears in numerous forms in songs, stories and fiction, most famously perhaps in Scott's best-selling narrative poem *The Lady of the Lake* (1810). The principle opposes the notion of insulated modern politicians, patrician aristocrats, self-appointed managers and unassailable members of a royal family to whom the languages and lives of most of their 'subjects' remain incomprehensible. To end the tyranny of false aristocracy is an imperative felt from Wallace through Burns to James Kelman, to Nan Shepherd writing about elemental realities in the Grampians, or The Proclaimers, singing that they find it incomprehensible to understand why any nation of people should willingly let 'someone else' rule over their whole country, and be obsequiously deferential to them.

With the Scottish parliament resumed in the late 20th century some measure of reclamation began. Walter Scott's character Mrs Howden in *The Heart of Midlothian* (1818) says this:

> When we had a king, and a chancellor, and parliament-men o' our ain, we could aye peeble them wi' stanes when they werena gude bairns – But naebody's nails can reach the length o' Lunnon.

It is salutary that these words are engraved on the Canongate wall beside the Scottish parliament building in Edinburgh.

Intrinsic to this egalitarian ideal is an understanding of languages and voices as various and relative. The languages, voices and speech of Scottish people, the fluency of our songs and the artifice of our writing, are another identifiable characteristic of Scottish literature generally. From the mix of languages Dunbar was familiar with at the court of James IV in the early 16th century, to the meticulous English prose published by the Enlightenment philosophers and the written and spoken Scots and Gaelic of their contemporaries in the late 18th century, all demonstrate this heterogeneity. Even while the written prose of the Enlightenment philosophers was determinedly English, by all accounts they usually spoke rich vernacular Scots fluently, and Adam Smith was equally fluent in Gaelic.

Scottish literature is predominantly a trilingual tradition, having been written or composed mainly in Gaelic, Scots and English. There is also significant poetry in French and major work in Latin. It is in that sense a polyphonic literature, as distinct from the English tradition that runs through the development of a single language from Chaucer to Shakespeare to Milton and on; and it is distinct from Irish literature, which is predominantly bilingual, composed in Irish Gaelic and English, although there is a strong, neglected tradition of Ulster Scots writing in the north. A particular sensitivity to the values of respect and understanding in different languages may be developed by the polyphonic condition of Scotland, rather than the ignorance, isolation and superiorism sometimes inculcated by monolingual identity. However, the danger of dividedness is also present. Divide and rule has always been our bane. Hostility between Gaelic, Scots and English-language writers was once typical; now, hopefully, it is no longer so. Incomprehensibility and ignorance lead to fear, prejudice and hostility. But when they can be remedied, they might prompt curiosity, learning, sympathy, and conversation across differences. The other side of dividedness is diversity.

How people speak is of singular importance in Scottish literature – regional accents, voices trained by virtue of class and received pronunciation, tones of voice and registers of eloquence and inarticulate frustrations are all crucial aspects of major works. Sometimes this is valued, sometimes it's a liability. In *The Heart of Midlothian*, Jeanie Deans's speech before Queen Caroline is a masterpiece of impassioned rhetorical eloquence in Scots, while her nephew, The Whistler, whose name registers his distance from the language of words, is beyond the scope of civil society and leaves for America and life among 'the savages' at the end of the book. Gaelic-speakers are lampooned in William Dunbar's poetry, and he identifies the language he writes in as 'Inglis', aligning himself with Chaucer. But Gavin Douglas, Dunbar's younger contemporary, explicitly states that he is writing in the language of the Scottish nation and that it should be called Scots, to distinguish it from Gaelic, on the one hand, and from English, on the other.

In the 20th century, writers from William McIlvanney to Liz Lochhead have described the emphatic distinction in childhood between the language of the school playground – Scots – and the language of the classroom – English. In Scotland in the early 21st century, American, urban Scots, Japanese, African, Afghan, Pakistani, Indian, European and Russian languages, idioms and family inheritances have been drawn upon to inform the writing of, for example, Andrew Greig, Alan Spence, Kokumo Rocks, Bashabi Fraser, James Meek, Suhayl Saadi, Anne Donovan and Ali Smith. In some parts of Scotland, Polish is as familiar a spoken language as Gaelic.

As the poet and translator Peter McCarey says in his essay, 'Language, Politics, Policy' (in his collection *Find an Angel and Pick a Fight*, 2013):

> Knowing who you are and where you are from is not only a matter of being able to say things to your friends without being understood by foreigners, useful though that can be at times. There are two main functions to speech: communication and identification. One function conveys messages and the other shows where the messages come from. One makes bridges and the other draws borders, often between two people who are trying to talk to each other. Both are vital. The importance of identity was always apparent – if only negatively – to those in power. The Gaelic language was outlawed in 18th-century Britain after a political revolt. Linguistic suppression since has become more subtle and more effective.

In the introduction to *The Faber Book of Twentieth-Century Scottish Poetry* (1994), Douglas Dunn quotes the proverbial saw, 'A language is a dialect with an army and navy.' I've always felt that gives far too much away to the fascist belief in the authority of military power and it's never seemed to me to be really true. Rather, I would say: *A language is a dialect with a literature.*

Dialects are forms of speech, effective structures of communication, but by definition, their provenance is limited to their location. When writers start to use such dialects in literature, they open their address to readers anywhere in the world. This transforms the experiences it describes. The lives of the local people about whom it is talking, the stories and songs that were for local circulation, are now to be transmitted into the writing itself and conveyed across borders, away from their places of origin. One example, taking place especially since the 20th century, is in the relation between speech and writing of the Shetland archipelago. Robert Alan Jamieson's novel *Da Happie Laand* (2010) ranges from Shetland locations to New Zealand and other islands in the South Pacific in a global context that pays close attention to local forms of communication. But the argument applies emphatically to the Scots language in all its dialects, throughout Scotland. There are two validities at work: that of speech and that of writing. When writing becomes literature, dialect becomes language.

At the core of all these instances is an endorsement of Scotland's diversity, a way of inverting the familiar cliché of divide-and-rule that has bedevilled Scottish history for long enough. I'm reminded of the last time Alastair Reid delivered his poem, 'Scotland' at a public event. The poem famously describes the elation of the poet, walking along the seashore after rain, when larks rise singing in the sky and grace inhabits the air like a halo on heather and hills, and, meeting a miserably scowling woman from the fish shop walking the other way, the 'sun-struck madman' poet cries out delightedly, 'What a day it is!' only to be told by the person beneath the bleak, wrinkling brow, 'We'll pay for it! We'll pay for it! We'll pay for it!' Having read his poem to its conclusion, Alastair set it on fire, held it up to burn, and declared that we'd paid enough, for far too long. Time to move on.

Imperial armies, navies and media often brought with them enforced impositions of language. English occluded local dialects the world over: a wonderful gift, in some ways, but in others, a usurpation. Yet there is redress. Understanding predicates interpretation. Judgements will also be judged. As Satan says in Book 1, line 106, of the English John Milton's epic poem, 'All is not lost'.

So far I've been describing common facts that apply generally but there is one further consideration: what happens when all is indeed lost, never to be recalled or recovered? Perhaps the deepest work of literature is to bring to our knowledge an understanding of tragedy. And the acknowledgement of language and speech, their inadequacy or failure in this condition, is crucial.

When King Lear is dying, he asks his two final questions and comes to two final realisations. He realises the common helplessness of mortality: his daughter Cordelia is dead and Lear cries out the question 'Why?' – 'Why should a dog, a horse, a rat, have life, / And thou no breath at all?'

In this anguish, the commonness of mortality does not bring living things together. It keeps separate the dead daughter and the despair of the witnessing father. This leads to the very last question: 'Do you see this?' And 'this' is so singular, so particular, we cannot pull back into generalisation, we cannot seek a common truth for solace. All last things are lonely, every dying, every final departure, is unique. Lear's final words immediately follow: 'Look on her, look, her lips, / Look there, look there!'

What is he looking at? What is he telling us to look at? Cordelia's dead lips, the place where all her breath and language have passed. It is this final, unspoken understanding that brings Lear's life to its end.

Lear comes to understand that he is no longer only the centre of a universe which he broke up in the first act, nor that is he only the specific man, 'more sinned against than sinning' – the central character in a story with others – but that he is only a man – a mortal being no different from any living thing in this respect.

Lear's story has taken him to this extremity of lonely understanding. He dies in its grief. But tragedy commemorates more than merely suffering. Every time we read or see the play, there is a strange quality of joy, a way of remembering, of embodying contradictory feelings and thoughts and beliefs and giving them substance, and the truth of this is not unique to Shakespeare. In Hugh MacDiarmid's poem 'The Watergaw', the poet's glimmering, possible knowledge of how mortality allows life to give meaning arrives through a vision held in words that prompt a recollection of 'the last wild look' on a dying man's face, and the thought that perhaps understanding through such memory may at last be beginning to dawn.

2

Big themes and new approaches

CERTAIN RELATED THEMES and topics seem to have particular provenance in Scottish literature. Many of these are familiar and contested: the ideal of egalitarianism and how the various languages of Scotland invoke that ideal. Writing and voices in Gaelic, Scots and English are all equally vital in our literature: in terms of literary value, no single one has imperial dominance. Then there is the practice of certain kinds of humour and playfulness, what makes some writers funny. And there is the idea of Scottish literature as something essentially connected to the country's geographical diversity, and that recognising this might be at the heart of the matter of the nation. Crucially, there is the question of freedom – freedom from oppressions, and freedom to do certain things outwith the constraints of a politically uniform mentality, the zombie mentality of absolute consistency.

This book is addressed primarily to English-language readers, students, teachers, residents or visitors curious about our literature, maybe coming to Scotland for the first time, or maybe native born-and-bred Scots still unfamiliar with the literature of the country but wanting to know something of its character, major themes, best writers, historical terrain and contemporary climate. Of course, to say that there are such main themes in a national literature is itself contentious. There are always people playing a flute or a fiddle or conducting an orchestra of their own, quite separate from anything we could describe as 'a main theme'. Some of them are great. But if most of Scotland's writers have been engaged in some way with Scotland's people, communities, languages, geographies, land and seascapes, political and historical conditions, it should be possible to describe some main themes. Other literatures have their own preoccupations so why shouldn't ours?

For instance, three major themes in American literature might be (1) the idea of the Frontier, (2) that of the non-conformist isolatos (Huck Finn lighting out for the territories, Ishmael and Ahab, Holden Caulfield in *The Catcher in the Rye*) or (3) the American dream and its failure: the story of the boy from the log cabin who ends up in the White House, President, a foundational myth of the egalitarian society, and its corrective counterpoint, in F. Scott Fitzgerald's *The Great Gatsby* or in the long story of Ernest Hemingway's disillusionment, the American dream as a recipe for disaster.

A central theme in English literature is that of colonial and imperial history and its microcosm in the good society and its discontents. Consider the trajectory from Shakespeare's history plays and *The Tempest* with its island-native Caliban and imperial magus Prospero, and John Donne describing his lover's body as 'My America, my new-found land', to the small-town worlds of Jane Austen and George Eliot, ultimately troubled by the romantic lovers, serious artists and committed political individuals who cut across social proprieties and families with property to protect, whether in the shape of the famously 'single' man Darcy in *Pride and Prejudice* or Ladislaw in *Middlemarch* or the title character in *Daniel Deronda*, who opens little England to a Europe that threatens to overwhelm her. Consider the novels of industrial England: Dickens's London is the heart of an empire from which comes tainted benefit. In the 20th century, consider D.H. Lawrence's working-class miners and their very specifically English society. And internationally, in Rudyard Kipling's *Kim*, consider the depiction of the imperial exploitation of wealth in an exotic context, and how, in the transitional work of Joseph Conrad, in *Heart of Darkness* and *Lord Jim*, how we read the imperial, colonial, racist world of the 19th century and read forward into the postcolonial world. Such works offer a depiction of imperialism that implies its own critique.

African literature in English, French and Gikuyu has its own major themes. From Nigeria, Chinua Achebe's novel *Things Fall Apart* (1958) describes a human tragedy specific to a colonial clash, and Wole Soyinka's novel *Season of Anomy* (1973) sets the myth of Orpheus and Euridice in the Nigerian Civil War. From Senegal, Ousmane Sembène's *God's Bits of Wood* (1960; translated 1995), and his novel *Xala* (1973) and the 1975 film based on it, describe complex societies in neo-colonial French West Africa, with corrupt politicians and civil servants and a novelist's understanding of people from all social strata. From Kenya, in English and then Gikuyu, Ngũgĩ wa Thiong'o's novels *Petals of Blood* (1977) and *Devil on the Cross* (1980) chart the digging deep into, and reconstruction out of, colonialism. South African literature, from Alan Paton's classic *Cry the Beloved Country* (1948) to the fiction of Nadine Gordimer and J.M. Coetzee, to the poetry of Dennis Brutus, deals directly with the matter of apartheid and the need for freedom from racist social oppression.

David Dabydeen and Nana Wilson-Tagoe, in *A Reader's Guide to West Indian and Black British Literature* (1987), have a chapter entitled 'Selected Themes in West Indian Literature' and list nine of them: (1) Anti-imperialism and Nationalism; (2) The Treatment of Race; (3) The Theme of Childhood; (4) The Treatment of Women / Women Characters; (5) The Theme of Migration; (6) The Rastafarian Theme; (7) Post-independence Critiques; (8) Carnival; (9) Calypso.

What this list makes clear is that some themes might be explored comparatively in any literature – for example, the representation of women or children or indeed men, how masculinity is represented – but there are themes which arise specifically from a particular history and culture (Rastafarianism, Carnival and Calypso), and there are themes which, while they have a universal reference, are going to be different in different cultures at different moments in history (the treatment of race, or the themes of migration, anti-imperialism and nationalism). Some are more important, more urgently in need of address in some nations and at certain times than in others. Literature is not exempt from these imperatives.

So here are seven major themes in Scottish literature. Some of them Scottish literature shares with other literatures around the world – people are people, language is language, songs are songs and stories are stories, wherever you go. But once again, it's worth emphasising the point that Scotland has its own unfinished history and the distinctiveness of that history has helped to form these distinctive themes: (1) Scotland: The Matter of the Nation; (2) The Idea of Kinship; (3) Resistance and Freedom; (4) Egalitarianism: Common Humanity; (5) Voice and Languages: Gaelic, Scots and English; (6) Geography: Terrain and Locations; (7) Humour and Play and their counterparts, Leanness and Austerity.

There are other approaches to Scottish literature that would highlight certain questions or areas of concern that our writers have addressed specifically. Many writers in many literatures address the same or similar questions and themes but there are differences in the emphases each writer brings to these questions.

Let's note another seven: (1) Time periods and what they might mean: The history of literature like that of any of the arts, is conveniently structured according to periods and movements, and some can be more accurately described than others. Medieval, Renaissance, Enlightenment, Romantic, Modernist, Postmodernist – these are all terms of reference more or less familiar and reliable to cultural historians internationally, though it might be noted that they are not universal. In some eastern cultures the priorities of individualism in the Romantic era are quite unfamiliar. (2) The Literature of War and of Religion: The two are connected. Every literature has addressed the themes of war and bloody conflict. Similarly, every literature has its libraries of the spirit: on the one hand, orthodoxies and doctrines, the rules, and on the other hand, understandings of what we call the 'spiritual' for want of a better term, the meanings. When Wilfred Owen looks on the consequences of war and asks, 'Was it for this the clay grew tall?' and Benjamin Britten sets his words to music in his *War Requiem*, there's no doubt about the way the question cuts across all national distinctions. (3) Children's Literature: What we encourage children to read is the key to everything else, and that's a reason to think about it seriously, as adults. (4) Sport: Is there a literature of sport? We'll return to this question. (5) Travel Writing: There's a history of writing about travelling through Scotland, and another history of writing about Scottish travellers in the world, the literature of the Scottish diaspora. (6) Languages: There's a neglected history of Scottish literature in Latin. And since at least the 1990s, there's a literature that has arisen in the context of (7) New Media.

Now, these aren't 'main themes' but they do open up to our enquiry forms of literature that might otherwise be neglected. So let's spend some time with them and see what we can find.

Start with the most basic frame, a spine that makes the subject vertebrate, a history. Time periods or international cultural movements such as Romanticism or Modernism are categories. They can be useful but they can also be misleading. They're almost always defined by a retrospective view: they were hardly ever described in such terms at the time the writers we associate with them were working. Therefore it's worth asking, what do certain literary terms mean, when we apply them to Scottish literature?

Medieval and Renaissance, for example, would be seen as historically consecutive terms in English literature, the first exemplified by Chaucer, the second by Shakespeare: supreme examples that reciprocate the validity of the terms. Chaucer's world-view is profoundly medieval, with all that implies of astronomical, mythological, religious, social and literary structures and assumptions. Shakespeare's is equally of the Elizabethan Renaissance and then of the Jacobean world. And yet if we think of Henryson, Dunbar, Douglas and Lyndsay, then of the 'Castalian Band' of poets associated with James VI, we find in Scottish literature that there is no such clear division of literary ethos. In many respects, from 1503–1513, the court of James IV (one hundred years before Shakespeare) could be described as a Renaissance court, rather than a medieval one. The essential text here is Andrea Thomas's *Glory and Honour: The Renaissance in Scotland* (2013).

The era of Enlightenment and Romanticism, from around 1750 to around 1840, is distinctively complex in Scottish literature. In English literature, this period is conventionally seen as a progression from the classical precision, snap and crackle of Pope to the individualistic radicalism and grand gestures of Shelley and his contemporaries. In Scottish literature, however, a more complex blend of these two cultural contexts is evident in, for example, Burns (certainly Romantic, but also a child of the Enlightenment) and Scott (certainly an Enlightenment writer, but also the novelist whose heroes and heroines include the Highland outlaw Rob Roy and the peasant cow-feeder's daughter Jeanie Deans).

A similar complexity can be understood in Scottish literature's relation to Modernism, to which we shall return.

These are merely examples of ways in which traditional, familiar categories might be usefully complicated by reading Scottish literature against the grain of the 'Great Tradition' of English literature. They show how far such a 'Great Tradition' is constructed by choices of preference and self-consciously retrospective definition.

Literary history itself is only one way of encountering great writers. Another is simply to roam around, without reference to historical periods, national traditions or transitional movements. But if this can be serendipitous and lead you to discoveries you could not have predicted, it can be hit-or-miss and arbitrary. Broader and deeper knowledge of the contexts of works of literature and the biographies of writers is usually a good thing.

The American poet William Carlos Williams once said, 'You should never explain a poem – but it always helps.' In Scottish literature, almost every demonstration that a writer is worth reading is an act of reclamation from neglect, and a challenge to an order of authority which already exists. Reading itself is one of the arts of resistance.

3

Mongrel nation: freedom, history and geography

SCOTLAND ITSELF IS a main theme in the literature of Scotland, from 'Deirdre's Farewell to Alba' to Dunbar's poem on the marriage of James IV and Margaret Tudor in 1503 to MacDiarmid's numerous poems that take 'Scotland' as their title. One of MacDiarmid's poems definitively sums up the whole question, 'Separatism':

> If there's a sword-like sang
> That can cut Scotland clear
> O' a' the warld beside,
> Rax me the hilt o't here!

However 'romantic' the metaphor seems, it is meaningful: 'For there's nae jewel till / Frae the rest o' earth it's free' – pause on that. It's true, isn't it? You see the value of something, anything, in its singularity, and yet, also, in its measurement against, and connectedness with, other things. MacDiarmid's hope is to give a 'starry separateness' to Scotland, that the country might be both valued accordingly and connected to reciprocal values internationally.

This 'separateness' might endorse political independence, yet national identity remains a central question even in ostensibly conservative texts. Scott's *Waverley* and John Buchan's recasting of the story as a native uprising in South Africa, in *Prester John*, leave the values of the rebels Fergus MacIvor and John Laputa intact, even if their cause in each novel seems defeated. The representation of the just ideal in literary terms has a preservative effect: we do not forget it.

So the theme of national identity and what it might mean has a long lineage in Scotland and in the work of Scotland's major writers, radical or conservative. The three novels of Lewis Grassic Gibbon's *A Scots Quair* were deliberately intended to address the whole matter of Scotland, from the farming community in *Sunset Song*, through the small town in *Cloud Howe*, to the industrial city in *Grey Granite*. His contemporary Neil Gunn, although most of his work describes the Highlands, also set novels in Edinburgh and Glasgow, and took an epic view of Scottish history through three novels, *Sun Circle*, *Butcher's Broom*, and *The Silver Darlings*. Once again, the whole vision is an all-in view of national identity and national potential. The significant precedent here is Walter Scott, writing about Scotland from the Borders to the archipelagos of Orkney and Shetland. One major 21st-century novel taking the historical scenario of

Scotland since the Second World War is James Robertson's *And the Land Lay Still*. The epic scale of these works of fiction was self-consciously intended to address the matter of the nation. And the nation, in Scotland, means differences. To know who and what we are we have to find out about others. These works encourage healthy curiosity. What stands in the way of that impulse of enquiry are the usurpers: oppressors, enemies, zombies. Even the dead are not safe from these enemies, when they win.

When Columba arrived in Scotland from Ireland, and when, before him, the Celtic warriors and lovers travelled between and throughout both countries, the foundations of a myth of kinship were laid down: kinship across differences. Let's call this a foundational myth of Scotland. The difference between peoples and the common things that connect us all are at the heart of it. Columba's legacy, through to the kingdom of Scotland in the time of Malcolm Canmore ('canmore' meaning 'great leader'), was to endorse the understanding that a nation is made up of different groups, languages, geographical areas, terrains, economies and cultural preferences. The early Celtic Church established this with the idea that the missionary was coming among people not to condescend to them and exploit their resources, but to live with others and give them his own expertise, freely. If Scotland is a major theme, the variousness of the nation's people is equally so. Liz Lochhead's poem 'Something I'm Not' seems to set forth difference in its title, but that title is actually the poem's first line, so it goes on: 'Something I'm Not // familiar with, the tune / of their talking…' and we begin to make the acquaintance of the poet's neighbours, a mother and her child, in a tentative, friendly way. They have come to Glasgow from somewhere far away, but the neighbourliness the poet expresses is encapsulated in the sympathetic question at the heart of the poem: 'How does she feel?' – and with that, a kinship of sympathy is established.

Sir David Lyndsay's *Ane Satyre of the Thrie Estaits* is essentially a play about the difference between people of various economic, professional and religious strata, but its comprehensive picture is a presentation of national complexity, a searching exploration of the corruptions of civic Scotland, and the dynamics that were to lead to the Reformation. Once again, the worst aspects of Scotland lie in the dividedness of the people; the best are to be found in a confident, knowledgeable familiarity with their diversity and relatedness, a compassion for the worst-off, and a practical, reforming zeal to condemn hypocrisy and improve the way things are.

William Lithgow, travelling from Scotland throughout Europe and as far as Constantinople, while always attached to the home base in Lanarkshire, stays open to the experience of foreign territories. His experience of otherness and his appetite for it is unlike anything else in literature. He places himself in the most vulnerable positions and suffers terribly sometimes, yet his sense of connectedness to the whole human story is a main force running through his astonishing book, *The Totall Discourse of The Rare Adventures & Painefull Peregrinations of long Nineteene Yeares Travayles from Scotland to the most famous Kingdomes in Europe, Asia and Africa* (1632).

Of all early 20th-century Scottish writers, perhaps Norman Douglas embodies the spirit of the myth of kinship most challengingly. His novel *South Wind* (1917) is utterly devoted to the life of pleasure on the island of Capri in the Mediterranean, and would seem as far removed from Scotland as possible. Douglas's devotion to hedonism is not merely self-indulgent narcissism but a necessary corrective to the self-denials of Calvinism. The same nation that produced John Knox and the 'Wee Free' Church, produced Ian Fleming, James Bond and his playgrounds in the Seychelles. There are many ways of being Scottish.

Kinship across difference is a deep myth, less obvious than the other early myth of Scottish identity: liberty, held in the image of the damned but defiant fighter. For a generation this was made familiar by the film *Braveheart* (1995) in which Mel Gibson's William Wallace stood against Patrick McGoohan's King Edward, both symbolic figures for Scotland and England. It's a biblical trope: David and Goliath. In the Bible, happily, David wins. When we meet Calgacus and his small army of warriors, resisting the encroaching, overwhelming might of imperial Rome, in the *Agricola* (98AD) of Tacitus, it's the same idea, but Rome overwhelms the resistance. It didn't quite happen that way, of course. Still, the nature of the opposition, the little guy against the bully, is perennially familiar. It may be projection to think that it underscores every one of the brief stanza-snaps in the kaleidoscope of martial disaster that is *The Gododdin*. The ideal of Liberty or Freedom (the former a Latin term, the latter Anglo-Saxon) – conceived as independence from English authority in the wars led by William Wallace and Robert the Bruce – was translated from historical event into literary artefact by John Barbour in *The Bruce* and Blind Harry in *The Wallace*, and into political rhetoric of the highest order in the *Declaration of Arbroath*. The posture recurs again and again. Perhaps its earliest articulation is in Sallust (Gaius Sallustus Crispus, 86–34BC), a statesman of the last century of the Roman Republic, who, in Chapter XXXIII, section 5 of his *Bellum Catilinae* (c.44BC), wrote:

> At nos non imperium neque divitias petimus, quarum rerum causa bella atque certamina omnia inter mortales sunt, sed libertatem, quam nemo bonus nisi cum anima simul amittit.

This translates as:

> We do not aim at power or wealth, for the sake of which wars and all

kinds of strife arise among mankind; we want only our liberty, which no honorable man relinquishes but with his life.

In the 18th century, William Hamilton of Gilbertfield rewrites Harry's *Wallace* in a contemporary idiom. Burns reads it fresh and writes in an autobiographical letter of 2 August 1787 to Dr John Moore: 'the story of Wallace poured a Scottish prejudice into my veins which will boil along there, till the flood-gates of life shut in eternal rest.'

He writes his own version of Bruce's address to the troops at Bannockburn, in 'Scots Wha Hae', providing an image of the defending Scots sending the invading army homeward to think again, that will reappear in the 20th century in the Corries' famous song, 'Flower of Scotland'. The danger, as usual, is cliché, but the corrective is there in that crucial sense of diversity. Scotland is not uniform. Geographical variety is one of the country's defining characteristics. Few nations contain so many vastly contrasting locations within such a short space of each other. Few cities are as different as Glasgow and Edinburgh, few archipelagos so different in character as Orkney and Shetland; every island in the Hebrides has an individual feel and sound to it. The acoustics are different. A map of the country opens up so many forms of terrain and landscape, different kinds of nature: the long plains of Caithness, the Alpine mountain ridges of Skye, the lush fields of Perthshire, Ross-shire and the eerie landscapes of the Borders, dramatic Dumfriesshire and the benign hills of Ayrshire, the Rhinns of Galloway, the historical densities of Argyll, the vast extending fields and sharp edges of Kincardinshire and Aberdeenshire.

And the relation between people, land and economy is crucial, not to be defined by sublime Romantic notions of the spectacular or picturesque. A comprehensive review of Scottish literature would have to take into full account the relation between writing and specific terrain, geographies of land, sea and imagination. And there are affinities between cultural priorities in different places and times, extending far beyond Scotland. The exhilarating, anti-Romantic realism of Duncan Ban MacIntyre's poem 'Praise of Ben Dorain' takes the form of a musical structure, a bagpipe pibroch, to describe the vigorous, crafty experience of hunting deer over the mountain slopes and through the woods. There is a shrewd balance or combination in the poem, of, on the one hand, respect for the spirit of other living creatures and our human place in the world beside them, and on the other, an understanding of the material reality that insists that the deer must be hunted, shot and used as good food. This calls to mind the words of the Nigerian Nobel laureate Wole Soyinka (as reported in *The Times Literary Supplement*, 11 April 1997, p.16), whose laconic reply to the question posed in a radio programme about the place of animals in Utopia, was: 'Mainly for hunting.' While he loves a quiet wander in the forest, 'it is marvellous when that peace is occasionally shattered by the sound of gunshot.'

Few literatures are so heavily populated by writers who show particular care for specific places: the Edinburgh of Dunbar, Fergusson, Scott, Spark, Garioch, MacCaig, Ian Rankin; the Glasgow of Catherine Carswell, Archie Hind, Morgan, Gray, Kelman; the Borders of the Ballads, Burns, Hogg, MacDiarmid; the Hebrides of MacLean, Crichton Smith or Marie Hedderwick; the north-east of Grassic Gibbon, Violet Jacob, Marion Angus; the Orkney of Mackay Brown, Muir, Linklater; the Shetland of William J. Tait, Stella Sutherland, Christine De Luca, Jen Hadfield and Roseanne Watt. Every school in Scotland might have a detailed map of their area showing all these literary links. The extent to which the superficialities of internationalised mass media and commercialism encroach upon such imaginative and linguistic sources of nourishment is obvious. But the legacy of this concern with the lived environment of people – most powerfully prioritised in the work of Patrick Geddes and Charles Rennie Mackintosh – is a deeply regenerating sensitivity and commitment to the human ecology. This is closely described in the critical study by Louisa M. Gairn, *Ecology and Modern Scottish Literature* (2008).

William McIlvanney once famously called Scotland a 'mongrel nation' and was cheered and praised for doing so. Edwin Morgan's exemplary lead in finding out what 'others' are all about is a key to all the arts: in study and discovery, you exercise that most valuable thing, the intrinsic optimism of curiosity.

4
Modernity and war: visions beyond violence

THE WALLACE OF William Hamilton of Gilbertfield (c.1665–1751) neither sentimentalises the violence of warfare, nor trivialises the ideals being fought for.

> Now all is death and wounds; the crimson plain
> Floats round in blood, and groans beneath its slain.
> Promiscuous crowds one common ruin share,
> And death alone employs the wasteful war.
> They trembling fly by conquering Scots oppress'd,
> And the broad ranks of battle lie defac'd;
> A false usurper sinks in ev'ry foe,
> And liberty returns with every blow.

Burns transforms this into his own anthem:

> By Oppression's woes and pains!
> By your Sons in servile chains!
> We will drain our dearest veins,
> But they *shall* be free!
>
> Lay the proud Usurpers low!
> Tyrants fall in every foe!
> LIBERTY's in every blow!
> Let us DO – OR DIE!!!

The word 'Usurper' – someone who is taking the place of someone else who should rightfully be there – is horribly resonant. Most memorably, it is the understated last word of the first section of James Joyce's *Ulysses* (1922). In the stance of resistance to imposed authority, there is a political continuity that runs across conspicuously different ideologies, from Harry's *Wallace* and Barbour's *Bruce* of the Catholic millennium, to the Protestant Reformers, through to the Catholic Jacobites, then on to the Protestant Covenanters once again. Pride may be a liability in any such configuration, but self-determination is its heart.

James Joyce, T.S. Eliot and Ezra Pound dedicated themselves to aesthetic priorities that would cleave away what Pound called the 'botched civilisation' of

Victorian sentimentalism, outworn hierarchies of perspective and the repetitive, soporific rhythms of the iambic pentameter. In Pound's phrase, the idea was to 'Make it new!' But MacDiarmid, Lewis Grassic Gibbon, Sorley MacLean and others, in the 1920s, 30s and early 40s, were dedicated not only to making it new but also to recovering and recuperating a vast neglected history of literary practice and lived experience from Scotland's past, especially in the 'subject' languages, Scots and Gaelic. For them, to make it new was to reclaim and reinvent the ancient. This is why the term 'Scottish Renaissance' is so appropriate: it was a regeneration, or as Edwin Morgan puts it, a 'Retrieving and Renewing'.

If MacDiarmid made the decisive break with a certain kind of familiar sentimentalism in his poems and essays of the 1920s, there are precedents for the unsentimental and hard-headed proto-modernist attitudes in earlier work from the 19th century. No-one is more the modern cultural relativist than Robert Louis Stevenson on his international travels; the experience of the industrial worker is voiced by John Davidson, who also supplies a Nietzschean analysis of the world in his Testaments; in Violet Jacob and Marion Angus we hear vernacular Scots voices articulating the experiences of women as the modern world of international trade and global warfare imposes itself upon them. Lewis Grassic Gibbon's modernist trilogy of novels ends in the city, like Joyce and Dos Passos, leaving the farm for the small town before entering the modern industrial world. The books are marching from one world war towards another. Fascism is the ethos they oppose.

If this is a main theme implicit in modern Scottish literature, how does it sound when it becomes explicit, when writers address directly the most unmistakable fact of modernity: that it is pervaded by unprecedented violence, rising fascism and war?

Across its history, Scottish literature has dealt with the subject, from the gory accounts of the Wars of Independence in the epics of Wallace and Bruce, to 20th-century novels, poems and songs about modern war, from Eric Linklater's classic novel *Private Angelo* (1946) to Edwin Morgan's provocative poem 'Twin Towers' (from *A Book of Lives*, 2007): 'The shock-waves were a tocsin for the overweening imperium.'

Among the best critical explorations of the questions raised here are to be found in Angus Calder's book of critical essays and reviews, *Disasters and Heroes: On War, Memory and Representation* (2004), Trevor Royle's anthology, *In Flanders Fields: Scottish Poetry and Prose of the First World War* (1990) and his historical studies *The Flowers of the Forest: Scotland and the First World War* (2006), *A Time of Tyrants: Scotland and the Second World War* (2011) and *Facing the Bear: Scotland and the Cold War* (2019). At least two poetry anthologies, Lizzie MacGregor's *Beneath Troubled Skies: Poems of Scotland at War 1914–1918*, and David Goldie and Roderick Watson's *From the Line: Scottish War Poetry 1914–1945* (both 2014), are also required reading.

There were many Scottish poets in both World Wars: private soldiers, officers, non-combatants, conscientious objectors. Marion Angus and Violet Jacob are only two of the women poets whose work represents the experiences of those who remained at home.

The English poets of World War 1, Siegfried Sassoon and Wilfred Owen, are very well known and the greatest modernist poem of the trenches is by the Welshman David Jones, *In Parenthesis* (1937). Less widely read but equally remarkable were the Scottish poets of the First World War. Like their English contemporaries, they were coming to terms with a new reality. John Buchan might be caricatured as an imperialist from his popular fiction but in 'On Leave' he demonstrates an understanding and sympathy with the soldier returning to a world irrevocably altered:

> I wasna the man I had been, –
> Juist a gangrel dozin' in fits; –
> The pin had faun oot o' the warld,
> And I doddered amang the bits.

With 'The stink o' the gas in my nose, / The colour o' bluid in my ee,' as the sun goes down in the West, the soldier attempts to make his peace with God. The Scots language, the use of the persona, the pathos inherent in the conventional verse form, all catch a moment of utter and fearful historical change.

W.D. Cocker (1882–1970), a journalist with the *Daily Record* who served with the Highland Light Infantry, was taken prisoner in 1917 and sent to work in a factory manufacturing barbed wire. His *Sonnets in Captivity*, written in English, keep a detached and formally distanced perspective: 'Endurance! That's the outstanding wonder! / What finely tempered steel we mortals are!' In 'The Call', he writes:

> They did not put off humanity when they put on a uniform.
> They could weep, too.
> They also had bad news in letters, and cried at night in their
>   dug-out or billet – those devoted lads.
> They were not soldiers; they were men,
> The best God ever created on this war-scarred earth.
> Not as the world calls soldiers.
> Military pomp, pride, pageantry and gorgeousness of arms –
> It moved them not...

The limpidity of the verse, the tight diction and the sharp line-breaks register the restraint of emotion and effective understatement.

Poets with immediate experience of the war included Roderick Watson Kerr (1893–1960), who, when his poems were first published, was immediately compared with Siegfried Sassoon. 'From the Line' begins:

> Have you seen men coming from the Line,
> Tottering, shuddering, as if bad wine
> Had drugged their very souls...

And Joseph Lee (1875–1949), a Dundee man who became editor of the *People's Journal*, enlisted with the Black Watch and saw battle in France, was writing and drawing pictures from the trenches before he was taken prisoner. 'The Green Grass' is blatant and bitter:

> The grass grows green on the long, long tracks
> That I shall never tread –
> Why are we dead?'

The family of Ewart Alan Mackintosh (1893–1917) came from Alness in Easter Ross, but he was born in Brighton, educated in London and Oxford, learned Gaelic and was awarded the Military Cross at the Battle of the Somme in 1916. Invalided home, he was offered a promotion, teaching cadets at Cambridge, but opted for further service and was killed in 1917. His earliest poems read like heroic glorifications of war but quickly he recognised the horror and waste he was witnessing, and began writing anguished parodies and Brechtian deflations. 'Departure of the 4th Camerons' begins: 'The pipes in the street were playing bravely / The marching lads went by...' but in 'Recruiting' he writes:

> Go and help to swell the names
> In the casualty lists.
> Help to make a column's stuff
> For the blasted journalists.

One of the most unforgettable poems of death in battle is 'When you see millions of the mouthless dead' by Charles Hamilton Sorley (1895–1915) who himself was killed in the Battle of Loos. Foreshadowing Hamish Henderson, Sorley's poem 'To Germany' begins with the recognition that all soldiers share a common experience: 'You are blind like us.' Yet it offers some hope that in peace, such commonalities might be replaced by the virtues of understanding sympathetically the differences that constitute cultural diversity:

> When it is peace, then we may view again

> With new-won eyes each other's truer form
> And wonder.

The thread that runs from the Scottish poets of the First World War on into what followed renews commitment to the realisation of hope in a nation of unrealised possibility.

Exactly this message is implicit in the words at the end of Lewis Grassic Gibbon's *Sunset Song*: 'They died for a world that is past, these men, but they did not die for this that we seem to inherit.' Or, what we do now, if it's the right thing, is the only real way to honour them, because whether we like it or not, we are history: we will become it, but we can make it too. Over to you, reader.

In the Second World War, Hamish Henderson wrote not only the beautifully sustained sequence *Elegies for the Dead in Cyrenaica* (1948) but also a number of ballads and songs that quickly passed into anonymous familiarity and were sung by soldiers on innumerable occasions without reference to their author. Corey Gibson's book, *The Voice of the People: Hamish Henderson and Scottish Cultural Politics* (2015), brings these two aspects together in a comprehensive overview of his achievement. Other major poets who came to prominence after the war remained connected by their experience of that war, often in North Africa: Sorley MacLean, Edwin Morgan, Robert Garioch, George Campbell Hay, G.S. Fraser. Not least among this company is Douglas Young: international scholar, translator, SNP Party Chairman in the 1940s, whose opposition to fascism combined with a stand against UK conscription of Scots led to two jail sentences, and whose *Naething Dauntit: Collected Poems*, edited by Emma Dymock (2016), warrants his reassessment.

Of course, the question of war has been addressed in different genres. Isobel Murray's *Scottish Novels of the Second World War* (2011) is essential reading. Plays such as Peter Arnott's *White Rose* (1985), about the only woman Russian fighter-pilot at the siege of Stalingrad, Gregory Burke's *Black Watch* (2006), or Gerda Stevenson's *Federer versus Murray* (2010), explore issues of camaraderie, heroism, self-sacrifice, solidarity and the idea of the family, asking the essential questions: What is at stake? What is it worth? What are we fighting for?

Throughout the Cold War, and since the 1990s, the rise of the era of Information Technology and 'globalisation', 'cosmopolitanism' or 'corporatisation', the gulf between rich and poor increased along with the commodification and desensitisation of the world. The work of artists and writers is to oppose that. This is the most subtle and extensive conflict of all and everyone is engaged, knowingly or otherwise. Many literary works explore the complexities of loyalty and betrayal in this context, including major novels by Allan Massie and Stuart Hood. A simple, sterner judgement comes from Hugh MacDiarmid, in this powerful summary of the military ethos in his poem on the Spanish Civil War, *The Battle Continues* (1957) and related work, such as 'England's Double Knavery':

> All soldiers are fools
> That's why they kill each other.
> The deterioration of life under the regime
> Of the soldier is a commonplace; physical power
> Is a rough substitute for patience and intelligence
> And co-operative effort in the governance of man;
> Used as a normal accompaniment of action
> Instead of a last resort it is a sign
> Of extreme social weakness. Killing
> Is the ultimate simplification of life.

This regime, which MacDiarmid characterises as the 'animus of war', is intended 'to enforce uniformity': 'To extirpate whatever the soldier / Can neither understand nor utilise'.

He knew what he was talking about and had enough experience to talk about it authoritatively. During the First World War, MacDiarmid served in the Royal Army Medical Corps in the British Army, in Salonika, in Greece, and witnessed death closely. His fury at the rise of fascism leading to the Spanish Civil War in 1936 and the escalation of Nazism in Germany, was expressed in poetry of indignation and exhaustion. In the 'Author's Note' to his autobiography *Lucky Poet* (1943), MacDiarmid quoted 'a forgotten poet of ancient Egypt' who wrote: 'I have seen violence, I have seen violence – / Give thy heart after letters…'

He had seen so many young men killed before that seeing another generation trooped out for the Second World War appalled him. And he knew how abhorrent it was – is – to begin to become indifferent to the increasing commonness of bad beliefs, to care less and less about the murderousness they lead to, and he saw it happening all around him. The focus of his anger was the uniformity enforced by militarism, fascism and imperialism, and this energised his creativity, his vision for a future in which the priorities of culture might be actively affirmed. The same could be said of the next generation of poets: Henderson, MacLean, and many others, a company of major Scottish writers recording the wars of the modern world with a vision of what might best come after them.

5

Genres and forms: crime, science fiction, children's literature, song

LITERATURE TAKES MANY shapes. It comes in different genres. The doyenne of crime fiction Val McDermid once countered the argument that genre fiction was not 'literature' by pointing out that literature was essentially something that made you care, something that sensitised you. If the driving force of politics and war is deeply and ultimately rooted in the desire for power and the rallying commands are for absolute authority or, 'reclaiming' your 'rights', then perhaps the energies and aptitudes that produce the most valuable works of art are essentially concerned with the enablement and clear exercise of differences, variations, multiplicities: more than one story, many ways of understanding.

Any good society balances standards of justice and egalitarian social practice with an encouragement of difference and diversity of practice. Any bad society tries to enforce the former by killing off the latter and policing forms of 'justice' that serve only the rulers.

Pause on that notion of diversity, the range of different forms and genres, and consider their literary or artistic effect. How does history speak of what has happened through the arts? How will the thoughtful minds of those who consider different ways of understanding come to an account? Thinking things through takes time and work, so perhaps we have to trust that the minds that help keep other minds alive are working unobtrusively, always, even now.

Philosophical aphorisms or extended enquiries, essays, multi-volume studies of history are in themselves a kind of storytelling. They are literature just as much as poems, fiction and plays. Good history well-written is as much a *literary* achievement as anything. If it's usually written by the winners, it's often better understood by the losers. The writing that allows film narratives or television programmes, either stand-alone drama or long-running series, to develop characters, relationships, social contexts, tension and ultimately meaning, is also literature. So is song.

The ballads are generally understood this way, and despite the commercial imperative, so are many songs caught up in the music industry, like those by some of the most famous names in Scotland since the 1960s: Frankie Miller (b.1949), Michael Marra (1952–2012), Annie Lennox (b.1954) and Eddi Reader (b.1959). One of the most popular songs of the 1980s and 1990s, 'I'm Gonna Be (500 miles)' by The Proclaimers, Craig and Charlie Reid (both b.1962), a comic, joyful declaration of love and commitment, has its own distinctly literary subtleties and ironies. The singer promises to be the man who will wake up next to, walk out alongside, and work hard to provide for, his beloved; but he also admits he's probably going to get drunk ('next to you'), and will be 'havering' (a good Scots word meaning, 'talking nonsense') 'to you' and when the money comes in, he'll 'pass almost every penny on to you'. The paradoxical certainty of hesitation in 'almost' is delightful. Commitment is qualified, but still the singer swears that he would walk a thousand miles to 'fall down at your door'. Whether his beloved would welcome the sight of him at that stage might be a moot point.

In his book *Literature and Oatmeal* (1935), William Power writes: 'Scotland is decidedly one of the not very numerous countries in which popular vernacular songs, as distinguished from narrative ballads, are to be counted as literature.' Popular songs, he says, were the oldest form if literature in Scots, 'made by the people for the people' and increasingly popular when anonymous singers with exceptional talents' gave them 'a touch of real artistry'. The singer Karine Polwart (b.1970), in her play *Wind Resistance* (2016), brings together songs, both traditional and specifically-authored and composed, stories, elements of autobiography and vitalising evocations of ecological understanding and appreciation of landscape and the living creatures who inhabit it. As a play, the work has a narrative arc through history, interrogating and affirming the principle of scientific and medical progress as something practically in need of a complementary understanding of living sympathy and intuitive sensitivities. Its combination of different media forms is intrinsic to its presentation of the necessity of interconnectedness. It scorns sentimentalism as much as it endorses deep feeling.

The popularity of different media idioms, drawing on various overlapping cultural strata, combined with the priorities of commercialism, have wrought their distortions and shaped the expressions of the national song tradition. Inevitably this is true of all cultures in all eras but it seems peculiarly visible in the second half of 20th-century Scotland. Norman Buchan's trusty pocket anthology *101 Scottish Songs* (1962) collects traditional ballads and familiar Burns songs with sparky children's playground rhymes, contemporary folk songs and the faux-anthems of an impotent nationalism: 'Ae Fond Kiss' and 'Scots Wha Hae' are followed by 'The Barnyards o' Delgaty', and 'The Wee Magic Stane' (about the removal of the Stone of Destiny from Westminster) is followed by Cliff Hanley's 'Scotland the Brave', in which the nation is hyperbolically glorified, with its soaring, resplendent reputation, its flags and pennants fluttering finely in the wind, symbolising a nation of great aspiration to match its natural beauties in river and mountain, a land to which the author's courageous heart is permanently pledged. The excessive exhilaration in the words of the song risks bathos, and succumbs to it, though for many generations it remained a sentimental touchstone.

It is followed by children's songs like 'Katie Bairdie', 'The Tod', 'Coulter's

Candy' and 'Ma Maw's a Millionaire' which come as welcome deflations of pomp:

> Ma Maw's a millionaire!
> Blue eyes an' curly hair!
> Sitting among the Eskimos,
> Playing a game o' dominoes,
> Ma Maw's a millionaire.

Performed through the 1960s and 1970s on radio and TV by such cultural luminaries as Andy Stewart and Joe Gordon, many of these songs were in family currency for more than one generation, whether they liked them or not. In the later 20th and 21st centuries, also through mass media and festivals, extraordinary Gaelic singers, from Dolina MacLennan to Karen Matheson and Julie Fowlis, reached a wider audience than had been possible in earlier periods. Within the dictates of popular commercialism and fashion, work of lasting quality was possible and sometimes thriving.

Reading against the grain, analysing what's intended to be accepted unquestioningly, is what good literary critics do, what literature itself encourages us all to do. Popularity is no guide. Some of the best literature, in its day, was not well-received. The poetry of William Blake, Melville's *Moby-Dick*, were not considered 'classics' in their time. On 22 November 1926, Hugh MacDiarmid's *A Drunk Man Looks at the Thistle* was published in an edition of 500 copies. Only 99 had been sold by the end of the year.

Yet one of the phenomena of modern literature has been the rise of established popular genre fiction, successful both in commercial terms and as literary forms in which a balance must be struck between the fulfilment of genre expectations and the renewal of novelty, books which are both reliable and unpredictable. There is a long tradition of popular genre work, from espionage novels by John Buchan, Ian Fleming and Alistair MacLean, science fiction by Naomi Mitchison, David Lindsay, Iain Banks, Ken MacLeod and Paul Johnston, in the western genre, Alan Sharp's film scripts for *The Hired Hand* (1971) and *Ulzana's Raid* (1972), and in Romantic fiction, from Annie S. Swan (1859–1943) to Dorothy Dunnett (1923–2001) and Jessica Stirling (another name for Hugh C. Rae, 1935–2014).

Crime fiction has a long pedigree in Scottish writing, arguably beginning in major authors such as Hogg and Stevenson but centrally occupying the golden period of the genre in work by Michael Innes (J.I.M. Stewart, 1906–94) such as *Lament for a Maker* (1938), with its recurring motif from William Dunbar, 'Timor Mortis Conturbat Me', and Josephine Tey (Elizabeth Mackintosh, 1896–1952), who set her novel *The Singing Sands* (1952) in Scotland, where the terrain itself is a significant component of the story. Tey's wry humour is worth savouring. In *The Singing Sands*, two of the characters have this memorable exchange:

> Grant, repeating Mr Tallisker's speech on comparative heavens, said that the Gaels were the only race who visualised Heaven as a country of the young; which was endearing of them.
> 'They are the only known race who have no word for no,' said Laura drily.
> 'That is a much more revealing characteristic than their notions of eternity.'

The biography by Jennifer Morag Henderson brings out the depth of Tey's interrogations of the assumptions which work against truth. Tey's novel *The Daughter of Time* (1951) is a salutary reminder of how quickly and deeply a lie can become established as fact in the public imagination.

Blending expectations familiar from the crime fiction genre with exotic locations, Alexander McCall Smith (b. 1948), in his novels featuring Mma Precious Ramotswe, *The No. 1 Ladies' Detective Agency* series, and in other books often set in Edinburgh, brings a poised, cleverly balanced style to bear on humorous, sometimes whimsical, situations, often spiced with serious implication. The sheer unexpectedness of the early novels sustains their charm. As genre fiction, after the scene is established, they trade on expectation, but the variety of his series novels (such as *The Sunday Philosophy Club* and *44 Scotland Street*) and the non-series novels such as *La's Orchestra Saves the World* suggests something of McCall Smith's range and calibre.

The early novels of Hugh C. Rae (the great-grandfather of Tartan noir), particularly *Skinner* (1965) and *A Few Small Bones* (1968), combine tight plotting and tense stylistic understatement. William McIlvanney (1936–2015), in mainstream novels, including *Docherty* (1975), delivers complex character-portraits and a depiction of community (Graithnock, based on Kilmarnock) at a particular historical moment, but he also occupies the crime genre with *Laidlaw* (1977) and its sequels *The Papers of Tony Veitch* (1983) and *Strange Loyalties* (1991). These are highly literate, politically engaged novels in which the genre opens the door to social exploration and moral judgement in bravura style. Frederic Lindsay (1933–2013) produced one of the most sinister, enigmatic crime novels in *Brond* (1983) and each of his subsequent books, some with the recurring main character Inspector Jim Meldrum, is cleverly paced and convincing. Christopher Brookmyre (b.1968) is a more effervescent writer whose writings bristle and fizz with irreverent humour and political bite, but they also make serious points about contemporary issues, including terrorism and international finance. Louise Welsh's *The Cutting Room* (2002), *The Bullet Trick* (2006) and *Naming the Bones* (2010) move through dark criminal underworlds but are more than strictly genre fiction. Her 'Plague Trilogy' novels use conventions of science fiction to explore the priorities of what might have been a good society, as opposed to a society of catastrophic failure. Similar application of generic expectations to political and social explorations is at work in the unflinchingly determined feminist self-possession of Denise Mina and the different series-novels of Val McDermid (b.1955), whose *My Scotland* (2019) traces not only the locations of her own life but those of her characters and the locations depicted in her fiction. The Inspector Rebus series of the most famous of modern Scottish crime novelists, Ian Rankin (b.1960), while satisfying 'police procedural' conventions, give a running commentary on the shifting ethos of late 20th-century Scotland, especially Edinburgh, over decades, as the Parliament was resumed and the political dynamics and criminal aspects of the economy changed.

Different priorities occupy writers in science fiction. Attention to the modern international scene informs fictional explorations of political ideas in the 'What if?' scenario proposed by the genre. Naomi Mitchison (1897–1999) was a pioneer in this field, as in others, with *Memoirs of a Spacewoman* (1962). The novels of Ken MacLeod (b.1954) clearly connect with contemporary issues, explicitly addressing religious, communist or anarchist political ideas, while Paul Johnston (b.1957) has a quintet of novels (1997–2001) set in a futuristic Edinburgh. Matthew Fitt (b.1968) in *But n Ben A-Go-Go* (2000) produced the first science fiction novel in Scots. Scotland after global warming is 300 feet under water and a virulent strain of sexually transmitted disease is rife, but the novel is compelling not only because of its social vision and its suspenseful quest narrative, but in the strangeness of the Scots language itself, used in this way. Many readers, after initial difficulty, report being swept into it eagerly.

There are major literary genres which might take entire book-length studies to themselves. Children's literature is one of them. The Association for Scottish Literary Studies published an annotated bibliography of children's fiction, *Treasure Islands: A Guide to Scottish Fiction for Young Readers aged 10–14* (2003, with supplements available online at the ASLS [now renamed ASL or Association for Scottish Literature] website).

Walter Scott and Robert Louis Stevenson wrote some works specifically for children which introduced the history and ethos of Scotland to new generations. Edinburgh-born R.M. Ballantyne (1825–94) was one of the quintessential literary figures of British imperialism, addressing an international readership of children and by that token, very much a historical figure. But in the last quarter of the 20th century and into the 21st, writing for children has become a major commercial industry in literary production. Certain novels are deliberately intended to address difficult issues like religious sectarianism and bigotry, and notwithstanding their planned didactic intention, some are terrific, like Theresa Breslin's *Divided City* (2005). The phenomenal early 20th-century success of

J.K. Rowling (b.1965) and the Harry Potter series of novels and films testifies to an appetite for new fiction that addresses tried-and-tested themes. Central to both novels and films are questions of childhood and adulthood, loneliness and company, independence and loyalty, courage in adversity, the qualities of friendship and caring for others. Yet their political implications are perhaps not as innocent as they seem. An immense popularity for stories set in an exotic fantasy-world in which magic is an antidote for a reality clearly related to the public-school ethos of *Tom Brown's Schooldays* (1857) has its ideological liabilities, no doubt. And what of the liabilities of their ancestry?

As Yeats put it in his poem 'The Stare's Nest by My Window' in 1922, 'We fed the heart on fantasies / The heart's grown brutal from the fare'. The perennial classic by Kenneth Grahame (1859–1932), *The Wind in the Willows* (1908), has had many manifestations in film, television and theatre. Writing about John Buchan (1875–1940), Marshall Walker commented in his book, *Scottish Literature Since 1707* (1996), that Buchan's heroes Richard Hannay, Sandy Arbuthnot and Sir Edward Leithen 'seem now like humanoid editions of Mole, Ratty, Badger and Toad at play on a Boy's Own Paper riverbank' and yet 'Buchan writes as committedly as William Golding about the fragility of civilisation.' Sandy Arbuthnot's speech about propaganda in *The Three Hostages* is to be taken seriously:

> He said that the great offensives of the future would be psychological, and he thought the Governments should get busy about it and prepare their defence… He considered that the most deadly weapon in the world was the power of mass persuasion.

Buchan wrote that in 1924. Not a bad prediction.

But there are other ways of seeing the world. Of many I might name I'd like to give the last word to Elizabeth Dodd, or more familiarly, Lavinia Derwent (1909–89), whose collected works were recommended and summed up in one word by those great, now sadly almost forgotten literary critics Heckenlooper and Voss: 'indispensable'. Many will have read her version of *The Tale of Greyfriar's Bobby* (1985) but her first books are paradigms of value: *Tammy Troot* (1945) and *Tammy Troot's Capers* (1947; both first read on the Children's Hour on Scottish Radio in the 1920s). They breathe the air of post-war liberty. 'The world cannae be a' bad, if we're still in it,' Auntie Lavinia almost wrote.

Song, genre fiction, science fiction, crime, thriller, spy or horror fiction, children's literature: as Val McDermid might put it, if they make you care, they're literature. They sensitise the world.

6

Scottish literature at play

BEAUTY IS IN the eye of the beholder and humour may be a matter of personal taste as well but there are evidently people who have a facility to write in ways that make readers happy, and sometimes even laugh out loud. There are different kinds of humour and comedy can serve more than one political purpose. To generalise: there are two main kinds of comic writing, overlapping but different: celebration and satire. In celebrative writing, the purpose is to enact and participate in something joyful; in satiric writing, the purpose is to share a critique. When the political world seems to have gone beyond satire and little enough seems worth celebrating, it's worth reminding ourselves what such work can do, a perennial refreshment. Satire can be wildly funny and celebration can be deadly serious, and the worst of it can be sanctimonious, but there are great writers – and great Scottish writers – who have worked throughout these areas.

Internationally, the comic writers that spring to my mind are pre-eminently Irish and North American: Oscar Wilde, Flann O'Brien, James Joyce, Mark Twain, Dorothy Parker, H.L. Mencken, S.J. Perelman, the Canadians Stephen Leacock and Tom Lehrer, the noir crime genre writers Raymond Chandler and Dashiell Hammett, and their modern successors, John D. MacDonald, Donald E. Westlake, Richard Stark, Sara Paretsky and Janet Evanovich. Consider Chandler: 'She had a face like a bucket of mud.' Or: 'He was as noiseless as a finger in a glove.' Or: 'She had a mouth like wilted lettuce.' Or the first sentence of Richard Stark's novel, *Firebreak* (2001): 'When the phone rang, Parker was in the garage, killing a man.' As Marshall Walker puts it in his book, *Comrades and Vexations* (2013): 'If the Irish invented the wisecrack, the Americans polished it.'

The Americans' comic exuberance – from Mark Twain on – has a firm foundation in social satire. In any sick society, healthily derisive laughter is normally in short supply. The utterly serious condemnation of racism in *Huckleberry Finn* is complemented by that novel's wonderful and sustained good humour, pathos and irony. In his journalistic writings about his travels in the world, such as *The Innocents Abroad*, Twain takes the idea of Voltaire's *Candide* and extends it: the wandering, wondering innocent encounters the wicked ways of the world and optimistically, naively, recounts his experiences. This is a plot-device that Iain Banks also puts to brilliant use in his novel *Whit* (1995).

Innocence is understood best by knowingness. Experience is its test, as well as its end. One of the most joyous demolitions of the Scottish cliché is the Canadian Stephen Leacock's 'Nonsense Novel' of 1911, *Hannah of the Highlands: or*

The Laird of Loch Aucherlocherty, where we read of Hannah singing as she paddles in the water, 'gathering lobsters in the burn that ran through the glen':

> It was here in the Glen that Bonnie Prince Charlie had lain and hidden after the defeat of Culloden. Almost in the same spot the great boulder still stands behind which the Bruce had lain hidden after Bannockburn; while behind a number of lesser stones the Covenanters had concealed themselves during the height of the Stuart persecution.
>
> Through the Glen Montrose had passed on his fateful ride to Killiecrankie; while at the lower end of it the rock was still pointed out behind which William Wallace had paused to change his breeches while flying from the wrath of Rob Roy.

In fact, 'most of the great events of Scotch history had taken place in the Glen, while the little loch had been the scene of some of the most stirring naval combats in the history of the Grampian Hills.' Historical tableau deftly established, our story closes in on Hannah, but not before the climate, weather conditions and general atmosphere are carefully annotated:

> It was a gloriously beautiful Scotch morning. The rain fell softly and quietly, bringing dampness and moisture, and almost a sense of wetness to the soft moss underfoot. Grey mists flew hither and thither, carrying with them an invigorating rawness that had almost a feeling of dampness.

And Hannah herself, 'the beautiful Highland girl' is 'a beautiful picture': 'Her bare feet were in the burn, the rippling water of which laved her ankles. The lobsters played about her feet, or clung affectionately to her toes, as if loath to leave the water and be gathered in the folds of her blue apron.' But before too long we are whirled into the conflict of the clans, the McWhinuses and the McShamuses, with Hannah caught in the crossfire. It does not end well. Our hero Oyster McShamus is found dead in the grass, soaked in 'whiskey' and Hannah is discovered lying 'among the sand and seaweed, her fair hair soaked in gasoline'.

From Twain to Leacock and on, the North American writers possess an exuberance perhaps less familiar to many writers in post-World War II Europe. Samuel Beckett's *Waiting for Godot* (1952) is funny, but it's funny in the face of cosmic emptiness and the absurdity of isolation, not teeming social presences and the surprise avalanche of anarchic energies.

Yet from James Joyce, Flann O'Brien and Beckett himself through to Roddy Doyle and others, the Irish writers are bright with comedy. With Joyce one is always aware that such comedy serves the purpose of a serious affirmation, social, humanly vulnerable, resilient, buoyant, endlessly exfoliating, deeply pleasing. With O'Brien, for all the sheer hilarity at times, there is also a deadly edge, an utterly inviting abyss beneath or just beside the exuberance. The verbal display and wit of these writers is characterised by social engagement but it also works in the pathos of a humanity lost in a Godless cosmos. Even the title of Doyle's novel *The Commitments* (1987) indicates the conflicting priorities of common human pleasure in music-making as against the prioritisation of commercialism in its exploitation.

What Scottish writers can we consider in this constellation?

Pre-eminently, there are Thomas Urquhart, Allan Ramsay, Robert Fergusson, Burns and Walter Scott. Neil Munro, in three long-running series of short stories, created the memorable comic characters Para Handy, the sly, gentle but tenacious Highland captain of the ship, the 'Vital Spark' and her crew, the long-suffering engineer Dan MacPhail, the infinitely oblique and patient first mate Dougie and the irrepressible cabin boy Sunny Jim; the laconic raconteur Erchie; and the sympathetic commercial traveller longing for domestic comfort, Jimmy Swan (a self-evidently Joycean character). MacDiarmid, in prose sketches like 'The Last Great Burns Discovery' and 'The Waterside' and in poems like 'Old Wife in High Spirits' and 'The Ross-Shire Hills' is very funny indeed. Compton Mackenzie's novel *Whisky Galore!* is a tour-de-force. Eric Linklater, in novels like *Magnus Merriman, Juan in America, Juan in China, Laxdale Hall* or *The Merry Muse*, keeps an irrepressible sense of humour scalpel-sharp and hedgehog-bristly. Muriel Spark's writing can be as funny as it is deadly. One of the central characters in James Robertson's novel, *To Be Continued...* is a clever, well-informed, and highly articulate toad.

For humour to work, there must sometimes be surprise. In *Solution 11–167: The Book of Scotlands* (2009) by Momus (Nick Currie, b.1960), over 150 'Scotlands' alternative to the one we inhabit are envisioned, folding in stories, depictions, propositions and statements, all anthologised in accordance with the promise emblazoned on the book's cover: 'Every lie creates a parallel world. The world in which it is true.' Whimsical, brutal, serious, this is the work of a flibbertigibbet mind, with the emphasis upon the gibbet. For example: 'Scotland 120: The Scotland which becomes the world's first successful post-industrial matriarchy.' Or 'Scotland 76: The mist-filled Scotland in which people chant Hugh MacDiarmid's poems over Side Two of David Bowie's *Low*.' Or 'Scotland 35: The Scotland in which you're not allowed to own more property than will fit into a rucksack.' The entries range from one short sentence to a few pages in length, some are interviews or dialogues, some are confessions, anecdotes or letters. All sit uneasily alone or leaning lopsided against each other, a tumble of references, sardonic, loving and probing. What does it amount to? What indeed.

On different ground, George MacDonald Fraser, in *The General Danced at Dawn* (1970) and the other stories about Private MacAuslin ('the dirtiest soldier in the world'), *McAuslan in the Rough* (1974) and *The Sheikh and the Dustbin* (1988) creates sympathetic, credible characters whose escapades prompt chortles, chuckles and even loud laughter. Fraser's better-known *Flashman* series (1969–2005) cover the years in the fictional life of their 'hero' from 1839 to 1894; he makes a final appearance in *Mr American* (1980), which is set immediately before the First World War. Flashman is last seen in a carriage making for Buckingham Palace, where he intends to relieve himself, as his bladder is not as good as it used to be. He will not be rushed, however, and is still shrewdly perceptive of the world around him, and flourishing, despite time's encroachments. The novels satirically recreate the Victorian world and the British Empire, across locations ranging from India and Afghanistan to Africa, the United States and South America. As the series progresses, the fortunes of British identity in the last three decades of the 20th century, the period in which the novels were written, affect the tone of humour, the portrayal of cowardice, hypocrisy, bullying and swagger, the futile and profligate waste of life dictated by imperial power, and the war-mongering of London governments. The first sentence of *Flashman in the Great Game* (1975) gives a good idea of the humour at work:

> They don't often invite me to Balmoral nowadays, which is a blessing: those damned tartan carpets always put me off my food, to say nothing of the endless pictures of German royalty and that unspeakable statue of the Prince Consort standing knock-kneed in a kilt.

One of Flashman's ancestors might have been Dugald Dalgetty, from Walter Scott's *A Legend of Montrose* (1819). Dalgetty is one of the great comic characters, a hardened mercenary soldier leading an expedition into enemy territory in one of the novel's sub-plots. Self-preservation is his necessary priority; he has his own integrity. His appetite and sense of the value of comfort are essential parts of his character. Every time he comes onto the page, you smile: he's one of the funniest, toughest, most enjoyable literary creations in fiction. In Chapter 2, on first riding up to a possibly hostile company of mounted soldiers, Dalgetty holds still and they look at each other warily:

> When they had stood at gaze for about a minute, the younger gentleman gave the challenge which was then common in the mouth of all strangers who met in such circumstances – 'For whom are you?'
> 'Tell me first,' answered the soldier, 'for whom are you? – the strongest party should speak first.'
> 'We are for God and King Charles,' answered the first speaker. – 'Now tell your faction, you know ours.'
> 'I am for God and my standard,' answered the single horseman.

'And for which standard?' replied the chief of the other party – 'Cavalier or Roundhead, King or Convention?'

'By my troth, sir,' answered the soldier, 'I would be loath to reply to you with an untruth, as a thing unbecoming a cavalier of fortune and a soldier. But to answer your query with beseeming veracity, it is necessary I should myself have resolved to whilk of the present divisions of the kingdom I shall ultimately adhere, being a matter whereon my mind is not as yet precisely ascertained.'

In other words, but marvellously indirectly, 'I'll tell you what side I'm on after I know who has won.' He finally introduces himself:

[M]y name is Dalgetty – Dugald Dalgetty, Ritt-master Dugald Dalgetty of Drumthwacket, at your honourable service to command. It is a name you may have seen in Gallo Belgicus, the Swedish Intelligencer, or, if you read High Dutch, in the Fleigenden Mercouer of Leipsic... a cavalier of fortune.

Later, in Chapter 6, after spending the night with his new acquaintances in a castle, Lord Menteith addresses him again:

'Captain Dalgetty,' said Lord Menteith, 'the time is come that we must part, or become comrades in service.'
'Not before breakfast, I hope?'

Scott is not often thought of as a comic writer but he can be very funny indeed. Iain Crichton Smith's *Murdo* stories (first collected in 1981) and the story 'Napoleon and I' are also funny but there is a dark threnody of seriousness, humour built upon fragility, vulnerability and frailty. Norman MacCaig is one of the funniest poets ever and Edwin Morgan combines celebration and festivity in a poem like 'Trio' and in concrete poems of visual puns, like the 'Siesta of a Hungarian Snake' or the 'Forgetful Duck'. Iain Banks is wild in the macabre appetite of his debut novel *The Wasp Factory* (1984), and *Espedair Street* (1987) is buoyant with humour, while *The Crow Road* (1992) begins with one of the funniest lines in fiction, which is nonetheless, in its own style, another way of saying what Robert Louis Stevenson says in *Kidnapped*, maybe the greatest opening line of any novel: 'I will begin the story of my adventures with a certain morning early in the month of June, the year of grace 1751, when I took the key for the last time out of the door of my father's house.' Banks's opening line in *The Crow Road* says the same thing but is less poignant and much faster: 'It was the day my grandmother exploded.'

Austere material conditions, the hardship of poverty and deprivation, can itself generate a kind of dark humour. When Marx called religion the opium of the people he was alerting us to the way in which immersive distraction from material reality can make us dozy about how things really are. Today, there's far more opium everywhere. Humour – like pleasure – can serve any political purpose. But it can, and in Scottish literature, frequently does, aid and abet a serious argument. It is not often merely trivial or dispensable. Rather, trivia become valuable, humour and pleasure can be savoured in every circumstance – from the mundane, daily routine to the sublime, exceptional, reified moment, from the physical facts of human creaturality to moments of spiritual elation, from crudity to sensuality, as in Thomas Urquhart's version of Rabelais or Sydney Goodsir Smith's complex sequence of love poems, *Under the Eildon Tree* (1948) or his verbally crazed novel, *Carotid Cornucopius* (1964). Satiric, reductive humour, black humour, is so frequently found in Scottish literature that it seems unnecessary even to start listing. The Scottish historian Angus Calder reminded us, in his book *Russia Discovered* (1976), how fantastically comic a writer Dostoevsky was. As William Blake puts it, all poets are of the Devil's party. Yet there's also a regenerating humour that runs right through Scottish literature, from Columba to Henryson to Duncan Ban MacIntyre and from Burns to MacDairmid, Morgan, Lochhead and on.

Even at its most serious, all art is play. In literature, language is always at play, in some sense, even in the most serious work. When language becomes exclusively serious, as in some church sermons or Burns supper speeches, it loses all interest in play, and dies. Bertolt Brecht was once asked, 'Are you in earnest? Are you a serious artist?' and he replied that no, he was never in earnest. He was always playing, just trying things out. All the arts – painting, sculpture, music of any kind, from lullabies to Schoenberg quartets – are playing. Even the most classical forms, sonnet, sonata, formal dance, involve movement. And in language, all writers are at play, especially poets.

Black humour is a kind of resilience but the general delight that literature and the arts give us, and the real threat they pose to authority, come about because every time we engage with them, we open up a silent space for contemplation where we do not know what will happen next. Art is a continually changing defiance of the dictatorial power of predestination. Politicians might think about this: the only diplomacy that really works is cultural diplomacy.

One of the most famous utterances of Sir William Thomson, Lord Kelvin (1824–1907), was this:

> When you can measure what you are speaking about, and express it in numbers, you know something about it; but when you cannot measure it, when you cannot express it in numbers, your knowledge of it is of a meagre and unsatisfactory kind; it may be the beginning of

knowledge, but you have scarcely, in your thoughts, advanced it to the stage of science.

This is wrong. All the arts refute it. Every work of art, especially the greatest works, are acts of intuition and intervention, cutting across history and changing it permanently. Things are not as they were. Numbers are never enough.

Weaponry and arms dealers thrive on numbers and wars come and go in the world. But the world is made better not because of them but because of Shakespeare, Beethoven, Picasso and their company: always free, but not directionless; and at their most serious, always at play.

7

Psychology, flyting, philosophy and speculation

IN ALI SMITH'S NOVEL *Autumn* (2016), an old man befriends a young woman, setting the tone of their relationship and giving her an imperative by which to live her life by asking whenever they meet, 'What are you reading?' When Smith appeared on radio 4's *Desert Island Discs* (2016) she let slip her habit of reading everything, all the time: 'The side of a pencil, the side of a bus...'

Reading is essentially no more nor less than critical evaluation, a continual appraisal of meaning and quality, which if we lapse from, allows the weeds in fast. The same might be said of any work we do towards the interpretation of art. In his indispensable book *Dear Sibelius: Letter from a Junky* (2008), Marshall Walker describes his boyhood friendship with the composer and principal conductor of the BBC Scottish Orchestra, Ian Whyte. Recognising the potential and growing musical appreciation in the boy, Whyte would greet him at every meeting, right up to the last encounter when he was in his hospital bed, with the question, 'Now what have you been listening to...?'

Because people are animals who depend upon learning, one generation failing to do this means it all has to start over again. Education is one word for how it's passed on. We have discussed genre fiction and 'the power of mass persuasion'. With literature, it helps to keep the remit open, to include all sorts of things as well as poems, fiction and plays, such as 'life writing': journals, letters, autobiography, speculative writing, including philosophy. This brings us to George Davie (1912–2007).

In his books *The Democratic Intellect* (1961) and *The Crisis of the Democratic Intellect* (1986), Davie focused on the history of tertiary education in Scotland. Davie argued that the basis of the generalist four-year Scottish degree encouraged a broad-based humanist understanding, as opposed to the dedicated specialisms more common in England. The notion of an education that encourages specialisation but maintains that any specialisation should be kept open, and not be closed off by privileges of jargon, class or economic advantage, informs Davie's books and retains potent political currency. It was linked to MacDiarmid and his assertive yoking together of Scottish Republican Nationalism with Communism – a radical idealism that makes sense in Scottish, rather than imperial British, terms. The aspiration of intellectual elitism maintained in society as an egalitarian right to which every person should have access remains profoundly significant in the early 21st century.

The social significance of Davie's educational thinking can be traced back through another literary genre: autobiography. Among the major Scottish figures in this tradition, James Boswell (1740–95) was not only the biographer of Samuel Johnson; it was his travel writing, his *Account of Corsica* (1768) that made him internationally famous and his London diaries that show us today the incipient significance of that city's maelstrom attraction, while his *Journal of a Tour to the Hebrides* (1775) is an essential corrective to that of his pontificating companion.

Elizabeth Grant (1797–1886) in her *Memoirs* (1898) gives a perceptive account of life in the Highlands, including encounters with Rob Roy and others, shrewd anecdotes and the sense of daily life in the context of what tourists saw – and see today – mainly as visual spectacle. Her writing crosses class barriers and her Irish journal national ones. In the 20th century, *My Scottish Youth* (1937) by R.H. Bruce Lockhart (1887–1970), head of the first British Mission to Russia's Bolshevik Government, contains a wealth of information about a pre-First World War Scotland, its local strengths and imperial ambitions. From a different perspective, first published during the Second World War, Hugh MacDiarmid's *Lucky Poet: A Self-Study in Literature and Political Ideas* (1943) is a rollercoasting juggernaut of flashing sharp angles of perspective, outrageous stories, high good humour, contentious notions, poignant moments, unexpected scenes and startling, sometimes shocking perceptions. A valuable complement to it is *Octobiography* (Montrose Standard Press, 1976), by Helen Cruickshank (1886–1975), a key figure in modern Scottish literature, friend and benefactor of MacDiarmid and many other writers, and a poet of distinction. Gavin Maxwell (1914–69), best known for *Ring of Bright Water* (1960), also wrote autobiographies, including *The House of Elrig* (1965), even more closely revealing his experience of wild animals and the elemental world. The autobiographies of Naomi Mitchison (1897–1999), *Small Talk: Memories of an Edwardian Childhood* (1973), *All Change Here: Girlhood and Marriage* (1973), *You May Well Ask: A Memoir, 1920–1940* (1979) and her wartime diaries *Among You Taking Notes* (1985) are richly detailed, presenting both her singular personality and her social and economic world.

If we keep in mind the relation between, on the one hand, individual character, idiosyncrasies of perspective and specialisation, and on the other, a social spectrum of wide and various forms of preference, as Davie suggests is or should be at the heart of education, we can see how keeping the literary remit open – and open to all the arts – constitutes a vital priority.

Such examples might be complemented by work devoted to food, drink, rituals and myths. Scottish classics of this kind would include the two compendium collections of recipes and good advice by F. Marian McNeill (1885–1973), *The Scots Kitchen: Its Traditions and Lore with Old-Time Recipes* (1929) and *The Scots Cellar: Its Traditions and Lore* (1956); her extended study of folklore and local festivals throughout Scotland was published as *The Silver Bough* (four volumes, 1957–68), the title answering the earlier anthropological magnum opus, *The Golden Bough: A Study in Magic and Religion* (1890) by another Scot, James Frazer (1854–1941).

Philosophy, autobiography, travel writing, writing on food, drink, myths and folklore – all these balance social behaviour and personal, internal consumption. So what of the internal mental world?

A singular contribution to psychology and medicine, very much of its time yet lastingly valuable, was made by R.D. Laing (1927–89), in case studies, speculative essays, quasi-fictional accounts and poems. The essential point Laing argued arose from the Freudian perception that a whole society might be described as mad, so that an individual categorised as insane might be the sanest character in a society which itself was 'insane'.

Think of *Hamlet*. Inexplicable impulses, strange behaviour, violent actions taken by young men or women in a family structure or society typified by constriction or oppression might be considered as the sanest response to such inimical force. The perception is social, personal, psychological, clinical but also intensely literary: it opens questions about what we see happening in the greatest of all tragedies, from ancient Greece through Shakespeare to a whole range of modern Scottish plays, and all great tragedy – indeed, all great comedy too – is based on the structure that has universal human application, the family, with all it entails of both support and constriction.

Introverted individuals might be the direct result of a bullying society. Folk are made silent, depressed and despondent by distant authorities empowered by force and mass media. There is one particularly Scottish answer to this conundrum: flyting. This is a distinct form of address with a long pedigree in Scottish literature. Flyting usually takes the form of a dialogue between poets, in which one hurls invective and abuse at the other, who then responds appropriately. An early example is that of William Dunbar and Walter Kennedy in the late 15th century. Another is that of Alexander Montgomerie and Patrick Hume of Polwarth, from the late 16th century. This is how it begins:

> Vyld venymous vipper, wanthreivinest of thingis,
> Half ane elph, half ane aip, of nature denyit,
> Thow flyttis and thow freittis, thou fartis and thow flingis;
> Bot this bargane, unbeist, deir sall thou buy it.

Or in my own English imitation:

> Vile venomous viper, most stunted of things,
> Half goblin, half monkey, unnatural beast,

> You leap, showing off, blasting farts, throwing flings;
> But this deal, you monster, you'll pay for at least!

In her edition of Montgomerie's poems, Helena Shire gives selections from his account of Polwarth's christening-party, a Peter Breughel-like fantasmagoria, ribald, saturnalian, teetering on the edge of terror. Mrs Shire supplies a note after the third stanza: 'Stanzas 4–7, a catalogue of diseases, are omitted' before resuming with stanza 8.

There are two kinds of flyting, one is playful, in which both practitioners know they are engaged in a competition of extremes. Linguistic energy, verbal precision, flamboyant rhetoric and wit are only some of the weapons put to use. In company, at parties, Norman MacCaig and Hugh MacDiarmid would sometimes launch into a flyting, starting with an occasional remark about a topic on which a response was sparked, escalating into a dazzling verbal display that might leave those present gasping. A visiting poet once witnessed such an encounter and afterwards remarked that he thought they were about to come to blows, physical violence. MacCaig told me that he replied, 'No, not at all. He's my best friend. We were just having some fun.'

The second type of flyting, though, is when it happens in deadly earnest. Tobias Smollett's attack on Admiral Knowles landed him in prison. An equally enraged and indignant work is MacDiarmid's book-length poem, *The Battle Continues* (1957), written in response to Roy Campbell's poem in praise of Franco and the Fascists in the Spanish Civil War, *Flowering Rifle* (1939). MacDiarmid opposes Campbell by praising the Spanish poet Federico García Lorca and all he stood for. He addresses Lorca:

> You will be remembered when your foes are forgotten.
> On the one side the People; on the other
> The vain titles and vicious wealth
> Of a worthless few. Chartres versus Versailles!

MacDiarmid describes Campbell's 'typical reader': 'A stout man, walking with a waddle' who, with his 'fat finger / Ticks off the feet in Campbell's lines / "Left, right! Left, right!"' Then he turns on Campbell himself: 'So you went for a soldier, did you, / Campbell? – a soldier in Spain? / The hero of a penny novelette / With the brain of a boy scout!'

In 2014 Alan Bissett published online one of the most fiercely sustained polemical poems, 'Vote Britain'. It moves through very serious issues indeed and uses extreme scorn and satire and ferocious comedy to prompt us to consider them. That combination of humour and seriousness is a literary skill, an approach or technique that runs back through MacDiarmid to Burns and

Fergusson all the way to Dunbar, and is another example of the democratic strain that characterises Scottish literature. This is how 'Vote Britain' begins:

> People of Scotland, vote with your heart.
> Vote with your love for the Queen who nurtured you, cradle to grave,
> Who protects you and cares for you, her most darling subjects, to whom you gave the glens she adores to roam freely through, the stags her children so dearly enjoy killing.
> First into battle, loyal and true. The enemy's scared of you.

More than 50,000 people read that poem or listened to it online in its first year of publication. That's a big audience. The impetus behind it was the drive towards Scottish independence. Another driving field of energy which has engaged beyond prediction is feminism. When Liz Lochhead published her first book, *Memo for Spring*, in 1972, its sales were phenomenal and her reputation was established. And yet, to her credit, there was never any question that she'd stay in a niche. Her development as a playwright as well as poet has enlivened her verse, especially the monologues, polemics and flytings.

If folk are to be open to the big questions and have some fun talking about them, the discussion needs to be snappy and sharp, and the whole world is the location in which the debate needs to take place, in popular culture and entertainment as much as in the most serious, esoteric or difficult arenas. Politics is normally the provenance of slippery, sneaky, snaky evaders of direct questions, the organised and impenetrable self-congratulators or the unapproachably smug and affluent. Radical thinking makes a different politics, informed by irreverence, imagination, honesty and respect for what matters. It gets us to the fundamental things. This is what close reading helps us to do. Or close listening.

When we open the maps to find the destination of a different Scotland, more democratic and less institutionally dominated, we know that even if the maps are wrong today, at least they show that the land is there. Whatever *actually* happens, or *can be made* to happen, change starts happening in the way you think about what *might* happen. That, also, is what literature helps us to do.

8

Religion and sport

RELIGION AND SPORT are not major themes in modern Scottish literature. That's surprising, perhaps, because they're major presences in Scottish life.

Looked at from distant countries, the United Kingdom seems distinctly characterised by two things, both of them absurd: the class system and the royal family. Focus more closely on Scotland and the two things that seem to pervade the lives of many people in one way or another are religion and sport. Deep contexts and questions of religious sectarianism are in the strata, conspicuous by their absence in most popular culture. One of the funniest and most horrible scenes in the film *T2: Trainspotting* (2017) is exceptional in this regard. Then there is the vastly disproportionate amount of attention given to 'sport'. How would it be if as much time on TV 'news' programmes and page-space in newspapers were given to serious accounts of the arts as is currently given to 'sport'? We'll leave that question hanging. Since our subject is literature, we should focus on that, and the odd thing is that our writers have dealt so infrequently with these subjects. The exceptions prove the rule.

There's a famous anonymous four-line mediaeval poem that describes 'The Bewteis of the Fute-Ball':

> Brissit brawnis and broken banis,
> Styf, discord and waistit wanis,
> Cruikit in eild, syne halt withal –
> Thir are the bewteis of the fute-ball.

That about sums it up. Then there's Dunbar's poem about the Friar of Tungland, John Damian Damiani, who seems to have made an early attempt at hang gliding (with feathered wings) from Stirling Castle and crunched to earth (Edwin Morgan picks him up in his *Sonnets from Scotland* sequence). Dunbar's younger contemporary Gavin Douglas, in his translation of Virgil's *Aeneid*, *The Eneados*, included vivid accounts of public sporting contests, a foot race, a boat race and a boxing contest from the funeral games section in Book 5. In 2014, when Glasgow hosted the Commonwealth Games, the Scottish Poetry Library and Glasgow University produced a little anthology of these episodes, in which Douglas's original, sinewy Scots was printed alongside an immediately accessible modern English translation by the Latin scholar David West.

David Lyndsay's *Satyre of the Three Estaits* is the major engagement with the religious and political world on the eve of the Reformation, and Walter Scott's *Old Mortality* explores fanaticism and moderation, while *Ivanhoe* is centrally about racism amongst Normans, Jews and Saxons, confronting codes of chivalry and the violence of jousting with social and religious prejudices that were sweeping through all of Europe, both at the time the novel was written and when it is set. Religion and politics are the same thing in these works, or at least, inextricable from each other. This was likewise the case in the disruption in the Church of Scotland in 1843, the subject of Robin Jenkins's novel, *The Awakening of George Darroch* (1985).

In the 20th century, as a young man, Hugh MacDiarmid considered converting to Catholicism, but then maintained a fierce atheism and materialism confirmed in the shocking, deeply consoling materialist elegy 'Crystals Like Blood' and explored thoroughly and remorselessly in his crucial poem, 'On a Raised Beach'. Marshall Walker's description of MacDiarmid in his book, *Scottish Literature Since 1707* (1996), is precise: he was 'sending out from the unforgiving disappointment of his atheism playful or intensely searching feelers to the space where God was.'

'Disappointment' isn't a word we easily associate with MacDiarmid, but it's accurate here. If his political effort was to redress the disappointing, mealy-mouthed half-heartedness of so many of his compatriots, there's a much deeper, more spiritual, materialist and philosophical context for his enquiry too. Darwin and Nietzsche lead straight into it. His early poem, 'The Fool' says it in brief:

> He said that he was God
> 'We are well met,' I cried,
> 'I've always hoped I should
> Meet God before I died.'
> I slew him then and cast
> His corpse into a pool,
> – But how I wish he had
> Indeed been God, the fool!

Fionn Mac Colla, Compton Mackenzie, George Mackay Brown and Muriel Spark all converted to Catholicism. Mackenzie's book *Catholicism and Scotland* (1936) is a valuable extended literary musing on the subject and Linden Bicket's *George Mackay Brown and the Scottish Catholic Imagination* (2017) is a fully-informed study of the subject with close reference to one of Scotland's major 20th-century writers. Yet the surprising fact remains that in the later 20th and early 21st centuries, there were almost no Catholic writers telling stories about the experience of Catholics in Scotland. Again, the exceptions prove the rule.

The title of Tom Leonard's poem 'The Good Thief', from *Six Glasgow Poems*

(1967), refers to the two thieves said to have been crucified on either side of Christ, the lesson being not to despair because one of them was saved, but not to be complacent either, because one of them was damned. However, the poem represents a speech ostensibly delivered by a supporter of Celtic football team to a companion who appears to have fallen, comatose with drink, on the floor of a bar. In the midwinter context of a New Year's Day game between the teams, Celtic (predominantly Catholic) and Rangers (predominantly Protestant), the two of them have been drinking heavily before going to the match, and the speaker notices that it's 'nearly three a cloke thinoo': winter dark is coming down. He concludes: 'good jobe they've gote thi lights': that is, the floodlights at the stadium.

Theresa Breslin's remarkable novel for young adults *Divided City* (2005) programmatically but with sharp effectiveness addresses religious sectarianism in Glasgow and takes us through a number of issues raised by religious bigotry, prejudices and commonplace assumptions that lead to incomprehension and violence. Liam McIlvanney's novel *All the Colours of the Town* (2009) and its sequel *Where the Dead Men Go* (2013) deal directly with Catholic-Protestant violence in Glasgow and Belfast, the interconnections between the two cities and the religious culture of both Scotland and Ireland, while taking the form of thriller or detective genre fiction, with the main character an investigative newspaper reporter. These are rare examples of novels that take religious sectarianism as a central subject.

The Irish novelist Colm Tóibín, in his book, *The Sign of the Cross: Travels in Catholic Europe* (1994), devotes one chapter to a sojourn in Scotland, in which he talks to a journalist about the mid-1990s literary urban scene: 'Do you mean, I asked him, that all of the writers, with their street credibility and their working-class heroes, are Protestants? Yes, he said. And do you mean that no one has ever raised this matter? Correct, he said. And do you mean that most people do not think this is a significant fact? Correct, once more.'

The one Catholic writer Tóibín made contact with was Thomas Healy, author of the novels: *It Might Have Been Jerusalem* (1991) and *Rolling* (1992), a book about boxing, *A Hurting Business* (1996), and a memoir, *I Have Heard You Calling in the Night* (2006). These books are raw and painful, full of loneliness, despair, resilience and hopelessness. Imagine Charles Bukowski entirely stripped of humour, and with appetite turned to compulsion. They are moving and significant, isolated instances.

There are a few further exceptions to note. The work of the poet Peter McCarey, which was published by small presses since the 1980s, until Carcanet Press published his *Collected Contraptions* (2011), arises from his Catholic Glasgow experience, though it does not depend upon it and rarely describes it specifically. James Kelman, whose novel *Kieron Smith, Boy* (2008), subtly and sensitively and with consummate skill, describes the experiences of a Protestant boy with a Catholic name, his family, friends and social circumstance. The same question of social displacement had arisen in Kelman's earlier novel *A Disaffection* (1989), whose main character is named Patrick Doyle.

And there is Edwin Morgan, who once commented that sport was probably the most difficult thing about which to write well, perhaps thinking of Alan Bold's sequence of poems about Scottish footballers, *Scotland, Yes! World Cup Football Poems* (1978). When challenged to produce the worst sporting poem ever written, Morgan obliged with *The South Sea Britherhood: A Poem from the Fort Baskerville Golf Club* published by David Hamilton's Partick Press (1989). However, Morgan also tackles the matter of spirituality – rather than religion – directly in two major works written at the end of the millennium: a sequence of poems entitled *Demon* (1999) and A.D.: *A Trilogy of Plays on the Life of Jesus Christ* (2000). The latter succeeded in offending senior representatives of both Catholic and Protestant churches. His poem 'Pelagius', from the book, *Cathures* (2002), affirms his belief in the Pelagian heresy: there is no such thing as original sin, and the future belongs to the future's generations, where they will do what they will, with 'only human grace'.

That sense of what is 'only human' informs the myth of kinship across differences which Morgan endorses. Perhaps there is an affinity with historical early Celtic Christianity, exemplified in the journey of St Columba from Ireland to Scotland in 563 AD. Only by being out of sight of Ireland could he do his work in Iona. In the last verse of Edwin Morgan's translation of Columba's poem, the 'Altus Prosator' or 'The Maker on High', Morgan gives Columba's description of heaven as a place into which we might ultimately enter into 'the dignity of all such diversity'. That phrase – 'the dignity of all such diversity' – is a rejection of uniformity and an affirmation that human variousness is a benison enabling human dignity. It's an affirmation that heaven is not a world of conforming to uniformity but of accepting variousness, which enables dignity. Securing such an understanding was heroic work, whether undertaken by a 6th-century Christian missionary or a 20th-century middle-class gay Scottish poet.

Des Dillon was born and grew up in a Catholic family in Coatbridge, one of the darkly sectarian post-industrial heartlands of Lanarkshire, and his fiction, plays and poems frequently address his experience directly. Sport and religion come together in his play *Singin' I'm No' a Billy, He's a Tim* (2005), written for three actors, a dialogue between two religion-and-sport fanatics locked up in a prison cell on the day of a football match between the teams each supports (Rangers and Celtic, again). The mediating figure is the turnkey, Harry, who keeps in the background but supplies a constant tone of human compassion as he speaks intermittently on the phone, asking about his grandson, in hospital undergoing an operation. The lurid language, wild humour, violent aggression and, finally, shared sympathy of the two main characters, infuse the overall structure of the play. It is a comedy, ultimately leading to reconciliation, so the idealistic hope presented at the end might seem formulaic. But there's nothing easy about what it presents.

Alex Gray's crime novel *Pitch Black* (2008) is a similar example of a work tackling a sports subject rarely directly addressed in literature. It's a generic 'police procedural', with Gray's recurring characters, Detective Chief Inspector Lorimer and his friend, the psychologist and criminal profiler Solomon Brightman. But the exploration of the novel takes us into the world of football in a way that readers with a healthy lack of interest in sport of any kind might find compelling.

Perhaps the one major novel centred crucially on football is Robin Jenkins's *The Thistle and the Grail* (1954). Harry Reid, former sportswriter and editor of *The Herald*, has an excellent introduction in the Birlinn edition (2006). The Thistle, the local football team in a dismal Lanarkshire town, is down on its luck. Players' morale is low as they have to deal with a hopeless president, a conniving policeman, a pious minister and their justly sceptical wives. They hold on to 'the beautiful game' as a last ideal. Then they start to win and their fortunes begin to turn, raising the expectations of their community. They set their hearts on the Grail, the Scottish Junior Cup. Being a Robin Jenkins novel, ambiguities abound: real hope and severe scepticism compete to pollute or temper the vision of the novel and nothing is carried through with simple conviction.

And maybe that's the answer to the question why there's so much more religion and sport (in one form or another) in Scottish social life than in our literature. These two strange forms of human activity are usually designed to produce confirmations. Pick a team. Cheer for the goals against the other side. Literature and the arts, at their best, help us ask questions, to find things out about the other sides, to see things from other points of view, to want better, and to work out how to make that betterment real. One side is never enough. Or to put it another way, literature is on the side of the open, multiple, mongrel, accommodative, endlessly possible world where borders are innumerable and each one is always made to be crossed. One team, or one church, one party, or one side, will never be enough.

9

Radio, film and TV

ONE OF THE most important cultural figures of modern Scotland, and probably one of the least familiar names, is Stuart Hood (1915–2011), novelist, translator and former Controller of BBC Television. Any consideration of talking about radio, film and TV, should keep him in mind. His work is centred on the interrelatedness of literature, media and politics. Walking out of an Italian POW camp into the countryside in 1943, he spent 11 months in an ancient peasant world of ploughing, planting, harvest and communal hospitality, but also working with the partisans, engaging in guerrilla warfare against the German troops. The most direct opposition to fascism gave him a lasting sense of human priorities. The sensitivity of his writing – particularly in his greatest novel, *A Storm from Paradise* (1985) – is measured against the absolutism of the fascism he fought against. It returns to Lewis Grassic Gibbon country in its rural, farming background but is imbued with a deep sense of the meaning of fascism only available in the late 20th century. His other novels centre on questions of loyalty and betrayal, most effectively in *The Upper Hand* (1987) and *The Brutal Heart* (1989). He once said, 'I was always interested in how politics is lived.' That's the key to understanding his work as a novelist, a broadcasting professional and a politically aware and committed individual.

When Hood wrote *On Television* (1980), *Fascism for Beginners* (1993) and edited *Behind the Screens: The Structure of British Television* (1994), he was acutely aware of the relations between fiction, mass media, persuasion, and the truths that must be told. Since his death, the power of social control in the selective dissemination of information, and the relation between online, screen and print media has become primary in the ethos of our time. Some of the dangers are discussed by Iain MacWhirter in his book, *Democracy in the Dark: The Decline of the Scottish Press and How to Keep the Lights On* (Saltire Society, 2014). The analyses provided in *The Media in Scotland*, ed. Neil Blane and David Hutchison (EUP, 2008) are very much in the spirit of Hood. The argument is brought up to date in Christopher Silver's brilliant *Demanding Democracy: The Case for a Scottish Media* (Word Power Books, 2015).

For John Reith (1889–1971) the BBC's job was 'to inform, educate, and entertain'. But consider Sir Alan Peacock (1922–2014), from 1984–86 Chairman of the Committee on the Financing of the BBC, rejecting Margaret Thatcher's proposal to fund the BBC by advertising and proposing a long-term strategy in which subscription would replace the licence fee. Essentially, he advised abandoning Reith's priorities and changing the BBC and all associated 'Heritage' industries away from educational priorities towards money-making. He has a special place in the story. Alongside him we might note the significance of Director General John Birt. In his 2002 autobiography he admitted how fiercely he aligned the corporation with the politically unionist agenda in the late 1990s and opposed devolution in broadcasting, insisting that BBC news 'bound Britain together'. When he put the case to the then Prime Minister of the United Kingdom Tony Blair, he grasped the argument immediately and agreed: 'Let's fight'.

This is a passage from Stuart Hood's essay 'The Backwardness of Scottish Television', in Karl Miller, ed., *Memoirs of a Modern Scotland* (London: Faber & Faber, 1970), worth considering in this light:

> By what criteria can we judge the quality of a country's television? One is the range and variety of programmes offered to the viewer. Another is the degree of freedom it enjoys to show and speak the truth. A third is its success in revealing a society to itself: on a primitive level by showing its citizens how they speak, behave, live, and on another higher level by revealing to them the mechanics of their society, how it functions politically, economically and culturally. All three criteria are linked. For it is not possible to deal in the truth unless there is a sufficiently wide spectrum of programmes to include those which honestly explore the nature of society. No society can be explored unless its broadcasters are free to ask honest questions and answer them. Unless broadcasters are allowed this minimum of freedom, self-revelation is impossible. All over the world there are societies, ranging from great modern capitalist or socialist states to small, emergent, underdeveloped ones, which have not achieved self-awareness because the dominant instruments of mass culture do not provide a mirror in which their citizens can see themselves truthfully. In most countries television is now the main disseminator of mass culture. In many of them it has either failed in its duties or been prevented from performing them.

In Ireland in Dublin in 1916, it was the Post Office; in Nigeria in the 1960s it was the radio; in Hood's time it was television, and today it's all these plus more: information control of the most far-reaching kind. Not revelation but distraction. Entrapment is the law.

Hood concludes his book with Thalia Tabary-Peterssen, *On Television* (1980) by noting:

> The future shape of the television industry will be determined by political decisions taken at government level. These decisions will be determined by how that government perceives television – as an industry

in which the market decides or as a medium which can provide a public service, supplying the Reithian trinity of information, education and entertainment. These are political issues that deserve to be addressed and discussed by viewers, trade unions, by political party branches. A society – to coin a phrase – gets the kind of television it deserves.

Since the 1970s, what might we single out as exemplary engagements with Scottish literature in radio and screen media?
Many fine writers produced original radio plays or adaptations of classics, and there were, once, various broadcast literary discussions and arts reviews. The medium is perfect for audio work focused on poetry as sound, literature and music, endorsing the literary validity of regional voices, forms of speech and the acoustics of locations. Literature means different things in soundscapes of different geographies, movements on land, river and sea. Think of what the external acoustics of Orkney are like, and what the indoor acoustics of Iona Cathedral are like. All poetry is about movement, one way or another. If Wordsworth's poems are mainly at a walking pace, 'The Birlinn of Clanranald' moves continually upon water, first by rowing, then by sailing, through storm, then finally rowing again. And after its opening episode in the pub, 'Tam o' Shanter' is mainly about riding – first slowly and unsteadily, then at full gallop. Radio is the perfect medium for evoking the sounds of such movements. It doesn't have to be hindered by visual or aural literalism.

Radio plays by writers such as Jessie Kesson, Iain Crichton Smith and Stewart Conn and adaptations by Catherine Lucy Czerkawska and especially Chris Dolan's adaptation of Stevenson's *Kidnapped* and Gerda Stevenson's radio version of Scott's *The Heart of Midlothian*, exemplify a vast and massively under-researched archive, not to mention the biographical and critical value of recorded interviews and accounts of the lives of major writers. One work of lasting value is the radio play *Carver* (1991) by John Purser (b. 1942), about the life of the great composer of polyphonic church music, Robert Carver (c.1485–c.1570). It was published by Methuen in *Best Radio Plays of 1991: The Giles Cooper BBC Award Winners* (1992).

In film, entire national iconographies have been fashioned and refashioned, most often by people who have neither lived in Scotland nor studied our history. If narrative fiction is the convention of what used to be called quaintly 'feature films' what about poem-films? And where are the film biographies of such crucial yet neglected Scots as John MacLean, or Tobias Hume? If they're made for cinema, they can be broadcast on TV.

There's a long history of representations of Scotland, from Laurel and Hardy's *Bonnie Scotland* (1935) to *Brigadoon* (1954) and on, but the list of films whose foundations in vision and writing might be accounted Scottish literature is a lot shorter. Examples might include *Red Road* (2006), co-written and directed by Andrea Arnold or the films of Bill Forsyth (b.1946), such as *Gregory's Girl* (1981) and *Local Hero* (1983), with its extensive location filming in Pennan on Scotland's east coast and Morar and Arisaig on the west coast. Ostensibly a comedy affirming old Scottish priorities over the exploitative materialism and power of American international finance, it opens ambiguities and asks questions about motivation and purpose that permit no easy answers, poised between seriousness and whimsy, dark adult themes and happy optimism. Forsyth's TV film *Andrina* (1981) was an impeccable adaptation of a short story by George Mackay Brown. Jonathan Murray's *Discomfort and Joy: The Cinema of Bill Forsyth* (2011) provides a thorough overview.

Another 'literary' scriptwriter is Alan Sharp (1934–2013), raised in Greenock. After writing two novels of a projected trilogy, *A Green Tree in Gedde* (1965) and *The Wind Shifts* (1967), he went to work in Hollywood. The film *Night Moves* (1975) relocated noir conventions to the post-Watergate era of disillusionment and cynicism, yet Sharp's novel of the film reads like the strange third in the trilogy, as if some of the characters from the earlier books had been transposed to a different ethos. In *Rob Roy* (1995), Sharp returned to Scotland with an epic adventure story, but *Dean Spanley* (2008) came as a complete surprise. Based on a novella by the Irish writer Lord Dunsany, the film, set in Edwardian England, begins as a whimsical, poignant comedy about a Dean of the Church who seems to have been reincarnated from a previous life as a spaniel, yet this startling proposition gives way subtly and gently to an exploration of ageing, the changing relation between a father and his son, and a meditation on and ultimately an affirmation of the vitality of life, despite the inevitability of mortality.

And so to TV. Troy Kennedy Martin (1932–2009) was of the same vintage as John McGrath. Born in Scotland, his early work included the police series *Z-Cars* (1962–78), *The Sweeney* (1975–78) and the serial *Reilly, Ace of Spies* (1983). Like Sharp, he also wrote for Hollywood, but his six-part television serial *Edge of Darkness* (1985) is his masterwork. The story takes the theme of power and corruption in the nuclear industry as it applies within and well beyond national boundaries and Westminster state politics. In a sense, it's a cross-medium sequel to John McGrath's play, *The Cheviot, the Stag and the Black, Black Oil* (1973), taking the subject of international commercial exploitation to a further stage of history. Scotland, England, Ireland and America are represented in the national identities of the main characters: each has different priorities. In the tensions and unfolding development, the relations between state-centred political authority and the brokers of international power are explored in the form of a thriller. In Stuart Hood's words, it is about 'how politics is lived'. The text of the scripts was published by Faber & Faber and the programmes made available on DVD, while an analysis of the work by John Caughie was published in the British Film Institute's 'Television Classics' series (2008). I'd call *Edge of Darkness* a classic of Scottish literature.

The playscripts and screenplays for television and film by John Byrne (b.1940) cross conventions of literary, visual and screen art forms, beginning with *The Slab Boys* (1978), followed by *Cuttin' a Rug* and *Still Life*, and then a fourth play, *Nova Scotia*. His two TV series, *Tutti Frutti* (1987) and *Your Cheatin' Heart* (1990) are full of wild humour, generous sympathies and tenderness. Like Hood, Forsyth, Sharp and Kennedy Martin, Byrne is a literary artist whose storytelling and depiction of characters and relationships are equal to those of our finest novelists.

The same might be said of Peter McDougall (b.1947). Glasgow-born, he worked in the shipyards before moving to London, where he began writing. His first television scripts were broadcast in the 1970s to critical acclaim and a shock of recognition. *Just Another Saturday* (1975) focused on a young man's experiences through the day and evening of an Orange Walk in his native city, while *Just a Boy's Game* (1979) recounted another single day experienced by two friends, a construction worker (played by Ken Hutchison) and a gang leader (played by the singer Frankie Miller) trying to move away from his violent past. The American director Martin Scorsese noted that the atmospheric filming was the Scottish equivalent of his own film *Mean Streets*. *Down Where the Buffalo Go* (1988), starring Harvey Keitel, documented an American officer's experience in the nuclear submarine base near Glasgow and remains an overwhelmingly downbeat account of the social dysfunction brought about in that awful era.

In the 21st century, almost nothing compares with these works, let alone the TV adaptations of great works of Scottish literature from the 1970s: *The Master of Ballantrae* (1962), *Sunset Song* (1971), *Weir of Hermiston* (1973), *Willie Rough* (1976), *Clay, Smeddum and Greenden* (1976), *Rob Roy* (1977), *Huntingtower* (1978), *The House with the Green Shutters* (1980), many of these made possible by another heroic figure too easily missed in Scottish literary histories: the drama producer for BBC Scotland, Pharic Maclaren (1923–80).

Joseph Goebbels once said,

> The essence of propaganda consists in winning people over to an idea so sincerely, so vitally, that in the end they succumb to it utterly and can never again escape from it.

Richard Strauss went to see Goebbels in Berlin in 1941, to be told,

> Franz Lehar has the masses – and you don't! The art of tomorrow is different from the art of yesterday. And you, Herr Strauss, are from yesterday!

But maybe that's where resistance always comes from.

10

New media

FIRST OF ALL, THERE's old media: newspapers and magazines. The American poet Ed Dorn used to run a paper of political-intellectual journalism called *Rolling Stock* in Ronald Reagan's America in the 1980s which, he said, was just about the only place where Marxist ideas could be published for a wider readership than specialists. Every issue's first page ran a banner title headline with an Old West locomotive coming straight at the reader with the strapline: 'If it moves – print it!'

Magazines, journals, periodicals of different kinds in different historical epochs, have been an essential part of literary and political culture internationally. Scotland's literature has been vitally nourished by such publications and by literary journalism in newspapers. The early 19th-century rivals, the Tory *Blackwood's Magazine* and the Whig *Edinburgh Review* are famous examples, and in the 20th century, *The Scottish Chapbook, The Scottish Nation, The Scottish Educational Journal, The Modern Scot, The Voice of Scotland, Lines Review, Chapman, Akros* and many others were constantly engaged in literary and cultural debates, where contemporary events and new publications were analysed and discussed, new poems and fiction were published, and writers could set out their wares. Of the many writers, publishers and champions who edited these periodicals, Joy Hendry of *Chapman* and Calum Macdonald and Tessa Ransford of *Lines Review* were exceptional both in the quality of their work and the longevity of their dedication and professionalism.

In 21st-century Scotland, new technology brings different possibilities yet the key questions remain: whose interests are being served? How does the technology help? What are its liabilities? Let me offer three different examples of valuable Scottish literary practice in new media, and then a fourth value.

Three e-publications suggest three very different forms of practice. The online journal *Glasgow Review of Books* for its lifetime did effectively what a published, paper-dependent magazine would do. Its technology wasn't tree-based but computer-reliant. Its 'Home Page' stated that it was

> a review journal publishing short and long reviews, review essays and interviews, as well as translations, fiction, poetry, and visual art. We are interested in all forms of cultural practice and seek to incorporate more marginal, peripheral or neglected forms into our debates and discussions.

At the time of writing, this periodical is no longer live, reminding us that there is an active lifespan for all these initiatives that doesn't last forever.

The emphases were on an international approach, the importance of translation, and the Glasgow base. The magazine was structured around 'threads', regularly publishing new poetry with a 'Translation Thursday' carrying reviews of translated work or new translations; and short fiction was also published regularly. There were reviews of books and literary festivals. Other 'threads' include ecology (using visual images as well as poetry and criticism). Since the *Review* was unfunded, the online format made the material both widely accessible and cost-effective.

I contributed in 2015, when there was a retrospective reassessment of 'Informationism', 21 years after the 'Informationist Primer' anthology *Contraflow on the Superhighway* (1994). The poet who gave the group its name, Richard Price, wrote:

> One of the features of Informationist poetry is its engagement with and deliberate mixing of different linguistic registers, and the interrogation of language's power-bearing qualities in the process.

That question of power, the interconnectedness and limitations of the 'information society' we inhabit today, was what concerned us, I think, most intuitively, back in the 1980s and especially the 1990s. The economist Paul Mason, in his book, *Postcapitalism* (2015), says this:

> Information is different from every previous technology. Its spontaneous tendency is to dissolve markets, destroy ownership and break down the relationship between work and wages. And that is the deep background to the crisis we are living through.

Online resources are essential to that crisis, and maybe, its resolution. Particular Scottish literary precedents were pre-eminently the late, epic, quotation-filled poems of Hugh MacDiarmid and the referentially wide-ranging poems of Edwin Morgan.

If the *GRB* was an online equivalent of a print-based periodical, even as it made use of new technology to help with dissemination and cost, a different enterprise was evident with Brian Johnstone and Andrew Jackson's *Scotia Extremis* website. Johnstone explained:

> It's a long time since I was last called an extremist – not since my student days, in fact – but from Burns Day this year I've been happy to consider myself as such, though entirely in the cause of poetry. For on that date the Perthshire-based poet Andy Jackson and myself launched a new poetry project, the online anthology *Scotia Extremis*.

The idea was to publish 'writing by a wide range of Scottish poets – from the well-known to almost the yet-to-be discovered': poems from the polarities of Scotland's psyche.

Taking their cue from Hugh MacDiarmid ('I'll ha'e nae hauf-way hoose, but aye be whaur extremes meet') the aim was to explore 'the soul of Scotland' through specially commissioned poems. In Johnstone's words:

> Each week the editors publish a brace of themed poems with a particular Scottish focus: people (past and present), places (real and imagined), culture (high and low), customs (ancient and modern) and more.

While the list represents the editors' interests they were also addressing what they saw as objectively intrinsic to Scotland's identity:

> Each theme is designed to represent what might be called an 'icon of Scotland', often of the sort that would be found in museums or arts centres, but equally often such as would not be out of place in the tartan gift shop, on the sports field, the national radio station or the local newsstand

Pairings included Burns Night and Up-Helly-Aa, Jenners and The Barras, Charles Rennie Mackintosh and Robert Adam, the Forth Bridge and the 'Bridge Over the Atlantic', Billy Bremner and Archie Gemmill, Celtic Connections and the White Heather Club, black bun and Black Bob. Many more unexpected, bizarre but mutually illuminating pairings were still to come. The invited poets remain ignorant of their partners, so that what gathers is an anthology which examines in poems, from a range of different angles, 'the interplay between extremes of the nation's culture'.

One virtue of the project was that it set its own limitation: it lasted one year, from Burns Day 2016 to spring 2017. There were over 1500 online followers and the number grew. Online technology is arguably what has made this project possible, though a selection of work appeared as a published book in 2018. Yet the excitement and curiosity was most immediate while the work was being enacted, and the book is a partial resource to return to and dwell upon.

The third example is Peter McCarey's *The Syllabary*: http://www.thesyllabary.com/: poetry as new technology arising uniquely in the computer era. In 2006, on his website, 'The Hyperliterary Exchange': http://hyperex.co.uk/reviewsyllabary.php, Edward Picot defined 'hyperliterature' as 'literature which makes use of the computerised/digital medium in such a way that it cannot be reproduced in print'. There are animations, sound-effects, nonlinear structures, interactivities, or combinations of these. Picot's own website: http://

www.edwardpicot.com/ links to other hyperliterature sites.

McCarey described the origins of *The Syllabary* as a list of monosyllabic words which formed the basis of his elaborations into short, dense and complex lyrical poems. The priority of syllables as opposed to metrical structures, sonnet or ballad forms for example, abandons rhyme and regulated rhythm for apparently random associations of sound. When you open the site, McCarey says,

> The simplest way to visualise what happens when you're in the programme is to imagine a set of concentric dials on the door of a safe. The outer dial is the initial, the second is the vowel, and the third is the terminal.

The dial turns, the letters form a sound, sometimes a recognisable word, and if there's a poem behind it, the screen pauses to display it. When there's a fix on a poem, what looks like an old portable typewriter's script takes form as you hear the poet's voice reading it. Then the dials shift again. Visually, the screen is layered with the dials, and then seemingly hand-written words or letter-clusters containing the syllables come and go, horizontally, and fade up into focus or back down to invisibility.

Edward Picot's conclusion is worth noting:

> Igor Stravinsky once wrote that 'The more constraints one imposes, the more one frees oneself of the chains that shackle the spirit...the arbitrariness of the constraint only serves to obtain precision of execution.' There are other ways of working, of course: but constraint and process certainly seem to suit McCarey. They have enabled him to produce a work of literature which is experimental, elaborate, simple, mathematically precise and deeply personal all at the same time.

And perfectly suited to online technology in a way no printed poem, or poem from the oral tradition, has ever been.

Paradoxically, the greatest 'futurist' of modern Scottish letters, Edwin Morgan, author of computer poems and hi-tech poem-jinks you'd think online technology was made for, never used a computer: his old typewriter stayed with him pretty much to the end and is now held in the Morgan archive at the Scottish Poetry Library. Yet Morgan knew well enough what the future might portend and in this context, it's also curious to reflect on the fact that he never published a major scholarly work, neither of literary history nor of close analysis of his favoured authors. He did, however, excel as a literary scholar in another form: the essay. With all the technological resources for information and the movement of data, the purpose of the essay remains an essential method of enquiry, whether in print or online.

Morgan's *Essays* (1974) and *Crossing the Border: Essays on Scottish Literature* (1990) prompt a further consideration of the essential need for prose criticism, literary, social, historical accounts, from the Enlightenment to contemporary political and literary analysis. Of many valuable works in this area from the 20th and 21st centuries, among the best are the collection *Scottish Scene: or, the Intelligent Man's Guide to Albyn* (1934) by Hugh MacDiarmid and Lewis Grassic Gibbon and 'The Voice of Scotland' series of books they commissioned early in that decade, including Victor McClure's *Scotland's Inner Man*, Compton Mackenzie's *Catholicism and Scotland*, Eric Linklater's *The Lion and the Unicorn*, William Power's *Literature and Oatmeal*, Willa Muir's *Mrs Grundy in Scotland* and Edwin Muir's *Scott and Scotland*.

More recently, Neal Ascherson (b. 1932), in *Stone Voices: The Search for Scotland* (2002), continued a tradition of considering literature, the arts, all forms of cultural production in Scotland, in the context of changing social, economic and political conditions. Cairns Craig, general editor of the 'determinations' series from Edinburgh University Press from 1987–97, was similarly committed to deep cultural engagement. This series included titles such as Craig Beveridge and Ronald Turnbull's *The Eclipse of Scottish Culture* (1989), *A Claim of Right for Scotland* (1989), edited by Owen Dudley Edwards, and Alexander Broadie's *The Tradition of Scottish Philosophy* (1990). More recently the series of 'Companions' to Scottish literature published by Edinburgh University and later the Association for Scottish Literary Studies take the spirit of critical enquiry further.

Angus Calder (1942–2008), historian and poet, was the author of major studies of the Second World War, *The People's War* (1969) and *The Myth of the Blitz* (1991), but his major work was *Revolutionary Empire: The Rise of the English-Speaking Empires from the Fifteenth Century to the 1780s* (1981). This is among the best Scottish books of the 20th century. In it, the responsibilities of the professional historian, an assiduous attention to recovered information about the conditions in which people of all kinds lived their lives, and the priorities of a cultural critic, who knows intimately the value of all the arts in the work of human imagination, are perfectly matched. Many literary critics are committed to the latter, many historians to the former, but few writers have brought them together with such lucidity and power. At over 900 pages, *Revolutionary Empire* is monumental, but never flags. It's one of the very few works to take a comprehensive account of the history of the English-speaking world in an international context which gives as much weight to considering the people of Scotland as it does to the people of more imperial centres of gravity. Calder's books of essays and literary appraisal dealing more closely with Scotland's culture and society bring unique insight and contagious engagement: *Revolving Culture: Notes from the Scottish Republic* (1994) and *Scotlands of the Mind* (2002).

To these names I would add the less familiar one of Thomas Docherty, author of *Aesthetic Democracy* (2006), *Universities at War* (2014) and *Complicity* (2016), books which engage fiercely with questions of philosophy, social purpose and morality. The first of these opens with the proposition: 'democracy is impossible in a polity that degrades the arts.' The second applies the argument to tertiary educational priorities in a world where financial wealth is the determining force, 'that has co-opted its countervailing authority, that of civilisation or, tragically, of the university.' The third is a devastating analysis of the relation between ethics and contemporary politics, with brilliant analyses of Shakespeare alongside a close reading of Edwin Morgan's poem for the opening of the Scottish parliament in 2004.

The work of Ascherson, Craig, Calder, Docherty and others is another example of a distinctive characteristic of Scotland: the priority, not only of perception, but of participation. Their examples show how the virtues of Scottish literature, like all other literatures and all the arts, are always with the open, never with things fixed, finally formed and closed. If new media excels in immediacy, essayists, historians and critics like these emphasise the necessity for its complement: incisive, reflective, serious thinking.

The online examples of Scottish literature in new media I began with are necessary practice, but they require the complement of the work that essays do. In her seminal book *Artful* (2012), Ali Smith asks: 'What is a screen?' And answers: 'A thing which divides.' But then she asks: 'Does an image on a screen form the same kind of surface as words on a page?' The answer to that is more complex.

11

Travel writing

TRAVEL WRITING EITHER by Scots themselves or visitors from elsewhere moving around within the country, forms a rich tradition crossing centuries. Its fascination is various: the expectations, prejudices and forms of analysis of the writers; the people, social conditions and ways of life encountered; the literary styles of travellers of different periods, quest-narratives, writers in search of something, sometimes finding it, sometimes left with hopes and questions, disappointments and affirmations. There are also works by Scots ranging through the world at large, from William Lithgow in the 17th century to Robert Louis Stevenson in the 19th century and further. And there is the writing of the Scots diaspora, people who have emigrated or are of Scots descent, now settled anywhere from Canada to New Zealand. Then there are the modes of transport available, and what they meant for ways of seeing and understanding. 'Better to travel hopefully than to arrive,' Stevenson is proverbially misquoted as saying – but it depends where you're going, and the territories and climates you have to travel through.

Writers have their own political priorities and persuasive intentions. Daniel Defoe visited Scotland as an English spy, Samuel Johnson came as an English superiorist. Wordsworth's sympathies were more open, characterised by the pathos of his own loneliness; his sister Dorothy's descriptions of what she sees are brilliantly precise. These visitors mainly walk; sometimes they're on horseback or in a carriage or boat. Robert Macfarlane, in *The Old Ways: A Journey on Foot* (2012) and other works returns to walking as the essential mode of travel for thinking and writing. And there is sailing. As Nick Thorpe says in *Adrift in Caledonia: Boat-hitching for the Unenlightened* (2006),

> Growing up in England, school history had taught me that the sea was a defensive barrier, policed by the navy to ensure that Britannia continued to rule the waves. To the explorers and traders in Scotland, however, it was predominantly a connection to the world – and crucially one which didn't involve kowtowing to Big Brother over the land border. Water was freedom and possibility.

Some of the earliest accounts are of new territory, experience of places unknown to readers, and first-time encounters for their authors. These have the virtue not only of delineating conditions of social life but also the curiosity and wonder of the pioneers: Donald Monro's *Description of the Occidental i.e. Western Islands of Scotland* (1549) and Martin Martin's *A Description of the Western Islands of Scotland* (c. 1695) and *A Voyage to St Kilda* (1698) are accounts of this kind.

In the 18th century, the purpose of visitors arriving from England is often directly political, to give an estimation of the resources, potential threats or compliances of a component part of what was now the United Kingdom. Thus, Defoe, in *A Tour through the Whole Island of Great Britain* (1724–26) highlights the virtues of Glasgow in the era prior to the Jacobite rising of 1745. In 'Letter 11' he comments that Scotland, by virtue of the Union with England, surrendered its parliament but has not lost the privilege of self-governing burghs making their own by-laws, which 'is now in many ways more advantageous to them than it was before, as their trade is like to be, in time, more considerable than before.' As a pro-Union spy, Defoe was satisfied that Scotland, which 'was before considered as a nation', now 'appears no more but as a province, or at best, a dominion.'

Thirty years after the Jacobite rising, Samuel Johnson, in *Journey to the Western Islands of Scotland* and James Boswell, in *Journal of a Tour to the Hebrides*, having travelled together in 1773, record their suffering discomfort and Johnson expressed his disdain for people still unable to speak English, but both are silent about the battlefield of Culloden. They pass within six miles of it and could not but have been sensitive to what had happened there. Similarly, they register something of the aura of Iona, which they visited eagerly. The best way to read both these journals is *To the Hebrides* (2007), edited by Ronald Black, which collates the two accounts and takes the reader through the journey, place by place, with Johnson's report immediately followed by Boswell's. The extensive annotation and editorial material gives the depth and detailed information only a Gaelic scholar could supply to complement the vivid writing of the travellers.

Written before, but published after, Culloden, *Letters from a Gentleman in the North of Scotland*, c.1726 (1754) by Edward Burt, bridges the cataclysm, and Thomas Pennant, in *Tour in Scotland* (1769; published 1771) and Thomas Thornton, in *Tour in the Highlands* (1786; published 1804), begin to see the country, and those parts of the country most remote from the cities, not only arising from the troubles of their history, but as valuable future destinations for the exercise of visual refreshment. Scenes of physical battle and bloodshed and landscapes redolent with spiritual meaning became mere items on the itinerary for a wide readership; it was not until the fiction of Walter Scott and James Hogg that the meaning of Culloden began to be confronted and explored more deeply in narrative fiction addressed to English-language readers.

Something intuitively keen, of course, is going on with Robert Burns, in his

Tour of the Borders (1787) and *Tour of the Highlands and Stirlingshire* (1787). There is certainly prejudice against the Highlanders but there is also an innate curiosity and sense of kinship with people of all sorts and landscapes of very different character from that of his native Ayrshire. And Alexander Campbell, in *A Journey from Edinburgh through parts of North Britain* (1802) brings together different kinds of writing, as if exploring Scotland for the first time. James Hogg, in *Highland Tours: Travels in the Scottish Highlands and Western Isles in 1802, 1803 and 1804*, is characteristically robust and often funny, as he meets people of all sorts and visits parts of Scotland that were new to him. Dorothy Wordsworth, in her *Recollections of a Tour Made in Scotland A.D. 1803*, and William, in his poems prompted by his tours in Scotland, are enlightened witnesses, whose observations and questions might be turned towards themselves as much as to what they meet north of the Border. Walter Scott exemplifies the same paradigm in *Northern Lights or a Voyage in the Lighthouse Yacht to Nova Zembla and the Lord Knows Where in the Summer of 1814*, where, as a native Scot, he is encompassing the furthest reaches of the archipelagic identity from which the nation is constructed.

Later in the 19th century, visitors from England and France have very different experiences. John Keats, in his poems and letters from Scotland of 1818, has much to say about the way in which the memory of Robert Burns is already being commercialised and the value of his poetry and character demeaned by exploitation. The Poet Laureate Robert Southey, in *Journal of a Tour in Scotland in 1819*, offers a refined account of his meeting the natives, while Queen Victoria, in her *Leaves from the Journal of Our Life in the Highlands* (1848–61) is superlative in praise of the territory now firmly in her domain. Her sense of the scenic attractiveness of Scotland is that of an amateur painter, but her awareness of the cultural distinctiveness of Scotland, not least its Gaelic component, prompts not repulsion but a maternal benevolence. Her journal shows both proprietorial authority and an awareness of something beyond her, something she knows she might wish to look after. By contrast, Jules Verne, in his *Voyage a reculons en Angleterre et en Écosse* (1859–60, translated as *Backwards to Britain*, 1992), tours Scotland with the curiosity of a fantasist unchained: everything is wondrous, and about to be turned in his fiction into something even more wondrous. And wonder of wonders – the coaches, ferries, all the public transport systems that he makes use of on his travels, run on time and connect with each other. Verne also wrote two novels set in Scotland, *Child of the Caverns* (1877), fancifully set in a labyrinth of coal mines deep beneath Loch Lomond and *The Green Ray* (1882), which takes us to the Hebrides.

A darker view typifies Robert Buchanan (1841–1901), whose *The Hebrid Isles: Wanderings in the Land of Lorne and the Outer Hebrides* (1882), recognises and describes the beauties of austerity and wilderness, and gives a sense of desolation that seems both man-made and godless. This is present too in his poems, especially the sonnet sequence depicting Loch Coruisk, in Skye. Here is one example, 'Desolate!' (Sonnet 6):

> Desolate! How the Peaks of ashen grey,
>   The smoky Mists that drift from hill to hill,
> The Waters dark, anticipate this day
>   That sullen desolation. O how still
>   The shadows come and vanish, with no will!
> How still the melancholy Waters lie
> How still the vapours of the under-sky
>   Mirror'd below, drift onward, and fulfil
> Thy mandate as they mingle!—Not a sound,
>   Save that deep murmur of a torrent near,
> Deepening silence. Hush! the dark profound
>   Groans, as some grey crag loosens and falls sheer
> To the abyss. Wildly I look around.
>   O Spirit of the Human, art Thou *here?*

Perhaps the most famous of all 'travel books' of Scotland is Stevenson's *Kidnapped* (1886). Here is an adventure which begins in the Lowlands, takes us east towards Edinburgh, then voyages around the coast of Scotland, up the east coast and round into the western seas, where shipwreck sends the heroes ashore near Mull and they journey on foot across Scotland, back to the capital. Geography (you can follow the maps) and post-Culloden history (understanding the full significance of that event) are woven deeply into the text. The Scotland travelled over here is unsettled, divided, everywhere uncomfortable, discomforting, questioning, interrogating assumptions of security and meaning at every level.

More conventional travel narratives of the period include Edward Topham, *Edinburgh Life 100 Years Ago: With An Account Of The Fashions And Amusements Of Society* (1886) and Daniel Turner Holmes, *Literary Tours in the Highlands and Islands of Scotland* (1909). But with George Eyre-Todd's *Scotland Picturesque and Traditional: A Pilgrimage with Staff and Knapsack* (1895), we come to the end of the era in which pedestrian travel, or travel by horse or coach or boat, was primary. After H.V. Morton, whose *In Search of Scotland* (1929) was followed by *In Scotland Again* (1933), we have A.A. Thomson, *Let's See the Lowlands* (1930), where the tour is taken by that relatively new invention, the motor car. Seeing, here, is done through the glass. The opening of Scotland through public transport and the private motor-car marks a transitional moment from the 1920s to the 1930s. George Eyre-Todd sets off walking with staff and knapsack, but A.A. Thomson putters around the

Lowlands in a car. This is a shift from experiencing the country and the people in physical proximity to seeing them through moving windows, as spectacle, without a sense of smell or hearing the sounds of birds, rivers, and wind in the grass and leaves. This is the moment when Scotland starts to be screened. Even though the movement of the images is made by the viewer rather that the spectacle itself, Scotland in screen media begins at this point.

Yet the deeper enquiries continued, with the poets Edwin Muir, in *Scottish Journey* (1935), Louis MacNeice, in *I Crossed the Minch* (1938) and Hugh MacDiarmid, in *The Islands of Scotland* (1939). These three books should be read together, for they complement and counterpoint each other in revealing ways. Muir is disillusioned with a Scotland characterised by poverty, ignorance and pessimism, almost in defiance of its awe-inspiring, purple landscapes. MacNeice is even more pessimistic as he encounters the Outer Hebrides, the oppressiveness of religious austerity, the ethos of rejection of and abstinence from the pleasures and experience of the arts. MacDiarmid sees clearly everything there is to deplore in social conditions and low expectations, but he delivers a new sense of what the islands of Scotland signify: an archipelagic identity of plural meanings, characterised by place and condition, weather, seasons, and forms of habitation and economy. Some things can be changed, but some arise from the deepest of human meanings, without romanticising or fabricating their value. That sense of value is most eloquently expressed in the poem 'Island Funeral', first published in this book. The closest work I can think of to this is *The Shoshoneans* (1966) by Edward Dorn, an account of a journey among native people in 1960s America that delivers a similar core sense of human dignity and cultural authority.

That sense of human connectedness – what's welcome and what should be resisted – has specific bearing in Scotland, across continents and centuries. Alistair MacLeod defines it in his novel, *No Great Mischief* (1999):

'You are from here,' said the woman.
'No,' said my sister, 'I'm from Canada.'
'That may be,' said the woman. 'But you are really from here. You have just been away for a while.'

12

Diaspora

OUR SURVEY OF travel writing in Scotland took us to the 1930s. Since then, a whole industry has grown up in the genre. Primarily anecdotal and light, George Scott-Moncrieff's *The Lowlands of Scotland* (1939), Halliday Sutherland's *Hebridean Journey* (1939) and T. Ratcliffe Barnett's *Scottish Pilgrimage in the Land of Lost Content* (1942) are exercises in travel writing whose pleasure is picaresque and unstrained. Moray McLaren, in *Stern and Wild: A New Scottish Journey* (1948), relates his return and rediscovery of Scotland, offering a series of questions about the country and what might be made of it, in the immediate aftermath of the Second World War. A.R.B. Haldane, in *The Drove Roads of Scotland* (1952), seems to be on a similar quest, but this book connects back explicitly to a previous economy and social context, where priorities arose from different needs. As such, it is part of the reconstruction of a modern Scotland that understands its past more thoroughly than superficial travel accounts normally allow.

James Campbell's *Invisible Country: A Journey Through Scotland* (1984) takes its cue from Edwin Muir. Campbell follows a similar trail, eager but gloomy in his appetite for meeting ignorant, indifferent or hostile people, generally unimpressed by local distinctions, especially when close to the cities. In the south, he meets few people who seem to know anything about the literature, culture or history of the country they live in. In the north, though, he uncovers the current traces of the Clearances in memorials that show how memory can be made public, with effort and dedication. And these are made not by the authorities but by descendants of those departed or oppressed since at least the 18th century, drawing upon not simply memories worth celebrating, but memories that give us, in the 21st century, reasons to condemn things that are as awful now as they were then.

Jaunty entertainment characterises another retracing of previous trails, in *A Walk to the Western Isles after Boswell & Johnson* (1993) by Frank Delaney, while Alastair Scott, in *Native Stranger: A Journey in Familiar and Foreign Scotland* (1995), sets the terms of his encounters in his title. But SNP MSP Michael Russell's *In Waiting: Travels in the Shadow of Edwin Muir* (1998) has a different function: this is a voluntary 'taking stock' of Scotland's resources, people and mood. It's an investigation that should be required of every one of our politicians, whether based in Edinburgh or London.

Particular motivation drives Iain Banks in *Raw Spirit: In Search of the Perfect*

Dram (2003), taking us along well-known and unfamiliar roads in Scotland, from distillery to distillery with coruscating perceptions tossed out in happy cascades. Andrew Greig's *By the Loch of the Green Corrie* (2010) follows a mission prompted by Norman MacCaig a short while before his death, to find and go fishing in a small loch in the north-west of Scotland. But Greig's real search is for things in the land itself that connect him with MacCaig and modern Scottish poetry more broadly. The book enacts a deep human need for things not easily disclosed in the modern world, wherever we are. And in the end, that's what all travel writing is for.

So what of travellers from Scotland, setting off to the wider world?

For hundreds of years, people from Scotland have settled in locations throughout the world and established their own lives and literatures across generations. James Hunter's book *Scottish Exodus: Travels Among a Worldwide Clan* (2005) describes his encounters with many people of the Clan MacLeod in America, South Africa, Australia, New Zealand and elsewhere. Exodus is a biblical term describing a movement of people to a new homeland. Diaspora, also a biblical term, describes the movement of people away from their homeland. For many who left Scotland, a new home was an ideal prospect, but for many, equally, the sense of leave-taking was not driven by choice and idealism, but economic necessity and brute force. In terms of Scottish literature, particular authors in many locations, writing in the context of different traditions, to a greater or lesser degree self-consciously, have identified their affiliations with Scotland.

The distinct tradition of poetry in Ulster Scots, in the north of Ireland, arose mainly on the foundations of the vernacular Scots tradition and the poems and songs of Burns. There are similar traditions in New Zealand and Gaelic traditions in Canada, the social context of which is nowhere more movingly described than in Alistair MacLeod's fine novel *No Great Mischief* (1999).

To name only a few of the writers of the 20th and 21st centuries for whom Scotland and Scottish literature are of personal and literary significance, there are Les Murray (1938–2019) and Chris Wallace-Crabbe (b. 1934) in Australia, Helen Adam (1909–93) in the Beat movement in America, Carlos Drummond de Andrade (1902–87) in Brazil, James K. Baxter (1926–72) and Bill Manhire (b. 1946) in New Zealand, Veronica Forrest-Thomson (1947–75) in Cambridge, Douglas Oliver (1937–2000) in Cambridge and Paris, John Sutherland (b. 1938) and Mick Imlah (1956–2009) in London.

In the West Indies, some Scots were deeply involved in slave-trading while some maintained an anti-slavery position of remarkable moral authority. The pastoral tradition established in the overlap between Scottish and English literature in the 18th and 19th centuries, especially through the work of James Thomson, Burns, John Clare and Wordsworth, is related to the work of two of the earliest poets writing of the West Indies: James Grainger (c.1721–1766), whose 'Sugar-Cane' describes the workings of a sugar plantation, and James Montgomery (1771–1854), whose desire to see the abolition of the slave trade was expressed in a four-part poem in heroic couplets published in 1809, 'The West Indies'. The adventures described in *Tom Cringle's Log* (1834) by Michael Scott (1789–1835) have less moral scruple but vividly evoke the West Indies its author knew at first hand.

Mary Seacole (1805–1881) was the daughter of a Scottish army officer and a free black woman. She was born in Jamaica and served as a nurse for the British Army during the Crimean war, after which a benefit Festival in her honour was held in 1857 in Royal Surrey Gardens. On the opening page of her autobiography, *Wonderful Adventures of Mrs Seacole in Many Lands* (1857), she wrote: 'I am a Creole, and have good Scotch blood coursing through my veins. Many people have traced to my Scottish blood that energy and activity which are not always found in the Creole race, and which have carried me to so many varied scenes: and perhaps they are right.'

The recognition of hybridity in personal and literary identity is one of the essential themes of West Indian culture and has a salutary presence in much that has been written about postcolonial literatures generally. One effect it helps bring about is the destabilising of hierarchic patriarchal lines of descent. In New Zealand, in the 1980s and 1990s, Keri Hulme emphasised her mixed background, coming from Maori, white New Zealand and Scots Orkney people, partly to question the idea of the superiority of secure racial identity. And in modern West Indian writers with Scots connections, this understanding of the complexity of identity is paramount, most explicitly in the novels of Wilson Harris, but also in the poetry and theories of 'nation-language' of Edward Kamau Brathwaite. Seamus Heaney, in *Stepping Stones* (2008), a book of interviews with Dennis O'Driscoll, draws attention to the affinity between this aspect of West Indian writing and Irish literature in ways that apply even more closely to Scottish literature, when you think of the relations between Gaelic, Scots and English: 'There were obvious parallels between the cultural and political situation in St Lucia [Derek Walcott's home island] in the second half of the 20th century and the situation in Ireland in the first half. In both places the writers were furnished with two languages, the vernacular of the home and the idiom of the school, and the choice between them had political implications.'

For Scotland, read three languages. And now, not only Gaelic, Scots and English, but Polish and Urdu and other languages brought by more recent settlers. The political question to which Heaney draws attention is crucial in Scotland as much as it was in Ireland:

> In Ireland in the 1920s, for example, you had a cultural nationalist critic like Daniel Corkery promoting a nativist line, saying that you

weren't a truly Irish writer if you couldn't find the heart of the matter in the crowd attending a Munster hurling final; the post-independence requirement therefore was to practise the government of the tongue and deny the imperial modes and matter. And in the 1960s these pressures were in operation elsewhere, with a poet like Edward Kamau Brathwaite turning from 'the voices of his education' in English to the voicing of the Afro-English of the Caribbean, tuning his lines to the African drum rather than the iambic metronome. It was a playing out in a different time and place of the conflict Joyce had designated in Ireland between the 'full stoppers and semi-colonials.' I was interested, at any rate, in [Derek] Walcott's refusal to renege on the inherited English strain and admired him for trying to let the whole problem play out in his work, and pay into it.

In other words, in Scottish terms, hybridity in language (the use of English as much as that of Scots and Gaelic) may be a strengthening component of our literary, cultural and indeed social identity. To do so it must be used not as a term of denigration, with overtones of racist or linguistic superiorism, but as a term of critical appraisal. Modern Scottish novels have contributed self-consciously to this process, among them, most notably, *Joseph Knight* (2003) by James Robertson, *The Quiet Stranger* (1991) by Robbie Kydd and *Illustrious Exile: Journal of my Sojourn in the West Indies* (2006) by Andrew O. Lindsay, which explores what might have happened had Burns in fact gone to Jamaica. The question has been taken further in scholarly studies of Burns's attitudes to slavery.

One of the best discursive explorations of the evolving presence of Scots at large is Billy Kay's *The Scottish World: A Journey into the Scots Diaspora* (2006), both a scholarly exposition and a personal account of discoveries. In the Prologue, Kay writes of how he came across a newsletter of the Caledonian Society of Hawaii from 1975, in which 'a young man from Ayrshire' lists various novelists whose work is recommended 'for Hawaiian readers', including Neil Gunn, Lewis Grassic Gibbon, George Douglas Brown, Iain Crichton Smith, Fionn Mac Colla, George Mackay Brown and William MacIlvanney. Kay adds to this:

> For too long we Scots were content to look to the past and perpetuate a romantic myth about the country. Attractive though the myth might be, it hinders the natural growth of the culture, for no one confronts the problems of the present in their thoughts and writing. The writers listed above are among those who tried honestly to be aware of the values of the past, but only as they touch the present and are relevant to the future. Books on tartan are fine, but books on people are better. Enjoy your reading and come to a closer understanding of Scotland at the same time.

In *Scottish Exodus* (2007), James Hunter draws attention to the darker side of the extensive emigration from Scotland:

> What will forever make emigration problematic, as far as Scots remaining in Scotland are concerned, is its unremittingly negative impact on the communities our hundreds of thousands of emigrants left behind.

Yet in the same book, he quotes Anne Grant writing in 1811, noting a sense of human connection through time that literature itself helps to reinstate, to the benefit of all:

> No Highlander ever once thought of himself as an individual... He considered himself...with reference to those who had gone before, and those who were to come after him.

Or as the Yoruba people of Nigeria might put it, the world of the living is always in the cradle of understanding, between both the world of the ancestors, and the world of the unborn.

Or as Malachy Tallack in *The Un-Discovered Islands* (2016) says of Hawaiki, described as 'the original home' of the Maori people:

> It is the place from which the spirit comes and to which it returns. It is the source and the destination. In some stories, it is also the place in which the very first human being was created, a kind of Eden, where gods still dwell.

Or in Hugh MacDiarmid's words in his poem 'Gairmscoile': 'we ha'e faith in Scotland's hidden poo'ers, / The present's theirs, but a' the past and future's oors.'

PART SIX

A Loose Canon

I

The idea of a canon

THE CONDUCTOR ANTONIO PAPPANO, on the BBC Radio 3 programme, *Music Matters*, on 1 May 2021, said this:

> The fact of the matter is society is identified by its culture… That's not by accident. This is something that's been honed and nurtured over hundreds of years. It doesn't happen just by itself. It needs encouragement, it needs people to stand up for it, people from the top echelon to stand up for it, because it's our identity. It's what we are.

He's using the word 'culture' in more than one sense. Go back to the Gaelic word with which we started this book and has recurred intermittently throughout its long course: the word is 'dùthchas' and it indicates the interconnections between land, people, and culture. In these interconnections, 'culture' is indeed something that 'doesn't happen just by itself' and the health of those living arises from the fluent activity in those interconnections. But sometimes that fluency is threatened or blocked, held in bias and thwart. Certain priorities of culture can be imposed and crush others. Certain priorities might be upheld and might even have to be defended. This is where the idea of a canon comes in.

Any construction of a canon of Scottish literature is an act of reclamation, a resistance to the canonical weight of English, or Anglo-American, or Anglophone literature(s), including post-imperial literatures in English. In this respect, the very idea of Scottish literature is intrinsically an assertion of the relativity of value.

This is not to oust one literary canon and replace it with another. Nor is it to enact a competition of ethnic or linguistic hierarchies. Rather, the recognition of Scottish literature is an expansion, correction and relativisation of literary value. Literature – all the arts – show us again and again, intrinsically, that there's always more than one story to be told, and more than one way to tell any story. I hope that what follows is responsive to that truth.

I hope the following list exemplifies inclusiveness. That isn't what a 'canon' usually does or tries to do. The word normally signifies a selection of books approved as the most important or indeed sacred, an inviolable choice, amounting to a collection of essential knowledge. It's usually as important for what it keeps out as for what it puts in. This is emphatically *not* a list of 'All You Need to Know' but rather offers a summary of some of the riches of Scottish literature in historical sequence and includes a selection of authors whose works open connections between Scottish literature and other disciplines and ways of approaching reality.

For example, I have included some works of philosophy, literary criticism and history, and the autobiography of the composer Alexander Campbell Mackenzie and a book about painting by the artist J.D. Fergusson. There might have been more inclusions of this kind, like the *Memoirs* (1949) of another composer, Frederic Lamond (1868–1948), or *Points in Time: An Autobiography* by the major artist William Johnstone (1897–1981), which has revealing things to say about Hugh MacDiarmid and F.G. Scott. There are always further reaches.

The list should amount to an indication rather than an attempt at essentialism or comprehensiveness. It is only temporarily fixed. It includes some things that may be considered inessential. It is here to be challenged, added to, subtracted from, made relative by future inclusion of other authors and works. It is here to prompt thought about how it should be extended and what should be excluded. Some readers might come across material which, to their thinking, should never have been included at all.

Perhaps the very idea of a canon of Scottish literature will be rendered unnecessary by an increasing familiarity with major works and authors and an easy confidence based on an understanding of their quality. Many of the texts listed here have been discussed in this book, or at least noted. Some have not. The value of listing them like this is simply to put in one place a sequence of names and works that are worth investigating and going back to. If they are not the 'essential works of Scottish literature' they might all prompt consideration of what that term means, what it connects with, how it has been informed and generated.

Most canon lists aim to be tight and essential. This one is loose and baggy, a promise of accommodation. I have been more inclusive of earlier work simply because it is more likely to be neglected and names from older eras are in greater need of retrieval. Many of our contemporaries who are not noted here will arrive in due course and others drift off as they may. Time will tell. The jury's out. Of those who are not named, not all have been excluded by mistake. More controversially, some names have been included to question canonicity itself and would not even be accepted as 'Scottish'. Partly this should prompt consideration of what constitutes a basis for the choice of inclusion or exclusion. Accidents of birth or belonging, deliberations of commitment, residence and decisive engagement are only a few of the possible reasons to identify an artist with a nation. But the list should also indicate authors and texts whose work triggers questions about ways of thinking about Scottish literature that otherwise might not have been asked. For example, I have included Wilson Harris but not William Shakespeare, Ben Jonson, Herman Melville, Joseph Conrad, Virginia Woolf or George Orwell, though all of them were related to Scotland and Scottish literary identity in various more or less important ways.

I have also resisted the temptation to include any of those thought-provoking 'aberrations' from Edwin Morgan's catalogue of items found in University Entrance papers in English Literature, 'A Hantle of Howlers' collected in his *Essays* (1974), such as Walter Scott's *Treasure Island* or Robert Louis Stevenson's *Waverley*.

I was tempted to include the novel *Loot and Loyalty* (1955) by the Polish poet and author Jerzy Peterkiewicz (1916–2007), as its subject is the professional mercenary and brilliant Scottish composer Tobias Hume (1569–1645). Peterkiewicz left Poland, took a degree from the University of St Andrews and worked closely with the Scottish poet Burns Singer on translating an anthology of Polish poems, so again there are definite connections. Noting him here must suffice.

Similarly, Frederick Douglass (1818–95) is rightly identified as an African American whose autobiographies, *A Narrative of the Life of Frederick Douglass, an American Slave* (1845), *My Bondage and My Freedom* (1855) and *Life and Times of Frederick Douglass* (1881, revised 1892), chart his journey from slavery to freedom. The National Library of Scotland's website (accessed 5 July 2021) identifies Scotland and Edinburgh as being influential after his visit there in 1846, noting that he was struck by the fact that he was treated as an equal in Scotland and was appointed 'Scotland's Antislavery Agent'. *Frederick Douglass and Scotland, 1846: Living an Antislavery Life* (2018) by Alasdair Pettinger tells the story in detail. However, I have included James McCune Smith, the first African American to take a medical degree from Glasgow University, whose residence in Scotland is noted, and whose lecture *The Destiny of the People of Color* (delivered as a lecture in 1841 and published in 1843) and writings on Douglass's work and the Haitian revolutionary Toussaint L'Ouverture have something further to give to Scotland's literary story. The point in these instances is to keep the conduits clear for approaches and considerations from new angles and contested territories. Keeping the question of nationality open, partial and unfinished, and reading McCune Smith alongside more traditionally canonical 19th-century Scottish authors alters our sense of the cultural context, while hopefully avoiding the dismal attempt at mere appropriation.

In a letter to the editor of *The Glasgow Herald* (7 January 1944) on the subject of 'Scottish Composers' John Blackwood McEwan said this:

> I assume that the word 'Scottish' applied to a composer has a significance which is more than merely geographical and that the musicians who are banded together under this designation have something individual to say and are able to say it in a way [...] peculiar to their race, associations, and outlook.

In the 21st century, we would not use the word 'race' and might say instead, 'their loosely grouped-together common background, history, home or sense of belonging, or personal investment and commitment' or some other description. In order to have meaning, a designation of national identity need not be rigorously exclusive, closely defined or absolutely foreclosed.

But that description is too tight to accommodate all the writers listed here. In the Editor's Note to *Poetry 1900–2000: One hundred poets from Wales* (2007), an anthology of Welsh poetry in English, Meic Stephens said this:

> [...] to have a body of English verse which can properly be called Welsh there must be some reference to the land and people, to the past as well as the present – otherwise, we shall produce merely a regional or provincial literature indistinguishable from that produced in parts of England. Like Irish and Scottish poetry, Welsh poetry in English should speak to the world, but it should also be rooted in the Welsh experience and have something to say about the country in which it is written. Even so, there is a healthy range of attitudes towards things Welsh [...]: how poets think of Wales is as pluralistic today as it has always been, and long may it be so.

Stephens was defending the provenance of Welsh poetry in English to be understood as positively Welsh. If poetry in the Welsh language is understood to be, intrinsically, of Wales, he was acknowledging that some defence was required to make the claim for Welsh poetry in English. We can begin happily enough with a linguistic inclusiveness that accommodates Gaelic, Scots and English. But one wonders: could a great Scottish novel be written in Polish? And what would its primary subject have to be before we could describe it as Scottish? For our purposes, the argument could open to include work that has no direct connection to Scotland, either as emerging from it or commenting on it. It might present aspects of Scotland refracted through different lenses and perspectives, oblique angles of approach, through geographical distance, with no literal or specific connection in the way of political history or biological ancestry. Janice Galloway's *Clara*, Alan Sharp's *Dean Spanley* and Compton Mackenzie's *Vestal Fire* and *Extraordinary Women* come to mind.

We cannot but remain open to, and indeed eager to know more about, the plurality of languages and other forms of identity that contribute to the mongrel singularity of the nation. That openness is as essential as the truth that we have to stop somewhere.

Ultimately, this list is simply an invitation.

2

What a canon is

A CANON IS a form of cultural empowerment. At times this power can be used badly, closing off options and limiting possibilities. At times it can work as effective resistance to foreclosure and oppression intended by others, however those 'others' may be defined. There are always others.

A canon can be a good thing because it prompts curiosity and can lead to worthwhile company. It can also be a bad thing because the others are sometimes out to exert their power over you or colonise you.

In any conflict of power, making use of both strengths and limitations helps; both knowing your own and understanding those of others. So, just as it can be an empowerment, a canon can also be a liability, as it is also in itself a limitation. It can give form to identity, and form can give power. Yet form means constriction, and power is always negotiated by position. One colleague suggested that I could produce a canon of Scottish literature in no more than a dozen authors. That's true, but it wouldn't get us much further than where we already are. A short list would have its uses but they would be very strictly limited.

On 25 January 2012, the front page story in *The Herald* newspaper in Glasgow told readers that the Scottish government had decided that Scottish literature would be a required subject in all schools in Scotland.

It must seem strange that a nation's literature had been so neglected in that nation's schools that it had to be argued for, yet the case of Scottish literature is singular.

After the Union of Crowns in 1603 and the Union of Parliaments in 1707, from the 18th century on, establishment of English as a subject for study in education, especially in the 19th and 20th centuries, coincided with the expansion of the British Empire. The central authority of London as economic power and English as the language of authority prized English literature, and later American literature, as most valuable in education.

These are broad generalisations, but they serve to introduce a condition which must be decidedly unusual to readers internationally. For a number of years up to 2012, I was involved in various meetings with the Scottish government, the Scottish Qualifications Authority, the Association for Scottish Literary Studies and others, in the negotiations for the establishment of Scottish literature as a required subject in the school curriculum in Scotland, an entitlement to which everyone growing up in Scotland should gainfully be introduced.

Sometimes those negotiations were vexed because of the historical and cultural contexts for the long-standing relationship between Scottish and English literatures and the institutional silencing of Scottish literature in education. The argument has to be maintained. Two concerns were raised repeatedly in formal meetings and casual conversations, and they form a Catch 22 problem (to use a proverbial phrase from a once-famous American novel).

The first concern is this: how are teachers to identify what is meant by the term 'Scottish literature'?

If you have never studied the subject, how do you know what it is or is not? Many schoolteachers of English in Scotland have studied English literature in their undergraduate degrees, and many will have read American, Irish and postcolonial literatures. Some will have studied Scottish literature but many will have no acquaintance with it whatsoever.

Until 2012, fine teachers might introduce Scottish literature to schoolchildren with deep knowledge and contagious enthusiasm, but the provision in schools was optional. Many other teachers might have no interest in teaching the literature of the country and were not required to do so. The 2012 government directive could thus be welcomed as a wonderful opportunity, or it might be resisted as an imposition from on high.

The second concern, arising from the idea that it is an imposition, was often expressed as the desire to keep the options as open as possible. Effectively this meant 'open' to what was familiar and established but with no responsibility for including Scottish work at all. Implicitly this signified an opposition to the very idea of a defined or prescribed canon of 'Major Texts' or a 'Great Tradition of Scottish Literature'.

To exclude the resource and empowerment of a canon might leave your options open to whatever you like but it can also generate self-doubt and a lack of confidence about what is agreed, while to insist upon a canon might be seen as coercive. Catch 22. Answering one question forecloses the other. And the catch works both ways.

So here's the twofold answer: The canon is always up for debate. And at its most irreducible it's something to build from, not to be excluded by.

In his magisterial but contentious study, *The Western Canon* (1994), Harold Bloom lists his own selection of major works from world literature – as far as he can – and includes 17 Scottish authors:

William Dunbar, *Poems*
James Boswell, *Life of Johnson*; *Journals*
Tobias Smollett, *The Adventures of Roderick Random*; *The Expedition of Humphry Clinker*
Robert Burns, *Poems*
Sir Walter Scott, *Waverley*; *Old Mortality*; *The Heart of Midlothian*;

Redgauntlet
Lord Byron, *Don Juan*; *Poems*
John Galt, *The Entail*
James Hogg, *The Private Memoirs and Confessions of a Justified Sinner*
Thomas Carlyle, *Selected Prose*; *Sartor Resartus*
James Thomson / 'Bysshe Vanolis', *The City of Dreadful Night*
John Davidson, *Ballads and Songs*
Robert Louis Stevenson, *Essays*; *Kidnapped*; *Dr Jekyll and Mr Hyde*; *Treasure Island*; *The New Arabian Nights*; *The Master of Ballantrae*; *Weir of Hermiston*
George Macdonald, *Lilith*; *At the Back of the North Wind*
David Lindsay, *A Voyage to Arcturus*
Edwin Muir, *Collected Poems*
Norman Douglas, *South Wind*
Hugh MacDiarmid, *Complete Poems*

Now, the values that inform this list are clear: these are recognised classics most well-informed English-speaking readers would acknowledge but it would be wrong to say it is sufficient. For example, it does not admit any Gaelic literature and there are no women.

If I were to offer a canon of Scottish literature what criteria would I want to endorse?

I should say that there must be representation: (1) of what we could demonstrate as 'literary merit' and of what helps us understand what that term might mean; (2) of women as well as of men; (3) of the three languages in which most Scottish literature has been composed – Gaelic, Scots and English – even if we can only approach the work through translations or with a glossary; (4) of Scottish people, or of Scotland, and the variety of identities that constitute those terms (geographical, historical, industrial, rural, residents and travellers, exiles and tradition-bearers) across centuries; (5) of accessibility and difficulty (some authors present more problems than others and contemporary readers may find the language of Dunbar, the extensive narratives of Scott or the extremisms of MacDiarmid particularly challenging): in other words, the construction of a canon would have to pay attention to its own limitations as well as its strengths, not to be constrained by fashion, and to estimate the extent of unknown regions.

These criteria are themselves up for debate. Scotland is a subject many writers deal with directly, and the anthology *Scotlands: Poets and the Nation* (2004), which I co-edited with Douglas Gifford, gathers poems which explicitly engage with questions of national identity, but there are many Scottish writers whose work deals with other things, such as John Henry Mackay. And others, such as Compton Mackenzie, who write sometimes about Scotland and sometimes not about Scotland at all.

Clearly, there are literary, artistic and cultural values that cannot be constrained to political and religious priorities. Secular priorities of free speech and toleration are reciprocated by works of literature and art. This is true even of literary and artistic works of political and religious determination and bias. *Paradise Lost* may have its intentions in politics and religion, but its literary quality is what keeps it valuable, readable and alive. It still offers challenges and affirmations beyond its historical or religious moment.

So, when does the assertion of canonical value act as progressive resistance, rather than reactionary constriction?

Resistance to the authorities who insist upon a canon is surely necessary when such insistence is limiting, distorting or misguided. Yet a counter-proposal introducing different priorities and preferences is effectively another canon. Canonicity itself is not dissolved or removed. Priorities themselves have their own historical moment. But the only way to reject any idea of canonicity would be to surrender the power of determining priorities and preferences altogether. Problematically, this practice always gives power to other decision-makers. It is always a surrender of power and usually a rejection of responsibility. This has been the defining characteristic of Scotland's political relation with England since 1707. It is exactly what has happened in Scotland for generations.

The Americans so often get the marketing right. In the early 21st century, the texts most familiar in Scottish schools for generations might have included *The Great Gatsby, Of Mice and Men, To Kill a Mockingbird, The Catcher in the Rye*. So why not *Kidnapped, Sunset Song, The Prime of Miss Jean Brodie, The Cone Gatherers*, 'The Two Drovers', 'Wandering Willie's Tale', 'Thrawn Janet', 'Clay', 'Smeddum', 'Greenden', *The Cheviot, the Stag and the Black, Black Oil, Mary Queen of Scots Got Her Head Chopped Off, Bondagers, The Strange Undoing of Prudencia Hart, Federer versus Murray* (and that's only a random handful of novels, stories and plays)?

From my experience teaching Scottish literature in New Zealand from 1986 to 2000, and delivering guest-lectures on the subject in Australia, Singapore, Samoa, China, India, the United States, France, Romania, Montenegro, Austria, Poland, Ireland, as well as in Scotland, where I was appointed to the established Chair of Scottish Literature at the University of Glasgow (the only such institutionally-established Chair in any of the Scottish universities), I know that a multi-faceted approach to Scotland's literary and cultural history effectively agrees with the deployment of a canonical 'spine'. Both the various approaches and the canonical spine are helpful just as they are always changing and open to challenge and debate. Maintaining that reciprocity is ultimately empowering.

So the spine is within the body of work the list below enumerates. In fact, there's more than one list of 'essential' works in there. But then, a spine is only a part of the bone structure and it doesn't go anywhere on its own. Inside it there's marrow, surrounding it sinew, muscle, flesh and blood, brain and what animates it all, whatever it's called, whatever it is that makes the clay grow tall. The spine is strong enough to keep the body vertebrate but the extent of the reach of the mind that body carries is illimitable. That reach is to touch and learn from, not to grip and drain out. And it seemed to me more useful here to allow the whole corpus to have a fulsome presence and be richly clothed. As Walt Whitman sings, in 'Song of Myself': 'I dote on myself, there is that lot of me and all so luscious' – why not let a canon be such a song of ourselves? Is a song not also a form of empowerment?

3
What a canon is for

TO AGREE ON co-ordinate points that allow a canon to be a prompt for further exploration and critical understanding is intrinsically a good thing. It works to resist monolithic, unchanging authority, but at the same time to affirm qualities and values that inform an authority that should be maintained. That balance is crucial.

If a canon becomes exclusive and self-enclosed, you're in trouble. Such things need to be blown apart from time to time. New growth and new readings of the past insist on that. So what I'm advocating is up for that challenge. That's why I'm calling it a 'loose' canon.

This is an idea of understanding what 'Scottish literature' might be. The proposition of a canon of Scottish literature ought to help counterbalance centuries of institutional neglect. And it should enable confident self-determination in channels of cultural transmission, both within and furth of Scotland.

The historical trajectory of this 'spine' of the subject, its full articulation and its supple interconnectedness, may be emphasised at particular points by regenerative moments of revaluation and revivification of past traditions. Allan Ramsay in the 18th century and Hugh MacDiarmid in the early 20th century deliberately set out to do this. They re-introduced older traditions of Scottish literature to their contemporaries, regenerating a longer view.

In 1724 Allan Ramsay published *The Ever Green*, an anthology of Scottish poetry drawing from the Bannatyne Manuscript of the 1500s. He intended to reawaken interest in older Scots poetry and present it to new generations of readers in the 18th century. He reproduced William Dunbar's 'Lament for the Makars', which lists writers Dunbar knew who had recently died, each verse ending with the Latin line, '*Timor mortis conturbat me*' or 'The terror of Death confounds me'. Finally, Dunbar foresees his own imminent death:

> Sen he has all my brethren tane,
> He will not let me leive alane;
> On Forss I maun his nixt Prey be,
> *Timor mortis conturbat me.*

> Sen for the Death Remeid is none,
> Best is that we for Death dispone;
> Aftir our Death, that live we may,
> *Timor mortis conturbat me.*

But after this, in his new anthology, Allan Ramsay adds a 'Postscript':

> Suthe I forsie, if Spae-craft had,
> Frae Hethir-Muirs sall ryse a Lad,
> Aftir twa Centries pas, sall he
> Revive our fame and Memorie.
>
> Then sall we flourish Evir Grene;
> All thanks to carefull *Bannatyne*,
> And to the Patron kind and frie,
> Quha lends the Lad baith them and me.
>
> Far sall we fare, baith Eist and West,
> Owre ilka Clyme by Scots possest;
> Then sen our Warks sall nevir die,
> Timor mortis non turbat me.

A note tells us that 'the Patron' was 'Mr William Carmichael, Brother to the Earl of Hyndford, who lent A.R. that curious MSS. collected by Mr George Bannatyne, Anno 1568, from whence these poems are printed.'

In the early 20th century, Hugh MacDiarmid's dervish energies to galvanise a Scottish Literary Renaissance took their inspiration from Patrick Geddes in the 1890s, publishing his own periodical anthology entitled *The Evergreen* and declaring the prospect of 'Renascence' in Scotland which would engage the cultural and political desire for liberation from 19th-century Anglocentrism and British imperialism. Geddes's title was a direct reference to Ramsay, and it was Geddes who chaired and introduced what was perhaps the first public reading MacDiarmid gave, from his first book of poems, *Sangschaw*, in Edinburgh, in October 1925. MacDiarmid's ambitions were revolutionary, on a global stage, but at their heart was the simplest and most essential vision of possibility: regeneration, embodied in youth, in actual women and men, in new generations and things still to come:

> I never set een on a lad or a lass
> But I wonder gin he or she
> Wi a word or a deed'll suddenly dae
> An impossibility

The resurgence of creative work in the 1980s and 1990s in Scotland coincided with a comprehensive revaluation of cultural production in literature, art and music through the same period. The purpose of having this depth of understanding is to provide something essential for 'vertebrate' identity – only by such understanding can the subject be compared and valued alongside other literatures.

Carla Sassi concludes her book, *Why Scottish Literature Matters* (2005), by affirming that Scottish literature does matter: 'this is beyond doubt – but it will have to be explained in other languages and to other cultures in order to survive.'

Why has it not been explained as comprehensively and confidently as other literatures – American, Irish, English, Australian or New Zealand literatures, say? Or French, Italian, Spanish, Catalan, Russian?

A great deal of work has been done, especially since the 1980s, but there remains a great deal more to do. The subject still needs to be more widely known and discussed with more confident curiosity. Interviewed on BBC2's *Newsnight* programme on 29 November 2011, I was asked by the broadcaster Gordon Brewer, 'Is there such a thing as Scottish literature?' Momentarily staggered by the inanity of this question, or perhaps the deliberate provocation of insult behind it, I was grateful when the novelist A.L. Kennedy, who was there with me, leant forward and replied:

> Is there such a thing as English literature or Irish literature or American literature? You don't want to claim any literature for a country because it's international and has to do with the commonality of human experience, but Scotland exists, as a cultural entity, as a historical entity... I want somebody to be able to sit in a Scottish school and think, I can succeed, being myself, from my country, using the language that I use, being the person that I am, and that's very difficult to do if you don't see images of your country in movies, if you don't see them on television in a widespread, meaningful and powerful way, if you're not reading Scottish texts or hearing the Scottish voice as a voice of success. And if you don't understand your history you're just going to keep on, as everybody says, repeating your mistakes.

In education, all literature has an essential value in helping to understand the various attitudes towards experience that people have and have had. Anyone who can, should be encouraged to read as widely as possible: authors such as Wole Soyinka, Emily Brontë, Bertolt Brecht, Gustave Flaubert, George Eliot, Tolstoy, Cervantes, Rabelais or Dante. You can learn things from these people. But nobody should undervalue the literature of their own people, written or composed in languages close to their own, and with reference to people, places, things and events that are familiar and local to them. As the Gaelic scholar Ronald Black once put it, '"We're rubbish, let's pretend to be someone else" has always been a powerful slogan in Scotland.' Ironically, for a long time, Scottish literature was probably valued more internationally than by Scots in Scotland.

This is the situation that we've been trying to change.

Anecdotes are not evidence but some of the stories I heard relating to the decision in 2012 to make a Scottish literature question compulsory in English examinations in Scottish schools were truly appalling. Allegedly, at one meeting of head teachers, the verdict was that there were no teachable plays by Scottish authors. At another meeting, I heard, the opinion was that no Scottish literature was of any quality at all, compared to English, Irish or American literature. These comments go well beyond, 'What is Scottish literature?' or 'Let's keep our options open.'

If these comments represent anyone's true opinions, then or now, their judgements are clearly based on ignorance, prejudice and political hostility – not only to me and the subject I profess but to every generation of schoolchildren that comes under their care.

Many of the writers and works named in this 'Loose Canon of Scottish Literature' will be well-known, but some will almost certainly be unfamiliar. Each one could be the subject of deep study and would repay, and indeed have repaid, scholarly enquiry, but collectively they can open the door for anyone, to a more extensive, diverse and complex terrain. The authors all write of things that have universal human provenance, but most of them also write of things that cannot be found elsewhere, things that pertain specifically to Scotland. Moreover, each one prompts further reading that complements and relativises their own centrality and status.

In the preface to his book, *Scottish Literature Since 1707* (1996), Marshall Walker wrote this:

> A literary canon implies 'great Books', but great books are not the only books, and who pronounces them great anyway? After all, even Shakespeare's inclusion in the canon has not always been secure. In 1814 Byron wrote to James Hogg, 'Shakespeare's name, you may depend on it, stands absurdly too high and will go down.' Yet the canon that was still is, albeit with its pores open to receive new and newly discovered works.

And he quotes and qualifies George Steiner: 'Democracy is, fundamentally, at war with the canonic', yet canonic reassertions are inevitable when standards are invoked or a culture looked at whole.

Hugh Kenner, in 'The Making of the Modernist Canon', in *Mazes: Essays* (1989), usefully complicates the idea:

> For a canon is not a list but a narrative of some intricacy, depending on places and times and opportunities. Any list – a mere curriculum – is shorthand for that.

In my 'narrative of intricacy', the diversity characteristic of Scottish literature is evident in language (Gaelic, Scots and English), form (poems, plays, fiction), representation of the experiences of women and men, religious and political commitment, regional predilection and choice, epochal significance in the international context (Medieval and Renaissance, Enlightenment, Romanticism, Modernism), the range of different cultural sensibilities, and so on.

Therefore there should be a balance between the representation of experiences specific to Scotland and the literary distinctiveness of their expression, or 'transnational' or 'universal' literary qualities.

The idea is both in some respects to confirm and in all respects to question the conventions of canon-formation. The intention is to open the prospect of reading Scottish literature in new ways, as well as the old ones.

4
A loose canon: significant authors and works of Scottish literature

1. Anonymous, 'Deirdre's Farewell to Alba' and other works from the three great cycles of Celtic stories and songs: (1) of the ancient gods and earliest men; (2) of the Red Branch, of Cuchulain and Skaaha, Deirdre and Naoise, Gráinne and Diarmuid; (3) of the Fianna or Féinn, the Fenian cycle, the coming of Christianity and Ossian after the Fianna
2. Tacitus (c.56–120 AD), *The Agricola*
3. Aneirin (fl.560s), *The Gododdin*, collected with many other important works of this era in *The Triumph Tree: Scotland's Earliest Poetry AD 550–1350* (1998), edited by Thomas Owen Clancy
4. Columba (c.520–597), 'Altus Prosator', collected with many other important works of the era in *Iona: The Earliest Poetry of a Celtic Monastery* (1995), edited by Thomas Owen Clancy and Gilbert Márkus
5. Adomnán (c.624–704), *Vita Columbae / The Life of Columba, Lex Innocentium / The Law of the Innocents*
6. Anonymous (c.700s?), *The Dream of the Rood* (Normally considered an 'Old English' poem but given its provenance on the Ruthwell Cross, let's be generous.)
7. Anonymous, *The Book of Kells* (9th century)
8. Anonymous, *The Book of Deer* (10th century)
9. Geoffrey of Monmouth (c.1100–c.1155), *The Life of Merlin* (Merlin of the Woods / Merlinus Sylvestris; or Merlin of Scotland / Merlinus Caledonius)
10. Jocelyn of Furness (fl.1175–1214), *The Life of St Kentigern* (Mungo)
11. Michael Scott (1175–1232), Works
12. Guillaume le Clerc (fl.1200), *Fergus of Galloway* (Written in Old French, author possibly William Malveisin, a royal clerk, later Bishop of Glasgow and then of St Andrews, under the patronage of Alan, Lord of Galloway. The knowledge displayed of the geography of southern Scotland is extensive, and Fergus himself is the son of Soumillot or Somerled, or Sorley, a farmer clearly connected to the Lord of the Isles, so who knows?)
13. Anonymous (post-1246), 'Quhen Alexander our King was dede…'
14. Thomas Rhymer (c.1220–98), *Sir Tristram*
15. Robert Baston (fl.1300–14), *The Battle of Bannockburn* (The circumstances of the poem's composition insist it should be here. See the 2004 translation by Edwin Morgan.)

16. Bernard of Arbroath (c.1260–c.1331), *The Declaration of Arbroath*
17. Anonymous, *Lives of the Scottish Saints*
18. Andrew of Wyntoun (c.1350–c.1425), *Originale Chronikyl of Scotland*
19. John Barbour (c.1320–95), *The Bruce*
20. Richard Holland (died c.1482), *The Buke of the Howlat*
21. 'Hutcheon of the Awle Ryale' (Sir Hugh of Eglintoun (?) died c.1381), Poems, especially 'The Pystil of Swete Susan'
22. John of Fordun (pre-1360–c.1384), *Chronica Gentis Scotorum / Chronicle of the Scottish People*
23. Walter Bower (1385–1449), *The Scotichronicon*
24. James I (1394–1437), *The Kingis Quair*
25. Gilbert Haye (c.1403–60), *The Buik of King Alexander the Conqueror*
26. Blind Harry (1440–93), *The Wallace*
27. Robert Henryson (c.1435–c.1505), Poems, especially 'The Testament of Cresseid', 'Orpheus and Euridices' and his versions of Aesop's *Fables*
28. William Dunbar (c.1460–c.1520), Poems, especially 'The Thistle and the Rose', 'The Twa Marriet Wemen and the Wedo', 'The Dance of the Seven Deidly Sins', 'Lament for the Makars'
29. John Mair (1467–1550), *Historia Majoris Britanniae / The History of Greater Britain*
30. Gavin Douglas (c.1474–c.1522), Poems, especially the translation of Virgil's *The Aeneid* as *The Eneados*
31. Anonymous, 'The Tale of Rauf Coilyear'
32. Anonymous, *The Ballads*
33. Anonymous, 'The Friars of Berwick'
34. James MacGregor (c.1480–1551), *The Book of the Dean of Lismore*
35. David Lyndsay (1490–1555), Poems, *Ane Satyre of the Thrie Estaits*
36. Anonymous, *Philotus*
37. William Lamb (c.1493–1555), *Ane Resonyng*
38. George Buchanan (1506–82), Poems, especially 'Epithalamium for the Dauphin of France and Mary', and plays, especially *Jephthes* and *The Baptist*, and *De Jure Regni apud Scotos*
39. Robert Wedderburn (1510–c.1555/60), Poems, especially (with his brothers James and John), *The Gude and Godly Ballates*, and (possibly) *The Complaynt of Scotland*
40. King James V (1512–42). Poems (attributed to him), especially 'Peblis to the Play', 'Chrystis Kirk on the Grene', 'The Gaberlunzieman', 'The Jolly Beggar'
41. John Knox (1514–1572). Works: especially 'The First Blast of the Trumpet Against the Monstrous Regiment of Women'
42. Alexander Scott (c.1515–c.1583). Poems
43. Robert Sempill (c.1530–1595). Ballads and poems, *The Sege of the*

Castel of Edinburgh
44. Mary Queen of Scots (1542–87). Poems
45. Alexander Hume (c.1556–1609), *Of the Day Estivall*
46. George Bannatyne (1545–1608), *The Bannatyne Mansucript*
47. John Stewart of Baldynneis (c.1545–c.1605). Poems, especially *Roland Furious*
48. Séon Carsuel / John Carswell (c.1522–72), *Foirm na n-Urrnuidheadh / The Book of Common Order*
49. Alexander Montgomerie (c.1555–97). Poems, especially *The Cherrie and the Slae*, 'The Solsequium' and 'The night is near gone'
50. William Fowler (1560–1612). Poems, especially 'The Tarantula of Love', and translations of Machiavelli
51. Mark Alexander Boyd (1563–1601). Poems, especially 'Cupid and Venus'
52. Domhnall mac Fhionnlagh nan Dan / Donald son of Finlay of the Poems (fl. end of the 16th century), 'Òran nan Comhachaig' / 'The Song of the Owl'
53. James Charles Stuart, King James VI and I (1566–1625), *Some Reulis and Cautelis, His Majesties Poeticall Exercises at Vacant Houres, Lepanto, Daemonologie, The True Law of Free Monarchies, Basilikon Doron, A Counterblaste to Tobacco*
54. David Murray (1567–1629). Poems, especially 'The Tragical Death of Sophonisba'
55. William Alexander (c.1567–1640), *Croesus, Darius, The Alexandrean, Julius Caesar* and 'Aurora' sonnet sequence
56. Patrick Gordon (c.1570s/80s–1650), *The Famous Valiant Historie of the renouned and valiant Prince Robert, surnamed the Bruce, King of Scotland, &c., and of sundrie other knights both Scots and English, done into heroic verse, Pernardo and Louissa* (verse romance)
57. Arthur Johnstone (c.1579–1641). Poems
58. John Barclay (1582–1681). *Argenis* ('bestselling' Latin novel)
59. William Lithgow (c.1582–after 1645). *The Totall Discourse of The Rare Adventures & Painefull Peregrinations of long Nineteene Yeares Travayles from Scotland to the most famous Kingdomes in Europe, Asia and Africa*
60. William Drummond of Hawthornden (1585–1649). Poems, especially 'Sonnet xxviii: Sound hoarse, sad Lute' and 'Song ii: Phoebus arise' and prose, especially 'A Cypresse Grove', 'A Speech on Toleration', 'A Letter on the True Nature of Poetry' and 'Conversations with Ben Jonson'
61. Sir William Mure of Rowallan (1594–1657). Poems, especially *The Joy of Teares, Dido and Aeneas, The True Crucifixe for True Catholicks, Caledons Complaint* and *The Cry of Blood and a Broken Covenant*

62. Robert Sempill (c.1595–c.1663). Poems, especially 'The Life and Death of Habbie Simson, Piper of Kilbarchan'; and his relations: James Sempill (1566–1625). *The Packman's Paternoster*; Francis Sempill (c.1630s–c.80s). Poems, especially 'The Banishment of Poverty'; Robert Semple (or Sempill) (1687–1789). Poems, especially 'Ramillies'
63. Sir Thomas Urquhart (1611–60), *The Jewel, Logopandecteision* and the translation of Rabelais, *Gargantua and Pantagruel*
64. James Graham, Marquis of Montrose (1612–50). Poems
65. Màiri nighean Alasdair Ruaidh / Mary MacLeod (c.1615–c.1707). Poems
66. Iain Lom MacDhòmhnaill / 'Bare' John MacDonald (c.1620–c.1716). Poems, especially 'Òran air Latha Blàir Inbhir Lóchaidh' / 'Song of the Day of Inverlochy'
67. Thomas Sydserf (c.1625–1689). Plays, translation of *Selenarchia: the government of the world in the moon: a comical history written by that famous wit and caveleer of France, Monsieur Cyrano Bergerac*; and pamphlets, including *The Prince of Tartaria, his Voyage to Cowper in Fife*; Sydserf was the author and publisher of one of the first Scottish newspapers, *The Mercurius Caledonius* (predated only by *The Scottish Dove* and *Mercurius Scoticus*).
68. George Mackenzie of Rosehaugh ('Bluidy Mackenzie', c.1636–91), *Aretina, or, The Serious Romance* (the first Scottish novel)
69. Ruaidhri MacMhuirich, 'An Clàrsair Dall' / Roderick Morrison, 'The Blind Harper' (c.1656–c.1714). Poems
70. Andrew Fletcher of Saltoun (1655–1716), *Political Writings and Speeches*
71. Seòras MacCoinnich / George MacKenzie (c.1655–c.1735). Poems, especially 'An Oba Nodha' / 'The Oobie Noogie'
72. Sìleas na Ceapaich / Cicely MacDonald of Keppoch (c.1660–c.1729). Poems, especially 'Alastair à Glengaradh' / Alexander from Glengarry' and 'An Aghaidh h-Oba Nodha' / 'Against the Oobie Noogie'
73. William Cleland (c.1661–89). Poems, especially 'Hallow my Fancie, Whither Wilt Thou Go?'
74. Màrtainn MacGilleMhàrtain / Martin Martin (c.1669–1718), *A Description of the Western Islands of Scotland*
75. Elizabeth Wardlaw (1677–1727). Poems and songs, especially 'Hardyknute'
76. Catharine Trotter (1679–1749). Plays, esp. *Agnes de Castro, Fatal Friendship, Love at a Loss, or, Most Votes Carry It, The Unhappy Penitent, The Revolution of Sweden*
77. Allan Ramsay, (1685–1758). Poems, especially 'Lucky Spence's Last Advice' and 'Wealth, or the Woody', *The Gentle Shepherd, The Tea-Table Miscellany* and *The Ever Green*

78. Alasdair mac Mhaighstir Alasdair / Alexander MacDonald (c.1695–c.1770). Poems, especially 'Birlinn Chlann Raghnaill' / 'The Birlinn of Clanranald'
79. Alexander Ross (1699–1784). Poems, especially *Helenore*
80. Robert Blair (1699–1746). Poems, especially *The Grave*
81. James Thomson (1700–48), *The Seasons* and 'Rule Britannia' from *The Masque of Alfred*
82. David Mallet (Malloch) (c.1702–65). Works: especially 'William and Margaret', and masques, especially *Mustapha, Britannia, Elvira*
83. William Hamilton of Bangour (1704–54). Poems and songs, especially 'The Braes of Yarrow'
84. David Hume (1711–76). Works: especially *A Treatise of Human Nature, An Enquiry Concerning Human Understanding*, 'The Science of Man', 'Dialogues Concerning Natural Religion', 'Of Miracles' and 'Of the Populousness of Ancient Nations'
85. Dùghall Bochanan / Dugald Buchanan (1716–68). Poems, especially 'Là a' Bhreitheanais' / 'The Day of Judgement'
86. John Skinner (1721–1807). Poems and songs, especially 'Tullochgorum' and 'The Christmas Bawing of Monimusk'
87. Tobias Smollett (1721–71). Poems, especially 'The Tears of Scotland' and novels, especially *Roderick Random, The Expedition of Humphry Clinker* and the translation of Miguel de Cervantes, *Don Quixote*
88. James Grainger (c.1721–1766). Poems, especially 'The Sugar-Cane'
89. John Home (1722–1808). *Douglas*
90. Adam Ferguson (1723–1816), *An Essay on the History of Civil Society*
91. Adam Smith (1723–90), *The Theory of Moral Sentiments, The Wealth of Nations*, 'The Four Stages of Society'
92. Donnchadh Bàn Mac an t-Saoir / Duncan Ban MacIntyre (1724–1812). Poems, especially 'Moladh Beinn Dòbhrain' / 'Praise of Ben Dorain'
93. James Hutton (1726–1797), *Theory of the Earth*
94. Jean Elliot (1727–1805). 'The Flowers of the Forest'
95. Seumus Mac an t-Saoir / James Macintyre (1727–99). poems, especially 'Òran Ollamh MacIain' / 'A Song to Dr Johnson'
96. William Falconer (1732–69). Poems, especially *The Shipwreck*
97. William Julius Mickle (1734–88). Poems and translations, especially 'There's Nae Luck Aboot the Hoose', 'Cumnor Hall' and translation of Camoens's *Lusiads*
98. James Beattie (1735–1803). Poems, especially 'To Mr Alexander Ross at Lochlee' and 'The Minstrel', the essay 'On Poetry and Music',

Scoticisms, Arranged in Alphabetical Order, Designed to Correct Improprieties of Speech and Writing, The Theory of Language

99. James Macpherson (1736–96), *The Poems of Ossian with an essay by Hugh Blair*
100. James Boswell (1740–95), *Journal of a Tour to the Hebrides, The Life of Samuel Johnson*
101. Isabel Pagan (c.1740–1821). Poems
102. Henry Mackenzie (1745–1831). *The Man of Feeling*
103. Alexander Fraser Tytler, Lord Woodhouselee (1747–1813), *Piscatory Eclogues, with Other Poetical Miscellanies of Phineas Fletcher, Essay on the Principles of Translation*
104. John Jamieson (1759–1838), *Etymological Dictionary of the Scottish Language* (1808)
105. Christian Carstaires (fl.1780s), *The Hubble-Shue*
106. Charles Keith (d.1807), 'Farmer's Ha'
107. John Mayne (1759–1836), 'Hallow-E'en' 'The Siller Gun'
108. Mungo Park (1771–1806), *Travels*
109. William Hamilton of Gilbertfield (c.1665–1751), translation of Blind Harry, *The Wallace*
110. Robert Fergusson (1750–74). Poems
111. Anne Grant of Laggan (1755–1838). Poems, memoirs
112. Robert Burns (1759–96). Poems, songs, journals and letters
113. Joanna Baillie (1762–1851). Plays
114. Uilleam Ros / William Ross (1762–c.91). Poems, especially 'Another Song'
115. Carolina Oliphant, Lady Nairne (1766–1845). Poems and songs
116. Alexander Wilson (1766–1813). Poems
117. James Hogg (1770–1835). Works: poems, especially 'Bonnie Kilmeny', and novels, especially *The Brownie of Bodsbeck, The Three Perils of Man, The Three Perils of Woman, The Private Memoirs and Confessions of a Justified Sinner*
118. Sir Walter Scott (1771–1832). Works: poems, especially *The Minstrelsy of the Scottish Border, The Lay of the Last Minstrel* and novels, especially *Waverley; or, 'Tis Sixty Years Since, The Tale of Old Mortality, Rob Roy, The Heart of Mid-Lothian, The Bride of Lammermoor, Ivanhoe, Redgauntlet*
119. James Montgomery (1771–1854). Poems, especially 'The West Indies'
120. John MacCulloch (1773–1835). *The Highlands and Western Isles of Scotland, in a series of letters to Sir Walter Scott*
121. Robert Tannahill *(1774–1810), Poems*
122. John Leyden (1775–1811). Poems, translations, *Tour of the Highlands and Western Islands of Scotland*

123. Jane Porter (1776–1850), *The Scottish Chiefs*
124. Thomas Campbell (1777–1844). Poems, especially 'Gertrude of Wyoming' and 'Lines on Revisiting a Scottish River'
125. Lord Cockburn (1779–1854), *Memorials of His Time* (1856), *Journal* (1874)
126. John Galt (1779–1839), *Annals of the Parish, The Entail*
127. Christian Isobel Johnstone (1781–1857), *Clan-Albin: A National Tale*
128. Susan Ferrier (1782–1854). Novels, especially *Marriage*
129. Thomas Dick Lauder (1784–1848), *Lochandhu, The Wolfe of Badenoch*
130. John Wilson (Christopher North), (1785–1854), *Margaret Lyndsay, The Foresters* and poems, especially 'The Isle of Palms' and 'The City of the Plague', and *Lights and Shadows of Scottish Life*
131. George Beattie (1786–1823). Poems, especially 'John o' Arnha''
132. George Gordon, Lord Byron (1788–1824). Poems
133. Thomas Hamilton (1789–1842), *The Youth and Manhood of Cyril Thornton*
134. Michael Scott (1789–1835), *Tom Cringle's Log, The Cruise of the Midge*
135. John Gibson Lockhart (1794–1854). *Peter's Letters to His Kinsfolk, Adam Blair*
136. Donald MacLeod (c.1794–c.1860s), *Gloomy Memories in the Highlands of Scotland versus Mrs Harriet Beecher Stowe's Sunny Memories in (England) a Foreign Land: or a Faithful Picture of the Extirpation of the Celtic Race from the Highlands of Scotland*
137. Thomas Carlyle (1795–1881). Works: especially 'Signs of the Times', *The French Revolution, Sartor Resartus*
138. William Drummond Stewart (c.1795–1871), *Altowan, Edward Warren*
139. Elizabeth Grant (1797–1885), *Memoirs of a Highland Lady*
140. David Macbeth Moir (1798–1851), *The Life of Mansie Wauch Tailor in Dalkeith*
141. Robert Pollok (1798–1827), *Tales of the Covenanters, The Course of Time*
142. Hugh Miller (1802–56). *The Old Red Sandstone, First Impressions of England and Its People, Essays, historical and biographical, political, social, literary and scientific*
143. Mary Seacole (1805–1881), *Wonderful Adventures of Mrs Seacole in Many Lands*
144. Lydia Mackenzie Falconer Miller (1812–76), *Passages in the Life of an English Heiress, or, Recollections of the Disruption Time in Scotland*
145. Uilleam MacDhunlèibhe / William Livingston (1808–70). Poems, especially 'Ireland Weeping'
146. J.S. Blackie (1809–95). Poems, essays and translations

147. William Miller (1810–72),'Wee Willie Winkie'
148. John Barr (1809–89). Poems
149. W.E. Aytoun (1813–65). Poems, especially *Lays of the Scottish Cavaliers*, short stories, especially 'How we got up the Glenmutchkin railway and how we got out of it'
150. James McCune Smith (1813–65). Works: especially *A Lecture on the Haytien Revolutions; with a sketch of the character of Toussaint L'Ouverture*, *The Destiny of the People of Color: A Lecture* and 'Introduction' to *My Bondage and My Freedom* by Frederick Douglass
151. Charles Mackay (1814–89), *Extraordinary Popular Delusions* and *The Madness of Crowds*
152. Catherine Helen Spence (1825–1910), *An Agnostic's Progress from the Known to the Unknown*, *A Week in the Future*
153. Màiri Nic a' Phearsain, Màiri Mhór nan Òran / Mary MacPherson, Big Mary of the Songs (1821–98). Poems and songs
154. William Alexander (1826–94), *Johnny Gibb of Gushetneuk*, *The Laird of Drammochdyle*
155. George Macdonald (1824–1905). Works: especially *Phantastes*, *Lilith*
156. R.M. Ballantyne (1825–94). *The Gorilla Hunters*, *The Coral Island*
157. Margaret Oliphant (1828–97), *A Beleaguered City*, *Kirsteen*
158. David Pae (1828–84). *Lucy, the Factory Girl*, *Mary Paterson or The Fatal Error*
159. Alexander Smith (1829–67). Poems, especially 'Glasgow', *Dreamthorp: Essays Written in the Country*, *A Summer in Skye*
160. Alasdair Gillesbaig MacGilleMhìcheill / Alexander Carmichael (1832–1912). *Carmina Gadelica*
161. John Gregorson Campbell (1834–91), *The Gaelic Otherworld* (*Superstitions of the Highlands and Islands of Scotland* and *Witchcraft* and *Second Sight in the Highlands and Islands*). edited by Ronald Black
162. James ('B.V.') Thomson (1834–82). Poems, especially *The City of Dreadful Night*, *Biographical and Critical Studies*, *Walt Whitman: The Man and the Poet*
163. William Black (1841–98), *A Daughter of Heth*, *A Princess of Thule*, *Macleod of Dare*, *In Far Lochaber*
164. James Logie Robertson ('Hugh Haliburton') (1846–1922). Poems
165. Robert Buchanan (1841–1901). Poems, *The Hebrid Isles: Wanderings in the Land of Lorne and the Outer Hebrides*
166. Alexander Campbell Mackenzie (1847–1935), *A Musician's Narrative*
167. James Young Geddes (1850–19?). Poems
168. Marion Bernstein (1846–1906). Poems

169. Jessie Russell (1850–1881). Poems
170. R.L. Stevenson (1850–94). Works: especially *Treasure Island, Strange Case of Dr Jekyll and Mr Hyde, Kidnapped, The Master of Ballantrae*, poems, essays, prayers and letters
171. Ian Maclaren (John Watson, 1850–1907), *Beside the Bonnie Brier Bush*
172. R.B. Cunninghame Graham (1852–1936). Works: especially *Scottish Stories, Thirteen Stories*
173. J.G. Frazer (1854–1941), *The Golden Bough*
174. Florence Caroline Dixie (1855–1905), *Across Patagonia, In the Land of Misfortune, Gloriana, or the Revolution of 1900*
175. William Sharp / Fiona MacLeod (1855–1905). Poems, *The Children of Tomorrow* (WS). *Pharais* (FM). *The Washer of the Ford* (FM). *Lyra Celtic: An Anthology of Representative Celtic Poetry* (WS). *From the Hills of Dream: Threnodies, Songs and Later Poems* (FM). *The Winged Destiny: Studies in the Spiritual History of the Gael* (FM)
176. James Pittendrigh MacGillivray (1856–1938). Poems, especially *Pro Patria, Bog Myrtle and Peat Reek*
177. Marjory Kennedy-Fraser (1857–1930), *A Life of Song*
178. John Davidson (1857–1909). Poems, especially 'A Runnable Stag', 'Thirty Bob a Week' and *The Testaments*
179. Annie S. Swan (1859–1943), *Aldersyde*
180. Arthur Conan Doyle (1859–1930), *The Sherlock Holmes Stories, The Lost World, The Brigadier Gerard* stories
181. S.R. Crockett (1859–1914). Novels, especially *The Raiders*
182. Kenneth Grahame (1859–1932), *The Wind in the Willows*
183. J.M. Barrie (1860–1937). Works: plays, novels and stories, especially *Sentimental Tommy, Tommy and Grizel, Auld Licht Idylls, Peter Pan, Farewell Miss Julie Logan*
184. J.J. Haldane Burgess (1862–1927). Poems
185. Helen Bannerman (1862–1946), *The Story of Little Black Sambo*
186. Violet Jacob (1863–1946). Poems, *Diaries and Letters from India 1895–1900*, and novels, especially *Flemington*, and *The House of Dun*
187. George Eyre-Todd (1862–1937), *Scotland Picturesque and Traditional: A Pilgrimage with Staff and Knapsack*
188. Neil Munro (1863–1930). Novels, stories and poems, especially *The New Road, Para Handy and The Vital Spark*
189. John Henry Mackay (1864–1933), *The Hustler* (1926). and poems, especially 'Morgen' / 'Morning'
190. Charles Murray (1864–1941). Poems, especially *Hamewith*
191. Marion Angus (1865–1946). Poems
192. Norman Douglas (1868–1952), *South Wind*

193. George Douglas Brown (1869–1902), *The House with the Green Shutters*
194. William Power (1873–1951), *The World Unvisited, Robert Burns and Other Essays, My Scotland, Literature and Oatmeal*
195. Lewis Spence (1874–1955). Poems, *The Magic Arts in Celtic Britain, The History of Atlantis, Celtic Spells and Charms*
196. J.D. Fergusson (1874–1961), *Modern Scottish Painting*
197. David W. Bone (1874–1959), *The Brassbounder*
198. John Buchan (1875–1940), *Prester John, The Thirty-Nine Steps, Witch Wood, A Prince of the Captivity, Sick Heart River*
199. Rachel Annand Taylor (1876–1960). Poems, especially 'The Princess of Scotland' and 'Ecstasy'
200. Ian Hay (1876–1952), *The First Hundred Thousand*
201. David Lindsay (1876–1945), *A Voyage to Arcturus, The Haunted Woman*
202. Frederick Niven (1878–1944), *Justice of the Peace*
203. John Maclean (1879–1923). Speech from the dock, 9 May 1918
204. Catherine Carswell (1879–1946), *Open the Door!*
205. John MacDougall Hay (1880–1919), *Gillespie*
206. Compton Mackenzie (1883–1972), *Sinister Street, Extraordinary Women, Water on the Brain, Whisky Galore, Thin Ice, Rockets Galore*
207. Richard Curle (1883–1968). *Wanderings: A Book of Travel and Reminiscence, Caravansery and Conversation*
208. William Laughton Lorimer (1885–1967), *The New Testament in Scots*
209. Andrew Young (1885–1971). Poems
210. F. Marian McNeill (1885–1973), *The Scots Kitchen, The Scots Cellar, The Silver Bough: A Four-Volume Study of the National and Local Festivals of Scotland*
211. Helen Burness Cruickshank (1886–1975). Poems, *Octobiography*
212. Lorna Moon (1886–1930), *Doorways in Drumorty, Dark Star*
213. Edwin Muir (1887–1959). Poems, *Autobiography, Scott and Scotland*
214. James Bridie (1888–1951). Works: plays and memoir, *One Way of Living*
215. Margaret Winefride Simpson (1888–c.1971). Poems
216. Patrick MacGill (1889–1963), *Songs of the Dead End, Children of the Dead End: The Autobiography of a Navvy, The Rat Pit*
217. Willa Muir (1890–1970), *Imagined Corners, Mrs Ritchie, Mrs Grundy in Scotland*
218. Neil M. Gunn (1891–1973), *Highland River, The Silver Darlings*
219. Rebecca West (Cicily Isabel Andrews, née Fairfield, 1892–1983). *The Judge, Black Lamb and Grey Falcon*
220. A.G. Macdonell (1895–1941), *England, Their England, Lords and*

Masters, My Scotland
221. Hugh MacDiarmid (C.M. Grieve, 1892–1978). Works: especially *Sangschaw, Penny Wheep, A Drunk Man Looks at the Thistle, Stony Limits* [including 'On a Raised Beach' and 'Lament for the Great Music'], *The Islands of Scotland, The Golden Treasury of Scottish Poetry Lucky Poet: A Self-Study in Literature and Political Ideas* and *In Memoriam James Joyce*)
222. Dot Allan (1892–1964), *Hunger March*
223. Nan Shepherd (1893–1981). Works: especially *The Quarry Wood*
224. George Blake (1893–1961), *The Shipbuilders*
225. Joe Corrie (1894–1968). Plays and Poems
226. William Jeffrey (1896–1946). Poems, especially *Fantasia Written in an Industrial Town*
227. Josephine Tey (Elizabeth MacKintosh, 1896–1952). Novels, especially *The Daughter of Time, The Singing Sands*
228. Edward Gaitens (1897–1966), *Dance of the Apprentices*
229. Naomi Mitchison (1897–1999). Works: especially *The Bull Calves, Lobsters on the Agenda*
230. Guy McCrone (1898–1877), *The Wax Fruit Trilogy*
231. William Soutar (1898–1943). Poems, *Diaries of a Dying Man*
232. Eric Linklater (1899–1974). Works: especially novels, *Juan in America, Magnus Merriman, Private Angelo, The Merry Muse, A Terrible Freedom*
233. Bruce Marshall (1899–1987). Novels, especially *Father Malachi's Miracle, Yellow Tapers for Paris: A Dirge*
234. Flora Garry (1900–2000). Poems
235. Lewis Grassic Gibbon (James Leslie Mitchell, 1901–35). Works: especially *A Scots Quair: Sunset Song, Cloud Howe, Grey Granite*; three short stories: 'Clay', 'Smeddum' and 'Greenden', *Spartacus, Stained Radiance, Gay Hunter*
236. Alexander McArthur (1901–47) and Herbert Kingsley Long, *No Mean City*
237. Joseph Macleod / Adam Drinan (1903–84). Poems
238. James Barke (1905–58), *Major Operation, The Land of the Leal, Immortal Memory, Bonnie Jean*
239. Ian Macpherson (1905–44), *Shepherds' Calendar, Wild Harbour*
240. Nancy Brysson Morrison (c.1906–86), *The Gowk Storm*
241. Fionn Mac Colla (1906–75). Works: especially *The Albannach, And the Cock Crew, Too Long in This Condition*
242. Robert McLellan (1907–85). Plays, poems, *The Isle of Arran*
243. Ian Fleming (1908–64). *Goldfinger, On Her Majesty's Secret Service*

244. Robert Kemp (1908–67). Plays and radio play scripts
245. Robert Garioch (1909–81). Poems, *Two Men and a Blanket*
246. Helen Adam (1909–93). Poems, play *San Francisco's Burning* and collages
247. Olive Fraser (1909–77). Poems
248. Mea Allan (1909–82), *Change of Heart*
249. Nigel Tranter (1909–2000), *Columba*, *The Montrose Trilogy*
250. George Bruce (1909–2002). Poems
251. George Friel (1910–75), *Mr Alfred M.A.*
252. Norman MacCaig (1910–96). Poems
253. Jane Duncan (Elizabeth Jane Cameron, 1910–76), the *My Friends* novels and autobiography, *Letter from Reachfar*
254. Ivan T. Sanderson (1911–73), *Animal Treasure*, *Caribbean Treasure*
255. Sorley MacLean (1911–96). Poems, especially *Dain do Eimhir*, *The Cuillin*, 'Hallaig', 'The Woods of Raasay', 'At Yeats's Grave' and 'Screapadal'
256. George Elder Davie (1912–2007), *The Democratic Intellect*, *The Crisis of the Democratic Intellect*
257. Margot Bennett (1912–80), *The Long Way Back*, *The Man Who Didn't Fly*, *Someone from the Past*, *The Furious Masters*
258. Robin Jenkins (1912–2005). Novels, especially *The Changeling*, *The Cone-Gatherers*
259. J.F. Hendry (1912–1986), *Fernie Brae*
260. Ena Lamont Stewart (1912–2006), *Men Should Weep*
261. David Daiches (1912–2005), *Robert Burns*, *Two Worlds*, *Critical Approaches to Literature*, *The Paradox of Scottish Culture: The Eighteenth Century Experience*
262. Douglas Young (1913–73), *Naething Dauntit: The Collected Poems*, *The Puddocks*, *The Burdies*, *Edinburgh in the Age of Walter Scott*
263. Gavin Maxwell (1914–69). *Ring of Bright Water*
264. George Campbell Hay (1915–84). Poems
265. Ewan MacColl (James Henry Miller, 1915–89). Songs and plays, especially *Johnny Noble*, *Uranium 235*, *Journeyman: An Autobiography*, *Agit-Prop to Theatre Workshop: political playscripts 1930–50*
266. Neil Paterson (1915–1995), *The China Run*
267. Sydney Goodsir Smith (1915–1975). Poems, especially *Under the Eildon Tree*, *Gowdspink in Reekie* and 'There is a tide' and the novel (if that's what to call it), *Carotid Cornucopius*
268. Jessie Kesson (1916–94). Novels and stories, especially *The White Bird Passes*

269. Ian Niall (John McNeillie) (1916–2002). *Wigtown Ploughman*, *No Resting Place*
270. Muriel Spark (1918–2006). Novels and poems, especially *The Prime of Miss Jean Brodie*
271. Joan Ure (Elizabeth Thoms Clark, 1918–1978). Plays and poems
272. William J. Tait (1918–92). Poems
273. Tom Scott (1918–95). Poems, especially *The Ship and Ither Poems*, *The Tree: An Animal Fable*, 'The Paschall Candle'
274. Elspeth Davie (1918–1995), *Creating a Scene*
275. Margaret Tait (1918–99). Poems, stories, writings and films
276. Dorothy K. Haynes (1918–1987), *Thou Shalt Not Suffer a Witch and Other Stories*
277. W.S. Graham (1918–86). Poems
278. Hamish Henderson (1919–2002). Poems and Songs
279. Christian Miller (1920–2012), *A Childhood in Scotland*
280. Edwin Morgan (1920–2010). Poems (see especially *The Second Life*, *From Glasgow to Saturn*, *The New Divan*, *Sonnets from Scotland*, *Virtual and Other Realities*, *Cathures*). *A.D.: A Trilogy of Plays on the Life of Jesus Christ*, *The Play of Gilgamesh*, *Collected Translations*
281. James Allan Ford (1920–2009). *A Judge of Men*
282. Alexander Scott (1920–89). Poems
283. George Mackay Brown (1921–96). Poems, novels and stories, especially *A Time to Keep*, *An Orkney Tapestry*, *Greenvoe*, *Magnus*
284. Wilson Harris (1921–2018). *Black Marsden*
285. Ruaraidh MacThòmais / Derick Thomson (1921–2012). Poems, especially 'Strath Nabhair' / 'Strathnaver'
286. William Neill (1922–2010). Poems
287. Alastair MacLean (1922–87). *When Eight Bells Toll*, *Where Eagles Dare*
288. Ivor Cutler (1923–2006). Works
289. Dorothy Dunnett (1923–2001), the Lymond Chronicles, The House of Niccolò, *King Hereafter*
290. Alexander Trocchi (1925–84), *Young Adam*, *Cain's Book*
291. Alastair Mackie (1925–95). Poems
292. Ian Hamilton Finlay (1925–2006). Poems, and garden: *Little Sparta*
293. Alastair Reid (1926–2014). Poems, especially *Weathering*, translations (especially of Pablo Neruda and Jorge Luis Borges), essays, and *Whereabouts: Notes on Being a Foreigner*
294. Agnes Owens (1926–2014), *Gentlemen of the West*, stories
295. R.D. Laing (1927–89). Works: especially *The Divided Self*
296. Gael Turnbull (1928–2004). Poems

297. Archie Hind (1928–2008). *The Dear Green Place*
298. James Burns Singer (1928–64). Poems, *Living Silver*
299. James Kennaway (1928–68). Novels, especially *Tunes of Glory*
300. Iain Mac a' Ghobhainn / Iain Crichton Smith (1928–98). Poems, essays, plays and novels, especially *Consider the Lilies* and *In the Middle*
301. Chaim Bermant (1929–98), *Jericho Sleep Alone*
302. Alasdair MacLean (1926–94). Poems, especially *From the Wilderness, Waking the Dead* and the memoir, *Night Falls on Ardnamurchan*
303. Dòmhnall MacAmhlaigh / Donald MacAulay (1930–2017). Poems
304. Neal Ascherson (b.1932). *Stone Voices: The Search for Scotland*
305. George Macbeth (1932–92). Poems, and prose: *My Scotland: Fragments of a State of Mind*
306. Troy Kennedy Martin (1932–2009), *Edge of Darkness*
307. Fredric Lindsay (1933–2013), *Brond*
308. Duncan Glen (1933–2008). Poems, *Autobiography of a Poet*
309. Alan Sharp (1934–2013), *A Green Tree in Gedde, Night Moves, Ulzana's Raid, Rob Roy, Dean Spanley*
310. Bill Douglas (1934–91), *The Trilogy*
311. Alasdair Gray (1934–2019). Novels, especially *Lanark, The Fall of Kelvin Walker*, essays, poems, plays
312. Gordon Williams (1934–2017), *From Scenes Like These, The Siege of Trencher's Farm*
313. Stuart MacGregor (1935–73). Poems, songs and novels, *The Myrtle and Ivy, The Sinner*
314. John McGrath (1935–2002) and 7:84 Theatre Company. Plays, especially *The Cheviot, the Stag and the Black, Black Oil*
315. Jeff Torrington (1935–2008), *Swing Hammer Swing*
316. Tom Buchan (1935–95). Poems, plays
317. Hugh C. Rae (1935–2014), *Skinner, A Few Small Bones*
318. Stewart Conn (b.1936). Poems, plays, essays
319. Tormod MacGill-Eain / Norman Maclean (1936–2017). Works: especially *The Leper's Bell: Autobiography of a Changeling*
320. William McIlvanney (1936–2015). Novels, especially *Remedy is None, Docherty, Laidlaw, The Papers of Tony Veitch*
321. Kenneth White (b.1936). Poems, essays
322. A.C. Jacobs (1937–94). Poems, especially *Nameless Country: Selected Poems*
323. Robin Fulton Macpherson (b.1937). Poems, especially *A Northern Habitat: Collected Poems 1960–2010*, translations, especially of Olav H. Hauge, Tomas Tranströmer and Harry Martinson, and essays
324. Alan Jackson (b.1938). Poems

325. Allan Massie (b.1938). Novels, especially *The Death of Men*
326. Donald Campbell (1940–2019). Poems, plays
327. John Byrne (b.1940), *The Slab Boys, Tutti Frutti*
328. Elspeth Barker (b.1940), *O Caledonia*
329. John Herdman (b.1941). Novels, stories, especially *Pagan's Pilgrimage, The Sinister Cabaret, My Wife's Lovers*
330. Carl MacDougall (b.1941), *The Lights Below, Someone Always Robs the Poor*
331. Tony Roper (b.1941), *The Steamie*
332. D.M. Black (b.1941). Poems
333. John Purser (b.1942), *There Is No Night: New and Selected Poems* and radio plays, especially *Carver*
334. Douglas Dunn (b.1942). Poems
335. Aonghas MacNeacail (b.1942). Poems and stories
336. Sue Glover (b.1943). Plays, especially *Bondagers*
337. Tom Leonard (1944–2018). Works: especially *Intimate Voices, Places of the Mind, Reports from the Present*
338. Maoilios Caimbeul / Myles Campbell (b.1944). Poems
339. James Kelman (b.1946), *Short Tales from the Night Shift, The Busconductor Hines, Kieron Smith, Boy*
340. Veronica Forrest-Thomson (1947–75), *Collected Poems and Translations*
341. Liz Lochhead (b.1947). Poems and plays, especially *Mary Queen of Scots Got Her Head Chopped Off* and *Medea*
342. Alan Spence (b.1947). Novels, plays, poems and stories, especially *Its Colours They Are Fine*
343. Janet Paisley (1948–2018). Poems, *White Rose Rebel, Warrior Daughter, Wildfire, Refuge*
344. Zoë Wicomb (b.1948), *David's Story, Playing in the Light, The One That Got Away, October*
345. Fearghas MacFhionnlaigh (b.1948). Poems, especially 'The Midge'
346. Meg Henderson (b.1948). Novels, especially *The Holy City*
347. Walter Perrie (b.1949). Poems
348. Ron Butlin (b.1949). Novels, especially *The Sound of My Voice*, stories, poems
349. Ann Marie Di Mambro (b.1950). Plays, especially *Tally's Blood*
350. Sharman Macdonald (b.1951). Plays
351. Frank Kuppner (b.1951). Poems, especially *A Bad Day for the Sung Dynasty*, and prose, especially *A Very Quiet Street*
352. Andrew Greig (b.1951). Poems, especially *Men on Ice* and *Surviving Passages*, and memoir: *At the Loch of the Green Corrie*

353. James Campbell (b.1951). *Invisible Country: A Journey through Scotland*
354. Brian McCabe (b.1951). Poems, stories and novel, *The Other McCoy*
355. Angus Peter Campbell (b.1952). Poems, fiction, especially *Invisible Islands*
356. Christopher Whyte (b.1952). Poems, novels, especially *The Gay Decameron*
357. Marcella Evaristi (b.1953). Plays
358. Gerrie Fellows (b.1954). Poems
359. Imtiaz Dharker (b.1954). Poems
360. Bashabi Fraser (b.1954). Poems
361. Dilys Rose (b.1954). Fiction
362. Val McDermid (b.1955). Fiction, especially *A Place of Execution*
363. Ian Stephen (b.1955). Poems, non-fiction, and *A Book of Death and Fish*
364. Carol Ann Duffy (b.1955). Poems
365. John Burnside (b.1955). Poems, fiction
366. Janice Galloway (b.1955). Novels, especially *The Trick is to Keep Breathing*, *Clara*
367. Anne Donovan (b.(c.)1956), *Buddha Da*
368. Peter McCarey (b.1956). Poems
369. George Gunn (b.1956). Poems, *The Province of the Cat*, *The Great Edge*
370. Elizabeth Burns (1957–2015). Poems
371. Robert Alan Jamieson (b.1958). Poems, novels
372. Chris Hannan (b.1958). Plays, especially *Shining Souls*, *Elizabeth Gordon Quinn*
373. Iain Banks (1954–2013). Novels, especially *The Wasp Factory*, *The Bridge*, *The Crow Road*
374. Irvine Welsh (b.1958). Novels, especially *Trainspotting*
375. James Robertson (b.1958). Novels, especially *And the Land Lay Still*
376. David Kinloch (b.1959). Poems
377. Meg Bateman (b.1959). Poems
378. Iain Bamforth (b.1959). Poems
379. Graham Fulton (b.1959). Poems
380. Donny O'Rourke (b.1959). Poems
381. Robert Crawford (b.1959). Poems
382. Gerda Stevenson (b.1956). Poems and plays, especially *Federer vs. Murray* and *Quines*
383. Maud Sulter (1960–2008). Works
384. Jackie Kay (b.1961). Poems, *Trumpet*, *Red Dust Road*

385. W.N. Herbert (b.1961). Poems
386. Kathleen Jamie (b.1962). Poems, essays
387. Ali Smith (b.1962), *Hotel World*, *Artful*, *Shire*, *Autumn*, *Winter*, *Spring*, *Summer*
388. Don Paterson (b.1963). Poems
389. Raymond Friel (b.1963). Poems
390. Angela McSeveney (b.1964). Poems
391. Duncan McLean (b.1964), *Bucket of Tongues*, *Blackden*, *Bunker Man*
392. Aminatta Forna (b.1964). *The Window Seat*, fiction
393. Alan Warner (b.1964), *Morvern Callar*, *These Demented Lands*, *The Sopranos*, *The Deadman's Pedal*
394. A.L. Kennedy (b.1965). Fiction, especially *Night Geometry* and the *Garscadden Trains* and non-fiction, especially *On Writing*
395. Alison Kermack (b.1966). Poems
396. Richard Price (b.1966). Poems, fiction
397. Roddy Lumsden (1966–2020). Poems
398. Stuart A. Paterson (b.1966). Poems
399. Ewan Morrison (b.1967), *Tales from the Mall*
400. Anne C. Frater (b.1967). Poems
401. Graeme Macrae Burnet (b.1967). Fiction, especially *His Bloody Project*
402. Matthew Fitt (b.1968). *Butt n Ben A-Go-Go*
403. Andrew O'Hagan (b.1968). *Our Fathers*
404. Douglas Stuart (b.1976). Fiction, especially *Shuggie Bain*
405. Hannah Lavery (b.1977). Poems and plays
406. Jenni Fagan (b.1977). Poems and fiction
407. Jenny Lindsay (b.1982). Poems
408. Darren McGarvey (b.1984). Works
409. Harry Josephine Giles (b.1986). Poems
410. Roseanne Watt (b.1991). Poems
411. Graeme Armstrong (b.1992). Fiction, especially *The Young Team*
412. Len Pennie or 'Miss Punny Pennie' (b.1999). Poems

5

After the Canon: What next? Where to?

SINCE THE 1990s at least, two things seem to have conditioned the context of Scottish literature, and what it is, generally and deeply: one is the rise of online technology, the other the awareness of ecological catastrophe. One offers opportunities for quick communication and liabilities of limiting sympathetic understanding. It gets information out fast but it's normally one-sided. Yet it also allows a global provenance for immediate communication as never before. The other conditions prevalent attitudes toward the whole earth and political power within economic systems defined by the opposed priorities of exploitation or replenishment. Within these contexts, questions of race, ethnicity, gender, sexuality, language, class, literary form, public communication platforms and exchanges, ego and vanity, education and self-effacement, all find forms of enquiry, expression, denigration and celebration. Foreclosures of opportunity, the ending or limiting of print publications, the cutting of educational resources of all kinds, the increasing scarcity of public intellectual engagement, whether through press, media, theatre, public hall or open lecture: all these go on incrementally, while new generations find values apt for their own time and era. The relation between national cultural distinctions and the global reality is constantly under revision.

Giving some sense of the range of possibilities, it's worth noting Elizabeth Rimmer Hannah Lavery (b.1977), poet, playwright, performer, director, whose autobiographical play *The Drift* toured Scotland in 2019, and whose *Lament for Sheku Bayoh* in 2020 was a response to a contemporary headline story deepened and sharpened by its deployment of traditional forms, with characters named 'Keener' and 'Singer', the Keen being the song of lament in Gaelic and many other cultures. Her poem, 'Scotland, you're no mine' defined a position of defiance against conventional, static, fixed national identity and reaffirmed the principle of openness not as a vague ideal but with specific points of reference: racists, cowards and reactionaries of all kinds might say she doesn't belong, but 'I am a limpet stuck on you'. It's a nice pun: 'stuck on' like superglue, but also like a dreamy lover. Jenny Lindsay (b.1982) likewise combines theatrical performance and poetry as verbal practice (rather than printed source of silent contemplation) in books including *The Things You Leave Behind* (2011), *The Eejit Pit* (2012), *Ire & Salt* (2015) and *This Script* (2019). Nalini Paul draws on roots and myths from India, Canada and Scotland, in collections such as *Skirlags* (2010) and *The Raven's Song* (2015), while stage performance and verse combine in *Beyond Mud Walls* (2016), bringing Scotland and India together through language, memory and the ambivalence of belonging and estrangement. In *Settle* (2016), Theresa Muñoz presents poems on immigration, contemporary technology and the benefits, constraints and ambiguous senses of exclusion and welcome. These poets' work demonstrates the dynamics of performative verse, rap, slam poetry, performance poetry, verbal pyrotechnics and fun crashing alongside the depth of deadly seriousness of issues increasingly understood as inescapable in the early 21st century. The poems and songs are made compelling by their skilful deployment of personal experience in highly crafted writing.

That blend and balancing of reflective, introspective verse and performative, theatrical forms of presentation is there too in the work of Len Pennie or 'Miss Punny Pennie' (b.1999), whose fame through online social media spread faster than a biological contagion, drawing both popular support and extremes of hostile denigration, during the COVID-19 pandemic of 2020. But Len Pennie was contagious health. As an advocate of the Scots language, in speech and writing, and of mental well-being as a correlative of linguistic self-confidence, she came from a long tradition of defiance of Anglophone, Anglocentric normativity. Her poem, 'I'm no havin children' is a playful and absolutely convincing assertion of the validity of the word 'weans' and by extension, the rightness of Scots, both as language and national self-determination.

Poets investing in performance run the necessary risk of becoming lost to the record. The moment is all. Accounts of the terrific impact of readings by Sandie Craigie (1963–2005) suggest that recordings do no justice to them, and print is cold by comparison. In print, Imtiaz Dharker (b.1954), confidently bringing the confluence of her Pakistani-Scottish resources into her work, delivered a worldview essentialised only in its humanity. As quality accumulates, the body of work by which individuals are recognised gathers both substance and range. In 2022, Peter McCarey's *Pogo* is a timely series of biting, bitter, antimonarchical squibs, funny, dangerous, nifty and necessary, as the hypocrisies of royalty reach new extents of exposure, while his *Orasho* is a book of observances and considerations, poems as barriers and bridges, coherences and fragments, amounting to redress, a warranty of justice, still touching but going beyond what everyday occurrence brings. The poems in both books do what only poems can do.

Harry Josephine Giles (b.1986), born in Walthamstow, growing up in Orkney, uses the language forms of that archipelago to overturn expectations of locality, conservatism and convention in exhilarating excursions through transgender identities. Roseanne Watt (b.1991) draws on tender but essentially secure roots in the Shetland archipelago, and while publishing strong poems in Scots and English in *Moder Dy / Mother Wave* (2019), is also an innovative musician and film-maker, combining words with moving images to complement, interrogate, riddle, cross and soak both genres with each other. Imagism arises between words and visualisation, with vulnerable, personal strengths transmitted through screened presences and aural landscapes.

Further poets might be named simply to indicate the range of dispositions at work, Elizabeth Rimmer, Lesley Benzie, Jock Stein, David Bleiman, each emphasising different priorities and questions about nature, morality, religion, languages, ways of living, histories of displacement and commitments of residence. All these authors are weathervanes of sorts, indicating where things are, and directions of travel. Increasingly understood as countering racism and superiorism is the broadening articulation of international ancestry and cultural complexity. Equally, writers might treasure their given local family and deep roots in one territory. Traditional literary genres are always there to be played with, experimented upon, deployed in varying degrees of invention, mixing writing and print, performance, declamation, celebration, combining the virtues of writing with those of theatre, film, music. Language itself is mixed, made up of impurities and diversities. This is as always, but perhaps more accepted as bringing potential benefit, so long as pluralism itself does not become a dulling convention. To be of any worth, literature, however defined, needs its cutting edge, to set against the dominance of uniformity, to oppose sterile conformity, to resist dictates of supremacy and rules of the establishment, to stay open, and never give in to the closed. Poetry keeps its outlaw status.

The mixing of generic expertise is exemplified by the novelist Louise Welsh's collaborations with the composer Stuart MacRae on operas such as *The Devil Inside* (2016, combining elements of Robert Louis Stenson's 'The Bottle Imp' and *Jekyll and Hyde*) and *Anthropocene* (2019). Such collisions of genre expectations are increasingly familiar. As a child, Jenni Fagan (b.1977) was adopted twice, grew up for some years living on a caravan park and was also homeless. A sense of the radical unreliability of 'safe ground' or 'home' animates her stories, novels and poems. She sang in punk and grunge bands, and the granular, vigorous resistance of those idioms can be felt in her writing. The *New York Times* described her as 'the Patron Saint of Literary Street Urchins'. Her novels *The Panopticon* (2012) and *The Sunlight Pilgrims* (2016) are unsettling, with aggressive narrative gear-shifts and twists, and *Luckenbooth* (2021), while centred on a multi-story tenement building, takes the reader through, down and up into different dimensions of history, violence and oppositional energy. Her poetry collections, *The Dead Queen of Bohemia* (2016), *There's a Witch in the Word Machine* (2018) and *Truth* (2019) enact similar themes of determined dislocation, creative threat and disturbance, in quick, sharp and curious verse, with no time for repose or complacency.

Edwin Morgan's Demon is at large, and roaming.

Another kind of genre-mix was the gauntlet thrown down by Darren McGarvey (b.1984), the rapper Loki, tightly controlled verbal elaborations found a wide audience as he set about encouraging teenagers to find expression for rage through words and music. He broadcast programmes about the consequences of deprivation on BBC Radio Scotland between 2004 and 2008, and published *Poverty Safari: Understanding the Anger of Britain's Underclass* (2017) as a partly autobiographical literary account of factual conditions.

In prose fiction, *Shuggie Bain* (2020) by Douglas Stuart (b.1976), a closely-observed, quasi-autobiographical novel about a young man growing up in working-class Glasgow with a mother to whom he is devoted and whose propensity to self-destruction is depicted with piercing compassion, won the 2020 Booker Prize and international acclaim. Presenting a similar social world in the Lanarkshire town of Airdrie, neighbouring Glasgow, *The Young Team* (2020) by Graeme Armstrong (b.1992) risked mixing racy dialogue and youthful exuberance with deadly serious presentations of a misogynist, abusive and self-abusive, economically devastated social world, where the main character faces the choices of escape, education and exile or the local entrapment of violence. Graeme Macrae Burnet (b.1967), in *His Bloody Project* (2015) and *Case Study* (2021) took a place within the crime fiction, or rather, 'noir' vision vogue and made it singular, by both drawing on literary tradition and blurring the lines between documentary realism and fictional fantasy (Hogg's *Confessions* is not far away).

In plays, poetry and fiction, the prospects of extending expression through the unprecedented international reach of online technology, the realignment of traditional genres and forms, the reassessment of linguistic efficacy and legitimacy, are everywhere evident. Such extension brings into question meanings we might normally take as given, what we assume are the 'facts' of national identity, or even of what literature is. And yet the premises that inform any manifestation of culture remain perennially present, as long as we care enough for the earth to sustain them: the gifts of being alive, physically, mentally, the gifts of geography and language (or geographies and languages), and ultimately of our apprehension of human potential. As far as the contemporary and the future can be spoken of meaningfully, the purpose is always assured: the extension – through time and over all terrain, seas and oceans – of consciousness, of the confidence of dream, of the sensitisation of the world.

PART SEVEN

Gazetteer of Scottish Literature: 101 Places to Visit

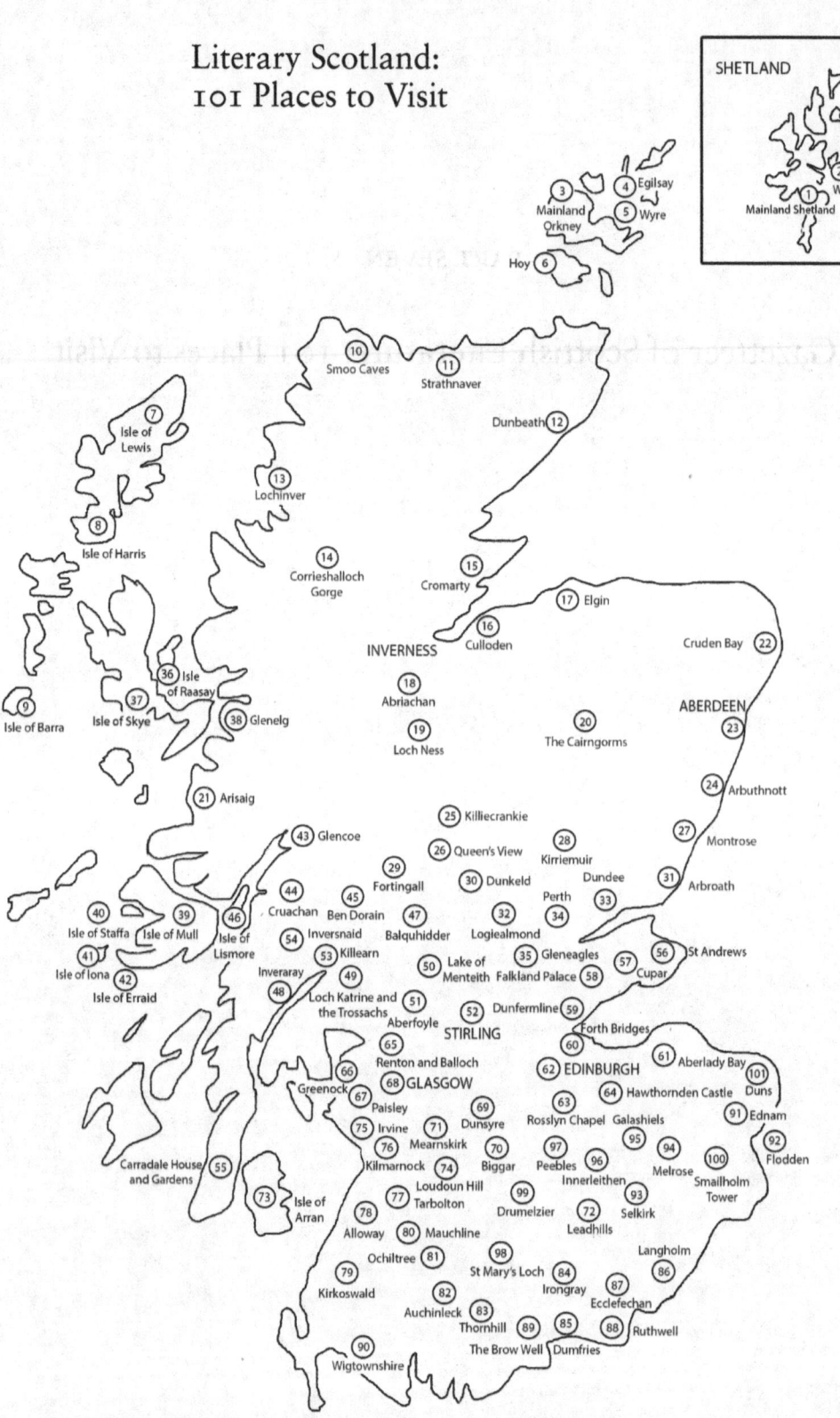

IN SCOTLAND, THERE are innumerable places to visit associated with great authors and their works. Writers' homes, birthplaces, graves, locations vividly described in novels and poems, theatres and writers' museums, libraries and visitors' centres, are to be found in almost every corner of the country. Scotland's landscapes and seascapes described in literature bring the reality of where and how people live into a vibrant presence. Many memorable characters in fiction and poems were based on real people whose homes, favoured places or graves may be seen. This list is a selection of places worth visiting. There are many more that might be added, so this is no more than a sampler. We are starting from the top, the far north, where Scotland rubs ocean-shoulders with Norway and Iceland, and we work our way south to the Borders, where England and Scotland become contested territories, the 'Debatable Lands'. But from Shetland to Selkirk, there is a coherent story across these diverse locations. The places to visit are described under the headings of 12 geographical areas in Scotland:

Shetland and Orkney (locations 1–6)
The Outer Hebrides (locations 7–9)
Highlands and Moray (locations 10–21)
Aberdeen and the East (locations 22–24)
Perthshire, Angus and Dundee (locations 25–34)
The Inner Hebrides, Argyll, Loch Lomond, Stirling and the Trossachs (locations 35–54)
The Kingdom of Fife (locations 55–60)
Edinburgh and the Lothians (locations 61–64)
Glasgow and The Clyde Valley (locations 65–72)
Ayrshire and Arran (locations 73–82)
Dumfries and Galloway (locations 83–90)
The Borders (locations 91–101)

Under each of these area headings I have listed a number of specific locations, each associated with an individual writer or writers, including landscapes or buildings described in novels and poems, and places where you will find a museum, library or visitor centre devoted to one or more major author. Each of these locations is numbered from 1 to 101, although in some cases, such as the entries for Edinburgh and Glasgow, there are many places listed under the one number.

While every effort has been made to be accurate in the descriptions of the places listed here, some may be closed for refurbishment or temporarily difficult to access for various reasons. To avoid disappointment, please check on the internet or with the local authority or institution in question directly before making your visit. Some of the places noted are in private ownership and may be opened to visitors only by prior arrangement.

Shetland and Orkney

1. Mainland Shetland: A good place to start reading is *A Shetland Anthology* (1998), edited by John J. Graham and Laurence I. Graham, along with *The Literature of Shetland* by Mark Ryan Smith (2014). On Mainland Shetland, Mavis Grind is one of the narrowest points of the isles and, with a very strong arm, you might be able to stand up to your ankles in the North Sea and throw a stone into the Atlantic. It is one of the locations in William J. Tait's magnificent poem 'A Day Atween Waddirs'. The township of Fladdabister in the south mainland is the scene of one of Rhoda Bulter's best known poems. The museum at Dunrossness was a crofthouse restored to its 19th-century condition and is the setting for Stella Sutherland's poem 'At da Croft Museum'. The Weisdale Valley is the location for John J. Graham's novels *Shadowed Valley* (1987) and *Strife in the Valley* (1992). The township of Sandness in the extreme west of the island was home to poet and novelist Robert Alan Jamieson and is the gravitational centre of his book of poems *Nort Atlantik Drift* (2007), while the oil terminal at Sullom Voe is the focus of his novel *Thin Wealth* (1986) and features in Ian Rankin's 'Rebus' crime novel *Black & Blue* (1997). Sumburgh Head is vividly described in Walter Scott's novel *The Pirate* (1822) and Eric Linklater's novel *The Dark of Summer* (1956) is partly set in Shetland.

2. Whalsay: On this island, Hugh MacDiarmid (C.M. Grieve), his wife Valda and their young son Michael lived from 1933 to 1942. The house they lived in is now a hostel, Grieve House Böd. The treeless terrain, stony beaches and tidal inlets of Whalsay and the nearby island of Little Linga are the land and seascapes of the central poem of MacDiarmid's career, 'On a Raised Beach' and many other fine poems of this period including 'Diamond Body: In a Cave of the Sea' as well as numerous stories, sketches and passages in his autobiography, *Lucky Poet* (1943). See also Alan Riach's essay, 'Infinite Whalsay', in the periodical *Archipelago*, no.8 (Winter 2013) and *MacDiarmid in Shetland* (1992) by Laurence Graham and Brian Smith.

3. Mainland Orkney: The foundational literary work of the Orkney archipelago is *The Orkneyinga Saga* (c.1200) and in the modern period, the best introduction to the Orkney archipelago is George Mackay Brown's *An Orkney Tapestry* (1969), a collection of stories, poems, dialogues, portraits and sketches giving a multi-faceted picture of the islands, their people and history. *The History of Orkney Literature* (2010) by Simon W. Hall is the essential literary guide. In his novels and numerous short stories, poems and sketches Mackay Brown describes the prehistoric monuments of Orkney, some predating the Pyramids of Egypt: the Standing Stones of Stenness, the Ring of Brodgar, Maes Howe and

Skara Brae. Brown wrote regularly for the local newspaper, *The Orcadian* and his collections of journalism are packed with affectionate descriptions of these and other Orkney places: *Letters from Hamnavoe* (1975), *Under Brinkie's Brae* (1979), *Rockpools and Daffodils: An Orcadian Diary, 1979–1991* (1992) and posthumously, *The First Wash of Spring* (2006). For many years, 3 Mayburn Court in Stromness was his home, where he regularly worked quietly through the mornings, with a card pinned to his door asking not to be disturbed, then often walked through the small town for his shopping, enjoying meeting visitors or friends for a beer in the nearby Braes Hotel or other local hostelries. He was a writer of international stature and a local resident, an unobtrusive celebrant of day-to-day rituals. From the porch outside his front door, the sea is a stone's throw away, seen through an alley, and the small streams that run down the slope behind Stromness give a murmuring music after rainfall. Brown wrote hauntingly of Stromness in his fiction and poems, calling it Hamnavoe. He is buried at the nearby Warbeth Cemetery, having chosen the words on his stone: 'Carve the runes, then be content with silence'. In the nearby capital of Orkney, Kirkwall, St Magnus Cathedral is named for the man who is the central character in Brown's most deeply impressive novel, *Magnus* (1973). It is the greatest building in the northern islands of Scotland. Unlike most buildings in the Highlands and Islands, this is architecture that does justice to its location.

Before it became a hotel, Merkister Hotel, by the Loch of Harray, was Merkister House, the home of novelist Eric Linklater, who is buried beside his wife Marjorie at St Michael's Churchyard nearby. Orkney is the scene of episodes in his novels *White-Maa's Saga* (1929) and *Magnus Merriman* (1934).

A very different Orkney writer was Margaret Tait, whose poems were first published by Hugh MacDiarmid in his journal *The Voice of Scotland* and are collected in *Subjects and Sequences: A Margaret Tait Reader* (2004) and *Poems, Stories and Writings* (2012). She was a film-maker of extraordinary invention and experimental vision, making a film-portrait of MacDiarmid (1964), a film version of the poem by Gerard Manley Hopkins, 'The Leaden Echo and the Golden Echo' (1955), 'Orquil Burn' (1955), tracing a small stream across the Orkney landscape, and the feature-length film *Blue Black Permanent* (1992)

4. Egilsay: George Mackay Brown's novel *Magnus* dramatises the life of Magnus Erlendsson, shockingly setting his individual biography against other contexts of violence and sacrifice in history, including that of Nazi Europe. Magnus was killed on the island of Egilsay in 1116 or 1117 and he is the subject of his own story, told in *Magnus' Saga: The Life of St Magnus, Earl of Orkney* (c.1250).

5. Wyre: Edwin Muir spent his childhood on his father's farm, The Bu, on the island of Wyre. It provided him with idyllic memories of childhood which were

heightened and intensified in symbolic significance when he encountered the squalor and poverty of industrial Glasgow, where he saw members of his family die, and later when he experienced the horrors of Fascism rising throughout Europe. The island and farming world he came from strengthens the vision in poems such as 'The Horses' and is an implicit counterpoint to the Cold War terrors of 'The Good Town'.

6. Hoy: Rackwick is an idyllic spot beautifully described by George Mackay Brown in his posthumous collection *Northern Lights: A Poet's Sources* (1999), in the 1950 poem 'Rackwick':

> The hidden valley of light.
> Sweetness from the clouds pouring.
> Songs from the surging sea.
> Fenceless fields, fishermen with ploughs
> And old heroes, endlessly sleeping
> In Rackwick's compassionate hills.

It was home for the composer Peter Maxwell Davies, and his favoured place. There are a number of collaborations between Davies and Brown and Davies's music inspired by Orkney includes *Orkney Wedding, With Sunrise* (1985) for orchestra and bagpipes, and the beautiful, lyrical piano pieces 'Yesnaby Sound' and 'Farewell to Stromness', which he played at Brown's funeral.

The Outer Hebrides

7. Isle of Lewis: On the outskirts of the town of Stornoway is Bayble, childhood home of poet and novelist Iain Crichton Smith (52 Upper Bayble); poet Derick Thomson was born nearby and both attended the Nicolson Institute, the famous Stornoway school. Both have numerous poems about Lewis and its people, in each of their volumes of *Collected Poems*.

In *The Old Ways* (2012), Robert MacFarlane recounts a boating trip, sailing from Lewis with the poet Ian Stephen, whose work is collected in *Mackerel and Creamola* (2001), *Providence II* (1994) and *Varying States of Grace* (1989), and whose epic novel, *A Book of Death and Fish* (2014) was widely praised.

Peter May set his trilogy of popular crime novels on Lewis, making full use of the topography and local customs: *The Black House* (2011), *The Lewis Man* (2012) and *The Chess Men* (2013).

8. Isle of Harris: In the south transept of St Clement's Church, Rodel, is the grave

of Mary Macleod / Màiri Nighean Alasdair Ruaidh, poet, composer and singer of the 16th and 17th centuries. Other Gaelic writers from the island include the religious poet John Morrison / Iain Gobha and Seamus MacLeod, novelist. An ancient carving of a birlinn or galley, a ship that would have been in familiar use with the people of the Lord of the Isles, can also be seen in St Clement's.

Luskentyre is the location of the cemetery mentioned by Norman MacCaig in his ferociously angry poem, 'Aunt Julia' and Scalpay is the island of his mother and his mother's people, described in the poem 'Return to Scalpay'.

A fond account of a 1930s Harris childhood is in Finlay J. MacDonald's three books of memoirs, *Crowdie and Cream* (1982), *Crotal and White* (1983), and *The Corncrake and the Lysander* (1985).

9. Isle of Barra: At Cille Bharra Cemetery, Eoligarry is the grave of Compton Mackenzie, author of the famous *Whisky Galore!* (1947) and the less well-known but far finer novel, *Thin Ice* (1956) and many others. His home was above the airport-beach at Eoligarry. Also highly recommended is *Tales of Barra Told by the Coddy* (1960), John MacPherson (1876–1955), for which Mackenzie wrote a Foreword.

Highlands and Moray

10. Smoo Caves: Walter Scott describes these three caves in his travel journal, *Northern Lights or a voyage in the Lighthouse Yacht to Nova Zembla and the Lord knows where in the summer of 1814*. This travel journal also includes Scott's account of his journeying throughout the northern islands of Orkney and Shetland.

11. Strathnaver: This is one of the most beautiful and saddest valleys in the world. Its emptiness is laden with the sense of missing people, more than a century after their evictions. Donald MacLeod describes what happened in his memoir of the Highland Clearances, *Gloomy Memories* (1857), the title an ironic reference to the American author Harriet Beecher Stowe's *Sunny Memories of Foreign Lands* (1854). MacLeod contrasts the conditions Stowe enjoyed as a guest of the Duke and Duchess of Sutherland at the lavish Dunrobin Castle which can be seen nearby. The memorial to MacLeod is by the roadside, across the River Naver from his birthplace, Rossal. The landowners' factor Patrick Sellar is vilified in memory for his brutality and hypocrisy. The Clearances are central in the novels *Butcher's Broom* (1934) by Neil Gunn, *And the Cock Crew* (1945) by Fionn Mac Colla and *Consider the Lilies* (1968) by Iain Crichton Smith and in Crichton Smith's poem 'Clearances', in Norman MacCaig's poems 'A Man in Assynt' and 'Two Thieves', and in John McGrath and the 7:84 Theatre Company's play, *The Cheviot, the Stag and the Black,*

Black Oil (1973). Among Gaelic poems contemporary with the Clearances are the coruscating 'Cumha a' Bhàillidh Mhòir' / 'Lament for the Great Factor' by Uisdean Ròs / Eugene Rose (or Ross) and the grief-drawn 'Fios chun a' Bhàird' / 'A Message from the Poet' by Uilleam MacDhunlèibhe / William Livingston. James Hunter's book *On the Other Side of Sorrow* (1995) takes a broad survey of poets and writers on the Clearances, writing in Gaelic, Scots and English.

12. Dunbeath: This was the favoured territory of the novelist Neil Gunn and Dunbeath Heritage Centre is sited in Gunn's old school. The Terrace, Gunn's birthplace, has a memorial plaque on the wall and there is a powerful sculpture by Alex Main of Kenn and the salmon from the novel *Highland River* (1937) at Dunbeath harbour. Dunbeath and other coastal towns here were home to large fishing fleets – now almost entirely gone, but vividly described in Gunn's epic novel *The Silver Darlings* (1941). There is also a Gunn Memorial Viewpoint above Dingwall near Strathpeffer where he latterly lived.

13. Lochinver: Norman MacCaig's summer home for many years surrounded him with the territory he wrote about in numerous poems, describing Suilven, Lochinver and Assynt, the people of the area he knew and whose company he enjoyed for a long time, including a close friend whose death is at the centre of his sequence of elegies, 'Poems for Angus'. The reversal of fortunes as the absentee landowners in the area were bought out by local people is told by John MacAskill in *We Have Won the Land: The Story of the Purchase by the Assynt Crofters' Trust of the North Lochinver Estate* (1999).

14. Corrieshalloch Gorge: The waterfall here (there is a viewpoint from a suspension bridge) is the subject of an astonishing poem by Norman MacCaig, 'Falls of Measach', which begins:

> The wind was basins slopping over.
> The river plunged into its ravine
> Like coins into a stocking. The day
> Was like the buzzard on the pine.

As a profound exercise in studying the relation between a work of literature and the specific location from which it arises, this place is worth visiting with the poem in mind, and, typically MacCaig, the poem is deeply revealing of the relation between language, imagination and specific location. In fact, MacCaig's poems deserve a whole gazetteer devoted to their locations. Though he was a primary school teacher in Edinburgh, he spent as many summers as he could in Lochinver and the area around Assynt. Andrew Greig's *At the Loch of the*

Green Corrie (2010) is an extended memoir centred on only one of MacCaig's favoured places, and Greig's expedition to discover it for himself.

15. Cromarty: Hugh Miller's Cottage is the birthplace of Hugh Miller, geologist, naturalist, pioneer ecologist, with collections of his geological specimens, manuscripts of his writings and personal belongings on display. Miller might be considered in the company of Carlyle, Ruskin, Matthew Arnold and J.S. Mill as moral and social thinkers of the late 19th century, the Victorian Sages.

16. Culloden: This is the place of the massacre of the soldiers supporting Prince Charles Edward Stuart in 1746, by 'Butcher' Cumberland and his Hanoverian troops. It was the culminating event (not described) in Walter Scott's first novel, *Waverley* (1814), as it was (horrifically detailed) in James Hogg's under-rated novel *The Three Perils of Woman* (1823). It features in numerous literary works, and in one of the most memorable of Iain Crichton Smith's poems, 'Culloden and After' from his collection *Thistles and Roses* (1961). At Struy in Strathglass, about 20 miles south-west of Inverness, a roadside memorial marks the site of the cottage where William Chisholm and Christiana Fergusson lived. After Chisholm's death at Culloden, Fergusson (fl.1740s) composed one of the most piercing laments, 'Cumha do dh'Uilleam Siseal' or 'Mo Rùn Geal Òg' / 'My fair young love'.

17. Elgin: The Cathedral here was founded in 1224 but in 1390 the notorious Wolf of Badenoch, son of King Robert II, after what he considered political and personal insults to his own authority, burned it to the ground in revenge, along with most of Elgin itself and neighbouring Forres. He was excommunicated by Bishop Alexander Bur. The medieval origins of the town are evident in the old cobbled market place and its narrow, surrounding streets, wynds and pends, and the ruins of the Cathedral itself. The epic historical novel *The Wolfe of Badenoch* (1827) by Sir Thomas Dick Lauder tells the story and depicts the devastation of Elgin and its Cathedral in spectacular style.

18. Abriachan: This little scattered township in the hills above Loch Ness, just south-west of Inverness, is where the novelist Jessie Kesson lived while recovering from her time in a mental hospital, before writing the modern classics, *The White Bird Passes* (1958), *Glitter of Mica* (1963), *Another Time, Another Place* (1983) and *Where the Apple Ripens* (1985).

19. Loch Ness: Adomnán in his *Life of Columba* (c.700) describes the saint's encounter with a water-monster from Loch Ness, often noted as the first appearance of what was to become familiar as the Loch Ness Monster. In an

act of astonishing and characteristic literary ventriloquism, Edwin Morgan gave voice to the creature in 'The Loch Ness Monster's Song', beginning with him – or her? who knows? – emerging from the watery deeps and curiously looking around: 'Sssnnnwhufffll?' and ending with her or his submergence once again: 'blm plm, / blm plm, / blm plm, / blp.'

20. The Cairngorms: This is a mountain range described and intimately explored by the modernist novelist Nan Shepherd in *The Living Mountain*, written in the 1940s but not published until 1977: 'under me the central core of fire from which was thrust this grumbling grinding mass of plutonic rock, over me blue air, and between the fire of the rock and the fire of the sun, scree, soil and water, moss, grass, flower and tree, insect, bird and beast, wind, rain and snow – the total mountain.' Robert Macfarlane has an excellent article in *The Guardian* (30 August 2008) about her and she is a vital presence in his book, *The Old Ways* (2012). Her novels, *The Quarry Wood* (1928) and *The Weatherhouse* (1930) are classics.

21. Arisaig: In the cemetery of Arisaig Church is the grave of Alasdair mac Mhaighstir Alasdair / Alexander MacDonald, the greatest Gaelic poet of the 18th century. A carved image in the stone of a sailing ship or 'birlinn' may be linked to his greatest poem, 'The Birlinn of Clanranald'.

Aberdeen and the East

22. Cruden Bay: The Irish writer Bram Stoker wrote *Dracula* (1897) while staying at the Kilmarnock Arms Hotel at Cruden Bay; in the novel, some of the rougher characters (ostensibly English locals in Whitby) speak broad Scots. Nearby Slains Castle, which was visited by Samuel Johnson and James Boswell in 1773, when it was inhabited, provided Stoker with a model for his Gothic imagination, as did nearby Whinnyfold, where he also stayed. Stoker set other fiction including *The Mystery of the Sea* (1902) in and around this area. But it is the ruined Slains Castle that haunts the memory. In it, you can almost hear Dracula whispering: 'My revenge is just begun. I spread it over centuries and time is on my side.'

23. Aberdeen: In front of the city Grammar School, there is a boldly assertive statue of Lord Byron, who attended the school till the age of ten, by the poet, sculptor and cultural activist Pittendrigh MacGillivray. MacGillivray's work is similar to that of his great contemporary Rodin. It was T.S. Eliot who insisted that Byron should best be considered as a Scottish poet, and in *Don Juan*, Cantos 10–11, Byron himself wrote: '…my heart flies to my head, // As Auld

Lang Syne brings Scotland, one and all, / Scotch plaids, Scotch snoods, the blue hills, and clear streams, / The Dee, the Don, Balgounie's Brig's blackwall, / All my boy feelings, all my gentler dreams / Of what I then dreamt, clothed in their own pall, / Like Banquo's offspring.' Byron's poignant 'Dark Lochnagar' is one of the loveliest evocations of the landscape of youth and one of the warmest and most beautiful of songs, especially as performed by Calum Kennedy. John Barbour, author of *The Bruce* (c.1376) was Archdeacon of St Machar's Cathedral, Aberdeen, and there is a memorial to him there. Writers have often been in two minds about Aberdeen, its prosperity, its granitic architecture and the stereotyped self-satisfaction and alleged frugality of its citizens. This ambivalence is notable in Alexander Scott's challenging descriptive poem 'Heart of Stone' composed to complement Alan Daiches's photography for a television programme in 1965, and in Lewis Grassic Gibbon's essay 'Aberdeen' from *Scottish Scene* (1934).

24. Arbuthnott: Lewis Grassic Gibbon (James Leslie Mitchell), the author of the novel *Sunset Song* (1932), grew up on the croft of Hillhead of Seggett and the farm of Bloomfield, and is buried in Arbuthnott Church, where an open book in sculpted stone in the corner of the cemetery carries the words, 'For I will give you the morning star…' The Howe o' the Mearns informs the novel, a vast, rolling, farming landscape extending all around this area, with a sense of the cold North Sea nearby and the presence of the priorities of seasonal change everywhere palpable. Of the two novels succeeding *Sunset Song* in the trilogy *A Scots Quair*, *Cloud Howe* (1933) is based on the town of Stonehaven and *Grey Granite* (1934) blends elements of Aberdeen, Dundee and Glasgow. The Lewis Grassic Gibbon Centre is a museum, café and bookshop devoted to his work.

Perthshire, Angus and Dundee

25. Killiecrankie: John Galt's *Ringan Gilhaize* (1823) is a violent and action-packed novel of religious extremism and the Covenanters, set mainly in the 1680s, which concludes with the Battle of Killiecrankie (1689). The site of the battle, in a dramatic, forested river-valley, with rock-bounded waterfall, has a visitor centre and walkway. For a poetic account of the battle, see 'Killiecrankie' by Iain mac Ailein / John MacLean (c.1655–1741), which begins with the breathless downhill rush of troops and 'Scotland and Ireland together' – it is collected in *The Harp's Cry: An Anthology of 17th Century Gaelic Poetry* (1994), edited by Colm O Baoill with translations by Meg Bateman.

26. Queen's View: Queen Victoria in her *Journals* wrote extensively and repetitiously of her rhapsodic response to the Scottish Highlands as a spectacle

to be viewed as a tourist, enjoying scenes of depopulated wilderness from which families who had been living there for generations had been violently evicted. This is reportedly her favourite view, when she visited in 1866, along Loch Tummel to the peak of Schiehallion. At 3,547 feet, 'Schiehallion!' is the toast that resoundingly ends Edwin Morgan's fantasia-poem composed of Scottish place-names, 'Canedolia'.

27. Montrose: The House of Dun was the ancestral home and birthplace of Violet Jacob, whose poems and novels, including the remarkable *Flemington* (1911), are often descriptive of the landscapes around Montrose while her travel writings and diaries from India illustrate the extent of her actual journeying and the liveliness of her enquiring mind. This is also the terrain of Jacob's contemporary, Marion Angus, who lived a much more locally-bound life, and whose poems, especially in *The Lilt and Other Verses* (1922) and *The Tinker's Road* (1924), represent the people of this area in deftly suggestive sketches of moments of crisis or reflection. Willa Muir's novels *Imagined Corners* (1931) and *Mrs Ritchie* (1933), and her memoir *Belonging* (1968), describe life in Montrose closely. The poet, suffragette and friend of many writers associated with the Scottish Renaissance movement of the 1920s, Helen Burness Cruickshank, was born in Hillside, and went to school in Montrose. Montrose was the town where, in the 1920s, Hugh MacDiarmid (C.M. Grieve) worked as a reporter on the local newspaper (a plaque on the wall of the newspaper building in the main street commemorates him), while living with his first wife, son and daughter at 16 Links Avenue, where much of his early writing was completed.

28. Kirriemuir: J.M. Barrie's birthplace is a museum with manuscripts and mementoes from his long involvement with the theatre and his classic plays *Quality Street* (1901), *The Admirable Crichton* (1902) and *Peter Pan* (1904). The little building in the narrow streets of the town, surrounded by the open fields of wide farming landscapes gives a strong impression of an imagination bursting to escape its material confinement. See also Moat Brae, Dumfries.

29. Fortingall: The Fortingall Yew is said to be the most ancient living thing in the world, between 2,000 and 5,000 years old. A story has it that Pontius Pilate was born in Fortingall, the son of a Roman centurion, and in Edwin Morgan's poem 'Pilate at Fortingall', from the sequence *Sonnets from Scotland* (1986), he is seen as an old man, returned to the village, washing his hands again and again, finding it impossible to absolve himself of his own guilty responsibility in the crucifixion of Christ. It was also here that James MacGregor, the vicar of Fortingall, compiled *The Book of the Dean of Lismore* between 1512 and 1542. This is an extremely important early Gaelic text with songs and heroic poems

apparently transmitted from the age of the ancient, pre-Christian mythical Celtic heroes such as Finn MacCoul and his son the bard Ossian.

30. Dunkeld: Gavin Douglas, who translated Virgil's *Aeneid* into the Scots language as *The Eneados* (1513) was Bishop of Dunkeld Cathedral. In the poem, he introduced his own descriptions of Scotland and Scotland's landscapes and weather into the Prologues to each Book. Near Dunkeld at Birnam, is the Beatrix Potter Centre and Garden, devoted to the works of the famous children's writer, creator of Jemima Puddle-Duck, Mr Jeremy Fisher, Mrs Tiggy-Winkle and Peter Rabbit. Potter spent summer holidays here in her youth and later wrote what was to become her first book, *The Tale of Peter Rabbit*, in Eastwood House, beside the River Tay.

31. Arbroath: It was from Arbroath Abbey that one of the most eloquent and passionate political documents in history was issued in 1320, the *Declaration of Arbroath*. A letter sent to the Pope at Avignon, written in the effort to legitimise the authority of King Robert the Bruce, the document defines one of the prevailing ideals of Scottish national identity: the sovereignty of the people (as opposed to the 'divine right' of royalty). There is a fine sculpture at the entrance to Arbroath by David Annand, showing the Abbot, the King and the Declaration being held aloft.

32. Logiealmond: Accessible via leafy byways from Perth and Crieff, this is a former quarry workers' village. Under the fictional name of Drumtochty it became famous as the setting of the best-selling collections of fictional sketches *Beside the Bonnie Brier Bush* (1894) and *The Days of Auld Langsyne* (1895). Writing under the nom de plume Ian Maclaren, their author the Rev John Watson created rose-tinted, backward-looking, whimsical sketches of country life on the fringes of the Perthshire highlands in the 1830s. These were sensationally popular in the USA and their first American editions (1896), bound in tartan and thistle livery, carried specially commissioned photographic illustrations of the locations and alleged principal characters of the stories.

33. Dundee: The William McGonagall Memorial is on the walkway of Riverside Drive, overlooking the Tay Bridge. The William McGonagall collection is in the Local History Centre of Dundee Central Library. The most radical Scottish poet between Burns and MacDiarmid was the Dundee man, James Young Geddes, but you will have to search for his works and the places associated with him. An excellent anthology of the poetry of Dundee and its hinterland is *Whaleback City* (2013), edited by W.N. Herbert and Andy Jackson. Herbert's own scintillating, elaborate, passionate, generous and clever poetry, in the

distinctive tonalities of Dundonian Scots, frequently circles back to and takes off from the city and references to locations abound in it. Other luminaries of the city include John Glenday, A.L. Kennedy, Don Paterson, and fine work about Dundee and its environs has been made by Matthew Fitt, Douglas Dunn, John Burnside, Kathleen Jamie and many others. Highlights of the anthology include Dunn's 'Tay Bridge' ('A sky that tastes of rain that's still to fall / And then of rain that falls and tastes of sky…'), Herbert's 'Ode to the New Old Tay Bridge', that begins: 'Twas in the clammy autumn of 2003 / I was commissioned by some madmen at the BBC / to write about you, rickety auld Tay railbridge / (a prospect as cheery as inhabiting a fridge)', Robert Crawford's 'Mary Shelley on Broughty Ferry Beach', Bashabi Fraser's 'From the Ganga to the Tay' (a long poem exploring relations between Scotland and India), Henry Marsh's 'Dundee, 1651' and Anne Stevenson's 'The Mudtower (Tayport, Fife, 1 January, 1975)'. Andrew Murray Scott's historical survey, *Dundee's Literary Lives: Volume 1: Fifteenth to Nineteenth Century* and *Volume 2: Twentieth Century* (both 2003), introduces the work of many literary figures, including visitors such as Charles Dickens and Oscar Wilde, and George MacKenzie (1636–91), the man who, with *Aretina, or The Serious Romance* (1660), a political allegory of 17th-century Scotland and the Civil War, has a claim to be Scotland's first novelist, and David Pae (1828–84), who, after a series of novels published serially in the second half of the 19th century, became known as Scotland's Anthony Trollope. Important 20th-century figures include Joseph Lee, Lewis Spence and William Montgomerie.

34. Perth: The William Soutar House at 27 Wilson Street was the home in which the poet retired to bed with the disease of spondylitis from 1930 till his death in 1943. The wall facing his bed was turned into a large window onto the garden by his father and Soutar kept journals of his dreams, diaries and accounts of his visitors, and continued to write some of the most memorable Scots-language poems of the 20th century from this location. The house has been home to a writer-in-residence and may be visited by appointment: contact the A.K. Bell Memorial Library in Perth, which has many items relating to Soutar and a theatre. There is an excellent film-biography of Soutar written and produced by Douglas Eadie, *The Garden Beyond* (1976).

35. Gleneagles: Not the famous luxury hotel but the centuries old, secluded House of Gleneagles on the other side of the A9, is the backdrop for one of Scotland's finest historical novels, Naomi Mitchison's *The Bull Calves*. Published in 1947 and set in 1747, this deals with the immediate impact of the Jacobite defeat at Culloden on the extended family of the Haldane Lairds of Gleneagles and their lands around Blackford. More recent novelists James Kennaway, Rosamunde Pilcher, Allan Massie and Ronald Frame have, in their different ways, explored lives of quiet desperation among the gentry and the genteel in rural Perthshire.

The Inner Hebrides, Argyll, Loch Lomond, Stirling and the Trossachs

36. The Isle of Raasay: Sorley MacLean's poem 'Hallaig' evokes the cleared township of that name and is engraved on a monument overlooking this spot. It is one of the most essential poems of the 20th century and visiting the place can help you understand it more deeply.

37. The Isle of Skye: 6 Penniechorrain, Braes, near Portree, was the home of Sorley MacLean and his wife René, and on the hill to the right of the road on the way to the small cluster of houses there, is a monument to the Battle of the Braes, with words by MacLean commemorating the confrontation in the 1880s that began the reclamation of land rights by the crofters in the face of absentee landowners. The great Skye-born poet of the crofters' battle for land rights was Mary Macpherson, known as Màiri Mhór nan Òran, Big Mary of the Songs. Southwest from Braes is the mountain range known as the Cuillins. Hugh MacDiarmid describes himself in his poem 'Direadh III' (published in his 1943 autobiography *Lucky Poet*) sitting on the summit of Sgurr Alasdair, lighting his pipe and looking around as if over all of Scotland, and concluding that the Inaccessible Pinnacle – among the highest points of the range – 'is not inaccessible'. In other words, the highest ambition needs to be encouraged if Scotland and the people of Scotland are to fulfil their potential. In his long poem-sequence, 'The Cuillin' (1939), Sorley MacLean evokes the mountains as a physical reality he climbed and knew intimately, but also as a permanent symbol of hope and aspiration. Surrounded by the Cuillin is Loch Coruisk. Robert Buchanan's 'Coruisken Sonnets' chillingly evoke the landscape in the loneliness of the Godless 19th-century universe, implicitly counterpointing the natural, elemental inhumanity of the scene with its familiarity as a famous Victorian tourist destination, frequently visited by boat as well as by hardy foot-travellers and depicted in a painting by J.M.W. Turner, commissioned as an illustration for 'The Lord of the Isles' in Walter Scott's *Poetical Works* (1831). On the other side of the island, near Tarskavaig, is Dunskaith, Skathach's Castle, a rocky island where the legendary Celtic hero Cuchulain learned the arts of war from the woman Skathach, and where he fathered a son, who as a young man hunts down his father, and, concealing his identity, engages him in mortal combat. Cuchulain kills his son and only then discovers who he was. The story occurs in the Ossianic heroic poems in *The Book of the Dean of Lismore* and there are versions in Lady Gregory's *Cuchulain of Muirthemne* (1902) and W.B. Yeats's poem 'Cuchulain's Fight with the Sea'. Skathach's story is the subject of a remarkable novel, *Warrior Daughter* (2009) by Janet Paisley.

38. Glenelg: Just south of Glenelg is Sandaig, the original location of Gavin Maxwell's Camusfearna, the home described in the classic account of his life with otters, *Ring of Bright Water* (1960).

39. Isle of Mull: Below Duart Castle is a memorial to the novelist William Black (1841–1898), author of the novel *Macleod of Dare* (1878), partly set on Mull. Nearby is a monument to Dugald Macphail, Gaelic poet and songwriter, author of the famous song 'An t-Eilean Mulleach' or 'The Isle of Mull'. The neglected narrative poem *Norman, A Legend of Mull: A Poem, in Five Duans* (1893) by Robert Cumming Macfee also evokes the island. Angela du Maurier (sister of the more famous Daphne), who stayed at Torosay Castle for almost a year during the Second World War, wrote *The Spinning Wheel* (1940), another novel partly set on Mull, and bought a farm at Achnacroish because she found the island so conducive to her writing.

40. Isle of Staffa: Fingal's Cave is the most famous of all locations associated with Fingal or Finn MacCoul, the Celtic (Irish and Scottish) hero, central character in the third of the cycles of Celtic tales. *The Fantastical Feats of Finn MacCoul* (2009) is a collection of stories by the distinguished folklorist Norah Montgomerie, who along with her husband the poet William Montgomerie also collected myths and legends in *The Folk Tales of Scotland* (1956). The cave also features in Jules Verne's novel *The Green Ray* (1882).

41. Isle of Iona: Here is Iona Cathedral but the whole island was home to Columba, whose hymn, the 'Altus Prosator', is translated by Edwin Morgan as 'The Maker on High' and whose biography was written by Adomnán in the 7th century. The 6th-century *Book of Kells*, now in the National Museum of Ireland, was probably made here on Iona, suggesting the profound interconnectedness of the ancient Celtic world, and the sea-commerce between Ireland and Scotland as it existed before our nations were politically redefined.

42. Isle of Erraid: This is where the overland journey made by David Balfour in *Kidnapped* begins, after he has escaped from the ship that has taken him from the east coast, around the north of Scotland, here, to the Inner Hebrides. Robert Louis Stevenson's novel is a circumnavigation of Scotland, from Edinburgh, around the country by sea, then across the country by land, from Erraid through Mull, Glencoe, across Rannoch Moor, Stirlingshire and back to where we began. David Balfour's beach – the spot where he supposedly was washed ashore – is a beautiful sandy bay in a rocky, tidal cove. You can walk there from and back to Mull at low tide if you time it carefully but the best way to arrive is under sail.

43. Glencoe: Site of the most notorious betrayal of hospitality in Scottish history in 1692, when soldiers accommodated by the villagers rose in the night under order and set about murdering their hosts, an event described in John Prebble's dramatic history book *Glencoe: The Story of the Massacre* (1966). This lowering valley has more recently been a favourite filming location for J. K. Rowling's *Harry Potter and the Prisoner of Azkaban* (2004), *Rob Roy* (1995), *Highlander* (1986), *Monty Python and the Holy Grail* (1975) and the James Bond extravaganza *Skyfall* (2012). Nearby Rannoch Moor was the subject of T. S. Eliot's one Scottish poem, an intense evocation of the landscape's persistent, contemporary, brooding power and echoing history: 'Here the crow starves, here the patient stag / Breeds for the rifle… / Memory is strong / Beyond the bone…'

44. Cruachan: The underground hydroelectric power station is the setting for the climax of the racy crime novel *A Big Boy Did It and Ran Away* (2003) by Christopher Brookmyre, where it is renamed Dubh Ardrain. Brookmyre's depiction of the resourcefulness of mischievous youngsters is as good as anything similar since John Buchan's wonderful novel *Huntingtower* (1922).

45. Ben Dorain: This imposing mountain on the right-hand side of the road as you drive north between Tyndrum and Glencoe was the subject of one of the greatest of all Gaelic poems, 'Praise of Ben Dorain', a celebration and vibrant evocation of a hunt for deer across the wooded slopes, by Duncan Ban MacIntyre. The Duncan Ban MacIntyre monument is about two miles up a side road from Dalmally railway station. Don't go there after heavy snow.

46. Isle of Lismore: The ruins of Achinduin mark the place where the compiler of *The Book of the Dean of Lismore* (early 16th-century) was based, although the Gaelic poems, songs and stories in the book were gathered in Perthshire and elsewhere, drawing on the Ossianic tales of Finn MacCoul and the Fianna. Lismore is also the crucial setting for most of Louise Welsh's novel *Naming the Bones* (2010), in which the island is implicitly and unemphatically described in contrast to the city of Glasgow and its university, both with dark secrets and false promises, inhabited by people engaged in dangerous acts of reclamation.

47. Balquhidder: In the church cemetery are the graves of Rob Roy MacGregor, his wife Helen and two of their sons, reminding us of their unusually happy endings after long lives. The outlaw hero and his family were made internationally famous by Walter Scott in his novel *Rob Roy* (1817).

48. Inveraray: The Neil Munro monument is in Glen Aray, just north of the town. Munro was born in Inveraray and his birthplace, Crombie's Land, now

known as Para Handy Cottage, has a plaque on the wall. His novels describe this part of Scotland, while his short stories, including the most-loved tales about Para Handy and the crew of the *Vital Spark*, give a vivid impression of Scotland's west coast and southern Highlands. Munro's comedy in the Para Handy stories is a counterpoint to his novels, where there is a tragic sense of the social changes thrust upon the Highlanders, which Munro knew at first hand. This pessimistic vision is close to that of his friend Joseph Conrad.

49. Loch Katrine and the Trossachs: This is the terrain of Walter Scott's narrative poem, *The Lady of the Lake* (1810), arguably the work which initiated literary tourism in the 19th century. A new edition with detailed map, notes and introduction was published by the Association for Scottish Literary Studies. Jules Verne was one of the tourists who came to the area in 1859, writing a travel memoir *Backwards to Britain* (English translation, 1992) and two astonishing novels set in Scotland, *The Underground City* (1877) and *The Green Ray* (1882). See Ian Thompson's *Jules Verne's Scotland in Fact and Fiction* (2011).

50. Lake of Menteith: Nearby Gartmore was the home of R.B. Cunninghame Graham and there is a memorial sculpture for him there. He and his wife Gabriella are buried in the ruins of Inchmahome Priory, on the island of Inchmahome, which can be reached across the Lake of Menteith by a small ferryboat. A commemorative plaque is in the ferry terminal building. On the island itself, in the priory, on the wall beside his wife's grave, Cunninghame Graham had a memorial placed, on which is the quotation, 'Los muertos abren los ojos a los que viven': an ambiguous phrase, meaning both, 'The dead open the eyes of those who live' and also, 'The dead open *their* eyes *on* those who live.' This was used as an epigraph by Hugh MacDiarmid to his short poem, 'Perfect' which adapts and combines lines from a short story by the Welsh writer Glyn Jones, and from the biography of Cunninghame Graham by A.F. Tschiffely which quotes the Spanish phrase, and also from a guide book to the western islands of Scotland by Seton Gordon: it is as if the significant images and oblique meaning in the poem come up onto the page through multiple layers of textual source material. The dead open their eyes on us – and open our own eyes as well.

51. Aberfoyle: The grave of the local minister Robert Kirk, author of *The Secret Commonwealth of Elves, Fauns and Fairies* (1691), is marked here but said to be empty, as he was spirited away to the underworld beneath the nearby Doon Hill, at the summit of which a strange tree in a clearing creates a peculiarly spooky aura. Walter Scott talks about Kirk's book in his *Letters on Demonology and Witchcraft* (1830) and James Robertson, in the novel *The Testament of*

Gideon Mack (2006) has more than one reference to Kirk and the mysterious underworld to which Kirk seems to have been sensitive.

52. Stirling: Writers who would have frequented Stirling Castle in the 15th and 16th centuries include William Dunbar and Sir David Lyndsay and the music of Scotland's greatest composer Robert Carver would have been heard in its halls. Burns was a later visitor who deplored the mess Stirling Castle had been left in after the departure of the Stuart dynasty in his poem 'Lines on Stirling': 'A Race outlandish fill their throne; / An idiot race, to honour lost; / Who know them best despise them most.' Just outside of Stirling stands the imposing Wallace Monument. The story of William Wallace, the Guardian of Scotland, was given racy literary treatment by Blind Harry in *The Wallace* (c.1477) and has exerted a profound influence on many writers over a long time, from Robert Burns in his reading of an 18th-century version of the poem, to Sydney Goodsir Smith's play *The Wallace* (1960) and Mel Gibson's film *Braveheart* (1995). The essential anthology opening doors to the poems and stories, the paintings and sculptures relating to Wallace that can be seen in numerous places in Scotland, is *The Wallace Muse: Poems and Artworks inspired by the Life and Legend of William Wallace*, edited by Lesley Duncan and Elspeth King (2005). Nearby, just west of Stirling, is Bannockburn, site of the most famous battle in Scottish history, in 1314, the culminating point of the Scottish Wars of Independence and the climax of John Barbour's poem, *The Bruce* (c.1376).

53. Killearn: The poet, playwright, historian and humanist scholar George Buchanan was born at The Moss, Killearn, and an obelisk at the centre of the village is dedicated to him.

54. Inversnaid: This was the scene of Wordsworth's poem 'To a Highland Girl' (1803) and of Gerard Manley Hopkins's poem 'Inversnaid' (1881) which describes the waterfall by the lochside, 'This darksome burn, horseback brown, / His rollrock highroad roaring down,' and ends in eternal praise of the uncultivated world: 'Long live the weeds and the wilderness yet.' Nearby, Rowardennan was the scene of the parting between Rob Roy and Bailie Nicol Jarvie, respectively representative characters of the Highlands and Lowlands, but also first cousins and therefore symbolic of the connectedness of all Scotland, in Walter Scott's novel *Rob Roy*.

55. Carradale House and Gardens, Kintyre: This was the home of the novelist, poet and political activist Naomi Mitchison. In the immediate aftermath of the Second World War, she campaigned tirelessly for better communal resources in the Highlands and Islands, novelising her own work in *Lobsters on the*

Agenda (1952) and describing her own family history in the novel *The Bull Calves* (1947).

The Kingdom of Fife

56. St Andrews: Britain's third oldest university has the whole of the historic town as its campus, 'a place eminently adapted to study and education' according to Dr Johnson. Notable alumni have included the poets William Dunbar, Gavin Douglas, Sir David Lyndsay, George Buchanan, James Graham Marquis of Montrose and Robert Fergusson. Another of its distinguished graduates, the folklore scholar Andrew Lang celebrated in nostalgic verse 'a little city worn and grey' and less solemnly the rigours of its golf links. He is buried among the graves surrounding the ruins of the cathedral. In the mid-1930s, St Andrews was a central location for the writers associated with the Scottish Literary Renaissance: James H. Whyte, a wealthy American who edited the key periodical of the time, *The Modern Scot*, owned and ran the Abbey Bookshop at 3 South Street and an art gallery in the former coastguard building at 5–11 North Street. Around this time, the composer F.G. Scott, poet Edwin Muir and his wife the novelist Willa Muir, art critic and cultural historian John Tonge and Hugh MacDiarmid, were intermittently residents of St Andrews. In the late 20th and early 21st centuries, a cluster of poets was centred at the university, including John Burnside, Robert Crawford, Douglas Dunn, Kathleen Jamie and Don Paterson.

57. Cupar: This is where the great play *Ane Satyre of the Thrie Estaits* (1552) by Sir David Lyndsay was first performed in its full-length version, over the course of an entire June day. The corner of Crossgate and Bonnygate was where the medieval market was held and nearby Castle Hill was where the play was put on.

58. Falkland Palace: Built in the early 16th century, Falkland Palace, with its gardens and surrounding medieval village, was the home of generations of Stewart kings and is associated with the playwright and poet Sir David Lyndsay.

59. Dunfermline: Abbot House Heritage Centre has particular connections with William Dunbar and Robert Henryson: both may have read their poems within these walls. Henryson may also have been a schoolmaster in Dunfermline Grammar School and was associated with the Benedictine Dunfermline Abbey.

60. Forth Bridges: The bridges across the Firth of Forth just north of Edinburgh

are spectacular to look at or to use, either by car or train. The train bridge features memorably in film adaptations of John Buchan's novel *The Thirty-Nine Steps* (1915), and, in a nightmare amalgamation of mechanical structure and unpredictable imagination, it forms the world of most of Iain Banks's novel *The Bridge* (1986). Head north-east along the coast and you'll reach Kinghorn, where a monument below the cliff marks the spot where King Alexander III is thought to have fallen to his death in 1286, prompting one of the oldest poems in Scots, recorded in the *Orygynale Cronykil of Scotland* by Andrew of Wyntoun: 'Quhen Alexander our kynge was dede'. Alexander's death left the kingdom leaderless and vulnerable, thus precipitating the conflicts that would lead to the Wars of Independence.

Edinburgh and the Lothians

61. Aberlady Bay, East Lothian: There is a monument here to the popular and prolific novelist Nigel Tranter, from whose novels many Scots learned their own history because for generations, Scottish history, literature and culture formed almost no part of the curriculum provision in Scottish schools. Tranter walked around the bay, composing his novels. The best of them include *Druid Sacrifice* (1993), *Columba* (1990), *The Bruce Trilogy: The Steps to the Empty Throne* (1969), *The Path of the Hero King* (1970) and *The Price of the King's Peace* (1971), *The Young Montrose* (1972) and *Montrose: The Captain General* (1973).

62. Edinburgh: Perhaps the essential Edinburgh novel is Muriel Spark's *The Prime of Miss Jean Brodie* (1961), which manages both to capture the hypocrisy, pretentiousness and potential for radicalism, and also to deploy a devastating and merciless sense of humour, all of which are essential aspects of Edinburgh's character. Some would say that Irvine Welsh's *Trainspotting* (1993) is closer to the reality of Edinburgh, or that Ian Rankin's Rebus crime novels show the city in its turn-of-the-century era and you can walk through Fleshmarket Close, the title of one of his novels, and see his handprint (next to that of J.K. Rowling) outside the City Chambers. Edinburgh's history has room for each of these visions, the genteel Brodie crème de la crème, the addicts of Leith, the underworld of Rankin, and many others too. Whatever your preference, Edinburgh is a literary centre, designated the first UNESCO City of Literature in 2004, home to the annual International Book Festival, and with its own Makar, or resident poet. Homes of authors include: 8 Howard Place, birthplace of Robert Louis Stevenson, and 17 Heriot Row, the Stevenson family home; 25 Drummond Place, home of Sydney Goodsir Smith; 4 Nelson Street, home of Robert Garioch; 39 Castle Street, home of Walter Scott; 160 Bruntsfield Place, birthplace of Muriel Spark;

and 7 Leamington Terrace, home of Norman MacCaig.

In the old town, the Royal Mile runs from the Castle down to the new Parliament Building and Holyrood Palace. The whole area is redolent with literary associations and there are various literary and other tours of the area, one atmospherically described in James Robertson's novel *The Fanatic* (2000). The entrance to the Castle is guarded by statues of William Wallace and Robert the Bruce, each respectively the hero of epic poems by Blind Harry and John Barbour. At the north-east corner of the Castle esplanade are the Outlook Tower, with the Camera Obscura and Ramsay Gardens: this was the home of Allan Ramsay in the 18th century and of Patrick Geddes in the 19th century. To your left as you go downhill, in Lady Stair's Close, is Lady Stair's House and the Writers' Museum, devoted mainly to the lives and works of Robert Burns, Walter Scott and Robert Louis Stevenson. Outside in the courtyard, named the Makars' Court, are memorial slabs with quotations from many Scottish writers. Just off the Royal Mile on George IV Bridge is the National Library of Scotland, which houses the John Murray Archive and puts on regular exhibitions of literary works and manuscripts. Opposite is the Central Library, with its Edinburgh Room and Scottish section, and just down the road is The Elephant House, a restaurant said to be one of the locations where J.K. Rowling began imagining and writing the internationally best-selling *Harry Potter* novels. Further along the road is Greyfriars Kirk where you can find the grave of the great Gaelic poet Duncan Ban MacIntyre. A small statue of Greyfriars Bobby, a wee dog renowned for its extraordinary loyalty, and the subject of children's novels by Lavinia Derwent (in 1985) and Eleanor Atkinson (in 1912) is in the street near the entrance to the cemetery. Back on the Mile, heading downhill, on your right is the High Kirk of St Giles, where there is a plaque for Gavin Douglas, who was Provost here in 1501, a plaque for Robert Fergusson, whose poem 'Auld Reekie' (the name for Edinburgh evoking its smokiness), and memorial windows to Burns and Stevenson. Beside the Kirk, cobblestones in the shape of a heart mark the site where the Heart of Midlothian, the name for Edinburgh's Old Tolbooth prison (Edinburgh's Bastille), once stood. It features centrally in Walter Scott's novel of that name. Behind the Kirk is Parliament House, where Scott and Stevenson both practised as advocates. Still further downhill on your left, is John Knox's House and the Scottish Storytelling Centre. Further down, still on your left, is Canongate Kirk, in which is the memorial stone for Robert Fergusson, commissioned by Robert Burns, and the grave of Robert Burns's Clarinda, Mrs Agnes MacLehose. Outside the cemetery, at the entrance gates on the Royal Mile, is a statue of Fergusson by David Annand. He is striding downhill as if heading towards The Scottish Poetry Library, which is across the road, in Crichton's Close. This is a major resource and a wonderful place to visit. And if you proceed to the new parliament building, ask there for a copy of the poem Edwin Morgan was commissioned to write for the occasion of its opening, which describes the building and itemises what is required by the people from our political representatives. Finally, you will see, brooding over Holyrood palace and parliament, the extinct volcano of Arthur's Seat on the summit of which, in a blue haze, the title character in James Hogg's novel *Confessions of a Justified Sinner* (1824) encountered his fearsome satanic doppelgänger.

Over on the other side of Princes Street Gardens, the New Town of Edinburgh is a creation of the Enlightenment. Go to George Meikle Kemp's spaceship-shaped monument to Walter Scott on Princes Street first, with John Steell's white Carrara marble statue of the writer, completed in 1844. This is the biggest monument to a writer anywhere in the world, populated with statues of characters from Walter Scott's novels. From the top, the view is panoramic. In the New Town, the Scottish National Portrait Gallery, on Queen Street, exhibits numerous portraits of great Scottish writers, including the iconic *Poets' Pub* by Alexander Moffat, with its group portrait of the major Scottish poets of the 20th century: Hugh MacDiarmid, Sorley MacLean, Norman MacCaig, Robert Garioch, Sydney Goodsir Smith, George Mackay Brown and Edwin Morgan. Many of them frequented Rose Street, the 'amber mile' of pubs running parallel to Princes Street. Poets, writers, intellectuals and artists of all kinds met in numerous pubs throughout the 1950s and 1960s, especially Milne's Bar, the Abbotsford and the Café Royal. The poets talking and drinking are accurately described in poems by Sydney Goodsir Smith, in *Kynd Kittocks's Land* (1965), and by George Mackay Brown, in his elegiac poem 'Norman MacCaig'. At the top of Leith Walk, commemorating Arthur Conan Doyle and his birthplace nearby, there is The Conan Doyle pub. If you proceed downhill into Leith itself, you'll find yourself in Irvine Welsh territory. Other pubs with particular literary associations in Edinburgh include Rutherford's, on Drummond Street in the Old Town, a dark pub familiar to Robert Louis Stevenson; Sandy Bell's Bar, Forrest Road, also in the Old Town, described in the novel *The Myrtle and Ivy* (1967) by Stuart MacGregor, the centre of the folk music revival and a regular watering-hole for poet and archivist Hamish Henderson. At 8 Young Street, The Oxford Bar, is a pub favoured by Ian Rankin, author of a series of popular police-crime novels with the central character John Rebus. Another popular phenomenon was the episodic novel *44 Scotland Street* (2004) by Alexander McCall Smith, first serialised in *The Scotsman* newspaper, about the inhabitants of a New Town tenement flat. This was followed by a series of novels, also set in Edinburgh, starting with *The Sunday Philosophy Club* (2004). On the outskirts of Edinburgh, at South Queensferry, is The Hawes Inn, described in Robert Louis Stevenson's *Kidnapped*. By the side of the main road running through Corstorphine is a large statue by Alexander Stoddart of Alan Breck Stewart and David Balfour, from *Kidnapped* and at Cramond, Cramond House may have been the model for the House of Shaws in *Kidnapped*.

63. Rosslyn Chapel: If you have read Dan Brown's tiresomely page-turning best-selling novel *The Da Vinci Code* (2003), this is an important destination for you. Of course, there is a lot more to it than that – but you'll have to find out for yourself what that might be.

64. Hawthornden Castle: Home of William Drummond, poet, who was visited here by London-based playwright and poet Ben Jonson in 1618. Jonson considered himself a Scot through ancestry at least, and the relation between Scottish identity and the gravitational attraction of London as location (for Jonson) and of the English language as poetic idiom (for Drummond) is a fascinating study. Their conversations are wonderful (though some say they are apocryphal). The Castle is built on a 15th-century ruin, with a 17th-century addition, and has been restored as a writer's retreat. There are older, man-made caves in the rock beneath the castle, where Robert the Bruce and before him, William Wallace, are said to have found shelter.

Glasgow and the Clyde Valley

65. Renton and Balloch: Cameron House Hotel, Balloch was formerly the home of novelist and poet Tobias Smollett and the Smollett Monument is a Tuscan Column in Renton, near Balloch.

66. Greenock: The house where the poet W.S. Graham was born at 1 Hope Street has a plaque on the wall, and above the industrial town is Loch Thom, which Graham describes in his unforgettable poem of that name, a haunting reflection on the fragility of memory and mortality. Then it goes beyond that literal location to deliver a universal, shiveringly accurate sense of human isolation and the trust we place in language to try to help each other.

In his shrewdly entertaining novels of small town society John Galt drew on his own experiences of life in Greenock and, further down the coast, Irvine. Greenock's riverside esplanade displays a Galt memorial fountain and he is buried in a local graveyard. Among his *Tales of the West* are *Annals of the Parish, The Provost, The Entail* and the *The Steamboat*.

Edwin Muir, in the novel *Poor Tom* (1932), George Blake, Alan Sharp and the dramatists Bill Bryden and Peter McDougall have all written powerfully about aspects of the growth and decay of Greenock as an industrial community.

67. Paisley: Among the many writers resident in Paisley, due west of Glasgow and south of the Clyde, Robert Tannahill, a younger contemporary of Burns,

wrote popular vernacular songs. He has a statue in the grounds of Paisley Abbey, and his cottage and grave are conserved. The direct descendant of his younger brother was the poet, translator and protest-song writer Andrew Tannahill, a friend and contemporary of Hugh MacDiarmid, who inherited the same tradition of Burns, and was equally a visionary of social justice. The same legacy informs many of the poets collected in the anthology *Radical Renfrew* (1990) edited by Tom Leonard, and the work of younger writers from the area such as Graham Fulton.

68. Glasgow: Perhaps the most essential novels set in Glasgow are Archie Hind's *The Dear Greeen Place* (1966) and Alasdair Gray's *Lanark* (1981), but the city is steeped in literary associations. The Cathedral was where Glasgow began, when the city was called Cathures, which is the name Edwin Morgan took as the title of a 2002 book of poems written while he was Poet Laureate of Glasgow. The Cathedral is described in Walter Scott's *Rob Roy*. The Necropolis, beside the Cathedral, is the Victorian cemetery, the city of the dead. Among its literary residents are William Miller, author of the nursery rhyme, 'Wee Willie Winkie'. The whole place features memorably at the end of Gray's *Lanark*.

South of the Cathedral, in the Merchant City, on the wall of a building in Candleriggs, is a plaque commemorating the Communist teacher John MacLean, whose life inspired tributes in poems and songs by Hugh MacDiarmid, Sorley MacLean, Hamish Henderson, Edwin Morgan, Andrew Tannahill, and many others, collected in *Homage to John MacLean*, edited by T.S. Law and Thurso Berwick (1973). In the pavement here, outside the Concert Hall and the Scottish Music Centre, engraved in the paving stones just along from this plaque, are four poems by Edwin Morgan commemorating the fruit and vegetable market that used to be located here and the people who lived and worked here. South and west, Cathkin Braes and Rutherglen were Morgan's earliest favoured territories: his first book of poems was *The Vision of Cathkin Braes* (1952). The East End of the city of Glasgow was traditionally working-class, homeland for the city's industrial poor. Robin Jenkins's novel *A Very Scotch Affair* (1968) is largely set in Bridgeton, regarded by some of the characters as a 'ghetto', Jenkins's *The Changeling* (1958) explores the tension between working-class and middle-class experience and expectations, between people who live in slums and those who live in more prosperous areas, and the further opposition between city-dwellers and the experience of life in the country.

South of the river, the Gorbals was the scene of perhaps the most famous of all literary depictions of Glasgow, Alexander McArthur and H. Kingsley Long's sensational novel *No Mean City* (1935). The tenement slums have been demolished. Near where they were is the Citizens' Theatre, whose resident company was founded by playwright James Bridie in 1943. The Gorbals was also the home of the fine writer of stories and the novel *Dance of the Apprentices* (1948), Edward Gaitens. Of the trilogy of memoirs by Ralph Glasser, *Growing Up in the Gorbals* (1986), *Gorbals Boy at Oxford* (1988) and *Gorbals Voices, Siren Songs* (1990), the first is a wonderfully evocative, poignant, critically clear-eyed account of childhood in this extraordinary world, while in the second, the distance between poverty and privilege is charted with fierce objectivity and in the third, the character of the place, family, friends and company the author came from, clearly reveals the persistent resources of value it was to him, as well as the oppressions and constraints it put upon him. Edwin Muir's novel *Poor Tom* (1932) is an autobiographical account of poverty-stricken life in the city, carefully plotted and dramatically effective. Returning to the city centre, George Square is populated by statues of Walter Scott, Robert Burns and Thomas Campbell, a Glasgow poet famous for many generations, who wrote critically of the industrial revolution and the pollution that came with it. Numerous writers studied at Glasgow School of Art, an astonishing architectural masterpiece designed by Charles Rennie Mackintosh, including John Byrne, Alasdair Gray, Stephen Mulrine and Liz Lochhead. Near Charing Cross stands the Mitchell Library, the largest public reference library in Europe. Travelling west along Woodlands Road towards Glasgow University, on the south side of Woodlands Road is the statue of Lobey Dosser, Sheriff of Calton Creek, taking his enemy the arch-villain Rank Bajin off to jail, on the back of his trusty two-legged horse El Fideldo. This is the only two-legged equestrian statue in the world, erected by public subscription, suggesting the affection in which Glasgow people continue to hold the creator of these characters, the genius cartoonist Bud Neill. The many writers, either students or teachers or both, associated with Glasgow University, include Robert Henryson, Alasdair mac Mhaighstir Alasdair, Adam Smith, James Boswell, Tobias Smollett, John Veitch, John Buchan, A.J. Cronin, James Bridie, Catherine Carswell, Edwin Morgan, Alexander Scott, Alexander Trocchi, Tom Leonard, Liz Lochhead, Alasdair Gray, James Kelman, Janice Galloway, Christopher Brookmyre, A.L. Kennedy and Louise Welsh. Embedded in the wall of the Randolph Stairwell under the university tower in the main university building, there is a sculpture portrait on a tablet of John Veitch, born in Peebles in 1829, who held the Chair of Logic and Rhetoric at Glasgow University from 1864 till his death in 1894. His border boyhood imbues much of his work as a poet and literary historian and critic, including *Tweed, and other Poems* (1875), *The History and Poetry of the Scottish Border* (1877), *The Feeling for Nature in Scottish Poetry* (1887), *Merlin* (1889) and *Border Essays* (1896). The tablet was created by John Oldrid Scott, son of Sir George Gilbert Scott, the architect of the University's main building. The inscription at its base reads: 'Through mystery to mystery, from God and to God.'

69. Dunsyre: At Stonypath, in Lanarkshire, 'Little Sparta' was the name Ian Hamilton Finlay gave to the garden and Temple to the Muses which he designed with his wife Sue, beginning in 1966. The gardens are intimately structured with neoclassical, subversively political sculptures and architectural works, as weaving paths take the visitor to unexpected views and unpredicted ways of seeing and reinterpreting the pastoral world and the violence in nature and mankind. Fairytales, myths and historical references populate the tranquillity of the rural setting with sharp-edged, subtle implications and provocations.

70. Biggar: Brownsbank Cottage, originally a farmworker's small, two-room house, was the home of Hugh MacDiarmid (Chris Grieve) and his wife Valda, from 1951 till their deaths, in 1978 and 1989, respectively. Here MacDiarmid was visited by Allen Ginsberg, Yevgeny Yevtushenko and other international literary luminaries. At first without running water or indoor plumbing, the ditches were dug with help from the actor Alex McCrindle, who went on to play General Dodonna in *Star Wars* (1977) and first uttered the words, 'May the force be with you!' The cottage is preserved in much the same condition as it was left, with MacDiarmid's collection of detective novels and Valda's native Cornwall memorabilia in their respective rooms and may be visited by appointment through Biggar Museum.

71. Mearnskirk: on the corner of the old Glasgow-Ayr high road, an obelisk stands commemorating the poet Robert Pollok (1798–1827), which notes: 'He soared untrodden heights / And seemed at home.' He was an immensely popular poet with his ten-volume epic, *The Course of Time* (1837) and his *Tales of the Covenanters* (posthumously published in 1895) was also widely read. If you're interested in poets who have fallen from contemporary vogue, Pollok is an intriguing figure. His manuscripts are held in Glasgow University's Special Collections department and, in his day, his major poem was likened to Milton.

72. Leadhills: Allan Ramsay, poet, anthologist and playwright, was born here and founded The Miners' Library in 1741. Rare books, 18th-century mining documents and local records are preserved here.

Ayrshire and Arran

73. Isle of Arran: Burns never described the view from Ayrshire of the Isle of Arran, with its striking mountainous skyline, but its landscape and natural resources had been celebrated as early as the 12th century in a lovely anonymous Gaelic lyric which ends, 'Arran is always delightful.' The island is rich in literary associations, from the tales of the Fianna, the ancient Celtic warrior band led by Finn MacCoul and his son, Ossian the bard, to the modern plays and poems

of Robert MacLellan, who also wrote the best introductory guide-book to the island. Arran is also the main location for the cult supernatural thriller *Deadlight* (1968) by Archie Roy.

74. Loudoun Hill: This is a striking visual landmark, imposing on the flat landscape on the edge of Ayrshire and Lanarkshire, looming like a sleeping lion. Loudoun Hill was the location of various battles, most memorably those described by John Barbour in *The Bruce* (c.1375), Blind Harry in *The Wallace* (c.1477), and Walter Scott in *Old Mortality* (1816). It is the focal point of Alan Riach's poem, 'At Loudoun Hill' in *This Folding Map* (1990), also in *Dream State: The New Scottish Poets*, edited by Donny O'Rourke (1994; revised edition 2001).

75. Irvine: Birthplace of novelist John Galt (1779–1839). A plaque on the wall of the building in Irvine High Street commemorates him. See also Greenock. Galt's immediate contemporary, also born at Irvine in 1779, John Allan, was the future foster father of Edgar Allan Poe. He emigrated, leaving for the United States in 1795, returning to Britain in 1815 with his adopted son. Poe went to school at the Irvine Parish Kirk Academy. It is said that the schoolmaster sent the young writer out to the local graveyard to practice his handwriting by copying inscriptions from the headstones.

76. Kilmarnock: The Kay Park Burns Monument and Museum is an arts venue for poetry and literary readings and entertaining educational lectures with a landmark statue of Robert Burns by W.G. Stevenson and a copy of the first edition of Burns's poems, the Kilmarnock Edition, on display with other manuscripts and related material. Kilmarnock is also fictionalised as Graithnock in novels by William McIlvanney, most vividly in the classic *Docherty* (1975) and the third of the Laidlaw trilogy, *Strange Loyalties* (1991).

77. Tarbolton: At Tarbolton is the Bachelors' Club, a 17th-century house at 28 Croft Street, where, in 1779, Burns learned to dance and play the fiddle. Burns and his friends met here regularly after establishing a literary and debating society, the Bachelors' Club, in 1780. He was initiated as a Freemason here in 1781. Period furniture helps convey a physical sense of what the domestic space Burns inhabited as a young man was like.

78. Alloway: The Robert Burns trail begins here, where he was born in 1759 in Burns Cottage, which was built by his father and was his home until 1766. The nearby Birthplace Museum houses numerous manuscripts, books and memorabilia. His father is buried in the cemetery of the Auld Kirk, the scene of the witches' dance in 'Tam o' Shanter', from which Tam gallops down to

the bridge over the river Doon, the original Brig o' Doon, to escape from the murderous 'hellish legion' who cannot cross running water. A marvellous sequence of paintings of 'Tam o' Shanter' by Alexander Goudie, that give full expression to both the comic and horrific aspects of the poem and its vertiginous speed, may be seen in Rozelle House Art Gallery nearby.

79. Kirkoswald: A few miles away, in the village of Kirkoswald, is Souter Johnnie's House, home of one of the characters named in the poem, the Souter or shoemaker. Many other models for Burns's characters and people Burns knew are buried in Kirkoswald cemetery.

80. Mauchline: On the upper floor of the Burns House is the room Burns took for Jean Armour in 1788 and there are various items of Burnsiana in the museum. Mauchline Kirkyard was the scene of the riotous poem, 'The Holy Fair' and many of Burns's friends and contemporaries are buried here, alongside four of his daughters. Nearby, Poosie Nancy's Tavern was the scene of his most anarchic song-sequence, 'Love and Liberty: A Cantata', also known as 'The Jolly Beggars'.

81. Ochiltree: This is the birthplace of novelist George Douglas Brown, author of the novel *The House with the Green Shutters* (1901), a tragedy of small-town Scottish commercial ambition causing family destruction in domestic slaughter of Greek proportion. His birthplace is marked with a plaque in Ochiltree main street, on a steeply sloping hill with broad views over the Ayrshire countryside beyond. George Douglas Brown is buried in Ayr cemetery.

82. Auchinleck: Auchinleck House was built in the late 1700s, a classical-style mansion based on designs by Robert Adam, one of Scotland's most famous architects, and remained for generations in the Boswell family, being owned by his father when the writer James Boswell lived here. When Boswell brought Dr Samuel Johnson to visit his father here, after their tour of the Hebrides in 1773, the Englishman famously argued over politics with Lord Auchinleck in the library. Boswell records that the house was host to much 'social glee'. A Boswell Book Festival at Auchinleck was launched in 2011.

Dumfries and Galloway

83. Thornhill: Closeburn is where The Crichope Linn ravine can be visited, following a signpost up a path on the road to the left of the main Thornhill to Dumfries road, just south of Thornhill. The ravine was described by Walter Scott in *Old Mortality*, in the climactic fight between the moderate hero Morton and the fanatic villain Balfour of Burley. Robert Burns also visited the nearby Closeburn Tower.

84. Irongray: In the cemetery of the church in the small village of Irongray lies the gravestone of Helen Walker, the original upon whom Walter Scott based his character Jeanie Deans, in *The Heart of Midlothian* (1818). Jeanie is one of the great women in fiction, refusing to lie to save her innocent sister Effie from the sentence of execution for murdering her own child, and choosing instead to walk barefoot to London to seek a pardon, which is delivered in the nick of time. The composer Hamish MacCunn's opera *Jeanie Deans* is based on Scott's novel.

85. Dumfries: Just north of Dumfries is Ellisland Farm: Robert Burns moved here in 1788 and one sunny afternoon, walking here on the banks of the River Nith, he composed the poem 'Tam o' Shanter' in a delighted spell of inspiration, before going indoors in the feverish grip of his imagination to commit it to paper in one sitting. Burns moved to Dumfries in 1791 to work as an Exciseman and died here in 1796, his widow Jean Armour staying on in their house till her death in 1834. Furniture he used may be seen in a favourite pub, The Globe Inn, and, if you're lucky, you may be invited to sit in the chair he is said to have sat in himself, but only if you recite a poem by heart while sitting there. The Robert Burns Centre is a film theatre and arts venue with regular poetry readings and the nearby Burns House contains relics and memorabilia. Burns was buried in St Michael's Churchyard but in 1815 his remains were relocated to the Mausoleum.

Also in Dumfries is Moat Brae, a Georgian mansion once owned by the Gordon family, where J.M. Barrie played as a little boy in the 1870s, and whose garden, he said, was 'enchanted land' in which he first imagined the adventures of Peter Pan. Its contours, trees, little twisting paths and angled slopes lean down towards the riverbank and, if you use your imagination, 'Neverland' is not far away.

86. Langholm: On Whita Hill is the Hugh MacDiarmid Monument by Jake Harvey, and MacDiarmid (C.M. Grieve) and his wife Valda are buried in Langholm cemetery. This beautiful little Borders town, the hills around and the rivers that run to a confluence in it, the Wauchope, the Esk and the Ewes, were the poet's childhood world. The composer F.G. Scott, a Hawick man, taught him at Langholm school; the post office building housed the Telford library he read his way through as a boy; and there is a 'Hugh MacDiarmid Walk' through the town. As a young man, he believed he could tell precisely where he was in Langholm simply from the sound of the running waters of the rivers. The road sign as you drive in says, not 'Welcome to...' but 'Here comes Langholm! Birthplace of Hugh MacDiarmid!' – a slogan devised by the local schoolchildren. Langholm features lovingly in many of MacDiarmid's poems, short stories, sketches and the essay, 'My Native Place' and in his autobiography, *Lucky Poet* (1943), where he recounts some outrageous goings-on at his school.

87. Ecclefechan: Here is the birthplace of Thomas Carlyle, a small stone house which effectively displays the humble conditions from which the high moral judgements of the mature Carlyle were developed. In his essays, such as 'Signs of the Times' and his classic satirical work, *Sartor Resartus* (1836) or, 'the Tailor Reclothed', he cuts through the hypocrisies of conventional Victorian society in heavy, self-consciously convoluted prose that was a significant influence on Herman Melville and many others. Latterly, Carlyle's opinions became increasingly inclined to brutal authoritarianism and racism but he remains one of the great Victorian sages, alongside Matthew Arnold, J.S. Mill and John Ruskin.

88. Ruthwell: At Ruthwell Church is the 18-foot high 8th-century Ruthwell Cross, on which runic characters and fragments of words from the anonymous ancient poem, 'The Dream of the Rood' are carved.

89. The Brow Well: This is where Robert Burns regularly immersed himself in cold water in the mistaken belief that it might improve his health not long before he died in 1796.

90. Wigtownshire: At St Medans is the Gavin Maxwell Monument, a fine sculpture of an otter in memory of Mij as decribed in Maxwell's popular work *Ring of Bright Water* (1960). Maxwell grew up in the village of Elrig, described in his autobiography, *The House of Elrig* (1965). In Wigtown, a pub on the main square is named after the sensational novel by Ian Niall (John McNeillie), *Wigtown Ploughman* (1939), whose *A Galloway Childhood* (1939), by contrast, is a fondly remembered, dreamlike, autobiography. Nearby, the Rhinns of Galloway are the location for James Barke's Tolstoyan classic of the lives of rural farmworkers, *The Land of The Leal* (1939). Barke's most famous works are a series of novels based on the life of Robert Burns, and their sequel, about Burns's widow Jean Armour. They remain popular, stylistically lucid and swift.

The Borders

91. Ednam: James Thomson, author of perhaps the most influential book of poems in the early 18th century, *The Seasons* (and of the song, 'Rule Britannia'), was born in the Old Manse at Ednam and is commemorated by the James Thomson obelisk, outside Kelso on the Ednam road. Another monument to Thomson, the Temple of the Muses, is on Bass Hill next the suspension bridge.

92. Flodden, Northumberland, England: 'The Flowers of the Forest' is an old tune traditionally associated with the Battle of Flodden in 1513, when James IV of Scotland, who had ruled his flourishing Renaissance court for ten years,

led his soldiers to destruction in 'Brankstone's deidly barrow' but it resonates through the Jacobite risings of the 18th century and the oppression of the Highlanders in the 19th century, the imperial violence of that and the 20th century and all the wars that are still with us. Words to the song were written and published in 1776 by Jean Elliot, who is buried in Bedrule kirkyard, near Jedburgh, in the Borders. Lewis Grassic Gibbon, at the end of his novel *Sunset Song*, insisted that words and music be printed as a lament for those killed in the First World War. You can go to the scene of the battle today, where there is a battlefield trail with interpretive boards, and the smallest visitor centre in the world, in a red telephone box in the village of Branxton. The Flodden Monument, erected in 1910, is approached from the village by the road past St Paul's Church, where an arch of the medieval church remains, set into the Victorian structure, dating from 1849. This is where James IV's body and many of the bodies of the men of his army were taken after the battle.

93. Selkirk: Walter Scott was the Sheriff of Selkirkshire and he worked regularly at the Selkirk Courthouse from 1800 to 1832. There is a statue of Scott in the market-square and at the far end of the High Street, another statue of the explorer of Africa, Mungo Park, whose *Travels in the Interior Districts of Africa: Performed in the Years 1795, 1796, and 1797* (1800) tell of his experience there. *Niger: The Life of Mungo Park* (1934) by Lewis Grassic Gibbon (James Leslie Mitchell) includes vivid scenes of Park's meeting and friendship with Scott.

94. Melrose: Melrose Abbey was founded in 1136 and partially rebuilt in 1385. It features vividly in Canto 2 of Walter Scott's poem *The Lay of the Last Minstrel*: 'If thou wouldst view fair Melrose aright, / Go visit it by the pale moonlight…' Rising beside Melrose are the Eildon Hills, where the Eildon Tree Stone marks the spot where Thomas the Rhymer is said to have been carried off by the Queen of Elfland, to spend years as if they were hours in the land of the ever-young. The wizard Michael Scott created the three Eildon hills by splitting them out of one hill with a fantastical spell described by James Hogg in his phantasmagorical novel *The Three Perils of Man* (1822). Rich in ballad, folklore and literary references, the Eildon Hills are also known as the location under which King Arthur and the Knights of the Round Table are currently resting. On the hill above Melrose is Scott's View: This is a picture-postcard prospect overlooking the bending River Tweed and the Eildon Hills, reputedly Scott's favourite panorama. Nearby at Bemersyde is an imposing red sandstone statue of William Wallace by John Smith of Darnick, commissioned by the Earl of Buchan and unveiled in 1814. Just outside of Melrose is Abbotsford, Scott's home, built between 1817 and 1822, which houses a magnificently curious

collection of historic relics gathered by Scott himself, from the outer doorlocks and door of the Heart of Midlothian (Edinburgh's famous jail, like the Paris Bastille, and the title of one of his greatest novels) to items from the battlefield of Waterloo. Armouries of guns and swords, a vast library of around 9,000 books, his writing desk and the little alcove in which he conducted private conversations: all give a palpable sense of Scott the man and the writer. He died here in 1832, on a warm, sunny afternoon, with all the windows open and hearing the sound of the nearby River Tweed. Nearby are the beautiful ruins of Dryburgh Abbey, in which are the graves of Scott, his wife Charlotte and son-in-law, John Gibson Lockhart.

95. Galashiels: There is a statue here of a Border Reiver, a man on horseback, with helmet and lance. This is a war memorial to borderers who lost their lives in the world wars of the 20th century, but it links them back to their ancestors, who rode across the Debatable Lands, raiding for sheep, cattle and other ready plunder. They have been described by the novelist George MacDonald Fraser historically in *The Steel Bonnets* (1971) and in fiction in his short, darkly evocative novel, *The Candlemass Road* (1993). Another novel evocative of their time and ethos, is *The Hanging Tree* (1990) by Allan Massie. But you should roam around in the anonymous Ballads themselves, each one like the last act of a Jacobean tragedy.

96. Innerleithen: *St Ronan's Well* is the title of a novel by Walter Scott, which appears to be a domestic comedy of manners, very much in the style of Jane Austen (with a constrained cast of characters, including a wonderful portrait of an innkeeper) but which deepens and darkens and moves into a far more dramatic and politically agitated arena than anything in Austen, climaxing in sudden and violent death in an open-air duel. The wells can be visited and the little town itself is unpretentious and enjoyable.

97. Peebles: The John Buchan Centre, in the Chambers Institution on the High Street, houses a collection of memorabilia, books, clothes, manuscripts and film posters relating to John Buchan and his sister Anna Buchan (O. Douglas), a prolific novelist whose first book, *Olivia in India* (1912) was followed by numerous others and whose memoir of her brother *Unforgettable, Unforgotten* (1945) is lucid, affectionate and revealing. Nearby, Traquair House is reputedly the oldest continuously-inhabited house in Scotland, dating from the 10th century, visited by numerous kings and queens including Mary Queen of Scots. This is said to be the model for the House of Tully-Veolan in Walter Scott's first novel, *Waverley*. The famous Bear-Gates were closed in 1746 after the disastrous conclusion of the Jacobite Rising of 1745 led by Prince Charles

Edward Stuart, and were promised not to be re-opened until the Stuarts ascend the throne once again. However, Grandtully Castle, Perthshire, also has a claim to be the model for Tully-Veolan.

98. St Mary's Loch: On the shore of the loch is Tibbie Shiel's Inn. By the roadside above is an imposing statue of James Hogg, the Ettrick Shepherd, seated and looking out over the loch and down to the Inn, where he and many friends once gathered for long, convivial conversations. They were great folk for binges of drink, food and conversation. The surrounding area by Yarrow Water is James Hogg territory, a constant presence in numerous novels, songs and poems, including *The Brownie of Bodsbeck* (1818), *The Three Perils of Man* (1822) and 'Kilmeny'. Hogg is buried in Ettrick Kirkyard.

99. Drumelzier: At the corner where the Powsail Burn runs into the River Tweed, the ancient bard Merlin is said to be buried. *Merlin* (1889) by the literary historian John Veitch includes poems describing the area. The Merlin of the title poem is the 6th-century Merlin Caledonius, otherwise known as Merlin Wylt or Merlin Silvestris (Merlin of the Woods), presumably a different character from the 5th-century Myrdin Emrys of Arthurian legend, who is associated with Snowdon in Wales. Of these two, 11th-century and later writers made the third figure, Merlin the Magician, a conflation of the Arthurian figure, who is said to have visited St Mungo in Glasgow and at Dumbarton Rock, and the historical Scottish poet, Merlin, whose life is described in Geoffrey of Monmouth's 12th-century *Vita Merlini*. There is a bewitching aura to the place that conflates history and myth. Strange things can happen here. One such event is described in Alan Riach's poem 'Drumelzier' in *Homecoming* (2009).

100. Smailholm Tower is a striking Border keep, a look-out tower commanding a bleak and forbidding panoramic vista. Nearby is Sandyknowe Farm, where Walter Scott, when he was a wee boy, lived with his uncle and aunt to recover from illness, and where tales and songs of the Borders were poured into his imagination and happily fermented for years to come.

101. In the public park of the Borders town of Duns, there is a memorial statue by F. Tritschier, unveiled in 1966 for the 700th anniversary of the birth of the philosopher Duns Scotus (1266–1308).

Further reading

Further discussion of the relation between Scottish literature and music is in John Purser, *Scotland's Music: A History of the Traditional and Classical Music of Scotland from Early Times to the Present Day* (revised edition, 2007). Scottish literature also comes well within the provenance of Duncan MacMillan, *Scottish Art: 1460–2000* (new edition, 2000) and Murdo Macdonald, *Scottish Art* (2000). Further discussion of the relation between Scottish poetry and painting, especially in the 20th century, is in *Arts of Resistance: Poets, Portraits and Landscapes of Modern Scotland* by Alexander Moffat and Alan Riach (2008). Revitalising consideration of some aspects of Anglophone Scottish literature in the 17th century in the context of the Anglophone literature of Ireland, Wales and England, is in John Kerrigan, *Archipelagic English: Literature, History, and Politics 1603–1707* (2008). Contextualising aspects of Scottish literature in the islands and coastal territories of the country runs throughout the series of journals *Archipelago*, 1–12 (2007–2019), edited by Andrew McNeillie, a selection from which is in *Archipelago: A Reader*, edited by Fiona Stafford and Nicholas Allen published by the Lilliput Press.

There are now a number of histories of Scottish literature. Extensive, balanced and even-handed coverage is in Roderick Watson, *The Literature of Scotland* (two volumes, 2007); argumentatively engaged readings are in Marshall Walker, *Scottish Literature Since 1707* (1996), Alan Riach, *Representing Scotland in Literature, Iconography and Popular Culture* (2005) and Douglas Gifford et al, *Scottish Literature* (2006); and wide-ranging, specialist scholarly expertise is paramount in the three-volume *Edinburgh History of Scottish Literature* published under the general editorship of Ian Brown (2007). There are many others to roam around in, each with its own merits and character. Older works are not necessarily superseded by newer ones.

A select bibliography of histories of Scottish literature

Blackie, John Stuart. *The Language and Literature of the Scottish Highlands* (Edinburgh: Edmonston and Douglas, 1876)

Brown, Ian (general editor). Clancy, Thomas Owen, Manning, Susan and Pittock, Murray (co-editors). *The Edinburgh History of Scottish Literature, Volume 1: From Columba to the Union, Volume 2: Enlightenment, Britain and Empire: 1707–1918, Volume 3: Modern Transformations: New Identities (from 1918)* (Edinburgh University Press, 2007)

Carruthers, Gerard. *Scottish Literature* (Edinburgh University Press, 2009)

Carruthers Gerard and MacIlvanney, Liam (editors). *The Cambridge Companion to Scottish Literature* (Cambridge University Press, 2012)

Craig, Cairns general editor; R.D.S. Jack, Andrew Hook, Douglas Gifford, co-editors. *The History of Scottish Literature Volume 1: Origins to 1660, Volume 2: 1660–1800, Volume 3: Nineteenth Century, Volume 4: Twentieth Century* (Aberdeen University Press, 1987–1988)

Crawford, Robert. *Scotland's Books: A History of Scottish Literature* (Harmondsworth: Penguin Books, 2007)

David, Craig *Scottish Literature and the Scottish People 1680–1830* (London: Chatto & Windus, 1961)

Fazzini, Marco (editor). *Alba Literaria: A History of Scottish Literature*, (Venice: Amos Edizione, 2005)

Gifford, Douglas, Dunnigan, Sarah and MacGillivray, Alan (editors). *Scottish Literature in English and Scots* (Edinburgh University Press, 2002)

Gifford, Douglas and McMillan, Dorothy (editors). *A History of Scottish Women's Writing*, (Edinburgh University Press, 1997)

Glen, Duncan. *Scottish Literature: A New History from 1299 to 1999* (Kirkcaldy: Akros Publications, 1999)

Gray, Alasdair. *A Short Survey of Classic Scottish Writing* (Edinburgh: Canongate, 2001)

Henderson, T.F. *Scottish Vernacular Literature: A Succinct History* (London: John Grant, 1910)

Korzeniowska, Aniela.*Translating Scotland: Nation and Identity* (Warsaw: University of Warsaw, 2008)

Lindsay, Maurice .*History of Scottish Literature* (London: Robert Hale, 1977)

MacLean, Magnus *The Literature of the Highlands* (1904; new edition, 1925)

MacNeill, Nigel (edited with additional chapter by John MacMaster Campbell).

The Literature of the Highlanders: Race, Language, Literature, Poetry and Music (Stirling: Eneas Mackay, 1892, second edition 1929)

Millar, John Hepburn. *A Literary History of Scotland* (London: T. Fisher Unwin, 1903)

Riach, Alan. *What Is Scottish Literature?* (Glasgow: Association for Scottish Literary Studies, 2008 [available as free PDF download])

Ross, John Merry. *Scottish History and Literature to the Period of the Reformation* (Glasgow: J. MacLehose & Sons, 1884)

Sassi, Carla. *Why Scottish Literature Matters* (Edinburgh: The Saltire Society, 2005)

Smith, G. Gregory. *Scottish Literature: Character & Influence* (London: David Nutt, 1896)

Smith, Sydney Goodsir. *A Short Introduction to Scottish Literature* (Edinburgh: Serif Books, 1951)

Speirs, John. *The Scots Literary Tradition: An Essay in Criticism* (London: Faber and Faber, 1940)

Thomson, Derick. *An Introduction to Gaelic Poetry* (London: Victor Gollancz, 1974)

Walker, Hugh. *Three Centuries of Scottish Literature* (London: Macmillan, 1893)

Walker, Marshall. *Scottish Literature since 1707* (London and New York: Longman, 1996)

Watson, Roderick. *The Literature of Scotland* (London: Macmillan, 1984)

Watson, Roderick. *The Literature of Scotland: Volume 1: The Middle Ages to the Nineteenth Century, The Literature of Scotland: Volume 2: The Twentieth Century* (London: Palgrave Macmillan, 2007)

Wittig, Kurt. *The Scottish Tradition in Literature* (Edinburgh: Oliver & Boyd, 1958)

Wood, H. Harvey *Scottish Literature* (London: Longmans, Green and Co., 1952)

Scottish Plays and Theatre History

Reassessment of the whole historical archive of Scottish drama has been so significant since the 1990s this subject warrants a reading list of its own.

Brown, Ian. *Scottish Theatre: Diversity, Language, Continuity* (Amsterdam-New York: Rodopi, 2013)

Brown, Ian. *History as Theatrical Metaphor: History, Myth and National Identities in Modern Scottish Drama* (London: Palgrave Macmillan, 2016)

Campbell, Donald. *Playing for Scotland: A History of the Scottish Stage 1715-1965* (Edinburgh: Mercat Press, 1996)

Findlay, Bill (editor) *A History of Scottish Theatre* (Edinburgh: Polygon, 1998)
Hutchison, David. *The Modern Scottish Theatre* (Glasgow: The Molendinar Press, 1977)
McMillan, Joyce. (editor Howard, Philip) *Theatre in Scotland: A Field of Dreams: Reviews*, (London: Nick Hern Books, 2016)
Reid, Trish.*Theatre & Scotland* (Houndmills: Palgrave Macmillan, 2013)
Smith, Donald et al. *The Scottish Stage: A National Theatre Company for Scotland* (Edinburgh: Candlemaker Press, 1994)
Stevenson, Randall and Wallace, Gavin (editors). *Scottish Theatre since the Seventies* (Edinburgh: Edinburgh University Press, 1996)

Edinburgh and International Companions to Scottish Literature

Under the general editorship of Ian Brown and Thomas Clancy, the Companions to Scottish Literature series was published first by Edinburgh University Press, then by the Association for Scottish Literary Studies. Rather than list them here by date of publication, I have ordered them according to (1) generic or historical studies and (2) studies of authors according to birthdate.

Genres and Periods

Scottish Traditional Literatures (eds. Sarah Dunnigan and Suzanne Gilbert, EUP, 2013)
Scottish Poetry (ed. Carla Sassi, Scottish Literature International, 2015)
Scottish Drama (ed. Ian Brown, 2011)
Scottish Women's Writing (ed. Glenda Norquay, 2012)
Scottish Literature 1400–1650 (ed. Nicola Royan, ASLS, 2018)
Scottish Romanticism (ed. Murray Pittock, 2011)
Twentieth-Century Scottish Literature (eds. Ian Brown, Alan Riach, ASLS, 2009)
Contemporary Scottish Poetry (eds. Matt McGuire and Colin Nicholson, EUP, 2009)

Authors

James Macpherson and the Poems of Ossian, ed. Dafydd Moore, ASLS, 2017)
Robert Burns (ed. Gerard Carruthers, EUP, 2009)
James Hogg (eds. Ian Duncan and Douglas S. Mack, EUP, 2012)
Sir Walter Scott (ed. Fiona Robertson, EUP, 2012)
John Galt (eds. Gerard Carruthers and Colin Kidd, ASLS, 2017)
Robert Louis Stevenson (ed. Penny Fielding, EUP, 2010)
Hugh MacDiarmid (eds. Scott Lyall and Margery Palmer McCulloch, EUP, 2011)

Lewis Grassic Gibbon (ed. Scott Lyall, ASLS, 2015)
Muriel Spark (eds. Michael Gardiner and Willy Maley, EUP 2010)
Edwin Morgan (ed. Alan Riach, ASLS, 2015)
Liz Lochhead (ed. Anne Varty, EUP, 2013)
James Kelman (ed Scott Hames, EUP 2010)
Irvine Welsh (ed. Berthold Schoene, EUP, 2010)

The Association for Scottish Literary Studies (ASLS) publishes many books and notes to assist the teaching of Scottish literature in schools and internationally. These range from short, accessible, detailed guides to individual authors and works in the 'Scotnotes' series, to specific teachers' notes with classroom applications, CD recordings of writers with commentaries, as well as scholarly annotated volumes of primary texts and an annual anthology of new writing from Scotland. The ASLS international committee has correspondents from Beijing to Boston. Check out the website at: http://www.asls.org.uk/

Endnote

Let me close this book with a short quotation from a visitor to Scotland, the Nigerian writer Ben Okri, who wrote this for the 'Diary' column of the periodical, *The New Statesman*, on 8 August 1986:

> It is another country. The air is sharper. The hills, stark in their solidity, sheer out in the lights. It is a country in which history breathes from the landscapes. My first impression of Edinburgh was of staircases which seemed to have been carved on boulders and cobbled streets which reminded me of courtyards in Paris and the South of France. It is a city of the imagination in which dwelled another city of frustrated yearnings... It is the only city I know where the old resides so solidly in the new, where the music of the place blasts out its ancient lore amid the living spaces of the inhabitants. Culture, during a time of political impotence, can become kitsch, but it can also function as continual declaration and resistance.

And even during times of political confidence, confirmation and self-determination, the work of culture, the arts and literature, continues to sensitise us to the world, to deliver news of permanent value, and to keep lively a constant and healthy resistance to all that would diminish the wealth of our complexity and purpose.

Acknowledgements

A GREAT DEAL of this book was first published in different form as essays in *The National*, the only daily newspaper in Scotland to support independence. I began writing for the paper in January 2016. I am lastingly grateful to its editor Callum Baird and deputy editors Roxanne Sorooshian and Jane Cassidy who saw most of them into print, to all the editorial team, and to the good readers whose comments have been so encouraging. I am very grateful to the close readers who criticised, prompted revisions and saved me from worse errors than those that remain, which are of course my own. I am especially grateful to Ronald Black, Ian Brown, Andrew McNeillie, John Purser, Ronald Renton, Fiona Paterson, Jamie Reid-Baxter, Theo van Heijnsbergen, Jennie Renton, Maddie Mankey, Kira Dowie and Eilidh MacLennan, and to my publisher, Gavin MacDougall.

Some passages in the essay on the Industrial Revolution are adapted from what I wrote in 'The Literature of Industrialisation' in *The Edinburgh History of Scottish Literature, Volume 2: Enlightenment, Britain and Empire (1707–1918)*, edited by Susan Manning (2007); some passages in the section on Robert Louis Stevenson are adapted from my essay 'Teaching Stevenson in the Creative Writing Class' in *Approaches to Teaching Robert Louis Stevenson*, edited by Caroline McCracken-Flesher (2011).

Many of the ideas and propositions I put forward in this book were devised through working in the Department of Scottish Literature at Glasgow University and I am grateful to my colleagues and to my students in the years since I started work there, on 1 January 2001.

This book was prompted by Paul Henderson Scott and the Saltire Society after an event at the Edinburgh International Book Festival one night in August 2005. I am so glad to have finally been able to make good on my promise to deliver it.

Index of author names

A

Abildgaard, Nicolai 226
Achebe, Chinua 392, 444, 579
Adam, Helen 634, 665
Adam, Henry 532
Adam, Robert 624, 703
Adomnán 30, 65, 66, 654, 683, 690
Aeschylus 180, 236
Aesop 118, 129, 655
Agate, James 325
Alexander, Michael 35, 36
Alexander, Mike 334
Alexander, William (c.1567–1640) 133, 656
Alexander, William (c.1826–94) 78, 330, 661
Allan, David 275
Allan, Dot 301, 347, 350, 664
Allan, John 702
Allan, Mea 665
Amis, Kingsley 478
Anderson, Alexander 330
Anderson, W.E.K. 278, 330, 386, 405
Aneirin 63, 654
Angus, Marion 162, 338, 343, 344, 356, 369, 409, 587, 589, 590, 662, 686
Annand, David 245, 687, 696
Anouilh, Jean 549
Apollinaire, Guillaume 422
Aquinas, Thomas 70, 71
Archer, William 325, 326
Arendt, Hannah 89
Ariosto, Ludovico 166
Aristophanes 527
Armour, Jean 703, 704, 705
Armstrong, Johnny 171
Arne, Thomas 236, 258
Arnold, Andrea 620
Arnold, Matthew 33, 304, 336, 683, 705
Arnott, Peter 530, 535, 536, 592
Ascherson, Neal 626, 627, 667
Astaire, Fred 432
Atwood, Margaret 511
Austen, Jane 37, 93, 270, 290, 300, 301, 579, 707

B

Baillie, Joanna 82, 298, 301, 363, 364, 365, 659
Ballantyne, James 276
Ballantyne, R.M. 338, 339, 598, 661
Balliol, John 79, 103, 345
Bamforth, Iain 568, 669
Banks, Iain (also Iain M. Banks) 269, 320, 500, 505, 506, 507, 508, 596, 600, 604, 633, 669, 695
Bannatyne, George 649, 650, 656
Bannerman, Helen 410, 662
Barbour, John 106, 108, 109, 585, 588, 655, 685, 693, 696, 702
Barclay, John 656
Barke, James 350, 471, 486, 664, 705
Barker, Elspeth 487
Barker, George 34
Barnett, T. Ratcliffe 633
Barr, John 327, 661
Barrie, J.M. 82, 338, 340, 341, 342, 343, 363, 364, 365, 662, 686, 704
Barrow, G.W.S. 78, 110
Barthes, Roland 474
Bartók, Béla 384
Bass, Charles 363
Baston, Robert 107, 108, 109, 112, 654
Bateman, Meg 52, 100, 159, 188, 359, 461, 561, 563, 564, 568, 669, 685
Bawcutt, Priscilla 127
Baxter, James K. 634
Bean, Alexander ('Sawney') 340
Beaton, Cardinal David 136
Beattie, George 660
Beaufort, Joan 113
Beckett, Samuel 286, 287, 367, 430, 473, 545, 601
Beethoven, Ludwig van 23, 198, 606
Bell, Andrew 199
Bell, Archibald 199
Bell, Barbara 288
Bell, Ian 297
Belli, Giuseppe 422
Belsches, Williamina 275
Benjamin, Walter 42, 89, 90, 91, 92, 93, 94, 203, 238, 320

Bennett, Margot 665
Bergengruen, Werner 382
Berlioz, Hector 288
Bermant, Chaim 667
Bernard (Abbot of Arbroath) 655
Bernstein, Marion 661
Berry, Chuck 563
Betty, William Henry West 239
Beveridge, Craig 626
Bicket, Linden 447, 613
Birt, John 618
Bissett, Alan 521, 610
Black, D.M. 668
Black, Ronald (Raghnall MacilleDhuibh) 52, 54, 55, 185, 192, 194, 195, 210, 212, 358, 491, 493, 497, 629, 651
Black, William 661, 690
Blackadder, Elizabeth 516
Blackie, John Stuart 64, 196, 332, 660
Blackwood McEwen, John 173
Blair, Duncan (An t-Urr. Donnchadh Blàrach) 312
Blair, Hugh 275, 659
Blair, Kirstie 339
Blair, Robert 658
Blair, Tony 618
Blake, George 338, 347, 350, 664, 698
Blake, William 328, 596, 605
Blane, Neil 617
Blind Harry 108, 257, 585, 655, 659, 693, 696, 702
Blok, Alexander 429
Bloom, Harold 485, 645
Boccaccio, Giovanni 269, 270, 410
Boece, Hector (Boethius) 145
Bogart, Humphrey 452
Bold, Alan 615
Boleyn, Anne 148
Bone, David W. 663
Borges, Jorge Luis 495, 666
Bosch, Hieronymus 534
Boswell, Alexander (Lord Auchinleck) 703
Boswell, James 35, 199, 608, 629, 645, 659, 684, 700, 703
Bottomley, Gordon 367
Boudicca 517
Bouok, William 232
Bower, Walter 107, 145, 655
Bowie, David 602

Bowman, Martin 530
Boyd, Mark Alexander 87, 158, 163, 165, 168, 656
Boyd, William 445, 488
Brandane, John (Dr John McIntyre) 367, 414
Braque, Georges 124
Brathwaite, Edward Kamau 635, 636
Brecht, Bertolt 82, 137, 312, 530, 605, 651
Bremner, Billy 624
Breslin, Theresa 598, 614
Brewer, Gordon 651
Bridie, James (Osborne Henry Mavor) 82, 369, 409, 413–415, 416, 463, 527, 663, 689
Britten, Benjamin 580
Broadie, Alexander 200, 203, 626
Broch, Hermann 386, 487
Brockie, Ian 306
Brontë, Charlotte 534
Brontë, Emily 534, 651
Brookmyre, Christopher 597, 691, 700
Broun, Dauvit 110
Brown, George Douglas (Kennedy King) 317, 345, 412, 471, 636, 663, 703
Brown, George Mackay 72, 73, 80, 88, 159, 448–451, 457, 474, 554, 558, 561, 587, 613, 620, 636, 666, 678, 679, 680, 697
Brown, Gordon 38
Brown, Ian 83, 336, 464, 465, 530, 535, 536, 542, 709
Brown, John 305
Browning, Robert 330
Bruce, George 665
Bruce, Robert 79, 103, 256
Bruckner, Anton 401
Brunton, Mary 298, 301
Brutus, Dennis 579
Bryden, Bill 248, 464, 528, 698
Buchan, Anna (O. Douglas) 347, 349, 707
Buchan, John 272, 293, 331, 347, 477, 478, 488, 489, 500, 583, 590, 596, 599, 663, 691, 695, 700, 707
Buchan, Norman 595
Buchan, Tom 466, 566, 667
Buchanan, Dugald (Dùghall Bochanan) 217, 218, 658
Buchanan, George 30, 83, 133, 145, 146, 152, 153, 156, 421, 422, 655, 693, 694

INDEX OF AUTHOR NAMES

Buchanan, Robert 330, 630, 661, 689
Bulter, Rhoda 678
Bunting, Basil 345
Bur, Alexander 683
Burel, John 133
Burgess, J.J. Haldane 662
Burke, Gregory 535, 537, 592
Burns, Elizabeth 561, 568, 669
Burns, John 486
Burns, Robert 25, 39, 87, 173, 199, 213, 245, 247, 249–257, 258, 275, 299, 350, 385, 410, 527, 630, 645, 659, 663, 665, 693, 700, 702, 703, 704, 705
Burnside, John 567, 669, 688, 694
Burt, Edward 629
Butlin, Ron 566, 668
Byrne, John 80, 464, 530, 621, 668, 700
Byrne, Michel 434,
Byron, George Gordon (Lord Byron) 22, 249, 258, 259, 260, 261, 262, 267, 277, 367, 406, 445, 477, 478, 646, 652, 660, 684, 685

C

Cadell, F.C.B. 65
Caesar, Julius 133, 223, 513, 656
Caimbeul, Alasdair 497
Caimbeul, Tormod 495, 499
Cairns, Gerard 543
Calder, Angus 18, 44, 283, 421, 589, 605, 626
Calder, George 332
Calder, Jenni 392
Calgacus 57, 60, 585
Calvino, Italo 495
Campbell, Alexander 311, 630
Campbell, Angus Peter (Aonghas Pàdraig Caimbeul) 359, 459, 490, 495, 498, 499, 569, 669
Campbell, Catherine 346
Campbell, Catriona Lexy (Catrìona Lexy Chaimbeul) 524
Campbell, Colin 312
Campbell, Donald 464, 528, 668
Campbell, James 311, 633, 669
Campbell, Marion 100
Campbell, Myles (Maoilios Caimbeul) 668
Campbell, Roy 610
Campbell, Thomas 327, 660, 700

Canmore, Malcolm (Malcolm III) 15, 103, 584
Cannon, Andy 465
Carlyle, Thomas 197, 267, 304, 305, 306, 307, 308, 324, 646, 660, 683, 705
Carmichael, Alexander (Alasdair Gilleasbaig MacGille Mhìcheil) 185, 357, 358, 661
Carmichael, John (Earl of Hyndford) 650
Carmichael, William 650
Carnegie, Andrew 536
Carpentier, Charlotte 276
Carrell, Christopher 449
Carruth, Jim 566
Carson, Ciaran 52
Carstairs, Christian 231, 242–244
Carswell, Catherine 299, 301, 308, 349, 369, 409, 410–411, 587, 663, 700
Carswell, Donald 410
Carswell, John (Séon Carsuel) 100, 490, 656
Cartimandua 517
Carver, Robert 86, 128, 132, 554, 619, 668, 693
Casanova, Giacomo 323, 502
Caughie, John 620
Chandler, Raymond 477, 478, 600
Chaplin, Charlie 453
Charteris, Robert 159
Chaucer, Geoffrey 59, 114, 120, 121, 122, 123, 131, 269, 270, 574, 581
Chekhov, Anton 44, 465, 549
Chisholm, Erik 229, 230, 369, 384, 409
Chisholm, William 683
Chomsky, Noam 132
Christianson, Aileen 412
Churchill, Winston 325
Clancy, Thomas Owen 61, 64, 542, 654
Clare, John 259, 634
Clarkson, Tim 57
Clark, Thomas A. 568
Clark, William 232
Cleland, William 657
Clifford, John / Jo 539
Cockburn, Henry (Lord Cockburn) 298, 302, 660
Cocker, W.D. 590
Cocteau, Jean 465, 534, 549
Cocteau Twins, The 196
Coetzee, J.M. 579

Cohen, A.P. 18
Coleridge, Samuel Taylor 198, 227, 251, 297
Coles, Cecil 330
Colquhoun, Donald 365
Colvin, Calum 226
Colvin, Sidney 322
Common, Thomas 324, 326
Congreve, William 83
Connolly, Billy 466
Connolly, James 333
Conn, Stewart 80, 464, 528, 553, 554, 619, 667
Conrad, Joseph 35, 290, 316, 343, 348, 352, 353, 354, 474, 479, 482, 579, 641, 692
Conran, Anthony 40
Constable, John 371
Corbett, John 142, 144
Corcoran, Neil 36
Corkery, Daniel 635
Corneille, Pierre 83, 146
Corrie, Joe 369, 413, 415, 416, 664
Corson, James C. 292
Cowan, Edward J. 78
Craig, Cairns 626, 627
Cranmer, Thomas (Archbishop of Canterbury) 148
Crawford, Robert 146, 149, 150, 152, 154, 155, 239, 567, 669, 688, 694
Crawfurd, Helen 333
Cregeen, Eric 311
Crichton, James 179, 341, 364, 686, 696
Crockett, S.R. 317, 323, 338, 340, 341, 342, 343, 349, 351, 662
Crofton Croker, Thomas 54
Cromwell, Oliver 232, 305, 480
Cronin, A.J. 350, 351, 700
Crosbie, William 425
Crozier, William 369, 409
Cruickshank, Helen Burness 162, 409, 608, 663, 686
Cumberland, Duke of ('Butcher' Cumberland, William Augustus) 264, 265, 683
Cumming, Mark 306
Cummings, E.E. 21
Cunningham, Allan 87, 259
Cunninghame Graham, R.B. 339, 348, 352, 353, 354, 389, 662, 692

Curle, Richard 663
Currie, Nick (Momus) 602
Cutler, Ivor 666
Czerkawska, Catherine Lucy 535, 619

D
Dabydeen, David 579
Daiches, David 665
Daiches, Alan 685
Dalí, Salvador 242
Damian, John (Damian Damiani) 612
Darwin, Charles 613
Davenport, Guy 21
Davidson, John 87, 267, 317, 328, 329, 330, 589, 646, 662
Davie, Donald 291
Davie, Elspeth 301, 487, 666
Davie, George 156, 572, 607
Davies, Peter Maxwell 680
Deane, Seamus 36
de Bergerac, Cyrano 503, 534
De Blácam, Aodh 52
Debussy, Claude 337
de Cagniol, Marie 154
de Cervantes, Miguel 180, 264, 280, 323, 490, 651, 658
Defoe, Daniel 628, 629
Deighton, Len 386
Delaney, Frank 52, 633
Deleuze, Gilles 71
de Linton, Bernard 109
De Luca, Christine 569, 587
de Luzarches, Robert 222
Democritus 417
de Montaigne, Michel 145
Dench, Judi 366
de Quincey, Thomas 298
de Rostand, Edmond 534
Derwent, Lavinia (Elizabeth Dodd) 599, 696
Dickens, Charles 37, 50, 290, 307, 315, 469, 579, 688
Dickinson, Emily 50
Dillon, Des 615
Di Mambro, Ann Marie 535, 668
di Prima, Diane 89
Dixie, Florence Caroline 322, 326, 662
Döblin, Alfred 487
Docherty, Thomas 627
Dolan, Chris 535, 619

Dollan, Agnes 333
Donald son of Finlay of the Poems (Dòmhnall mac Fhionnlaigh nan Dàn), 87, 183, 656
Donaldson, William 330
Donizetti, Gaetano 287
Donne, John 579
Donn, Rob (Rob Donn MacAoidh) 189, 218, 219, 220
Donovan, Anne 575, 669
Dorn, Edward 24, 71, 162, 194, 245, 563, 622, 632
Dos Passos, John 589
Dostoevsky, Fyodor 346, 605
Douglas, Archibald A.H. 112
Douglas, Bill 667
Douglas, Gavin 29, 87, 114, 128–132, 135, 137, 153, 197, 574, 612, 655, 687, 694, 696
Douglas, Joe 529
Douglas, Norman 355, 585, 646, 662
Douglass, Frederick 642, 661
Doyle, Arthur Conan 39, 326, 327, 331, 478, 662, 697
Doyle, Roddy 601, 602
Drake, Francis 258
Drummond de Andrade, Carlos 634
Drummond, William of Hawthornden 153, 154, 168–170, 174, 656, 698
Dryden, John 156
Duffy, Carol Ann 159, 444, 568, 669
Dunbar, William 39, 59, 86, 87, 98, 103, 114, 124–127, 128, 131, 132, 135, 137, 160, 176, 242, 250, 345, 384, 421, 553, 573, 574, 581, 583, 587, 596, 609, 611, 612, 645, 646, 649, 655, 693, 694
Duncan, A.A.M. 112
Duncan, Jane (Elizabeth Jane Cameron) 665
Duncan, John 45, 226
Duncan, Lesley 566, 693
Dundas, Henry 23
Dunn, Catriona 546
Dunn, Douglas 36, 247, 557, 575, 668, 688, 694
Dunnett, Dorothy 596, 666
Dylan, Bob 173, 563
Dymock, Emma 499, 541, 592

E
Eadie, Douglas 333, 688
Eastwood, Clint 293
Eatough, Graham 539
Edmonds, Rosemary 502
Edward I 103, 104
Eliot, George 37, 50, 290, 315, 381, 382, 445, 503, 579, 651
Eliot, T.S. 33, 39, 84, 241, 289, 324, 328, 362, 380, 386, 400, 425, 426, 588, 684
Elliot, Jean 87, 394, 658, 706
Eriugena, Johannes Scotus 69
Erlendsson, Magnus 679
Erskine, David Stuart (Earl of Buchan) 706
Erskine, Ruaraidh of Marr 490, 543
Euripides 146, 180, 236, 367, 531, 560
Evanovich, Janet 600
Evans, B. Ifor 489
Evaristi, Marcella 535, 669
Eveling, Stanley 528
Eyre-Todd, George 324, 326, 631, 662

F
Falconer, William 660
Faulkner, William 24
Faust, Johann 321, 422, 534
Fellows, Gerrie 561, 569, 669
Ferguson, Adam 28, 202, 275, 658
Ferguson, J.A. 365
Ferguson, Samuel 52
Fergusson, Christiana 217, 683
Fergusson, J.D. 45, 63, 124, 125, 380, 641, 663
Fergusson, Robert 25, 39, 87, 213, 220, 245–248, 249, 251, 422, 602, 659, 694, 696
Ferrier, Susan 298, 299, 300, 301, 349, 660
Findlater, Jane 349
Findlater, Mary 349
Findlay, Bill 530
Finlay, Ian Hamilton 152, 248, 533, 566, 666, 701
Fischer, Bram 392
Fisher, Gregor 144
Fitt, Matthew 485, 598, 670, 688
Fitzgerald, F. Scott 578
Flaubert, Gustave 289, 290, 651
Fleming, Ian 331, 476, 477, 585, 596, 664
Fleming, Mary 134

Fleming, Tom 144, 527, 529
Fletcher, Andrew (of Saltoun) 197, 480, 657, 659
Fonda, Henry 82
Forbes, William (of Pitsligo) 233, 276
Ford, James Allan 666
Ford, John 293
Ford, P.I. 146
Forgaill, Dallán 66
Forna, Aminatta 521, 670
Forrest, Edwin 239
Forrest-Thomson, Veronica 562, 563, 634, 668
Forsyth, Bill 620
Fowler, William 163, 165, 656
Fowlis, Julie 196, 596
Francis of Valois 150
Franco, Francisco 610
Franklin, Benjamin 201
Fraser, Bashabi 561, 566, 575, 669, 688
Fraser, George MacDonald 602, 707
Fraser, G.S. 84, 433, 592
Fraser, Olive 665
Fraser, Simon of Lovat 343
Frater, Anne (Anna) 159, 359, 461, 670
Frazer, J.G. 324, 326, 391, 609, 662
Freud, Sigmund 271, 369, 563
Frew, Dallas 399
Friel, Brian 45, 542
Friel, George 469, 472, 665
Frye, Northrop 29
Fulton, Graham 569, 667, 669, 699

G
Gade, Niels 229
Gairn, Louisa M. 587
Gaitens, Edward 350, 664, 700
Gallacher, Tom 528
Galloway, Alan 654
Galloway, Fergus 654
Galloway, Janice 301, 349, 505, 507, 669
Galsworthy, John 389, 549
Galt, John 293-297, 315, 398, 646, 660, 685, 698, 702
Gandhi, Mahatma 326
Garden, Mary 337
Gardiner, Michael 447
Garioch, Robert 88, 146, 147, 148, 159, 247, 421, 422, 423, 425, 427, 433, 439, 561, 587, 592, 665, 695, 697
Garrick, David 263
Garry, Flora 664
Gaskill, Howard 230
Gaughan, Dick 252, 395
Geddes, Patrick 321, 409, 587, 650, 696
Geddes, W.D. 158
Gemmill, Archie 624
Genet, Jean 530
Geoffrey of Monmouth 57, 654
George, Stefan 86
Gibbon, Lewis Grassic (James Leslie Mitchell) 24, 28, 34, 39, 80, 93, 247, 316, 369, 394-398, 401, 409, 446, 447, 471, 485, 583, 587, 589, 592, 617, 626, 636, 664, 685, 706
Gibson, Corey 438, 592
Gibson, Mel 37, 585, 693
Gide, André 271, 272
Gifford, Douglas 48, 447, 646, 709
Gillies, Duncan (Donnchadh MacGillìosa) 522
Ginsberg, Allen 473, 701
Giraudoux, Jean 549
Girodet, Anne-Louis 226
Gish, Nancy 35
Gladstone, William Ewart 476
Glasser, Ralph 486, 529, 700
Glenday, John 567, 688
Glen, Duncan 667, 711
Glover, Sue 535, 668
Glover, Thomas 515
Goebbels, Joseph 306, 621
Gogol, Nikolai 23, 530
Goldie, David 589
Golding, Arthur, 129
Golding, William 340, 505, 599
Gordimer, Nadine 579
Gordon, Joe 596
Gordon, Patrick 656
Gorky, Maxim 23, 416
Gorman, Rody 359, 459, 460, 461, 569
Goudie, Alexander 703
Goya, Francisco 198
Graham, James (Marquis of Montrose) 174, 657, 694
Graham, John J. 678
Graham, John of Claverhouse 156
Graham, Laurence I. 678

Graham, W.S. 36, 88, 426, 430, 431, 432, 554, 666, 698
Grahame, Kenneth 599, 662
Grainger, James 634, 658
Gramsci, Antonio 437
Grant, Alexander 79
Grant, Anne 637
Grant, Anne of Laggan 659
Grant, Elizabeth 608, 660
Gray, Alasdair 29, 93, 376, 481, 482, 484, 485, 489, 514, 537, 587, 667, 699, 700
Gray, Alex 616
Greenhorn, Stephen 539
Green, R. 146
Green, Roger Lancelyn 323
Greer, Germaine 159
Gregor, Walter 54
Gregorson Campbell, John 53, 54, 358, 661
Gregory, Augusta (Lady Gregory) 54, 55, 81, 335, 689
Greiffenhagen, Maurice 410
Greig, Andrew 563, 575, 634, 668, 682, 683
Greig, David 530, 535, 538, 539, 563
Grierson, Herbert 306, 425
Grieve, Chris (see also MacDiarmid, Hugh) 369, 376, 412, 428, 664, 678, 686, 701, 704
Grieve, Dorian 380
Grieve, Michael 678
Gunn, George 569, 669
Gunn, Kirsty 520
Gunn, Neil M. 316, 367, 369, 399, 400, 401, 402, 404, 409, 446, 454, 471, 536, 554, 583, 636, 663, 681, 682
Guthrie, Tyrone 529

H
Hadfield, Jen 569, 587
Hadley Williams, Janet 144
Haggard, Henry Rider 323
Hailes, Lord 163
Haldane, A.R.B. 633
Hall, Simon W. 678
Hamilton, Alex 514
Hamilton, David 615
Hamilton, Elizabeth 327
Hamilton, Janet 327
Hamilton, Thomas 660

Hamilton, William of Bangour 658
Hamilton, William of Gilbertfield 257, 586, 588, 659
Hammett, Dashiell 600
Handel, George 263, 264
Hanley, Cliff 595
Hannan, Chris 535, 669
Hardie, Charles Martin 275
Hardie, Keir 332, 353, 373
Hardy, Oliver 619
Hardy, Thomas 286, 471
Harris, Wilson 635, 641, 666
Harrower, David 530, 535
Hart, Francis Russell 307, 308, 340, 341, 342, 347
Harvey, Jake 704
Hauge, Olav H. 667
Hauser, Kaspar 323
Havergal, Giles 468
Hawthorne, Nathaniel 319
Hay, George Campbell (Deòrsa mac Iain Dheòrsa) 84, 88, 152, 346, 359, 362, 426, 430, 432–436, 439, 554, 592, 665
Hay, Ian 663
Hay, John Macdougall 317, 346, 347, 356, 412, 432, 471, 663
Hay, Sheena 346
Haydn, Joseph 198, 258
Haye, Gilbert 655
Haynes, Dorothy K. 487, 666
Hayward, Brian 365
Healy, Thomas 614
Heaney, Marie 52, 223
Heaney, Seamus 35, 36, 37, 52, 376, 471, 635
Hedderwick, Marie 587
Heidegger, Martin 71
Hemingway, Ernest 349, 578
Henderson, George 53
Henderson, Hamish 84, 89, 196, 418, 433, 437–438, 439, 592, 666, 697, 699
Henderson, Jennifer Morag 597
Henderson, Meg 668
Hendry, J.F. 665
Henry de Bohun, Sir 107
Henryson, Robert 39, 87, 98, 103, 114, 118–123, 128, 129, 135, 161, 176, 250, 319, 428, 581, 605, 655, 694, 700
Heraclitus 71

Herbert, W.N. 247, 567, 670, 687, 688
Herdman, John 487, 668
Hesiod 422
Hesketh, Barrie 465
Hesketh, Marianne 465
Heylin, Clinton 173
Hikmet, Nazim 374
Hind, Archie 481, 482, 483, 484, 587, 667, 699
Hitler, Adolf 306, 520
Hogg, James 89, 173, 259, 268–272, 276, 293, 298, 299, 315, 316, 319, 320, 342, 359, 398, 445, 509, 587, 596, 629, 630, 646, 652, 659, 674, 683, 697, 706, 708
Holland, Richard 655
Holmes, Daniel Turner 331, 478, 662
Home, John 82, 223, 231, 237–241, 244, 658
Homer 21, 50, 160, 207, 322, 453
Hood, Stuart 592, 617, 618, 620, 621
Hook, Andrew 235, 239, 240
Hopkins, Anthony 366, 479
Hopkins, Gerard Manley 449 538, 679, 693
Howard, Philip 144
Hugh of Eglinton, Sir (Hucheone of the Awle Royale) 59, 655
Hugo, Victor 291, 302
Hulme, Keri 635
Hume, Alexander 656
Hume, David 28, 197, 199, 200, 201, 202, 203, 237, 238, 658
Hume, Patrick of Polwarth 609
Hume, Tobias 619, 642
Hunter, Andy 171
Hunter, James 192, 332, 634, 637, 682
Hunt, Tristram 501
Hutcheson, Francis 201, 202
Hutchison, David 80, 532, 617
Hutchison, Ken 621
Hutton, James 28, 197, 202, 658
Huxley, Aldous 401

I
Ibsen, Henrik 138, 325, 364, 365, 549
Imlah, Mick 569, 634
Ingres, Jean-Auguste-Dominique 226
Innes, Kirstin 517, 521
Innes, Michael (J.I.M. Stewart) 596
Ionesco, Eugene 473
Irving, Washington 54

J
Jackson, Alan 566, 667
Jackson, Andrew 569, 623, 687
Jackson, Linda 518
Jacob, Arthur 355
Jacob, Violet 87, 162, 369, 352, 355, 369, 409, 587, 589, 590, 662, 686
Jacobs, A.C. 667
James, Henry 35, 39, 290, 309, 316, 318
Jamesone, George 154
Jamie, Kathleen 88, 159, 247, 561, 566, 568, 569, 670, 688, 694
Jamieson, John 199, 659
Jamieson, Robert Alan 569, 575, 669, 678
Jeffares, A. Norman 36
Jeffrey, William 664
Jenkins, Robin 78, 443–444, 445, 447, 536, 613, 616, 665, 699
Jocelyn of Furness 68, 654
John of Fordun 655
John the Baptist 133, 146, 148, 149
Johnson, Edgar 275, 286
Johnson, Samuel 35, 36, 37, 192, 199, 220, 221, 246, 259, 263, 608, 628, 629, 633, 645, 659, 684, 694, 703
Johnston, Duncan (Donnachadh Maclain) 311
Johnston, Henry Erskine 239
Johnston, Paul 596, 598
Johnstone, Arthur 30, 151, 154, 155, 156, 158, 422, 656
Johnstone, Barbara 154
Johnstone, Brian 623, 624
Johnstone, Christian Isobel 306, 660
Johnstone, Iain 465
Johnstone, William 17, 369, 409, 641
Johnstone, William Borthwick 275
Jones, David James ('Gwenallt') 40, 42, 59, 86, 590
Joyce, James 24, 36, 46, 50, 63, 84, 93, 289, 325, 375, 377, 378, 380, 382, 404, 431, 534, 588, 600, 601, 664
Jung, Carl 271

K
Kafka, Franz 93, 386, 469
Kane, David 80
Kant, Immanuel 200, 201
Kapuściński, Ryszard 22

INDEX OF AUTHOR NAMES

Kavanagh, Patrick 471
Kavanagh, Paul 132
Kay, Billy 636
Kay, Jackie 88, 159, 248, 535, 561, 562, 564, 568, 569, 669
Kean, Charles 239
Keats, John 22, 198, 251, 562, 630
Keitel, Harvey 621
Keith, Charles 196, 659
Kelly, Fergus 314
Kelly, Muireann 546
Kelman, James 319, 333, 350, 376, 398, 464, 481, 513, 514, 515, 573, 587, 614, 615, 668, 700
Kemble, John Philip 239
Kemp, Robert 464, 527, 529, 531, 665, 697
Kennaway, James 481, 667, 688
Kennedy, A.L. 301, 349, 500, 503–504, 651, 670, 688, 700
Kennedy, Andrew 553
Kennedy, Calum 685
Kennedy, Walter 98, 609
Kennedy-Fraser, Marjory 662
Kenner, Hugh 652
Kermack, Alison (Alison Flett) 568, 670
Kerouac, Jack 473
Kerrigan, John 709
Kerr, Roderick Watson 591
Kesson, Jessie 469, 470, 472, 619, 665, 683
Kinloch, David 567, 669
Kinsella, Thomas 52
Kipling, Rudyard 326, 477, 579
Kirk, Robert 53, 54, 55, 171, 174, 175
Knowles, Charles (Admiral Knowles) 264, 610
Knox, John 134, 143, 527, 572, 585, 655, 696
Kolson, Rognvald 72
Kuppner, Frank 518, 519, 668
Kurosawa, Akira 60
Kydd, Robbie 636
Kyllour, John 133

L
Laing, R.D. 271, 609, 666
Lamb, William 196, 369, 655
Lamond, Frederic 641
Landseer, Edwin 39
Lang, Alison 524, 526

Lang, Andrew 53, 174, 322, 323, 324, 326, 694
Lang, John 323
Langhorne, John 275
Lauder, Harry 161
Lauder, Thomas Dick 660, 683
Laurel, Stan 619
Law, John 129
Lawrence, D.H. 273, 290, 299, 410, 476, 579
Leacock, Stephen 600, 601
Leask, W.K. 158
Leavis, F.R. 289
le Carré, John 165
le Clerc, Guillaume 654
Lee, Joseph 591, 688
Lehar, Franz 621
Lehrer, Tom 600
Lenin, Vladimir 23, 349, 372, 467
Lennox, Annie 527
Leonard, Tom 248, 327, 376, 514, 557, 558, 559, 613, 668, 699, 700
Leopardi, Giacomo 328
Lermontov, Mikhail 23, 228
Le Roy Ladurie, Emmanuel 536
Leslie, John 145
Lewis, C.S. 117
Lewis, Jeremy 264
Lewis, Saunders 375
Leyden, John 659
Linacre, Thomas 152
Lindsay, Andrew O. 636
Lindsay, David 485, 596, 646, 663
Lindsay, Frederic 597
Lindsay, Jenny 670, 671
Lingard, Joan 301
Linklater, Andro 391
Linklater, Eric 73, 253, 301, 402–408, 475, 587, 589, 602, 626, 664, 678, 679
Linklater, Marjorie 408
Lithgow, William 28, 176, 177, 178, 179, 584, 628, 656
Littlewood, Joan 413, 416, 549
Litvak, Lily 536
Livingston, William (Uilleam MacDhunlèibhe) 311, 334, 660, 682
Livingstone, Duncan (Donnachadh MacDhunléibhe) 357, 360, 361
Livingstone, Lachlan 311

Lochhead, Liz 40, 88, 159, 367, 368, 376, 464, 483, 527, 530, 531, 537, 538, 557, 559, 560, 561, 563, 564, 568, 569, 575, 584, 605, 611, 668, 700
Lockhart, John Gibson 279, 298, 660, 707
Lockhart, R.H. Bruce 608
London, Jack 316, 326, 350
Long, Herbert Kingsley 664
Long, Michael 390
Lorca, Federico García 250, 530, 610
Lorimer, William Laughton 616, 663
Lorne Gillies, Anne 217
Lumet, Sidney 82
Lumsden, Roddy 569, 670
Lyall, Roderick 144
Lynch, Benny 536
Lyndsay, David 80, 82, 133, 135–144, 146, 157, 176, 238, 247, 416, 529, 573, 581, 584, 612, 655, 660, 693, 694

M
Macafee, Caroline 129
MacAlpin, Kenneth 15, 103
MacAonghais, Pòl 495, 545
MacAskill, John 682
MacBeth, George 477
MacBhàtair, Aonghas 492
MacCaig, Norman 30, 86, 88, 152, 159, 190, 191, 192, 196, 202, 421, 422, 423, 424, 430, 439, 470, 491, 558, 561, 587, 604, 610, 634, 665, 681, 682, 683, 696, 697
MacCodrum, Iain (John) 190, 211
MacCoinneach, Uilleam 543
MacColl, Evan (Eòghann MacColla) 313
MacColl, Ewan (James Henry Miller) 369, 413, 415, 416, 418, 549, 665
Mac Colla, Fionn (Tom MacDonald) 51, 404, 405, 406, 454, 613, 636, 664, 681
MacCormick, John (Iain MacCormaic) 543, 545
MacCoul, Finn 50, 183, 687, 690, 691, 702
MacCulloch, John 659
MacCunn, Hamish 28, 288, 289, 337, 349, 704
MacDiarmid, Hugh (Christopher Murray Grieve) 15, 23, 28, 33, 34, 35, 36, 37, 40, 42, 47, 53, 56, 58, 59, 63, 84, 86, 88, 99, 112, 113, 125, 146, 150, 155, 156, 159, 160, 177, 197, 201, 202, 228, 240, 241, 250, 253, 272, 316, 324, 326, 328, 332, 333, 337, 343, 353, 362, 367, 368, 369–382, 383, 384, 385, 386, 388, 389, 391, 397, 399, 401, 404, 407, 409, 410, 411, 412, 416, 421, 425, 426, 427, 428, 431, 432, 438, 440, 441, 473, 478, 480, 488, 490, 509, 534, 558, 561, 563, 565, 567, 568, 569, 577, 583, 587, 589, 592, 593, 596, 602, 607, 608, 610, 613, 623, 624, 626, 632, 637, 641, 646, 649, 650, 664, 678, 679, 686, 687, 689, 692, 694, 697, 699, 701, 704
MacDonald, Alexander (Alasdair MacDhòmhnaill) 312
MacDonald, Alexander (Alasdair mac Mhaighstir Alasdair) 25, 87, 195, 205, 658, 684
Macdonald, Angus 192
MacDonald, Cicely of Keppoch (Sìleas na Ceapaich) 87, 194, 195, 657
MacDonald, Donald (Dòmhnall Ruadh Chorùna) 357, 358
Macdonald, Finlay J. 486, 681
MacDonald, George 307, 324
MacDonald, James 311
MacDonald, James (of Sleat) 211
MacDonald, John 311
MacDonald, John D. 600
MacDonald, John (Iain Dubh mac Iain mhic Aileain) 189, 190
MacDonald, John (Iain MacDhòmhnaill) 183, 184, 657
MacDonald, Keith Norman 196
MacDonald, Lachlan 311
Macdonald, Murdo 709
Macdonald, Norman Malcolm 495
MacDonald, Norman (Tormod Calum Dòmhnallach) 498, 546
Macdonald, Patricia 192
MacDonald, Ramsay 397
MacDonald, Robert David 530
Macdonald, Sharman 535, 668
Macdonell, A.G. 663
MacDougall, Carl 500, 502, 668
MacFadyen, John 312
MacFarlane, Malcolm 313
Macfarlane, Robert 628, 680, 684
Macfarquhar, Colin 199

INDEX OF AUTHOR NAMES

MacFhionnlaigh, Fearghas 359, 459, 668
MacGill, Patrick 349, 663
MacGillivray, James Pittendrigh 369, 662, 684
MacGregor, James 98, 655, 686
MacGregor, Lizzie 589
MacGregor, Stuart 667, 697
Machiavelli, Niccolò 656
Mac'ill'eathain, Donaidh 545
MacInnes, John 192, 311
MacIntyre, Donald 334
MacIntyre, Duncan Ban (Donnchadh Bàn Mac-an-t-Saoir) 25, 40, 48, 87, 155, 189, 205, 213, 259, 332, 334, 586, 605, 658, 691, 696
Macintyre, James (Seumas Mac an t-Saoir) 217, 220, 246, 658
Macintyre, Lorn 465
MacIntyre, Martin (Màrtainn Mac an t-Saoir) 498
MacÌomhair, Dòmhnall Iain 492, 497
MacIver, Donald John (Dòmhnall Iain MacÌomhair) 497
Mackay, Charles 322, 324, 326, 661
Mackay, John Henry 355, 646, 662
Mackay, Mary (Marie Corelli) 324, 325, 326
Mackay, Peter (Pàdraig MacAoidh) 253, 418, 429, 458, 461
Mackenzie, Agnes Mure 59, 110, 112
Mackenzie, Alexander Campbell 641, 661
MacKenzie, Colin (Cailein T MacCoinnich) 493
Mackenzie, Compton 389–391, 470, 602, 613, 626, 643, 646, 663, 681
Mackenzie, Donald W. 311
Mackenzie, George of Rosehaugh ('Bluidy Mackenzie') 657
Mackenzie, George (Seòras MacCoinnich) 194, 195, 688
Mackenzie, Henry 213, 249, 250, 275, 659
Mackenzie, Kenneth (Coinneach) 323
Mackenzie, Simon 544
Mackie, Alastair 666
Mackintosh, Ewart Alan 591
MacLaren, Archibald 274
Maclaren, Ian (John Watson) 317, 338, 340, 341, 662, 687
Maclaren, Pharic 621
MacLaverty, Bernard 488
Maclean, Alasdair 554, 667

MacLean, Alistair 476, 479, 596
Maclean, Calum I. 192, 196
Maclean, John 332, 333, 349, 437, 467, 551, 619, 663, 685, 699
MacLean, Mary (Màiri NicGill-Eathain) 495
Maclean, Norman (Tormod MacGill-Eain) 486, 522, 667
MacLean, Sorley (Somhairle MacGill-Eain) 50, 84, 88, 101, 216, 247, 359, 362, 385, 395, 422, 425–427, 428, 429, 432, 554, 558, 561, 589, 592, 665, 689, 697, 699
MacLellan, William 112, 378
MacLennan, Dolina 334, 596
MacLeod, Alistair 632, 634
MacLeod, Anne 495
MacLeod, Christina (Ciorstai Nicleòid) 357, 361
MacLeod, Donald 310, 660, 681
Macleod, Finlay (Fionnlagh MacLeòid) 545
Macleod, James (Seumas MacLeòid) 491
Macleod, John (Iain M. MacLeòid) 545
Macleod, Joseph (Adam Drinan) 664
MacLeod, Ken 506, 596, 598
Macleod, Mary (Màiri Nighean Alasdair Ruaidh) 183, 185, 187, 188, 197, 657, 681
Macleod, Michelle 541, 542, 544, 545
MacLeod, Norman (of Bernera) 185
MacLeod, Rev Dr Norman 490, 541
MacLeod, Seamus 681
MacLeòid, Iain F. 522
MacMhuirich, Niall 194
MacMillan, Duncan 709
MacMillan, Hector 464, 528, 530
MacMillan, James 229, 384
MacNeacail, Aonghas 359, 459, 499, 553, 554, 555, 556, 668
MacNeice, Louis 36, 632
MacNiven, Charles 311
MacNiven, Duncan 311
MacPhail, Dugald (Dhùgall MacPhàil) 313
Macpherson, Ewan 223
MacPherson, Ian 485, 664
MacPherson, Iain S. 253
Macpherson, James 25, 213, 220, 222–226, 227, 229, 230, 239, 240, 262, 659
MacPherson, John 681
MacPherson, Mary (Màiri Nic a' Phearsain, Màiri Mhòr nan Òran) 87, 310, 324, 326, 332–336, 661, 689

Macpherson, Robin Fulton 667
Macrae, Donald 333
MacWhirter, Iain 617
Maeterlinck, Maurice 336, 337
Main, Alex 399, 682
Mair, John 655
Maitland, William 134
Major, John 506
Malcolm X 112
Mallet (Malloch), David 236, 258, 658
Malveisin, William 654
Mandela, Nelson 438
Manhire, Bill 634
Manning, Susan 542
Manson, John 380, 386
Manson, Peter 569
Marlowe, Christopher 129
Márquez, Gabriel García 495
Marra, Michael 594
Marshall, Bruce 486, 664
Martin, Martin (Màrtainn MacGilleMhàrtain) 189, 192, 629, 657
Martin, Troy Kennedy 80, 248, 416, 620, 667
Martinson, Harry 667
Mary of Guise 135, 137, 143
Mason, Paul 623
Massie, Allan 513, 592, 668, 688, 707
Matheson, Karen 333
Matheson, Kay 596
Maxwell, Douglas 532
Maxwell, Gavin 608, 665, 690, 705
Mayakovsky, Vladimir 374, 439
Mayne, John 327, 659
May, Peter 680
McArthur, Alexander 664, 699
McCabe, Brian 669
McCall Smith, Alexander 597, 697
McCance, William 369
McCarey, Peter 222, 567, 568, 575, 614, 624, 625, 669, 672
McCartney, Nicola 535
McClure, Victor 626
McCrone, Guy 664
McCulloch, Archibald (Gilleasbh MacCuillaich) 543
McDermid, Val 301, 594, 598, 599, 669
McDougall, Peter 621, 698
McEwan, John Blackwood 394, 642

McGonigal, James 442
McGoohan, Patrick 585
McGrath, John 82, 248, 333, 463, 466, 529, 549, 620, 667, 681
McGrath, Tom 528
McGregor, Ewan 473
McIlvanney, Liam 614
McIlvanney, William 350, 575, 587, 597, 667, 702
McKay, John 539
McKenna, Catherine Anne 488
McKim, Anne 112
McLaren, Moray 633
McLean, Linda 535, 670
McLeish, Robert 416
McLellan, Robert 463, 465, 467, 664
McLeod, Wilson 100, 499, 541
McLuhan, Marshall 21
McManus, Arthur 333
McMillan, Joyce 143, 144
McMillan, Roddy 464
McNeill, F. Marian 64, 608, 663
McNeillie, Andrew 41, 471, 472, 709
McNeillie, John (Ian Niall) 41, 471, 666, 705
McOmish, David 158
McTaggart, William 65
Meek, Donald E. 312, 332, 334, 490, 491
Meek, James 575
Melville, Andrew 154, 163
Melville, Elizabeth 159, 160, 161, 162, 165
Melville, Herman 50, 317, 319, 347, 554, 641, 705
Mencken, H.L. 600
Menteith, Alexander (Alexander Stuart/Earl of Menteith 108, 192, 604
Merlin 57, 58, 59, 67, 654, 700, 708
Meyer, Kuno 60
Mickle, William Julius 658
Mill, J.S. 304, 683, 705
Miller, Christian 487, 488, 666
Miller, Frankie 594, 621
Miller, Hugh 306, 324, 528, 554, 660, 683
Miller, Karl 618
Miller, Lydia Mackenzie Falconer 660
Miller, William 339, 661, 699
Mills, Elizabeth 324
Mills, George 339
Milne, Lennox 527

Milton, John 59, 251, 330, 472, 574, 576, 701
Mina, Denise 598
Mitchell, Ian 401
Mitchison, Naomi 369, 389, 391, 392, 393, 596, 598, 608, 664, 688, 693
Moffat, Alexander 409, 568, 697, 709
Moffat, Alistair 58, 59, 103
Moir, David Macbeth 660
Moireach, Iain (John Murray) 193, 493
Molière, (Jean-Baptiste Poquelin) 527, 530, 531, 560
Monk, Seonag 526
Monnickendam, Andrew 306
Monro, Donald 629
Monroe, Marilyn 534
Montale, Eugenio 374
Montesquieu (Charles-Louis de Secondat), 201
Montezuma 323
Montgomerie, Alexander 87, 163, 165, 609, 610, 656
Montgomery, Catriona 461
Montgomery, James 635, 659
Montgomery, Mary (Màiri NicGumaraid) 497
Montgomery, Morag 461
Moody, Dwight L. 339
Moon, Lorna 663
Moore, Dafydd 230
More, Thomas 148
Morgan, Edwin 40, 61, 62, 66, 68, 69, 70, 84, 88, 108, 112, 128, 135, 157, 159, 168, 169, 176, 241, 242, 244, 247, 390, 392, 421, 433, 437, 438–442, 443, 450, 455, 456, 469, 470, 483, 513, 516, 530, 533, 534, 535, 537, 559, 560, 561, 562, 564, 568, 569, 572, 587, 589, 592, 604, 605, 612, 615, 623, 625, 626, 627, 642, 654, 666, 674, 684, 686, 690, 697, 699, 700
Morison, Roderick (Ruaidhri MacMhuirich) 184, 657
Moro, Aldo 513
Morrison, Blake 36
Morrison, John (Iain Gobha) 681
Morrison, Mairi (Màiri Nic'IlleMhoire) 547
Morrison, Nancy Brysson 486, 664
Morrison, Neil (Niall Moireasdan) 313
Morton, H.V. 631
Motion, Andrew 36

Motteux, Pierre 180
Muir, Edwin 34, 35, 36, 58, 87, 369, 383, 384–388, 399, 409, 448, 518, 587, 626, 632, 633, 646, 663, 679, 694, 698, 700
Muir, Thomas 332, 536
Muir, Willa 162, 349, 369, 386, 399, 409, 410, 411, 412, 626, 663, 686, 694
Munro, George 464
Munro, Neil 340, 342, 343, 350, 353, 602, 662, 691, 692
Munro, Rona 530, 535
Murdoch, John 332, 333, 334
Mure, William (of Rowallan) 656
Murray, Charles 344, 662
Murray, David 656
Murray, Donald S. 496, 546
Murray, Isobel 470, 592
Murray, James 199
Murray, John 696
Murray, John (Iain Moireach) 493, 544
Murray, Jonathan 620
Murray, Kylie 70
Murray, Les 247, 634
Mussolini, Benito 437

N
Napier, James 54
Neat, Timothy 311, 438
Neill, William 666
Neilson, Anthony 532, 537
Neruda, Pablo 250, 374, 427, 558, 666
Newton, Michael 192
NicDhòmhnaill, Màiri Anna 523
NicLeòid, Norma 523
Nietzsche, Friedrich 254, 306, 324, 340, 369, 374, 541, 613
Niven, Frederick 663
Nostradamus (Michel de Nostradame) 323

O
Ó Baoill, Colm 188, 685
O'Brien, Flann 20, 600, 601, 602
O'Casey, Sean 82, 413
O'Driscoll, Dennis 635
O'Grady, Standish 335
O'Hagan, Andrew 488, 670
Oliphant, Carolina 301, 659
Oliphant, Margaret 301, 308, 476, 661
Oliver, Douglas 634

Olson, Charles 14, 40, 71
Orage, A.R. 17
O'Rourke, Donny 421, 669, 702
Orwell, George 305, 401, 490, 641
Ossian 25, 45, 50, 51, 57, 60, 66, 220, 221, 222, 223, 224, 225, 226, 227, 228, 229, 230, 239, 240, 262, 335, 336, 405, 654, 659, 687, 702
Otway, Thomas 239
Ovid 129, 152, 154
Owen, Wilfred 394, 580, 590
Owens, Agnes 481, 514, 666

P
Pae, David 661, 688
Pagan, Isabel 659
Paisley, Janet 517, 518, 568, 668, 689
Pappano, Antonio 640
Paretsky, Sara 600
Park, Mungo 397, 510, 659, 706
Parnell, Charles Stewart 332, 354
Pascal, François Gérard Simon 226
Paterson, Don 247, 569, 670, 688, 694
Paterson, Neil 487, 665
Paterson, Stuart 465, 670
Paton, Alan 579
Paxman, Jeremy 501
Payne, John Howard 239
Peacock, Alan 617
Peacock, Charlotte 411
Pearson, John 477
Peckinpah, Sam 60, 474
Pennant, Thomas 629
Peploe, Denis 428
Peploe, James Reid 476
Peploe, Samuel 65
Perelman, S.J. 600
Perrie, Walter 668
Peterkiewicz, Jerzy 642
Pettinger, Alasdair 642
Picasso, Pablo 124, 242, 373, 383, 606
Pichot, Amédée 239
Picot, Edward 624, 625
Pilditch, Jan 410, 411
Pindar 422
Pirandello, Luigi 549
Pitcairne, Archibald 156, 157, 158, 232
Pittock, Murray 542
Poe, Edgar Allan 291, 325, 538, 702

Poet, Francis 546
Pollock, R.F. 367, 368
Pollok, Robert 660, 701
Polwart, Karine 595
Pope, Alexander 198
Porter, James 229, 230
Porter, Jane 660
Pound, Ezra 17, 27, 29, 33, 84, 131, 163, 164, 289, 362, 382, 538, 562, 588, 589
Powell, Nick 539
Power, William 46, 48, 197, 249, 250, 301, 305, 352, 353, 595, 626, 663
Pow, Tom 566
Prebble, John 324, 480, 691
Price, Richard 567, 568, 623, 670
Proust, Marcel 39, 166
Prynne, J.H. 37, 559, 562
Puccini, Giacomo 516
Purcell, Henry 129
Purser, John 48, 52, 63, 64, 67, 80, 171, 229, 230, 380, 554, 566, 619, 668, 709

Q
Quasimodo, Salvatore 374

R
Rabelais, François 129, 179, 180, 182, 605, 651, 657
Racine, Jean 83, 146, 530, 534
Raeburn, Henry 477
Rae, Hugh C. (Jessica Stirling) 596, 597, 667
Raffles, Gerry 549
Ramsay, Allan 25, 35, 39, 82, 87, 153, 159, 171, 197, 207, 231–236, 237, 238, 244, 248, 251, 527, 602, 649, 650, 657, 696, 701
Rankin, Ian 272, 522, 587, 598, 678, 695, 697
Reader, Eddi 594
Reagan, Ronald 622
Redpath, Jean 355
Reekie, Tony 465
Reid, Alastair 576
Reid, Alexander 527
Reid, Charlie 594
Reid, Craig 594
Reid, Jim 355
Reid, Jimmy 516, 535

Reid, Marion Kirkland 302, 303
Reid, Steven J. 158
Reid, Thomas 201
Reid, Trish 76, 537, 538, 539
Reid-Baxter, Jamie 134, 146, 147, 148, 149, 150, 162
Reith, John 617, 618
Renan, Ernest 336
Rennie Mackintosh, Charles 124, 587, 624, 700
Renoir, Pierre-Auguste 553
Rhymer, Thomas 48, 103, 104, 329, 480, 527, 654, 706
Riach, Alan 18, 44, 678, 702, 708, 709
Richards, David 274
Ritchie, Aileen 535
Roberts, Kate 40
Robertson, Angus (Aonghas MacDhonnchaidh) 491
Robertson, Gill 465
Robertson, James 89, 92, 95, 153, 174, 509, 512, 518, 584, 602, 636, 669, 696
Robertson, Jeannie 438
Robertson, Robin 569
Robeson, Paul 248
Robinson, Mary 25
Rochead, John Thomas 213
Rocks, Kokumo 575
Rodin, Auguste 684
Rogers, Byron 56
Rolfe, Frederick (Baron Colvo) 156
Rolfe, J.C. 111
Rommel, Erwin 432
Roper, Tony 528, 668
Rorie, David 340
Rose, Eugene (Uisdean Ròs) 313, 682
Rose, Reginald 82
Ross, Alexander 658
Ross, Neil 60
Ross, William (Uilleam Ròs) 219, 220, 493, 659
Roth, Joseph 511
Rothko, Mark 236, 237
Rousseau, Jean-Jacques 201, 249, 304
Rowe, Nicholas 239
Rowling, J.K. 350, 599, 691, 695, 696
Royle, Trevor 217, 589
Roy Stuart, John (Iain Ruadh Stiùbhart) 217
Ruddiman, Thomas 153, 197
Runciman, Alexander 226

Ruskin, John 304, 683, 705
Russell, Jessie 328, 662
Russell, Michael 633

S
Saadi, Suhayl 521, 575
Sabatini, Rafael 176
Said, Edward 248
Sallust (Gaius Sallustus Crispus) 111, 585
Sanderson, Ivan T. 665
Sankey, Ira D. 339
Sartre, Jean-Paul 272
Sassi, Carla 651, 711
Sassoon, Siegfried 590, 591
Saurat, Denis 381, 409
Schoenberg, Arnold 605
Schubert, Franz 229
Schumann, Clara 507
Schumann, Robert 507
Scorsese, Martin 621
Scot, John 158
Scott, Alastair 633
Scott, Alexander (c.1515–1583) 88, 655
Scott, Alexander (c.1920–89) 528, 573, 666, 685, 700
Scott, Benedick 464
Scott, Francis George 28, 164, 369, 383, 384, 386, 409, 436, 641, 694, 704
Scott, Ian 539
Scott, Michael 270, 527, 635, 654, 660, 706
Scott, Ridley 474
Scott, Tom 666
Scott, Walter 22, 28, 34, 37, 39, 53, 54, 80, 87, 89, 104, 112, 125, 171, 173, 174, 197, 198, 201, 203, 213, 249, 259, 260, 262, 267, 268, 269, 272, 273–292, 293, 297, 298, 300, 301, 302, 306, 311, 315, 316, 319, 320, 323, 347, 348, 349, 355, 357, 359, 363, 364, 365, 367, 383, 387, 397, 401, 402, 443, 444, 445, 469, 513, 538, 573, 581, 583, 587, 598, 602, 603, 604, 613, 619, 629, 630, 642, 645, 659, 665, 678, 681, 683, 689, 691, 692, 693, 646, 695, 696, 697, 699, 700, 702, 703, 704, 706, 707, 708
Scott-Moncrieff, George 633
Scotus, Duns (Johannes) 70, 71, 708
Scullion, Adrienne 541
Seacole, Mary 635, 660

Sellar, Patrick 681
Sembène, Ousmane 579
Sempill, Francis 657
Sempill, James 657
Sempill, Robert (elder) 655
Sempill, Robert the Younger 251, 657
Semple, Robert 657
Seneca 146, 152
Shakespeare, William 21, 22, 29, 39, 47, 50, 59, 77, 83, 93, 122, 123, 142, 143, 144, 160, 163, 168, 180, 233, 236, 237, 238, 242, 288, 290, 366, 376, 381, 390, 432, 454, 465, 490, 534, 539, 562, 565, 574, 577, 578, 581, 606, 609, 627, 641, 652
Shapiro, James 77
Sharp, Alan 341, 596, 620, 621, 643, 667, 698
Sharp, Elizabeth 336
Sharp, William (Fiona Macleod) 336, 662
Sharpe, Patrick 163
Shelley, Mary 285, 688
Shelley, Percy Bysshe 22, 188, 198, 493, 581
Shepherd, Nan 301, 349, 369, 399, 411–412, 664, 684
Sheridan, Richard Brinsley 83
Shiel, Tibbie (Isabella) 268, 708
Shire, Helena 5, 610
Shire, Helena Mennie 511
Shirley, Rob 492
Sibbald, James 275
Sibelius, Jean 388, 607
Siddons, Sarah 238, 239, 241
Silver, Christopher 617
Silver, R.S. 464
Silver, Sally 287
Simpson, Habbie 251
Simpson, Margaret Winefride 663
Sinclair, Donald (Dòmhnall Mac na Ceàrdaich) 361, 385, 543
Singer, James Burns 642, 667
Skaaha 45, 517, 654
Skinner, John 658
Slater, Oscar 518
Smellie, William 199
Smith, Adam 28, 201, 202, 213, 574, 658, 700
Smith, Alexander 327, 328, 661
Smith, Ali 391, 510, 511, 575, 607, 627, 670
Smith, Brian 678
Smith, Ian Crichton (Iain Mac a' Ghobhainn) 51, 80, 88, 159, 283, 359, 421, 425, 448, 451–457, 465, 474, 493, 494, 543, 545, 554, 561, 587, 604, 619, 636, 667, 680, 681, 683
Smith, James McCune 642, 661
Smith, John of Darnick 706
Smith, Mark Ryan 678
Smith, Sydney Goodsir 88, 159, 406, 425, 427–430, 527, 561, 605, 665, 693, 695, 697
Smollett, Tobias 198, 236, 263, 264, 265, 266, 267, 301, 610, 645, 658, 698, 700
Smyth, Alfred P. 72
Sophocles 236, 531
Sorley, Charles Hamilton 591
Soutar, William 40, 369, 383–384, 388, 409, 664, 688
Southey, Robert 630
Sowerby, Kathrine 569
Soyinka, Wole 250, 392, 579, 586, 651
Spark, Muriel 269, 272, 319, 443, 444–447, 511, 512, 587, 602, 613, 666, 695
Spearing, A.C. 114
Speght, Thomas 122
Spence, Alan 515, 516, 529, 535, 575, 668
Spence, Catherine Helen 661
Spence, Lewis 53, 663, 688
Spenser, Edmund 26
Squire, Charles 52
St Columba 15, 30, 63, 64, 65, 66, 67, 71, 87, 100, 152, 222, 480, 584, 605, 615, 654, 690
St John 399
St Kentigern or Mungo 57, 67, 68, 708
St Magnus 72, 448, 679
St Margaret 67
St Molaise 67
St Patrick 50, 51, 57, 66, 222, 405
Stafford, Fiona 225, 226, 230, 239, 709
Stalin, Joseph 23, 563
Stanislavski, Konstantin 367
Stark, Richard 600
Steinbeck, John 471
Stephen, Ian 4496, 569, 669, 680
Stephens, Meic 643
Stevens, Wallace 86
Stevenson, D.E. 476
Stevenson, Gerda 80, 159, 561, 569, 592, 619, 669
Stevenson, Robert 277

INDEX OF AUTHOR NAMES

Stevenson, Robert Louis 35, 39, 40, 53, 80, 87, 174, 245, 267, 269, 272, 277, 315–321, 322, 323, 324, 326, 331, 348, 349, 355, 364, 398, 476, 506, 596, 589, 598, 604, 619, 628, 631, 642, 646, 662, 690, 695, 696, 697
Stevenson, Ronald 384, 388
Stevenson, W.G. 702
Stewart, Alan Breck 316, 323, 697
Stewart, Andy 453, 596
Stewart, Dugald 201, 203
Stewart, Ena Lamont 369, 416, 467, 665
Stewart, John of Baldynneis 163, 166, 656
Stewart, Margaret 134
Stewart, William Drummond 660
Stewart, William Grant 54
Stoker, Bram 39, 684
Storey, John 499
Stott, Ken 536
Stowe, Harriet Beecher 310, 660, 681
Strauss, Richard 355, 621
Stravinsky, Igor 124, 373, 625
Strindberg, August 138, 465, 549
Stuart, Charles (Bonnie Prince Charlie) 39, 207, 219, 301, 323, 354, 601, 683, 707, 708
Stuart, Henry (Lord Darnley) 134, 146
Stuart, Mary (Mary Queen of Scots) 133, 134, 135, 143, 145, 146, 150, 151, 153, 165, 344, 480, 530, 531, 536, 656, 707
Sutherland, Halliday 633
Sutherland, John 634
Sutherland, Luke 521
Sutherland, Stella 587, 678
Swan, Annie S. 476, 596, 662
Sweeney, William 28
Swinton, John 332
Swinton, Tilda 536
Sydserf, Thomas 657
Sym, Robert 298
Synge, J.M. 48, 82, 336

T

Tacitus, Publius Cornelius 60, 145, 152, 585, 654
Tait, Margaret 666, 679
Tait, William 146
Tait, William J. 587, 666, 678
Tallack, Malachy 637
Tannahill, Robert 659, 698
Tate, Nahum 129, 237
Tavener, Alan 64
Taylor, C.P. 82, 386, 527, 528
Taylor, Rachel Annand 663
Tennyson, Alfred 362, 476
Tey, Josephine (Elizabeth Mackintosh) 596, 597, 664
Thom, William 327
Thomas, Andrea 132, 145, 146, 152, 153, 581
Thomas, Dylan 423
Thomas, R.S. 56, 160, 471
Thomson, A.A. 631
Thomson, David 173
Thomson, Derick (Ruaraidh MacThòmais) 88, 99, 192, 230, 359, 434, 458, 459, 497, 666, 680
Thomson, George 28
Thomson, James 25, 155, 198, 214, 236, 258, 634, 658, 705
Thomson, James ('B.V.') 87, 317, 328, 559, 646, 661
Thomson, William (Lord Kelvin) 605
Thornton, Thomas 629
Thorpe, Nick 628
Tóibín, Colm 614
Tolstoy, Leo 23, 250, 291, 455, 502, 651
Topham, Edward 631
Torrington, Jeff 667
Tranströmer, Tomas 667
Tranter, Nigel 104, 476, 479, 480, 665, 695
Tremblay, Michel 530
Trevlyn, Valda 375
Tritschier, F. 708
Trocchi, Alexander 473, 474, 475, 666, 700
Trollope, Anthony 308, 688
Trotter, Catharine 657
Tudor, Elizabeth 143, 148, 150, 165, 168, 463
Tudor, Margaret 125, 128, 583
Turnbull, Gael 666
Turnbull, Ronald 626
Turner, J.M.W. 226, 381, 689
Twain, Mark 325, 330, 600, 601
Tytler, Alexander Fraser (Lord Woodhouselee) 659

U

Ulanova, Galina 534

Ungaretti, Giuseppe 374
Ure, Joan 533, 666
Urquhart, Fred 469, 470, 472
Urquhart, Thomas 129, 176, 178, 179, 180, 182, 197, 602, 605, 657

V
Vaughan-Hughes, Gerald 474
Vegius, Mapheus 129
Veitch, John 57, 58, 700, 708
Vellacott, Philip 367
Venables, Terry 474
Verne, Jules 630, 690, 692
Victoria (Alexandrina Victoria, Queen) 310, 354, 630, 685
290, 311
Villon, François 321, 345
Virgil 29, 129, 131, 146, 152, 153, 197, 207, 612, 655, 687
Voltaire (François-Marie Arouet) 201, 304, 600
Vyver, Bertha 325

W
Waddell, Bertha 465, 466
Waddell, Jenny 466
Walcott, Derek 35, 59, 152, 635, 636
Waldo Emerson, Ralph 305
Walker, Helen 704
Walker, Marshall 18, 76, 247, 442 484, 599, 600, 607, 613, 652, 709
Wallace, Stuart 196
Wallace, William 106, 108, 109, 115, 257, 258, 480, 572, 573, 585, 586, 589, 601, 693, 696, 698, 706
Wallace-Crabbe, Chris 634
Walter, Bruno 23
Walter, William Grey 534
Wardlaw, Elizabeth 657
Warner, Alan 511, 512, 670
Warner, Marina 53
Warren, Robert Penn 20
wa Thiong'o, Ngũgĩ 579
Watson, James 251
Watson, Moray 489, 491, 493, 494, 495, 523, 542, 543
Watson, Roderick 407, 589, 591, 709
Watt, Eilidh 497
Watt, Roseanne 569, 587, 670, 672
Waugh, Evelyn 445

Webber, Andrew Llyod 135
Wedderburn, James 133, 655
Wedderburn, John 133, 655
Wedderburn, Robert 133, 655
Wells, H.G. 326
Welsh, Irvine 263, 272, 319, 443, 473, 499, 500–501, 669, 695, 697
Welsh, Louise 597, 673, 691, 700
West, David 129, 130, 612
Westlake, Donald E. 600
West, Rebecca (Cicily Isabel Andrews, née Fairfield) 663
White, Kenneth 566, 667
Whitman, Walt 24, 93, 250, 328, 429, 648, 661
Whittock, Martyn 52
Whyte, Christopher 519, 520, 669
Whyte, Henry 490
Wicomb, Zoë 668
Wilde, Oscar 35, 316, 465, 600, 688
Williams, Gordon 475, 474, 667
Williams, Ralph Vaughan 381
Williams, William Carlos 21, 28, 34, 40, 70, 582
Wilson, Alexander 659
Wilson, James 78, 345
Wilson, John (Christopher North) 298, 660
Wilson, Rab 569
Wilson, Susan R. 385
Wilson, Thomas 67
Wilson-Tagoe, Nana 579
Witherspoon, John 78
Woffington, Margaret (Peg) 237
Woolf, Virginia 641
Wordsworth, Dorothy 628, 630
Wordsworth, William 37, 59, 198, 227, 250, 251, 298, 388, 619, 628, 630, 634, 693
Wyntoun, Andrew of 59, 104, 655, 695

Y
Yeats, W.B. 21, 34, 46, 47, 54, 55, 81, 82, 84, 169, 324, 335, 375, 377, 385, 425, 426, 435, 545, 599, 689
Young, Douglas 152, 527, 592, 665
Young Geddes, James 87, 328, 661, 687

Z
Zohn, Harry 89
Zola, Émile 471, 563

Luath Press Limited

committed to publishing well written books worth reading

LUATH PRESS takes its name from Robert Burns, whose little collie Luath (*Gael.*, swift or nimble) tripped up Jean Armour at a wedding and gave him the chance to speak to the woman who was to be his wife and the abiding love of his life. Burns called one of the 'Twa Dogs' Luath after Cuchullin's hunting dog in Ossian's *Fingal*. Luath Press was established in 1981 in the heart of Burns country, and is now based a few steps up the road from Burns' first lodgings on Edinburgh's Royal Mile. Luath offers you distinctive writing with a hint of unexpected pleasures.

Most bookshops in the UK, the US, Canada, Australia, New Zealand and parts of Europe, either carry our books in stock or can order them for you. To order direct from us, please send a £sterling cheque, postal order, international money order or your credit card details (number, address of cardholder and expiry date) to us at the address below. Please add post and packing as follows: UK – £1.00 per delivery address; overseas surface mail – £2.50 per delivery address; overseas airmail – £3.50 for the first book to each delivery address, plus £1.00 for each additional book by airmail to the same address. If your order is a gift, we will happily enclose your card or message at no extra charge.

Luath Press Limited
543/2 Castlehill
The Royal Mile
Edinburgh EH1 2ND
Scotland
Telephone: 0131 225 4326 (24 hours)
Fax: 0131 225 4324
email: sales@luath.co.uk
Website: www.luath.co.uk

www.ingramcontent.com/pod-product-compliance
Lightning Source LLC
Chambersburg PA
CBHW010718300426
44114CB00023B/2890